T0214425

Lecture Notes in Artificial Intelligence   11238

Subseries of Lecture Notes in Computer Science

More information about this series at http://www.springer.com/series/1244

Guillermo R. Simari · Eduardo Fermé
Flabio Gutiérrez Segura
José Antonio Rodríguez Melquiades (Eds.)

Advances in Artificial Intelligence – IBERAMIA 2018

16th Ibero-American Conference on AI
Trujillo, Peru, November 13–16, 2018
Proceedings

 Springer

Editors
Guillermo R. Simari ⓘ
Universidad Nacional del Sur
Bahía Blanca, Buenos Aires, Argentina

Flabio Gutiérrez Segura
Universidad Nacional de Piura
Castilla-Piura, Peru

Eduardo Fermé ⓘ
University of Madeira
Funchal, Portugal

José Antonio Rodríguez Melquiades
Universidad Nacional de Trujillo
Trujillo, Peru

ISSN 0302-9743   ISSN 1611-3349   (electronic)
Lecture Notes in Artificial Intelligence
ISBN 978-3-030-03927-1   ISBN 978-3-030-03928-8   (eBook)
https://doi.org/10.1007/978-3-030-03928-8

Library of Congress Control Number: 2018960666

LNCS Sublibrary: SL7 – Artificial Intelligence

This Springer imprint is published by the registered company Springer Nature Switzerland AG
The registered company address is: Gewerbestrasse 11, 6330 Cham, Switzerland

Preface

IBERAMIA 2018, the 16th Ibero-American Conference on Artificial Intelligence, was held in Trujillo (Perú) held during November 13–16, 2018, organized by the Universidad Nacional de Trujillo and the Sociedad Peruana de Inteligencia Artificial. IBERAMIA is the biennial Ibero-American Conference on Artificial Intelligence. The conference is sponsored by the main Ibero-American Societies of Artificial Intelligence (AI) and gives researchers from Portugal, Spain, and the Latin America countries the opportunity to meet with AI researchers from all over the world. This volume presents the proceedings of the conference.

Since its first edition in Barcelona during 1988, IBERAMIA has continuously expanded its scope to become a well-recognized international conference where the AI community shares the results of their research. Springer's *Lecture Notes in Computer Science* has published the works accepted for the conference since 1998 when the sixth edition of IBERAMIA took place in the city of Lisbon, Portugal. The organizational structure of IBERAMIA 2018 follows the standard of the most prestigious international scientific conferences. The scientific program this year led to fruitful debates among the researchers on the main topics of AI. As customary, the program of the conference was organized in several tracks and each one was coordinated by area chairs in charge of the reviewing process following the general rules of assigning each submitted paper to three members of the Program Committee (PC).

The tracks organized for this edition were the following:

- Knowledge Engineering, Knowledge Representation and Reasoning under Uncertainty
- Multiagent Systems, Game Theory and Economic Paradigms, Game Playing and Interactive Entertainment, Ambient Intelligence
- Machine Learning Applications, Machine Learning Methods, Cognitive Modeling, Cognitive Systems
- Planning and Scheduling, Robotics, Vision
- Natural Language Processing, Human–Computer Interaction, AI in Education, NLP and Knowledge Representation, NLP and Machine Learning, NLP and Text Mining, Humans and AI, Human-Aware AI
- General AI, Knowledge Engineering, AI and the Web Applications, Computational Sustainability and AI, Heuristic Search and Optimization

The criterion to select these tracks was based on their current relevance in the field. IBERAMIA 2018 received 92 papers with widespread contributions from Latin America and the rest of the world; from that initial set of submissions 41 of them were accepted through a process that involved the collaboration of three reviewers per paper. When necessary, additional reviews were requested to obtain a clear decision on a particular work. The full list of area chairs, PC members, and additional reviewers can be found after this preface.

We would like to express our sincere gratitude to all the people who helped to bring about IBERAMIA 2018. First and foremost, to the contributing authors that provided the works of the highest quality to the conference and for their cooperation in the preparation of this volume. We also want to give special thanks to the area chairs and the members of the PC and the reviewers for the quality of their work, which undoubtedly helped in the selection of the best papers for the conference. Without the expert guidance and continuous support of the IBERAMIA Executive Committee and secretariat that shepherd our work, nothing would have been possible. In particular, we acknowledge the enormous help of Federico Barber and Francisco Garijo.

The use of the EasyChair conference management system provided the support for all the tasks involved in the submission and review of the papers and the preparation of the proceedings. We would like to express our thanks to the sponsors of the conference since without their contribution the conference would not have been possible.

Lastly, it is necessary to remark that IBERAMIA 2018 was possible through the work and dedication of the Organizing Committee from the Universidad de Trujillo. We wish to express our gratitude to all the people who helped in the organization of this significant event.

November 2018

Guillermo R. Simari
Eduardo Fermé
Flabio Gutiérrez Segura
José Antonio Rodríguez Melquiades

Organization

Program Committee

Program Chairs

Guillermo R. Simari	Universidad Nacional del Sur, Argentina
Eduardo Fermé	Universidade da Madeira, Portugal

Track Chairs

Blai Bonet	Universidad Simón Bolívar, Colombia
Marcelo Errecalde	Universidad Nacional de San Luis, Argentina
Eduardo Fermé	Universidade da Madeira, Portugal
Vicente Julian	Universitat Politècnica de València, Spain
Paulo Novais	Universidade do Minho, Portugal
Aline Villavicencio	Federal University of Rio Grande do Sul, Brazil

Program Committee Members

Alberto Abad	IST/INESC-ID
Enrique Marcelo Albornoz	Research Institute for Signals, Systems and Computational Intelligence, sinc(i), UNL-CONICET
Laura Alonso Alemany	Universidad Nacional de Córdoba, Colombia
Matías Alvarado	Centro de Investigacion y de Estudios Avanzados del IPN
Javier Apolloni	Universidad Nacional de San Luis, Argentina
Luis Avila	INGAR_CONICET
Wilker Aziz	University of Amsterdam, The Netherlands
Javier Bajo	Universidad Politécnica de Madrid, Spain
Federico Barber	Universitat Politècnica de València, Spain
Roman Barták	Charles University, Czech Republic
Néstor Becerra Yoma	Universidad de Chile, Chile
Olivier Boissier	Mines Saint-Etienne, Institut Henri Fayol, France
Rafael Bordini	PUCRS
Antonio Branco	Universidade de Lisboa, Portugal
Facundo Bromberg	UTN-Mendoza y CONICET
Benjamin Bustos	Universidad de Chile, Chile
Pedro Cabalar	University of A Coruna
Leticia Cagnina	Universidad Nacional de San Luis, Argentina
Carlos Carrascosa	GTI-IA DSIC Universidad Politecnica de Valencia, Spain

Henry Carrillo	Universidad Sergio Arboleda, Colombia
Amedeo Cesta	National Research Council of Italy
Carlos Chesñevar	Universidad Nacional del Sur, Argentina
Helder Coelho	Universidade de Lisboa, Portugal
Silvio Cordeiro	Aix-Marseille University, France
Luís Correia	Universidade de Lisboa, Portugal
Anna Helena Reali Costa	University of São Paulo, Brazil
Ângelo Costa	University of Minho, Portugal
Andre de Carvalho	University of São Paulo, Brazil
Mariano De Paula	INGAR, CONICET
Jorge Dias	University of Coimbra, Portugal
Néstor Darío Duque Méndez	Universidad Nacional de Colombia, Colombia
Alejandro Edera	Instituto de Biología Agrícola Mendoza, CONICET, Universidad Nacional de Cuyo, Argentina
Amal El Fallah Seghrouchni	LIP6, Pierre and Marie Curie University, France
Hugo Jair Escalante	INAOE
Florentino Fdez-Riverola	University of Vigo, Spain
Eduardo Fermé	Universidade da Madeira, Portugal
Antonio Fernández-Caballero	Universidad de Castilla-La Mancha, Spain
Rafael Ferreira	Federal Rural University of Pernambuco, Brazil
Edgardo Ferretti	National University of San Luis, Argentina
Guillem Francès	University of Basel, Switzerland
Joao Gama	University of Porto, Portugal
Pablo Gamallo	University of Santiago de Compostela, Spain
Rosario Girardi	UFMA
Sergio Alejandro Gomez	Universidad Nacional del Sur, Argentina
Jorge Gomez-Sanz	Universidad Complutense de Madrid, Spain
Paulo Guerra	Federal University of Ceara, Brazil
Waldo Hasperué	UNLP
Carlos Daniel Hernández Mena	Universidad Nacional Autónoma de México, Mexico
Carlos A. Iglesias	Universidad Politécnica de Madrid, Spain
Jean-Michel Ilie	LIP6, Pierre et Marie Curie University, France
Vitor Jorge	UFRGS
Jason Jung	Chung-Ang University, South Korea
Ergina Kavallieratou	University of the Aegean, Greece
Fabio Kepler	Federal University of Pampa, Brazil
Laura Lanzarini	III LIDI
Joao Leite	Universidade NOVA de Lisboa, Portugal
Nir Lipovetzky	The University of Melbourne, Australia
Patricio Loncomilla	Universidad de Chile, Chile
José Gabriel Lopes	.
Adrián Pastor Lopez-Monroy	Instituto Nacional de Astrofísica, Óptica y Electrónica

Juan Antonio Rodriguez Aguilar	IIIA-CSIC
Ricardo Rodríguez	F.C.N.yN.-UBA
Paolo Rosso	Technical University of Valencia, Spain
Aiala Rosá	UDELAR
Jose M. Saavedra	Orand S.A.
Miguel A. Salido	Technical University of Valencia, Spain
Elci Santos	University of Madeira, Portugal
Ichiro Satoh	National Institute of Informatics
Pierre-Yves Schobbens	University of Namur, Belgium
Emilio Serrano	Universidad Politécnica de Madrid, Spain
Efstathios Stamatatos	University of the Aegean, Greece
Vera Lúcia Strube de Lima	Independent
António Teixeira	University of Aveiro, Portugal
Ivan Varzinczak	University of Artois and CNRS, France
Rene Venegas Velasquez	Pontificia Universidad Católica de Valparaíso, Chile
Rodrigo Verschae	Kyoto University, Japan
Rosa Vicari	Universidade Federal do Rio Grande do Sul, Brazil
Esau Villatoro-Tello	Universidad Autónoma Metropolitana, Mexico
Rodrigo Wilkens	UCL
Dina Wonsever	Universidad de la República, Uruguay
Neil Yorke-Smith	Delft University of Technology, The Netherlands
Marcos Zampieri	University of Wolverhampton, UK
Leonardo Zilio	Université catholique de Louvain, Belgium
Alejandro Zunino	CONICET-ISISTAN, UNICEN

Additional Reviewers

Alvarez Carmona, Miguel Ángel
Bugnon, Leandro
Chiruzzo, Luis
Freitas, Fred
Hernandez Farias, Delia Irazu
Manso, Luis

Martínez, César
Nogueira, Rita
Peterson, Victoria
Ronchetti, Franco
Rosso Mateus, Andres Enrique

Organizing Committee

Organization Chair

Flabio Gutiérrez Segura   Universidad Nacional de Piura, Peru

Organization Vice-chair

José Antonio Rodríguez   Universidad Nacional de Trujillo, Peru
Melquiades

Organizing Committee Members

Nicolas Kemper Valverde	Presidente de la Sociedad de Inteligencia Artificial
Julio Peralta Castañeda	Secretario de la FFCCYMM Universidad Nacional de Trujillo, Peru
Carlos Castillo Diestra	Universidad Nacional de Trujillo, Peru
Jorge Gutiérrez Gutiérrez	Universidad Nacional de Trujillo, Peru
José Cruz Silva	Universidad Nacional de Trujillo, Peru
Edwin Mendoza Torres	Universidad Nacional de Trujillo, Peru
Iris Cruz Florian	Universidad Nacional de Trujillo, Peru
Ricardo Guevara Ruíz	Universidad Nacional de Trujillo, Peru
Yenny Sifuentes Díaz	Universidad Nacional de Trujillo, Peru
José Peralta Lujan	Universidad Nacional de Trujillo, Peru
Juan Salazar Campos	Universidad Nacional de Trujillo, Peru
Sofia Pedro Huamán	Universidad Nacional de Trujillo, Peru
José Díaz Pulido	Universidad Nacional de Trujillo, Peru
David Bravo Escalante	Universidad Nacional de Trujillo, Peru
Antony Gómez Morales	Universidad Nacional de Trujillo, Peru
Ana Maria Li García	Universidad Nacional de Trujillo, Peru
Edwar Lujan Segura	Universidad Nacional de Trujillo, Peru
Yaneth Alva Alva	.
Ricardo Vásquez Melon	.
Gustavo Rodríguez	.

Contents

Machine Learning Applications, Machine Learning Methods, Cognitive Modeling, Cognitive Systems

Planning and Scheduling, Robotics, Vision

Natural Language Processing, Human-Computer Interaction, AI in Education, NLP and Knowledge Representation, NLP and Machine Learning, NLP and Text Mining, Humans and AI, Human-Aware AI

Knowledge Engineering, Knowledge Representation and Reasoning under Uncertainty

Querying Probabilistic Temporal Constraints for Guideline Interaction Analysis: GLARE's Approach

Antonella Andolina[1], Luca Anselma[2(✉)], Luca Piovesan[3],
and Paolo Terenziani[3]

[1] ITCS Sommeiller, Corso Duca degli Abruzzi 20, 10129 Turin, Italy
antoando@libero.it
[2] Dipartimento di Informatica, Università di Torino,
Corso Svizzera 185, 10149 Turin, Italy
anselma@di.unito.it
[3] DISIT, Università del Piemonte Orientale "A. Avogadro", Alessandria, Italy
{luca.piovesan,paolo.terenziani}@uniupo.it

Abstract. The treatment of patients affected by multiple diseases (*comorbid* patients) is one of the main challenges of the modern healthcare, involving the analysis of the interactions of the guidelines for the specific diseases. However, practically speaking, such interactions occur *over time*. The GLARE project explicitly provides knowledge representation, temporal representation and temporal reasoning methodologies to cope with such a fundamental issue. In this paper, we propose a further improvement, to take into account that, often, the effects of actions have a *probabilistic distribution in time*, and being able to *reason* (through constraint propagation) and to *query probabilistic temporal constraints* further enhances the support for interaction detection.

Keywords: Probabilistic temporal constraints · Temporal reasoning
Guideline interaction analysis · Decision support system

1 Introduction

Clinical practice guidelines are the major tool that has been introduced to grant both the quality and the standardization of healthcare services, on the basis of *evidence-based* recommendations. The adoption of computerized approaches to acquire, represent, execute and reason with Computer–Interpretable Guidelines (CIGs) provides crucial additional advantages so that, in the last twenty years, many different approaches and projects have been developed to manage CIGs (consider, e.g., the book [1] and the recent survey [2]). One of such approaches is GLARE (Guideline Acquisition, Representation and Execution) [3], and its successor METAGLARE [4]. By definition, clinical guidelines address specific pathologies. However, *comorbid* patients are affected by more than one pathology. The problem is that, in comorbid patients, the treatments of single pathologies may interact with each other, and the approach of proposing an ad-hoc "combined" treatment to cope with each possible comorbidity does not scale up. In the last years, several computer-based approaches have started to

© Springer Nature Switzerland AG 2018
G. R. Simari et al. (Eds.): IBERAMIA 2018, LNAI 11238, pp. 3–15, 2018.
https://doi.org/10.1007/978-3-030-03928-8_1

face this problem and also GLARE has been extended to cope with comorbid patients. In this paper we focus on interaction detection. In [5] we developed an ontology for interactions, and complemented it with detection algorithms. Interactions between CIGs occurs *over time*. Indeed, the effects of two actions taken from different guidelines can practically conflict only if the times of execution of such actions are such that their effects overlap in time. In [6] we proposed an explicit treatment of temporal constraints and of temporal reasoning in GLARE. However, such previous approaches disregard the fact that temporal constraints may have different *probabilities*, and such probabilities may be important for physicians to correctly analyze and manage interactions.

Our running example considers drug interactions. Several aspects influence the absorption of a drug, and therefore its effects. In particular, they are influenced by the methods of administration (e.g., enteral, parenteral, transcutaneous...) of the drug, by its mechanisms of absorption and elimination, and by the targets of the administered substance. The fields in medicine that study such mechanisms are the pharmacokinetics and pharmacodynamics. It integrates a pharmacokinetic and a pharmacodynamic model component into one set of mathematical expressions that allows the description of the time course of effect intensity in response to administration of a drug dose. Deriving from such mathematical expressions the probabilities of the effects of a drug along time is difficult. As an approximation, we have considered the models of the plasma concentrations of the drugs, their half-life (i.e., the time to reduce the substance amount in the blood of 50%) and the type of the effect, and we approximate the probabilities with the help of an expert.

Example 1. Consider, for instance, a patient affected by gastroesophageal reflux (GR) and by urinary tract infection (UTI). The CIG for GR may recommend calcium carbonate administration (CCA; assumed to be punctual at the chosen temporal granularity), to be administered within three hours. CCA has the effect of decreasing gastric absorption (DGA). Considering as *granularity units of 15 min*, DGA can start after 1 unit with probability 0.4, after 2 with probability 0.4, and after 3, with probability 0.2. Additionally, the duration of DGA may be 4 units (probability 0.1), 5 (0.3), 6 (0.4), 7 (0.1), or 8 (0.1). The CIG for UTI may recommend Nalidixic acid administration (NAA), to be administered within two hours. NAA has as effect Nalidixic acid gastric absorption (NAGA), starting after 1 unit (probability 0.4) or 2 (probability 0.6). The duration of NAGA may be 1 (probability 0.05), 2 (0.05), 3 (0.15), 4 (0.15), 5 (0.25), 6 (0.25), 7 (0.05), 8 (0.05). ∎

In order to support physicians in the study of the interaction between CCA and NAA, one must take into account not only the temporal constraints, but also their probabilities. This is essential in order to answer physician's queries such as:

(Q1) *If I perform on the patient CCA in unit 1 or 2 (i.e., in the following 30 min), and NAA in units 1 or 2 (i.e., in the following 30 min), what is the probability that the effects of such two actions intersect in time (i.e., what is the probability of the interaction between CCA and NAA)?*

In the following, we sketch our ongoing approach to support physicians in the management of probabilistic temporal interaction detection. This is the first approach in the literature managing such a challenging task. Specifically, to the best of our knowledge, our approach is the first one that:

(1) Introduces *probabilistic quantitative temporal constraints*, and provide a *constraint propagation algorithm* to reason with them
(2) Identifies a comprehensive *query language* operating on such constraints
(3) Provides a support to *evaluate the queries*
(4) Proposes the introduction of such mechanisms (which are domain independent) in the analysis of *temporal interactions* between guidelines.

Notably, while contribution (1) already appeared in a recent work [7], results (2–4) are entirely new contributions of this paper.

2 Background and Related Work

Temporal Constraints and Temporal Reasoning. Informally speaking, temporal constraints are limitations of the possible time of occurrence of events. *Quantitative* temporal constraints involve *metric time* and are very frequent in many application domains. They include *dates* (e.g., "John arrived on 10/10/99 at 10:00"), *durations* (e.g., "John worked for 3 h") and *delays* (e.g., "John arrived 10 min after Mary"). *Qualitative* temporal constraints concern the relative position of events (e.g., "John arrived at work after Mary (arrived)"). Notably, in many cases, temporal constraints are *not exact* (e.g., "John arrived between 10 and 30 min after Mary"). A plethora of approaches has been developed within the AI community to deal with quantitative temporal constraints (see, e.g., the survey in [8]). However, all of them agree that, given a set of temporal constraints, *temporal reasoning* is fundamental for different tasks, including to check their *consistency*, to find a *scenario* (i.e., a solution: an instantiation of all events such that all constraints are satisfied), to make explicit the *tightest* implied constraints, and\or to *answer queries* about the (explicit plus implied) constraints. Notably, while in several task (e.g., in scheduling) the goal is to find a *scenario*, in others, such as *decision support* (which is the context of our work), the *minimal network* (representing the tightest temporal constraints) must be determined, to provide users with a compact representation of all the possible solutions (since the choice of a specific solution must be left to the users).
A well-known and widely used framework to cope with quantitative temporal constraints is STP (Simple Temporal Problem [9]). In STP, constraints have the form $P_i[l, u]P_j$, where P_i and P_j denote time points, and l and u (l $\leq$ u) are integer numbers, stating that the *temporal distance between P_i and P_j ranges between l and u*. In most AI approaches, temporal reasoning is based on two operations on temporal constraints: *intersection* and *composition*. Given two constraints C1 and C2 between two temporal entities A and B, temporal intersection (henceforth $\cap$) determines the most constraining relation between A and B (e.g., A[20,40]B $\cap$ A[30,50]B $\rightarrow$ A[30,40]B). On the other hand, given a constraint C1 between A and B and a constraint C2 between B and C, composition (@) gives the resulting constraint between A and C (e.g., A[20,40] B @ B[10,20]C $\rightarrow$ A[30,60]C).

In STP, constraint propagation can be performed taking advantage of the possibility of representing temporal constraints as a graph, and applying Floyd-Warshall's *all-pairs shortest path* algorithm (see below, where $\lambda(i,j)$ denotes the constraint between two time points i and j).

```
for k:=1 to n do
  for i:=1 to n do
    for j:=1 to n do
      λ(i,j)= λ(i,j) ∩ (λ(i,k) @λ(k,j))
```

As discussed in [9], Floyd-Warshall's algorithm is *correct* and *complete* on STP, operates in cubic time, and provides as output the **minimal network** of the input constraints, i.e., the tightest equivalent STP, or an inconsistency (in case a negative cycle is detected).

In the last two decades, many approaches have realized that, in many domains, "crisp" temporal constraints are not enough, since *preferences* or *probabilities* have to be considered. An important mainstream of research in this area (in which our approach is located) has focused specifically on the representation of *"non-crisp" temporal constraints*, and on the **propagation** of such constraints. Concerning **qualitative** constraints, in their seminal work Badaloni and Giacomin [10] have defined a new formalism in which the "crisp" qualitative temporal relations in Allen's Interval Algebra are associated with a degree of *plausibility,* and have proposed temporal reasoning algorithms to propagate such constraints. Ryabov et al. [11] attach a *probability* to each of Allen's basic interval relations. A similar probabilistic approach has been proposed more recently by Mouhoub and Liu [12], as an adaptation of the general probabilistic CSP framework. *"Non-crisp" quantitative temporal constraints* have been considered by Khatib et al. [13], that extended the STP and the TCSP framework [9] to consider temporal *preferences*. An analogous approach has been recently proposed in [14]. However, until now, no approach has been developed to cope with both *quantitative temporal constraints* and *probabilities*, and to perform *query answering* on them.

CIG Interaction Detection. In short, our approach is *the only approach in the CIG literature focusing on the **temporal** detection of CIG interactions.* Indeed, most of the CIG approaches to comorbidities do not even focus on interaction detection: they simply assume that the possible interactions are identified a-priori by physicians, and focus on how to merge the CIGs in such a way that the interactions are avoided or managed. As a remarkable exception, [15] exploits ontological knowledge and domain-independent general rules to support the *automatic detection of interactions* between (the effects of) medical actions. However, in [15] *no temporal analysis* is performed to check whether such interactions can effectively occur during the treatment of a specific patient. In our GLARE approach, a similar methodology has been devised, extending it with the possibility of *performing the temporal analysis of interactions* [6], and a methodology to support physicians in their management [16]. However, our temporal approach in [6] only considers "crisp" temporal constraints, so that the approach can only warn physicians whether an interaction certainly occurs, possibly occurs, or cannot occur, while physicians in several cases would prefer a "finer" support, considering also the probability of such occurrences. This is the task of the work in this paper.

3 Representing and Reasoning with Probabilistic Temporal Constraints

In [7] we proposed an extension of *quantitative* (i.e., metric) temporal constraints of STP [9] to support the possibility to associate preferences between alternative constraints in the form of probabilities. The distances between two points (denoting the starting\ending points of events) are a **convex** and **discrete** set of alternatives, from a minimum to a maximum distance. A probability is associated with each distance.

Definition 1. Probabilistic Quantitative Temporal Constraint (PQTC). Let $t_i, t_j \in Z$ be time points. A PQTC between t_i and t_j is a constraint of the form $t_i <(d_1, p_1), ..., (d_n, p_n)> t_j$, where (i) $p_1, ..., p_n \in \Re$ are probabilities ($0 \leq p_1 \leq 1, ..., 0 \leq p_n \leq 1$), (ii) $d_1, ..., d_n \in Z$ are distances, and (iii) $\Sigma\, p_1, ..., p_n = 1$.   ∎

The intended *meaning* of a constraint $t_i <(d_1, p_1), ..., (d_n, p_n)> t_j$ is that the *distance* $t_j - t_i$ between t_j and t_i is d_1 with probability p_1, or ... or d_n with probability p_n.

Note. In PQTCs, we assume that the distances $d_1, ..., d_n$ are ordered.

A PQTC $t_i <(d_1, p_1), ..., (d_n, p_n)> t_j$ can be graphically represented by an directed arc labelled $<(d_1, p_1), ..., (d_n, p_n)>$ connecting two nodes N_i and N_j, representing the time points t_i and t_j respectively.

Definition 2. Probabilistic Temporal Network (PTN). Given a set $V = \{t_1, ..., t_n\}$ of time points, a Probabilistic Temporal Network (over V) is a set of probabilistic quantitative temporal constraints over V. It can be graphically represented by a directed graph.   ∎

Figure 1 shows the graphical representation of the PTN modelling Example 1. S(X) and E(X) stand for the start and the end of a durative event X.

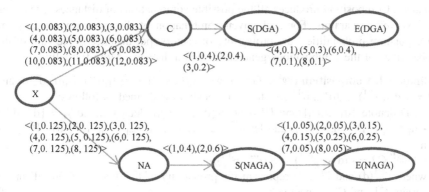

Fig. 1. PTN of Example 1. (Colour image online)

3.1   Temporal Reasoning on PTNs

Our representation model is basically an extension of STP [9] (considering discrete values for the distances) to include probabilities. We can thus perform STP-like temporal reasoning, adopting Floyd-Warshall's algorithm. However, we had to adapt it to apply to PTNs, by properly instantiating the operators $\cap$ and @ in the algorithm Floyd-Warshall's algorithm with two new operators ($\cap^P$ and @^{P}) operating not only on distances, but also on probabilities. Considering distances only, both our intersection and composition operators work as the STP operators. However, they also evaluate the probabilities of the output distances. For technical (computational complexity) reasons, we assume the probabilistic independence of the constraints.

The operator *intersection* $\cap^P$ is used to "merge" two constraints $C1 = <(d_1,p^{d1})$, ..., $(d_n,p^{dn})>$ and $C2 = <(d'_1,p^{d'1}),...,(d'_m, p^{d'm})>$ *concerning the same pair of time points*. The set intersection between the two input sets of distances is computed as in STP. The probabilities of each distance belonging to both input constraints are multiplied, and the resulting probabilities are then normalized to sum-up to 1. The formal definition is given below.

Definition 3. Intersection ($\cap^P$). Given two PQTCs $C1 = <(d_1,p^{d1}),..., <(d_n,p^{dn})>$ and $C2 = <(d'_1,p^{d'1}),...,(d'_m, p^{d'm})>$ their intersection is defined as follows:

let $\{d''_1,...,d''_k\} = \{d_1,...,d_n\} \cap \{d'_1,...,d'_m\}$, then

$C1 \cap^P C2 = Normal(< d''_1, P^{C1}(d''_1) \cdot P^{C2}(d''_1)),..., (d''_k, P^{C1}(d''_k) \cdot P^{C2}(d''_k)) >)$

where $P^{C1}(d)$ and $P^{C2}(d)$ represent the probability of the distance d in the constraint C1 and C2 respectively, and $Normal(<(d_1,p_1),...,(d_n,p_n)>) = <(d_1,p_1 /(p_1 + ...+p_n)),..., (d_n,p_n /(p_1 + ...+p_n))>$ ∎

Example 2. *NAA<(2, 0.02), (3, 0.05), (4, 0.09), (5, 0.15), (6, 0.19), (7, 0.25), (8, 0.17), (9, 0.05), (10, 0.03)>E(NAGA)* $\cap$ *NAA<(8, 0.1), (9, 0.2), (10, 0.4), (11, 0.3)>E(NAGA)→ NAA<(8, 0.132), (9, 0.775), (10, 0.093)>E(NAGA)* ∎

The composition operator @^{P} is used to infer the constraint between two time points t_i and t_j, given the constraint C1 between t_i and t_k and the constraint C2 between t_k and t_j. As in STP, output distances are evaluated as the pairwise sums of the input distances. Composition produces all the possible combinations of distances taken from the involved constraints. For each given combination of distances we multiply the corresponding probabilities; the probability of each output distance is the sum of the probabilities of the combinations generating such a distance. More formally:

Definition 4. Composition (@^{P}). Given two PQTCs $C1 = <(d_1,p^{d1}),...,(d_n,p^{dn})>$ and $C2 = <(d'_1,p^{d'1}),...,(d'_m, p^{d'm})>$, their composition is defined as follows:

let D denote $\{d_1,...,d_n\}$ and D' denote $\{d'_1,...,d'_m\}$, let $\{d''_1,...,d''_r\} = \{d'': d'' = d_i + d_j \wedge d_i \in D \wedge d_j \in D'\}$, and let $p^{d''} = \Sigma_{d \in D,d' \in D': d+d'=d''+d'=d''} (P^{C1}(d) \cdot P^{C2}(d'))$, then

$C1$ @^{P} $C2 = <(d''_1, p^{d''1}), ..., (d''_r, p^{d''r})>$,

where $P^{C1}(d)$ and $P^{C2}(d')$ represent the probability of the distance d and d' in the constraint C1 and C2 respectively. ∎

Example 3. For example, the composition of the constraint between NAA and the start of NAGA with the one between the start and the end of NAGA gives as result the constraint between NAA and the end of NAGA:

NAA<$(1, 0.4)$, $(2, 0.6)$>S(NAGA) @ S(NAGA)<$(1, 0.05)$, $(2, 0.05)$, $(3, 0.15)$, $(4, 0.15)$, $(5, 0.25)$, $(6, 0.25)$, $(7, 0.05)$, $(8, 0.05)$>E(NAGA) $\rightarrow$ NAA<$(2, 0.02)$, $(3, 0.05)$, $(4, 0.09)$, $(5, 0.15)$, $(6, 0.19)$, $(7, 0.25)$, $(8, 0.17)$, $(9, 0.05)$, $(10, 0.03)$>E(NAGA) ∎

Finally, temporal reasoning on a PTN is achieved by Floyd-Warshall's algorithm in Fig. 1, in which ∩ and @ are replaced by our operators ∩^{P} and @^{P} respectively. It computes the minimal network, i.e., the strictest temporal constraints (and their probabilities) between each pair of temporal entities (nodes in the PTN).

Example 4. In the *minimal network*, the constraint between S(DGA) and S(NAGA) is: S(DGA)<$(-13, 0.000003)$, $(-12, 0,00006)$, $(-11, 0.0005)$, $(-10, 0.00218)$, $(-9, 0.0067)$, $(-8, 0.01618)$, $(-7, 0.0328)$, $(-6, 0.05775)$, $(-5, 0.08877)$, $(-4, 0.11784)$, $(-3, 0.1353)$, $(-2, 0.13862)$, $(-1, 0.12964)$, $(0, 0.10739)$, $(1, 0.07651)$, $(2, 0.04689)$, $(3, 0.025239)$, $(4, 0.01167)$, $(5, 0.00444)$, $(6, 0.00127)$, $(7, 0.000234)$, $(8, 0,00002)$>E(NAGA). ∎

4 Querying Probabilistic Temporal Constraints

We provide users with facilities to query the minimal network. We propose the syntax of our query language in *Backus-Naur Form* (augmented with the meta-symbol $^+$ to denote non-empty lists), and then we describe our query answering mechanism.

The basic entities on which query operates are events E. They may be instantaneous (E_I; e.g., NAA) or durative (E_D; in such a case, they are started and ended by an instantaneous event – e.g., S(DGA), E(DGA)).

$$\mathbf{E} :: \, = \, \mathbf{E_D} | \mathbf{E_I}$$

Queries may concern *qualitative relations* (R) between such events. Since we consider both instantaneous and durative events, we consider the relations in Vilain's algebra [17], which include Allen's relations (R_D), but also relations between instantaneous events (R_I), and relations between instantaneous and durative (R_M). We add the relation INTERSECT, which is important in the interaction detection task.

R ::= R₁ | Rₘ | R_D
R₁ ::= < | = | > | ≤ | ≥ | ≠ | <=>
Rₘ ::= •BEFORE|•STARTS|•DURING|•ENDS|•AFTER
      R_D ::= BEFORE|MEETS|OVERLAPS|ENDED-BY|CONTAINS|
      STARTS|EQUAL|STARTED-BY|DURING|ENDS|
      OVERLAPPED-BY|MET-BY|AFTER|DISJOINT|INTERSECTS

We support both "simple" (Q_S) and hypothetical (Q_H) queries. In turn, "simple" queries can be divided into (i) extraction (Q_E), (ii) qualitative probabilistic (Q_P), and (iii) Boolean probabilistic (Q_B) queries.

$$Q :: = Q_S | Q_H$$

$$Q_S :: = Q_E | Q_P | Q_B$$

Extraction Queries. Trivially, given a set of pairs of events, such queries give as output the probabilistic temporal constraints between each pair, taken from the minimal network.

$$Q_E :: = \{ <E, E >^+ \}?$$

Example 5. For example, the query (Q2) asks for the temporal constraints (and their probabilities) between the start of DGA and the start of NAGA.

(Q2): *{S(DGA),S(NAGA)}?*   ∎

Qualitative Probabilistic Queries. They ask the probability of a qualitative temporal relation between two events.

$$Q_P :: = \mathbf{prob}(A_R)?$$

$$A_R :: = E_I \, R_I \, E_I | E_I \, R_M \, E_D | E_D \, R_D \, E_D$$

Example 6. Physicians can ask (given the constraints in Example 1) what is the probability that the effects of CCA and NAA intersect in time (i.e., what is the probability of the interaction between CCA and NAA) through the query (Q3).

(Q3) *Prob(DGA(INTERSECT)NAGA).*   ∎

Boolean Probabilistic Queries. These queries ask whether the probability of a qualitative relation A_R (as above) is $<, >, =, \leq, \geq$ or $\neq$ with respect to a given probability P.

$$Q_B :: = \mathbf{Prob}(A_R)\mathbf{Op}\, P?$$

Example 7. The query (Q4) asks whether the probability that DGA starts before NAGA are greater than 0.5.

(Q4) **(Prob(*S(DGA)* > *S(NAGA)*)) > 0.5)**   ∎

Hypothetical Queries. Such queries are "simple" (i.e., extraction, qualitative probabilistic or Boolean probabilistic) queries to be answered in the context in which a set of PQTCs (denoted by C^+ in the BNF below) is assumed.

$$Q_H:: = Q_S \text{ if } \{C^+\}$$

Example 8. The query (Q1) in the introduction can be expressed as:

(Q1') *Prob(DGA(INTERSECT)NAGA) if {X_0<(1,0. 5),(2,0. 5)>CAA, X_0<(1,0.5), (2,0.5)>NAA}*   ∎

4.1   Query Evaluation

The minimal network of the PTN (henceforth MN) must be available to answer queries. Thus, if it is not available, it must be computed, as discussed in Sect. 3.

(1) Extraction queries. Given the MN, such queries can be answered by returning to the user the constraints in the MN concerning the events specified in the query.

Example 9. The output of query Q2 is the constraint shown in Example 4.   ∎

(2) Qualitative probabilistic queries. To evaluate a probabilistic query, we first have to define the probabilities of the relationships between instantaneous events.

Given two any instantaneous events e_1 and e_2, and given the temporal constraint $e_1 < (d_1, p_1), \ldots, (d_k, p_k) > e_2$, we indicate with $\varphi(d_i)$ the probability of the distance d_i (i.e., $\varphi(d_i) = p_i$). The probabilities are evaluated as below. For example, since $e_1 < (d_1, p_1), \ldots, (d_k, p_k) > e_2$ states that the possible distances of e_2 with respect to e_1 are $d_1, \ldots, d_k$, e_2 precedes e_1 for all the distances $d_i \in \{d_1, \ldots, d_k\}$ such that $d_i > 0$. Therefore the probability **Prob$(e_2 > e_1)$** is the sum of the probabilities of such distances.

Definition 5. Given a constraint $e_1 < (d_1, p_1), \ldots, (d_k, p_k) > e_2$

  Prob$(e_2 > e_1)$ = $\Sigma_{d_i > 0} \, \varphi(d_i)$ if $\exists d_i \in \{d_1, \ldots, d_k\}$ such that $d_i > 0$ (0 otherwise)

  Prob$(e_2 = e_1)$ = $\varphi(0)$ if $0 \in \{d_1, \ldots, d_k\}$ (0 otherwise)

  Prob$(e_2 < e_1)$ = $\Sigma_{d_i < 0} \, \varphi(d_i)$ if $\exists d_i \in \{d_1, \ldots, d_k\}$ such that $d_i < 0$ (0 otherwise) ∎

Example 10. Given the MN in Example 4, Prob(S(DGA) > S(NAGA)) = 0.166273.   ∎

The probabilities of "ambiguous" relationships between instantaneous events can be simply evaluated on the basis of the definition above, as the sum of the probabilities of the alternative basic relationships that constitute them.

Definition 6.

  Prob$(t_2 \geq t_1)$ = **Prob$(t_2 > t_1)$** + **Prob$(t_2 = t_1)$**

  Prob$(t_2 \neq t_1)$ = **Prob$(t_2 > t_1)$** + **Prob$(t_2 < t_1)$**

  Prob$(t_2 \leq t_1)$ = **Prob$(t_2 < t_1)$** + **Prob$(t_2 = t_1)$**   ∎

The probabilities of atomic temporal relations between two durative events e_1 and e_2 can consequently be evaluated as shown in Definition 7 (the probabilities of the qualitative relations between an instantaneous and a durative event can be defined in a similar way, and are omitted for the sake of brevity).   ∎

Definition 7.

$Prob(e_i(BEFORE)e_j) = Prob((end(e_i)+1) < start(e_j))$

$Prob(e_i(MEETS)e_j) = Prob((end(e_i)+1) = start(e_j))$

$Prob(e_i(OVERLAPS)e_j) = Prob(start(e_i) < start(e_j)) \cdot Prob(end(e_i) \geq start(e_j)) \cdot Prob(end(e_i) < end(e_j))$

$Prob(e_i(ENDED\text{-}BY)e_j) = Prob(start(e_i) < start(e_j)) \cdot Prob(end(e_i) = end(e_j))$

$Prob(e_i(CONTAINS)e_j) = Prob(start(e_i) < start(e_j)) \cdot Prob(end(e_i) > end(e_j))$

$Prob(e_i(STARTS)e_j) = Prob(start(e_i) = start(e_j)) \cdot Prob(end(e_i) < end(e_j))$

$Prob(e_i(EQUAL)e_j) = Prob(start(e_i) = start(e_j)) \cdot Prob(end(e_i) = end(e_j))$

$Prob(e_i(STARTED\text{-}BY)e_j) = Prob(start(e_i) = start(e_j)) \cdot Prob(end(e_i) > end(e_j))$

$Prob(e_i(DURING)e_j) = Prob(start(e_i) > start(e_j)) \cdot Prob(end(e_i) < end(e_j))$

$Prob(e_i(ENDS)e_j) = Prob(start(e_i) > start(e_j)) \cdot Prob(end(e_i) = end(e_j))$

$Prob(e_i(OVERLAPPED\text{-}BY)e_j) = Prob(start(e_i) > start(e_j)) \cdot Prob(start(e_i) \leq end(e_j)) \cdot Prob(end(e_i) > end(e_j))$

$Prob(e_i(MET\text{-}BY)e_j) = Prob((end(e_j)+1) = start(e_i))$

$Prob(e_i(AFTER)e_j) = Prob((end(e_j)+1) < start(e_i))$

$Prob(e_i(INTERSECTS)e_j) = Prob(start(e_j) \leq start(e_i)) \cdot Prob(start(e_i) \leq end(e_j)) + Prob(start(e_i) \leq start(e_j)) \cdot Prob(start(e_j) \leq end(e_i)) - Prob(start(e_i) \leq start(e_j)) \cdot Prob(start(e_i) \leq end(e_j)) \cdot Prob(start(e_j) \leq start(e_i)) \cdot Prob(start(e_j) \leq end(e_i)))$. ∎

Example 11. Given the MN for the constraints in Example 1, Prob(DGA(DURING) NAGA) = 0.085, and Prob(DGA(INTERSECT)NAGA) = 0.995 ∎

(3) **Boolean probabilistic queries**. Given the MN, such queries can be answered by evaluating the probability of the qualitative relation (as above), and comparing it with the probability in the query.

(4) **Hypothetical queries**. To answer hypothetical queries:

(1) First, the "hypothesized" temporal constraints in $\{C^+\}$ are added to the MN (through the intersection with previous temporal constraints; see Sect. 3.1)

(2) Temporal reasoning is performed (through Floyd-Warshall's algorithm), producing a new MN

(3) The probability of the conditions (left part of the query) is evaluated in the new MN, as discussed above.

Example 12. The evaluation of the query (Q4) above requires the addition of the constraints $\{X_0 <(1, 0.5),(2, 0.5) > CAA, X_0 < (1, 0.5),(2, 0.5)> NAA\}$ into the MN, and a new propagation. The result of the query is: **0.9943**.

5   Probabilistic Temporal Detection of Interactions

Though our temporal approach is domain-independent, we designed it with specific attention to the GLARE application. When executing multiple guidelines on a comorbid patient, physicians can adopt GLARE's facilities to study possible interactions between treatments. During the acquisition phase the temporal constraints and their probabilities are acquired jointly by expert physicians and knowledge engineers. Several aspects influence the absorption of a drug and its effects. Pharmacokinetics and pharmacodynamics study such mechanisms. It integrates a pharmacokinetic and a pharmacodynamic model component into a set of mathematical expressions that allows the description of the effect intensity in time w.r.t. the administration of a drug dose. Deriving from such mathematical expressions the probabilities of the effects of a drug along time could be difficult. As a first approximation, we considered the models of the plasma concentrations of the drugs, their half-life (i.e., the time to halve the drug amount in the blood) and the type of the effect, and we have approximated the probabilities with the help of medical experts.

At each time during the execution, physicians can trigger GLARE's interaction analysis mechanism to check whether interactions may arise among the next actions to be executed in the guidelines. Probabilistic temporal reasoning is used to check not only whether interactions are temporally possible, but also their probabilities. The output of temporal reasoning is a complex network of PQTCs. For example, in the case of our running example, we have a set of constraints like the one in Example 4 above, one for each pair of instantaneous events (or starting\ending points of durative events). Obviously, the MN is hard to understand. Thus, we consider our query language an essential support for physicians. To facilitate them, we also provide a graphical interface, which makes the formulation of queries more user-friendly. Indeed, the physicians working in the GLARE project asked us for a temporal support to cope with two main situations:

(1) *They are already executing one or more therapies on a patient. Focusing on the next actions, they analyze whether interactions are temporally possible.*
(2) *They are going to choose among alternative therapies in a guideline, and they want to analyze the alternatives to check whether they may interact with the other therapies currently in execution for the patient.*

Situation (1). In such a context, queries in general, and "INTERSECTS" queries (hypothetical or not) in particular, are very helpful. Notably, probabilities are very important, since physicians tend to accept interactions having low probabilities (indeed, all drugs, even considered in isolation, have a list of –not highly probable– undesirable side effects). In such a context, also hypothetical temporal queries are very useful: physicians exploit such a facility to check whether they can decrease the probabilities of interactions by executing actions at "proper" times. In our running example, the query Q1 can be expressed by physicians (through a graphical interface) as Q1' in Example 8, and the output would be the probability **0.9943**. Given the high probability, physicians may still try to see whether, choosing specific execution times for some actions, such a probability can be decreased. For example, physicians might ask a query like Q5 (to check the probability of interaction in case NAA is executed in the first 30 min, and CAA between two and three hours from the current time):

(Q5) **Prob(DGA(INTERSECTS)NAGA)**
    if $\{X_0 <(1, 0.5),(2, 0.5) > NAA, X_0 < (9, 0.25),(10, 0.25), (11, 0.25),(12, 0.25)>$ CAA}

The output probability is **0.02455**, suggesting to the physicians that the probability of interaction sharply decreases if they delay the execution of CAA. Notably, using "crisp" temporal constraints, physicians could only know that an interaction may occur, both in case CAA is executed within the first 30 min, and in case it is executed after two or three hours.

Situation (2). From the point of view of our support, situation (2) is similar to situation (1) above. Simply, physicians have to iterate the checking process on each one of the alternatives that they think can be appropriate for the patient at hand.

6   Conclusions and Future Work

Dealing and reasoning with temporal information in CIGs is an important issue [2]. In our previous works we coped with temporal reasoning problems and in particular with temporal indeterminacy in the areas of CIGs [6, 18] and relational databases [19, 20]. In this paper, we have proposed the first approach for reasoning and query answering about probabilistic quantitative temporal constraints, and its application within the GLARE project, for the analysis of the interactions between guidelines. Preliminary tests conducted with the physicians cooperating in the GLARE project show that they appreciate a probabilistic approach (with respect to "traditional" "crisp" approaches, that can only say whether an interaction is certain, possible or impossible). The development of "physician-friendly" graphical facilities to acquire, treat and query probabilistic temporal constraints, and a more extensive evaluation with other physicians are two of the main goals of our future work.

References

1. Ten Teije, A., Miksch, S., Lucas, P. (eds.): Computer-Based Medical Guidelines and Protocols: A Primer and Current Trends. IOS Press, Amsterdam (2008)
2. Peleg, M.: Computer-interpretable clinical guidelines: a methodological review. J. Biomed. Inform. **46**, 744–763 (2013)
3. Terenziani, P., Molino, G., Torchio, M.: A modular approach for representing and executing clinical guidelines. Artif. Intell. Med. **23**, 249–276 (2001)
4. Bottrighi, A., Terenziani, P.: META-GLARE: a meta-system for defining your own computer interpretable guideline system - architecture and acquisition. Artif. Intell. Med. **72**, 22–41 (2016)
5. Piovesan, L., Anselma, L., Terenziani, P.: Temporal detection of guideline interactions. In: Proceedings of HEALTHINF 2015, Part of BIOSTEC 2015, pp. 40–50 (2015)
6. Anselma, L., Piovesan, L., Terenziani, P.: Temporal detection and analysis of guideline interactions. Artif. Intell. Med. **76**, 40–62 (2017)
7. Terenziani, P., Andolina, A.: Probabilistic quantitative temporal reasoning. In: Proceedings of Symposium on Applied Computing, pp. 965–970. ACM (2017)
8. Schwalb, E., Vila, L.: Temporal constraints: a survey. Constraints **3**, 129–149 (1998)
9. Dechter, R., Meiri, I., Pearl, J.: Temporal constraint networks. Artif. Intell. **49**, 61–95 (1991)
10. Badaloni, S., Giacomin, M.: The algebra IAfuz: a framework for qualitative fuzzy temporal reasoning. Artif. Intell. **170**, 872–908 (2006)

11. Ryabov, V., Trudel, A.: Probabilistic temporal interval networks. In: Proceedings of TIME 2004, pp. 64–67. IEEE (2004)

12. Mouhoub, M., Liu, J.: Managing uncertain temporal relations using a probabilistic interval algebra. In: Proceedings of IEEE International Conference on Systems, Man and Cybernetics, pp. 3399–3404 (2008)

13. Khatib, L., Morris, P., Morris, R., Rossi, F.: Temporal constraint reasoning with preferences. In: Proceedings of IJCAI 2001, pp. 322–327. Morgan Kaufmann (2001)

14. Terenziani, P., Andolina, A., Piovesan, L.: Managing temporal constraints with preferences: representation, reasoning, and querying. IEEE Trans. Knowl. Data Eng. **29**, 2067–2071 (2017)

15. Zamborlini, V., da Silveira, M., Pruski, C., ten Teije, A., van Harmelen, F.: Towards a conceptual model for enhancing reasoning about clinical guidelines. In: Miksch, S., Riaño, D., ten Teije, A. (eds.) KR4HC 2014. LNCS (LNAI), vol. 8903, pp. 29–44. Springer, Cham (2014). https://doi.org/10.1007/978-3-319-13281-5_3

16. Piovesan, Luca, Terenziani, Paolo: A constraint-based approach for the conciliation of clinical guidelines. In: Montes-y-Gómez, Manuel, Escalante, Hugo Jair, Segura, Alberto, Murillo, Juan de Dios (eds.) IBERAMIA 2016. LNCS (LNAI), vol. 10022, pp. 77–88. Springer, Cham (2016). https://doi.org/10.1007/978-3-319-47955-2_7

17. Vilain, M.: A system for reasoning about time. In: Waltz, D.L. (ed.) Proceedings of AAAI 82, Pittsburgh, PA, 18–20 August 1982, pp. 197–201. AAAI Press (1982)

18. Anselma, L., Bottrighi, A., Montani, S., Terenziani, P.: Managing proposals and evaluations of updates to medical knowledge: theory and applications. J. Biomed. Inform. **46**, 363–376 (2013)

19. Anselma, L., Piovesan, L., Terenziani, P.: A 1NF temporal relational model and algebra coping with valid-time temporal indeterminacy. J. Intell. Inf. Syst. **47**, 345–374 (2016)

20. Anselma, L., Stantic, B., Terenziani, P., Sattar, A.: Querying now-relative data. J. Intell. Inf. Syst. **41**, 285–311 (2013)

An AI Approach to Temporal Indeterminacy in Relational Databases

Luca Anselma[1(✉)], Luca Piovesan[2], and Paolo Terenziani[2]

[1] Dipartimento di Informatica, Università di Torino,
Corso Svizzera 185, 10149 Turin, Italy
anselma@di.unito.it
[2] DISIT, Università del Piemonte Orientale "A. Avogadro", Alessandria, Italy
{luca.piovesan,paolo.terenziani}@uniupo.it

Abstract. Time is pervasive of the human way of approaching reality, so that it has been widely studied in many research areas, including Artificial Intelligence (AI) and *relational* Temporal Databases (TDB). Indeed, while thousands of TDB papers have been devoted to the treatment of determinate time, only few approaches have faced temporal indeterminacy (i.e., "don't know exactly when" indeterminacy). In this paper, we propose a new AI-based methodology to approach temporal indeterminacy in relational DBs. We show that typical AI techniques, such as studying the *semantics* of the *representation formalism*, and adopting *symbolic manipulation* techniques based on such a semantics, are very important in the treatment of indeterminate time in relational databases.

Keywords: Temporal data · Data representation and semantics
Query semantics · Symbolic manipulation

1 Introduction

Time is pervasive of our way of dealing with reality. As a consequence, time has been widely studied in many areas, including AI and DBs. In particular, the scientific DB community agrees that time has a special status with respect to the other data, so that its treatment within a *relational* database context requires dedicated techniques [1, 2]. A plethora of dedicated approaches has been developed in the area of temporal relational databases (TDB in the following; see, e.g., [3, 4]). Different data models, and algebraic operations to query them, have been introduced in the literature. However, to the best of our knowledge, no TDB approach has explicitly identified the fact that, while adding time to a relational DB, one adds ***implicit knowledge*** (i.e., the semantics of time) in it. This is particularly true in case temporal indeterminacy is considered (i.e., "*don't know exactly when*" indeterminacy [5]), since no TDB approach makes all the alternative cases explicit. In this paper we argue that, since a high degree of implicit information is present in temporally indeterminate DB data, a temporal indeterminate DB is indeed close to a (simplified) knowledge base, so that AI techniques are important to properly cope with it. In this paper, we propose an AI-based methodology to deal with temporal indeterminacy:

© Springer Nature Switzerland AG 2018
G. R. Simari et al. (Eds.): IBERAMIA 2018, LNAI 11238, pp. 16–28, 2018.
https://doi.org/10.1007/978-3-030-03928-8_2

(i)   We formally define and extend the *snapshot semantics* [2] to cope also with temporal indeterminacy,

(ii)   We propose a 1NF **representation model** for *"interval-based"* temporal indeterminacy

(iii) We analyse the **semantics** of the representation model, showing that (at least) two alternatives are possible

(iv)   We define the relational algebraic operators (which perform **symbolic manipulation** on the model) to query the representational model, for both the alternative semantics, showing that only with one of them it is possible to devise a relational algebra which is both *closed* with respect to the model and *correct* with respect to the semantics.

Result (iv) enforces the core message of our approach: in TDBs, the representational model contains *implicit* (temporal) information. Thus, AI techniques could \should be used to analyse its *semantics*, and devise *algebraic operators* that perform *symbolic manipulation* on the representational model, *consistently* with the devised semantics.

2   Background

Most TDB approaches focus on individual occurrences of facts, whose time of occurrence (**valid time** [2]) is exactly known. However, in many real-world cases, the exact time of occurrence of facts is not known, and can only be approximated, so that *temporal indeterminacy* (i.e., in the TDB context, *"don't know exactly when"* indeterminacy [5]) has to be faced. Temporal indeterminacy is so important that "support for temporal indeterminacy" was already one of the eight explicit goals of the data types in TSQL2 consensus approach [2]. Despite its importance, and differently from the area of AI, in the area of TDBs only few approaches coping with temporal indeterminacy have been devised (see the surveys in [5, 6]).

Dyreson and Snodgrass [7] cope with valid-time indeterminacy by associating a period of indeterminacy with a tuple. A period of indeterminacy is a period between two indeterminate instants, each one consisting of a range of granules and of a probability distribution over it. However, in [7], no relational algebra is proposed to query temporally indeterminate data. Dekhtyar et al. [8] introduce temporal probabilistic tuples to cope with a quite specific form of temporal indeterminacy, concerning instantaneous events only, and provide algebraic relational operators. Anselma et al. [9, 10] identify different forms of temporal indeterminacy, and propose a family of achievable representational models and algebrae. However, such an approach is semantic-oriented, abstract and not in 1NF (thus not suitable for a direct implementation). A 1NF approach for a form of temporal indeterminacy has been proposed in [11], but no semantics for the model has been presented.

3   Snapshot Semantics for Temporal Relational Databases

A premise is very important, when starting a discussion about the *semantics* of temporal DBs. Indeed, seen from an AI perspective, a "traditional" non-temporal database is just an elicitation of all and only the facts that are true in the modeled mini-world. In such a sense, the semantics of a non-temporal DB is "trivial", since the DB does not contain any implicit data\information. Since the data is explicit, no "AI-style" reasoning mechanism is required, and query operators are used just to *extract* the relevant data from a DB. However, such an "easy" scenario changes when *time* is introduced into DBs, to associate each fact with the time when it holds (usually called *valid time* [2]). Roughly speaking, in such a case, eliciting explicitly all true facts would correspond to elicit, for each possible unit of time, all the facts that hold at that unit. Despite the extreme variety of TDB approaches in the literature, almost the totality of them is based, explicitly or (in many cases) implicitly, on this idea, commonly termed "*snapshot semantics*": a TDB is a set of "standard" (non-temporal) DBs, each one considering a snapshot of time, and eliciting all facts (tuples) that hold at that time (see, e.g., the "consensus" BCDM semantics, which is the semantics for TSQL2 and for many other TDB approaches [2]). Of course, for space and time efficiency reasons, no approach in the literature directly implements TDBs making all such data explicit: representational models are used to encode facts in a more compact and efficient form. Notably, this is a dramatic departure from "traditional" DB concepts: a *temporal* DB is no more an elicitation of all facts that hold in the modelled mini-world, but a compact *implicit* representation of them. Therefore, in this paper, we propose that the following "AI-style" methodological requirements must be taken into account. First,

(M1) *a semantics for making explicit the intended meaning of the representational models must be devised.*

In such a context, the algebraic query operators cannot simply select and extract data (since some data are implicit). Making all data explicit before\while answering queries is certainly not a good option (for the sake of space and time efficiency). Thus

(M2) *algebraic operators must operate on the (implicit) representation*
(M3) *algebraic operators must provide an output expressed in the given representation (i.e., the representation formalism must be closed with respect to the algebraic operators)*
(M4) *algebraic operators must be correct with respect to the semantics of the representation*

In the rest of this section, we provide a new "*functional*" way to describe the snapshot semantics for *determinate* time TDBs, that we later extend to *indeterminate* time in Sect. 4, as a starting point to realize the above AI-style methodology.

3.1   Data Semantics of Determinate Time DBs: A "Functional" Perspective

We first introduce the notion of tuple, relation, and database. We then move to the definition of time, and define the notion of (semantics of) a temporal database.

Definition 1. (non-temporal) Database, Relation, Tuple. A (non-temporal) relational database *DB* is a set of relations over the relational schema $\sigma = (R_1{:}s_i,\ldots, R_k{:}s_j)$ where

$s_i, ..., s_j \in S$ are the sorts of $R_1, ..., R_k$, respectively. A relation $R(x_1, ..., x_k){:}s$ of sort $s \in S$ is a sequence of attributes $x_1, ..., x_k$ each with values in a proper domain $D_1, ...D_k$. An instance $r(R{:}s)$ of a relation $R(x_1, ..., x_k)$ of sort $s \in S$ is a set $\{a_1, ..., a_n\}$ tuples, where each tuple a_i is a set $<v_1, ..., v_k>$ of values in $D \times ... \times D_k$.   ■

Notation. In the following, we denote by DB_σ the domain of all possible database instances over a schema σ.   ■

In AI, the ontology of time has attracted a lot of attention, and many different possibilities have been investigated. Some approaches, for instance, consider both points and intervals as basic time units (see, e.g., [12]), while in other approaches time points exist only as interval boundaries (see, e.g., [13]). Another important distinction regards time density: time can be represented as discrete, dense or continuous. Finally, time can be linear or branching. The review in [14] discusses in detail such aspects and compares the approaches coping with time in ontologies.

On the other hand, most TDB approaches, including TSQL2 [2], and the BCDM "consensus" semantics [2], simply assume that time is linear, discrete and bounded, and term *chronon* the basic time unit.

Definition 2. Temporal domain D_T. We assume a limited precision for time, and call *chronon* the basic time unit. The domain of chronons is finite, and totally ordered. The domain of valid times D_T is given as a set $D_T = \{c_1, ..., c_k\}$ of chronons.   ■

In the *snapshot semantics* [2], a TDB is a set of conventional (non-temporal) databases, one for each chronon of time. We formalize such a semantics through the introduction of a function, relating chronons with (non-temporal) databases.

Definition 3. Temporal database (semantic notion). Given a relational schema $\sigma = (R_1{:}s_i, ..., R_k{:}s_j)$ a temporal database DB^T is a function $f_{\sigma,DT}{:}\ D_T \rightarrow DB_\sigma$ ■

Analogously, a temporal relation r^T is a function from D_T to the set of tuples of r^T that hold at each chronon in D_T.

Definition 4. Time slice. Given a temporal database DB^T and a temporal relation r^T in DB^T, and given a chronon $c \in D_T$, we define the time slice of DB^T (denoted by $DB^T(c)$) and of r^T (denoted by $r^T(c)$) the result of the application of the functions DB^T and r^T to the chronon c.   ■

Example 1. Let us consider a simple database DB_1^T modeling patient symptoms. DB_1^T contains a unique relation SYM of schema <Patient, Symptom, Value> and contains two facts:

(f1) John had high fever from 10 to 12
(f2) Mary had moderate fever from 11 to 13

(in the example, we assume that chronons are at the granularity of hours, and hour 1 represents the first hour of 1/1/2018). The TDB (semantic notion) modeling such a state of affairs is the following (for clarity and simplicity, we omit the chronons in D^T for which no tuple holds, and we omit the name of the relation(s)).

10 → {<John, fever, high>}
11 → {<John, fever, high>, <Mary, fever, moderate>}
12 → {<John, fever, high>, <Mary, fever, moderate>}
13 → {<Mary, fever, moderate>}

In this example $DB_1^T(10) = SYM^T(10) = \{ <John, fever, high > \}$ ■

Notably, Definition 3 above is a purely "semantic" definition. Other definitions of the snapshot semantics for TDBs, such as the one in the "consensus" BCDM [2] model, are more "operational" and are closer to actual representations[1].

3.2 Query Semantics

In TDBs, the *semantic of queries* is commonly expressed in terms of ***relational algebraic operators***. Codd designated as complete any query language that was as expressive as his set of five relational algebraic operators: relational union ($\cup$), relational difference (–), selection (σ_P), projection (π_X), and Cartesian product ($\times$). Though different approaches have generalized such operators to cope also with TDBs, there is a common agreement that such operators should be a *consistent extension* of standard Codd's operators, and that they should be *reducible* to them in case time is removed (see, e.g., [2, 15]). In other words, temporal algebraic operators should behave exactly as Codd's non-temporal ones, at each point (chronon) of time. Given our definitions above, such a requirement can be formally stated as below.

Definition 5. Relational algebraic operators on determinate time databases ("semantic" notion). Denoting by Op^C a Codd's operator, and by Op^T its corresponding temporal operator, Op^T must be defined in such a way that the following holds:

$$\forall c \in D_T \left(Op^T(r^T, s^T) \right)(c) = Op^C(r^T(c), s^T(c)))$$ ■

(In Definition 5 above, we assume that r^T and s^T are temporal relations in a temporal database DB^T, and that Op is a binary operator. $r^T(c)$ represents the *time slice* of r^T at the chronon c. The definition of unary operators is analogous).

Of course, the "purely semantic" definition above is highly inefficient, as snapshots of the underlying relations at each single chronon have to be computed. Thus, more "operational" definitions of algebraic operators have been proposed in the literature. Notably, however, the "commonly agreed" BCDM definition of the semantics of algebraic operators is consistent with Definition 5 above.

3.3 Implementations of (Determinate Time) Temporal Databases

Different realizations of determinate time TDBs have been proposed in the literature. All of them (except few "pioneering" approaches) respect the above data and query semantics, and provide an efficient implementation for it. The large majority of such approaches enforce at least two key requirements to achieve efficiency: (i) *1NF is used to represent data, (ii) temporal algebraic operators directly manipulate the representation*.

---

[1] Indeed, the most common way of presenting the semantics of a temporal database is the one in BCDM, in which each tuple is paired with all the chronons when it holds. In BCDM, temporal databases directly associate times with tuples, so that the semantics of Example 1 above would be modeled as follows: {<John, fever, high, {10,11,12}>, <Mary, fever, moderate, {11, 12, 13}>.

In Sect. 4 we extend the semantic framework introduced so far to provide the general semantics of temporal indeterminacy in TDBs. Then, in Sect. 5, we move to a representational model, considering the requirements (i) and (ii) above, and following the methodological requirements (M1–M4) identified in Sect. 3.

4 Snapshot Semantics of Temporal Indeterminacy in TDB

In TDBs, the notion of temporal indeterminacy is usually paraphrased as *"don't know exactly when"* indeterminacy (consider, e.g., the Encyclopedia survey in [5]): facts hold at times that are *not exactly* known. An example is reported in the following:

Example 2. As a running example, let us consider a simple database DB_1^{IT} modeling patient symptoms. The database contains a unique relation SYM^{IT} of schema <Patient, Symptom, Value> and models two facts:

(f1) John had high fever at 10 and 11, and possibly at 12, or 13, or both.
(f2) Mary had moderate fever at 12 and 13, and possibly at 11.

(In the example, we assume that chronons are at the granularity of hours, and hour 1 represents the first hour of 1/1/2018).

4.1 Data Semantics of Indeterminate Time DBs

Of course, we can still retain the definition of the temporal domain D_T provided in Sect. 3. However, the definition of an indeterminate temporal database is different: informally speaking, an indeterminate TDB is simply a set of alternative determinate-time TDBs, each one encoding one of the different possibilities. Technically speaking, such a definition requires the introduction of a set of functions.

Definition 6. Indeterminate temporal database (semantic notion). Given a relational schema $\sigma = (R_1:s_i,..., R_k:s_j)$, an indeterminate temporal database DB^T is a set $S(DB^{IT}) = \{f^1, ..., f^k\}$ of functions $f^i_{\sigma,DT} : D_T \rightarrow DB_\sigma$ ∎

Analogously, a temporally indeterminate relation r^{IT} is a set $S(r^{IT})$ of functions from D_T to the set of tuples of r^T that hold at each chronon in D_T.

As an example, eight functions are necessary to cover all the alternative possibilities (henceforth called *scenarios*) for Example 2.

Example 2 (cont). The indeterminate temporal database DB^{IT} (semantic notion) modeling Example 2 consists of a unique relation SYM^{IT} and is shown in the following (for the sake of brevity, we denote with "J" the tuple <John, fever, high> and with "M" the tuple <Mary, fever, moderate>).

f^1	f^2	f^3	f^4
$10 \rightarrow \{J\}$	$10 \rightarrow \{J\}$	$10 \rightarrow \{J\}$	$10 \rightarrow \{J\}$
$11 \rightarrow \{J\}$	$11 \rightarrow \{J\}$	$11 \rightarrow \{J\}$	$11 \rightarrow \{J\}$
$12 \rightarrow \{M\}$	$12 \rightarrow \{J,M\}$	$12 \rightarrow \{M\}$	$12 \rightarrow \{J,M\}$
$13 \rightarrow \{M\}$	$13 \rightarrow \{M\}$	$13 \rightarrow \{J,M\}$	$13 \rightarrow \{J,M\}$

f^5	f^6	f^7	f^8
$10 \rightarrow \{J\}$	$10 \rightarrow \{J\}$	$10 \rightarrow \{J\}$	$10 \rightarrow \{J\}$
$11 \rightarrow \{J,M\}$	$11 \rightarrow \{J,M\}$	$11 \rightarrow \{J,M\}$	$11 \rightarrow \{J,M\}$
$12 \rightarrow \{M\}$	$12 \rightarrow \{J,M\}$	$12 \rightarrow \{M\}$	$12 \rightarrow \{J,M\}$
$13 \rightarrow \{M\}$	$13 \rightarrow \{M\}$	$13 \rightarrow \{J,M\}$	$13 \rightarrow \{J,M\}$ ∎

For the technical treatment that follows, it is useful to introduce the notion of *scenario* slice, which "selects" a specific scenario.

Definition 7. Scenario slice. Given an indeterminate temporal database $DB^{IT} = \{f^1,...,$ $f^k\}$ and a temporal relation $r^{IT} \in DB^{IT}$, and given any $f \in \{f^1,...,f^k\}$, we define the *scenario* slice f of DB^{IT} (denoted by DB_f^{IT}) and of r^{IT} (denoted by r_f^{IT}) the determinate temporal database and the determinate temporal relation obtained by considering only the alternative f for DB^{IT} ∎

Example 3. For example, considering Example 2 above, and the scenario f^1, $DB_{f1}{}^{IT} = SYM_{f1}{}^{IT} = \{10 \rightarrow \{J\}, 11 \rightarrow \{J\}, 12 \rightarrow \{M\}, 13 \rightarrow \{M\}\}$. ∎

4.2 Query Semantics

Of course, for the algebraic query operators, we can still retain all the general requirements discussed so far for determinate time. However, we have to generalize the above approach, to consider the fact that a set of *alternative* (determinate) temporal databases (*scenarios*) are involved. Therefore, given two temporally indeterminate relations r^{IT} and s^{IT}, binary temporal algebraic operators must consider, at each chronon, all the possible combinations of the scenarios $f_r \in S(r^{IT})$ of r^{IT} and $f_s \in S(s^{IT})$ of s^{IT}.

Definition 8. Relational algebraic operators on indeterminate temporal databases ("semantic" notion). Denoting by Op^C a Codd's operator, and by Op^{IT} its corresponding temporal operator for indeterminate time, Op^{IT} must be defined in such a way that the following holds

$$\forall c \in D_T \left(Op^T \left(r^T, s^T \right) (c) = \bigcup_{f_r \in S(r^{IT}) \wedge f_s \in S(s^{IT})} Op^C(f_r(c), f_s(c)) \right)$$

∎

(In Definition 8, r^{IT} and s^{IT} are temporal relations in a temporally indeterminate database DB^{IT}, and Op is a binary operator. $f_r(c)$ represents the *time slice* at the chronon c of the scenario f_r of r^{IT}. The definition of unary operators is simpler).

We regard Definition 8 as one of the major results of this paper: until now, no approach in the TDB community has been able to clarify the semantics of temporal algebraic operators on indeterminate time in terms of their Codd's counterparts. But, obviously, this is just *data* and *query semantics*: a direct implementation of the data model and algebraic operators defined so far would be highly inefficient, as regard both space and time. As a consequence, "compact" representational models and operators on them should be identified. We address this issue in the next section.

5 Possible "Compact" Approaches to Temporal Indeterminacy

The most frequently adopted representational model to cope with (valid) time in a compact and 1NF way is the interval-based representation (consider, e.g., the TSQL2 "consensus" representational model [2]). A time interval (compactly modelled by a starting and an ending time) is associated with each temporal tuple, to denote that the (fact represented by the) tuple holds in each chronon in the interval. In the indeterminate time context, such an interval-based representation has also been used, e.g., in [7, 11, 16–18]. As in such approaches, we associate four temporal attributes (say T1, T2, T3, and T4) with each temporal tuple, to compactly represent the intervals when it certainly and possibly holds.

Definition 9. Temporally indeterminate Database, Relation, Tuple (representational model). A temporally indeterminate relational database DB^{IT} is a set of (temporally indeterminate) relations over the relational schema $\sigma = (R_1{:}s_i,\ldots, R_k{:}s_j)$ where $s_i,\ldots, s_j \in S$ are the sorts of $R_1,\ldots, R_k$, respectively. A relation $R(x_1,\ldots, x_k|T1, T2, T3, T4){:}s$ of sort $s \in S$ is a sequence of non-temporal attributes $x_1,\ldots, x_k$ each with values in a proper domain $D_1,\ldots D_k$, and temporal attributes $T1, T2, T3, T4$ *with domain* D_T. An instance $r(R{:}s)$ of a relation $R(x_1,\ldots, x_k|T1, T2, T3, T4){:}s$ is a set $\{t_1, \ldots, t_n\}$ tuples, where each tuple t_i is a set $<v_1,\ldots,v_k|t_1, t_2, t_3, t_4>$ of values in $D_1 \times \ldots \times D_k \times D_T$ $D_T \times D_T \times D_T$. ■

Example 4. In the temporally indeterminate context, the relation SYM (called SYM^{IT}) may be represented with the schema <Patient, Symptom, Value| T_1, T_2, T_3, T_4>. Tuples of SYS are shown in Examples 5 and 7 below ■

Intuitively and *roughly* speaking, the semantics of such a compact 1NF "interval-based" representation of temporal indeterminacy is the following:

(sem1)   the fact represented by the tuple $<v_1, \ldots, v_k|t_1, t_2, t_3, t_4>$ occurs possibly in the (chronons in the) time intervals $[t_1, t_2)$ and $[t_3, t_4)$, and certainly in the time interval $[t_2, t_3)$.

We now show that an "informal" semantics like (sem1) above is not enough: it must be fully formalized as a starting point for devising a "proper" representational model and algebra, following the methodological requirements M1–M4 above.

5.1 "Single Occurrence" Semantics

A first way of interpreting the "ambiguous" semantics (sem1) above is formally described in Definition 10 below. For the sake of space constraints, in Definition 10 we adopt a compact notation to represent scenarios: given a temporally indeterminate tuple with non-temporal part v, we denote by $v([c_1, c_2])$ the scenario $\{c_1 \to \{v\}, c_1 + 1 \to \{v\}, ..., c_2 \to \{v\}\}$.

Definition 10. Representation semantics (sem1'). The semantics of an indeterminate time tuple $<v|t_1, t_2, t_3, t_4>$ in the representational model in Definition 9 is the set of scenarios

$$\{v([t_2, t_3 - 1]), v([t_2, t_3]), v([t_2, t_3 + 1]), v([t_2, t_3 + 2]), ..., v([t_2, t_4 - 1]),$$
$$v([t_2 - 1, t_3 - 1]), v([t_2 - 1, t_3]), v([t_2 - 1, t_3 + 1]), v([t_2 - 1, t_3 + 2]), ..., v([t_2 - 1, t_4 - 1]),$$
$$v([t_2 - 2, t_3 - 1]), v([t_2 - 2, t_3]), v([t_2 - 2, t_3 + 1]), v([t_2 - 2, t_3 + 2]), ..., v([t_2 - 2, t_4 - 1]), ...,$$
$$v([t_1, t_3 - 1]), v([t_1, t_3]), v([t_1, t_3 + 1]), v([t_1, t_3 + 2]), ..., v([t_1, t_4 - 1])\}$$

∎

In Definition 10, we formalize that the fact v occurred in a ***convex*** (i.e., with no gap) time interval, which includes all the chronons in $[t_2, t_3)$, and may extend forward until chronon t_4 (excluded) and backward until chronon t_1. This is, probably, the most intuitive notion of temporal indeterminacy in TDBs: each tuple represents ***a single occurrence*** of a fact, and temporal indeterminacy concerns the starting and ending chronons of it. In such a context, it looks natural to impose $t_1 \leq t_2 < t_3 \leq t_4$, thus granting that there is at least one chronon in which the fact certainly occurs (see, e.g., [7]).

Example 5. Given the temporally indeterminate relation SYM^{IT}, with the semantics (sem1') above, the fact

(f2) Mary had moderate fever at 12 and 13, and possibly at 11 can be represented by the tuple <Mary, fever, moderate|11, 12, 14, 14>.

The semantics of such a tuple consists of two possible scenarios:

$$\begin{array}{ll} & 11 \to \{M\} \\ 12 \to \{M\} & 12 \to \{M\} \\ 13 \to \{M\} & 13 \to \{M\} \end{array}$$ ∎

Notably, if we assume the semantics (sem1'), the fact (f1)

(f1) John had high fever at 10 and 11, and possibly at 12, or 13, or both cannot be represented in the representational model: as a matter of fact, the tuple

<John, fever, high|10, 10, 12, 14>

would be interpreted as the compact representation of the semantics below:

$$10 \rightarrow \{J\} \qquad 10 \rightarrow \{J\} \qquad 10 \rightarrow \{J\}$$
$$11 \rightarrow \{J\} \qquad 11 \rightarrow \{J\} \qquad 11 \rightarrow \{J\}$$
$$12 \rightarrow \{J\} \qquad 12 \rightarrow \{J\}$$
$$13 \rightarrow \{J\}$$

while the scenario $<10 \rightarrow \{J\}, 11 \rightarrow \{J\}, 13 \rightarrow \{J\}>$ would not be part of the semantics of the representation. Indeed, if we assume (sem1'), each tuple represents a single occurrence of a fact, while the latter scenario above represents two separate occurrences, one at $[10,12)$, and one at $[13,14)$.

Of course, the specification of the semantics is fundamental also for the definition of the algebraic operators. In particular, we must grant that such operators (i) are correct wrt the semantics, and (ii) are closed wrt the representational model.

Notably, if we assume the semantics (sem1') for the representational model in Definition 9, there is no way to satisfy both requirements (i) and (ii)[2]. A trivial counterexample is discussed in the following, considering algebraic difference.

Example 6. Consider the difference between two relations $r1^{IT}$ and $r2^{IT}$ having the same schema $(A_1, ..., A_k | T_1, T_2, T_3, T_4)$. Let $r1^{IT} = \{<a_1, ..., a_k | 1, 3, 5, 7>\}$ and $r2^{IT} = \{<a_1, ..., a_k | 3, 3, 8, 8>\}$ (i.e., the two tuples are value-equivalent, and the tuple in $r2^{IT}$ is determinate, starts at 3 and ends at 7). In such a case the result of the difference $r1^{IT} -^{IT} r2^{IT}$ should be a fact $a_1,...,a_k$ which may not occur, or occurs in $\{2\}$, or in $\{1, 2\}$. A tuple with such a semantics cannot be represented in the given representation. Thus, this example suffices to show that (the semantically correct) difference is not closed with respect with the given formalism (with the semantics (sem1') above). ∎

5.2 "Independent Chronons" Semantics

A different way of interpreting the "rough" semantics (sem1) above is provided in Definition 11 where, for the sake of space constraints, we adopt the following compact notation to represent scenarios: given a temporally indeterminate tuple with non-temporal part v, we denote by $v(\{c_1, c_2, ..., c_k\})$ the scenario $\{c_1 \rightarrow \{v\}, c_2 \rightarrow \{v\}, ..., c_k \rightarrow \{v\}\}$; furthermore, we denote by $P^S(A)$ the power set of a set A.

Definition 11. Representation semantics (sem1'). The semantics of an indeterminate time tuple $<v | t_1, t_2, t_3, t_4>$ in the representational model in Definition 9 is the set of scenarios $v(\{t_2, t_2 + 1, t_2 + 2, ..., t_3 - 1\} \cup T \setminus T \in P^S(\{c \setminus c \in ([t_1, t_2) \cup [t_3, t_4))\})$ ∎

In such a semantics, there is no notion of single occurrence at all. v certainly holds in each chronon in $[t_2, t_3)$ (if any), and may hold in each one of the chronons c in $[t_1, t_2)$

---

[2] Notably, it is possible to show that it is not possible to define correct algebraic operators closed with respect to the representational model also in case one admits the possibility that facts in the TDBs do not necessarily occur, i.e., imposing $t_1 \leq t_2 \leq t_3 \leq t_4$ in the representational model. We cannot show such a generalization here, for the sake of space constraints.

and in $[t_3, t_4)$, independently of each other. In such a context, it is natural to impose $t_1 \leq t_2 \leq t_3 \leq t_4$, so that the fact may also not be certain in a chronon, in case $t_2 = t_3$.

Example 7. Given the temporally indeterminate relation SYM^{IT}, with the semantics (sem1') above, the fact (f1)

(f1) John had high fever at 10 and 11, and possibly at 12, or 13, or both is represented in the representational model by the tuple

<John, fever, high|10, 10, 11, 13>

which has the semantics discussed above (in short, the fact may hold at $\{10, 11\}$, or at $\{10, 11, 12\}$, or at $\{10, 11, 13\}$, or at $\{10, 11, 12, 13\}$).   ∎

With such a semantics for the representational model, it is possible to define correct and closed algebraic operators as follows:

Definition 12. Algebraic operators for indeterminate time (independent chronons semantics). Let r and s denote relations of the same sort and $<v|t_1, t_2, t_3, t_4>$ a tuple with non-temporal part v and temporal part t_1, t_2, t_3, t_4.

$$r \cup^{IT} s = \{<v|t_1, t_2, t_3, t_4 > \,|<v|t_1, t_2, t_3, t_4 > \,\in r \vee <v|t_1, t_2, t_3, t_4 > \,\in s\}$$

$$r \times^{IT} s = \{<v_r \cdot v_s|\, t_1, t_2, t_3, t_4 > \,|\exists t_1', t_2', t_3', t_4' \exists t_1'', t_2'', t_3'', t_4'' (<v_r|t_1', t_2', t_3', t_4' > \,\in r$$
$$\wedge <v_s|t_1'', t_2'', t_3'', t_4'' > \,\in s \wedge t_1 = \max\left(t_1', t_1''\right) \wedge t_4 = \min\left(t_4', t_4''\right) \wedge t_1 \leq t_4 \wedge$$
$$\text{let } t_s = \max\left(t_2', t_2''\right) \wedge t_e = \min\left(t_3', t_3''\right)$$
$$\text{if } t_s \leq t_e \text{ then } t_2 = t_s \wedge t_3 = t_e \text{ else } t_2 = t_3 = t \text{ where } t \text{ is any value in } [t_1, t_4)\}$$

$$\pi_X^{IT}(r) = \{<v|t_1, t_2, t_3, t_4 > \,|\exists v_r, t_1, t_2, t_3, t_4(<v_r|t_1, t_2, t_3, t_4 > \,\in r \wedge v = \pi_X(v_r))\}$$

$$\sigma_P^{IT}(r) = \{<v|t > \,|<v|t > \,\in r \wedge P(v)\}$$

$$r -^{IT} s = \{<v|\, t_1, t_2, t_3, t_4 > \,|(\exists v, t_1, t_2, t_3, t_4(<v|t_1, t_2, t_3, t_4 > \,\in r \wedge$$
$$\neg\exists t_1', t_2', t_3', t_4'(<v|t_1', t_2', t_3', t_4' > \,\in s)))\vee$$
$$(\exists t_1', t_2', t_3', t_4' \exists t_1'', t_2'', t_3'', t_4''(<v|t_1', t_2', t_3', t_4' > \,\in r \wedge <v|\, t_1'', t_2'', t_3'', t_4'' > \,\in s$$
$$\wedge t_1, t_2, t_3, t_4 = \text{difference}\left(\left[t_1', t_4'\right), \left[t_2', t_3'\right), \left[t_1'', t_4''\right), \left[t_2'', t_3''\right)\right))))\}$$

where difference can be defined by the following function (where s is a function that returns the starting point of an interval and e returns the ending point, and the function *Nor* is used to reformat the output in case $t_2 > t_3$, i.e.,

$$\text{Nor}(<t_1, t_2, t_3, t_4 >) = <t_1, t_2, t_3, t_4 > \text{ if } t_1 \leq t_2 \leq t_3 \leq t_4,$$
$$\text{Nor}(<t_1, t_2, t_3, t_4 >) = <t_1, t, t, t_4 > \text{ where } t_1 \leq t \leq t_4 \text{ if } t_2 > t_3)$$

difference (p1, n1, p2, n2)

(1) if (p1 $\subseteq$ n2) then return $\varnothing$
(2) else if (p1 $\cap$ n2 = $\varnothing$) then return {Nor(<s(p1), s(n1-p2), e(n1-p2), s(p1)>)}
(3) else if (p1 $\supset$ n2) then return {Nor(<s(p1), s(n1-p2), e(n1-p2), s(n2)>), Nor(<e(n2), s(n1-p2), e(n1-p2), e(p1)>)}
(4) else return {Nor(<s(p1-n2), s(n1-p2), e(n1-p2), e(p1-n2)>)}   ∎

The difference function accepts as parameters two time intervals for the minuend (p1 and n1) and two time intervals for the subtrahend (p2 and n2). p1 and p2 are the possible intervals, i.e., they contain the chronons that are in at least one scenario, and n1 and n2 are the necessary –certain– intervals, i.e., they contain the chronons that are in every scenario (thus n1 $\subseteq$ p1 and n2 $\subseteq$ p2). The function operates along the following idea (for space constraints, we will not go into the details): if a chronon is both in the minuend and in the subtrahend, and in the subtrahend such a chronon is (i) necessary (i.e., it belongs to n2), it will not be in the result, (ii) only possible (i.e., it belongs to p2 but not to n2), it will be possible in the result. From (i) and the fact that n1 $\subseteq$ p1, descends line (1) of the difference function, from (ii) descends line (2), from (i) and (ii) and the fact that n2 $\not\subseteq$ p1 descends line (3), from (i) and (ii) and the fact that n2 $\subseteq$ p1 descends line (4) and, in particular, since n2 $\subseteq$ p1 the minuend "breaks" into two (pairs of) intervals.

Property. The algebraic operators in Definition 12 are correct (with respect to the semantics defined so far) and are closed with respect to the representational model.

6 Conclusions and Future Work

In this paper, we propose an innovative approach in which a semantic-based AI-style methodology is proposed to cope with temporal indeterminacy in TDBs. Specifically:

(1) We propose a new semantic definition for indeterminate time in TDBs, in which the semantics of algebraic operators can be expressed in terms of their Codd's counterparts (thus formally providing a "_snapshot semantics_" for indeterminate time TDBs).
(2) We propose a new AI-style methodology to the treatment of TDBs, using it to develop a semantically-grounded 1NF approach (data model plus algebra) to cope with "interval-based" temporal indeterminacy.

Indeed, in this paper we have shown that, when introducing the temporal dimension, TDBs have to cope with **implicit** information, which has to be **symbolically manipulated** by algebraic operators to answer queries. As a consequence, we propose an innovative AI-based methodology to cope with time in relational DBs. We are confident that our methodology can be fruitfully applied to other types of temporal information in TDBs (e.g., implicit representation of periodically repeated data [19, 20]), and possibly of other forms of indeterminacy, thus leading to a new AI stream of research to cope with _indeterminate\implicit_ data in relational DBs.

References

1. Snodgrass, R.T.: Developing Time-Oriented Database Applications in SQL. Morgan Kaufmann Publishers Inc., San Francisco, CA, USA (2000)
2. Snodgrass, R.T.: The TSQL2 Temporal Query Language. Kluwer (1995)
3. Wu, Y., Jajodia, S., Wang, X.S.: Temporal database bibliography update. In: Etzion, O., Jajodia, S., Sripada, S. (eds.) Temporal Databases: Research and Practice. LNCS, vol. 1399, pp. 338–366. Springer, Heidelberg (1998). https://doi.org/10.1007/BFb0053709
4. Liu, L., Özsu, M.T. (eds.): Encyclopedia of Database Systems. Springer, Heidelberg (2009)
5. Dyreson, C.: Temporal indeterminacy. In: Liu, L., Ozsu, M.T. (eds.) Encyclopedia of Database Systems, pp. 2973–2976. Springer, Boston (2009)
6. Jensen, C.S., Snodgrass, R.T.: Semantics of time-varying information. Inf. Syst. 21, 311–352 (1996)
7. Dyreson, C.E., Snodgrass, R.T.: Supporting valid-time indeterminacy. ACM Trans. Database Syst. (TODS) 23, 1–57 (1998)
8. Dekhtyar, A., Ross, R., Subrahmanian, V.: Probabilistic temporal databases, I: algebra. ACM Trans. Database Syst. (TODS) 26, 41–95 (2001)
9. Anselma, L., Terenziani, P., Snodgrass, R.T.: Valid-time indeterminacy in temporal relational databases: a family of data models. In: Proc. TIME, pp. 139–145. IEEE (2010)
10. Anselma, L., Terenziani, P., Snodgrass, R.T.: Valid-time indeterminacy in temporal relational databases: semantics and representations. IEEE Trans. Knowl. Data Eng. 25, 2880–2894 (2013)
11. Anselma, L., Piovesan, L., Terenziani, P.: A 1NF temporal relational model and algebra coping with valid-time temporal indeterminacy. J. Intell. Inf. Syst. 47, 345–374 (2016)
12. Hobbs, J.R., Pan, F.: An ontology of time for the semantic web. ACM Trans. Asian Lang. Inf. Process. 3, 66–85 (2004)
13. Baumann, R., Loebe, F., Herre, H.: Axiomatic theories of the ontology of time in GFO. Appl. Ontol. 9, 171–215 (2014)
14. Ermolayev, V., Batsakis, S., Keberle, N., Tatarintseva, O., Antoniou, G.: Ontologies of time: review and trends. IJCSA 11, 57–115 (2014)
15. McKenzie Jr., L.E., Snodgrass, R.T.: Evaluation of relational algebras incorporating the time dimension in databases. ACM Comput. Surv. 23, 501–543 (1991)
16. Anselma, L., Bottrighi, A., Montani, S., Terenziani, P.: Extending BCDM to cope with proposals and evaluations of updates. IEEE Trans. Knowl. Data Eng. 25, 556–570 (2013)
17. Anselma, L., Stantic, B., Terenziani, P., Sattar, A.: Querying now-relative data. J. Intell. Inf. Syst. 41, 285–311 (2013)
18. Anselma, L., Piovesan, L., Sattar, A., Stantic, B., Terenziani, P.: A comprehensive approach to "now" in temporal relational databases: semantics and representation. IEEE Trans. Knowl. Data Eng. 28, 2538–2551 (2016)
19. Terenziani, P.: Irregular indeterminate repeated facts in temporal relational databases. IEEE Trans. Knowl. Data Eng. 28, 1075–1079 (2016)
20. Terenziani, P.: Nearly periodic facts in temporal relational databases. IEEE Trans. Knowl. Data Eng. 28, 2822–2826 (2016)

Development of Agent Logic Programming Means for Heterogeneous Multichannel Intelligent Visual Surveillance

Alexei A. Morozov$^{(\boxtimes)}$ and Olga S. Sushkova

Kotel'nikov Institute of Radio Engineering and Electronics of RAS,
Mokhovaya 11-7, Moscow, Russia
`morozov@cplire.ru`, `o.sushkova@mail.ru`
`http://www.fullvision.ru`

Abstract. Experimental means developed in the Actor Prolog parallel object-oriented logic language for implementation of heterogeneous multichannel intelligent visual surveillance systems are considered. These means are examined by the instance of a logic program for permanent monitoring of people's body parts temperature in the area of visual surveillance. The logic program implements a fusion of heterogeneous data acquired by two devices: (1) 3D coordinates of the human body are measured using a time-of-flight (ToF) camera; (2) 3D coordinates of the human body skeleton are computed on the base of 3D coordinates of the body; (3) a thermal video is acquired using a thermal imaging camera. In the considered example, the thermal video is projected to the 3D surface of the human body; then the temperature of the human body is projected to the vertices and edges of the skeleton. A special logical agent (i.e., the logic program that is written in Actor Prolog) implements these operations in real-time and transfers the data to another logical agent. The latter agent implements a time average of the temperature of the human skeletons and displays colored 3D images of the skeletons; the average temperature of the vertices and edges of the skeletons is depicted by colors. The logic programming means under consideration are developed for the purpose of the implementation of logical analysis of video scene semantics in the intelligent visual surveillance systems.

1 Introduction

In this paper, the basic ideas of using the Actor Prolog object-oriented logic language for the multichannel/multimedia data analysis are described by the example of processing of 3D video data acquired using Kinect 2 (Microsoft, Inc.) and 2D thermal imaging video acquired using the Thermal Expert V1 camera (i3system, Inc.). The distributed logic programming means of Actor Prolog are discussed by the example of two communicating logical agents that analyze 3D video data and implement a fusion of these data with the thermal video.

© Springer Nature Switzerland AG 2018
G. R. Simari et al. (Eds.): IBERAMIA 2018, LNAI 11238, pp. 29–41, 2018.
https://doi.org/10.1007/978-3-030-03928-8_3

The fusion of the thermal imaging video with 3D video data and the data of other kinds is a rapidly developed research area [1,2,15,16]. In this paper, the problem of remote measurement of human body parts in the video surveillance area is considered as an example. In the first section, the architecture and basic principles of the Actor Prolog logic programming system are considered. In the second section, a set of built-in classes of the Actor Prolog language are considered that were developed by the authors for the acquisition and analysis of 3D video data. In the third section, an example of a logical agent that inputs 3D data on the body surface of the people under the video surveillance and implements a fusion of this data with the thermal imaging video is discussed. In the fourth section, the basic principles and means for the communication of the logical agent in the Actor Prolog language are considered.

2   The Architecture of the Actor Prolog Logic Programming System

Actor Prolog is a logic programming language developed in the Kotel'nikov Institute of Radio Engineering and Electronics of Russian Academy of Sciences [3–7]. Actor Prolog was designed initially as an object-oriented and logic language simultaneously, that is, the language implements classes, instances, and inheritance; at the same time, the object-oriented logic programs have model-theory semantics. The Actor Prolog language supports means for definition of data types (so-called domains), the determinancy of predicates, and the direction of data transfer in the subroutine arguments [14]. These means are vital for the industrial applications of the logic programming because the experience demonstrated that it is very difficult to support and debug big and complex logic programs without these means. Actor Prolog is a parallel language; there are syntax means in the language that support creation and control of communicating parallel processes. These syntax means of the language provide the model-theory semantics of the logic programs as well, but only when certain restrictions are imposed on the syntax and structure of the programs [6].

A distinctive feature of the Actor Prolog logic programming system is in that the logic programs are translated in Java code and executed by the standard Java virtual machine [9,11]. This scheme of logic program execution was developed, mainly, to ensure the stability of the programs and prevent possible problems with the memory management. Another important feature of this scheme is in that it ensures high extensibility of the logic language; one can easily add necessary built-in classes to the language.

One can add a new built-in class to the Actor Prolog language in the following way. During the translation of the logic program, it is converted to the set of Java classes. There are special syntax means in the language to declare some automatically generated Java classes as descendants of external Java classes that were created manually by the programmer. Thus, it is enough to implement a new built-in class in Java and link it with the logic program in the course of translation to make this class the built-in class of Actor Prolog. Currently, a set of built-in classes of Actor Prolog are implemented totally in pure Java; other built-in classes are Java interfaces with open source libraries implemented in C++. The examples of the former classes are: the *Database* class that implements a simple data management system; the *File* class that supports reading and writing files; the *WebResource* class that implements data acquisition from the Web. The examples of the latter classes are: the *FFmpeg* class that links Actor Prolog with the FFmpeg open source library for video reading and writing; the *Java3D* class that implements 3D graphics; the *Webcam* class that supports video data acquisition. The authors consider the translation to Java as an architectural solution that helps to develop and debug rapidly new built-in classes. The speeding-up of the software life cycle is caused by the fact that the Java language, in comparison with the C++ language, prevents the appearance of the bugs linked with the incorrect memory access and out-of-range array access that can be very difficult for detection.

3 Built-In Classes Supporting the Intelligent Visual Surveillance

A set of built-in classes for 2D and 3D video acquisition and analysis is implemented in the Actor Prolog logic programming system. These built-in classes were developed mainly in the course of experimenting with the methods of intelligent video surveillance.

In this paper, new means of the Actor Prolog language are described that were developed for 3D data acquisition and analysis using the Kinect 2 device. These means and specialized built-in classes of Actor Prolog were created for the experimenting with the 3D intelligent visual surveillance [12,13]. The developed means are based on the same ideas as the means for the 2D video analysis:

1. The low-level and high-level video processing stages are separated.
2. The low-level video processing stage is implemented in special built-in classes that encapsulate all intermediate data matrices.
3. The high-level video processing stage is implemented by the logical rules; the data is processed in the form of graphs, lists, and other terms of the logic language.

The data processing scheme was adapted to the following properties of 3D video data:

1. The data are heterogeneous (multimodal). For instance, the Kinect 2 device provides several data streams simultaneously; there are: the frames describing 3D point clouds; the infrared imaging frames; the conventional colored (RGB) frames; the frames that describe coordinates of human skeletons; etc.
2. The size of 3D video data is usually huge; a typical personal computer is not powerful enough to store in real time all raw data of Kinect 2 to the hard disk. Thus, a preferable scheme of 3D data processing includes preliminary real-time analysis of the data and storing/networking the intermediate results of the analysis.

There are two built-in classes in Actor Prolog that support 3D video acqui-sition and analysis: *Kinect* and *KinectBuffer*. The former class implements communication between the logic program and the Kinect 2 device. The latter class implements low-level analysis as well as reading and writing 3D data files. The definitions of these classes including the definitions of data types (domains) and predicates are placed in the "Morozov/Kinect" package of Actor Prolog.

The *KinectBuffer* class is the most important element in the 3D data processing scheme. The instance of the *KinectBuffer* class can be used in the following modes: data acquisition from Kinect 2; reading data from the file; playing 3D video file; writing data to the file. The playing-3D-video-file and reading-from-the-file modes differ in that in the former mode the *KinectBuffer* class reads data and transfers them to the logic program in real-time; in the reading-from-the-file mode, the programmer has to control reading of every frame of the video.

The *operating_mode* attribute of the *KinectBuffer* class is to be used to select the operating mode of the instance of the class: *LISTENING*, *READING*, *PLAYING*, or *RECORDING* correspondingly. The *KinectBuffer* class can be used alone to read/write 3D videos; however one has to use it in connection with the *Kinect* class to acquire data from the Kinect 2 device. In this mode, one has to create an instance of the *Kinect* class and transmit it to the constructor of the *KinectBuffer* class instance; the *input_device* attribute is to be used as the argument of the constructor. An example of the logic program that reads and processes 3D video data from the file is considered in the next section.

4   Acquisition and Fusion of 3D and Thermal Imaging Video Data

Let us consider an example of the logic program that reads and implements a simple analysis of 3D video data that were acquired using ToF camera of the Kinect 2 device. Fragments of source code written in Actor Prolog will be demon-strated below with comments; of course, the source code is reduced, because the purpose of the example is just to describe the scheme of the data processing using the *Kinect* and *KinectBuffer* classes.

Let us define the *3DVideoSupplier* class that is a descendant of the *Kinect Buffer* class. The *operating_mode* attribute has the *PLAYING* value that indicates that the data are to be read from the "My3DVideo" file in the playing-3D-video-file mode.

```
class '3DVideoSupplier' (specialized 'KinectBuffer'):
name            = "My3DVideo";
operating_mode  = 'PLAYING';
```

In the course of the creation of the *3DVideoSupplier* class instance, it down-loads a lookup table from the "MyLookUpTable.txt" file. This lookup table establishes the correspondence between the 3D coordinates measured by the ToF camera and 2D coordinates on the 2D thermal imaging video. After that, the reading from the file is activated using the *start* predicate of the *KinectBuffer* class.

```
goal:-!,
    set_lookup_table("MyLookUpTable.txt"),
    start.
```

The *KinectBuffer* class supports 2D and 3D lookup tables. It is supposed that the lookup table is computed and stored in the text file in advance during the calibration of the video acquisition system. The 2D lookup table is a matrix K of the same size as the Kinect 2 infrared video frame. Each cell (i, j) of the matrix contains coordinates x and y on an image T; in the example under consideration, T is the thermal image. Thus, the T image is to be projected to 3D surfaces investigated using the ToF camera. The 3D lookup table is also a matrix, but the cell of this matrix contains quadratic polynomial coefficients that are necessary for computation of the coordinates on the T image, but not the (x, y) coordinates themselves. Each cell (i, j) of the matrix contains six coefficients p_1, p_2, p_3, q_1, q_2, and q_3. The coordinates on the T image are computed using the quadratic polynomial depending on the inverse value of the distance $d(i, j)$ in meters between the ToF camera and the surface of the object to be investigated:

$$x = p_1(1/d)^2 + p_2(1/d) + p_3 \tag{1}$$

$$y = q_1(1/d)^2 + q_2(1/d) + q_3 \tag{2}$$

In the example, the thermal image is projected to the 3D surface during the processing of every frame of 3D video. The *frame_obtained* predicate is invoked automatically in the instance of the *KinectBuffer* class when a new frame of 3D video is read from the file. The programmer informs the *KinectBuffer* class that s/he is going to process this frame using the *commit* predicate. After that, all the predicates of the *KinectBuffer* class operate with the content of this particular flame until the *commit* predicate is called again. The logic program gets the *Time*1 time of the frame in milliseconds using the *get_recent_frame_time* predicate. Then the number of corresponding thermal imaging frame is calculated using this information. The *texture_time_shift* attribute contains a value of the temporal shift between the 3D and thermal videos. The *texture_frame_rate* attribute contains the frame rate of the thermal imaging video.

```
frame_obtained:-
    commit,!,
    get_recent_frame_time(Time1),
    Time2== Time1 - texture_time_shift,
    FileNumber== texture_frame_rate * Time2 / 1000,
```

Suppose the thermal imaging video is converted to the separate frames. The *frame_obtained* predicate computes the name of the corresponding JPEG file using the number of the frame. Then it uses the *load* predicate to read the frame and stores it to the image instance of the *BufferedImage* built-in class. The *get_recent_scene* predicate of the *KinectBuffer* class is called; this predicate creates a 3D surface on the base of the ToF camera data and projects given texture to this surface. The texture is transferred to the predicate by the second argument *image* that contains an instance of the *BufferedImage* class. The lookup table loaded above is used for the implementation of the texture projection. The created 3D surface is returned from the *get_recent_scene* predicate via the first argument. This argument has to contain an instance of the *BufferedScene* built-in class. The *BufferedScene* built-in class implements storing and transferring 3D data. In particular, the content of the *BufferedScene* class instance can be inserted into the 3D scene displayed by the means of the Java3D graphics library. In the example under consideration, the *set_node* predicate is used for this purpose that replaces the "MyLabel" node of the 3D image created using the *graphics_window* instance of the *Java3D* built-in class.

```
ImageToBeLoaded == text?format(
    "%08d.jpeg",?round(FileNumber)),
image ? load(ImageToBeLoaded),
get_recent_scene(buffer3D,image),
graphics_window ? set_node(
    "MyLabel",
    'BranchGroup'({
        label: "MyLabel",
        allowDetach: 'yes',
        compile: 'yes',
        branches: [buffer3D]
    })),
```

The *get_recent_mapping* predicate of the *KinectBuffer* built-in class operates approximately in the same way as the *get_recent_scene* predicate. The difference is in that it does not create a 3D surface and the results of the projection of the texture to the 3D surface are returned in a form of a convenient 2D image. In the example, the *get_recent_mapping* predicate stores the created image to the *buffer2D* instance of the *BufferedImage* built-in class. The *get_skeletons* predicate of the *KinectBuffer* class returns a list of the skeletons detected in the current frame. The skeletons are graphs that contain information about coordinates of the human body, head, arms, and legs. In the logic program, the graphs are described using the standard simple and compound terms: lists, structures, underdetermined sets, symbols, and numbers [12,13]. In the example, the skeletons and thermal images are transferred to another logical agent that implements further analysis and fusion of the data. The routine of the data transfer between the logical agents will be considered in the next section. Note that the image to be transferred from the *buffer2D* instance of the *BufferedImage* class is converted to the term of the *BINARY* type. The *get_binary* predicate of the *BufferedImage* class is used for this purpose.

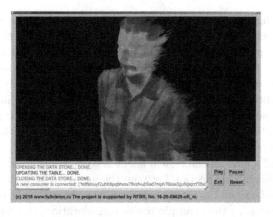

Fig. 1. An example of a logical agent that collects and transfers heterogeneous multi-channel data (3D video data and thermal imaging data).

```
get_recent_mapping(buffer2D,image),
get_skeletons(Skeletons),
communicator ? notify_all_consumers(
    Skeletons,buffer2D?get_binary()).
```

The results of the fusion of 3D and thermal imaging data implemented by the logical agent under consideration are demonstrated in the Fig. 1.

In the next section, a scheme of communication between the logic programs (the logical agents) based on the *Database* and *DataStore* built-in classes and the mechanism of the remote predicate calls are discussed.

5   A Link Startup and Communication Between the Logical Agents

The remote predicate calls are a special feature of the Actor Prolog language that was developed to support distributed/decentralized logic programming. The idea of this mechanism is in that any object of the logic program (the logical agent) can be transferred to another logical agent; after that, the new owner of the object can invoke remotely and asynchronously the predicates of the object [14]. Note that in terms of Actor Prolog the object is a synonym of the world and the instance of a class. The complication of the development of this mechanism was in that Actor Prolog has a strong type system and, therefore, the type system of the language did not provide a possibility for the agents to link and communicate dynamically without a preliminary exchange of the information about the types of the data to be transferred. Usually, the languages with strong type systems require an exchange of data type definitions on the stage of compilation of the agents, but in the Actor Prolog language, another solution was elaborated. In the distributed version of Actor Prolog, a combined type system was developed, that is, the strong type system was partially softened in the case when the inter-agent data exchange is performed. To be more precise, the types of the arguments in the remote predicate calls are compared by structure, but not by names; moreover, the check of that the external object implements a required predicate is postponed until this predicate call is to be actually performed. In all other cases, the standard static type check is implemented in the language. The combined type system unites the advantages of the strong type system that is used for generation of reliable and fast executable code and the possibility of the dynamic type check during the inter-agent data exchange.

An instance of a class of the logical agent is to be transferred to other agents somehow to establish a connection between the agents. The instance of the class can be transferred via an operating system file, a shared database, or just in a text form by E-mail. In the example under consideration, the built-in database management system of Actor Prolog is used for this purpose. This system is implemented by the *Database* and *DataStore* built-in classes of the language.

Let us define the *Main* class that will implement two roles in the logic program: the execution of the logic program begins with the creation of an instance of the *Main* class in accordance with the definition of the language; the instance of the class is to be transferred to another agent to establish a link and for the communication in the example under consideration.

The *Main* class contains several slots (that is, the class instance variables). The *datastore* slot contains an instance of the *DataStore* built-in class. The *database* slot contains an instance of the 3DDataSources class that is a descendant of the *Database* built-in class. The *video_supplier* slot contains an instance of the 3DVideoSupplier class that was considered in the previous section. The *consumers* slot contains an instance of the *ConsumersList* class that is a descendant of the *Database* built-in class; the *consumers* database keeps a list of external logical agents that requested information from the agent under consideration.

```
class 'Main' (specialized 'Alpha'):
datastore = ('DataStore',
                name="AgentBlackboard.db",
                sharing_mode='shared_access',
                access_mode='modifying');
database  = ('3DDataSources',
                place= shared(
                    datastore,
                    "3DDataSources"));
video_supplier = ('3DVideoSupplier',
                communicator=self);
consumers     = ('ConsumersList');
```

The *Database* built-in class implements a simple database management system that provides storing and searching the data of arbitrary structure; the operations of this kind are standard for the Prolog-like logic languages. One might say that the convenient relational databases are a special case of the Prolog databases when the database is used only for storing the data of the structure type, that is, the records with a name and a list of arguments. Note that the *Database* class is destined for storing data in the main memory of the computer, that is, for the management of the temporary data. The temporary data can be stored to the file or loaded from the file if necessary.

A database management mechanism of a more high level is to be used to control data that are shared between several logic programs. This mechanism is implemented in the *DataStore* built-in class. The *DataStore* class can coordinate and control the operation of one or several instances of the *Database* class. For instance, one can read from or write to the file the content of several instances of the *Database* class at once. Another useful mechanism of the *DataStore* class is supporting shared data access, that is, it can link the instances of the *Database* class with the operating system files and automatically transfer the updates of the data in the memory of one logic program to the memory of other logic programs. The data integrity is guaranteed by the standard mechanism of transactions. These instruments of the *DataStore* class are used in the example under consideration.

In the code above, the constructor of the *DataStore* class instance accepts the following input arguments: the *name* attribute that contains the name of the "AgentBlackboard.db" file that is to be used for the shared data storage; the *sharing_mode* attribute that assigns the shared mode of the data access (the *shared_access* mode); the *access_mode* attribute that indicates that the logic program demands the privileges for shared data modification (the *modifying* mode).

The constructor of the 3*DDataSources* class instance accepts the *place* argument that contains the *shared(datastore,* "3*DDataSources*") structure with two internal arguments. This argument indicates that the instance of the 3*DData Sources* database will operate under the control of the *DataStore* class and the content of the database has the "3DDataSources" unique identifier in the namespace of the *DataStore* class instance. Using the analogy with the relational databases, "3DDataSources" is the name of a generalized relational table in the "AgentBlackboard.db" shared database.

In the course of the creation of the *Main* class instance, a sequence of operations on the shared data will be performed. The *open* predicate initiates the access to the "AgentBlackboard.db" shared data file. After that, a transaction will be opened with the data modification privileges. All the records in the "3DDataSources" database will be deleted and the *Main* class instance will store itself in the database. Then the transaction will be completed by the *end_transaction* predicate and the access to the "AgentBlackboard.db" database will be ended by the *close* predicate.

```
goal:-
     datastore ? open,
     database ? begin_transaction('modifying'),!,
     database ? retract_all(),
```

```
database ? insert(self),
database ? end_transaction,
datastore ? close.
```

The instance of the *Main* class becomes available for other logical agents after the storing to the shaded database. In particular, an external agent can read this instance from the database and invoke the *register_consumer* predicate in the world to receive the information about the temperature of the people in the scope of the visual surveillance system. The external agent has to send himself as the argument of the *register_consumer* predicate. The *register_consumer* predicate of the former agent will store it to the *consumers* internal database.

```
register_consumer(ExternalAgent):-
    consumers ? insert(ExternalAgent).
```

During each call of the *frame_obtained* predicate of the class $3DVideo$ *Supplier*, the *notify_all_consumers* predicate is called. This predicate uses the search with backtracking to extract one-by-one the receivers from the *consumers* database and send them the data set.

```
notify_all_consumers(Skeletons,Image):-
    consumers ? find(ExternalAgent),
        notify_consumer(
            ExternalAgent,Skeletons,Image),
        fail.
notify_all_consumers(_,_).
```

The *notify_consumer* predicate implements the remote call of the predicate *new_frame* in the *ExternalAgent* external world.

```
notify_consumer(ExternalAgent,Skeletons,Image):-
    [ExternalAgent] [<<] new_frame(Skeletons,Image).
```

The syntax notation of this clause has the following semantics. The $<<$ infix indicates that so-called informational direct message is to be used for the data transfer. The informational direct message is a kind of asynchronous messages supported by the Actor Prolog language [6]. The square brackets in the $[<<]$ expression indicate that this message must not be buffered, that is, the message is to be discarded if the receiver is not processed it before the receiving the next message. The square brackets in the $[ExternalAgent]$ expression indicate that the remote call of the *new_frame* predicate is to be performed immediately during the execution of the command under consideration; otherwise the remote call will be suspended and afterward canceled during the backtracking of the *notify_all_consumers* predicate.

The receiving logical agent will accept and process the message *new_frame* (*Skeletons, Image*). In the example, the receiving agent has to analyze the *Skeletons* graph describing the skeletons of the people observed by the intelligent video surveillance system. The vertices and edges of the graph with the

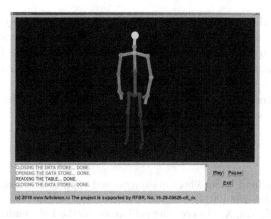

Fig. 2. A logical agent that estimates the average temperature of the human body parts during the unrestricted movements of people in the video scene.

TRACKED status (that means that the ToF camera observes them directly) will be selected and compared with the *Image* thermal imaging frame. The intensities of the pixels at the thermal image that correspond to the coordinates of the graph edges are averaged. The intensities of vertices and average intensities of edges are stored in a special table. In the course of the processing of new frames, a time average of the intensities of vertices and edges stored in the table will be implemented. The purpose of this processing is in that one estimates the average temperature of the human body parts during the unrestricted movements of the people in the video scene (see the Fig. 2).

The principles of analysis and fusion of heterogeneous multichannel video data by the means of the object-oriented logic programming were discussed by the example. A set of built-in classes of the Actor Prolog language for the database management as well as acquisition and distributed processing of 2D and 3D video data were considered. The complete text of the example considered in this paper is published in the installation package of the Actor Prolog that is freely available in the Web Site [10]. The source codes of the built-in classes considered in the paper are available on GitHub [8].

6   Conclusions

In the Actor Prolog project, mean and tools for 2D and 3D video data acquisition and processing are developed and implemented including the means for the fusion of 3D data collected using a ToF camera and a thermal imaging camera. In the authors' opinion, the main result of the project is in that the logic language is adopted for the effective processing of the big arrays of heterogeneous data. This is provided thanks to the object-oriented architecture of the Actor Prolog logic programming system that supplies the encapsulation of the big data arrays in the instances of specialized built-in classes. The developed logical means open new prospects in the area of intelligent visual surveillance, namely, they enable to implement semantic analysis of the video scenes, that is, conduct logical inference on the base of heterogeneous data describing the context of the human actions, objects, and events observed by the intelligent video surveillance system.

Acknowledgement. This research was supported by the Russian Foundation for Basic Research (grant number 16-29-09626-ofi-m).

References

1. Gade, R., Moeslund, T.B.: Thermal cameras and applications: a survey. Mach. Vis. Appl. **25**(1), 245–262 (2014)
2. Han, S., Gu, X., Gu, X.: An accurate calibration method of a multi camera system. In: Fei, M., Ma, S., Li, X., Sun, X., Jia, L., Su, Z. (eds.) LSMS/ICSEE -2017. CCIS, vol. 761, pp. 491–501. Springer, Singapore (2017). https://doi.org/10.1007/978-981-10-6370-1_49
3. Morozov, A., Obukhov, Y.: An approach to logic programming of intelligent agents for searching and recognizing information on the Internet. Pattern Recogn. Image Anal. **11**(3), 570–582 (2001)
4. Morozov, A.A.: Actor Prolog. Programmirovanie **5**, 66–78 (1994). in Russian
5. Morozov, A.A.: Actor Prolog: an object-oriented language with the classical declarative semantics. In: Sagonas, K., Tarau, P. (eds.) IDL 1999, pp. 39–53. France, Paris (1999)
6. Morozov, A.A.: Logic object-oriented model of asynchronous concurrent computations. Pattern Recogn. Image Anal. **13**(4), 640–649 (2003)
7. Morozov, A.A.: Operational approach to the modified reasoning, based on the concept of repeated proving and logical actors. In: Salvador Abreu, V.S.C. (ed.) CICLOPS 2007, Porto, Portugal, pp. 1–15 (2007)
8. Morozov, A.A.: A GitHub repository containing source codes of Actor Prolog built-in classes (2018). https://github.com/Morozov2012/actor-prolog-java-library
9. Morozov, A.A., Polupanov, A.F.: Intelligent visual surveillance logic programming: implementation issues. In: Ströder, T., Swift, T. (eds.) CICLOPS-WLPE 2014, pp. 31–45. No. AIB-2014-09 in Aachener Informatik Berichte, RWTH Aachen University, June 2014
10. Morozov, A.A., Sushkova, O.S.: The intelligent visual surveillance logic programming Web Site (2018). http://www.fullvision.ru
11. Morozov, A.A., Sushkova, O.S., Polupanov, A.F.: A translator of Actor Prolog to Java. In: Bassiliades, N., et al. (eds.) RuleML 2015 DC and Challenge. CEUR, Berlin (2015)
12. Morozov, A.A., Sushkova, O.S., Polupanov, A.F.: Object-oriented logic programming of 3D intelligent video surveillance: the problem statement. In: ISIE, pp. 1631–1636. IEEE Xplore Digital Library, Washington (2017)
13. Morozov, A.A., Sushkova, O.S., Polupanov, A.F.: Object-oriented logic programming of 3D intelligent video surveillance systems: the problem statement. RENSIT **2**(9), 205–214 (2017)
14. Morozov, A.A., Sushkova, O.S., Polupanov, A.F.: Towards the distributed logic programming of intelligent visual surveillance applications. In: Pichardo-Lagunas, O., Miranda-Jiménez, S. (eds.) MICAI 2016. LNCS (LNAI), vol. 10062, pp. 42–53. Springer, Cham (2017). https://doi.org/10.1007/978-3-319-62428-0_4

15. Nakagawa, W., et al.: Visualization of temperature change using RGB-D camera and thermal camera. In: Agapito, L., Bronstein, M.M., Rother, C. (eds.) ECCV 2014. LNCS, vol. 8925, pp. 386–400. Springer, Cham (2015). https://doi.org/10.1007/978-3-319-16178-5_27
16. Rangel, J., Soldan, S., Kroll, A.: 3D thermal imaging: fusion of thermography and depth cameras. In: International Conference on Quantitative InfraRed Thermography (2014)

A Distributed Probabilistic Model for Fault Diagnosis

Ana Li Oña García$^{(\boxtimes)}$, L. Enrique Sucar, and Eduardo F. Morales

Instituto Nacional de Asrofísica Óptica y Electrónica,
Sta. María Tonantzintla, Puebla, Mexico
{anali,esucar,emorales}@inaoep.mx

Abstract. Fault diagnosis in complex systems is important due to the impact it may have for reducing breakage costs or for avoiding production losses in industrial systems. Several approaches have been proposed for fault diagnosis, some of which are based on Bayesian Networks. Bayesian Networks are an adequate formalism for representing and reasoning under uncertainty conditions, however, they do not scale well for complex systems. For overcoming this limitation, researchers have proposed Multiply Sectioned Bayesian Networks. These are an extension of the Bayesian Networks for representing large domains, while ensuring the network inference in an efficient way. In this work we propose a distributed method for fault diagnosis in complex systems using Multiply Sectioned Bayesian Networks. The method was tested in the detection of multiple faults in combinational logic circuits showing comparable results with the literature in terms of accuracy, but with a significant reduction in the runtime.

Keywords: Fault diagnosis · Complex systems
Multiply Sectioned Bayesian Networks

1 Introduction

Fault detection is an important part of each engineering system, and it is often a prerequisite for commissioning, so systems must be robust to different types of faults which translates into high levels of reliability.

Research in this field has been focused on the application of different statistics techniques or Artificial Intelligence (AI), focusing efforts to timely detect abnormal behaviors from the analysis of the data of the sensed variables which translates into reduced repair costs.

A complex system is a system formed out of many components whose behavior is emergent, i.e., the behavior of the system cannot be simply inferred from the behavior of its components. A measure for assessing the complexity of such system is the amount of information necessary to describe its behavior [1]. Examples of complex systems include human economies, climate, nervous systems, and modern energy or telecommunication infrastructures.

© Springer Nature Switzerland AG 2018
G. R. Simari et al. (Eds.): IBERAMIA 2018, LNAI 11238, pp. 42–53, 2018.
https://doi.org/10.1007/978-3-030-03928-8_4

Several approaches have been proposed for fault detection, but not all take into account the uncertainty of real-world systems. In practice, model uncertainties and measurement noise can complicate fault detection, so the developed methods must be robust to these conditions. Bayesian Network (BN), represent an adequate formalism for the representation and reasoning under uncertainty conditions [19].

In [12], the authors proposed an algorithm for sensor validation by representing the relationships between the variables by using a Bayesian Network and the validation process is based on probabilistic propagation. The authors estimate the values of the variables, identifying the apparent fault from the expected value and the actual value of the analyzed variable. This work does not take into account, however, the complexity of the model domain and the distributed nature of its different components.

Multiply Sectioned Bayesian Networks (MSBNs), proposed by [26], are presented as an alternative for the modeling of large domain problems. MSBN identify domain partitions in smaller sub-domains that communicate with each other from shared information and where the inference process of the global network is performed efficiently.

In this work we focused on extending the work presented in [12] to a distributed approach, using the Multiply Sectioned Bayesian Network theory, for detection of multiple faults in complex systems. The proposal is tested by applying it to fault detection of combinational logic circuits.

The method was tested for 3 circuit examples, simulating the failed behavior of some of its components. The results show that, in terms of precision, our proposal has a behavior similar to the method proposed in [12], but it also results in a reduced runtime, and offers the possibility of modeling large domain problems for which the original method is intractable.

The remainder of this paper is organized as follows. First, in Sect. 2 the related work is presented. Section 3 describes the main concepts related to MSBN. In Sect. 4, we show the distributed method of fault diagnosis based on the proposal presented in [12]. In Sect. 5, we show our experimental study for fault diagnosis applied to combinational logic circuits. Finally, Sect. 6 presents some conclusions and future work.

2   Related Work

The methods of sensor validation (or more generally, the process of data validation) consist for two main stages: the detection of data faults and the correction of these failed data. The detection of defective data identifies dubious values or errors in the data, and the correction process provides methods to deal with problematic data [20]. In each category, different tools and methods exist in the scientific literature, and we will focus on the methods of fault detection as the main objective of our investigation.

In the state of the art related to fault detection, there are simple methods based on tests or physical or mathematical models, classifying the data in valid, invalid or missing [2,4]. These works, however, require knowledge of the observed phenomenon, what is not applicable to real problems, and where you do not have all the information of the study object.

Other studies in Artificial Intelligence have investigated the use of Artificial Neural Networks (ANNs) for sensor validation. Some of the network architectures use Multilayer Perceptrons for the estimation of some variables from other known [7,9,14,17].

In another work, [16], the authors use Multilayer Perceptrons to estimate variables, based on their values from previous epochs, for which they compare two approaches for the fault detection process. The first approach is based on the use of a set of Neural Networks for learning on-line, and the second approach is based on the use of Kalman filters [10]. The study reveals that neural online learning architectures have potential for estimation purposes in a sensor validation scheme.

Another technique proposed is Self-Organizing Maps. In these works the data are grouped into clusters of related data [3,22]. The detection of a fault is based on a measure of distance to the closest cluster.

Other works combine different Artificial Intelligence techniques. For example, in [18], the authors proposed a fault detection method using ANNs and Support Vector Machines (SVM) with Genetic Algorithms (GA).

All of these approaches that are based on the use of ANNs are limited by the need to learn the model from the complete information of the variables. It is necessary to use alternative techniques to predict the values of the variables in the presence of incomplete information or uncertain data.

Other works, such as those proposed in [8,11], introduce the use of Fuzzy Logic for the task of fault detection. The main limitation of using Fuzzy Logic is the need for expert knowledge to learn the membership functions.

Another technique used for the validation of sensor data, and which are robust to the uncertainty of the data, are probabilistic methods. The authors of [13] proposed sensor validation algorithms that combine different probabilistic methods, including Bayesian Networks. On the contrary, [21] proposed the validation of data using Sparse Bayesian Learning (SBL) and a Relevance Vector Machine (RVM), which is an SVM specialization.

Our research is an extension of the work presented in [12], for the validation of sensors in complex systems in the presence of uncertainty. The method consists of two fundamental stages: the apparent fault detection stage and the fault isolation stage.

In the fault detection stage, apparent faults are detected by comparing the current value with the predicted value through the propagation of beliefs, considering the rest of the variables as the evidence. This process is repeated for all variables, identifying those whose value differs from the value predicted as apparent faults.

In the fault isolation stage, from the apparent faults identified in the first stage and based on the property of the Markov Blanket (MB), an additional

Bayesian Network composed of two levels is created. The root nodes represent the real faults, and the nodes in the lower level represent the apparent faults.

The main advantage of this work is that it does not require fault data that can be difficult to obtain and is scarce, but it does not take into account the complexity of models in the inference process. In [6], the author demonstrated that the inference mechanism in the Bayesian Networks with multiple connections is a *NP-hard* problem, so that increasing the complexity (in terms of the connectivity of the network) of the problem modeled as a Bayesian Network increases the computational cost of probabilistic inference. That is why in the work presented in [12], the size of the domain of the problem is an important aspect, both in the probabilistic model obtained in the fault detection stage and in the Bayesian Network that is built in the fault isolation stage.

3   Multiply Sectioned Bayesian Networks

Multiply Sectioned Bayesian Networks (MSBNs) were proposed by [26] for the representation of large domain networks. An MSBN M is a set of Bayesian subnets that together defines a Bayesian Network (BN). M represents probabilistic dependence of a domain partitioned into sub-domains [25]. This technique constitutes an extension of the junction tree technique [15], where each node in the tree is formed by the clustering of a group of variables from the original network, and probabilistic inference is made on this new structure where each grouping acts as a unit for the passage of messages.

To ensure exact inference, MSBNs must satisfy the following tree conditions. The mathematical principles, as well as the definitions, are extracted from the work presented in [24].

(a) The subnets must satisfy a *hypertree* condition.

Definition 1. *Let $G = (V, E)$ be a connected graph sectioned into subgraphs $G_i = (V_i, E_i)$ such that the G_i's can be associated with a tree Ψ with the following property: Each node in Ψ is labeled by a G_i and each link between G_k and G_m is labeled by the interface $V_k \cap V_m$ such that for each i and j, $V_i \cap V_j$ is contained in each subgraph on the path between G_i and G_j in Ψ. Then Ψ is a hypertree over G. Each G_i is a hypernode and each interface is a hyperlink.*

(b) Variables shared between subnets must form a *d-sepset*.

Definition 2. *Let G be a directed graph such that a hypertree over G exists. Let x be a node that is contained in more than one subgraph and $\pi(x)$ be its parents in G. Then x is a d-sepnode if there exists one subgraph that contains $\pi(x)$. An interface I is a d-sepnode if every $x \in I$ is a d-sepnode.*

(c) The structure of an MSBN is a multiply sectioned DAG (MSDAG) with a hypertree organization.

Definition 3. *A hypertree MSDAG $G = \bigsqcup_i G_i$, where each G_i is a DAG, is a connected DAG such that (1) there exists a hypertree Ψ over G, and (2) each hyperlink in Ψ is a d-sepset.*

Under these conditions an MSBN is defined as:

Definition 4. *An MSBN M is a triplet (V, G, P). $V = \bigcup_i V_i$ is the domain where each V_i is a set of variables, called a subdomain. $G = \bigsqcup_i G_i$ (a hypertree MSDAG) is the structure where nodes of each DAG G_i are labeled by elements of V_i. Let x be a variable and $\pi(x)$ be all parents of x in G. For each x, exactly one of its occurrences (in a G_i containing $\{x\} \cup \pi(x)$) is assigned $P(x|\pi(x))$, and each occurrence in other DAGs is assigned a uniform potential. $P = \prod_i P_i$ is the joint probability distribution (jpd), where each P_i is the product of the potentials associated with nodes in G_i. A triplet $S_i = (V_i, G_i, P_i)$ is called a subnet of M. Two subnets S_i and S_j are said to be adjacent if G_i and G_j are adjacent.*

Figure 1 shows a trivial example of MSBN with three sections or subnets. The dashed nodes correspond to the variables shared between subnets.

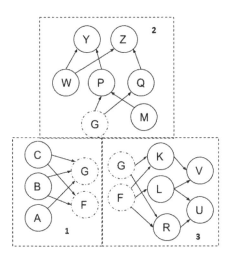

Fig. 1. A example of MSBN with three sections. Each section represents a sub-domain of the problem. The dashed nodes are the variables shared between adjacent sections.

The use of MSBN is limited to problem domains capable of breaking down into smaller subdomains. Many complex systems meet this condition so it is possible to apply this technique.

4   Distributed Fault Detection Method

In this section we briefly describe the proposed method from extending the work presented in [12] to a distributed approach with the use of the MSBN technique. To organize the work, the following subsections are divided, taking into account the two stages proposed by the authors of [12]: fault detection and fault isolation.

4.1   Fault Detection Stage

In the fault detection stage, a MSBN is constructed, representing the relationships between the variables of the domain to be validated, and partitioned into sections that satisfy the conditions described in the previous section (partitions are created from localization principles inherent to each problem domain). For the construction of the MSBN, we use the research tool WebWeavr-IV [23]. The four main steps for its construction are summarized below:

(a) Bayesian Networks construction for each section (individual agent level). For this step the necessary parameters include:
   - a set of variables;
   - a graph that represents the relations of independence between the variables; and
   - a set of conditional probability distributions.
(b) Knowledge representation at the agent society level. In this stage the structure for communication between adjacent sections is defined. For this task we define:
   - organization of sections or agents;
   - public variables between adjacent sections; and
   - hypertree condition check.
(c) Model verification. This stage includes obtaining the junction tree associated with each section, including:
   - global acyclicity test and
   - d-sepnode test.
(d) Compilation into Linked Cluster Trees. This structure is responsible for ensuring efficient communication between the adjacent sections through message passing.

For more details related to the construction and inference process of MSBNs see [26].

In general, the apparent fault detection algorithm consists of the following steps:

```
1: Obtaining the MSBN that represents the domain of the problem to validate
2: for new evidence do
3:     for each section do
4:         for each variable to be validated (usually all) do
5:             Propagate the probabilities to obtain the posterior probability distri-
             bution of the variable given the new evidence. The propagation process involves
             communication between adjacent sections
6:             Compare the predicted value (maximum posterior probability) with
             the current value of the variable and decide if there is an error
7:         end for
8:     end for
9: end for
```

The output of the algorithm consists of a list S of variables with apparent faults related to the section or sections to which they belong in the case of being shared variables.

4.2   Fault Isolation Stage

In the fault isolation stage, new Bayesian Networks are built relative to the sections of the model to be validated. These new Bayesian Networks consist of two levels. The nodes in the first level represent, for all variables, the events with real faults, and the nodes in the second level represent the apparent faults in all the variables. The relationship between the two levels corresponds with the Extended Markov Blanket (EMB) for each variable.

The EMB of one variable is defined as the parents, children, and other parents of their children, including the variable. In [12] the authors showed that it is enough to find matches between the apparent faults and the Extended Markov Blanket to isolate the real faults. Considering as new evidence the apparent faults identified in the previous stage, the probabilities associated with the real faults of each variable are updated.

For the case where apparent faults are identified in shared variables, the isolation network is formed from the union of the isolation networks corresponding to each section to which the shared variable belongs. Figure 2 represents the isolation network obtained for Sect. 1 of the example described in Fig. 1.

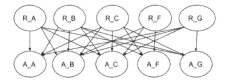

Fig. 2. Isolation network corresponding to Sect. 1 of the example of Fig. 1. The nodes (variables) at the upper level, R_i, correspond to the real faults, and the ones in the lower level, A_i, to the apparent faults.

5   Experiments and Results

In this section we tested the distributed algorithm of sensor validation for fault detection in combinational logic circuits. Initially, we will describe the main steps followed to obtain the models of MSBNs, then we will present the used evaluation metrics, and finally, we will describe the obtained results.

5.1   Integration of MSBNs in Combinational Logic Circuits

The case studies used to test our proposal correspond to combinational logic circuits formed by several components (subnets or sections) that communicate with each other. Each component is formed by a set of logical gates: AND, OR and NOT. Figure 3 depicts a simple example of a circuit partitioned in five components.

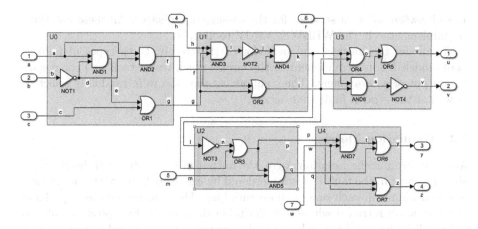

Fig. 3. Combinational logic circuit partitioned into 5 components.

For the work with the MSBNs we use the WEBWEAVR-IV toolkit [23], both for the creation of Bayesian networks at the local level, and for communication between the adjacent sections globally.

Each component is modeled as a Bayesian Network where each node represents the input and output variables of each logic gate within the circuit. For the parameters learning of the BN, the normal behavior of the circuit was simulated with the incomplete information of the variables represented by the BNs. Figure 4, shows a BN from component U0 in Fig. 3.

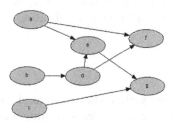

Fig. 4. Bayesian Network that represents the relationship between the variables of component U0 of Fig. 3.

After defining the sections at the local level, the communication structure is defined at the section level, establishing the variables shared between adjacent sections and verifying the hypertree condition. The model is also verified with the global aciclicity test and d-sepset tests. The last step in the construction of the model is the inference in all the MSBN that consists of two fundamental steps: the inference at global level using the junction tree technique and the inference to guarantee the global consistency from the construction of the Linked Cluster

Trees between adjacent sections for the passage of messages. All these functions are implemented in the WEBWEAVR-IV toolkit.

To model the unsuccessful behavior of the circuit, three types of failures were modeled: some component of the circuit stuck to 0, stuck to 1, or negate the output of a component. The components that fail were randomly selected, as well as the type of fault that occurs.

5.2 Evaluation Metrics

After performing the isolation stage, the output of our system will be the variables involved in the fault detection ordered by the probability of the occurrence of a real failure in each one of those variables. This can be seen as a problem of information retrieval where it is desirable that, in the first positions of this ordered list, the variables with real faults are found which would be the relevant variables.

To test the behavior of our research, we used two evaluation metrics proposed in the information retrieval work: P@5 and MAP [5]. P@5 is the precision at the 5-th position in the ranking of results. Mean Average Precision (MAP) is the Mean of the Average Precision scores for a group of queries, and average precision is the average of the precision scores at the rank locations of each relevant variable. This metric takes into account the order in which the variables are returned and is defined as:

$$MAP = AVG \left(\frac{\sum_{i=1}^{n} P(i) * rel(i)}{|relevant\_variables|} \right) \tag{1}$$

where n is the number of retrieved variables, $P(i)$ is the precision of the first i variables, and $rel(i)$ is a binary function indicating if variable at i-position is relevant or not.

5.3 Results

For the experiments we tested with 3 different examples of logic circuits. To each example, 20 cases of failures were made, 50% simple faults and 50% multiple faults (two and three simultaneous failures). Each test case corresponds to the abnormal behavior of one or more components of the circuit and consists of 100 instances.

Table 1 shows a summary of the test examples. The results are shown independently of the sectioning performed on each example.

To evaluate the effectiveness of our proposal we will compare it with the work presented in [12], which we will call baseline.

Table 2 shows the results of the P@5 and MAP for the three test cases. As shown in the results for example 1 and 2, the results are the same, which makes sense because the main difference of our proposal with the baseline is the representation and the way of making the inference, which translates into reduced runtime as the complexity of the problem to be modeled increases. For

Table 1. Summary of the logic gates and the variables of each test example.

Example	OR gates	AND gates	NOT gates	Variables
1	8	6	4	25
2	20	24	8	97
3	96	75	44	391

Table 2. Comparison of our proposal vs. [12] (baseline) in P@5 and MAP for the three combinational logic circuits of Table 1.

Example	1		2		3	
	P@5	MAP	P@5	MAP	P@5	MAP
Baseline	0.9417	0.5788	0.8917	0.6113	-	-
Our proposal	0.9417	0.5788	0.8917	0.6113	0.8802	0.5771

example 3, given the complexity of the problem, it is not possible to obtain a solution for the case of the work presented in [12].

Table 3 shows the results of the two metrics used for the detection of simple and multiple faults. The best results, in terms of P@5, are obtained for the detection of simple faults, where in most cases the variable with fault is returned within the first 5 positions of variables with the highest probability of having a real fault.

Table 3. Comparison between simple and multiple faults in terms of P@5 and MAP.

Example	1		2		3	
	P@5	MAP	P@5	MAP	P@5	MAP
Simple faults	1	0.575	0.9	0.5583	1	0.5409
Multiple faults	0.8833	0.5826	0.864	0.6643	0.7262	0.5931

Table 4 shows the comparison in terms of execution time of the work presented in [12] vs. our proposal. The times are indicated in minutes. This analysis includes the learning of the parameters, the fault detection stage and the fault isolation stage. The time reduction of the proposed algorithm is considerable, and as the complexity of the problem increases, the difference becomes even more evident. In Example 3, given the size of the problem, it is not possible to obtain a solution with the baseline method.

Table 4. Comparison between the average execution time of [12] (baseline) vs. our proposal. The times are indicated in minutes.

Example	1	2	3
Baseline	0.1173	23.717	-
Our proposal	0.0325	9.07	4368.9

6   Conclusions

We proposed a distributed extension of the work presented in [12], for the multiple faults detection in complex systems. For this, we use MSBNs, that is a technique for representing large domains that it is possible to partition into smaller sub-domains. The proposed method was tested for the detection of faults in combinational logic circuits. Based on the experiments, we can conclude that the proposed method maintains the effectiveness in terms of accuracy with respect to the original work while significantly reducing the execution time which makes it possible to deal with larger domain models.

As future work, we will apply this approach to other domains, in particular for diagnosis of wind turbines, which include discrete and continuous variables.

Acknowledgement. This work was sponsored by CEMIE-Eolico (CONACYT and SENER) and INAOE. The first author gratefully acknowledges CONACyT for her master scholarship 611489.

References

1. Bar-Yam, Y.: Dynamics of Complex Systems, vol. 213. Addison-Wesley, Reading (1997)
2. Bertrand-Krajewski, J.L., Winkler, S., Saracevic, E., Torres, A., Schaar, H.: Comparison of and uncertainties in raw sewage cod measurements by laboratory techniques and field UV-visible spectrometry. Water Sci. Technol. **56**(11), 17–25 (2007)
3. Böhme, T., Cox, C., Valentin, N., Denoeux, T.: Comparison of autoassociative neural networks and kohonen maps for signal failure detection and reconstruction. Intell. Eng. Syst. Through Artif. Neural Netw. **9**, 637–644 (1991)
4. Branisavljević, N., Kapelan, Z., Prodanović, D.: Improved real-time data anomaly detection using context classification. J. Hydroinformatics **13**(3), 307–323 (2011)
5. Chowdhury, G.G.: Introduction to Modern Information Retrieval. Facet Publishing, London (2010)
6. Cooper, G.F.: The computational complexity of probabilistic inference using Bayesian belief networks. Artif. Intell. **42**(2–3), 393–405 (1990)
7. Eryurek, E., Upadhyaya, B.: Sensor validation for power plants using adaptive backpropagation neural network. IEEE Trans. Nuclear Sci. **37**(2), 1040–1047 (1990)
8. Goebel, K., Agogino, A.: An architecture for fuzzy sensor validation and fusion for vehicle following in automated highways. In: Proceedings of the 29th International Symposium on Automotive Technology and Automation (1996)

9. Guo, T.H., Nurre, J.: Sensor failure detection and recovery by neural networks. In: Seattle International Joint Conference on Neural Networks, IJCNN 1991, vol. 1, pp. 221–226. IEEE (1991)
10. Haykin, S.S., et al.: Kalman Filtering and Neural Networks. Wiley, Hoboken (2001)
11. Holbert, K.E., Heger, A.S., Alang-Rashid, N.K.: Redundant sensor validation by using fuzzy logic. Nuclear Sci. Eng. **118**(1), 54–64 (1994)
12. Ibargüengoytia, P.H., Vadera, S., Sucar, L.E.: A probabilistic model for information and sensor validation. Comput. J. **49**(1), 113–126 (2005)
13. Ibarguengoytia, P., et al.: Any time probabilistic sensor validation. Ph.D. thesis, University of Salford, UK (1997)
14. Khadem, M., Alexandro, F., Colley, R.: Sensor validation in power plants using neural networks. In: Neural Network Computing for the Electric Power Industry, pp. 51–54 (1993)
15. Lauritzen, S.L., Spiegelhalter, D.J.: Local computations with probabilities on graphical structures and their application to expert systems. J. Roy. Stat. Soc. Ser. B (Methodol.) **50**, 157–224 (1988)
16. Napolitano, M.R., Windon, D.A., Casanova, J.L., Innocenti, M., Silvestri, G.: Kalman filters and neural-network schemes for sensor validation in flight control systems. IEEE Trans. Control Syst. Technol. **6**(5), 596–611 (1998)
17. Rajakarunakaran, S., Venkumar, P., Devaraj, D., Rao, K.S.P.: Artificial neural network approach for fault detection in rotary system. Appl. Soft Comput. **8**(1), 740–748 (2008)
18. Samanta, B.: Gear fault detection using artificial neural networks and support vector machines with genetic algorithms. Mech. Syst. Sig. Process. **18**(3), 625–644 (2004)
19. Sucar, L.E.: Probabilistic Graphical Models - Principles and Applications. Advances in Computer Vision and Pattern Recognition. Springer, Heidelberg (2015). https://doi.org/10.1007/978-1-4471-6699-3
20. Sun, S., et al.: Literature review for data validation methods. Sci. Technol. **47**(2), 95–102 (2011)
21. Tipping, M.E.: Sparse Bayesian learning and the relevance vector machine. J. Mach. Learn. Res. **1**(Jun), 211–244 (2001)
22. Valentin, N., et al.: A neural network-based software sensor for coagulation control in a water treatment plant. Intell. Data Anal. **5**(1), 23–39 (2001)
23. Xiang, Y.: Webweavr-iv research toolkit (2006)
24. Xiang, Y.: Comparison of multiagent inference methods in multiply sectioned Bayesian networks. Int. J. Approx. Reason. **33**(3), 235–254 (2003)
25. Xiang, Y., Jensen, F.V., Chen, X.: Inference in multiply sectioned Bayesian networks: methods and performance comparison. IEEE Trans. Syst. Man Cybern. Part B (Cybern.) **36**(3), 546–558 (2005)
26. Xiang, Y., Poole, D., Beddoes, M.P.: Multiply sectioned Bayesian networks and junction forests for large knowledge-based systems. Comput. Intell. **9**(2), 171–220 (1993)

Semantic Representation for Collaboration Trajectories in Communities of Practice

Matheus Pereira[1(✉)], Rosa Maria Vicari[1], and João Luis Tavares da Silva[2]

[1] PPGC/UFRGS, Porto Alegre, Brazil
{mpereira,rosa}@inf.ufrgs.br
[2] UNIFTEC, Caxias do Sul, Brazil
joaoluis.tavares@gmail.com

Abstract. In communities of practice (CoP), learning occurs through constant interactions of their participants. The social aspect is fundamental for the construction of knowledge. This work uses semantic web technologies and ontologies to structure and represent the interactions of CoPs participants around a dynamic user profile. This user profile describes a set of dispersed properties and relationships in CoPs, allowing collaborative trajectories recovery in these learning environments.

Keywords: Communities of practice · Semantic web · Ontologies
User profile · Collaboration trajectory

1 Introduction

Communities of Practice consist in groups of people who share a common interest and learn through continuous interactions [1]. The learner is an active agent that establishes relations, produces and socializes knowledge [2]. The social character of a CoP is fundamental to the knowledge construction process. It is through user interactions that bonds are created, experiences are shared, and the knowledge is explicited. For this reason, this work investigates how the dynamics of CoPs can be represented to describe collaboration trajectories in the context of learning, and try to answer the following question: is it possible to build a knowledge base capable of capturing the dynamic and distributed aspect of the interactions in communities of practice?

In order to answer this research question, we propose the use of semantic web technologies and ontologies to describe the relationships among the CoPs, their collaboration tools, contents and participants. The construction of this knowledge base will be explored to define a user profile that evolves while the participants interact and learn through regular exchanges. This dynamic profile allow us to represent collaboration trajectories, which map a group of properties and describe the forms of relationships that may occur in communities of practice, according to the 3C Collaboration Model [4].

© Springer Nature Switzerland AG 2018
G. R. Simari et al. (Eds.): IBERAMIA 2018, LNAI 11238, pp. 54–66, 2018.
https://doi.org/10.1007/978-3-030-03928-8_5

2   Background

User profile is the process of managing and maintenance information associated with the user [5]. Studies involving information retrieval [6], content recommendation [7], adaptive virtual learning environments [5] and intelligent tutor systems [8] concentrate their efforts on this development. Knowledge, goals, interests, experiences and context are some of the information represented in user models. Intelligent tutoring systems handle user profile looking for recognizing student difficulties to offer guidance that facilitates their learning process [9].

In the CoPs context, the user interactions will be captured in order to follow, trace and analyze their learning path. The purpose of this approach is to identify the collaboration degree and the intensity of relations about CoPs participants in collaborative activities. The dynamic user profile consists of the semantic representation of the user interactions and involves the information sources relationship to their activities in the community. The capture and description of these actions will be used to represent the user collaboration trajectory in a given community.

Several researches use semantic web technologies to formalize user profiles [7,10,13], communities of practice [11,12] and collaboration in online communities [14,15]. These technologies associated with ontological representations promote structural, syntactic and semantic interoperability of information. The reuse of ontologies like FOAF (*Friend of a Friend*) and SIOC (*Semantically-Interlinked Online Communities*) also contribute to promote the information interoperability [13,15]. FOAF ontology [17] allows representing people and their social relationships. SIOC ontology [16] provides a vocabulary to represent online communities and user-generated content.

In this work, we have applied semantic web technologies and an ontological representation, reusing FOAF and SIOC, in order to achieve a profile interoperability. This approach extends the possibilities of acquisition and information exchange, and allows services sharing between applications. In addition, it is fundamental to provide computational structures that manipulate and make it possible to extract knowledge about the stored information in an autonomous way. As a result, services using ontologies, are capable of extending their capacity to build knowledge, to perform inferences, to retrieve content from different servers, to stimulate the relationship between users and to engage individuals in a permanent learning environment [7].

3   Communities of Practice Platform

The Communities of Practice Platform CoPPLA [2], used in this experiment, consists of a set of communication and collaboration tools for the instrumentation of CoPs. These tools include manipulation of texts, images, web pages, links, events, discussion forums and spaces for learning experiences. Participants have the ability to create and manage their communities as a space to share knowledge involving learning activities. Projects developed with the CoPPLA involve knowledge exchange through the conduction of collaborative learning activities. The CoPPLA environment provides the support for network interactions and the sharing of practices with collective access for simultaneous exchanges between participants. Figure 1 shows the view of a content in a CoP (center), its domain (top), its participants (right) and some of its collaboration and communication tools (left menu).

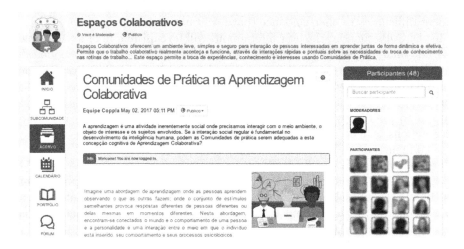

Fig. 1. View of a shared content in a community of practice

3.1 CoPPLA Ontology

In [2], a communities of practice framework is proposed with the objective of providing a semantic knowledge representation model for any CoP Platform (*CoPPLA*). In [3], a reference ontology was proposed in order to describe a general user profile in CoPs. This model focus on communities representation, its participants, interest profile and domain. The user profile has an identity, interactions, interests, roles and skills, classified in two levels: static and dynamic profile. In [18], an expanded CoPPLA ontology was conceived through studies on the real model of CoPs to represent the knowledge in a web CoP platform. The relationships proposed are derived from actions that users can perform in the CoPs. The schema also includes FOAF and SIOC concepts.

In this ontology (Fig. 2), the semantic structure of a community of practice (*CommunityOfPractice*) is a subclass of a community (*sioc.Community*). The community has a set of practices (*has_practices, Practice*) related to a domain of interest (*related_domain, Domain*). An online community (*sioc.Community*) has associated users (*has_user, sioc.UserAccount*) and a user is an extension of the semantic representation of SIOC online user. In addition, the user is associated with an FOAF representation (*account_of, foaf.Person*). The users (*sioc.UserAccount*) create content (*has_creator, sioc.Item*) in the CoPs' spaces for collaboration (*sioc.Container*). In these spaces the actions (*Action*) of the participants (*agent, foaf.Person*) happen. These actions may be related to interaction (*InteractionAction*), search (*SearcAction*), organization (*Organize-Action*), update (*UpdateAction*) or access (*ConsumeAction*) to the CoP content.

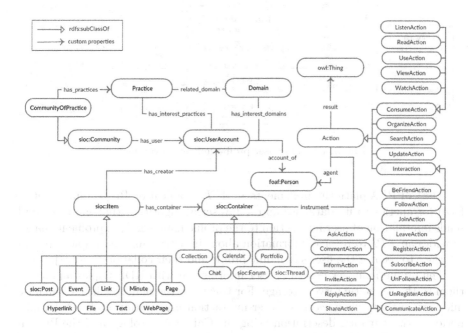

Fig. 2. Current CoPPLA ontology.

The user activity in a CoP is the result of an action that is part of a relationship set of the CoPPLA platform. These actions can be specialized in actions of consumption (*ConsumeAction*), organization (*OrganizeAction*), search (*SearchAction*), updating (*UpdateAction*) and interaction (*Interaction*). Therefore, the action class (*Action*) is fundamental to this work since the dynamic profile, the interaction history and the collaboration trajectory are built from the user's actions.

4 Dynamic User Profile Manager

The dynamic profile manager organizes the dispersed interaction information inside the CoPs into a user profile with associated semantics. With the help of a semantic server, this profile allows to execute a series of queries and inferences evidencing complex relationships between the participants and the knowledge distributed in the environment. As shown in Fig. 3, the profile manager operates between the communities of practice platform and the semantic server.

The manager is implemented over the *Tornado Python* web framework. Communication between the CoPPLA platform and the profile manager happens through *REST* (REpresentational State Transfer) interfaces and data in *JSON* (JavaScript Object Notation) format.

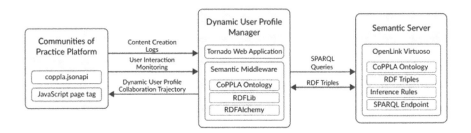

Fig. 3. Dynamic user profile manager overview

The CoPPLA platform implements an *API* (Application Programming Interface) for queries to its database and a Javascript algorithm that monitors and sends information of user interaction to the profile manager. The profile manager provides an *API* to receive information about user tracking and implements an interface to recover the user's dynamic profile and their collaboration trajectory.

The profile manager describes user information with RDF triples and sends them to the semantic server storage. For this task, the manager has a semantic middleware that, when receiving user interaction information in JSON format, performs the semantic description using the CoPPLA ontology and the Python libraries *RDFLib* and *RDFAlchemy*. Lastly, the semantic server is implemented on the *Openlink Virtuoso* universal server. The semantic server stores the set of RDF triples resulting from the mapping process and semantic description, is responsible for queries and inferences, and provides a *SPARQL endpoint* for external access. Virtuoso and SPARQL make up the semantic server data layer core, allowing semantic descriptions to be exposed and consulted on the web.

4.1   Acquisition of User Actions

Web analytics is the process that involves collecting, measuring and monitoring aspects of user behavior, combined and transformed into data that may be analyzed [19,20]. When applied to education, the Web analytics techniques are known as Learning Analytics (LA) and Educational Data Mining (EDM) [21]. These techniques are essential for capturing information related to the interaction of participants in learning environments.

In this work, user actions are a subset of the actions (*Action*) described in the CoPPLA ontology. This subset includes access actions (*ConsumeAction*), search (*SearchAction*), and content update (*UpdateAction*). It also includes interaction actions (*InteractAction*) following and unfollowing other users and themes

(*FollowAction, UnfollowAction*), participating or stop participating in a community (*JoinAction, LeaveAction*) and communication actions (*CommunicateAction*), sharing content (*ShareAction*) and participating in chats (*CommentAction, AskAction, ReplyAction*). The user profile manager obtains this information using Web analytics techniques in two distinct forms: queries to the communities of practice platform database to acquire information related to the collaboration actions available on the server; and Scripts to follow user interaction and capture information related to content access, sending and receiving messages, searches and contexts where actions occur individually.

4.2 Mapping and Semantic Description

When receiving data from user interaction in JSON format, the manager triggers the middleware responsible for the mapping process and semantic description of the collaborative actions, associating a set of RDF triples to each collaborative action in the community. A comment in the forum of a community of practice, for example, has its semantic description associated with the *SIOC.Post* class. All content shared on the platform generates a set of triples containing title, description, date and time, location published and the participant responsible for the content. A creation event (*ShareAction*) is also associated with the content.

A community of practice concept (*CommunityOfPractice*) consists of a set of spaces for collaboration where participants are able to share news, interact, hold discussions, and maintain organized the collective and individual productions. The spaces mapped in this work are collection, calendar, portfolio, forum and tasks. These spaces are described with classes that are specializations of *SIOC.Container* class and serve as instrument (*instrument*) for the actions (*Action*) in the platform. Every action has an agent (*FOAF.Agent*) that executes it and a context (*context*), date and time (*startTime, endTime*) in which it takes place. An action may include the community where it occurred (*location*) and the collaboration tool used (*instrument*) by the agent. The manager has the ability to infer the location and collaboration tool used from the context where the action occurred and from the relationships described in the CoPPLA ontology (*has_container, container_of, is_part_of_community, is_composed_of_container*).

From this mapping, collaboration scenarios with associated semantics are represented, for example: in a community (*CommunityOfPractice*), a participant (*FOAF.Person*) accesses the collection of the community (*Collection*) and shares (*ShareAction*) a text (*Page*). A second user (*FOAF.Person*) views this content (*ConsumeAction*) and leaves a comment (*CommentAction*) for its creator. The creator in turn responds to the comment (*ReplyAction*) and decides to follow the publications of the other user (*FollowAction*).

5 User Profile and Collaboration Trajectory

The dynamic profile is the result of user actions on the platform. The semantic description of these actions increases the expressiveness and the ability to represent the information, allowing reasoning and inferences that may be explored to find complex relationships distributed in the environment. A simple information that can be retrieved from this representation is the **user interaction history**. This result can be obtained by means of an all-action query (*Action*) where the agent is an user in question. The representation capacity and the dynamic aspect of the profile becomes apparent when it is possible to associate information to its history, such as the number of views of a particular content, the number of users that interacted in the same context, and related subjects and contents.

According to the *3C Model* [4], in order to collaborate, individuals must exchange information (**Communication**), operate together in a shared environment (**Cooperation**) and organize themselves (**Coordination**), assigning responsibilities and supervising each other. Therefore, collaboration includes reciprocity and interdependency between pairs. Based on this definition, this work models an **user collaboration trajectory** as a *historical set of communication actions among participants of CoPs in the same context*. The availability of different tools for collaboration, as well as the ability to share and access content in CoPs, provide the necessary resources for communication and cooperation actions. Coordination occurs implicitly by organizing tools and CoPs structures and the commitments, conventions and vocabularies defined by the participants themselves during communication.

The identification of collaboration in communities of practice is done through a semantic query to relate users only in contexts where more than one participant has interacted by means of communication actions (*CommunicateAction*). Using a semantic query for retrieving communication actions in the same context, the relations between the participants become apparent. This query highlights users who interacted with each other, while describing the path taken by the participant when navigating in the environment. In this way, the collaboration trajectory of a user is inferred from the relationships among participants on the same content, be it through sharing or discussions about a resource.

6   Experiment: A Collaboration Scenario

We have built several scenarios to validate this work. In the great part of these scenarios, the semantic server retrieves static information and the topics of interest from users, the communities of practice, the collaboration tools, the shared content, their related information such as title, description, creation date, agent responsible for sharing and location, the topics marked in the publications, and the sharing actions corresponding to the creation of each content.

The semantic description of a general CoPPLA use case allows us to represent the progressive and dynamic aspect of the user profile built from the interactions and relationships distributed in the platform. A semantic queries usage is proposed to find static user information and explicit relations. Moreover, these queries takes advantage of ontologies, semantic web technologies and the user profile to discover indirect relations and information resulting from reasoning processes over the RDF triples. Three queries snippets and its results will be presented below from the perspective of the user *John*.

User Personal Information: The Query 1 searches for John's static profile information described with the *SIOC:UserAccount* and *FOAF:Person* classes, including their topics of interest. The query selects predicates (*?Predicate*, *?Value*) related to the user and his online account, as showed in Table 1. The user information described with associated semantics contributes to the interoperability of the CoPPLA platform. An external agent with access to the SPARQL endpoint can performs this query and will be able to interpret the results even without knowing how CoPPLA platform works internally. Navigating to the description of the predicate *FOAF:topic_interest*, for example, the agent, human or software, may verify that it is something for which the user has an interest. The same holds true for any property with a formal description.

Query 1. John's personal information.

```
SELECT DISTINCT ?predicate , ?value WHERE {
  {
    ?user foaf:account ?account .
    ?user ?predicate ?obj
  } UNION {
    ?account a sioc:UserAccount .
    ?account ?predicate ?obj
  }
  OPTIONAL { ?obj rdfs:label ?label . }
  BIND ( IF(?label , ?label , ?obj) AS ?value ) .
  FILTER ( ?user = <http://Plone/author/john> )}
```

Table 1. John's personal information semantically described.

Predicate	Value
http://xmlns.com/foaf/0.1/topic_interest	Internet of things
http://xmlns.com/foaf/0.1/topic_interest	Semantic web
http://xmlns.com/foaf/0.1/topic_interest	Recommender systems
http://xmlns.com/foaf/0.1/birthday	10–29
http://xmlns.com/foaf/0.1/gender	male
http://xmlns.com/foaf/0.1/age	53
http://xmlns.com/foaf/0.1/lastName	Smith
http://xmlns.com/foaf/0.1/firstName	John

User Interactions: This query proposes to relate the participants of communities of practice according to their interactions in the same context. The query considers all users actions, including those do not result in information accessible by their peers, such as content access and search. This query implies some level of interaction between users, however, does not allow to affirm that there was collaboration between the participants of communities of practice. Access by different users to the same resource, for example, is part of these results (Table 2), but can not be considered a collaborative action, even if users benefit from the content when accessing it.

Query 2. John's interactions with other participants.

```
SELECT DISTINCT ?context ?john_action ?user2 ?action2
WHERE {
    ?action coppla:context ?context .
    ?action coppla:agent ?user .
    ?action rdf:type ?type1 .
    ?type1 rdfs:label ?joao_action .
    ?action coppla:startTime ?datetime .
    ?context coppla:title ?context_title .
    ?other_action coppla:context ?context .
    ?other_action coppla:agent ?other_user .
    ?other_action rdf:type ?type2 .
    ?type2 rdfs:label ?action2 .
    ?other_user foaf:firstName ?user2 .
    FILTER( ?user = <http://Plone/author/joao> &&
    ?user != ?other_user )
} ORDER BY(?datetime)
```

Table 2. John's interactions with other participants.

Context	john_action	user2	action2
Collaborative Filtering	Consume Action	Rosa	Comment Action
Collaborative Filtering	Share Action	Rosa	Comment Action
Collaborative Filtering	Follow Action	Rosa	Comment Action
FOAF/SIOC Ontologies	Consume Action	Matheus	Comment Action
FOAF/SIOC Ontologies	Consume Action	Matheus	Follow Action
FOAF/SIOC Ontologies	Consume Action	Rosa	Reply Action
FOAF/SIOC Ontologies	Consume Action	Matheus	Share Action
Collaborative Filtering	Reply Action	Rosa	Comment Action
FOAF/SIOC Ontologies	Reply Action	Matheus	Comment Action
FOAF/SIOC Ontologies	Reply Action	Rosa	Reply Action
FOAF/SIOC Ontologies	Reply Action	Matheus	Share Action
OBAA Pattern	Consume Action	Clara	Comment Action
OBAA Pattern	Consume Action	José	Reply Action
OBAA Pattern	Comment Action	José	Reply Action
OBAA Pattern	Comment Action	Clara	Share Action

Communication Actions: Looking forward to identifying collaboration in communities of practice, this query attempts to relate users in contexts where more than one participant has interacted through communication actions (*CommunicateAction*), subclass of action (*Action*) on the CoPPLA ontology. This query definition allow us to follow the **collaboration trajectory** from the perspective of individual users, but also, the association with the other collaborative activities in the various contexts of a CoP, representing the collective production of the participants and the community of practice, displaying its practice and domain. In this way, the collaboration trajectory of a user is inferred from the relationships between the participants in the same content, either through sharing or discussions about the resource (Table 3).

Query 3. John's interactions with other participants.

```
SELECT DISTINCT ?context ?user1 ?action1 ?user2 ?action2
WHERE {
    ?action rdf:type ?type .
    ?type rdfs:subClassOf* coppla:CommunicateAction .
    ?action coppla:context ?context .
    ?context coppla:title ?context_title .
    ?action coppla:agent ?user .
    ?user foaf:firstName ?user1 .
    ?action rdf:type ?type1 .
    ?type1 rdfs:label ?action1 .
    ?action coppla:startTime ?datetime .
    ?other_action coppla:context ?context .
    ?other_action rdf:type ?type2 .
    ?type2 rdfs:subClassOf* coppla:CommunicateAction .
    ?other_action coppla:agent ?other_user .
    ?other_user foaf:firstName ?user2 .
    ?other_action rdf:type ?type2 .
    ?type2 rdfs:label ?action2
    FILTER( ?user = <http://Plone/author/john> &&
    ?user != ?other_user )}
```

7   Results and Discussion

This work propose a mapping of relationships among CoPs, collaboration tools, participants and their interactions, proposing a semantic representation for the dynamically constructed knowledge in CoPs. The proposed solution establishes services for the acquisition, persistence and recovery of interactions in CoPs. A semantic server stores the RDF triples described with the CoPPLA, FOAF and SIOC ontologies, allowing the execution of semantic queries and inferences. These queries retrieve information from the users and their dispersed interactions in the various collaboration tools of a CoP. This information can be used to find interests, historical interactions, and collaboration trajectories in CoPs.

Table 3. Example of John's collaboration trajectory.

Context	user_1	type_action_1	user_2	type_action_2
Collaborative Filtering	John	Share	Rosa	Comment
Collaborative Filtering	John	Reply	Rosa	Comment
FOAF/SIOC Ontologies	John	Reply	Matheus	Comment
FOAF/SIOC Ontologies	John	Reply	Rosa	Reply
FOAF/SIOC Ontologies	John	Reply	Matheus	Share
OBAA Pattern	John	Comment	Clara	Comment
OBAA Pattern	John	Comment	Clara	Share
OBAA Pattern	John	Comment	Jose	Reply

The first contribution of this work was the adequacy of ontologies and the use of semantic web technologies to formalize the environment information. From the CoPs knowledge formalization, the information interoperability was improved and semantic queries and automatic processing became possible to be performed. The user profile with associated semantics is able to store information that was previously scattered among different CoP collaboration tools. The ability to track user interactions, capturing different aspects of their interactions, and representing them with semantic value allows to combine, reuse, and share the knowledge dynamically constructed during exchanges between participants.

Semantic queries have the ability to retrieve information related to the static and dynamic aspects of the participants. The proposed representation is capable of organize information that is linked to both the user and their relationship network. Thus, the dynamic profile is updated according to the user's actions and with their colleagues actions. To these actions it is possible to associate the context and the moment in which they occurred, the participants involved, the type of action executed and the collaboration tools used. These information, organized from an individual perspective, allows the retrieval of **interaction histories and collaboration trajectories**. This may be explored to understand how knowledge is built on CoPs and allows the construction of new collaboration tools based on the behavior pattern of each participant.

Future work intends to evolve the user profile and aspects related to the performance, security and privacy of semantic queries. The use of the semantic web also allows the execution of federated queries that can access resource descriptions on external semantic bases. Thereby, it is possible to search for new relationships and combine information to generate new knowledge. Finally, the organization of the user actions in a formal representation allows the execution of complex queries, retrieving and combining information, including incomplete ones, to discover new knowledge. From this information, it is possible to create interactive dashboards combining user actions, contexts, other participants who interacted in the same resource, related materials and related topics. The dynamic user profile evolves as the interactions occur in the CoPs and may be explored to adapt the platform and to improve recommendation systems.

References

1. Wenger, E.: Communities of practice: learning as a social system. Systems Think. **9**(5), 2–3 (1998)
2. Ribeiro, A.M., Silva, J.L., Boff, E., Viccari, R.M.: Dos ambientes de aprendizagem às comunidades de prática. Simpósio Brasileiro de Informática na Educação 22 (2011)
3. Da Silva, J.L., Ribeiro, A.M., Boff, E., Primo, T.T., Viccari, R.M.: A reference profile ontology for communities of practice. Int. J. Metadata Semant. Ontol. **7**(3), 185–196 (2012)
4. Fuks, H., Raposo, A.B., Gerosa, M.A., Lucena, C.J.: Applying the 3C model to groupware development. Int. J. Coop. Inf. Syst. **14**(02n03), 299–328 (2005)
5. Brusilovsky, P., Millán, E.: User models for adaptive hypermedia and adaptive educational systems. In: Brusilovsky, P., Kobsa, A., Nejdl, W. (eds.) The Adaptive Web. LNCS, vol. 4321, pp. 3–53. Springer, Heidelberg (2007). https://doi.org/10. 1007/978-3-540-72079-9_1
6. Ghorab, M.R., Zhou, D., OConnor, A., Wade, V.: Personalised information retrieval: survey and classification. User Model. User Adapt. Interact. **23**(4), 381–443 (2013)
7. Primo, T.T., Vicari, R.M., Bernardi, K.S.: User profiles and learning objects as ontology individuals to allow reasoning and interoperability in recommender systems. In: Global Engineering Education Conference (EDUCON), pp. 1–9. IEEE (2012)
8. Käser, T., Klingler, S., Schwing, A.G., Gross, M.: Beyond knowledge tracing: modeling skill topologies with bayesian networks. In: Trausan-Matu, S., Boyer, K.E., Crosby, M., Panourgia, K. (eds.) ITS 2014. LNCS, vol. 8474, pp. 188–198. Springer, Cham (2014). https://doi.org/10.1007/978-3-319-07221-0_23
9. Fenza, G., Orciuoli, F.: Building pedagogical models by formal concept analysis. In: Micarelli, A., Stamper, J., Panourgia, K. (eds.) ITS 2016. LNCS, vol. 9684, pp. 144–153. Springer, Cham (2016). https://doi.org/10.1007/978-3-319-39583-8_14
10. Plumbaum, T., Wu, S., De Luca, E.W., Albayrak, S.: User modeling for the social semantic web. In: de Gemmis, M., De Luca, E.W., Di Noia, T., Gangemi, A., Lukasiewicz, T. (eds.) Proceedings of the Second International Conference on Semantic Personalized Information Management: Retrieval and Recommendation - Volume 781 (SPIM 2011), vol. 781, pp. 78–89. Aachen (2011). CEUR-WS.org
11. Tifous, A., El Ghali, A., Dieng-Kuntz, R., Giboin, A., Christina, C., Vidou, G.: An ontology for supporting communities of practice. In: Proceedings of the 4th International Conference on Knowledge Capture, pp. 39–46. ACM (2007)
12. Chikh, A., Berkani, L.: Communities of practice of e-learning, an innovative learning space for e-learning actors. Procedia - Soc. Behav. Sci. **2**(2), 5022–5027 (2010)
13. Fernandez, M., Scharl, A., Bontcheva, K., Alani, H.: User profile modelling in online communities (2014)
14. Caballé, S., Daradoumis, T., Xhafa, F., Juan, A.: Providing effective feedback, monitoring and evaluation to on-line collaborative learning discussions. Comput. Hum. Behav. **27**(4), 1372–1381 (2011)

15. Conesa, J., Caballé, S., Gañán, D., Prieto, J.: Exploiting the semantic web to represent information from on-line collaborative learning. Int. J. Comput. Intell. Syst. **5**(4), 653–667 (2012)
16. Bojars, U., et al.: SIOC core ontology specification (2007)
17. Brickley, D., Miller, L.: FOAF vocabulary specification (2012)
18. Da Silva, J.L.T., Ribeiro, A.M., Reategui, E.: Tecnologias semânticas aplicadas a representação de conhecimento educacional em comunidades de prática (2016)
19. Hasan, L., Morris, A., Probets, S.: Using Google analytics to evaluate the usability of E-Commerce sites. In: Kurosu, M. (ed.) HCD 2009. LNCS, vol. 5619, pp. 697–706. Springer, Heidelberg (2009). https://doi.org/10.1007/978-3-642-02806-9_81
20. Beasley, M.: Practical Web Analytics for user Experience: How Analytics can Help you Understand Your Users. Newnes, Oxford (2013)
21. Baker, R.S., Inventado, P.S.: Educational data mining and learning analytics. In: Larusson, J.A., White, B. (eds.) Learning Analytics, pp. 61–75. Springer, New York (2014). https://doi.org/10.1007/978-1-4614-3305-7_4

Completeness by Modal Definitions

Levan Uridia[1(✉)] and Dirk Walther[2]

[1] Razmadze Institute of Mathematics, Tbilisi, Georgia
l.uridia@freeuni.edu.ge
[2] Fraunhofer IVI, Dresden, Germany

Abstract. In this paper, we develop a framework for obtaining completeness results for extensions of modal logics. A modal language is extended by fresh modalities, which are then specified using definitions formulated in the original logic. When adding the modal definitions to the axiom system, completeness of the extended logic is guaranteed by the main result of the paper. We demonstrate the technique by applying it to extensions of the modal logic S5.

1 Introduction

We show how to obtain Kripke completeness for certain extensions of modal logics. We consider extensions of a modal logic L with *modal definitions* of the form

$$\boxplus p \leftrightarrow \varphi(p),$$

where '$\boxplus$' is a fresh box-modality, and p is a proposition occurring in φ. That is, the modality $\boxplus$ is defined in terms of φ in which $\boxplus$ does not occur. We state the conditions on φ under which we obtain Kripke completeness of the extended logic. We pose as an interesting open problem to find a syntactic characterisation of modal definitions that give rise to what we call relational semantics. The related problem of characterising elementary formulas (i.e., modal formulas that define a first-order frame property) has been studied extensively; see, e.g., [5,8, 14,18]. However, elementarity is neither a necessary nor sufficient criterion for a modal formula to be used in relational modal definitions.

The idea to add modal definitions to existing normal modal logics is quite common, e.g., for (dynamic) epistemic logics. The following formulas are examples of modal definitions: $E_A p \leftrightarrow \bigwedge_{a \in A} \Box_a p$ is the axiom for 'everyone knows' in epistemic logic, i.e., every agent in the group A knows p [13]; $[!\varphi]p \leftrightarrow (\varphi \rightarrow p)$ is the reduction axiom for the announcement operator $[!\varphi]$ in Public Announcement Logic [4,17]; $\Box_{\mathsf{S4}} p \leftrightarrow \Box_{\mathsf{K4}} p \wedge p$ is a definition of an S4-box modality in terms of a K4-box modality [11]; $[\varphi]_K p \leftrightarrow [\top]_K p \vee (\varphi \wedge [\top]_K(\varphi \rightarrow p))$ was used as the definition of the modal operator 'Modest Enrichment (Type B)' in [12]; and $[\varphi]p \leftrightarrow \Box p \vee (\varphi \wedge \Box(\varphi \rightarrow p))$ is the reduction axiom used for the epistemic logic S5^r for reasoning about knowledge under hypotheses in [19].

We show that we can obtain a finite axiomatisation of normal modal logics extended with relational modal definitions in a straightforward way. We illustrate

© Springer Nature Switzerland AG 2018
G. R. Simari et al. (Eds.): IBERAMIA 2018, LNAI 11238, pp. 67–79, 2018.
https://doi.org/10.1007/978-3-030-03928-8_6

this technique with one extensions of the modal logic S5. In Sect. 4, we recall the logic S5^r, which extends S5 with a modal operator '[·]' that can be parameterised with a hypothesis. The modality $[\varphi]$ represents the knowledge state under the hypothesis φ. The formula $[\varphi]\psi$ states that 'under the hypothesis φ, the agent knows ψ'. If φ happens to be true at the current world and the agent knows that φ implies ψ, then the agent knows ψ; otherwise, i.e., if φ is false, the agent knows only what it would know anyway, i.e. without any assumptions. We give a new completeness proof for the logic S5^r based on techniques developed in Sect. 3.

The paper is organised as follows. In the following section, we review standard definitions of modal logic and modal definability. In Sect. 3 we introduce the notion of relational modal definitions and pose the problem of finding a syntactic characterisation for it. Additionally, we show how to obtain completeness for modal logics extended with a relational modal definition as new axiom schema. We illustrate this technique with extensions of the modal logic S5 in Sect. 4. Finally, we conclude the paper in Sect. 5.

2   Preliminaries

In this section, we briefly review some standard definitions for modal logic and modal definability, cf. [7]. First, we fix a signature $\langle \Pi, M \rangle$ consisting of countable sets Π and M of symbols for propositions and modalities, respectively. The *propositional modal language* $\mathcal{L}$ for this signature consists of formulas φ that are built up inductively according to the grammar:

$$\varphi ::= p \mid \neg\varphi \mid \varphi \wedge \varphi \mid \Box_m\varphi,$$

where p ranges over proposition symbols in Π and m over modality symbols in M. The logical symbols '$\top$' and '$\bot$', and the additional connectives such as '$\vee$', '$\rightarrow$' and '$\leftrightarrow$' and the dual modalities '$\Diamond_m$' with $m \in M$ are defined as usual, i.e.: $\top := p \vee \neg p$ for some atomic proposition p; $\bot := \neg\top$; $\varphi \vee \psi := \neg(\neg\varphi \wedge \neg\psi)$; $\varphi \rightarrow \psi := \neg\varphi \vee \psi$; $\varphi \leftrightarrow \psi := (\varphi \rightarrow \psi) \wedge (\psi \rightarrow \varphi)$; and $\Diamond_m\varphi := \neg\Box_m\neg\varphi$.

A subset L of the propositional modal language $\mathcal{L}$ is a *modal logic* iff it contains all propositional tautologies, is closed under substitution, modus ponens and modal replacement (MREP) $\frac{p \leftrightarrow q}{\Box_m p \leftrightarrow \Box_m q}$, for $m \in M$. The modal logic L is called *monotonic* iff it contains the formulas (C) $\Box_m(p \wedge q) \rightarrow \Box_m q$, for $m \in M$, and L is *normal* iff it additionally contains the formulas (S) $\Box_m p \wedge \Box_m q \rightarrow \Box_m(p \wedge q)$ and (T) $\Box_m\top$. Alternatively, it is also sufficient to state normal modal logics contain the formulas (K) $\Box_m(p \rightarrow q) \rightarrow (\Box_m p \rightarrow \Box_m q)$ and are closed under (NEC) $\frac{p}{\Box_m p}$ (i.e., instead of stating (C), (S), (T) and (MREP)). The smallest normal modal logic is commonly denoted with K.

The relational semantics for the propositional modal language $\mathcal{L}$ is based on labelled graphs (Kripke structures) for the signature of $\mathcal{L}$. That is, the points are labelled by propositions from Π and the edges are binary relations, one for every modality in M. Formally, an M-*frame* is a tuple $\mathfrak{F} = (W, \{R_m\}_{m \in M})$, where W is a non-empty set of worlds and each $R_m \subseteq W^2$ is a binary relation over W labeled with a symbol m, for every $m \in M$. Formally R_m is a shorthand for (R_m, m). A *Kripke structure for* $\langle \Pi, M \rangle$ is a pair $\mathfrak{M} = (\mathfrak{F}, V)$ consisting of an M-frame $\mathfrak{F} = (W, \{R_m\}_{m \in M})$ together with a valuation function V : $\Pi \to 2^W$ assigning to every proposition p in Π a set $V(p)$ of worlds. A Kripke structure $\mathfrak{M} = (\mathfrak{F}, V)$ is said to be *based on the frame* $\mathfrak{F}$. We also refer to a Kripke structure as a 'model'. We denote the class of all Kripke structures for $\langle \Pi, M \rangle$ as $\mathcal{K}_{\langle \Pi, M \rangle}$, or simply $\mathcal{K}$ if the signature is understood. Later we will use $\mathcal{C}$ to denote a class of models.

An interpretation of formulas from $\mathcal{L}$ is given by means of a *satisfaction relation* '$\models$', which is a binary relation between pointed models and formulas. A pointed model is a pair $\langle \mathfrak{M}, w \rangle$, where $\mathfrak{M} = (W, \{R_m\}_{m \in M}, V)$ is a model from the class $\mathcal{C}$ of all models and w a world from W. The satisfaction relation is defined inductively on the structure of formulas φ as:

- $\langle \mathfrak{M}, w \rangle \models p$ iff $w \in V(p)$;
- $\langle \mathfrak{M}, w \rangle \models \neg\psi$ iff $\langle \mathfrak{M}, w \rangle \not\models \psi$;
- $\langle \mathfrak{M}, w \rangle \models \psi \wedge \chi$ iff $\langle \mathfrak{M}, w \rangle \models \psi$ and $\langle \mathfrak{M}, w \rangle \models \chi$;
- $\langle \mathfrak{M}, w \rangle \models \Box_m \psi$ iff for all $v \in W$ with $(w, v) \in R_m$, $\langle \mathfrak{M}, v \rangle \models \psi$.

A formula φ is said to be *true* at w in $\mathfrak{M}$ iff $\langle \mathfrak{M}, w \rangle \models \varphi$; φ is *satisfiable* iff there is a pointed model $\langle \mathfrak{M}, w \rangle$ at which it is true; φ is *valid in* $\mathfrak{M}$ (written '$\mathfrak{M} \models \varphi$') iff $\langle \mathfrak{M}, w \rangle \models \varphi$ for all w in $\mathfrak{M}$; φ is *valid on* $\mathfrak{F}$ (written '$\mathfrak{F} \models \varphi$') iff φ is valid in all models based on $\mathfrak{F}$; and φ is *valid* in the class $\mathcal{C}$ of models (written '$\models_\mathcal{C} \varphi$') iff it is valid in every model from $\mathcal{C}$.

The set of $\mathcal{L}$-formulas that are valid in all models from a class $\mathcal{C}$ of models is called the *$\mathcal{L}$-theory* $\mathsf{Th}_\mathcal{L}(\mathcal{C})$ of $\mathcal{C}$, i.e.:

$$\mathsf{Th}_\mathcal{L}(\mathcal{C}) := \{\varphi \in \mathcal{L} \mid \text{for every } \mathfrak{M} \text{ from } \mathcal{C}, \varphi \text{ is valid in } \mathfrak{M}\}.$$

A modal logic L is said to be *Kripke complete w.r.t.* $\mathcal{C}$ iff $L = \mathsf{Th}_\mathcal{L}(\mathcal{C})$. In what follows, we will also just say 'complete'. For instance, K is complete w.r.t. the class of all models, and $\mathsf{S4}$ is complete w.r.t. the class of models which are based on frames that are pre-orders (i.e., frames with reflexive and transitive relations). A modal logic L is *complete w.r.t. a class $\mathcal{F}$ of frames* iff L is complete w.r.t. the class of models that are each based on a frame from $\mathcal{F}$. Not all normal modal logics are complete w.r.t. a class of frames.

The relationship to first-order logic is made precise by the so-called *standard translation* $\mathrm{ST}(\cdot)$, which assigns to a modal formula φ a corresponding first-order formula $\mathrm{ST}_x(\varphi)$ with one free variable x. The signature of the first-order language contains unary predicate symbols P and binary predicate symbols R_m, one P for every $p \in \Pi$ and one R_m for every $m \in M$. The translation function $\mathrm{ST}(\cdot)$ is inductively defined as follows:

$$\begin{aligned}
\mathrm{ST}_x(p) &:= P(x) \\
\mathrm{ST}_x(\neg\varphi) &:= \neg\mathrm{ST}_x(\varphi) \\
\mathrm{ST}_x(\varphi \wedge \psi) &:= \mathrm{ST}_x(\varphi) \wedge \mathrm{ST}_x(\psi) \\
\mathrm{ST}_x(\Box_m\varphi) &:= \forall y(R_m(x, y) \to \mathrm{ST}_y(\varphi))
\end{aligned}$$

where y is a fresh variable for every occurrence of a box-modality.

A Kripke structure $\mathfrak{M} = (W, \{R_m\}_{m \in M}, V)$ for $\langle \Pi, M \rangle$ can be seen as a first-order structure interpreting the formulas $\mathrm{ST}_x(\varphi)$. While a predicate symbol R_m

is interpreted as the same called binary relation over W that is interpreting the modality m in M, a predicate symbol P is interpreted as the subset $V(p)$ of W, where p is the proposition symbol from Π that corresponds to P. Neither constants nor function symbols are introduced by the standard translation. In the first-order structure $\mathfrak{M}$, however, we introduce a dedicated constant c_w for every world $w \in W$ and we interpret c_w as w. At the level of pointed models $\langle \mathfrak{M}, w \rangle$, the relationship between φ and $\mathrm{ST}_x(\varphi)$ is such that:

$$\langle \mathfrak{M}, w \rangle \models \varphi \text{ iff } \mathfrak{M} \models \mathrm{ST}_x(\varphi)[x \mapsto c_w],$$

where $[x \mapsto c_w]$ substitutes every occurrence of the free variable x in $\mathrm{ST}_x(\varphi)$ with the constant c_w. Note that $\mathrm{ST}_x(\varphi)[x \mapsto c_w]$ is a sentence, i.e. a first-order formula without free variables.

When considering the notion of validity on frames $\mathfrak{F}$, we have that φ corresponds to the monadic second-order formula $\forall \boldsymbol{P} \forall x\, \mathrm{ST}_x(\varphi)$ as follows:

$$\mathfrak{F} \models \varphi(\boldsymbol{p}) \text{ iff } \mathfrak{F} \models \forall \boldsymbol{P} \forall x\, \mathrm{ST}_x(\varphi),$$

where $\boldsymbol{p}$ are the propositions from Π that occur in φ and $\boldsymbol{P}$ the corresponding unary predicates.

For modal formulas φ that are commonly considered as axioms, such as the formulas of the axioms (K), (T), (4), etc., there exists a first-order equivalent of the second-order formula $\forall \boldsymbol{P} \forall x\, \mathrm{ST}_x(\varphi)$. A modal formula that defines a first-order frame property is also said to be *elementary*. For instance, (4) is elementary as it is valid on all frames with transitive relations and the class of transitive frames can be defined with first-order formulas $\forall xyz(R(x,y) \wedge R(y,z) \rightarrow R(x,z))$, one for every relation R in the frame. However, there are modal formulas that are non-elementary, among them are the Löb formula $\Box(\Box p \rightarrow p) \rightarrow \Box p$ and the McKinsey formula $\Box \Diamond p \rightarrow \Diamond \Box p$. The Sahlqvist formulas define a set of elementary modal formulas [18], but it does not cover all elementary formulas. The problem of determining whether or not a modal formula is elementary is undecidable [8]. Conversely, there are elementary frame classes that are not modally definable, e.g. the class of irreflexive and the class of antisymmetric frames.

3   Modal Definitions

In this section, we show for certain extensions of modal logics how to obtain Kripke completeness w.r.t. a specific class of models. Later, in the next section, we apply this technique to extensions of the modal logic S5.

By *extending a modal logic L with a formula φ* we mean obtaining a modal logic L' as a set of formulas that is minimal w.r.t. $\subseteq$, that contains all tautologies over the symbols for propositions occuring in $L \cup \{\varphi\}$, that contains all formulas from $L \cup \{\varphi\}$ and that is closed under substitution, modus ponens and modal replacement. It can readily be seen that $L \cup \{\varphi\}$ is not necessarily a modal logic. Moreover, an extension of a modal logic that is Kripke complete w.r.t. a class $\mathcal{C}$ of models is not necessarily complete w.r.t. $\mathcal{C}$ itself nor any other class of models. We are interested in studying formulas of a specific form (modal definitions)

that, when used to extend a modal logic, yield a modal logic that is complete
w.r.t. a specific class of models.

Before formulating the completeness result, we introduce the notion of modal
definitions.

Definition 1. *Let $\mathcal{L}$ be a propositional modal language over the signa-*
ture $\langle \Pi, M \rangle$. Let $\varphi(\boldsymbol{p})$ be a formula in $\mathcal{L}$, where $\boldsymbol{p}$ are the propositions occurring
in φ. Let '+' be a fresh symbol for a unary modality not in M, and $\boxplus$ the box-
version of this modality. A modal definition *in $\mathcal{L}$ is a formula of the form*

$$\boxplus p \leftrightarrow \varphi(\boldsymbol{p}),$$

where $\boldsymbol{p}$ contains p.

The box-modality $\boxplus$ is defined in terms of a modal formula in which $\boxplus$ does
not occur. Notice that the modal definition $\boxplus p \leftrightarrow \varphi(\boldsymbol{p})$ itself is a formula in the
propositional modal language over the extended signature $\langle \Pi, M \cup \{+\} \rangle$. For
the sake of simplicity, we consider $+$ to be a unary modality symbol. We leave
generalising Definition 1 and the results below to polyadic modality symbols for
future work. Moreover, we will only consider the modal definitions for the box-
version of $+$. The results for the dual modality can be obtained in a similar
way.

In this paper, we only consider modal definitions $\boxplus p \leftrightarrow \varphi(\boldsymbol{p})$, where the box-
modality $\boxplus$ does not occur in $\varphi(\boldsymbol{p})$. It is interesting, however, to also consider
the more general setting, where this restriction may be weakened. For instance,
the axiom for common knowledge and the axiom for the star-programme of PDL
are not covered by Definition 1. We leave this for future work as well.

A modal definition is interpreted in models $\mathfrak{M} = (\mathfrak{F}, V)$ that are based on
$M \cup \{+\}$-frames $\mathfrak{F} = (W, \{R_m\}_{m \in M} \cup \{R_+\})$, i.e., frames that are extended with
a binary relation R_+ to interpret the new box-modality $\boxplus$. The semantics of $\boxplus$
can be defined in the usual way as for any other box-modality:

- $\langle \mathfrak{M}, w \rangle \models \boxplus \psi$ iff for all $v \in W$ with $(w, v) \in R_+$, it holds that $\langle \mathfrak{M}, v \rangle \models \psi$.

We want to interpret $\boxplus$ as specified in the modal logic L' obtained from the modal
logic L extended with a modal definition of $\boxplus$. To this end, we have to confine
outselves to the models from $\mathcal{C}(L')$, i.e., all models from $\mathcal{K}_{\langle \Pi, M \cup \{+\} \rangle}$ in which
all formulas of L' are valid. It is now interesting to investigate the relationship
between the modal definition of $\boxplus$ and the properties of the relation R_+ in the
models from $\mathcal{C}(L')$.

Example 1. Let $\mathcal{L}$ be a propositional modal language over $\langle \Pi, M \rangle$. Additionally,
let '+' be a fresh symbol for a modality not in M. Finally, let $L \subseteq \mathcal{L}$ be a modal
logic.

The modal definition $\alpha_1 = \boxplus p \leftrightarrow p$ yields that R_+ is the identity relation.

Another simple example of a modal definition is $\boxplus p \leftrightarrow \square_m p$, for some $m \in M$.
Here we have that R_+ equals R_m in every model. Consider two more examples:
$\boxplus p \leftrightarrow p \vee \neg p$ and $\boxplus p \leftrightarrow p \wedge \neg p$. In the former case, R_+ is the empty relation,
whereas in the latter the modal definition does not yield any relation.

As the examples show, not all modal definitions yield a relational semantics for the logic extended with the newly defined modality. Taking the standard translation of a formula φ that is used in a definition $\boxplus p \leftrightarrow \varphi(\boldsymbol{p})$ results in the second-order formula $\forall \boldsymbol{P} \forall x \, \mathrm{ST}_x(\varphi)$, where the predicates in $\boldsymbol{P}$ correspond to the propositional variables in $\boldsymbol{p}$. We are interested in elementary formulas, i.e., those formulas φ for which there exists a first-order formula that is equivalent to the second-order formula $\forall \boldsymbol{P} \forall x \, \mathrm{ST}_x(\varphi)$, that additionally yield a relational semantics for the new modality $+$. It is a non-trivial problem to give a syntactic characterisation of such formulas φ that are suitable for defining fresh modalities.

In this paper, we will not solve this problem, but we will show how such modal definitions can be used to obtain an axiomatisation of the extended logic. To this end, we introduce the notion of 'relational modal definition'.

Definition 2. *Let $\mathcal{L}$ be a propositional modal language over the signature $\langle \Pi, M \rangle$. Let $\varphi(p, p_1, \ldots, p_n)$ with $n \geq 0$ be a formula in $\mathcal{L}$, where $p, p_1, \ldots, p_n$ are the propositions occurring in φ. Let '$+$' be a fresh symbol for a unary modality not in M, and $\boxplus$ the box-version of this modality.*

A modal definition $\boxplus p \leftrightarrow \varphi(p, p_1, \ldots, p_n)$ is called a relational modal definition *if there exists a first-order formula $\Psi_+(x, y)$ with two free variables x and y using only predicates that occur in $\mathrm{ST}_x(\varphi(p, p_1, \ldots, p_n))$ such that for every $\psi \in \mathcal{L}$, it holds that for all pointed models $\langle \mathfrak{M}, w \rangle$,*

$$\langle \mathfrak{M}, w \rangle \models (\forall y)(\Psi_+(x, y) \Rightarrow \mathrm{ST}_y(\psi)) \ \textit{iff} \ \mathfrak{M} \models \mathrm{ST}_x(\varphi(\psi, p_1, \ldots, p_n))[x \mapsto c_w].$$

We note that elementarity is not a sufficient condition for modal formulas being suitable for a relational modal definition. For instance, the modal formula $\Diamond_m \top$ is elementary as it is valid on all frames in which the relation R_m is serial and the class of serial frames can be defined with first-order formulas $\forall x \exists y (R(x, y))$, one for every relation R in the frame. However, it can readily be seen that there is no first-order formula corresponding to $\boxplus p \leftrightarrow \Diamond_m \top$ in the sense of Definition 2. Another example is the formula $\Diamond_m \Box_m \bot$ which together with Axiom (4) states the reachability of a world without successors from any world. Furthermore, elementarity is not a necessary condition either; see, e.g., the reduction axiom for $\mathbf{S5}^r$ in the following section which yields a relational modal definition despite it being non-elementary.

Let $\Psi_+(x, y)$ be the first-order formula with two free variables x and y corresponding to a relational modal definition. Given a model $\mathfrak{M} = (\mathfrak{F}, V)$ with $\mathfrak{F} = (W, \{R_m\}_{m \in M})$, we uniquely construct the model $\mathfrak{M}_+ = (\mathfrak{F}_+, V)$, where the underlying frame $\mathfrak{F}_+$ is obtained from $\mathfrak{F}$ by adding the binary relation $R_+ \subseteq W \times W$ defined as:

$$(v, w) \in R_+ \ \textit{iff} \ \mathfrak{M} \models \Psi_+(x, y)[x \mapsto c_v, y \mapsto c_w].$$

For a class $\mathcal{C}$ of models, we denote with $\mathcal{C}_+$ the class consisting of the models $\mathfrak{M}_+$, where $\mathfrak{M}$ ranges over the models in $\mathcal{C}$.

Formulas from the extended language $\mathcal{L}_+$ can be translated to formulas in $\mathcal{L}$ in a straightforward way.

Definition 3. *Let $\mathcal{L}$ and $\mathcal{L}_+$ be propositional modal languages over the signatures $\langle \Pi, M \rangle$ and $\langle \Pi, M \cup \{+\} \rangle$, respectively, where $+$ is a fresh unary modality not in M. The translation function $^*\colon \mathcal{L}^+ \to \mathcal{L}$ for the relational modal definition $\boxplus p \leftrightarrow \varphi_+(p, p_1, \ldots, p_n)$ is inductively defined as follows:*

- $p^* = p$;
- $(\varphi \vee \psi)^* = \varphi^* \vee \psi^*$;
- $(\neg \varphi)^* = \neg \varphi^*$;
- $(\Box_m \varphi)^* = \Box_m \varphi^*$, *for $m \in M$*;
- $(\boxplus \psi)^* = \varphi_+(\psi^*, p_1, \ldots, p_n)$.

Lemma 1. *Let $\mathcal{L}$ and $\mathcal{L}_+$ be propositional modal languages over the signatures $\langle \Pi, M \rangle$ and $\langle \Pi, M \cup \{+\} \rangle$, respectively, where $+$ is a fresh unary modality not in M. Let $L \subseteq \mathcal{L}$ be a normal modal logic, and obtain $L_+ \subseteq \mathcal{L}_+$ from L by adding a relational modal definition $\boxplus p \leftrightarrow \varphi(p, p_1, \ldots, p_n)$ as an only axiom schema for $\boxplus$.*

Then for every $\psi, \chi \in \mathcal{L}_+$, it holds that:

(i) if $\psi \leftrightarrow \chi \in L_+$, then $\boxplus \psi \leftrightarrow \boxplus \chi \in L_+$; and
(ii) $\psi \in L_+$ iff $\psi^* \in L$.

Proof. We first show Item *(i)*. Due to the reduction axiom it suffices to show that if $\psi \leftrightarrow \chi \in L_+$, then $\varphi(\psi, p_1, \ldots, p_n) \leftrightarrow \varphi(\chi, p_1, \ldots, p_n) \in L_+$. We show this by induction on the structure of φ. Recall that $\varphi(p, p_1, .., p_n)$ is a formula of the language $\mathcal{L}$, i.e., not containing $\boxplus$. We use the following as induction hypothesis. For every $\varphi(p, p_1, .., p_n) \in \mathcal{L}$ and every two formulas $\psi, \chi \in \mathcal{L}_+$ with $\psi \leftrightarrow \chi \in L_+$, it holds that $\varphi(\psi, p_1, \ldots, p_n) \leftrightarrow \varphi(\chi, p_1, \ldots, p_n) \in L_+$. For the base case, we distinguish two cases. *Case 1* $\varphi(p, p_1, .. p_n) = q$ where q is a propositional letter distinct from p. For this case $\varphi(\psi, p_1, \ldots, p_n) = q = \varphi(\chi, p_1, \ldots, p_n)$ and indeed $q \leftrightarrow q \in L_+$. *Case 2* $\varphi(p, p_1, .. p_n) = p$. For this case after substitution we get $\varphi(\psi, p_1, \ldots, p_n) = \psi$ and $\varphi(\chi, p_1, \ldots, p_n) = \chi$ and by assumption $\varphi \leftrightarrow \chi \in L_+$. Now assume for every formula before some constructive step k the inductive claim holds. Let $\varphi(p, p_1, .., p_n)$ be the formula constructed on step k. Then either $\varphi(p, p_1, .., p_n) = \varphi_1(p, p_1, .., p_n) \wedge \varphi_2(p, p_1, .., p_n)$ or $\varphi(p, p_1, .., p_n) = \neg \varphi_1(p, p_1, .., p_n)$ or $\varphi(p, p_1, .., p_n) = \Box_m \varphi_1(p, p_1, .., p_n)$ for some formulas $\varphi_1(p, p_1, .., p_n), \varphi_2(p, p_1, .., p_n)$ constructed on previous steps. For each case by inductive assumption we have that substitution keeps the equivalence. Let us check this only for the last case other cases are similar. So assume that $\varphi(p, p_1, .., p_n) = \Box_m \varphi_1(p, p_1, .., p_n)$. By inductive assumption we know that $\varphi_1(\psi, p_1, .., p_n) \leftrightarrow \varphi_1(\chi, p_1, .., p_n) \in L_+$. Hence $\Box_m(\varphi_1(\psi, p_1, .., p_n) \leftrightarrow \varphi_1(\chi, p_1, .., p_n)) \in L_+$ since $L_+ \supseteq L$. By properties of box modality we obtain $\Box_m \varphi_1(\psi, p_1, .., p_n) \leftrightarrow \Box_m \varphi_1(\chi, p_1, .., p_n) \in L_+$.

Consider Item *(ii)*. We show by induction on the structure of $\varphi \in \mathcal{L}$ that $\vdash_{L_+} \varphi \leftrightarrow \varphi^*$. The only non-trivial case is when $\varphi = \boxplus \beta$. We omit the other cases. Suppose that $\varphi = \boxplus \beta$. Then by the induction hypothesis it holds that $\vdash_{L_+} \beta \leftrightarrow \beta^*$. By Item *(i)* we obtain that $\vdash_{L_+} \boxplus \beta \leftrightarrow \boxplus \beta^*$. Due to the reduction axiom, we have that $\vdash_{L_+} \boxplus \beta^* \leftrightarrow \varphi(\beta^*, p_1, \ldots, p_n)$. Hence $\vdash_{L_+} \boxplus \beta \leftrightarrow \varphi(\beta^*, p_1, \ldots, p_n)$. By Definition 3 we obtain $\boxplus \beta \leftrightarrow (\boxplus \beta)^*$.

As a result we obtain that $\varphi \in L_+$ iff $\varphi^* \in L_+$, and since $\varphi^* \in \mathcal{L}$ and the logic L_+ is defined without further axioms or rules involving the symbol $+$, it follows that $\varphi^* \in L$. The other direction of *(ii)* is immediate since the logic L_+ extends L.

Lemma 2. *Let $\mathcal{L}_+$ be a propositional modal language over the signature $\langle \Pi, M \cup \{+\}\rangle$, where $+$ is a fresh unary modality not in M. Let L_+ be the logic in the language $\mathcal{L}_+$ obtained from L by adding a modal definition $\vdash \boxplus p \leftrightarrow \varphi(p, p_1, .., p_n)$ as an only axiom schemata involving $\boxplus$.*

Then for every $\psi \in \mathcal{L}_+$, it holds that $\langle \mathfrak{M}_+, w\rangle \models \psi$ iff $\langle \mathfrak{M}, w\rangle \models \psi^*$.

Proof. The proof proceeds by induction on the structure of the formula ψ. For ψ being a proposition in Π, the lemma is immediate since both models have the same valuation function. The Boolean cases and the case for the box-modalities $\square_m$ with $m \in M$ are standard. Let $\psi = \boxplus \alpha$. Assume that $\langle \mathfrak{M}_+, w\rangle \models \boxplus \alpha$. This is equivalent to the implication $(\forall v)((w, v) \in R_+ \Rightarrow \langle \mathfrak{M}_+, v\rangle \models \alpha)$. By the induction hypothesis this is equivalent to $(\forall v)(\mathfrak{M} \models \Psi(w, v) \Rightarrow \langle \mathfrak{M}, v\rangle \models \alpha^*)$. By Definition 2, this is equivalent to $\mathfrak{M} \models \mathrm{ST}_x(\varphi(\alpha^*, p_1, \ldots, p_n))[x \mapsto c_w]$, and by Definition 3 to $\langle \mathfrak{M}, w\rangle \models (\boxplus \alpha)^*$.

Theorem 1. *Let $\mathcal{L}$ and $\mathcal{L}_+$ be propositional modal languages over the signatures $\langle \Pi, M\rangle$ and $\langle \Pi, M \cup \{+\}\rangle$, respectively, where $+$ is a fresh unary modality not in M. Let $L \subseteq \mathcal{L}$ be a normal modal logic that is sound and complete w.r.t. a class $\mathcal{F}$ of Kripke frames. Obtain $L_+ \subseteq \mathcal{L}_+$ from L by adding a relational modal definition $\boxplus p \leftrightarrow \varphi(p, p_1, \ldots, p_n)$ as an only axiom schema for $\boxplus$.*

Then the logic L_+ is sound and complete w.r.t. the class $\mathcal{F}_+$.

Proof. Completeness. Assume $\nvdash \varphi$ in the logic L_+. By Lemma 1, we have that $\nvdash \varphi^*$ in the logic L. As L is complete w.r.t. $\mathcal{F}$, there is a model $\mathfrak{M}$ based on a frame in $\mathcal{F}$ and a world w in $\mathfrak{M}$ such that $\langle \mathfrak{M}, w\rangle \not\models \varphi^*$. By Lemma 2, it follows that $\langle \mathfrak{M}_+, w\rangle \not\models \varphi$. Hence, $\mathcal{C}_+ \not\models \varphi$.

4   The Modal Logic S5^r

In this section, we recall the multi-modal logic S5^r from [19] together with the completeness result w.r.t. a particular class of models called *basic structures*. The language of S5^r is the language of propositional logic extended with modal operators parameterised with S5^r-formulas. Formally, this is done as follows.

Definition 4 (Syntax of S5^r). *Let Π be a countable set of propositions. Formulas φ of the language $\mathcal{L}$ are defined inductively over Π by the following grammar:*

$$\varphi, \psi ::= p \mid \neg\varphi \mid \varphi \vee \psi \mid [\varphi]_K \psi,$$

where p ranges over propositions in Π and $_K$ is a part of modality symbol indicating that we deal with knowledge modality.

The logical symbols '$\top$' and '$\bot$', and additional operators such as '$\wedge$', '$\rightarrow$', '$\leftrightarrow$', and the dual modalities '$\langle\varphi\rangle_K$' are defined as usual.

Modal formulas are commonly evaluated in models containing a binary relation over the domain, one for each modality in the modal language. In this case, however, every binary relation is determined by the valuation of the atomic propositions in the domain. Therefore, it is sufficient to consider models without relations, which we call *basic structures*. Formally, a basic structure $\mathfrak{M}$ is a tuple $\mathfrak{M} = (W, V)$, where W is a non-empty set of *worlds* and $V : \Pi \rightarrow 2^W$ a *valuation function* mapping every atomic proposition p to a set of worlds $V(p)$ at which it is true. The relations that are required to evaluate the modalities are defined alongside the satisfaction relation. But first we introduce an auxiliary notion, a binary operation '$\otimes$' on sets yielding a binary relation. Let X and Y be two sets. Let $X \otimes Y$ be a binary relation over $X \cup Y$ such that

$$X \otimes Y = X^2 \cup (X \times Y) \cup Y^2. \tag{1}$$

We illustrate this notion with an example.

Example 2. Let $X = \{x_1, x_2\}$ and $Y = \{y_1, y_2, y_3\}$ be two sets. Then, according to (1), $X \otimes Y$ is a binary relation over $X \cup Y$ that is composed of the relations X^2, $X \times Y$ and Y^2 by taking their union. It holds that $X^2 = \{(x_1, x_2), (x_2, x_1)\} \cup \mathsf{id}(X)$, $X \times Y = \{(x_1, y_1), (x_1, y_2), (x_1, y_3), (x_2, y_1), (x_2, y_2), (x_2, y_3)\}$ and $Y^2 = \{(y_1, y_2), (y_2, y_1), (y_1, y_3), (y_3, y_1), (y_2, y_3), (y_3, y_2)\} \cup \mathsf{id}(Y)$. Then the relation $X \otimes Y = X^2 \cup (X \times Y) \cup Y^2$ contains two fully connected clusters X^2 and Y^2, and directed edges between every point in X to every point in Y. Figure 1 below gives a graphical representation of $X \otimes Y$ (leaving out the reflexive and symmetric edges).

We are now ready to introduce the semantics of S5^r. It differs from the semantics of Public Announcement Logic [10,17] in that the model does not change during the evaluation of formulas.

Definition 5 (Semantics of S5^r). *Let $\mathfrak{M} = (W, V)$ be a basic structure. The logical satisfaction relation '$\models$' is defined by induction on the structure of S5^r-formulas as follows: For all $p \in \Pi$ and all $\varphi, \psi \in \mathcal{L}$,*

- *$\langle\mathfrak{M}, w\rangle \models p$ iff $w \in V(p)$;*
- *$\langle\mathfrak{M}, w\rangle \models \varphi \vee \psi$ iff $\langle\mathfrak{M}, w\rangle \models \varphi$ or $\langle\mathfrak{M}, w\rangle \models \psi$;*
- *$\langle\mathfrak{M}, w\rangle \models [\varphi]_K\psi$ iff for all $v \in W$ with $(w, v) \in R_\varphi$, it holds that $\langle\mathfrak{M}, v\rangle \models \psi$;*

where $R_\varphi = (W \setminus \llbracket\varphi\rrbracket_\mathfrak{M}) \otimes \llbracket\varphi\rrbracket_\mathfrak{M}$ as defined in Eq. (1) and $\llbracket\varphi\rrbracket_\mathfrak{M} = \{x \in W \mid \langle\mathfrak{M}, w\rangle \models \varphi\}$ is the extension of φ in $\mathfrak{M}$.

We say that a S5^r-formula φ is *satisfiable* if there is a model $\mathfrak{M}$ and a world w in $\mathfrak{M}$ such that $\langle\mathfrak{M}, w\rangle \models \varphi$; φ is *valid in $\mathfrak{M}$* if $\langle\mathfrak{M}, w\rangle \models \varphi$ for all w in $\mathfrak{M}$; and φ is *valid* if φ is valid in all models. We will refer to the relation R_φ as being *determined* by φ and a model.

According to the semantics, a formula determines a binary relation in a model. The following proposition states the properties of such relations.

Proposition 1. *Let φ be an $S5^r$-formula and let $\mathfrak{M} = (W, V)$ be a basic struc-*
ture. Then, the relation R_φ determined by φ and $\mathfrak{M}$ (cf. Definition 5) is a one-
step total preorder, i.e., R_φ satisfies the following conditions:

- *R_φ is transitive: $\forall xyz(R_\varphi(x,y) \land R_\varphi(y,z) \to R_\varphi(x,z))$;*
- *R_φ is total: $\forall xy(R_\varphi(x,y) \lor R_\varphi(y,x))$; and*
- *R_φ is one-step: $\forall xyz(R_\varphi(x,y) \land \neg R_\varphi(y,x) \land R_\varphi(x,z) \to (zR_\varphi y))$.*

Instead of 'preorder' also the term 'quasiorder' is often used in the literature.
Note that totality implies reflexivity and that a symmetric total preorder is an
equivalence relation. The proposition is readily checked as any relation R_φ in a
model determined by φ is defined using the operation '$\otimes$', which always yields
a so-called 'one-step total preorder'. As the domain of a model is non-empty, it
contains at least one point and, thus, the smallest relation R_φ is the edge of a
single reflexive point.

Proposition 2. *The relation R_φ for every formula $\varphi \in S5^r$ is characterised by*
the following condition: $R_\varphi(w, v)$ iff $w \in [\![\varphi]\!]$ implies that $v \in [\![\varphi]\!]$.

Figure 1 illustrates the relation R_φ in a model $\mathfrak{M}$. The domain of $\mathfrak{M}$ is partitioned into two clusters, the worlds in each of which are fully connected (reflexive
and symmetric edges within the clusters are not shown). Between the clusters
there are outgoing directed edges from worlds in the cluster on the left- to worlds
in the cluster on the right-hand side, but not vice versa. Revisit Example 2 to
see in detail how R_φ is computed (where $X = W \setminus [\![\varphi]\!]_{\mathfrak{M}}$ and $Y = [\![\varphi]\!]_{\mathfrak{M}}$).

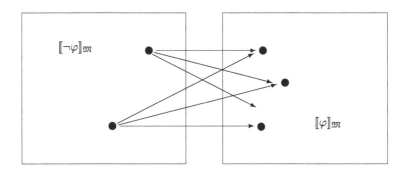

Fig. 1. Model $\mathfrak{M}$ with relation R_φ

Consider the following example, which illustrates the effect that hypotheses
can have on an agent's knowledge.

Example 3. Let $\mathfrak{M} = (W, V)$ be a basic structure with $W = \{x, y\}$, $V(p_h) = V(p_c) = \{x\}$ and $V(p_u) = \{x, y\}$. Intuitively, the three propositions p_h, p_c
and p_u stand for hypothesis, conclusion and universal or already established
knowledge, respectively. Then, $[p_h]_K p_u$ is true at x and y in $\mathfrak{M}$. In fact, we have
that $\langle \mathfrak{M}, x \rangle \models [\varphi]_K p_u$ for every $S5^r$-formula φ, because p_u holds everywhere
in $\mathfrak{M}$. But $[p_h]_K p_c$ holds only at x and not at y, because $\langle \mathfrak{M}, x \rangle \models p_h$ and p_h
implies p_c everywhere in $\mathfrak{M}$.

We conclude this section with a discussion on how S5^r could possibly be used to reason about the knowledge of multiple agents; see, e.g., [13,16] for standard references. Syntactically, S5^r is a single-agent logic. That is, it does not provide us with syntactic markers to distinguish agents such as a different modality for each agent as in the modal epistemic logic S5$_n$. Consequently, there is no way to distinguish different agents other than by what they know. In S5^r we can represent the individuality of agents in the hypothesis itself. For instance, in order to represent what the agents a and b know, we can use different hypotheses p_a and p_b, which are atomic propositions labelling the states which the agents a and b, respectively, consider possible. Thus $[p_a]_K\varphi$ states 'a knows φ' and $[p_b]_K\psi$ states that 'b knows ψ'.

4.1 Axiomatisation

We now present a sound and complete axiomatisation of S5^r from [19]. The axiom system consists of all propositional tautologies and the following axioms:

(K) $[\varphi]_K(p \to q) \to ([\varphi]_K p \to [\varphi]_K q)$
(T) $[\top]_K p \to p$
(4) $[\top]_K p \to [\top]_K[\top]_K p$
(B) $p \to [\top]_K \neg[\top]_K \neg p$
(R) $[\varphi]_K p \leftrightarrow [\top]_K p \vee (\varphi \wedge [\top]_K(\varphi \to p))$.

The first four axioms are similar to the axioms known from the modal epistemic logic S5 characterising any modality $[\varphi]_K$ in our logic S5^r as epistemic operator that can be used to represent what is known under the hypothesis φ.

The axioms (T), (4), and (B) are for the modality $[\top]_K$ only, whereas we need additional instances of the axioms (K) and (R), namely the ones for each modal parameter φ (cf. Definition 4). The reduction axiom (R) states that every modality $[\varphi]_K$ is definable in terms of the basic modal operator $[\top]_K$, which corresponds to the S5-box or the universal modality. As it was already mentioned in the introduction, Axiom (R) corresponds to the definition of the modal operator 'Modest Enrichment (Type B)' in [12].

Theorem 2 ([19]). *The system S5^r is sound and complete w.r.t. the class of basic structures.*

We note that the completeness proof that we present here is different from the canonical model proof envisioned in [19].

Proof. We first show soundness. The axioms (K), (T), (4), and (B) are sound w.r.t. basic structures. We show that the reduction axiom is also valid. Let $\mathfrak{M} = (W, V)$ be a basic structure and let w be a world in it. Suppose that $w \models [\varphi]_K\psi$. For every $v \in W$, it holds that if $R_\varphi(w, v)$, then $\langle\mathfrak{M}, v\rangle \models \psi$. By Proposition 2 we obtain that for every $v \in W$, if $w \in [\![\varphi]\!] \Rightarrow v \in [\![\varphi]\!]$, then $\langle\mathfrak{M}, v\rangle \models \psi$. We now show that $\langle\mathfrak{M}, w\rangle \models [\top]_K\psi \vee (\varphi \wedge [\top]_K(\varphi \to \psi))$. We distinguish two cases. In the first case, it holds that $w \notin [\![\varphi]\!]$. The implication $w \in [\![\varphi]\!] \Rightarrow v \in [\![\varphi]\!]$ holds for every $v \in W$. Hence, for every $v \in W$, we have that $\langle\mathfrak{M}, v\rangle \models \psi$. This implies that $\langle\mathfrak{M}, w\rangle \models [\top]_K\psi$. In the second case, it holds that $w \in [\![\varphi]\!]$. Then $\langle \mathfrak{M}, w \rangle \models \varphi$ and also $\langle \mathfrak{M}, w \rangle \models [\top]_K(\varphi \to \psi))$. This is because only R_φ-successors of w satisfy φ and every R_φ-successor of w satisfies ψ. Therefore, every world where φ is true also satisfies ψ. The converse direction can be shown similarly.

For showing completeness, it suffices to show that the reduction axiom $[\varphi]_K\psi \leftrightarrow [\top]_K\psi \vee (\varphi \wedge [\top]_K(\varphi \to \psi))$ is a relational modal definition defining the relation R_φ (cf. Theorem 1). Let $\Psi_\varphi(x,y) = \mathrm{ST}_x(\varphi) \Rightarrow \mathrm{ST}_y(\varphi)$ be a formula with the two free variables x and y. We want to show that $(\forall y)(\Psi_\varphi(x,y) \Rightarrow \mathrm{ST}_y(\psi))$ is equivalent to $\mathrm{ST}_x([\top]_K\psi \vee (\varphi \wedge [\top]_K(\varphi \to \psi)))$. The standard translation $\mathrm{ST}_x([\top]_K\psi \vee (\varphi \wedge [\top]_K(\varphi \to \psi)))$ is a disjunction of the formulas $(\forall y)(\mathrm{ST}_y(\psi))$ and $(\mathrm{ST}_x(\varphi) \wedge (\forall y)(\mathrm{ST}_y(\varphi) \Rightarrow \mathrm{ST}_y(\psi))$. We show that for a model $\mathfrak{M}$ and a world w, it holds that $(\forall y)(\mathrm{ST}_x(\varphi) \Rightarrow \mathrm{ST}_y(\varphi)) \Rightarrow \mathrm{ST}_y(\psi)[x \leftarrow c_w]$ iff $(\forall y)(\mathrm{ST}_y(\psi)) \vee (\mathrm{ST}_x(\varphi) \wedge (\forall y)(\mathrm{ST}_y(\varphi) \Rightarrow \mathrm{ST}_y(\psi))[x \leftarrow c_w]$.

5   Conclusions

In this paper we present a method for obtaining Kripke completeness of Kripke complete modal logics extended with a special kind of axioms which we call relational modal definitions. The notion of relational modal definition ensures that the newly defined modality has a relational semantics. The method applies to several existing modal logics, e.g., variants of dynamic epistemic logic. As an illustration we show completeness of the multi-modal logic S5^r. The logic S5^r was introduced as a logic of hypotheses [19]. We think that it is an interesting non-trivial problem to give an explicit syntactic characterisation of the class of all relational modal definitions. Similar questions have been addressed in [20] and [9], although to the best of our knowledge no such characterisation has been given yet. Here we have considered some instances of relational modal definitions, e.g., classes of formulas constructed in a manner similar to Sahlqvist formulas. The first author was partially supported by Shota Rustaveli National Science Foundation of Georgia (SRNSFG) grant number YS17-71.

References

1. Baltag, A., Smets, S.: Group belief dynamics under iterated revision: fixed points and cycles of joint upgrades. In: Proceedings of TARK 2009, pp. 41–50. Morgan Kaufmann Publishers Inc., San Francisco, CA, USA (2009)
2. Baltag, A., Moss, L.S., Solecki, S.: The logic of public announcements, common knowledge, and private suspicions. In: Proceedings of TARK 1998: the 7th Conference on Theoretical Aspects of Rationality and Knowledge, pp. 43–56. Morgan Kaufmann Publishers Inc., San Francisco, CA, USA (1998)
3. Barwise, J.: Three views of common knowledge. In: Yardi, M.Y. (ed.), Proceedings of the Second Conference on Theoretical Aspects of Reasoning About Knowledge, pp. 365–379. Morgan Kaufman, San Francisco (1988)
4. van Benthem, J., Liu, F.: Dynamic logic of preference upgrade. J. Appl. Non-Class. Log. **17**(2), 157–182 (2007)
5. van Benthem, J.: Modal frame classes revisited. Fundam. Inform. **18**, 307–317 (1993)

6. van Benthem, J.: Rational dynamics and epistemic logic in games. In: International Game Theory Review, vol. 9, pp. 13–45 (2007). Erratum reprint, vol. 9, no. 2, pp. 377–409

7. Blackburn, P., de Rijke, M., Venema, Y.: Modal Logic. Cambridge University Press, Cambridge (2001)

8. Chagrova, L.A.: An undecidable problem in correspondence theory. J. Symb. Log. **56**, 1261–1272 (1991)

9. Conradie W., Palmigiano A., Sourabh S., Zhao Z.: Canonicity and relativized canonicity via pseudo-correspondence: an application of ALBA. In: Working paper, Delft University of Technology (2015)

10. van Ditmarsch, H., van der Hoek, W., Kooi, B.: Dynamic Epistemic Logic Synthese Library: Studies in Epistemology, Logic, Methodology, and Philosophy of Science, vol. 337. Springer, Dordrecht (2007). https://doi.org/10.1007/978-1-4020-5839-4

11. Esakia, L.: Weak transitivity - a restitution. In: Logical Investigations, vol. 8, pp. 244–255 (2001). in Russian

12. Esakia, L.: Around provability logic. Ann. Pure Appl. Log. **161**(2), 174–184 (2009). Festschrift on the occasion of Franco Montagna's 60th birthday

13. Fagin, R., Halpern, J.Y., Moses, Y., Vardi, M.Y.: Reasoning about Knowledge. The MIT Press, Cambridge (1995)

14. Goldblatt, R.I., Thomason, S.K.: Axiomatic classes in propositional modal logic. In: Crossley, J.N. (ed.) Algebra and Logic. LNM, vol. 450, pp. 163–173. Springer, Heidelberg (1975). https://doi.org/10.1007/BFb0062855

15. Lewis, D.: Convention: A Philosophical Study. Harvard University Press, Cambridge (1969)

16. Meyer, J.-J.C., van der Hoek, W.: Epistemic Logic for AI and Computer Science, Cambridge Tracts in Theoretical Computer Science, vol. 41. Cambridge University Press, Cambridge (1995)

17. Plaza, J.A.: Logics of public communications. In: Proceedings of the 4th International Symposium on Methodologies for Intelligent Systems, pp. 201–216. Oak Ridge National Laboratory, ORNL/DSRD-24 (1989)

18. Sahlqvist, H.: Completeness and correspondence in the first and second order semantics for modal logics. In: Proceedings of the 3rd Scandinavian Logic Symposium, pp. 110–143. North-Holland Publishing Company (1975)

19. Uridia, L., Walther, D.: An epistemic logic with hypotheses. In: van Ditmarsch, H., Lang, J., Ju, S. (eds.) LORI 2011. LNCS (LNAI), vol. 6953, pp. 286–299. Springer, Heidelberg (2011). https://doi.org/10.1007/978-3-642-24130-7_21

20. Venema, Y.: Canonical pseudo-correspondence. In: Zakharyaschev, M., Segerberg, K., de Rijke, M., Wansing, H. (eds.), Advances in Modal Logic, vol. 2, pp. 421–430. CSLI Publications (1998)

Multiagent Systems, Game Theory and Economic Paradigms, Game Playing and Interactive Entertainment, Ambient Intelligence

Potential Fields in Smoke Dispersion Applied to Evacuation Simulations

Bruna A. Corrêa, Diana F. Adamatti$^{(\boxtimes)}$, and Alessandro de L. Bicho

Centro de Ciências Computacionais (C3),
Universidade Federal do Rio Grande (Furg),
Avenida Itália, Km 8, S/N, Rio Grande, RS, Brazil
dianaadamatti@furg.br

Abstract. We often visit places with a large concentration of people, such as malls, football stadiums, restaurants or nightclubs. Through the media, there are often reports of emergency's cases in these places. It is known that in a fire situation, one of the main causes of deaths is the inhalation of smoke. Therefore, it is essential that at the start of emergency situations people leave quickly to avoid possible injuries. We have investigated the dispersion of smoke in closed places and simulate the crowds' behavior in these situations. This paper aims to present a new proposal to model the smoke dispersion in closed environments using the concept of potential fields joined to cellular automata. To validate the work, a behavioral model for the simulation of people evacuation using the multiagent approach was implemented.

Keywords: Potential fields · Smoke dispersion · Multiagent systems
Evacuation simulation

1 Introduction

Many studies have been carried out to understand the behavior of smoke in closed places in order to escape people in places where there is fire. In an emergency situation, fires can be classified as accidental or intentional, with the dispersion varying according to the material that suffers the combustion process [7].

In a fire associated with the combustion phenomenon, four dangerous situations appear in general: heat, flames, insufficiency of oxygen and smoke. Of these four factors, smoke is one that causes very serious damage to people life [7]. Considering a fire situation in an environment in which it does not have any type of alarm or signaling, when people smell the smoke, they will instinctively look for the nearest exit. However, the smoke will hinder the vision causing tearing, in addition to causing respiratory symptoms such as coughing and suffocation. Smoke can cause panic, because it occupies a large volume of the environment, making it difficult for people to move in an evacuation [7]. There is great importance in conducting studies of the behavior of smoke to prevent deaths in fires caused by their inhalation.

© Springer Nature Switzerland AG 2018
G. R. Simari et al. (Eds.): IBERAMIA 2018, LNAI 11238, pp. 83–95, 2018.
https://doi.org/10.1007/978-3-030-03928-8_7

Building projects should include active and passive measures to facilitate the escape of people, but prior simulation of an emergency situation minimizes the chances of fatality. Therefore, the objective of this paper is to propose a model to simulate the dispersion of smoke in an environment using potential fields and cellular automata. Cellular automata represent evolutionary systems that from an initial random configuration, each component of the system has its evolution based on the current situation of its neighbors and a set of rules that are the same for all components [12]. Potential field is an array or field of vectors that represent the space. The main idea of this method is to establish a potential field of attractive forces around the target point and a potential field of repulsive forces around obstacles. The sum of all forces determines the subsequent direction and velocity of the movement [4], and a new potential field is established called the artificial potential field [14].

In this work, a new application for potential fields is proposed, being joined to cellular automata to describe the dispersion of the smoke in a closed environment. We simulate an emergency situation causing the crowd evacuation in which each person is modeled as an autonomous agent using multiagent simulation [13].

The paper is organized as follows. In the next section the related works to the proposed method are presented. The details of the model are introduced in Sect. 3. The simulation results are analyzed in Sect. 4. At last the final considerations is given.

2   Related Works

Pessoli [6] proposes a methodology to simulate the transport of light pollutants under the action of wind fields in complex environments. The method consists of dividing the advective diffusion equation into two components, one laminar and other tubular. The internal modules of the model are programmed in C, for the external modules it was used the MATLAB® interpolation tool and for the calculation of the wind fields in the entire environment was used a CFD (Computational Fluid Dynamics).

The potential fields method has been commonly used in obstacle prevention because its modelling is simple. However, the method brings substantial deficiencies. Koren and Borenstein [4] present a rigorous mathematical analysis to identify the problems inherent in the potential fields method. As a result, the authors define a differential equation that combines the robot and the environment in a unified system.

Silva et al. [10] show the importance of respecting the indications of the ABNT[1] standard for emergency situations. For validate it, two scenarios were modeled using NetLogo software: a scenario where it uses real data from the Kiss nightclub in Santa Maria/RS (Brazil), at the time of the tragedy in 2013; and a second scenario for the Kiss nightclub respecting the ABNT standard. Considering the data obtained from the evacuations in the two scenarios, it was

---

[1] ABNT: Associação Brasileira de Normas Técnicas (Brazilian Association of Technical Standards).

possible to note that the application of emergency exit signs, together with the number of doors and their correct dimensions, make evacuation considerably more effective.

Helbing et al. [3] model the evacuation of pedestrians in a panic situation using particle systems. It uses a social forces model that influences the behavior of pedestrians to investigate the mechanisms of panic and interference by uncoordinated movement in crowds.

Zheng et al. [15] propose a model to study the dynamics of evacuation of pedestrians with influence of fire and the smoke dispersion. The direction of smoke dispersion is from top to bottom, which leaves less size to pedestrians movement, and pedestrians' movement behavior is divided into three stages: normal walking, curved walk and crawling. The influence of fire and smoke on the movement of pedestrians is modeled by the field of fire floor and the field of smoke floor.

Hardt et al. [2] propose a computational model for real-time simulation of the large-scale flow of smoke or gas in large environments, depending of a given configuration of obstacles and a field of winds. A discrete approach was adopted for wind transport and diffusion mechanisms, allowing simple and efficient simulation.

The work of Pax and Pavón [5] proposes an architecture of agents for internal scenarios, looking for performance and flexibility in the individual behavior of the agents. It keeps the crowd effects and allows the modeling of rich and heterogeneous behaviors for each agent.

In this section some related models to the proposal of this paper were presented. A specific discussion will be given in Sect. 4.1.

3   The Model

3.1   The Potential Fields Model

Considering a simple case, we can assume an element (e.g., a robot or an agent) being a point that is influenced by the potential field $2D$. If we assume a differentiable potential field function $U(q)$, we can find the related artificial force $F(q)$ acting at the position $q = (x, y)$ [9]. We have:

$$F(q) = -\nabla U(q), \text{ where } \nabla U(q) = \left[\frac{\partial U}{\partial x}, \frac{\partial U}{\partial y} \right] \tag{1}$$

denotes the gradient vector of U in the q position. The potential field that acts on the element is the sum of the attractive field with the repulsive field:

$$U(q) = U_{att}(q) + U_{rep}(q). \tag{2}$$

The attractive potential can be defined as a parabolic function:

$$U_{att}(q) = \frac{1}{2} k_{att} \cdot \rho_{goal}^2(q), \tag{3}$$

where k_{att} is a positive scale factor and $\rho_{goal}(q)$ indicates the Euclidean distance $\|q - q_{goal}\|$. Since this potential is differentiable:

$$F_{att}(q) = -\nabla U_{att}(q) = -k_{att}.\rho_{goal}(q)\nabla\rho_{goal}(q) = -katt.(q - q_{goal}). \quad (4)$$

The repulsive potential should be strong when the element is close to the obstacle, but it should not influence when the element is far from the obstacle. We can define it as:

$$U_{rep}(q) = \begin{cases} \frac{1}{2}k_{rep}\left(\frac{1}{\rho(q)} - \frac{1}{\rho_0}\right)^2 & \text{, if } \rho(q) \leq \rho_0 \\ 0 & \text{, if } \rho(q) > \rho_0 \end{cases}. \quad (5)$$

The k_{rep} constant is a scaling factor, $\rho(q)$ is the distance of q to the obstacle and ρ_0 is the distance of influence of the obstacle. The repulsive potential function U_{rep} is positive or zero, and it tends to infinity when the element approaches the obstacle. If the boundary of the obstacle is convex and differentiable in parts, $\rho(q)$ is differentiable everywhere in the free configuration space. We can define a repulsive force as:

$$F_{rep} = -\nabla U_{rep}(q), \quad (6)$$

$$F_{rep} = \begin{cases} k_{rep}\left(\frac{1}{\rho(q)} - \frac{1}{\rho_0}\right)\frac{1}{\rho^2(q)}\frac{q-q_{obstacle}}{\rho_0} & \text{, if } \rho(q) \leq \rho_0 \\ 0 & \text{, if } \rho(q) > \rho_0 \end{cases}. \quad (7)$$

In this way, the resultant force is:

$$F(q) = F_{att}(q) + F_{rep}(q), \quad (8)$$

which acts on the element and it is influenced by attractive and repulsive forces, directing the element away from the obstacles towards to the target [9].

3.2 The Potential Field Model Adapted for Smoke Dispersion

This work creates a model to simulate the dispersion of smoke in an environment using the concept of potential fields associated with cellular automata. From this model, we simulated an emergency situation causing an evacuation of people based on multiagent system. The Fig. 1 shows the diagram of the methodology and the following subsections present their steps.

Potential fields are typically used for agent movement models. In this work, a new application for the concept is proposed, being used to describe the dispersion of the smoke in a closed environment. For that, it was necessary to make some adjustments in the equations of the potential fields, then it could be used in this new application. In the original definition of potential fields, it is considered only a possible target for the agent to reach and obstacles can be more than one in the environment. In our application, the equations were modified so that it was possible to have a single obstacle (fire) with several possible targets (doors). With this, the obstacle generates a force of repulsion while each target generates

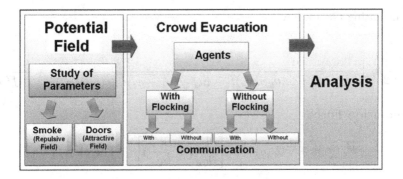

Fig. 1. Proposed methodology.

its force of attraction. Considering the Vector Agent position being $\vec{q} = (q_x, q_y)$, the Vector Target position being $\vec{a} = (a_x, a_y)$ and the Vector Obstacle position being $\vec{o} = (o_x, o_y)$, the artificial potential field for the dispersion of the smoke is obtained through the following equations:

Attractive Potential

$$U_a(q) = \frac{1}{2}k_a \frac{1}{\| \vec{q} - \vec{a} \|^2}. \tag{9}$$

The k_a constant is how much the field deforms near the target point.

Attraction Force

$$\vec{F}_a(q) = -\nabla U_a(q) = -\left[\frac{\partial U_a}{\partial q_x}\hat{i} + \frac{\partial U_a}{\partial q_y}\hat{j}\right] = -\left[A_a\hat{i} + B_a\hat{j}\right]. \tag{10}$$

Calculating A_a, we have:

$$A_a = \frac{1}{2}k_a \left[\frac{2a_x - 2q_x}{[(q_x - a_x)^2 + (q_y - a_y)^2]^2}\right]. \tag{11}$$

Calculating B_a, we have:

$$B_a = \frac{1}{2}k_a \left[\frac{2a_y - 2q_y}{[(q_x - a_x)^2 + (q_y - a_y)^2]^2}\right]. \tag{12}$$

Repulsive Potential

$$U_r(q) = \begin{cases} C_r \ , \text{ if } d(q,o) \leq inf \\ 0 \ , \text{ if } d(q,o) > inf \end{cases}, \tag{13}$$

$$\text{where } C_r = \frac{1}{2}k_r \left(\frac{1}{d(q,o)} - \frac{1}{inf}\right)^2. \tag{14}$$

The k_r constant is how much the field deforms near the obstacle point, $d(q,o)$ is the Euclidean distance of the agent to the obstacle and inf is the distance of influence of the obstacle.

Calculating C_r, we have:

$$C_r = \frac{1}{2}k_r\left[\frac{1}{(o_x - q_x)^2 + (o_y - q_y)^2} - \frac{2}{inf\sqrt{(o_x - q_x)^2 + (o_y - q_y)^2}} + \frac{1}{inf^2}\right].$$

(15)

Repulsion Force

$$\overrightarrow{F}_r(q) = -\nabla U_r(q) = -\left[\frac{\partial U_r}{\partial q_x}\widehat{i} + \frac{\partial U_r}{\partial q_y}\widehat{j}\right]. \quad \text{Therefore,}$$

(16)

$$\overrightarrow{F}_r(q) = -\left[\frac{\partial C_r}{\partial q_x}\widehat{i} + \frac{\partial C_r}{\partial q_y}\widehat{j}\right] = -\left[D_r\widehat{i} + E_r\widehat{j}\right].$$

(17)

Calculating D_r, we have:

$$D_r = \frac{1}{2}k_r\left[\frac{2o_x - 2q_x}{[(o_x - q_x)^2 + (o_y - q_y)^2]^2} + \frac{2}{inf}\left(\frac{1}{2[(o_x - q_x)^2 + (o_y - q_y)^2]^{\frac{3}{2}}} - 2q_x + 2o_x\right)\right].$$

(18)

Calculating E_r, we have:

$$E_r = \frac{1}{2}k_r\left[\frac{2o_y - 2q_y}{[(o_x - q_x)^2 + (o_y - q_y)^2]^2} + \frac{2}{inf}\left(\frac{1}{2[(o_x - q_x)^2 + (o_y - q_y)^2]^{\frac{3}{2}}} - 2q_y + 2o_y\right)\right].$$

(19)

Resultant Force

$$\text{Finally, } F(q) = -\sum_{i=1}^{n}\overrightarrow{F}_{a_i}(q) + \overrightarrow{F}_r(q).$$

(20)

The model potential field is defined from its attracting points which are the exit doors and a repulsive point that is the origin of the fire. The smoke is generated at the point of repulsion, it starting gradually and moves according to the vectors generated by the potential field. Table 1 shows the steps of the smoke dispersion, that is an approximation of Fick's Second Law [8], where Fick's Laws are diffusion mass transport equations. The second Fick law associated to potential fields defines the rules used in the cellular automata necessary to define how smoke can spread through of building.

3.3 Calibrating Parameters for the Simulations

The Table 2(a) shows some simulations using one door and the focus of the smoke, varying the parameters door constant (k_a), smoke constant (k_r), and smoke influence (inf), which are part of the equations of the potential field. Analyzing each column of Table 2(a), it is possible to see that there is no change

Table 1. Smoke dispersion rules.

1st step	2nd step	3rd step
Each tick generates the smoke at the starting point of the fire (black patch), which is defined by the user.	Smoke spreads 1/8 of its intensity to its neighbors (Moore's Neighborhood).	Smoke disperses half (1/2) of its intensity to the patch that its potential field vector is pointing to.

in the size of the smoke dispersion by varying the parameters k_a and k_r. However, when analyzing each line of Table 2(a), it is possible to see that there is a change in the size of the smoke dispersion by varying the parameter inf, and it is possible to say that the most relevant variable in the formation of the smoke is the influence of the smoke. In this way, an average value for the variables was chosen for our experiments: door constant equal to 5, smoke constant equal to 5, and smoke influence equal to 5. After defining the values of the constant parameters, the smoke dispersion was simulated with 1, 2, 3 and 4 doors, in ticks 11, 15, 21 and 25, as shown in Table 2(b).

3.4   Crowd Evacuation Model

In order to simulate a crowd emergency situation with the dispersion of smoke, the NetLogo software was used to implement the case study. The simulation environment implemented by Silveira [11] in the NetLogo was used, which is an simple evacuation model where an environment with a crowd is created, and people leave by the nearest door using Euclidean Distance. The environment has a square configuration, with 61 × 61 grid, as shown in Table 3, which it is possible to choose the agents or the vectors of the potential field to be shown, but it is always possible to see the dispersion of smoke. In the modeled environment, people are created in random positions and move randomly until they recognize the smoke. When this happens, agents identify the closest exit, calculated by the Euclidean Distance. These agents have the ability to communicate with others when they feel the smoke in the environment (this ability could be ON or OFF).

4   Results Analysis

In the simulations performed with the model some parameters were their values fixed and some parameters varied their values, as shown in Table 4. The initial

Table 2. (a) Simulations with one door and the focus of smoke, varying the parameters door constant k_a, smoke constant k_r and influence of smoke inf. (b) Simulations with 1–4 doors, in ticks 11, 15, 21 and 25.

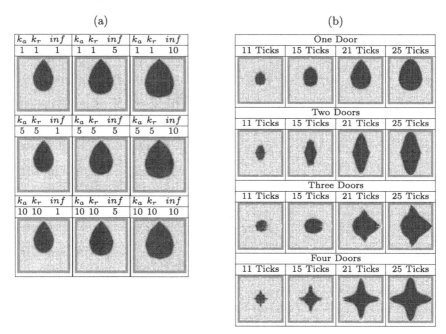

Table 3. Interfaces.

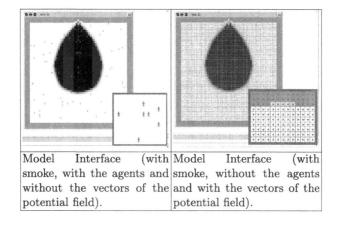

| Model Interface (with smoke, with the agents and without the vectors of the potential field). | Model Interface (with smoke, without the agents and with the vectors of the potential field). |

population size in the simulations was chosen, and it increases gradual, to facilitate the analysis of the results. For each configuration of values, five simulations were performed, and the average, the standard deviation and the percentage of people that left or died in relation to the initial amount of people in the environment were calculated.

Table 4. Parameters.

Parameter	Value	Parameter	Value
door_size	5	people	**on**
time_in_smoke	20 ticks	vision	5
xsmoke	30	ysmoke	30
smoke_increment	0.4	difusion_coefficient	0.4
constant_door1	5	constant_door3	5
constant_door2	5	constant_door4	5
smoke_constant	5	smoke_influence	5
Potential Vectors	**off**	-	-
Parameters		**Values**	
initial_population		35, 150 and 600 agents	
amount_doors		1, 2, 3 and 4 doors	
communication		**ON e OFF**	

In this section, we analyze the results obtained from the simulations to evaluate the influence of communication in an emergency situation with different populations of people in an environment. The focus of our work is to understand the used techniques, without a concern about computational performance. In the Table 5(a), (b) and (c) are the values obtained from these simulations.

In a general way, it is possible to see that the more doors, the lower the percentage of dead, as established by the Brazilian standard NBR 9077 [1]. With a population of 35 agents (Table 5(a)) having communication and three or four doors the values of people who left were better, but as it is a small population, people are far from each other to communicate. An example, which we can see in the Table 5(a), when we have four doors, with communication came out 83% of the people, while without communication came 79%. When analyzing the Table 5(b) with 150 agents, in the simulations with communication, people's exit results are better, with this it is understood that communication has more impact in the process of evacuation people. An example, which we can see in the Table 5(b), when we have four doors, with communication 82% of people left and without communication 77% of people left. And with 600 agents (Table 5(c)), it is possible to see that in the simulations when there are many people in the environment, we obtained better results when we have four doors without communication, because there are many people in the simulation and they simply

Table 5. Simulations: (a) population **35 agents**, (b) population **150 agents**, and (c) population **600 agents** (L: people who have left; D: people who died; %: percentage of people who left or died in relation to the total number of people).

(a)

Population 35 agents					
With Com.			Without Com.		
Doors Amount: 1					
$\bar{x}$	σ	%	$\bar{x}$	σ	%
L 7.6	1.82	22%	11.4	2.88	33%
D 27.4	1.82	78%	23.6	2.88	67%
Ticks 78.8	2.59	-	79.6	4.28	-
Doors Amount: 2					
$\bar{x}$	σ	%	$\bar{x}$	σ	%
L 20.2	2.49	58%	20.2	3.03	58%
D 14.8	2.49	42%	14.8	3.03	42%
Ticks 73.8	3.19	-	76.0	3.08	-
Doors Amount: 3					
$\bar{x}$	σ	%	$\bar{x}$	σ	%
L 23.2	1.92	66%	22.0	5.29	63%
D 11.8	1.92	34%	13.0	5.29	37%
Ticks 76.0	4.30	-	77.2	3.27	-
Doors Amount: 4					
$\bar{x}$	σ	%	$\bar{x}$	σ	%
L 29.2	2.59	83%	27.8	1.10	79%
D 5.8	2.59	17%	7.2	1.10	21%
Ticks 77.2	5.63	-	78.8	4.44	-

(b)

Population 150 agents					
With Com.			Without Com.		
Doors Amount: 1					
$\bar{x}$	σ	%	$\bar{x}$	σ	%
L 48.0	5.79	32%	43.4	5.08	29%
D 102.0	5.79	68%	106.6	5.08	71%
Ticks 80.2	1.30	-	82.4	2.19	-
Doors Amount: 2					
$\bar{x}$	σ	%	$\bar{x}$	σ	%
L 101.4	5.13	68%	93.0	2.74	62%
D 48.6	5.13	32%	57.0	2.74	38%
Ticks 78.6	1.52	-	78.2	0.84	-
Doors Amount: 3					
$\bar{x}$	σ	%	$\bar{x}$	σ	%
L 94.0	2.55	63%	90.4	3.58	60%
D 56.0	2.55	37%	59.6	3.58	40%
Ticks 79.4	1.67	-	79.6	1.52	-
Doors Amount: 4					
$\bar{x}$	σ	%	$\bar{x}$	σ	%
L 122.6	5.64	82%	115.6	5.94	77%
D 27.4	5.64	18%	34.4	5.94	23%
Ticks 81.0	1.58	-	83.6	2.07	-

(c)

Population 600 agents					
With Com.			Without Com.		
Doors Amount: 1					
$\bar{x}$	σ	%	$\bar{x}$	σ	%
L 106.8	9.58	18%	101.8	3.83	17%
D 493.2	9.58	82%	497.8	4.21	83%
Ticks 75.8	3.56	-	83.6	1.14	-
Doors Amount: 2					
$\bar{x}$	σ	%	$\bar{x}$	σ	%
L 218.6	12.44	36%	232.8	8.17	39%
D 361.4	51.72	60%	367.2	8.17	61%
Ticks 75.2	5.54	-	81.0	1.00	-
Doors Amount: 3					
$\bar{x}$	σ	%	$\bar{x}$	σ	%
L 246.6	49.08	41%	271.2	22.11	45%
D 333.4	13.39	56%	321.6	6.50	54%
Ticks 77.0	9.64	-	84.0	0.71	-
Doors Amount: 4					
$\bar{x}$	σ	%	$\bar{x}$	σ	%
L 315.2	10.18	53%	359.6	8.08	60%
D 284.8	10.18	47%	240.4	8.08	40%
Ticks 71.0	13.34	-	85.0	0.71	-

leave the environment, before identifying the fire or be warned from the fire. An example, which we can see in the Table 5(c), when we have four doors, without communication 60% of people left, while with communication 53% of people left.

4.1   Smoke Dispersion Methods Comparison

Zheng et al. [15] simulate the evacuation dynamics of pedestrians with the influence of fire and the smoke dispersion. The smoke dispersion is from top to bottom, as time goes on, less space as to people walk in the environment as a normal way. In this way, this work considers three ways to people movement: normal walking, curved walk, and crawling. The Fig. 2(a) shows the simulation performed, where, in the middle of the room happens the fire in the red color; the smoke in shades of gray (the stronger the more smoke); people in a normal walking are in blue; people in a curved walk are in green; and people in crawling are in cyan. There are two evacuation doors on the left at the room.

Using our model to represent the same scenario presented in [15], we obtained the results presented in the Fig. 2(b), where the smoke is represented in shades of gray and two doors on the left in yellow; and the potential field vectors are in red. It is possible to see that our approach could reproduce the smoke dispersion for this scenario, with a more "realist" way, because the form of smoke is less symmetric (drop form), differently of the results in [15], which only uses the neighborhood to disperse the smoke.

Hardt et al. [2] simulate in real time the large-scale smoke or gas flow in large environments, where there are one obstacle (yellow circle) and a wind field. The Fig. 3(a) shows the sequence of laminar wind images, using a diffusion coefficient equal to 0.2.

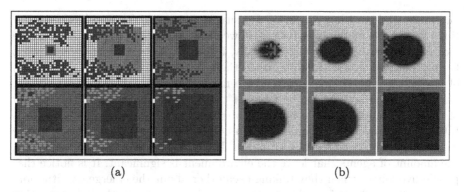

Fig. 2. (a) The results of the work in [15]. (b) Our results using the same scenario. (Color figure online)

Using our model to represent the same scenario in [2], we obtain the results presented in Fig. 3(b), that shows the images sequence of the smoke with diffusion coefficient equal to 0.2. In this model, the obstacle is the blue circle, and the attractor is the door in the right side of the environment (in yellow). Our scenario has just one attractor to cause the dissipation of smoke, whereas the proposed method in [2] uses a wind field (whole field acts as attractors, using a flow velocity). Therefore, the smoke shape is different: the dispersion in our model is wider in the initial point and finer at the end point, near the door.

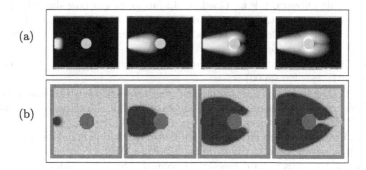

Fig. 3. (a) The results in [2]. (b) Our results using the same scenario. (Color figure online)

5   Final Considerations and Further Works

This paper presented a new model to simulate the dispersion of smoke in closed environments, using potential fields associated to the concept of cellular automata, and modeling an emergency situation using multiagent-based simulation. The results of our experiments showed that using the potential fields in the modeling of smoke dispersion, generally, brings a good approximation of what happens in reality. For example, when there is a single door and a single focus of fire that generates smoke, it tends to move toward the door forming a drop, having its rounded part in the focus of the fire and narrowing in the vicinity of the door. Modeling the evacuation of people in an emergency situation was taken into consideration communication between people, to know if its influence is significant in an emergency situation. If the people know about the smoke, the amount of agents that leave the environment is significant. It is notice that people live longer when they talking each other about the emergency situation.

As future work, we intend to generate complex scenarios with obstacles within the environment (e.g., with walls, tables, and chairs), add emergency signals (according NBR 9077 [1]), and model real scenarios such as the Kiss Nightclub [10]. Other improvements will be proposed in the concept of potential fields to model the agents movement, as well as apply the concepts of roadmaps (path planning). In this way, people will not only look for the nearest path but rather the safest. Finally, another work is ensured the conservation of mass in the smoke dispersion.

References

1. Associação Brasileira de Normas Técnicas (ABNT), Rio de Janeiro, RJ: ABNT: NBR 9077 - Saídas de emergência em edifícios (2001)
2. Hardt, K., de Oliveira, L.P.L., Goedert, J.: Smoke or gas flow simulation in large environments with obstacles considering the effect of wind arrays. In: Proceedings of the 5th EUROSIM Congress on Modelling and Simulation, pp. 1–8. ESIEE Paris, Marne la Vallée, France (2004)
3. Helbing, D., Farkas, I., Vicsek, T.: Simulating dynamical features of escape panic. Nature **407**, 487–490 (2000)
4. Koren, Y., Borenstein, J.: Potential field methods and their inherent limitations for mobile robot navigation. In: Proceedings of the IEEE International Conference on Robotics and Automation, vol. 2, pp. 1398–1404 (1991)
5. Pax, R., Pavón, J.: Agent architecture for crowd simulation in indoor environments. J. Ambient Intell. Hum. Comput. **8**(2), 205–212 (2017)
6. Pessoli, L.: Modelagem da dispersão de poluentes leves em ambientes complexos. Master's thesis, Universidade do Vale do Rio dos Sinos, São Leopoldo, RS (2006)
7. Seito, A.I., et al. (eds.): A Segurança Contra Incêndio no Brasil. Projeto Editora, São Paulo, SP (2008)
8. Serra, R., Villani, M.: A CA model of spontaneous formation of concentration gradients. In: Umeo, H., Morishita, S., Nishinari, K., Komatsuzaki, T., Bandini, S. (eds.) ACRI 2008. LNCS, vol. 5191, pp. 385–392. Springer, Heidelberg (2008). https://doi.org/10.1007/978-3-540-79992-4_50
9. Siegwart, R., Nourbakhsh, I.R., Scaramuzza, D.: Introduction to Autonomous Mobile Robots, 2nd edn. MIT Press, London (2011)

10. Silva, V.M., Scholl, M.V., Corrêa, B.A., da Costa Junior, M.J.Z., Adamatti, D.F.: Multi-agent simulation of a real evacuation scenario: kiss nightclub and the panic factor. In: Belardinelli, F., Argente, E. (eds.) EUMAS 2017. LNCS, vol. 10767, pp. 268–280. Springer, Berlin (2017). https://doi.org/10.1007/978-3-030-01713-2_19
11. Silveira, A.G.: A people evacuation model (2015). Simulação Social: Teoria e Aplicações, Prog. de Pós-Grad. em Modelagem Computacional (PPGMC/Furg)
12. Wolfram, S.: Statistical mechanics of cellular automata. Rev. Mod. Phys. **55**, 601–644 (1983)
13. Wooldridge, M., Jennings, N.R.: Intelligent agents: theory and practice. Knowl. Eng. Rev. **10**(2), 115–152 (1995)
14. Zhang, Q., Chen, D., Chen, T.: An obstacle avoidance method of soccer robot based on evolutionary artificial potential field. Energy Procedia **16**(Part C) 1792–1798 (2012)
15. Zheng, Y., Jia, B., Li, X.G., Jiang, R.: Evacuation dynamics considering pedestrians' movement behavior change with fire and smoke spreading. Saf. Sci. **92**, 180–189 (2017)

MAS Modeling of Collaborative Creative Processes

Luis de Garrido and Juan Pavón[✉]

Universidad Complutense Madrid, 28040 Madrid, Spain
pontmare@hotmail.com, jpavon@fdi.ucm.es

Abstract. The main purpose of this work is to model collaborative creative process as multi-agent systems. This will allow the generation of a computational model that can be simulated for assessment of different methods and the analysis of their characteristics, or to create tools that support collaborative creative processes. This paper illustrates how this modeling is done with one example of group brainstorming, Symbolic Brainstorming, which includes many of the features that are common in this type of creative processes. The use of agents to model each of the actors allows modeling heterogeneous individuals, as well as a diversity of interactions and workflows.

Keywords: Multi-agent systems (MAS) · Computational creativity
Symbolic brainstorming · Agent-based simulation · JADE · INGENIAS

1 Introduction

Developing computational models of the collaboration of persons in creative processes, such as brainstorming, will allow their simulation. This can be useful on one side to find those aspects and relevant components that contribute to creative problem solving. Also, and taking into account these factors, a general structure can be sketched to model a computer system capable of solving problems in a creative way, or supporting persons in a collaborative creative process, for instance, to facilitate the workflow of contributions of the participants and the evolution of the creative process.

There are not too many attempts to model collective creative processes, and this is more discussed in theoretical terms, such as in [9]. Some computational models are too specific, such as [4] using genetic algorithms, which can be useful to study a concrete issue, but not very flexible to cope with complex configuration or changing requirements. More practical are those efforts oriented to create tools that support the creative process, such as [3]. Agents can be helpful for this task, as discussed in [6] and shown in [11], an agent-based bot-communication platform designed where agents can share artistic practices with each other, or in [8], where two agents create an artifact by evolving the same artifact set in turns. Our approach intends to be more general, so we use an agent modeling framework, INGENIAS [12], in order to specify computational models of collaborative creative processes, which can be either simulated to study the process, or be the basis to generate a tool to facilitate the automation of the process.

This paper starts from a review of different methods that are commonly applied to incentive creativity. They can be characterized by certain workflows where different

© Springer Nature Switzerland AG 2018
G. R. Simari et al. (Eds.): IBERAMIA 2018, LNAI 11238, pp. 96–107, 2018.
https://doi.org/10.1007/978-3-030-03928-8_8

entities (e.g., individuals) can perform some activity on their own and through interactions among them can get new inputs and contrast ideas in order to generate new ones. These methods can be formalized as computational models for many reasons. On the one hand, in order to analyze exhaustively each method, determine their basic mechanisms and thus improve their effectiveness. On the other hand, once we know their structure and the reason for their effectiveness, we can model artificial systems that assist in the creative process, increasing the speed and quantity of creative ideas that can be generated.

This is done by using multi-agent systems, as agents can model the individual entities and their interactions, as well as different forms of organization and the resulting workflows. This modeling is performed by using the INGENIAS methodology and tools [12]. This methodology has been chosen as it provides computational representation of relevant concepts such as goal, agent, workflow, interaction, and organization, among others that are used in the modeling process. Also, because it facilitates the automatic generation of code for the JADE platform [1], which is a standard for implementing the multi-agent system.

The rest of the paper is organized as follows. The next section describes some collaborative creative methods, more specifically, Brainstorming, as this is a well-known technique. A particular case, Symbolic Brainstorming, will be used as an example to illustrate how to make the agent-based modeling of the creative process. This is described in Sect. 3 with enough detail in order to identify the main entities that take part in the process, their tasks, and how do they interact. This facilitates the definition of the multi-agent system model that is presented in Sect. 4 by using INGENIAS modeling language. This kind of modeling can be applied to other collaborative creative processes, and the conclusions, in Sect. 5, discuss what can be learnt from this experience and future lines of research.

2   Overview of Collaborative Creative Methods

Throughout history, the human being has been generating a set of strategies with the aim of solving problems in a creative way with the greatest possible efficiency. The increase in the size of the human network and the complexity resulting from its social relations has forced us to look for alternative, creative solutions to solve many of the problems that usually arise.

It is difficult to make a classification of the techniques that allow the creative resolution of problems, since there are as many strategies as human groups can be formed, and at the same time many of them are variations of the same subject. However, with a purely practical purpose, among the most relevant we can mention:

- Generate parallels with known problems [10].
- Problem solving [16].
- Brainstorming, and different variants [13].
- Lateral thinking [14].
- Parallel thinking [2].
- Extract a problem out of its usual context [15].
- Symbolic Brainstorming [5].

In this work we focus on collaborative techniques, and in this sense Brainstorming is probably the oldest and best known technique of creative problem solving, as it can be applied for a diversity of problems, for generating a large amount of good, new and fresh ideas. The method can be complemented with other techniques, and must necessarily be followed by a process of analysis of the ideas that are generated. Therefore, each session of Brainstorming actually has two consecutive sessions:

1. Generation of ideas session.
2. Ideas evaluation session.

2.1   Generation of Ideas Session

To be effective, a Brainstorming session should count with the participation of about 7–10 people, and a person to act as secretary and moderator.

At the beginning of the process the secretary-moderator introduces the problem that must be solved, and provides all kinds of available information. He then gives the floor to the group members in such a way that everyone must quickly provide several ideas to solve the problem that has been presented. The secretary-moderator takes note of all the ideas, writing them in large letters on a blackboard (so that all the members of the group can read them at all times) and ensures that all the members of the group contribute with several ideas, giving the word to each of them, according to a certain order, or arbitrarily.

For a Brainstorming to be effective, five basic rules must be followed:

1. Eliminate criticism. When the ideas arise, no critical comments are allowed, as this would prevent them from continuing to be generated. Therefore all the ideas are written down, as they are generated, and the evaluation (or adverse judgment) is reserved for later. Since our childhood we have been trained to be instantly analytical, practical and convergent in our thinking, so this rule is difficult to follow, but it is crucial to be creative. In fact, creating and judging at the same time is like pouring hot and cold water into the same glass.
2. Absolute freedom. The freedom to generate ideas is very important, and wild thoughts, or ideas that might seem impossible or unimaginable, are especially valued. In fact, in each session there should be some idea that is crazy enough to be able to cause embarrassment, stupefaction or even laugh to the whole group. It must be borne in mind that practical ideas are often born of others that are impracticable, absurd or impossible. Thinking outside the limits of the usual, of the normal, new and great solutions can arise. Some wild ideas are transformed into practices. The more energetic the idea, the better the results can be, since it is easier to perfect an idea than to issue a new one.
3. Generate many ideas. In a first phase, the most important thing is to generate a large number of ideas so that later they can be reviewed. The larger the number of ideas, the easier it is to choose between them. There are two reasons to seek for a lot of ideas. First, because it has been observed that obvious, habitual, worn, impracticable ideas come first to mind, so it is likely that the first 20 or 25 ideas are not fresh

or creative. Second, the longer the list, the more ideas there will be to choose, adapt or combine. In some sessions, the objective is set to get a certain number of ideas, of the order of 50 or 100, before finishing the meeting.

4. Multiplier effect. The goal of Brainstorming is both to generate new ideas, and to improve the ones exposed. In addition to contributing their own ideas, participants can suggest improvements to others' ideas or get a better idea from others. That is, participants can use the ideas of others as a stimulus to modify or improve them. Sometimes, changing only one aspect of an impractical solution can make it a great solution. Each human brain has developed differently, so it has a different structure. Each response to both external and internal stimuli is establishing a series of neuronal connections. The most stimulated neural networks consolidate their structure little by little with respect to other less used networks. Therefore, synaptic connections are facilitated to the detriment of others. With the passage of time each brain has strengthened some connections over others, so that a certain way of reasoning is established by responding to both external and internal stimuli. Therefore, a particular brain has more ability to solve a certain problem in a known way, while it has more difficulties in solving other problems that may require the use of other synaptic pathways. Therefore, each brain tends to follow a certain cognitive path when solving a problem, so the solutions usually follow the same pattern. On the other hand, if other people provide us with complementary information, the cognitive procedure is enriched and can take new roads or new routes that would not otherwise easily follow. Therefore the feedback of several human brains is always enriching because it favors that each individual brain follows cognitive structures slightly different from those that would follow when thinking alone.

5. Relaxed and cheerful atmosphere. As it has been noted in many sessions, creativity flows better when participants are relaxed, enjoying, playing and feeling free, without coercion of any kind. Even when the problem to be solved is of enormous seriousness or transcendence, the sessions should be relaxed. As an aid and encouragement to creativity, it is often good to start with a ten-minute warm-up session, where an imaginary problem is addressed. Thinking about an imaginary problem frees people and makes them happy, so they can address the real problem in better conditions.

The cognitive explanation for the creative efficacy of this situation is that when the brain does not have tasks directed by external stimuli it is reconfigured and adopts an operating state called "by default". In this state the cognitive capacity adopts previously established automatic mechanisms of functioning, but since there are no external stimuli, it simply activates again and again internally generated or random mechanisms. So to speak, the brain starts to "toy" by training automated strategies with random interior stimuli. Much of this invented neuronal activity does not make sense apparently since it does not aim to solve external problems. However, the activity is very intense and at a certain moment can find a partial or total solution to a certain conscious problem with which the brain was busy previously. In other words, the automated, random, incessant and unconscious activity of the brain when it has no external stimuli is able to find alternative ways and solutions to a given problem, which has not been solved in a conscious way or has been solved in a trivial way, not very creative.

The relaxed environment means that the brain functions in a "mind wandering" way, stimulating the default mode network and taking the creative problem to an unconscious level, in which the automatic and spontaneous cognitive mechanisms take place Kühn et al. [7]. In a computational plane this means that there must be a stage of mass generation of solutions in parallel, including bottom-up, top-down and random mechanisms. In other words, each time the computer system has not been able to solve problems above expectations, it should generate random information, invented by the system itself, and merge it with the information initially provided.

2.2   Evaluation Session

The day after having realized the session of generation of ideas (and never the same day) the group has to meet again. First, they have to share the ideas thought from the previous session. Afterwards, the group evaluates each of the ideas and develops those more promising to be able to put into practice.

During the evaluation sessions, wild ideas become practical or are used to suggest realistic solutions. The emphasis has to be placed on the analysis and real world issues. Sometimes the ideas found that are believed useful are divided in three groups:

- Ideas of immediate utility. Ideas that can be used immediately.
- Areas to explore more widely. Ideas that should be elaborated and discussed more widely.
- New approaches to the problem. Ideas that suggest new points of view to solve the problem.

Keep in mind that the evaluation session is not performed the same day as the brainstorming session. This makes the evaluation of ideas in the session more open (without the fear of immediate evaluation) and allows an incubation time of more ideas and a time to think about the ideas that have arisen.

3   Computational Modeling for Creative Problem Solving

The structure of brainstorming suggests that a computational system based on its structure should be composed of several agents, each of which has a different structure (and a different behavior) and therefore processes the information in a different way. Each agent communicates with the others in a common space that accumulates the information generated. Based on the information that is generated at each moment, each agent can decide to work in a linear way, analyzing the information and deducting new information, or in a random way, to a greater or lesser degree.

It is important to give the system a certain degree of "consciousness". The system must have a certain feedback mechanism. The human creative process develops on a conscious level when the problem is new and learns to solve it. When the problem is complex, it is solved in an unconscious plane, which has an "echo" in a conscious plane every time it is fed back, new information is added, or when the problem "suddenly" has been solved.

Usually humans have increased the conscious and unconscious feedback through the realization of diagrams, sketches, graphics and other means that stimulate a new direction to follow, and at the same time generate a "conscious" plane of the problem to solve. The diagrams and sketches have two key aspects for creativity. On the one hand, they are "fuzzy", that is, they can be interpreted in different ways. A sketch can be as ambiguous as you want, and therefore, at the same time you do it, the sketch itself establishes new search paths. If one draws a cross, it may be that the lines used to draw it have come by chance a little curved. And those curves can be the origin of a type of cross completely unknown until now. In addition, the sketches generate an agglutinating structure of all the parties, forming a coherent whole, with determined compositional rules that were not known at the beginning of the process. In short, the realization of a sketch of an idea what it does is not to represent that idea, but above all to suggest new ideas and establish internal "agglutinating" structures of the different parts of that idea. Undoubtedly, this aspect is essential for the design of a creative system, and it is surely complex to model. Somehow, graphic and abstract representations must be created in different parts of the process (especially at the beginning of the process) capable of interacting with the design process that is taking place at that moment.

The representation of knowledge is done by entities with an *object-attribute-value* structure. The objects (for example, a chair object), are composed of several attributes, and in turn of several objects (for example, arms, legs, seats, backs, etc.) in an indeterminate and flexible number. It is important to note that the values of the attributes may be fuzzy and may have values including counters. In addition, each object may have a huge number of attributes, often random, or that apparently have nothing to do with the object in question.

The computer system must have several agents (one of them must continually propose random ideas) that propose complete objects, or modify the value of the attributes of existing objects, or propose new attributes to objects that are being generated. In this way the different agents are continuously generating objects, or shaping those that already exist according to the information that is generated at each moment. After the first stage of the process several objects will have been generated, apparently with attributes and maybe incongruous or random values. In the second part of the process, graphic attributes will be associated to each object based on associations of the agents. In the third part of the process the generated solutions will be evaluated and values of the most important attributes will be satisfied, based on a process of successive refinement of the same solution.

4 A Case Study: Symbolic Brainstorming

Symbolic Brainstorming [5] is used for the creation of architectural forms. It is based on asking the participants to associate several symbols to the problem or parts of the problem to be solved. It is a very effective method in design problems in which visual and formal components are important. This is taken in this section as an example to show how to model as a multi-agent system this method for collaborative creation.

In principle the organization has two groups of participants, the facilitators (in this case, one Moderator) and the team members (one of them acting as Secretary, and 7 to 10 participants). This is the starting point to model the collaborative creation process with INGENIAS as a multi-agent system (MAS). The MAS is conceived as one organization where different agents play specific roles. In this case, there are two groups of agents in the organization, as shown in Fig. 1.

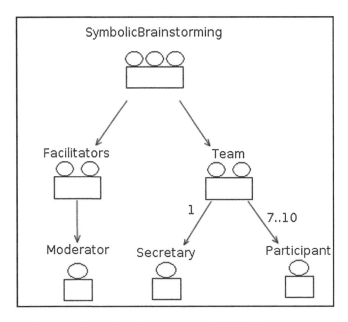

Fig. 1. Organization for Symbolic Brainstorming (*INGENIAS organization model: The rectangle with three circles on top represents an organization, with two circles a group, and with one, an agent*)

The environment of these agents consists of the elements that they use for their activity in the brainstorming process, and this is represented in the Environment diagram in Fig. 2. In this case, agent resources are a blackboard to share their ideas, and drawings that each of the participants create and share. The moderator writes on the blackboard and the participants and moderator see that. The secretary takes notes to generate a report of each session.

The Symbolic Brainstorming is structured in three main stages, and each one is specified in INGENIAS with a workflow diagram and the description of interactions among the agents.

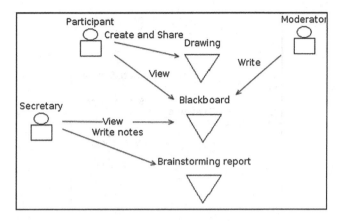

Fig. 2. Tools for Symbolic Brainstorming (*INGENIAS Environment model: the triangle represents a resource*)

4.1 First Session: Identify Characteristics and Associate Symbols

In the first session the different participants must identify several qualities or characteristics of the problem to be solved, and they must associate symbols with these characteristics.

Taking the example of the design of a chair, to generate ideas, each participant must emphasize some characteristic of the chair and should suggest a form. For instance, the characteristic "comfort", or the characteristic "rest", or the characteristic "rotation", and draw some sketches of symbols associated with these characteristics. For example, the characteristic "rest" can be associated with the "symbol of a spring", the characteristic "comfort" can be associated with the "symbol of a cloud", etc. The identified symbols can suggest new symbols to the rest of the participants. There is no order and any participant can participate at any time and as many times as they wish. The most suitable size is about 10 people, with an approximate duration of one hour. The secretary (moderator) of the session must collect all the symbols and symbolic ideas generated, and must deliver a copy of them to each participant. The task that each agent performs in this stage (*Sketch a drawing of a concept*) is specified with an INGENIAS Goal-Task diagram, as shown in Fig. 3.

How all agents interact in this session is defined with several INGENIAS diagrams. First, a goal-tasks diagram as the one in Fig. 4 shows that the agents participate in a workflow with different roles (in this case, Control and Collaborator). This workflow, called "First session" in the diagram, consists of several tasks, which are executed sequentially (*Define Goal, Sketch concepts*, and *Share diagrams*). The first task is where the main goal (Design a chair) is defined by proposal of the moderator. Then, the Sketch concept task will generate Drawings, which will be later distributed with the Share drawing task.

Other diagrams are needed, especially those for defining the interactions. In INGENIAS they provide all the information to generate the source code on JADE

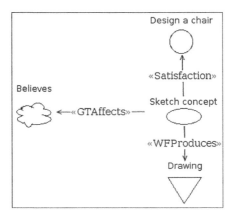

Fig. 3. Specification of the task *Sketch a drawing of a concept (INGENIAS goal-task model: The task is represented as an oval, and its purpose is to satisfy the goal, in this case, design a chair. The task is affected and may change the mental state of the agent, which is represented by a set of believes. The result of the task is producing some drawings)*

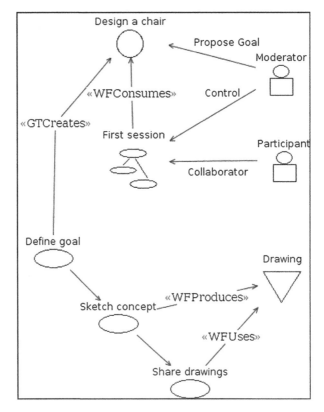

Fig. 4. Workflow for the first session *(INGENIAS goal-task model: Here there is a new symbol to represent a workflow, which is named as First session. A workflow is defined as a sequence of tasks, where each task can produce some resource, which is used as input for another task.)*

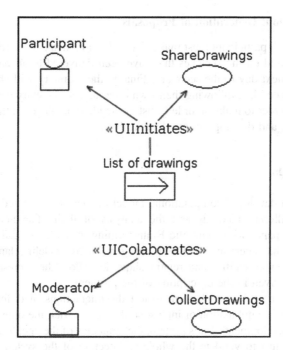

Fig. 5. Interaction of a Participant to provide a list of drawings to the Moderator (*INGENIAS interaction model: Each interaction is defined by one initiator, in this case a Participant agent, and one or more Collaborators, in this case the Moderator agent. In this example the interaction is made of one message, a FIPA Inform with the list of drawings that the Participant agent provides in the execution of its task Share drawings. The Moderator is waiting for this message in its task CollectDrawings*).

platform to implement FIPA messages exchange. An example of one interaction is shown in Fig. 5.

Similarly, the other sessions are modeled with their corresponding workflow and interactions diagrams. The development of these diagrams will allow to identify the tasks that the agent has to perform and the types of interactions that need to implement. They are generated as FIPA messages on the JADE platform.

4.2   Second Session: Discussion on Generated Ideas

In the second stage, the next day, a critical session must be held, in which all the formal ideas generated the previous day are discussed. Participants can generate complementary ideas based on these criticisms. At the end of the session one or several valid ideas must be achieved. The secretary will collect all the ideas or generated forms, and deliver them to the participants.

4.3   Third Session: Generation of Proposals

In a third stage each participant must make a slightly more detailed sketch of the object to be designed based on the sketches that have been delivered to all participants, and deliver them the next day to the secretary. Finally, the secretary will choose which is the most appropriate idea, following their own criteria. The secretary can choose more than one idea, in order to make an orderly list of the ideas, and choose the ones that are more appropriate, and develop or complement them.

5   Conclusions

The possibility to develop a computational model that can be executed will allow the assessment of different methods and the analysis of their characteristics. This is illustrated in this paper with Symbolic Brainstorming, a real case study with enough complexity. This has been specified with an agent-based modeling language, INGE-NIAS, which provides entities and relationships that allow the representation of the concepts that are given in the description of the problem.

This model is useful as a platform to test the interactions of different agents, to provide them with a combination of inputs, so they can enrich the objects they create. At this stage of development of this system, the strategies of the agents are defined in a very simple way just to validate the whole architecture of the system. They are not specified with INGENIAS, so they are manually implemented as part of the behavior of the agents. INGENIAS generates the code to implement the workflows using JADE message exchange mechanisms, which is important to have the structure of the agent-based application. The next step of the work is to develop different agent behaviors for generating ideas and adapting their creative process with the inputs during the work-flows that are depicted here.

Acknowledgements. This work has been partially supported by the project "Collaborative Ambient Assisted Living Design (ColoSAAL)", which is funded by Spanish Ministry for Economy and Competitiveness under grant TIN2014-57028-R.

References

1. Bellifemine, F.L., Caire, G., Greenwood, D.: Developing Multi-Agent Systems with JADE. Wiley, Hoboken (2007)
2. De Bono: Six Thinking Hats. Penguin UK (2017)
3. Corneli, J., Jordanous, A.: Implementing feedback in creative systems: a workshop approach. In: Proceedings of the First International Conference on AI and Feedback, vol. 1407 (2015). CEUR-WS.org
4. Gabora, L.: Meme and variations: a computer model of cultural evolution. In: Nadel, L., Stein, D.L. (eds.) 1993 Lectures in Complex Systems, pp. 471–486. Addison Wesley (1995)
5. De Garrido, L.: Aplicaciones de la Inteligencia Artificial en la composición de objetos arquitectónicos. Tesis Doctoral. Escuela Técnica Superior de Arquitectura. Universidad Politécnica de Valencia (1989)

6. Gomez-Sanz, J.J., Fuentes-Fernández, R.: Understanding agent-oriented software engineering methodologies. Knowl. Eng. Rev. **30**(4), 375–393 (2015)
7. Kühn, S., Ritter, S.M., Müller, B.C., Baaren, R.B., Brass, M., Dijksterhuis, A.: The importance of the default mode network in creativity—a structural MRI study. J Creat Behav **48**(2), 152–163 (2014)
8. Linkola, S., Hantula, O.: On collaborator selection in creative agent societies: an evolutionary art case study. In: Liapis, A., Romero Cardalda, J.J., Ekárt, A. (eds.) EvoMUSART 2018. LNCS, vol. 10783, pp. 206–222. Springer, Cham (2018). https://doi.org/10.1007/978-3-319-77583-8_14
9. Maher, M.L.: Computational and collective creativity: who's being creative? In: International Conference on Computational Creativity, ICCC 2012, pp. 67–71 (2012)
10. Martin, M., Voigt, K.I.: What do we really know about creativity techniques? A review of the empirical literature. In: The Role of Creativity in the Management of Innovation, pp. 181–203 (2017)
11. Pagnutti, J., Compton, K., Whitehead, J.: Do you like this art I made you: introducing techne, a creative artbot commune. In: Proceedings of 1st International Joint Conference of DiGRA and FDG (2016)
12. Pavón, J., Gómez-Sanz, J.J., Fuentes, R.: The INGENIAS methodology and tools. In: Agent-Oriented Methodologies, pp. 236–276. IGI Global (2005)
13. Rawlinson, J.G.: Creative Thinking and Brainstorming. Routledge (2017)
14. Stirrups, R.: Thinking laterally. Lancet Neurol. **16**(2), 113 (2017)
15. Sloane, P.: The Leader's Guide to Lateral Thinking Skills: Unlock the Creativity and Innovation in You and Your Team. Kogan Page Publishers (2017)
16. Wopereis, I., Derix, E.: Seeking creativity: a case study on information problem solving in professional music. In: Kurbanoğlu, S., Boustany, J., Špiranec, S., Grassian, E., Mizrachi, D., Roy, L., Çakmak, T. (eds.) ECIL 2016. CCIS, vol. 676, pp. 428–436. Springer, Cham (2016). https://doi.org/10.1007/978-3-319-52162-6_43

Multi-agent Systems that Learn to Monitor Students' Activity

Rubén Fuentes-Fernández[1]([⊠]) and Frédéric Migeon[2]

[1] Research Group on Agent-based, Social and Interdisciplinary Applications (GRASIA), Universidad Complutense de Madrid, Madrid, Spain
ruben@fdi.ucm.es
[2] Institut de Recherche en Informatique de Toulouse (IRIT), Toulouse, France
frederic.migeon@irit.fr
http://grasia.fdi.ucm.es

Abstract. Learning activities make use today of a variety of software tools, like Learning Management Systems (LMSs), online social networks, and forums. They enhance the experience by facilitating interactions among participants and with resources. These interactions can be used as a source of information on how the process is working for individual students or groups, and therefore to provide them a tailored support. However, lecturers can only do this monitoring in very simple ways, as their time is limited, tools generate large amounts of data, and students have very different profiles. In order to improve this situation, this work proposes the use of semi-automated assistants to analyse these data, able to learn from the lecturers' expertise on what situations are relevant. The Assistant for Learning Activities (ALA) is an Adaptive Multi-Agent System (AMAS) that raises alerts when some events appear in data. Its architecture includes two groups of agents. The core are the agents that learn and classify the data to generate the alerts. There can be multiple groups of these agents to identify different types of alert. A second group of agents wraps and transforms data from sources to feed the first group. The ALA setup uses a prototypical training based on information from previous courses. Then, it learns and adjusts for a specific course using the lecturers' feedback on the alerts it generates. The paper reports the currently undergoing validation of the ALA knowledge based on the information from the institutional LMS of a Spanish university.

Keywords: Students' monitoring · Learning analytics
Semi-automated assistant · Supervised learning
Adaptive multi-agent system

1 Introduction

Education is in continuous change as a consequence of the evolution of its social context. Over the last decades, as society becomes more involved with information technologies, so are its educational institutions [15,16]. Tools like Learning

G. R. Simari et al. (Eds.): IBERAMIA 2018, LNAI 11238, pp. 108–119, 2018.
https://doi.org/10.1007/978-3-030-03928-8_9

Management Systems (LMSs), Online Social Networks (OSNs), Version Control Systems (VCSs), or forums, are of common use in courses today. However, misconceptions and the lack of extensive practice and suitable support tools hinder some of the potential benefits that these technologies can bring to educational activities. Some problems that appear in this context are an increased workload for lecturers and the difficulties to monitor student evolution [22].

Though information technologies in education have made easier some interactions, they also demand from lecturers extra effort. Lecturers need to pay attention to their traditional activities with students (e.g. classes and tutorship), and additionally carry out with tools administrative tasks (e.g. create assignments), developing specifics contents (e.g. tutorials and tests), and monitor students' activities (e.g. when they are using the online contents).

Fields like *learning analytics* [9] and *educational data mining* [18] pursue making a higher use of the information from learning activities, which is frequently obtained from software tools. This would improve the monitoring and assessment of multiple aspects, like students' performance, acquisition of competences, or time required for tasks. Nevertheless, the actual use of these techniques is not easy for the learning community, as it involves specialised knowledge of disciplines such as Data Mining, Big Data, Statistics, or Programming [20].

There have been some efforts aimed at facilitating a broader use of these data by learning communities. These have been mainly focused on providing ready-to-use tools [9,18,20]. Nevertheless, this approach offers little room for a community to explore new specific issues of interest, as tools are usually closed solutions for their users. Alternatively, some works have tried to reduce this entrance step by providing repositories of properties that can be analysed and wrappers for information sources. Users choose among these properties those of their interest. Properties are defined using modelling languages that are more user-friendly than the languages of common analysis tools. An example of this approach is the work in [5], which works on the acquisition of teamwork competences using the framework for *social properties* from [11]. This does not deal with the difficulties to build the wrappers to access and transform the data from information sources. Moreover, users still have to decide how the intended properties appear in data, which again requires expertise in analysis techniques.

In order to reduce the gap between the data and the properties to study, our work proposes using Multi-Agent Systems (MAS) able to learn directly from the data and feedback of users. The Assistant for Learning Activities (ALA) has an architecture based on three groups of agent: a pipeline to wrap and preprocess information sources; Adaptive MASs (AMASs) [6,21] to learn from data and feedback, and raise alerts; and user-interface agents.

This MAS architecture closely follows the organization of the MASSA system [23], originally used for intelligent gene annotation. It isolates the components that depend on the programming interfaces of the external information sources and the format of raw data in the *pipeline layer*. This layer feeds the *alerts layer*, which comprehends the AMASs that learn the alerts. The *interface layer* does not appear in MASSA. It adds user-friendly processing of data and alerts, like the elaboration of digests about the observed activity.

The implementation of the ALA architecture as a MAS facilitates the change of producer-consumer relationships among its components, as well as the introduction and modification of agents. This allows, for instance, the setup of a new learning AMAS when users decide to consider a new alert, without disrupting the functioning of the rest of the system.

This work is illustrated with the discussion of the validation of the current alerts in the ALA. The data come from courses in the Faculty of Informatics in a Spanish university using Moodle[1]. They have been used to train the system, and then validate its alerts with users.

The rest of the paper is organized as follows. Section 2 introduces the basis of learning with AMAS according to [21]. Section 3 describes the ALA's architecture. Then, Sect. 4 reports the results of the evaluation with the ALA, that Sect. 5 compares with related work. Finally, Sect. 6 discusses some conclusions on the approach and future work.

2   Background

AMAS [6] are a particular type of MAS [13]. Their agents are cooperative and their mutual interactions are largely governed by the goal of solving functional inadequacies. These inadequacies are called Non Cooperative Situations (NCSs). There are several types of NCS, like *incomprehension* or *ambiguity* regarding stimulus; *incompetency* and *unproductiveness* to choose actions from knowledge; or *uselessness* when the agent thinks that it cannot take any useful action. To solve them, an agent can act in three ways. It can *tune* its inner parameters, *reorganize* its interactions with the environment and other agents, and produce *openness*, i.e. create other agents. With these elements, the cooperation in an AMAS is assured by design, as all agents are willing to anticipate and solve any NCS that appear.

The AMAS approach has been the basis to create a learning system for classification called ALEX (Adaptive Learner by EXperiments) [21]. It relies on three types of agent:

- *Percept agents* get observations from the environment. One of these agents is linked to only one information source, and thus to only one value at a given moment.
- *Context agents* take inputs from several percept agents. They identify when these inputs are in a given range. With that information they propose an action or category with certain confidence.
- *Input agents* receive the output of context agents and, according to them, choose an action.

---

[1] http://moodle.org.

In order to adjust its behaviour, the ALEX gets feedback from a tutor. The feedback corresponds to the intended output that the input agent should provide in the presence of certain inputs to percept agents.

In this context, several NCSs can appear and agents are provided with actions to solve them. For instance, when the input agent has no proposal, there can be or not feedback from the tutor. If there is, the input agent creates a new context agent to recognise the current inputs from percept agents, and gives as output the current feedback. If there is no feedback, the input agent keeps the last identified action. Another NCS happens when the input agent receives simultaneously action proposals from several context agents. In this case, if proposals differ from feedback, context agents need to change their contexts to exclude this situation. If proposals agree with the feedback, the context agents with lower confidences should try to exclude the current situation from their contexts.

With this approach, ALEX is able to learn a classifier. It separates the points (i.e. groups of observations from the environment) with a hyperplane that determines the actions or categories of points. Each group of observations provided to an ALEX system as input constitutes a complete description of its context (e.g. every source at every moment). That is, there is not a notion of some temporal relationship (e.g. before or after) among different groups of observations. The system learns from the continuous feedback, so there is no need to separate training and classifying processes.

The agents in an ALEX system are light computationally. This allows having large numbers of them, and therefore deploying several of such systems to work simultaneously on multiple alert types or observation time windows.

This approach is the basis of the learning components of the ALA. For every alert that users need to identify on data, the ALA includes an ALEX system which input agent provides that alert.

3   The ALA Architecture

The ALA architecture follows the organization for knowledge-based MAS developed in [23] to a large extent. It adopts common practices in MAS engineering [13], so its components are encapsulated in autonomous agents that interact through the exchange of messages. These agents also control resources such as external programs and databases. Figure 1 shows the main ALA components.

The ALA organizes its agents in three layers: the *pipeline layer* carries out the acquisition and preprocessing of data; the *alerts layer* processes data based on users' knowledge; and the *interface layer* mainly provides post-processing services to present the information from the other two layers in a user-friendly way. The first two layers correspond to those in [23], though the ALA replaces the rule-based components in the original work by ALEX instances (see Sect. 2). The third layer is original for the ALA.

The *pipeline layer* includes four types of agent: *wrapper*, *transformation*, *model*, and *event* agents. *Wrapper agents* receive *information* and *events* from the *applications* used in the learning activities. Among these applications are

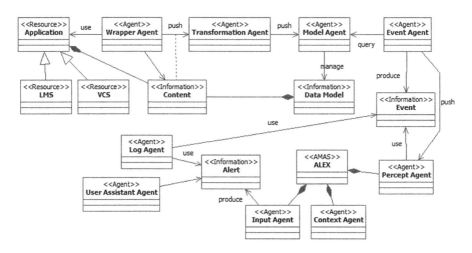

Fig. 1. ALA architecture.

currently *LMSs* and *VCSs*, which are accessed using their logs. *Transformation agents* take the input from wrappers to perform further transformations and composition on data, like normalization of values, feature extraction, or anonymization of private data when needed. *Model agents* link the data from previous agent types to create *data models* and support querying them. Finally, *event agents* provide a simple subscription-notification mechanism for *events* based on [10]. As currently the ALA works on applications logs, these agents are responsible for providing this information to the rest of the system according to the timestamps from those logs.

The *alerts layer* is composed of several *ALEX* systems. There is an ALEX system for every different type of *alert*, as the learning components need to be able to separate with a hyperplane the positive and negative instances of the context regarding the alert. The *event agents* of the *pipeline layer* are connected to the *percept agents* of some of the ALEX systems. In some cases, the alert output of an ALEX system can be used as an input by another ALEX system.

The *interface layer* directly interacts with users. It includes *log agents* to store information related to a given alert in *repositories*. When an alert happens, it stores the events provided by *event agents*, and the *alert* raised. The *user assistant agent* receives the previous notifications and generates *digests* about activity. This can summarize, for instance, the alerts raised over a certain period of time or for a given set of students, or selecting only current alerts of interest.

Lecturers study this information to decide when alerts apply or not to their courses. They provide positive or negative feedback to identify whether a raised alert is correct or not respectively.

4 Evaluation

The case study refers to a course of Software Engineering (SE) at the Complutense University of Madrid, Spain. SE is a mandatory yearly subject at the Faculty of Informatics, in the second year of its four-year degrees. This course is aimed at teaching the basis of project management in the first semester, and software architectures in the second one. The first semester includes, among other topics, project planning, risk management, teamwork, and requirements elicitation. The second semester includes the basis of software modelling, design patterns, and software multi-layer architectures.

The course is structured around a project that students carry out through the whole academic year. In it, they practice in large teams the topics of the course. These teams usually gather 5–8 students. The course also includes lectures in the classroom, practical sessions in the laboratories, individual practical assignments, and group discussions. The final score of students in the course comprehends the evaluation of the project (40% of the final mark), a compulsory final exam (50%), and other evaluable activities (10%).

The experiment considered two different groups A and B. Group A corresponds to a double degree in Mathematics and Informatics, where students attend simultaneously to both degrees. Group B corresponds to a standard Informatics Engineering degree. Besides their studies, both groups also differ in their students. Group A is a reduced group with a maximum of 25 students, while B is a common group with around 60 students. The double degree has a higher admittance mark, so its students usually have on average higher marks than those of other degrees, and almost none of them leave their courses. Available datasets correspond to academic years 2014–2015 (group B with 72 students), 2015–2016 (group A with 21 students), and 2016–2017 (group A with 25 students and group B with 59 students).

Over the previous years, lecturers and students have become more involved with online tools to carry out and manage the course works. This follows current trends in the related industry, as it facilitates collaboration in teams thanks to the distribution of tasks and staff, and the later integration of their results. Besides, they use tools focused on the learning activities, mainly the university LMS. Its main uses are as a repository of course materials, to gather assignments, and to deliver notifications.

Despite their impact in course dynamics, these practices have not change too much the way lecturers monitor and assist their students. Though lecturers expected being able to get a more accurate picture of the students' activities using the information tools provided, examining these data proved to be an overwhelming task. For instance, the logs of the university LMS (i.e. Moodle), which are XML with only the login and access times to the different contents, are over 1 MB for group A and 1.5 MB for group B in the academic year 2016–2017. This is only part of the information available. Moodle itself includes forums for discussions, and there are also other tools like VCSs, project management applications, and e-mail.

In this situation, issues like students' difficulties with the course leading to abandonment, problematic dynamics in teams, or need for additional support in some topics, frequently go unnoticed. Lecturers only realize them when it is too late to take any measure. However, and at least in some cases like abandonment or problematic teams, the activities of students could show early signs of these problems, and these can appear in their activities in tools.

The ALA research is intended to deal with these issues. Our experiments with these courses try to check several hypotheses: (a) relevant events in student's activity show early signs in that activity before the event appears; (b) these early signs can be traced to the student's activity in online tools; (c) there are recurrent patterns in the correspondence between early signs and events.

In order to make a first test on these hypotheses, the experiment focused on abandonment. It was organized as follows.

The datasets from the academic years 2014–2015 and 2015–2016 were used for training, and the datasets from the academic year 2016–2017 for testing. The datasets only include the logs from the LMS used in the course. Additional information to validate findings include which students made the final exam, and the list of assistance to class.

The hypothesis (a) was that before leaving the course, students change their activity patterns in it. To gain some insights into the issue of how early these signs appear, the experiment tested different time windows. Hypothesis (a) translates in (b) to changed behaviours in the LMS. Regarding (c), abandonment patterns of the first two academic years should be applicable to the last year.

In order to reduce the number of events to consider in the analysis, these were grouped in a weekly base. For instance, a student had a login event in a given week when that student had a login event some day of that week.

The architecture of the ALA used in the experiment was the same shown in Sect. 3. The *pipeline layer* included a *wrapper agent* for the LMS logs, *transformation agents* to add categories to log events (e.g. access to lectures, forums, or assignments), and a *model agent* to be able to query by user, time, and type of log event. Finally, *event agents* provided information on every student each week of the academic year. The *alerts layer* included just one ALEX system. The only type of alert to detect was whether some student was about to leave the course. The *interface layer* only included a *log agent* to record the input information related to the alerts.

Table 1 summarizes the main figures of the experiment. Abandonment figures represent the students that did not complete the project (i.e. *before exams*), completed it but did not make the June exam (i.e. *June exam*), or completed the project and failed in the June exam, but did not go to the September exam (i.e. *September exam*).

The manual detection rate indicates the lecturers' expectation on how many students would make the exam in June. They obtained these figures considering the assistance to classrooms and laboratories.

The ALA only used the logs from the LMS. The first version considered when the student made a login in the system (i.e. *with login*). The second version took

Table 1. Abandonment detection rates considering access to the LMS.

2015–2016	Group A	Group B
Students	25	59
Abandonment before exams	0	22
Detection rate - Manual	0	16, 57%
Abandonment in June exam	0	3
Fail in June exam	0	17
Abandonment in September exam	0	3
Fail in September exam	0	10
Detection rate - ALA with login	0	17, 61%
Detection rate - ALA with section access	0	17, 61%

into account the different lessons the student accessed (i.e. *with section access*). There were no differences in detection between the two versions of the ALA. Both offered the same detection rate of 61%.

The ALA detected all the abandonments that lecturers also identified, plus one extra student that also abandoned before the June exam. The system did not make neither false positives nor false negatives.

Students who completed the project but did not make the exams went unnoticed both by lecturers and the ALA. Probably, they made the decision when preparing the exams, and then there was no extensive information on their activities from the LMS.

Tested time windows ranged from 1 month to the whole course without differences in detection. In this case, this can be explained by the fact that almost every 1–2 weeks, there are new materials in the LMS for the SE course. These are used in the classroom, so students following the course should access the LMS to get them with that frequency.

Regarding training, the information from the previous academic years was effective for 2015–2016. No additional training was needed.

The ALA results show the feasibility of providing lecturers semi-automated assistance to detect some relevant events related to their students. The ALA and lecturers detections rates were very similar, but the use of the ALA largely reduced the lecturers' workload.

5   Related Work

This work is related to two main lines of research: analysis of learning activities and semi-automated tools to support it.

The analysis of learning activities appears mainly under the fields of *learning analytics* [9] and *educational data mining* [18]. Though there is a wide range of works, most of them were done by experts in data analysis and not intended for the direct use of the learning community in courses. Making these techniques affordable for everyday use is an open issue in the area [18].

Though the ALA is currently using classification, this has not been the only technique used in this context. Others like clustering, outlier detection, pattern matching, association rules, or text mining have also been used [9,14,18]. Nevertheless, the suitable technique depends on the problem context, for instance regarding result understanding or number of available examples. There is no single technique able to work well in all these aspects in all the potential learning settings.

Regarding ease to be understood, these techniques can provide useful insights on learning, but need to be usable by the final user (sometimes the lecturer), both regarding training and understanding of results [17]. Some techniques are better to provide explanations on decisions. For instance, decision trees give an intuitive explanation of the classification based on the considered attributes and values (e.g. [4]).

As for data, a common problem for analytics with educational datasets is the usually low number of available records [24]. This demands techniques able to learn from few examples (e.g. support vector machines [8]), or learning from feedback to grow the datasets (e.g. instance-based learning).

Regarding tools, literature mainly focuses on the study of standard applications that mediate the learning activities, such as LMSs and VCSs (e.g. [2]). The common conclusion is that lecturers need to make an important effort with these tools in order to get insights in learning [18]. There are some works [3] that try to fill this gap, for instance integrating these analytics and data mining techniques into intelligent tutoring systems. Nevertheless, most of them are mainly focused on visualization (e.g. [19]), or offer little room to modify systems according to specific needs (e.g. [7]), as their architectures are closed and use non-standard formats for data. Available works on open architectures and particularly in MASs [12] offer solutions for this problem. The ALA architecture already adopts some of them.

6   Conclusions

Our research in the ALA tries to provide an effective user-oriented support to carry out learning analytics and data mining in the everyday classroom. It facilitates introducing different sources of information and analysis techniques for this purpose. The focus of the presented work was on early detection of students' abandonment of courses. The use of the ALA offers the advantages of reducing the lecturers' workload and can guarantee the desired frequency of checks on students' activities.

The ALA's architecture currently incorporates works on systems with intelligent components for data analysis [23], and a general learning classifier [21]. All this work is based on MASs, a paradigm that offers relevant advantages regarding flexibility, scalability, and distribution in the development of intelligent systems [12,13].

The selected classification system, ALEX [21], offers good tradeoffs regarding training from few examples and with noise, and time required for that training. It supports continuous learning, so it is able to work from the early beginning of the course. The feedback on classification is an intuitive way for users to adjust its behaviour. Only the explanations can be difficult to grasp for users. Beyond the alert and the input data that cause it, the definition of the hyperplane that separates positive and negative examples is the only explanation. Nevertheless, this is a problem shared with many other classification techniques.

In the experiments, the ALA performance in detection was equivalent to that of lectures, 61%. This was achieved using only basic data on students' access to the LMS. The system was also able to use successfully the training from previous groups for the academic year 2015–2016, showing that some patterns are recurrent.

Regarding the future work, the ALA research has several open issues. First, detection rates are yet quite low. A higher diversity of information sources and a different design of online materials could help to provide more fine-grained information about learning activities. This requires further study on the information needed to detect relevant events. Second, the system has used only information from one course, SE. Other courses in the same academic year have influence on the students' performance. Additional experiments need to work at the level of all the courses where students are enrolled simultaneously. Third, the ALA is currently working offline from the logs of tools. Its architecture can evolve to work on timely events, as it already includes a subscription-notification mechanism based on [10], which is also based on MASs. There is also needing to provide mechanisms that support information fusion from a mixture of technologies. This can be done extending our architecture in the vein of the work for context-aware workflows in [1]. Finally, explanations on alerts are key for the adoption of these systems. Explanations based on graphical visualizations of data and examples can be useful to address this issue.

Acknowledgment. This work has been done in the context of the individual grant "Subprograma de Movilidad del Programa Estatal de Promoción del Talento y su Empleabilidad, en el marco del Plan Estatal de Investigación Científica y Técnica y de Innovación" (grant PRX17/00613) supported by the Spanish Ministry for Education, Culture, and Sports, the projects "RISE Women with disabilities In Social Engagement (RISEWISE)" (grant 690874) supported by the European Commission in the Horizon 2020 programme, "Collaborative Design for the Promotion of the Well-Being in Inclusive Smart Cities (DColbici3)" (grant TIN2017-88327-R) supported by the Spanish Ministry for Economy and Competitiveness, MOSI-AGIL-CM (grant S2013/ICE-3019) supported by the Autonomous Region of Madrid and co-funded by EU Structural Funds FSE and FEDER, "Manage Your Time - Learning Method of Time Management and Organizational Autonomy in Multiple Projects (GesTie)" (grant 258 - 2018-19) supported by the Universidad Complutense de Madrid, and the "Programa de Creación y Consolidación de Grupos de Investigación" (UCM-BSCH GR35/10-A).

References

1. Alfonso-Cendón, J., Fernández-de Alba, J.M., Fuentes-Fernández, R., Pavón, J.: Implementation of context-aware workflows with multi-agent systems. Neurocomputing **176**, 91–97 (2016)
2. Arnold, K.E., Pistilli, M.D.: Course signals at Purdue: using learning analytics to increase student success. In: Proceedings of the 2nd International Conference on Learning Analytics and Knowledge, pp. 267–270. ACM (2012)
3. Baker, R.S.: Educational data mining - an advance for intelligent systems in education. IEEE Intell. Syst. **29**(3), 78–82 (2014)
4. Bhaskaran, S.S., Lu, K., Aali, M.A.: Student performance and time-to-degree analysis by the study of course-taking patterns using J48 decision tree algorithm. Int. J. Model. Oper. Manag. **6**(3), 194–213 (2017)
5. Blanco, D., Fernández-Isabel, A., Fuentes-Fernández, R., Guijarro, M.: Using multi-agent systems to facilitate the acquisition of workgroup competencies. In: Bajo-Pérez, J., et al. (eds.) Highlights on Practical Applications of Agents and Multi-Agent Systems. AISC, vol. 156, pp. 223–230. Springer, Heidelberg (2012). https://doi.org/10.1007/978-3-642-28762-6_27
6. Bonjean, N., Mefteh, W., Gleizes, M.P., Maurel, C., Migeon, F.: ADELFE 2.0. In: Cossentino, M., Hilaire, V., Molesini, A., Seidita, V. (eds.) Handbook on Agent-Oriented Design Processes, pp. 19–63. Springer, Heidelberg (2014). https://doi.org/10.1007/978-3-642-39975-6_3
7. Burns, H., Luckhardt, C.A., Parlett, J.W., Redfield, C.L.: Intelligent Tutoring Systems: Evolutions in Design. Psychology Press, Abingdon (2014)
8. Camba, J., David, R.E., Betan, A., Lagman, A., Caro, J.D.: Student analytics using support vector machines. In: 2016 7th International Conference on Information, Intelligence, Systems & Applications (IISA 2016), pp. 1–6. IEEE (2016)
9. Elias, T.: Learning analytics: Definitions, processes and potentials. https://pdfs.semanticscholar.org/732e/452659685fe3950b0e515a28ce89d9c5592a.pdf
10. Fernández-De-Alba, J.M., Fuentes-Fernández, R., Pavón, J.: Architecture for management and fusion of context information. Inf. Fusion **21**, 100–113 (2015)
11. Fuentes-Fernández, R., Gómez-Sanz, J.J., Pavón, J.: Modelling culture through social activities. In: Dignum, V., Dignum, F. (eds.) Perspectives on Culture and Agent-based Simulations. SPS, vol. 3, pp. 49–68. Springer, Cham (2014). https://doi.org/10.1007/978-3-319-01952-9_4
12. Garijo, F., Gómes-Sanz, J.J., Pavón, J., Massonet, P.: Multi-agent system organization: an engineering perspective. In: Pre-Proceeding of the 10th European Workshop on Modeling Autonomous Agents in a Multi-Agent World (MAAMAW 2001) (2001)
13. Gómez-Sanz, J.J., Fuentes-Fernández, R.: Understanding agent-oriented software engineering methodologies. Knowl. Eng. Rev. **30**(4), 375–393 (2015)
14. Guijarro-Mata-García, M., Guijarro, M., Fuentes-Fernández, R.: A comparative study of the use of fuzzy logic in e-learning systems. J. Intell. Fuzzy Syst. **29**(3), 1241–1249 (2015)
15. Kirkwood, A., Price, L.: Learners and learning in the twenty-first century: what do we know about students' attitudes towards and experiences of information and communication technologies that will help us design courses? Stud. High. Educ. **30**(3), 257–274 (2005)
16. Laurillard, D.: Rethinking University Teaching - A Conversational Framework for the Effective Use of Learning Technologies. Routledge, London (2002)

17. Papamitsiou, Z., Economides, A.A.: Learning analytics and educational data mining in practice: a systematic literature review of empirical evidence. J. Educ. Technol. Soc. **17**(4), 49 (2014)
18. Romero, C., Ventura, S.: Educational data mining: a survey from 1995 to 2005. Expert Syst. Appl. **33**(1), 135–146 (2007)
19. Ruipérez-Valiente, J.A., Muñoz-Merino, P.J., Leony, D., Kloos, C.D.: Alas-ka: a learning analytics extension for better understanding the learning process in the Khan academy platform. Comput. Hum. Behav. **47**, 139–148 (2015)
20. Siemens, G., Long, P.: Penetrating the fog: analytics in learning and education. EDUCAUSE Rev. **46**(5), 30 (2011)
21. Verstaevel, N., Régis, C., Gleizes, M.P., Robert, F.: Principles and experimentations of self-organizing embedded agents allowing learning from demonstration in ambient robotic. Procedia Comput. Sci. **52**, 194–201 (2015)
22. Waycott, J., Bennett, S., Kennedy, G., Dalgarno, B., Gray, K.: Digital divides? Student and staff perceptions of information and communication technologies. Comput. Educ. **54**(4), 1202–1211 (2010)
23. Xavier, D., Crespo, B., Fuentes-Fernández, R.: A rule-based expert system for inferring functional annotation. Appl. Soft Comput. **35**, 373–385 (2015)
24. Xing, W., Guo, R., Petakovic, E., Goggins, S.: Participation-based student final performance prediction model through interpretable genetic programming: integrating learning analytics, educational data mining and theory. Comput. Hum. Behav. **47**, 168–181 (2015)

RETRACTED CHAPTER: Encouraging the Recycling Process of Urban Waste by Means of Game Theory Techniques Using a Multi-agent Architecture

Alfonso González-Briones[1]([⊠]) [iD], Pablo Chamoso[1] [iD], Sara Rodríguez[1] [iD], Angélica González-Arrieta[1] [iD], and Juan M. Corchado[1,2,3] [iD]

[1] BISITE Digital Innovation Hub, University of Salamanca, Edificio Multiusos I+D+i, 37007 Salamanca, Spain
{alfonsogb,chamoso,srg,angelica,corchado}@usal.es
[2] Department of Electronics, Information and Communication, Faculty of Engineering, Osaka Institute of Technology, Osaka 535-8585, Japan
[3] Pusat Komputeran dan Informatik, Universiti Malaysia Kelantan, Karung Berkunci 36, Pengkaan Chepa, 16100 Kota Bharu, Kelantan, Malaysia

Abstract. The increase in population has caused the amount of waste generated in cities to increase, generally in large cities. It is necessary to develop solutions to reduce the amount of waste and to be able to recycle most of it, avoiding wasting natural resources. Thanks to the treatment of these wastes, it is possible to obtain information to reduce costs and reduce the amount of waste generated, allowing a large quantity of them to be recycled. It is necessary to develop solutions to reduce the amount of waste, and to be able to recycle most of it, avoiding wasting natural resources. One of the main advantages of the Internet is its ability to connect people in remote locations and in real time. This has allowed the emergence of numerous collaborative applications, previously unthinkable, that are capable of solving traditional problems. This paper aims to address the problem of waste treatment by encouraging recycling among the different users involved in the system. This objective is approached from a perspective in which participants are rewarded for the amount they recycle, in order to encourage their participation and involvement in the recycling process. A framework that integrates gamification methodologies and multi-agent technology is presented with a case study demonstrating the benefits of the developed system. More specifically, a case study has been carried out simulating the functionality of this system by recreating the conditions of a real urban environment. The case study has made it possible to evaluate the effectiveness of the gamification system for citizen incentive in the recycling process.

Keywords: Game theory · Social computing · Ambient intelligence Multi-agent systems

This work has been supported by the Spanish Government throughthe project SURF (grant TIN2015-65515 -C4-3-R) and FEDER funds.

The original version of this chapter was retracted: The retraction note to this chapter is available at https://doi.org/10.1007/978-3-030-03928-8_42

G. R. Simari et al. (Eds.): IBERAMIA 2018, LNAI 11238, pp. 120–131, 2018.
https://doi.org/10.1007/978-3-030-03928-8_10

1   Introduction

One of the main ones affecting society is the large amount of waste and residues that are produced and that often do not have a place to keep them in a sustainable way. This problem affects equally any type of population, having a greater incidence in the largest populations and increasing due to the high number of consumer activities and processes. This increase, together with an inefficient form of waste management (open burning or storage in garbage dumps, among others), causes problems such as water, soil and air pollution, which causes health problems and environmental damage, including political and social conflicts.

The current solution to this problem is the implementation of a mechanism that allows us to recycle this waste. Many regions or cities have waste treatment plants that allow the treatment and recycling of urban waste generated in urban areas [2]. When these recycling centres were set up, only a small percentage of the waste that can currently be treated is used, being only waste such as oil, tyres, recycled electronic products. In order for these plants to be able to carry out their function, it was necessary to develop a network for the collection and transport of waste from the urban nucleus to the plant. However, this network is not common and there are various methods, for example, in the European Union. One of the most commonly used methods for this is the deployment of a series of containers organised by colour for the specific collection of waste according to its characteristics. Another of the methods most widely used in the EU is the establishment of establishments that allow the deposit of waste and packaging for recycling. These methods have made it possible to recycle many tons of waste that were previously completely disposed of in landfills, with numerous benefits for both human beings and the environment.

These measures have had a high degree of acceptance and have allowed many tons of recyclable materials that ended up in landfills without any reuse to be reused. The rate of glass recycling in the European Union reached 73% in 2013 according to The European Container Glass Federation (FEVE) [0]. The recycling rate for paper/cardboard is around 83%, plastic around 34.3% and wood around 37.7% [24]. This shows that the glass and paper/cardboard recycling model works well, but a higher recycling rate for the remaining materials needs to be achieved.

This paper proposes a way to increase the rate of waste recycling through a more active involvement of users in the recycling chain. The way to encourage this participation and increase the amount of recycled waste is to give benefits to the citizens who participate more actively. This concept is known as gamification, and it is the technique that will allow the recycling process to be stimulated and carried out in a more dynamic way so that satisfactory results can be achieved. For this reason, this paper presents a system that uses the concept of gamification to increase the recycling rate of waste through greater citizen participation. This system is based on a multi-agent system that allows the management of all the processes involved and allows the promotion of citizen participation by increasing the number of wastes collected in the recycling chain.

The multi-agent of this system use CAFCLA (Context-Aware Framework for Collaborative Learning Applications) as a basis for its technical and social features implementation [7,8]. The system has the capacity to learn from citizens' actions to provide new, more efficient solutions to increase recycling rates and citizen participation.

This article is organized as follows: Sect. 2 describes the state of the art of multi-agent systems and gamification, Sect. 3 describes the proposal, Sect. 4 presents the results and Sect. 5 conclusions.

2   Recycling Background

This section reviews the state of the art of the main methods implemented in the European Union, showing the characteristics, advantages and disadvantages of each of these methods. It also details the current state of each of the techniques used by the proposed system within the problem of waste recycling, and how these techniques are ideal for increasing citizen participation.

2.1   Tradicional RRecycling Methods in the EU

In 1982, the first glass container was installed in Spain. That year the collaboration between the Autonomous Communities, the local authorities and the manufacturers of glass containers for the recycling of this material began. In 1994, Directive 94/62/EC lays down the framework within which all the legislation of each of the countries of the European Community is to be developed. To avoid the disposal of large quantities of waste and residues that can be recycled, different methods were developed to collect these materials so that they can be recycled. One of these first methods was the implementation of containers for the collection of glass. In Spain, in 1982, the collaboration between the Autonomous Communities, local authorities and manufacturers of glass containers for the recycling of this material began. In 1994, Directive 94/62/EC established a framework within which all the legislation applied in each of the countries of the European Community was developed.

Within the European Community, two methods stand out that stand out above the rest. The first one consists of the deployment of different containers in the metropolis which are identified by colors so that each of them can deposit their respective waste. Although this method is used in many countries of the European Union, there is no standardization about colors for each container as we can see in the following examples.

- In Spain there are three containers: blue for paper and cardboard, yellow for plastic waste and green for glass, there are also specific containers for organic waste and clean points for the collection of other waste such as oil, tires and electronic waste.
- In France there are five containers with different colors and symbols to distinguish it at first sight. In addition, there is an annual planning to follow, which sets the days to throw away the garbage, usually two days a week.

– In Italy the recycling system is also by colors, although the color of the containers varies with respect to Spain and France. The citizen who does not recycle can also receive a fine and the collection of waste also follows a planning. In Norway, the system is similar, with one container for organic waste and another for paper and cardboard. The plastic is placed in a special bag that is placed next to the paper and cardboard container. The glass is left in special containers-res next to the supermarkets.

In some of these countries there is a specific waste collection calendar and there is the possibility of being fined in case of non-recycling.

The second method that has greater acceptance has been implemented in countries such as Germany, Sweden and Denmark and is known as Deposit Refund System (DRS). This method works by paying a tax when citizens buy a container. This tax is returned when the container is returned in perfect condition in a series of established places that have machines to make said deposit. Citizens receive a ticket that can be exchanged for cash, receiving €0.25 for each container. This method in some countries like Germany is found together with the method of containers by colors.

Both methods have a high degree of reception, providing a good mechanism to recycle a large amount of waste. However, they are not as complete as they should be to provide the desired effectiveness. Both models have a series of disadvantages and disadvantages.

One of the disadvantages of the DRS is that the type of containers are limited, being able to collect water containers, soft drinks and beers, both plastic and metal containers. The rest of the containers are not accepted. This amount of packaging is only 8% of the containers, while in the model of colored containers, through the yellow and blue containers, about 80% of the waste can be managed. Another disadvantage of this method is that often the collection sites are in supermarkets, so that citizens can only go to deposit their containers when these stores are open.

Another problem associated with the DRS is that the citizen may not obtain reimbursement of the tax paid when buying the containers if they are not returned in good conditions. They are often rejected by the machine due to small dents. So there is no real guarantee to recover the money.

Once the problem has been identified, it has been identified that the collection of waste for recycling is an imposition in the container model and that in the DRS system the money paid for each container was simply recovered when they are acquired.

2.2 Gamification

The games have been an entertainment form and a playful way to pass the time, although many times the mechanism of the games has been used to be used in activities and educational tasks. These games, better known as educational games, use the mechanics and strategies of traditional games with an educational purpose used for learning, understanding or social impact, addressing both the cognitive and affective dimensions. For this, dynamics and concepts are used that stimulate and make more attractive the interaction of the player with the learning process.

Gamification uses these strategies with a different purpose to the playful side of games and more focused on the learning process. The incorporation of the gamification in this work will allow a playful form to increase the number of users that recycle as well as the amount of recycled waste. This concept will be incorporated into the mobile application that will allow users to visualize their results, obtaining rewards when they do well and receive penalties otherwise. This will allow higher levels of user commitment and stimulate the development of habits that contribute favorably to the environment. This technique has been used in different fields such as energy optimization [6,8,29–32], has not been used in proposals as in this work is presented [21].

2.3 VO System for Data Capture, Action Learning and Decision Making

Multi-agent systems (MAS) have been widely used in a variety of contexts because of their characteristics and capabilities to model behavior, simulate situations or solve problems that are difficult or impossible for an individual agent to solve. The characteristics of the MAS allow the agents that form them to communicate, coordinate and cooperate to carry out different tasks. For this reason, they have been applied in works with such varied objectives as the obtaining of genes with behavior patterns associated to a particular disease [10,11,15,19], detection of drivers under the influence of drugs [1], facial image classification according to gender and age [1], energy optimization [25–27], job recommendation [28]. The autonomy of agents within architectures based on virtual organizations of agents allows them to interact with each other, while interacting with other organizations, without the need for action on the part of the user. These organizations have the capacity to perceive and react to changes in the environment, which makes them an ideal approach for capturing data, learning behavior patterns and making decisions for certain actions that may occur [16,18]. This allows the virtual organizations of agents to apply to different proposals within the field of recycling, from the simulation of behaviors, the learning of behaviors associated with recycling, the efficient management of waste within the supply chain to the learning of actions of user behavior.

The use of agents in this area has not been widely used, although the proposal made by Meng et al. [13] in which a system of agents simulates behavior and decision making in scenarios of established conditions. However, although behavior is simulated in various conditions, it does not encourage citizen participation in recycling processes. Another proposal like the one presented by Mishra et al. a multi-agent system was shown that makes autonomous judgments for the effective recycling of waste [14]. These agents were efficiently coordinated for categorization of waste, transport, waste recycling, waste management and reusable product allocation. The system will make effective judgments in the future. The proposed framework, therefore, will contribute to effective decision-making, from the collection of scrap to the distribution of recycled components and manufacturing using the environment of the ecological supply chain.

The adoption of virtual organizations of agents is motivated by the ability to model problems with the characteristics presented in this, the possibility of programming agents to learn actions and recognize patterns of behavior [3,4,23]. The virtual Organizations of agents allow the integration of different devices, distributed services, applications making possible to develop distributed systems implemented in different environments for the common administration. Necessary features for a system that needs to manage the waste collection service distributed within Smart City, but also, the user must accumulate the benefits obtained along with the benefits that may have been obtained in another city or urban environment. In addition, this architecture allows applications and services that can be communicated in a distributed manner, even from mobile devices, regardless of the programming language or operating system they use. The previous typology will be used together with the model proposed by Rodríguez et al. [17], whose main novelty lies in the capacity of dynamic and adaptive planning to distribute tasks among the member agents of the organization in the most effective way possible.

3   Proposed Architecture

In this section the technical part of the architecture is shown, describing the most relevant aspects to be displayed in a Smart city.

3.1   Infrastructure Required for the VO Architecture

The system to be developed needs to obtain all the information about each recycling process from each of the users, so it is necessary to deploy the infrastructure that obtains the information related to factors such as the type and amount of waste deposited, who is the user who carries out the deposit, the state of the containers, degree of occupation of the nearest waste treatment plant.

However, this infrastructure should not imply high installation costs, nor imply a change in the current methodology that implies a readaptation to the recycling model. Therefore, the changes to adapt the methodology to the current infrastructure focuses on incorporating a series of devices in the containers (i) a QR code reader to identify the users. (ii) GPS locator. (iii) Sensor for the measurement of the amount of material introduced by the citizen. (iv) Volumetric sensor that measures the filling status of the container. (v) NarrowBand IOT (NB-IoT) comunication technology, to transmit data to the VO of agents.

The use of NB-IOT should require sending data over long distances. A LPWAN network using ICM bands has been chosen to be able to send this information between 5 and 10 Km in urban areas and up to 50 Km in rural areas. (vi) Solar panel that feeds the sensors and actuators of the container allowing for energy independence.

The way of interaction with the platform is simple, a user introduces a waste bag in the indicated container, the software part of the system generates a data structure whose information is: user id, type of waste, quantity of waste, container id, location of the container, container filling status. This data structure is sent via the MQTT protocol using the NB-IoT network to a local station. Sending is done from each local station that acts as MQTTT Broker for sending the data structure in JSON format through REST services.

3.2   VO Architecture

Due to the complexity of managing a container network in an urban environment, it is necessary for the system to be able to adapt to an indefinite number of containers, and it may undergo changes such as an increase or decrease in containers at certain times. This adaptability is provided by developing the architecture as a virtual organization of agents. Agent used-vehicle VOs enable highly dynamic architecture design using real-time self-adaptive capabilities. The architecture is developed as a Belief-desire-intention (BDI) agents model. This model allows agents to make autonomous decisions based on beliefs, desires and intentions, and its functionalities are modeled as REST services. This approach to the architecture provides a high degree of flexibility to change agent behavior at runtime and increased error recovery capabilities. As the proposed system requires the deployment of an associated infrastructure which may undergo changes such as increasing the number of containers, changing the location of containers, etc., it is necessary for the management system to be a highly dynamic platform employing self-adapting capabilities at runtime. This allows an agent's behavior to be determined by the goals it wishes to achieve (amount of waste to be recycled, participation percentage, etc.), while taking into account the goals of other agents and any changes that may arise in the environment. The core of the architecture is a group of deliberative agents that act as controllers and administrators of all applications and services3. The functionalities of the agents are not within their structure, but modeled as services. This approach provides greater error-recovery capability and greater flexibility to change agent behavior at runtime [19,20,2].

The architecture based on virtual organizations of agents distributes the functionality between the organizations, and these in turn between the agents that compose them according to their roles. The architecture consists of three organizations as can be seen in Fig. 1.

- Infrastructure VO. This virtual organization is formed by basic agents that act as Middleware between the users and the system. Each container is associated with an agent that is responsible for generating a data structure (quantity, type of waste deposited, user that recycles, state of filling of the container, degree of occupation of the nearest waste treatment plant). These agents through LPWAN send the information to the Data capture and transmission VO agents.

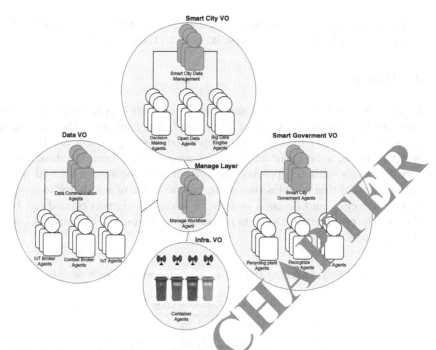

Fig. 1. Proposed architecture based on virtual agent organizations.

- Data capture and transmission VO. The agents in this layer are responsible for capturing data from the infrastructure deployed in the Smart City. IoT agents communicate with the agents deployed in the Infrastructure VO to build the data structure that collects the data about the waste deposit in a container, which is sent in JSON format through REST services. IoT Bro-ker is in charge of performing the NGSI-to-NGSI (Next Generation Services Interface) conversion between IoT agents and the Context Bro-ker agents, and the data is collected by Data Communication agents that transmit it for analysis to Smart City Intelligence VO.
- Smart City Intelligence VO. Once the data structures of each recycling pro-cess has been received, it is checked whether the container is full and thus make the decision to send a truck to collect the waste. In the following stage, Big Data Engine Agents analyzes the data through Complex Event Process-ing (CEP) for the recognition of patterns, for the system has Open Data agents that incorporate mechanisms for the incorporation of data that may be relevant for the analysis, such as information about the temperature or the weather forecast so that more information is available for decision making.
- Smart Govermenet VO. In this VO, the results obtained from the analysis carried out in the Smart City Intelligence VO are managed for the collection of containers that are full, the deployment of a greater number of containers if an area does not have the necessary ones or the more frequent sending of containers. A larger number of garbage collection trucks. This layer is

responsible for rewarding or penalizing the user with the decrease or increase in the rate of garbage that must be paid to the local government.

4 Results

In order to validate the effectiveness of the system it is essential to be able to compare the results in terms of recycling before and after the application of the system. In order to make this comparison, the experiment has been divided into two parts, a first part in which information has been obtained about the recycling rates without applying the system, and the second part in which the system, in addition to collecting data, has provided of its ability to gamify this task of recycling and decision making. The case study was carried out between the months of June and December 2017 and each stage of the experiment lasted three months.

Table 1. Quantity (Kg) of waste collected from each container

	Before system	After system
Plastic container	1,731.24	2,023.82
Paper/cardboard	2,214.15	2,625.98
Glass container	1,595.07	1,851.88
Plastic container	1,731.24	2,023.82
Total	5,540.46	6,501.68

The system was implemented in an urbanization with a population of around 4,500 inhabitants, in which the infrastructure deployed on traditional containers was deployed in fifty-four containers, with the collaboration of the city's urban waste collection company. In the part of the experiment in which the system was used, each user had a mobile application with which he could be identified each time he was going to deposit waste in the recycling containers. The identification was made by reading the QR code that identifies the container and identifies the user in such a way that the opening of the waste deposit and the weighing of the container are enabled. Once each user is identified, the container's deposit is opened so that the waste can be deposited, this deposit calculates the amount of waste deposited through the volumetric sensor and prepares the data structure that is sent through the local relay antenna deployed using LPWAN. The data structure is collected by the agents of the virtual organization for the reception of the information and through the analysis of the information obtained makes decisions such as, for example, sending a truck to empty the container if it is full. Another of the decisions made by the agents is the updating of the user profile (updating of the accumulated bonuses or penalties). If the user reaches the objectives proposed by the local management unit, the user will be given a bonus or penalized if he does not. In the present experiment it was proposed to increase the amount of waste by 21%. Users who reach the target obtained a €5 reduction in the monthly waste rate (€53). At the end of the experiment, the amount of waste deposited in the containers was measured in such a way as to measure the efficiency of the system, as shown in Table 1. In which we see a 17.2% increase.

One of the possibilities that the developed architecture allows is the development of sociological studies, which allows to know more about how the recycling process is carried out and to be able to create awareness campaigns based on this knowledge.

5 Conclusions

The present proposal makes use of an innovative approach based on Virtual Organizations (VO) of agents that allows increasing the participation of users in recycling processes (increase of users and increase in the amount of recycled residues). The proposal uses gamification algorithms which, thanks to the bonuses and penalizations, force an interaction with the users. The VO allow managing the control of the infrastructure developed for the control of the deposit of waste made by each user and the rest of related factors (amount of waste, type of waste deposited, user that recycles, state of filling of the container, occupation rate of the nearest waste treatment plant).

In the case of the study in which the proposal was validated, the submitted proposal based on gamification and virtual organizations has been validated. Regarding the data prior to the implementation of the proposal in the pilot project, citizen participation has been 32.2% and the amount of waste has increased by 17.2%. At the level of social study, it has been possible to identify the groups of people who have had the most participation in the experiment. It is proposed in the next version of this work to make partial achievements, so that the benefit for each user depends on the amount of waste deposited.

References

1. Briones, A.G., González, J.R., de Paz Santana, J.F.: A drug identification system for intoxicated drivers based on a systematic review. ADCAIJ: Adv. Distrib. Comput. Artif. Intell. J. **4**(4), 83–101 (2015)
2. Chamoso, P., De la Prieta, F., De Paz, F., Corchado, J.M.: Swarm agent-based architecture suitable for internet of things and smartcities. In: Omatu, S., et al. (eds.) Distributed Computing and Artificial Intelligence. AISC, vol. 373, pp. 21–29. Springer, Cham (2015). https://doi.org/10.1007/978-3-319-19638-1_3
3. Costa, Â., Barberá, S.M.H., Cámara, J.P., Novais, P., Inglada, V.J.J.: Persuasion and recommendation system applied to a cognitive assistant. ADCAIJ: Adv. Distrib. Comput. Artif. Intell. J. **5**(2), 89–99 (2016)
4. De La Prieta, F., Navarro, M., García, J.A., González, R., Rodríguez, S.: Multi-agent system for controlling a cloud computing environment. In: Correia, L., Reis, L.P., Cascalho, J. (eds.) EPIA 2013. LNCS, vol. 8154, pp. 13–20. Springer, Heidelberg (2013). https://doi.org/10.1007/978-3-642-40669-0_2

5. Eurostat, Statistics Explained: Waste statistics (2018). http://ec.europa.eu/eurostat/statistics-explained/index.php/Waste_statistics. Accessed 19 Dec 2017

6. García, Ó., Alonso, R.S., Prieto, J., Corchado, J.M.: Energy efficiency in public buildings through context-aware social computing. Sensors **17**(4), 826 (2017)

7. García, Ó., Alonso, R.S., Tapia, D.I., Corchado, J.M.: CAFCLA: a framework to design, develop, and deploy am I-based collaborative learning applications. In: Recent Advances in Ambient Intelligence and Context-Aware Computing, pp. 187–209. IGI Global (2015)

8. García, O., Chamoso, P., Prieto, J., Rodríguez, S., de la Prieta, F.: A serious game to reduce consumption in smart buildings. In: Bajo, J., et al. (eds.) PAAMS 2017. CCIS, vol. 722, pp. 481–493. Springer, Cham (2017). https://doi.org/10.1007/9-3-319-60285-1_41

9. González Briones, A., Chamoso, P., Barriuso, A.L.: Review of the Main Security Problems with Multi-Agent Systems used in E-commerce Applications (2016)

10. González, A., Ramos, J., De Paz, J.F., Corchado, J.M.: Obtaining relevant genes by analysis of expression arrays with a multi-agent system. In: Overbeek, R., Rocha, M., Fdez-Riverola, F., De Paz, J. (eds.) Practical Applications of Computational Biology and Bioinformatics. AISC, vol. 375, pp. 137–146. Springer, Cham (2015). https://doi.org/10.1007/978-3-319-19776-0_15

11. González-Briones, A., Ramos, J., De Paz, J.F., Corchado, J.M.: Multi-agent system for obtaining relevant genes in expression analysis between young and older women with triple negative breast cancer. J. Integr. Bioinform. **12**(4), 1–14 (2015)

12. González-Briones, A., Villarrubia, G., De Paz, J.F., Corchado, J.M.: A multi-agent system for the classification of gender and age from images. Comput. Vis. Image Underst. (2018). https://doi.org/10.1016/j.cviu.2018.01.012

13. Meng, X., Wen, Z., Qian, Y.: Multi-agent based simulation for household solid waste recycling behavior. Resour. Conserv. Recycl. **128**, 535–545 (2018)

14. Mishra, N., Kumar, V., Chan, F.T.: A multi-agent architecture for reverse logistics in a green supply chain. Int. J. Prod. Res. **50**(9), 2396–2406 (2012)

15. Oliveira, T., Neves, J., Novais, P.: Guideline formalization and knowledge representation for clinical decision support. ADCAIJ: Adv. Distrib. Comput. Artif. Intell. J. **1**(2), 1–11 (2012)

16. Prieto, J., Mazuelas, S., Bahillo, A., Fernández, P., Lorenzo, R.M., Abril, E.J.: On the minimization of different sources of error for an RTT-based indoor localization system without any calibration stage. In: 2010 International Conference on Indoor Positioning and Indoor Navigation (IPIN), pp. 1–6 (2010)

17. Rodríguez, S., de Paz, Y., Bajo, J., Corchado, J.M.: Social-based planning model for multiagent systems. Expert Syst. Appl. **38**(10), 13005–13023 (2011)

18. Román, J.A., Rodríguez, S., de la Prieta, F.: Improving the distribution of services in MAS. In: Bajo, J., et al. (eds.) PAAMS 2016. CCIS, vol. 616, pp. 37–46. Springer, Cham (2016). https://doi.org/10.1007/978-3-319-39387-2_4

19. Silva, A., Oliveira, T., Neves, J., Novais, P.: Treating colon cancer survivability prediction as a classification problem. ADCAIJ: Adv. Distrib. Comput. Artif. Intell. J. **5**(1), 37–50 (2016)

20. Silveira, R.A., Comarella, R.L., Campos, R.L.R., Vian, J., de la Prieta, F.: Learning objects recommendation system: issues and approaches for retrieving, indexing and recomend learning objects. ADCAIJ: Adv. Distrib. Comput. Artif. Intell. J. **4**(4), 69–82 (2015)

21. Silveira, R.A., da Silva Bitencourt, G.K., Gelaim, T.Â., Marchi, J., de la Prieta, F.: Towards a model of open and reliable cognitive multiagent systems: dealing with trust and emotions. ADCAIJ: Adv. Distrib. Comput. Artif. Intell. J. **4**(3), 57–86 (2015)
22. Tapia, D.I., Alonso, R.S., De Paz, J.F., Corchado, J.M.: Introducing a distributed architecture for heterogeneous wireless sensor networks. In: Omatu, S., et al. (eds.) IWANN 2009. LNCS, vol. 5518, pp. 116–123. Springer, Heidelberg (2009). https://doi.org/10.1007/978-3-642-02481-8_16
23. Tapia, D.I., Fraile, J.A., Rodríguez, S., Alonso, R.S., Corchado, J.M.: Integrating hardware agents into an enhanced multi-agent architecture for Ambient Intelligence systems. Inf. Sci. **222**, 47–65 (2013). https://doi.org/10.1016/j.ins.2011.05.002. The European Container Glass Federation (2017). FEVE PR recycling 2013. http://feve.org/wp-content/uploads/2016/04/Press-Release-EU.pdf. Accessed 19 Dec 2017
24. Wood woRking INdustry RecycliNG (2017). Waste statistics. https://ec.europa.eu/growth/tools-databases/eip-raw-materials/en/content/wood-working-industry-recycling. Accessed 19 Dec 2017
25. González-Briones, A., Prieto, J., Corchado, J.M., Demazeau, Y.: EnerVMAS: virtual agent organizations to optimize energy consumption using intelligent temperature calibration. In: de Cos Juez, F., et al. (eds.) HAIS 2018. LNCS, vol. 10870, pp. 387–398. Springer, Cham (2018). https://doi.org/10.1007/978-3-319-92639-1_32
26. González-Briones, A., Chamoso, P., De La Prieta, F., Demazeau, Y., Corchado, J.M.: Agreement technologies for energy optimization at home. Sensors **18**(5), 1633 (2018)
27. González-Briones, A., De La Prieta, F., Mohamad, M.S., Omatu, S., Corchado, J.M.: Multi-agent systems applications in energy optimization problems: a state-of-the-art review. Energies **2018**, 11 (1928)
28. González-Briones, A., Rivas, A., Chamoso, P., Casado-Vara, R., Corchado, J.M.: Case-based reasoning and agent based job offer recommender system. In: Graña, M., et al. (eds.) SOCO 18-CISIS 18-ICEUTE 18 2018. AISC, vol. 771, pp. 21–33. Springer, Cham (2019). https://doi.org/10.1007/978-3-319-94120-2_3
29. Rivas, A., et al.: Semantic analysis system for industry 4.0. In: Uden, L., Hadzima, B., Ting, I.-H. (eds.) KMO 2018. CCIS, vol. 877, pp. 537–548. Springer, Cham (2018). https://doi.org/10.1007/978-3-319-95204-8_45
30. Briones, A.G., et al.: Use of gamification techniques to encourage garbage recycling. a smart city approach. In: Uden, L., Hadzima, B., Ting, I.-H. (eds.) KMO 2018. CCIS, vol. 877, pp. 674–685. Springer, Cham (2018). https://doi.org/10.1007/978-3-319-95204-8_56
31. Casanedo, I.S., Nieves, E.H., González, S.R., Martín, M.T.S., Briones, A.G.: Machine learning predictive model for industry 4.0. In: Uden, L., Hadzima, B., Ting, I.-H. (eds.) KMO 2018. CCIS, vol. 877, pp. 501–510. Springer, Cham (2018). https://doi.org/10.1007/978-3-319-95204-8_42
32. González-Briones, A., et al.: GarbMAS: simulation of the application of gamification techniques to increase the amount of recycled waste through a multi-agent system. In: De La Prieta, F., Omatu, S., Fernández-Caballero, A. (eds.) DCAI 2018. AISC, vol. 800, pp. 332–343. Springer, Cham (2019). https://doi.org/10.1007/978-3-319-94649-8_40

State Machines Synchronization for Collaborative Behaviors Applied to Centralized Robot Soccer Teams

Jose Guillermo Guarnizo[1(✉)] and Martin Mellado[2]

[1] Grupo de Estudio y Desarrollo en robótica, Universidad Santo Tomás,
Bogotá, Colombia
jose.guarnizo@usantotomas.edu.co
[2] Instituto AI2, Universitat Politècnica de València, Valencia, Spain
martin@ai2.upv.es

Abstract. In robot soccer, collaborative behaviors are necessary to establish team coordination. In centralized architectures with global perception, the team coordination is carried out by a making decision system, where the team strategy is programmed out. Finite state machines are an alternative for the making decision systems design in order to assign players roles and behaviors, depending on the game conditions. In this paper a team strategy for robot soccer architectures with global perception and centralized control is proposed, through the use of synchronized state machines for collaborative behaviors among the players by using a synchronization function in some determinate states. This function is used to synchronize one machine state which selects the behavior of one player, with other state which selects the behavior of another player. The synchronization is used, for instance, to coordinate a pass between two players looking for a goal, or blocking an opposite goal by an opposite defender player. Synchronized state machines presented better results than strategies with state machines non-synchronized on different matches played.

Keywords: Multi-agent systems · Robot soccer · Architecture
Finite state machine · Synchronization

1 Introduction

Robot soccer is considered a multi-robot system that includes uncertainties and hostile environment, where robots are working in a coordinated manner on a real challenging problem. Coordination is an important issue for robot soccer, since undesirable behaviors can arise in uncoordinated teams, for example, teammates blocking the ball, obstructing each other or failing to block opposing players [1]. In robot soccer, strategy is defined as the plan of the robot soccer team expecting to win a match, tactic is defined as the organization of the team for the game. Roles are defined as a list of behaviors to perform by the robot. Behaviors are the basic sensorimotor skills of the robot, such as shoot the ball, to block an opponent or to intercept the ball [2].

Robot soccer leagues are divided into two main categories. One is the centralized leagues, using one decision-making body, with global perception and global motion

© Springer Nature Switzerland AG 2018
G. R. Simari et al. (Eds.): IBERAMIA 2018, LNAI 11238, pp. 132–144, 2018.
https://doi.org/10.1007/978-3-030-03928-8_11

control [3]. The other corresponds to the distributed leagues, which use fully autonomous robots, with local perception and autonomous control [4]. Many studies have been published on robot soccer strategies, looking for team coordination. Some other are focused on machine learning, for example using case-based approach for coordinated action selection in distributed robot soccer teams [5]. Or presenting a novel model of reinforcement learning algorithm applied to learning behavior [6]. In [7] is used fuzzy neural networks to task planning and action selection. In [8] is training the decision-making system by Bayesian SOM. Other papers proposed learning machine algorithms using robot soccer strategies for validation purpose [9].

One way to design robot soccer strategies is by using different computational models, such as coordination graphs for role assignment [10]. Finite state machines to switch tactics combined with Petri Net Plans for tasking execution are presented in [11]. Other example of using hierarchical state machines for robot soccer architectures is presented in [12]. Other research uses finite state machines for tactic selection and behavior selection [13]. Collaborative Filtering techniques combined with set-plays are also presented [14]. The use of Hierarchical Finite State Machines is presented in [15]. Synchronization has been used in different robot soccer distributed architectures in order to coordinate autonomous robots [16], focused on communication protocols. Other example of synchronization in computational models for robot soccer architectures is presented in [17], introducing the concept of Multi Robot Plans. In [18] a team strategy is modeled based on the discrete events system theory. In [19] it is proposed dynamic role assignment based on action utility prediction.

In [20] a robot soccer strategy based on tactics, roles and behaviors is presented, which uses a hierarchical state machines. Nevertheless the state machines are based on the game conditions, without a feedback of the behaviors selected by their teammates. This strategy was used to control the operation mode in an islanded ac microgrid [21]. Subsequently, in [22] a robot soccer strategy based on roles was proposed, in this work one role is assigned to each player and a behavior is assigned depending on game conditions, however a behavior feedback selected by their teammates is neither presented. This situation is similar to other strategies related above where synchronization is not presented. In this paper, is proposed a strategy for centralized robot soccer architectures based on a hierarchical finite state machine for tactic selection, dynamic roles assignment and behaviors selection. The behavior selection layer is performed by synchronized state machines, for the purpose of coordinate collaborative behaviors between players. In this case, the behavior selected by one player depends on a function activated by a state of its teammate. This model is designed for a robot soccer team with two-wheeled robots, with a central computer used for computational processes. This strategy is tested using the SimuroSot 5 vs. 5 league simulation platform, and programmed using C++. The proposed strategy has different advantages such as easy programming and low computational costs, and is scalable and easily adaptable to changes in the decision-making system.

2 Hierarchical Team Architecture Using Synchronization Functions

In centralized architecture there is a top-view vision system, which provides full global knowledge of the game field, showing the position of the players and the ball. The image processing is performed by the host computer. Coordinates of each robot and the ball are supplied to the decision-making body which selects the tactic, roles and behaviors. Once behaviors are selected, the decision-making body calculates and transmits the signals control for each robot. State machines have often been used in the robot soccer domain, as an alternative for team architectures. In this paper is proposed a decision-making system based on hierarchical state machine, which is divided into levels. The highest level is presented in Fig. 1(a), where a hierarchical finite state machine (HFSM) selects a tactic from a set of n predefined tactics $T = \{t1, t2, ..., tn\}$, using environmental conditions Ev as transitions.

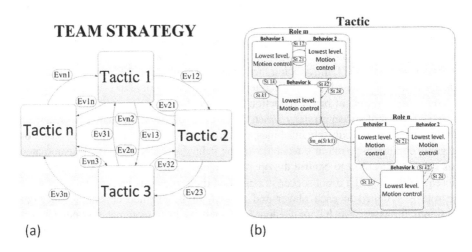

Fig. 1.   (a). Highest level of HFSM. (b). Behavior selection using synchronization function.

Once the tactic has been selected, the next layers are activated. At this level one role is assigned to each player. Players with roles perform specific behaviors controlled by a lower layer of the state machine, using environmental conditions St as transitions. To carry out the behaviors, the lowest layer, namely the motion control layer is activated. Once the tactic has been selected, it is assigned a set of roles $R = \{r1, r2, ..., rm\}$ to a finite number of agents $A = \{a1, a2, ..., am\}$, such that i $\neq$ j$\rightarrow$Ri $\neq$ Rj. Note that there is the same number of agents and roles. One role has been assigned to each agent, without repeating roles. There is a set of behaviors $B = \{b1, b2, ..., bk\}$, which will be performed by the agents. Each role r has been associated to one or more behaviors that will be executed by agent a in the game, according to game conditions. There is a set of characteristics $G = \{g1, g2, ..., gp\}$ that describes the changes in the game field. The highest level of the HFSM uses set G to select T, and then is used set G to assign R to

A. Subsequently, the second layer of the HFSM selects one behavior *bk* to be executed by each *a*. Control of the robot motion is implemented in the lowest layer of the HFSM. The procedure is performed as follows:

ALGORITHM 1   DECISION SYSTEM OF THE STRATEGY

---

1. *Hierarchical state machine* **reads** set *G* and **assigns** tactic *t*.
2. Given *t* selected in step 1, *C* **assigns** one role *r* to each agent *a*, ensuring that complete set *R* is assigned to complete set *A*.
3. *Hierarchical state machine* **reads** set *G* and assigns behaviors *b* to each agent *a*, depending on the role *r* assigned in step 2, and set *G*.
4. The set of behaviors *B* are controlled by robot motion control, and this is carried out by the lowest level of the hierarchical state machine.
5. On the soccer field, set *A* **executes** behaviors associated with set R, which was assigned in step 2, modifying set *G*.
6. When conditions are triggered, **repeat** step 1.

It is proposed synchronization functions to feedback the state of the other player to synchronize collaborative behaviors between players. As is shown in Fig. 1(b), the player with the role *m* triggers the behavior *k* when the conditions *St2k* or *ST1k* are triggered. The player with the role *n* may trigger the behavior *1* when the condition *St1 k* is activated and the agent with the role *m* plays its respective behavior *k* and the condition of the role *m* triggers the function *fm n(Stk1)*. This happens when the player with the role *m* players its behavior *k*. This strategy is implemented in a robot soccer team with five wheeled robots. One is the goalkeeper, which is the only constant role.

Two parameters have been chosen for tactic selection. The first one refers to ball localization on the game field. For this purpose the field is divided into three different zones defined as follows: The defensive zone is the zone where the goalkeeper of the own team is located. The middle zone is in the half of the playing field, and the offensive zone is where the opponent's goal post is located. Ball zone corresponds to the zone where the ball is located. It is defined the ball possession as the minimal distance between a robot and the ball, where the robot can shoot the ball. This distance is obtained experimentally as an appropriate distance at which a robot can shoot the ball.

Four tactics are defined as follows:

- Defensive defense tactic: This is selected when the ball is located in the defensive zone or the middle zone, and one's own-team does not keep ball possession.
- Defensive attack tactic: This is selected when the ball is located in the defensive zone or the middle zone, and own-team keeps ball possession.
- Offensive defense tactic: This is selected when the ball is located in the offensive zone, and own-team does not keep ball possession.
- Offensive attack tactic: This is selected when the ball is presented in the offensive zone, and own-team keeps ball possession.

Four tactics correspond to states, whereas the environmental conditions (ball zone, and ball possession), correspond to the transitions. For role assignment, there are five players per team. One of them is the goal-keeper *ap*, which keeps a constant role. Thus, there is a finite number of agents *A = a1; a2; a3; a4* that perform a set of roles

$R = rad;$ $rpd;$ $rs;$ ra, where rad corresponds to active defender, rpd corresponds to passive defender, rs is supporter, and ra is attacker. The decision-making body executes the algorithm to assign roles, depending on the tactic previously selected. It is important to highlight that the role assignments is similar between defensive tactics (defensive defense and defensive attack tactics), and offensive tactics (offensive defense and offensive attack tactics).

For defensive tactics, the role assignment is reaches by both defensive defense and defensive attack tactics. Once each tactic is activated, the role selection algorithm is carries out. In these tactics, the player closest to the ball becomes the active defender rad, and this player attempts to take the ball. The second nearest player to the ball becomes the passive defender rpd, which blocks an opponent player. The third nearest player to the ball is the attacker ra, which goes to the offensive zone, waiting for the ball. The last player becomes the supporter rs, which goes to offensive zone.

For the offensive tactics, the role assignment is reaches by both offensive defense and offensive attack tactics. Similarly, once each tactic is activated, the role selection algorithm is carries out again. The player nearest to the ball becomes the attacker ra, and this player attempts to take possession of the ball, in order to score a goal. The second nearest player to the ball becomes the supporter rs, which supports the attacker. The third nearest player to the ball is the active defender rad, which is in the middle zone in case of counter attack. The last one is the passive defender rpd, which supports the active defense.

2.1   Behavior Selection

Many roles were implemented to execute different behaviors, depending on the tactic chosen. Goalkeeper is the only static role in this strategy. The behaviors of the goalkeeper are presented in Fig. 2. There is a goalkeeper zone, which is an area in front of the own-team's goal post. When goalkeeper behavior is triggered, the player checks its location. If it is within the goalkeeper zone, the robot localizes and follows the ball in a line running parallel to the goal line. If the player is not located in the goalkeeper zone, the robot must become properly located and subsequently checks its location and continues playing.

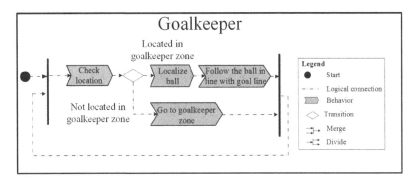

Fig. 2. Goalkeeper behaviors.

For the tactic defensive defense, the active defender role goes by the ball as is shown in the Fig. 3(a). Firstly, the ball is located. If the ball is in the goalkeeper zone, the robot follows the ball outside, to avoid own-goals or block the goalkeeper. If the ball is outside of the goalkeeper zone, the active defender goes to catch the ball. The Fig. 3(b) shows the behaviors in the tactic defensive attack. Once the tactic is activated the ball is located. If the ball is inside the goalkeeper zone, then the active defender follows the ball outside. If the ball is not located in the goalkeeper zone, then the active defender checks the ball possession, if it has ball possession, the robot shoots the ball to offensive zone. If it has not the ball possession, the active defender tries to catch the ball. In the Fig. 3(c) is presented the behaviors of the active defender for both offensive tactics. There is an active defender zone, which corresponds to a zone behind the half-way line. When the tactics are activated, the active defender checks its location, if it is not inside the active defender zone, the robot goes to its zone. If the robot is located in its zone, the player follows the ball in line with the half-way line.

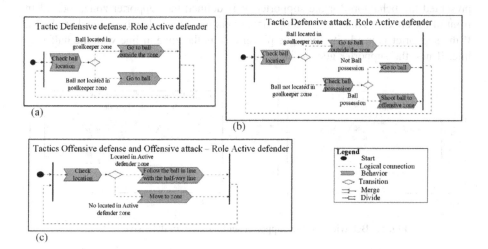

Fig. 3. Active defender behaviors

The behaviors of the role passive defender for both defensive tactics are shown in the Fig. 4(a). In these tactics, the passive defender checks its nearest opponent and goes to block without touch the player, in order to prevent possible opponent passes avoiding collisions with the player. In the Fig. 4(b) are shown the behaviors of the passive defender for both offensive tactics. For this purpose there is a passive defender zone, behind the active defender zone, where the passive defender covers the other side that the active defender blocks. Thus, when the offensive tactics are activated, the passive defender check its location, if the robot is not located in its respective zone, it goes to its zone. If the robot is located in its respective zone, the player covers in line with the half-way line the other side where the ball is located.

For the defensive tactics, the behaviors of the supporter and attacker are presented in the Fig. 5. In the case of the attacker (Fig. 5(a)), there is an attacker zone in the

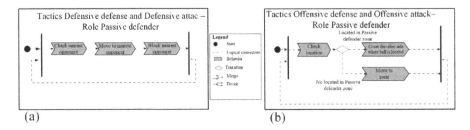

Fig. 4. Behaviors of passive defender.

offensive zone, where the robot follows the ball in line with the half-way line, waiting for the ball. Thus, when the defensive tactics are activated, coordinates of attacker are checked, if the robot is in the attacker zone, the robot follows the ball in line. If the attacker is not properly located, the robot goes to its zone. In the Fig. 5(b), it is presented the behaviors for the supporter. It is defined the supporter zone, located in front of the attacker zone, where supporter covers the other side where attacker blocks. If the supporter is inside its zone, the player covers the zone in line with the half-way line. If not, the supporter goes to its zone.

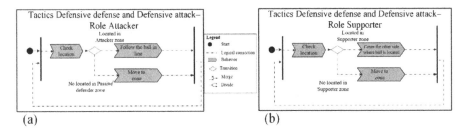

Fig. 5. Behaviors of the supporter and attacker in defensive tactics.

2.2   Synchronization Functions in Coordinate Attack Behaviors

For the tactic offensive attack, the main purpose of the attacker is to shoot the ball to opponent's goal post, seeking score a goal. As is shown in the Fig. 6(a), ball possession is checked in the attacker, if the attacker not has the ball possession, player goes to catch the ball. If the robot has the ball possession, it is checked if there is an opponent player different from the goalkeeper, which blocks the trajectory to opponent's goal post. If the trajectory is blocked, attacker activates a synchronization function to supporter, in order to coordinate a ball pass. In the Fig. 6(b), is presented the behaviors of the supporter. Initially, the supporter checks if the attacker activates the synchronization function. If there is not activated, supporter works as is described in the Fig. 5 (b). If the synchronization function is activated, the supporter receives a ball pass of the attacker, when the tactic changes and new role assignment is reached, supporter becomes the new attacker.

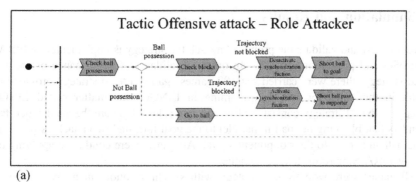

(a)

(b)

Fig. 6. Behaviors of the supporter and attacker in offensive attack tactic

In the Fig. 7, are shown the different zones presented to perform the different roles (goalkeeper zone, active defender zone, passive defender zone, attacker zone, supporter zone and lateral zones).

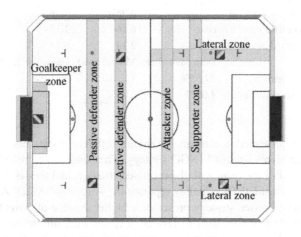

Fig. 7. Zones in game field.

3 Simulation and Results

In order to test and validate the proposed model, the strategy is implemented in FIRA's SimuroSot and programing in C++. In order to validate the performance of the proposed strategy, there were carried out 100 games against a team strategy provided by default in the simulator and programming in LINGO (hereinafter called LINGO strategy). LINGO strategy consists of five constant roles which are the goalkeeper, two defenders that blocking the ball in parallel to the goal line, and two attackers which go to the ball and shoot to their opponent's goal. All games were conducted applying the rules of FIRA SimuroSot 5 vs. 5 League.

All games were won by the strategy with synchronization, in many cases with ample goal difference. In Table 1 is presented the comparison of the different results obtained in the 100 games by each team. The average of goals scored, the average of ball possession and the average of successful passes is significantly higher in the team with the proposed strategy. This is because a greater number of collaborative behaviors, due to the synchronization between attacker and supporter. It should also be noted that in all games the ball remained in the offensive zone in the many of cases. The variations of goals scored, successful passes or ball possession observed in different games are due to an incremental odometry error induced by the simulator. However, it shown that team with the strategy proposed presented a better adaptation to game conditions than LINGO strategy. In all games was observed that team with LINGO strategy shown different behaviors that produce faults or own-goals.

Table 1. Comparison of the parameters of 100 games against team with LINGO strategy

Parameters		Local	Opponent
Goals average		5.66	1.8
Standard deviation		2.49	1.53
Ball possession average		64.87%	35.13%
Standard deviation		5.98%	5.98%
Successful passes average		6.56	1.12
Standard deviation		2.14	0.88
	Defensive zone	Middle zone	Offensive zone
Ball location	27.53%	12.30%	60.17%
Standard deviation	7.09%	3.06%	6.89%

In Table 2 is presented a comparison among different results obtained in games between different teams against LINGO strategy. The comparison includes the results previously reported of the team with the proposed strategy, and the results obtained by other strategies against LINGO strategy reported in [9, 15, 18–20, 22]. As can be seen the team with the proposed strategy presented a higher average of goals by game than the strategies previously published in [18–20, 22], the goal difference is higher than reported in [15], the only strategy which presented considerably higher average of goals is the strategy presented in [9] however, this work is focused on machine learning. Strategies which reported ball possession showed similar percentages. N.R. corresponds to data not reported. Goals av., refers to goals average. Ball poss., refers to ball possession. Standard deviation is similar in the cases when it was reported is similar (excepting [20], where were only performed 10 games), this is because an incremental error of odometry induced by the simulator, in order to perform more realistic simulations.

Table 2. Comparison of results reported of other strategies against team with LINGO strategy

Teams	Games played	Games			Goals average		Ball possession	
		Won	Tied	Lost	Local	Opp.	Local	Opp.
Sync.	100	100%	0	0	5.88	1.8	64.87%	35.13%
					S.D.	S.D.	S.D.	S.D.
					2.49	1.53	5.98%	5.98%
[20]	10	100%	0	0	3	1	72.3%	27.7%
					S.D.	S.D.	S.D.	S.D.
					0.82	0.82	7.09%	7.09%
[18]	10	70%	10%	20%	5.5	4.2	N.R	N.R
					S.D.	S.D.	S.D.	S.D.
					2.01	2.53	N.R	N.R
[19]	10	100%	0	0	5.1	3.7	71.7%	28.3%
					S.D.	S.D.	S.D.	S.D.
					N.R	N.R	N.R	N.R
[15]	50	100%	0	0	6.1	2.8	67%	37%
					S.D.	S.D.	S.D.	S.D.
					N.R	N.R	N.R	N.R
[9]	50	100%	0	0	9.74	1.78	N.R	N.R
					S.D.	S.D.	S.D.	S.D.
					2.21	1.22	N.R	N.R
[22]	100	100%	0	0	5.29	2.17	68.3%	31.7%
					S.D.	S.D.	S.D.	S.D.
					1.93	1.33	8.3%	8.3%

In the Fig. 8 is presented an example of synchronization of behaviors between attacker and supporter, including a change in the roles. In the Fig. 8(a) the player 2 (attacker) detects that an opponent player blocks the trajectory of the ball to the goal, player 1 (supporter) accompanies. In the Fig. 8(b) player 2 activates the synchronization function and sends the ball to player 1, who, in turn goes to catch the ball. When player 2 do not have ball possession a new tactic is selected and new roles are assigned, player 1 becomes attacker and player 2 becomes supporter. In the Fig. 8(c) the new attacker catches the ball and try to score a goal, meanwhile player 2 supports.

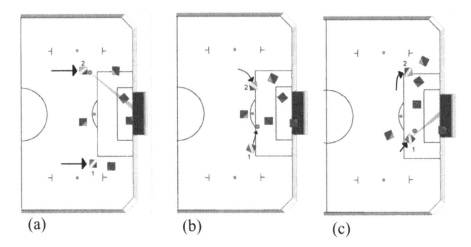

(a)   (b)   (c)

Fig. 8. Example when an opponent player blocks the goal, with synchronization function.

4   Conclusions and Future Works

Finite state machines for multi-agent coordination in centralized robot soccer architectures allow an intuitive design of the strategy keeping in mind the league rules. Given that robot soccer is a multi-agent system, coordination among player is necessary and given that, synchronization function merge as alternative to improve the performance of collaborative behaviors such as successful passes. The proposed strategy was compared with other reported strategies that played games against a basic strategy provided by the simulator. The strategy proposed showed better results that those strategies, excepting one case where machine learning where implemented. Even though the use of computational models as finite state machines have displayed satisfactory results in coordination in robot soccer, the use of synchronization functions among players allow to obtain better results in cooperative behaviors that other similar strategies that not use synchronization functions obtaining, for example, more goals scored, more number of successful passes or more percentage of ball possession. The Synchronization functions usage do not represent any increasing in strategy complexity, neither a relevant increasing in source code or computation cost. Likewise these synchronization functions can be also applicable to other architectures, such as distributed architectures or using other computational models.

In future works will be proposed synchronization function implemented in distributed strategies seeking better results in cooperative behaviors. As well nondeterministic finite state machines and probabilistic finite state machines to design coordination strategies and the making decision systems in robot soccer leagues.

Acknowledgements. This work has been funded by "Decimosegunda convocatoria interna para el fomento de la investigación - FODEIN 2018" at Universidad Santo Tomás, Bogotá Colombia, entlited "Localización y mapeo por medio de redes inalámbricas de datos aplicado a roots móviles colaborativos", project code: 1836001.

References

1. Stulp, F., Utz, H., Isik, M.: Implicit coordination with shared belief: a heterogeneous robot soccer team case study. Adv. Robotics **24**(7), 1017–1036 (2010)
2. Drogoul, A., Collinot, A.: Applying an agent-oriented methodology to the design of artificial organizations: a case study in robotic soccer. Auton Agent Multi-Ag **1**(1), 113–129 (1998). https://doi.org/10.1023/A:101009862392
3. Stone, P., Veloso, M.: A layered approach to learning client behaviors in the robocup soccer server. Appl. Artif. Intell. **12**, 165–188 (1998)
4. Marsella, S., Tambe, M., Adibi, J., Al-onaizan, Y., Kaminka, G., Muslea, I.: Experiences acquired in the design of RoboCup teams: a comparison of two fielded teams. Auton. Agent Multi-Ag. **4**(1), 115–129 (2001). https://doi.org/10.1023/A:1010027016147
5. Ros, R., Arcos, J.L., Lopez de Mantaras, R., Veloso, M.: A case-based approach for coordinated action selection in robot soccer. Artif. Intell. **137**(9–10), 1014–1039 (2009)
6. Cunha, J., Serra, R., Lau, N., Lopes, L.S., Neves, A.: Batch reinforcement learning for robotic soccer using the Q-batch update-rule. J. Intell. Robot. Syst. **80**(3), 385–399 (2015). https://doi.org/10.1007/s10846-014-0171-1
7. Jolly, K.G., Sreerama, R., Vijayakumar, R.: Intelligent task planning and action selection of a mobile robot in a multi-agent system through a fuzzy neural network approach. Eng. Appl. Artif. Intel. **23**(6), 923–933 (2010). https://doi.org/10.1016/j.engappai.2010.04.001
8. Chen, B., Zhang, A., Cao, L.: Autonomous intelligent decision-making system based on Bayesian SOM neural network for robot soccer. Neurocomputing **128**, 447–458 (2014)
9. Hwang, K.S., Chen, Y.J., Lee, C.H.: Reinforcement learning in strategy selection for a coordinated multirobot system. IEEE Trans. Syst. Man. Cybern. A Syst. Hum. **37**(6), 1151–1157 (2007)
10. Wang, J., Wang, T., Wang, X., Meng, X.: Multi-robot decision making based on coordination graphs. In: Mechatronics and Automation International Conference on, pp. 2393–2398 (2009)
11. Kontes, G., Lagoudakis, M.G.: Coordinated team play in the four-legged robocup league. In: 19th IEEE International Conference on Tools with Artificial Intelligence, pp. 109–116 (2007)
12. Guarnizo, J.G., Mellado, M.: Robot soccer strategy based on hierarchical finite state machine to centralized architectures. IEEE Lat. Am. Trans. **14**(8), 3586–3596 (2016)
13. Lou, Y., Chen, B., Shi, H.: Decision making model based on state assessment and hierarchical FSM in robot soccer. In: Automatic Control and Artificial Intelligence (ACAI 2012)
14. Abreu, P.H., Castro, D., Almeida, F., Mendes-Moreira, J.: Improving a simulated soccer team's performance through a memory-based collaborative filtering approach. Appl. Soft Comput. **23**, 180–193 (2014). https://doi.org/10.5772/56189
15. Lou, Y., Chen, B., Shi, H. Decision making model based on state assessment and hierarchical FSM in robot soccer. In: International Conference on Automatic Control and Artificial Intelligence (ACAI 2012), Xiamen, pp. 756–759 (2012)
16. Stone, P., Veloso, M.: Task decomposition, dynamic role assignment, and low bandwidth communication for real-time strategic teamwork. Artif. Intell. **110**(2), 241–273 (1999)
17. Palamar, P.F., Ziparo, V.A., Iocchi, L., Nardi, D., Lima, P.: Teamwork design based on petri net plans. In: Robot Soccer World Cup XII, RoboCup 2008, pp. 200–211 (2008)
18. Cardoso, P., Molina, L., Freire E.O., Carvalho, E.A.N.: A methodology to designing strategies for robot soccer based on discrete event systems formalism. In: Brazilian Robotics Symposium and Latin American Robotics Symposium, Fortaleza, pp. 143–149 (2012)

19. Yang, M., Jia, Y.: Action utility prediction and role task allocation in robot soccer system. In: 12th International Conference on IEEE Control Automation Robotics and Vision (ICARCV), Guangzhou, pp. 112–117 (2012)
20. Guarnizo, J.G., Mellado, M., Low, C.-L., Blanes, F.: Architecting centralized coordination of soccer robots based on principle solution. Adv. Robot. **29**(15), 989–1004 (2015)
21. Diaz, N.L., Guarnizo, J.G., Mellado, M., Vasquez, J.C., Guerrero, J.M.: A robot-soccer-coordination inspired control architecture applied to islanded microgrids. IEEE Trans. Power Electron. **32**(4), 2728–2742 (2017)
22. Guarnizo, J.G., Mellado, M.: Centralized robot soccer architecture based on roles. RIAI **13** (3), 370–380 (2016). https://doi.org/10.1016/j.riai.2016.05.005

Adaptive and Intelligent Mentoring to Increase User Attentiveness in Learning Activities

Ramón Toala[1,2]([⊠]) [iD], Filipe Gonçalves[1]([⊠]) [iD], Dalila Durães[3,4]([⊠]) [iD], and Paulo Novais[1]([⊠]) [iD]

[1] Algoritmi Research Centre/Department of Informatics, University of Minho, Braga, Portugal
id7410@alunos.uminho.pt, fgoncalves@algoritmi.uminho.pt, pjon@di.uminho.pt
[2] Technical University of Manabí, Portoviejo, Manabí, Ecuador
[3] Department of Artificial Intelligence, Technical University of Madrid, Madrid, Spain
d.alves@alumnos.upm.es
[4] CIICESI, ESTG, Polytechnic Institute of Porto, Felgueiras, Portugal

Abstract. In the past decades intelligent mentoring systems have rapidly increased. In e-learning environment there has been an exponential growth in technological development environments and number of users that are addressed, hence an intelligent mentoring system should capture the user's attention in order to improve results when focused in (e)learning tasks (i.e. serve both as a support of presence lessons and for distance form of studies – e-learning). It is important to note that the process of teaching-learning requires an interaction between the different actors involved: the tutor, the student, the expert domain and the learning environment or interface. In this paper we propose an innovative approach of an intelligent mentoring system that monitors the user's biometric behaviour and measures his/her attention level during e-learning activities. Additionally, a machine learning categorisation model is presented that monitors students' activity during school lessons. Nowadays computers are used as important working tools in many places, where we intend to use non-invasive methods of intelligent orientation through the observation of the user's interaction with the computer.

Keywords: Adaptive systems · Learning
Intelligent mentoring systems · Attention

1 Introduction

Currently, one of the main problems related to learning is the amount of attention that students dedicates to the execution of a proposed task. The level of attention of each person is increasingly affected by the evolution of the use of the Internet and social networks. These two factors have a high impact on attention,

© Springer Nature Switzerland AG 2018
G. R. Simari et al. (Eds.): IBERAMIA 2018, LNAI 11238, pp. 145–155, 2018.
https://doi.org/10.1007/978-3-030-03928-8_12

as they offer lots of information regarding general interest, negatively influencing students' attention. Based on this information, the manager could prevent undesirable situations and improve the users' attention. It is crucial to improve the learning process and to solve problems that may occur in an environment using new technologies [4].

Attention is a complex process through which an individual is able to continuously analyse a set of stimuli and, within a sufficiently short period of time, choose one to focus on. Most people can only focus on a very small group of stimuli at a time, preventing the user from focusing on a set of stimuli concerning noticeable information.

Adaptive learning can be a powerful learning tool. Learning skills are vital to school success and employment and are becoming increasingly important for social communication.

Over the last few decades, researchers and developers have worked to create and improve educational technologies. These technologies were transported from the simple aid of teaching to promote high-level reasoning in the academic field. By monitoring student's behaviour, it is possible to improve the effectiveness of mentoring systems by giving students relevant materials in order to enable their evolution and by providing appropriate feedback and scaffolding [8]. The main goal of Intelligent Tutoring Systems (ITS) is to make these technologies adaptable to students, taking into account their individual characteristics and needs.

In this paper we present an non-invasive approach for an mentoring system based on the behaviour biometric analysis of the work during high-end tasks. More specifically, the system monitors and analyses the mouse dynamics, keystroke dynamics and task activity in order to determine the student's performance.

2   Related Work

The rapid evolution of the last decades of information and communication technologies has benefited all areas of knowledge. According to [10], ICT has been applied in Education very late. From these technologies emerged the Virtual Environments of Learning (e-learning), in which the students interact as if they were in a real environment. These environments are combined with other applications that provide intelligent tutorials and are called Virtual Environments with Smart or Intelligent Tutoring.

These Intelligent Tutorials aim to adapt to the student's profile, applying techniques which best adapt to each student, in order to obtain better learning results. Currently there are a number of such tutors, however they do not fully achieve the desired goals since they do not consider an important element that affects student learning: their emotional state. Some of these tutors only assess the emotional state of the student at the end of the work sessions, which alone is not enough to improve learning.

2.1 ITS

In the educational field it is important to have an adaptive and intelligent system to improve learning. Adaptive systems consist of a system that is different for different students or groups of students, taking into account the accumulated information of an individual or groups of students over time. Intelligent System consists of a system that applies Intelligent Environments (AmI) techniques in order to provide better and greater support to users of educational systems [2]. However, what is observed in most of these systems is that they are either adaptive or intelligent. Examples of adaptive system are AHA [1] and WebCOBALT [15], which uses very simple techniques that scarcely can be classified as "intelligent". Examples of intelligent systems are German Tutor [7] or SQL-Tutor [11], yet, these systems provide the same solutions for different types of students [2].

The ITS must consider the curriculum, the effective state of the students, their learning style and adapt the tasks and the type of presentations in order to obtain better results.

2.2 Attention

Attention is the capacity to focus clearly on one of the various subjects or objects. Attention implies mental concentration on an object through observation or listening, which means the ability or power to concentrate mentally.

The concept of attention can be defined as the transformation of a large set of scattered and unstructured data into a small set of acquired data where key information is preserved. In Computer Science, attention means that there is an input that filters and chooses the most important data in data processing and this is a key mechanism of behavioural control for tasks. This type of process is related to planning, decision-making, and prevention of new situations, however there are limited computation capabilities [9,14]. Attention implies mental concentration on a given object through observation or careful and meticulous listening, which is the ability or power to mentally concentrate.

3 Framework

The architecture of the developed system (shown in Fig. 1) is divided into three main parts: the lowest level with the devices that generate the data; the intermediate level where the ITS cloud is located; and the highest level, the client system.

At the lower level, the devices that generate the raw data (e.g. soft sensors) describe the students' interaction with both the mouse and the keyboard. The raw data generated is stored locally until it synchronises with the ITS web server in the cloud at regular intervals. In this layer, each event is encoded with the corresponding required information (i.e. timestamp, coordinates, type of click, key pressed, etc.).

The intermediate level is subdivided into five layers: the storage layer, the analytic layer, the classification profile layer, the emotion classification layer, and the adaptive model interaction. In the storage layer, a MongoDB database stores the data received from users when it is synchronised. MongoDB, in addition to being a data storage engine, also provides native data processing tools such as Map Reduce and the Aggregate Pipeline. Both procedures can operate in a shared collection (partitioned on several machines with horizontal scaling).

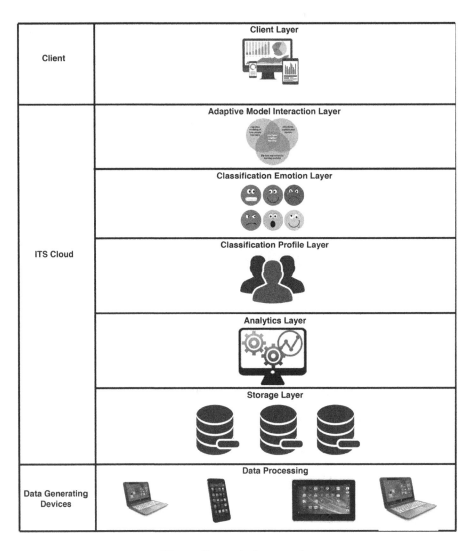

Fig. 1. System's framework.

In the analytical layer, some processes were developed that aim to prepare the received data, such as removing outlines (for example, the backspace key being continuously pressed to delete a character set is not a regular key press), so that this data is evaluated according to the presented metrics. In addition, the system receives this information in real time and calculates, at regular intervals, the values of behavioural biometrics and the estimation of the general level of attention of each student. These are powerful tools for performing analytic and statistical analysis in real-time, which is useful for ad-hoc querying, pre-aggregated reports, and more. MongoDB provides a large set of aggregation operations that process data records and return corrected results, allowing the use of these operations in the data layer to simplify application code and limit resource requirements.

In the classification profile layer, all user indicators are interpreted. Based on the preprocessed data and on the construction of the metadata that will support decision making, the system will classify the user's profile. When the system presents a large enough set of study cases, it is possible to make classifications accurately. The classifier, in real time, will classify the data received from the different levels of attention, creating the learning profile of each student. With these results, it is possible to obtain a profile of the learning style.

The classification emotion layer has all users' emotional data and the construction of metadata that will support decision making. The system will sort the user's emotional profile and, when the system has a high set of data, it makes it possible to make ratings accurately. Note that mouse movements and keyboard usage patterns also help predict the mood of the user.

The adaptive model interaction is based both on the classification profile layer and the classification emotion layer, which adjusts the level of difficulty of tasks for the user in real-time.

Finally, a web application is available at the client layer where students can visualise the tasks they must complete. Moreover, for the managers (teachers), the user's attention information is displayed at the client layer. The graphical user interface present at this layer consists of a module that allows the creation of graphics (CHART) and allows the creation of virtual teams (ROOM or Classes) so that the administrator can intuitively visualise the students' behaviour.

4   Behavioural Features

Based on the framework described in Sect. 3, a set of behavioural features are monitored and preprocessed by the proposed system. Through these features, it enables the development of a classification model capable of determining the task at hand executed by the user, given the influence of the user's biometric behaviours. For this study, Keystroke Dynamics, Mouse Dynamics and Attention Performance Metrics were selected to this end. To monitor students' performance, behavioural information was collected from a group of students during high-end tasks in a school environment.

4.1   Mouse Dynamics

Mouse dynamics describe an individual's behaviour with a computer-based pointing device (e.g. mouse or touch-pad). Recently, mouse dynamics have been proposed as a behavioural biometric, under the premise that mouse behaviour is relatively unique among different people. The motions of the user's hand and by extension the movements of the computer mouse have a direct relation with the psychological – sentimental condition of the user. To be more specific, the way by which the mouse is moved (orbit, speed, intervals of immobility, direction) can demonstrate the user's condition [4, 6, 12]. Based on this concept, the following features are gathered through the monitoring of the mouse dynamics:

- Click Duration (cd) - time spent between key up events, whenever this time interval is inferior to 200 ms;
- Distance Between Click (dbc) - total distance travelled by the mouse between two consecutive clicks;
- Duration Distance Clicks (ddc) - time between consecutive key up and key down events;
- Distance Point to Line Between Clicks (dplbc) - computes the distance between two consecutive key up and key down events;
- Mouse Velocity (mv) - velocity at which the cursor travels;
- Mouse Acceleration (ma) - acceleration of the mouse at a given time;

4.2   Keystroke Dynamics

Another way of monitoring the user's performance in human-computer interaction (HCI) is based on keystroke analysis. The way a user types may indicate his/her state of mind. Pressing rapidly the keyboard could mean an altered state, anger or stress for instance, while taking too much time may mean sadness or fatigue. Keystroke dynamics, which measure an individual's typing rhythms, have been the subject of considerable research over the past few decades and their use for emotion recognition has shown promising results [3, 5, 13]. In this study, keystroke dynamics are used to analyse the attentiveness of a student. The following keystroke dynamics features are monitored:

- Key Down Time (kdt) - time spent between the key down and key up events;
- Time Between Keys (tbk) - timespan between two consecutive key up and key down events;

4.3   Attention Performance

Aside from the mentioned behavioural features, which describe the interaction of the student with the computer, the system also registers the application usage by recording the timestamp in which each student switched to a specific application, by recording the user's ID, timestamp and application name. By default, applications that are not considered work-related is count negatively towards the quantification of attention. The following attention performance features are monitored:

- Activity Timer - time between the start and the completion of the task;

- Main App. Total Time Usage - total time spent in the task solver application (i.e. the Adobe Photoshop app.)
- Main Application Percentage Usage - usage percentage of the task solver application;

5   Methods and Results

In order to validate the proposed system, we have implemented it at the Caldas das Taipas High School, located in the northern of Portugal. For this purpose, a group of volunteer students (9 girls and 13 boys) from the last year of the high school vocational course, whose average age was 17.6 (SD = 1.4) was selected. On different days, students had a class where they accessed to an individual computer and two hours where given to complete a task using Adobe Photoshop application. All involved participants presented computing proficiency and the rooms were equipped with similar computers, each participant was randomly assigned to.

In addition to the biometrics features captured (referred to in Sect. 4), each case study was labelled with the respective activity (i.e. video, image, text and audio). Moreover, based on the biometric features recorded from different soft sensors, the distribution of each feature (e.g. mean, median, standard deviation, etc.) are presented in different scales. In order to solve this problem, it was necessary to apply feature scaling (i.e. normalisation techniques). In this study, the two methods used were max-min normalisation and Z-score normalisation. Min-max normalisation technique is a normalisation strategy which linearly scales a feature value to the range [0,1], based on the minimum and maximum values of the set of observed values. In other words, the minimum value of the feature value is mapped to 0 while the maximum value is mapped to 1. As for Z-score, this technique is a stand-in for the actual measurement, and they represent the distance of a value from the mean measured in standard deviations. This distribution technique is useful when relating different measurement distributions to each acting as a "common denominator".

With this, several machine learning categorisation methods were used to predict the student's activity, through the analysis of his/her behaviour in HMI. Several classifiers were trained and tested in order to determine the most efficient method to categorise the student's activity, where the most applied methods in the scientific literature were taken into account. The set of classification methods trained and tested were: Support Vector Machine, Nearest Neighbour, Naive Bayes, Neural Network and Random Forest.

As for the validation method, a split validation method was used in order to determine the classification performance, where 2/3 of the study cases were used for training the classifiers while the remaining 1/3 was used to test it. Table 1 presents the set of results for the classifiers performance.

Looking upon the outcome, some conclusion can be taken into account: (1) according to the trained and tested classification methods, the Random Forest method presents overall the best performance, with a correct percentage of

Table 1. Comparative analysis of machine learning categorisation performance.

	Raw	Min-max normalisation	Z-score
Support Vector Machine	37.5%	43.75%	37.5%
Nearest Neighbour	43.75%	62.5%	43.75%
Naive Bayes	68.75%	75%	68.75%
Neural Network	31.25%	56.25%	56.25%
Random Forest	81.25%	87.5%	87.5%

classifications of 87.5%, while Support Vector Machine presents the worst performance; (2) through the application of Feature Scaling techniques, the performance of the applied classifiers showed an improvement between [6.25%–25%], where the greatest improvement is verified in the neural network classifier; (3) the performance of the classifiers is dependent on the quality of the features and the total number of case studies analysed (i.e. 48 case studies).

Given the set of conclusions, the Random Forest method was selected to categorise student's activity. Additionally, this model was optimised through the application of hyper-parameter optimisation. In other words, in order to optimise the Random Forest's classification performance, it was required to find the optimal number of leafs/features (i.e. between [1–11] leafs/features) and number of trees (in this study it was modelled between [1–500] trees) that best suit the model and minimises the validation error function. For this, an exhaustive grid search was used, where a set of parameter values for each model are trained and validated. In the end, the model with the lowest error rate was the selected one. Figure 2 presents the set of results from this process, where it shows that the model displays a average minimised error when the number of decision trees is 80. As for the number of leafs/features for each decision tree, 9 was the number that presented the best performance. Moreover, the features relevance of the model is presented, where the Activity Timer (alltime) is by far the most important one to predict the student's activity, followed by the Duration Distance Clicks (ddc), Time Between Keys (tbk), Key Down Time (kdt), Distance Point to Line Between Click (dplbc) and Distance Between Click (dbc).

The respective confusion matrix of the Random Forest's model is presented in Table 2, where only the Video activity presents an misclassification of 40% of total cases (i.e. 2/5 cases were misclassified as Audio editing activity).

Table 2. Random forest: confusion matrix

	Audio	Image	Text	Video	Correct prediction (%)
Audio	2	0	0	0	100%
Image	0	6	0	0	100%
Text	0	0	3	0	100%
Video	2	0	0	3	60%

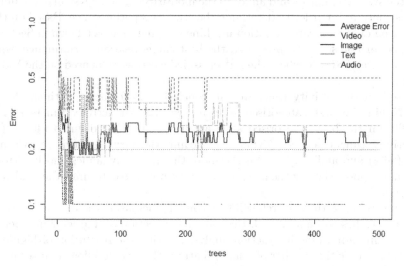

(a) Random Forest: Error vs Trees based on the different labels/activities

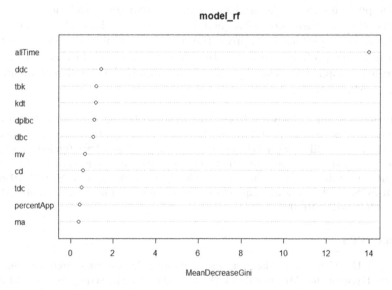

(b) Random Forest: Features Relevance in Activity Classification

Fig. 2. Random forest classifier analysis.

6   Conclusions and Future Work

This work proposes an non-invasive approach for a mentoring system based on the behaviour biometric analysis of the work during high-end tasks. More specifically, the system monitors and analyses the mouse dynamics, keystroke dynamics and task activity in order to determine the student's performance. Based on the application of several categorisation machine learning models (shown in Sect. 5), the Random Forest model presented the best categorisation performance, with a success rate of 87.5%, where the missclassified cases were focused on the Video activity.

Based on the activity timer we can conclude: (1) for activity timers lower than 75 min the best categorised style is text; (2) for activity timers higher than 90 min the best categorised style are image (60%) and audio (40%); (3) for activity timers between 75 min and 90 min the best categorised style are video (80%) and audio (20%). Furthermore the mouse dynamics and keystroke dynamics support slightly the machine learning model to determine the student's activities.

As future work, the research will focus on: (1) increasing the number of available case studies to be analysed, through the collection of a greater number of cases of human-machine interaction analysis, during the resolution of high-end tasks (2) increase the number of quality features that would allow a better monitoring of student's performance (e.g. features related to body posture, touch intensity with the mouse, etc.) (3) detailed analysis of the features that influence the performance of the student's (e.g. through the correlation analysis of students' class performance with their biometric behaviours);(4) definition of different student profiles to improve the adaptive learning mechanisms of the platform (i.e. by profiling students into different behaviour clusters, better measures can be applied for each specific profile, improving intelligent mentoring systems performance).

Acknowledgement. This work has been supported by: SENESCYT - Universidad do Minho and Secretaría de Educación Superior, Ciencia, Tecnología e Innovación within the Project: SENESCYT-SDFC-DSEFC-2017-2855-O; Part-funded by ERDF–European Regional Development Fund and by National Funds through the FCT–Portuguese Foundation for Science and Technology within project NORTE-01-0247-FEDER-017832. The work of Filipe Gonçalves is supported by a FCT grant with the reference ICVS-BI-2016-005.

References

1. Bra, P.D., Calvi, L.: Aha! an open adaptive hypermedia architecture. New Rev. Hypermedia Multimedia **4**(1), 115–139 (1998). https://doi.org/10.1080/13614569808914698
2. Brusilovsky, P., Peylo, C.: Adaptive and intelligent web-based educational systems. Int. J. Artif. Intell. Educ. **13**(2–4), 159–172 (2003). http://dl.acm.org/citation.cfm?id=1434845.1434847
3. Carneiro, D., Novais, P.: Behavioral biometrics and ambient intelligence: new opportunities for context-aware applications. State Art AI Appl. Ambient Intell. **298**, 68 (2017)
4. Durães, D., Bajo, J., Novais, P.: Assess and enhancing attention in learning activities. In: Auer, M.E., Guralnick, D., Simonics, I. (eds.) ICL 2017. AISC, vol. 715, pp. 803–811. Springer, Cham (2018). https://doi.org/10.1007/978-3-319-73210-7_93

5. Gomes, M., Oliveira, T., Silva, F., Carneiro, D., Novais, P.: Establishing the relationship between personality traits and stress in an intelligent environment. In: Ali, M., Pan, J.-S., Chen, S.-M., Horng, M.-F. (eds.) IEA/AIE 2014. LNCS (LNAI), vol. 8482, pp. 378–387. Springer, Cham (2014). https://doi.org/10.1007/978-3-319-07467-2_40

6. Gonçalves, F., Carneiro, D., Novais, P., Pêgo, J.: EUStress: a human behaviour analysis system for monitoring and assessing stress during exams. In: Ivanović, M., Bădică, C., Dix, J., Jovanović, Z., Malgeri, M., Savić, M. (eds.) IDC 2017. SCI, vol. 737, pp. 137–147. Springer, Cham (2018). https://doi.org/10.1007/978-3-319-66379-1_13

7. Heift, T.: Web delivery of adaptive and interactive language tutoring: revisited. Int. J. Artif. Intell. Educ. **26**(1), 489–503 (2016). https://doi.org/10.1007/s40593-015-0061-0

8. Kegel, C.A., Bus, A.G.: Online tutoring as a pivotal quality of web-based early literacy programs. J. Educ. Psychol. **104**(1), 182 (2012)

9. Mancas, M.: Computational attention towards attentive computers. Presses Universitaires de Louvain (2007)

10. Méndez Pozo, G.: Una arquitectura software basada en agentes y recomendaciones metodológicas para el desarrollo de entornos virtuales de entrenamiento con tutoría inteligente. Ph.D. thesis, Informatica (2008)

11. Mitrovic, A.: An intelligent SQL tutor on the web. Int. J. Artif. Intell. Educ. **13**(2–4), 173–197 (2003). http://dl.acm.org/citation.cfm?id=1434845.1434848

12. Pimenta, A., Carneiro, D., Novais, P., Neves, J.: Monitoring mental fatigue through the analysis of keyboard and mouse interaction patterns. In: Pan, J.-S., Polycarpou, M.M., Woźniak, M., de Carvalho, A.C.P.L.F., Quintián, H., Corchado, E. (eds.) HAIS 2013. LNCS (LNAI), vol. 8073, pp. 222–231. Springer, Heidelberg (2013). https://doi.org/10.1007/978-3-642-40846-5_23

13. Rodrigues, M., Gonçalves, S., Carneiro, D., Novais, P., Fdez-Riverola, F.: Keystrokes and clicks: measuring stress on e-learning students. In: Casillas, J., Martínez-López, F., Vicari, R., De la Prieta, F. (eds.) Management Intelligent Systems. Advances in Intelligent Systems and Computing, vol. 220, pp. 119–126. Springer, Heidelberg (2013). https://doi.org/10.1007/978-3-319-00569-0_15

14. Tamiz, M., Karimi, M., Mehrabi, I., Ghidary, S.S.: A novel attention control modeling method for sensor selection based on fuzzy neural network learning. In: 2013 First RSI/ISM International Conference on Robotics and Mechatronics (ICRoM), pp. 7–13. IEEE (2013)

15. Yano, Y., Mitsuhara, H., Ochi, Y.: An adaptive web-based learning system with a free-hyperlink environment. In: Barker, P., Rebelsky, S. (eds.) Proceedings of EdMedia: World Conference on Educational Media and Technology 2002, pp. 1349–1350. Association for the Advancement of Computing in Education (AACE), Denver (2002). https://www.learntechlib.org/p/9991

Machine Learning Applications, Machine Learning Methods, Cognitive Modeling, Cognitive Systems

Analysis of Encoder Representations as Features Using Sparse Autoencoders in Gradient Boosting and Ensemble Tree Models

Luis Aguilar[1]([envelope]) [iD] and L. Antonio Aguilar[2]([envelope]) [iD]

[1] Academic Department of Mathematics, National University of Piura,
Urb. Miraflores s/n, Castilla Apartado Postal 295, Piura, Peru
laguilari@unp.edu.pe
[2] Computer and System School, Antenor Orrego Private University,
Av. América Sur 3145 Urb. Monserrate, Trujillo, Peru
laguilarg@upao.edu.pe

Abstract. The performance of learning algorithms relies on factors such as the training strategy, the parameter tuning approach, and data complexity; in this scenario, extracted features play a fundamental role. Since not all the features maintain useful information, they can add noise, thus decreasing the performance of the algorithms. To address this issue, a variety of techniques such as feature ex-traction, feature engineering and feature selection have been developed, most of which fall into the unsupervised learning category. This study explores the generation of such features, using a set of k encoder layers, which are used to produce a low dimensional feature set F. The encoder layers were trained using a two-layer depth sparse autoencoder model, where PCA was used to estimate the right number of hidden units in the first layer. Then, a set of four algorithms, which belong to the gradient boosting and ensemble families were trained using the generated features. Finally, a performance comparison, using the encoder features against the original features was made. The results show that by using the reduced features it is possible to achieve equal or better results. Also, the approach improves more with highly imbalanced data sets.

Keywords: Unsupervised learning · Sparse autoencoders · Feature generation
Gradient boosting models · Ensemble models

1 Introduction

In a supervised learning setting, algorithms use a set of feature vectors x_i to predict a set of targets y_i, which can be discrete (classification) or continuous (regression). Typically xi is grouped into a design matrix $X^{(m,\ n)}$ where m represents the total observations and n the number of features. Algorithms use the learned features to predict new values $\hat{y}$ from unseen data. In this context, features play an important role in the algorithm's performance, due to the ability to increase or decrease it. Thus, learning the appropriate set of features becomes a crucial task in the majority of practical applications.

© Springer Nature Switzerland AG 2018
G. R. Simari et al. (Eds.): IBERAMIA 2018, LNAI 11238, pp. 159–169, 2018.
https://doi.org/10.1007/978-3-030-03928-8_13

Therefore, it is necessary to apply some techniques or transformations to the original features in order to improve them. Such techniques are usually grouped into feature engineering, feature extraction and feature selection. Although certain debate exists about the formalism of feature engineering, there is no doubt of its effectiveness as observed in many machine learning competitions. An example of this is described in [1], where a set of diverse features were generated in order to improve the final model score.

Feature engineering can be defined as an iterative process, where a set of new features are generated using a set of transformations, which can be very simple, like obtaining the mean, or could involve a more complex set of calculations. Usually the quality of the obtained features is related to the practitioner's prior knowledge over the problem domain. The lack of this prior knowledge represents an issue in the feature generation process. To address this problem, different techniques have been proposed to generate features in an automatic fashion [2, 3]. In this context, algorithms are typically used to generate and evaluate the new features.

Some of those techniques involve the application of unsupervised algorithms such as autoencoders, which are a type of unsupervised neural network. They were introduced by Hinton [4] in 1986. Since then, many variants have been proposed, including sparse autoencoders [5], variational autoencoders [6] and denoising autoencoders [7]. These architectures introduce different variations to the original autoencoder model, but they are generally composed of two types of layers, namely encoder and decoder. The encoder has the function to learn a compress representation of the data. Typically, the encoder has k units such as $k < n$, where n represents the number of features in the data. This ensures that the encoder learn a compact representation of the data, similarly to what can be achieved with PCA. Meanwhile the decoder layer reconstructs the representation learned by the encoder to its original form [8].

The complexity of the autoencoders to generate features are related to factors such as the type of architecture used, the parameter tuning strategy, the preprocessing techniques and the data complexity. In this context, the encoder units are learning a certain type of fix features $A \in H$, where H represents the total feature space. Therefore, it is possible to assume that there are other feature spaces F that could also be explored as features by introducing variations to the number of units in the encoder layer. This represents the main topic of this study. But instead of using the common reconstructions from the decoder layer, the encoder layer is being used to learn and generate new features from the original data, using a different subset of encoder units. Using these new representations, a set of learning algorithms which belong to the gradient boosting and ensemble families are being trained. The results show that using this approach enables to explore other feature spaces F. Also, the new features are less dimensional than the original ones, obtaining similar or better auc scores, even in the presence of highly imbalanced data sets.

2   Main Idea and Motivation

Autoencoders are applied in diverse application domains. For example, due to their innate capability to maintain the local variability in lower dimensions, they can be used in feature embeddings [9]. In feature extraction tasks, they are capable of creating new features, which can be used as training data for classifiers [10]. Also, they are very efficient when applied to extract features from high dimensional data [11]. Another interesting application of autoencoders is related to data augmentation [12]. Finally, autoencoders can be used to automatize the feature generation process [13]. In all the applications discussed, the encoder units are capable of generating a new rich set of representations.

However, these representations correspond to a fix number of units in the encoder layer. Moreover, they are the result of a very careful and laborious tuning process, which correspond to the autoencoder architecture design. But if a different number of units were used in the encoder layer, then the learned representations would significantly change. In fact, a totally new set of features would be obtained. This makes us asking, which set of obtained features are better [14]. Using this fact, it is possible to hypothesize the existence of a more general feature space H. In this context, the encoder layer is learning an optimal subset $A \in H$.

Therefore, if variations are made to the encoder layer, then it is possible to obtain a new set of features F. However, there are diverse types of variations and criteria that can be implemented. For example, in [15], from a set of hidden layers, only the highest activations were kept. Also, multiple layers and other algorithms can be implemented to learn features as shown in [16]. Finally, it is also possible to introduce kernel techniques to control the learned representations [17]. However, in this study, variations to the number of encoder units are instead been made, resulting in different k-encoder layers.

However, in order to explore F a set of assumptions has to be made: (i) F must not be an infinite space, and (ii) there has to be a reasonable number of original n features to generate F. It is also important to pay attention to the autoencoder architecture used to explore F. For example, if a single encoder layer is used, it would be equivalent to a PCA reduction. Therefore, it is necessary that the autoencoder will be at least two layers in depth to guarantee a set of more complex features. This idea is illustrated in Fig. 1.

Also, the defined autoencoder in Fig. 1 must maintain sparsity in the learned representations. Therefore, a series of L1 and L2 regularizations, which can guarantee these criteria are been applied to the autoencoder layers.

Once the k-encoders learn F, it is possible to transform the original data using the learned representations from the k-encoders. Section 3 will provide a detailed approach describing the implementation of the main idea proposed here.

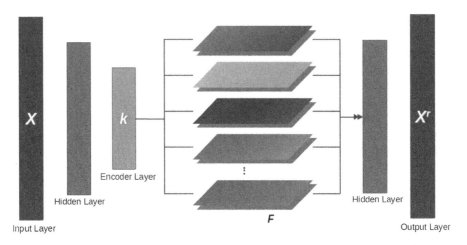

Fig. 1. Feature space F generated by the k different encoder layers.

3 Design Approach

3.1 Base Sparse Autoencoder

In order to consider the approach described in Sect. 2, a base sparse autoencoder [5] B_a will be implemented. This sparse autoencoder B_a will be used to train the different k-encoder layers. Since the architecture defined in Fig. 1 is composed by a two-layer depth sparse autoencoder, it is necessary to determine the number of units in the respective layers. Let be p the number of units in the first layer and k the number of units in the k-encoder layers. Then the number of hidden units p can be defined as follows:

$$p = \sum_{i=1}^{n} c_{var(i)} > \varepsilon \qquad (1)$$

Where the total hidden units p is determined by the total principal components c_i obtained from the data set X_i, which maintain a variance greater than ϵ. In this context, ϵ becomes a parameter that must be tuned. We choose to keep $\epsilon = 0.9$. This means that the total number of units p will be equivalent to the total components that maintain a variance equal to 90%. Using (1) also acts as a filter to discard features that could represent noise or are irrelevant.

Once p is defined, it is possible to determine the total number of k-encoders units as follows:

$$k = \{1, \ldots, p - 1\} \qquad (2)$$

Using (2), k is being constrained to explore a representative finite space from F. Meanwhile (1) is removing unnecessary features from X_i. To guarantee the sparsity in B_a, a set of L1 and L2 regularizations will be applied to the layers. The activation functions used are: relu for the first layer, tanh for the encoder layer, relu for the first layer of the decoder and finally sigmoid for the output layer. Also, the weights are being initialized using a normal glorot distribution (3). Finally, to guarantee the reconstruction from the original X_i, KL divergence (4) is used as a loss function.

$$stdev = \sqrt{\frac{2}{u_i + u_o}} \qquad (3)$$

$$KL(q \| p) = \sum_d q(d) * \log\left(\frac{q(d)}{p(d)}\right) \qquad (4)$$

It is important to note that the number of k-encoders to be generated will be restricted by three factors: (i) the total number of features n in X_i, (ii) the number of units p obtained applying (1) on X_i and (iii) the number of k encoder units generated from (2). This means that per each data set X_i a set of k-encoder layers will be generated, varying only in the number of units k. Using the definition of B_a, the architecture can be summarized in Fig. 2.

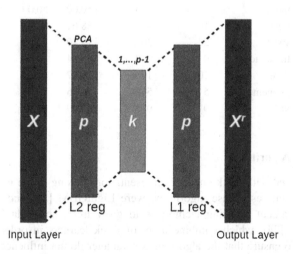

Fig. 2. Architecture representation of the B_a sparse autoencoder.

Libraries scikit-learn [18] and Keras [19] were used to implement B_a.

3.2   Data Sets

In order to test the proposed approach, library PMLB [20] was used. This library contains a well-known easily accessible benchmark data set repository. The repository can be used for regression and classification tasks. In this experiment, the data sets were restricted to only binary classification tasks. It also included both balanced and imbalanced data sets.

From the repository, a total of 13 data sets were selected. Each data set was partitioned into training (80%), development (10%) and test (10%), respectively. This partition was used during training both the sparse autoencoders B_a and the algorithms. Also, to guarantee the reproducibility of the results, a constant random seed was maintained in each split during all the experiment. Table 1 shows the data sets alongside their respectively properties.

Table 1. Data sets description.

Data Sets	# Features	# Instances	Class balance (%)	
			Positive	Negative
mushroom	22	8124	48.20	51.80
twonorm	20	7400	49.96	50.04
ring	20	7400	50.49	49.51
agaricus-lepiota	22	8145	48.09	51.91
parity5+5	10	1124	50.44	49.56
threeOf9	9	512	46.48	53.52
monk1	6	556	50.00	50.00
vote	16	435	38.62	61.38
spect	22	267	79.40	20.60
tic-tac-toe	9	958	65.34	34.66
flare	10	1066	17.07	82.93
phoneme	5	5404	29.35	70.65
xd6	9	973	33.09	66.91

3.3 Trained Algorithms

Algorithms trained with the k-encoder representations belong to the gradient boosting and ensemble families. These algorithms were LightGBM [21] and CatBoost [22], which apply gradient boosting techniques to grow trees, and Ada Boost [23] and Random Forest [24], which combine a set of week learners in order to boost their performance. To ensure that the algorithm's parameter do not influence the results, no parameter tuning was implemented. Therefore, their default configuration with a constant random seed was used during training with the k-encoder features and with the original ones.

3.4 Training Methodology

Using the definition described in (1) and (2) the right number of p units and k-encoder layers were determined for each data set X_i. Then each k-encoder layer was trained using a sparse architecture. Once the training was complete, the different k-encoders were used to transform the original features into their new feature representation F for each X_i. This process was carried out a total of ten times per each data set X_i. Then both the ensemble and gradient boosting algorithms were trained using the generated features and the original ones. Also, the auc score was averaged for the transformed test features per each data set X_i. Finally, the hardware used was an Intel core i5-6200U CPU – 2.30 GHz laptop with 8 GB RAM and running Ubuntu 16.04 LTS 64-bit.

4   Results

The experiment was performed ten times on the data sets. The table below shows the average auc test scores obtained by each algorithm, alongside with the number of p units and the best encoder layer (b_k).

The results in Table 2 indicate that each algorithm obtain their maximum auc score from different k-encoders. Also, LightGBM and CatBoost do not present much improvement from the k-encoder representation. In fact, in most cases the auc scores are equal or slightly better. However, it must be noted that these results are achieved using just a smaller number of features than the original ones, which indicates that the obtained features are relevant. On the other hand, AdaBoost and Random Forest have received a more significant improvement over their auc scores, especially Ada Boost, which achieves an average auc score greater than the normal Ada Boost model. Also, there are two remarkable cases where all the algorithms benefit greatly from the encoder representations: the spect and flare data sets.

Table 2. ROC scores from transformed test data using the best encoder layers (b_k).

Data sets	p	b_k	Ada Boost		b_k	Random forest		b_k	LightGBM		b_k	CatBoost	
			Enc	Norm		Enc	Norm		Enc	Norm		Enc	Norm
mushroom	13	12	0.97	1.00	7	**1.00**	1.00	9	**1.00**	1.00	8	**1.00**	1.00
twonorm	18	16	**0.97**	0.97	17	**0.96**	0.95	16	0.97	0.98	16	**0.98**	0.98
ring	18	17	0.90	0.96	12	0.89	0.93	16	0.92	0.97	16	0.91	0.97
agaricus-lepiota	13	11	0.95	1.00	9	**1.00**	1.00	11	**1.00**	1.00	9	**1.00**	1.00
parity5+5	9	6	**0.65**	0.43	8	**0.72**	0.57	6	0.69	1.00	6	0.68	1.00
threeOf9	9	5	**0.82**	0.81	8	0.81	0.96	5	0.84	1.00	7	0.81	1.00
monk1	6	5	**0.75**	0.70	3	0.79	0.93	5	0.88	1.00	5	0.86	1.00
vote	10	2	**1.00**	1.00	8	**1.00**	1.00	9	**1.00**	1.00	6	**1.00**	1.00
spect	14	8	**0.78**	0.53	1	**0.75**	0.68	8	**0.73**	0.58	3	**0.70**	0.68
tic-tac-toe	8	6	0.69	0.79	5	0.70	0.90	4	0.69	1.00	3	0.68	1.00
flare	7	5	**0.62**	0.55	1	**0.62**	0.59	2	**0.64**	0.59	5	**0.65**	0.59
phoneme	4	1	**0.73**	0.71	3	0.71	0.85	3	0.71	0.85	1	0.71	0.83
xd6	9	4	**0.88**	0.76	7	0.94	1.00	8	0.95	1.00	8	0.95	1.00
Total avg			*0.82*	*0.79*		*0.85*	*0.87*		*0.85*	*0.92*		*0.84*	*0.93*

When analyzing the impact of the different k-encoders over the auc performance, two cases must be noted. First, there is a point where the maximum auc score is achieved. Then, when more k-encoders units are added, the performance begins to

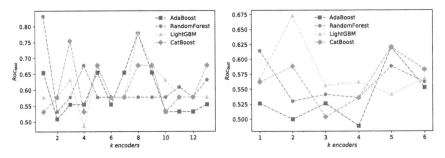

Fig. 3. Trained k-encoders on spect (left) and flare (right) data sets.

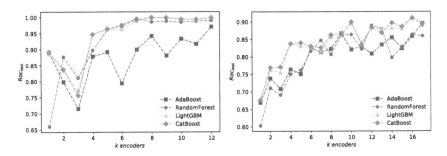

Fig. 4. Trained k-encoders on mushroom (left) and ring (right) data sets.

gradually decrease or oscillate. This pattern is more predominant with the spect and flare data sets, as observed in Fig. 3. However, this is totally the opposite with other data sets, where it seems that adding more k-encoder units improve the auc performance as seen in Fig. 4. Taking this into consideration, it is necessary to train all the k-encoders, in order to find a suitable set of features for a particular learning algorithm.

Table 3. Training time in balanced data sets.

Data sets	mushroom	twonorm	ring	agaricus-lepiota	parity5 +5	threeOf9	monk1
Total features	22	20	20	22	10	9	6
Training instances	6499	5920	5920	6516	899	409	444
K-encoders trained	12	17	17	12	8	8	5
Training time (s)	39.44	66.20	84.73	77.66	33.38	33.73	19.42

Table 4. Training time in imbalanced data sets.

Data sets	vote	spect	tic-tac-toe	flare	phoneme	xd6
Total features	16	22	9	10	5	9
Training instances	348	213	766	852	4323	778
K-encoders trained	9	13	7	6	3	8
Training time (s)	36.97	57.21	37.23	36.03	30.94	51.21

Another factor to consider is the time taken to train the k – encoders. This is illustrated in Tables 3 and 4 for the balanced and imbalanced data sets. In both cases, the k-encoders also reflect the new low dimensionally obtained features. Also, observing the results in both tables, the data sets which take more time to train the k-encoders are usually the ones that have more features. The number of training instances also have impact on the training time.

5   Conclusions

The proposed approach allows us to observe how the different k-encoder features F impacted the performance of the gradient boosting and ensemble algorithms. Also, the proposed approach improved greatly the performance in two highly imbalanced data sets, such as flare and spect. The proposed approach also allowed us to obtain better results using less dimensions than the original features.

It was also observed that in some cases, using a reduced number of k-encoders was enough to generate a good set of features F. At the same time, there were cases in which adding more k-encoders further improved the performance. Therefore, both cases are strongly related to the particular characteristics of the data sets. However, this approach should be able to generate useful features in the presence of balanced and imbalanced data sets.

When analyzing the average performance obtained by the algorithms, Ada Boost was the one which beneficiated the most of the proposed approach. In fact, a normal Ada model only obtains a 79% average auc score, in contrast with the 82% using the proposed approach.

It is also important to note that each algorithm selected a different k-encoder, which means that each k-encoder feature will have a different relevance for each algorithm. Therefore, to put this approach into practice, all the k-encoders must be trained in order to find the best representation suited for a particular algorithm.

During the experiments a limitation in the proposed approach for the k-encoder generation was found. If the number of units p for a particular data set are equal to 1, then (2) will become 0, thus, the k-encoders cannot be generated. Finally, it was observed that the addition of regularization techniques such as L1 and L2 to the layers improved significantly the results.

References

1. Martínez-Romo, J.C., Luna-rosas, F.J., Mora-gonzález, M., De Luna-ortega, C.A.: Optimal feature generation with genetic algorithms and FLDR in a restricted-vocabulary speech recognition system. In: Bio-Inspired Computational Algorithms and Their Applications, pp. 235–262 (2012). https://doi.org/10.5772/36135
2. Cheng, W., Kasneci, G., Graepel, T., Stern, D., Herbrich, R.: Automated feature generation from structured knowledge. In: Proceedings of the 20th ACM International Conference on Information and Knowledge Management, CIKM 2011, p. 1395 (2011). https://doi.org/10.1145/2063576.2063779
3. Katz, G., Shin, E.C.R., Song, D.: ExploreKit: automatic feature generation and selection. In: Proceedings - IEEE 16th International Conference on Data Mining (ICDM), pp. 979–984 (2016). https://doi.org/10.1109/ICDM.2016.0123
4. Rumelhart, D.E., Hinton, G.E., Williams, R.J.: Learning representations by back-propagating errors. Nature **323**, 533–536 (1986). https://doi.org/10.1038/323533a0
5. Ng, A.: Sparse autoencoder. In: CS294A Lecture Notes, pp. 1–19 (2011). http://web.stanford.edu/class/cs294a/sae/sparseAutoencoderNotes.pdf
6. Kingma, D.P., Welling, M.: Auto-encoding variational Bayes, pp. 1–14 (2013). https://arxiv.org/abs/1312.6114
7. Vincent, P., Larochelle, H., Bengio, Y., Manzagol, P.-A.: Extracting and composing robust features with denoising autoencoders. In: Proceedings of 25th Annual International Conference on Machine Learning, ICML 2008, pp. 1096–1103 (2008). https://doi.org/10.1145/1390156.1390294
8. Baldi, P.: Autoencoders, unsupervised learning, and deep architectures. In: Guyon, I., Dror, G., Lemaire, V., Taylor, G.W., Silver, D.L. (eds.) ICML Unsupervised and Transfer Learning, pp. 37–50 (2012). JMLR.org
9. Yu, W., Zeng, G., Luo, P., Zhuang, F., He, Q., Shi, Z.: Embedding with autoencoder regularization. In: Blockeel, H., Kersting, K., Nijssen, S., Železný, F. (eds.) ECML PKDD 2013. LNCS (LNAI), vol. 8190, pp. 208–223. Springer, Heidelberg (2013). https://doi.org/10.1007/978-3-642-40994-3_14
10. Bosch, N., Paquette, L.: Unsupervised deep autoencoders for feature extraction with educational data. In: Deep Learning with Educational Data Workshop at the 10th International Conference on Educational Data Mining (2017)
11. Meng, Q., Catchpoole, D., Skillicom, D., Kennedy, P.J.: Relational autoencoder for feature extraction. In: Proceedings of International Joint Conference Neural Networks, May 2017, pp. 364–371 (2017). https://doi.org/10.1109/ijcnn.2017.7965877
12. DeVries, T., Taylor, G.W.: Dataset augmentation in feature space, pp. 1–12 (2017). https://arxiv.org/abs/1702.05538v1
13. Yousefi-azar, M., Varadharajan, V., Hamey, L., Tupakula, U.: Autoencoder-based feature learning for cyber security applications. In: International Joint Conference on Neural Networks 2017 (IJCNN), pp. 3854–3861 (2017). https://doi.org/10.1109/IJCNN.2017.7966342
14. Bengio, Y., Courville, A., Vincent, P.: Representation learning: a review and new perspectives. IEEE Trans. Pattern Anal. Mach. Intell. **35**, 1798–1828 (2013). https://doi.org/10.1109/TPAMI.2013.50
15. Makhzani, A., Frey, B.: k-sparse autoencoders (2013). https://arxiv.org/abs/1312.5663
16. Ju, Y., Guo, J., Liu, S.: A deep learning method combined sparse autoencoder with SVM. In: 2015 International Conference on Cyber-Enabled Distributed Computing and Knowledge Discovery, pp. 257–260. IEEE (2015). https://doi.org/10.1109/CyberC.2015.39

17. Kampffmeyer, M., Løkse, S., Bianchi, F.M., Jenssen, R., Livi, L.: Deep kernelized autoencoders. In: Sharma, P., Bianchi, F. (eds.) Image Analysis. SCIA 2017. LNCS, vol. 10269, pp. 419–430. Springer, Cham (2017). https://doi.org/10.1007/978-3-319-59126-1_35
18. Pedregosa, F., et al.: Scikit-learn: machine learning in Python. J. Mach. Learn. Res. **12**, 2825–2830 (2011)
19. Chollet, F.: Keras. GitHub Repos (2015). https://keras.io/
20. Olson, R.S., La Cava, W., Orzechowski, P., Urbanowicz, R.J., Moore, J.H.: PMLB: a large benchmark suite for machine learning evaluation and comparison. BioData Min. **10**, 36 (2017). https://doi.org/10.1186/s13040-017-0154-4
21. Ke, G., Meng, Q., Wang, T., Chen, W., Ma, W., Liu, T.-Y.: LightGBM: a highly efficient gradient boosting decision tree. Adv. Neural. Inf. Process. Syst. **30**, 3148–3156 (2017)
22. Dorogush, A.V., Ershov, V., Yandex, A.G.: CatBoost: gradient boosting with categorical features support. In: Workshop on ML System, NIPS 2017, pp. 1–7 (2017)
23. Hastie, T., Rosset, S., Zhu, J., Zou, H.: Multi-class AdaBoost. Stat. Interface **2**, 349–360 (2009). https://doi.org/10.4310/SII.2009.v2.n3.a8
24. Breiman, L.: Random forests. Mach. Learn. **45**, 5–32 (2001). https://doi.org/10.1023/A:1010933404324

Furnariidae Species Classification Using Extreme Learning Machines and Spectral Information

E. M. Albornoz[1]([✉]), L. D. Vignolo[1], J. A. Sarquis[2], and C. E. Martínez[1]

[1] Instituto sinc(i), Universidad Nacional del Litoral - CONICET, Santa Fe, Argentina
{emalbornoz,ldvignolo,cmartinez}@sinc.unl.edu.ar
[2] Instituto Nacional de Limnología, Universidad Nacional del Litoral - CONICET, Santa Fe, Argentina
juandres.sarquis@gmail.com

Abstract. Automatic bird species classification and identification are issues that have aroused interest in recent years. The main goals involve more exhaustive environmental monitoring and natural resources managing. One of the more relevant characteristics of calling birds is the vocalisation because this allows to recognise species or identify new ones, to know its natural history and macro-systematic relations, among others. In this work, some spectral-based features and extreme learning machines (ELM) are used to perform bird species classification. The experiments were carried on using 25 species of the family Furnariidae that inhabit the Paranaense Littoral region of Argentina (South America) and were validated in a cross-validation scheme. The results show that ELM classifier obtains high classification rates, more than 90% in accuracy, and the proposed features overperform the baseline features.

Keywords: Birds classification · Spectral information
Auditory representation · Extreme learning machines

1 Introduction

The presence of avian species is usually perceived through vocalisations, one the most noticeable characteristics of calling birds [34]. The census of bird species allows to estimate the biodiversity in a habitat due to they respond quickly to changes, are relatively easy to detect and may reflect changes at lower trophic levels (e.g. insects, plants) [9,28]. With the improvement of technological devices, more and more birds data can be collected in almost any habitat. Nevertheless, some problems arise as poor sample representation in remote regions, observer bias [26], defective monitoring [7], and high costs of sampling on large spatial and temporal scales, among others.

Bird vocalisations field has influenced the ethology [20], taxonomy [37] and evolutionary biology [31]. In addition, ecosystems monitoring is benefits from

© Springer Nature Switzerland AG 2018
G. R. Simari et al. (Eds.): IBERAMIA 2018, LNAI 11238, pp. 170–180, 2018.
https://doi.org/10.1007/978-3-030-03928-8_14

vocalisation identification because it allows registering and processing the recordings, and improving the data collection in the field [41]. Gather data in disjoint or large areas is essential for conducting reliable studies.

Passeriformes produce complex songs and can adapt their content over time: depending on the audience [10] or to match it with that of their neighbours [32]. Even, they can take possession of new songs or syllables during their lifetime [29]. Specifically, the Furnariidae family has several songs and some species show similar structures in their songs, manifested in introductory syllables or in the trill format. More complexity is added because the environmental conditions (humidity, wind, temperature, etc.) may alter the recording process, modifying the features that are present in the structure of songs and in the calls (e.g. frequency, duration, amplitude, etc.) [19,47]. Consequently, researchers use recordings from known databases, in order to avoid errors and distortions in analyses and results. As the scientific community validates these registrations (attributes, labels, etc.), they are more credible than "home-made" records despite these can be also affected by environmental conditions. Some works describe vocalisation changes in certain Furnariidae species [5,35,46], however, it is novel to evaluates several vocalisations of Furnariidae species from South America simultaneously [4]. In this work, the analysed Furnariidae species inhabit the Paranaense Littoral region (see Fig. 1). Many recent studies on bird vocalisations report that this region has become in an interesting place for this task [5].

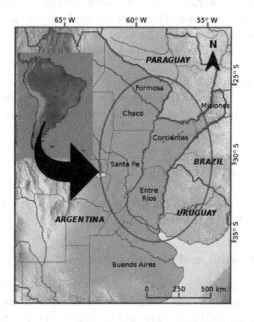

Fig. 1. Paranaense Littoral region (Argentina). Taken from [4].

The classification scheme can be defined as a pipeline of three steps: preprocessing, feature extraction and classification. The first one depends strongly on the recording process and involves filtering, segmentation and enhancement of audio signals. Regarding feature extraction, time- and frequency-based information was employed [25,34]. In addition, characteristics originally developed for speech analysis were used for bird call recognition: mel frequency cepstral coefficients (MFCCs) [16] and standard functionals (mean, standard deviation, kurtosis, etc.) computed over these [13,36]. Various techniques have been applied to bird call classification: Gaussian mixture model (GMM) [38], support vector machines (SVM) [4], random forest (RF) [8], among others. An interesting strategy based on the pairwise similarity measurements, computed on bird-call spectrograms, was evaluated in [25], where the authors used different classifiers to recognise four species. In [13], thirty-five species were classified using a SVM classifier and six functionals were obtained from each MFCC. A different approach was proposed in [42], where a classifier based on hidden Markov models (HMMs) was used to recognise bird calls through their temporal dynamics. Previous works developing full-automatic methods for vocalisation recognition can be examined in [17,23,40], and the current relevance of this topic is shown in some recent works [16,36]. However, to address the vocalisation recognition of species belonging to the Furnariidae family is novel.

This study proposes to use Extreme Learning Machines classifier with spectral-based parameterisations for Furnariidae species classification. The model needs to be able to perform properly using data from three different databases. The main contributions of this work are the compilation of an interesting set of songs for 25 species of the Furnariidae family, to address the complex classification of species taken from the same family, a novel use of spectral-based and auditory inspired features for this task, and a novel approach using the ELM network.

The following section introduces the data, the features extraction process and the classifier. Section 3 deals with the experimental setup, presents the results an its discussions. Finally, conclusions are summarised and future work is proposed in the last section.

2   Materials and Methods

This section resumes the speech database, the baseline systems on the task and our approach to feature extraction.

2.1   Bird Call Corpus and Baseline System

To obtain a suitable number of vocalisations for training the classifiers and evaluating the performance, records from three well-known databases were selected and processed to obtain 751 recordings of Furnariidae species. Some of these were selected from the *Xeno-canto*[1] database [24,33,34], others were taken from the

---

[1] http://www.xeno-canto.org/.

Birds of Argentina & Uruguay: A Field Guide Total Edition corpus [12,27,30], and finally, several recordings were taken from *The Internet Bird Collection*[2] [1].

This set of audio signals, obtained from different data sources, involves an additional complexity that the model should be able to handle.

Similar to [4], the state-of-art (for speech signals) feature sets are obtained from the recordings using the *openSMILE* toolkit [14]. It calculates 6373 acoustic features using diverse functionals over low-level descriptor (LLD) contours, and with these we computed the three feature set used as baseline sets. A full description can be found in [43].

2.2 Mean of Log-Spectrum

The Mean of Log-Spectrum (MLS) coefficients is a set of features calculated from spectral data for different frequency bands. They were defined to extract relevant information from speech signals and were firstly used in the analysis and classification of spoken emotions (in clean and noisy conditions [2,3]). The MLS coefficients are defined as the average of the signal spectrogram

$$S(k) = \frac{1}{N} \sum_{n=1}^{N} \log |v(n,k)|, \tag{1}$$

where k is a frequency band, N is the number of frames in the signal and $v(n,k)$ is the discrete Fourier transform of the signal in the frame n. For the computation, the spectrograms were obtained with Hamming windows of 25 ms.

2.3 Mean of the Log-auditory Spectrum

In the same way as previously, we propose to analyze the recordings by means of a related set of features based on the auditory spectrogram. The representation of the sound signal at the cochlear level and auditory cortical areas has been studied as an alternative to classical analysis methods, given its intrinsic selective tuning to relevant natural sound [44]. In [45], a model based on neurophysiological investigations at various stages of the auditory system was proposed. This model has two consecutive stages: an early auditory spectrogram with the activity of auditory nerve fibres (Fig. 2), and a model of the primary auditory cortex used to process the spectrogram and find the spectro-temporal receptive fields. The first stage uses a bank of 128 cochlear (bandpass) filters in the range [0–4000] Hz, with the central frequency of the filter at location x on the logarithmic frequency axis (in octaves) is defined as $f_x = f_0 2^x (\text{Hz})$, where f_0 is a reference frequency of 1 kHz. This frequency distribution proved to be satisfactory for the discrimination of acoustic clues in speech and further reconstruction of the signals [11]. Using the first stage output, a set of features is built using the mean of the log auditory spectrogram (MLSa) [3], as

$$S_a(k) = \frac{1}{N} \sum_{n=1}^{N} \log |a(n,k)|, \tag{2}$$

---

[2] http://ibc.lynxeds.com/.

where k is a frequency band, N is the number of frames in the utterance and $a(n, k)$ is the k-th coefficient obtained by applying the auditory filter bank to the signal in the frame n.

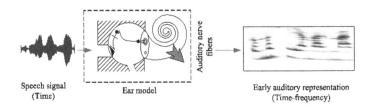

Speech signal
(Time)   Ear model   Early auditory representation
                                             (Time-frequency)

Fig. 2. Scheme of the used auditory model.

2.4   Extreme Learning Machines

The ELM is a kind of artificial neural network with one hidden layer [22] and its main peculiarity respecting to classical models is the training algorithm. It does not need parameter tuning and the hidden neurons are randomly initialised. Consequently, the training time is significantly reduced with respect to other training methods that use complex optimisation techniques.

Formally, let be J hidden units with F inputs and P output units. The hidden layer output is given by

$$h_j = \Phi(\mathbf{v}_j^T \mathbf{x} + b_j), \tag{3}$$

with Φ as a non-linear activation function, $\mathbf{v}_j$ the input weights and b_j the bias for the j-th hidden unit. The hidden-layer output, also known as projected features, can be expressed as $\mathbf{H} = [\mathbf{h}_1, \ldots, \mathbf{h}_N]^T$. Rewriting the equation in a matrix form, with $\mathbf{W} = [\mathbf{w}_1, \ldots, \mathbf{w}_P]$, $\mathbf{w}_p \in \mathbb{R}^J$ and $p = 1, \ldots, P$ as the output layer weights, the ELM output is

$$\tilde{\mathbf{Y}} = \mathbf{HW}. \tag{4}$$

If the function Φ satisfy certain properties (infinitely differentiability and random hidden weights) it can be shown that for any pair of inputs $(\mathbf{X}, \mathbf{Y})$ exists a number $J < N$ such $||\tilde{\mathbf{Y}} - \mathbf{Y}|| < \epsilon$ for any small ϵ [22]. This means that the ELM can approximate the target $\mathbf{Y}$ as much as we want by adjusting only the number of hidden units and the output weights. The optimisation problem for $\mathbf{W}$ can be written as

$$\underset{\mathbf{W}}{\text{minimise}}\ ||\mathbf{HW} - \mathbf{Y}||_2, \tag{5}$$

which is a least square optimisation problem. The smallest norm solution is given by

$$\hat{\mathbf{W}} = \mathbf{H}^\dagger \mathbf{Y}, \tag{6}$$

where $\mathbf{H}^\dagger$ is the Moore-Penrose pseudoinverse [6]. This solution for the optimisation problem is greatly fast comparing with the classical classifiers as SVM or backpropagation multi-layer perceptrons. More mathematical details of the ELM algorithm and several comparison with other neural nets can be seen in [21,22].

3   Results and Discussions

In this section the experiments are presented and discussed. At first, a directly comparable work is introduced. Then, the experimental scheme and the results using ELM are showed.

In a previous work [4], this Furnariidae set (25 species) was classified using 206 records, all the experiments were performed in a cross-validation scheme. Three features sets were evaluated:

- *Baseline:* a set of means and variances computed for the first 17 MFCCs, their deltas and acceleration over the entire song (102 features),
- *MFCC+Fun:* a set of functionals computed only from the MFCCs (531 features),
- *Full-Set:* a set of 6373 state-of-the-art features defined for speech processing (INTERSPEECH 2013 ComParE Challenge [39]).

For the determination of performance, two figures of merit are used: the Accuracy is calculated as the mean recognition rate and the Unweighted Average Recall (UAR) is obtained as the average of the class-specific recalls achieved by the system. The baseline for the bird song identification task was defined based on previous works [13,15]. In Table 1 the best results are showed, using Random Forest (RF) using 100 trees, support vector machines (SVM) and the two best MLP architectures: one hidden layer with a number of neurons set as $(Num.\ of\ inputs + Num.\ of\ outputs)/2$ (MLP1) and one hidden layer with a number of neurons set equal to the number of inputs (MLP2). It is important to remark that the best UAR result (82.21) was reached using the linear forward selection (LFS) [18] on the *Full-Set* and MLP1, however, it can not be exactly reproduced here for comparison (see [4]).

In the present work, 25 Furnariidae species (751 records) are classified using ELM. The three sets of features presented previously are evaluated using ELM, and compared with MLS+ set (328 features) and MLS++ set (346 features). The MLS+ includes 200 MLS and 128 MLSa coefficients, while the MLS++ added 18 speech-related features (13 MFCCs, pitch, energy, zero-crossing rate, short-term energy entropy and short-term spectral entropy). For all the experiments, a 6-fold cross-validation scheme was performed and for each case, the data were normalised using the percentile 5 and 95 from training partition. The average results for the best configurations are presented in Tables 2 and 3. Table 2 shows that the spectral features (MLS and MLSa) improved the accuracy reached by the previous parameterisations, although the UAR is similar as with baseline set. As the MLS+ and MLS++ obtain similar results, it is possible to say that MFCC and the other prosodic values are not too much useful here. Obviously, both spectral representations are very useful for this issue and it is necessary

Table 1. Summary of best results taken from [4], (* MLP1, ** MLP2)

Feature vector	RF100	SVM	MLP
	Accuracy		
Baseline	80.10	84.95	86.89**
MFCC+Fun	83.01	85.92	**89.32***
Full-Set	80.10	83.50	74.27*
	UAR		
Baseline	67.00	74.07	79.21**
MFCC+Fun	70.43	75.18	**80.85****
Full-Set	65.24	72.46	61.90*

Table 2. Summary of best results using ELM classifiers.

Feature vector	Accuracy [%]	UAR [%]
MLS+	93.22	84.89
MLS++	**93.61**	84.25
Baseline	91.48	**84.97**
MFCC+Fun	84.55	73.43
Full-Set	82.59	65.56

to explore them more to find the optimal set of characteristics, making feature selection (e.g. with LBS) or incorporating new ones.

As the set of records is notably unbalanced, we propose an experiment to evaluate the balance by repetition. Its utilisation is very extended [39] and it consists in augmenting the minority classes repeating their records. Table 3 shows the results using the balanced data, where the *MLS+* reaches the same percentage as in previous experiment. While it is not possible to conclude that this balance is useful for the system, it is possible to say that it increases the computational cost for the training.

Table 3. Summary of best results using ELM classifiers, balanced.

Feature vector	Accuracy [%]	UAR [%]
MLS+	**93.22**	**84.89**
MLS++	92.13	81.69
Baseline	85.60	78.83
MFCC+Fun	86.43	75.94
Full-Set	86.66	71.75

4   Conclusions

Monitoring bird species allows to surveillance the environmental due to it reflects important ecosystem processes and human activities. This work addresses the bird call classification problem using spectral-based features, and compares the performance with previous proposals. Species from the Furnariidae family which inhabit the Paranaense Littoral region were analysed, and although they are well-known in the community, to focus the study on a big group from the same family is very novel.

Results shows that spectral information seems to be really useful to reach a high performance in this application, even considering diverse recordings sources what hinders the task. The sets of features which obtain the best rates here, were previously defined for speech-related tasks, consequently it would be interesting to define more specific features.

This approach could be improved for developing autonomous tools that allow ornithologists to know which species are present in particular areas in order to do ecological monitoring and management. Specifically, it could to help the labelling of Furnariidae recordings, while it could be used for remote and simultaneous monitoring in different areas.

In future research, these spectral parameterisations will be studied further with other classification schemes as deep neural networks that exploit also the local variability along the records. In this sense, an interesting approach is to use the spectral information as images to feed well-known nets as the AlexNet (to perform transfer learning) or to train a new net using spectral information from several bird families. Also, a more in-depth analysis of specific filter banks is needed to process bird song records an to obtain more useful information.

Acknowledgements. The authors wish to thank to *Agencia Nacional de Promoción Científica y Tecnológica* (ANPCyT)(with PICT-2015-977), *Universidad Nacional del Litoral* (with CAID-PJ-50020150100055LI and CAID-PJ-50020150100059LI) and *Consejo Nacional de Investigaciones Científicas y Técnicas* (CONICET), from Argentina, for their support.

References

1. The internet bird collection. Ref. Rev. **26**(8), 42–43 (2012)
2. Albornoz, E.M., Milone, D.H., Rufiner, H.L.: Spoken emotion recognition using hierarchical classifiers. Comput. Speech Lang. **25**(3), 556–570 (2011)
3. Albornoz, E.M., Milone, D.H., Rufiner, H.L.: Feature extraction based on bio-inspired model for robust emotion recognition. Soft Comput. **21**, 5145–5158 (2017)
4. Albornoz, E.M., Vignolo, L.D., Sarquis, J.A., Leon, E.: Automatic classification of furnariidae species from the paranaense littoral region using speech-related features and machine learning. Ecol. Inform. **38**, 39–49 (2017)
5. Areta, J.I., Pearman, M.: Species limits and clinal variation in a widespread high andean furnariid: the buff-breasted earthcreeper (upcerthia validirostris). Condor **115**(1), 131–142 (2013)

6. Ben-Israel, A., Greville, T.N.E.: Generalized Inverses: Theory and Applications, 2nd edn. Springer, New York (2001). https://doi.org/10.1007/b97366
7. Betts, M., Mitchell, D., Diamond, A., Bêty, J.: Uneven rates of landscape change as a source of bias in roadside wildlife surveys. J. Wildlife Manag. **71**(7), 2266–2273 (2007)
8. Breiman, L.: Random forests. Mach. Learn. **45**(1), 5–32 (2001)
9. Burkart, R., Bárbaro, N., Sánchez, R., Gómez, D.: Eco-Regiones de la Argentina. Administración de Parques Nacionales (APN). Secretaría de Recursos Naturales y Desarrollo Sostenible, Presidencia de la Nación Argentina (1999)
10. Byers, B.E.: Geographic variation of song form within and among chestnut-sided warbler populations. The Auk, pp. 288–299 (1996)
11. Chi, T., Ru, P., Shamma, S.A.: Multiresolution spectrotemporal analysis of complex sounds. J. Acoust. Soc. Am. **118**(2), 887–906 (2005)
12. Contreras, J.R., Agnolin, F., Davies, Y.E., Godoy, I., Giacchino, A., Ríos., E.E.: Atlas ornitogeográfico de la provincia de Formosa. Vazquez Mazzini (2014)
13. Dufour, O., Artieres, T., Glotin, H., Giraudet, P.: Clusterized mel filter cepstral coefficients and support vector machines for bird song identification. In: Soundscape Semiotics - Localization and Categorization. InTech Open Book (2014)
14. Eyben, F., Weninger, F., Gross, F., Schuller, B.: Recent developments in openSMILE, the Munich open-source multimedia feature extractor. In: 21st ACM International Conference on Multimedia, pp. 835–838. Barcelona, Spain, October 2013
15. Fagerlund, S.: Bird species recognition using support vector machines. EURASIP J. Appl. Sig. Process. **2007**(1), 64–64 (2007)
16. Ganchev, T.D., Jahn, O., Marques, M.I., de Figueiredo, J.M., Schuchmann, K.L.: Automated acoustic detection of vanellus chilensis lampronotus. Expert Syst. Appl. **42**(15–16), 6098–6111 (2015)
17. Giannoulis, D., Benetos, E., Stowell, D., Rossignol, M., Lagrange, M., Plumbley, M.D.: Detection and classification of acoustic scenes and events: an IEEE AASP challenge. In: Proceedings of the Workshop on Applications of Signal Processing to Audio and Acoustics (WASPAA)
18. Gütlein, M., Frank, E., Hall, M., Karwath, A.: Large-scale attribute selection using wrappers. In: IEEE Symposium on Computational Intelligence and Data Mining, CIDM 2009, pp. 332–339. IEEE (2009)
19. Harris, C.M.: Absorption of sound in air versus humidity and temperature. J. Acoust. Soc. Am. **40**(1), 148–159 (1966)
20. Hesler, N., Mundry, R., Dabelsteen, T.: Does song repertoire size in common blackbirds play a role in an intra-sexual context? J. Ornithol. **152**(3), 591–601 (2011)
21. Huang, G., Huang, G.B., Song, S., You, K.: Trends in extreme learning machines: a review. Neural Netw. **61**, 32–48 (2015)
22. Huang, G.B., Zhu, Q.Y., Siew, C.K.: Extreme learning machine: theory and applications. Neurocomputing **70**(1–3), 489–501 (2006). https://doi.org/10.1016/j.neucom.2005.12.126
23. ICML International Conference on Proceedings of 1st Workshop on Machine Learning for Bioacoustics - ICML4B (2013). http://sabiod.univ-tln.fr
24. Joly, A., et al.: LifeCLEF 2014: multimedia life species identification challenges. In: Kanoulas, E., et al. (eds.) CLEF 2014. LNCS, vol. 8685, pp. 229–249. Springer, Cham (2014). https://doi.org/10.1007/978-3-319-11382-1_20
25. Keen, S., Ross, J.C., Griffiths, E.T., Lanzone, M., Farnsworth, A.: A comparison of similarity-based approaches in the classification of flight calls of four species of north american wood-warblers (parulidae). Ecol. Inform. **21**, 25–33 (2014)

26. Laje, R., Mindlin, G.B.: Highly structured duets in the song of the south American Hornero. Phys. Rev. Lett. **91**(25), 258104 (2003)
27. Leon, E.J., et al.: Song structure of the golden-billed saltator (saltator auranti-irostris) in the middle parana river floodplain. Bioacoustics **24**(2), 145–152 (2015)
28. Louette, M., Bijnens, L., Upoki Agenong'a, D., Fotso, R.: The utility of birds as bioindicators: case studies in equatorial africa. Belgian J. Zool. **125**(1), 157–165 (1995)
29. Marler, P.: Three models of song learning: evidence from behavior. J. Neurobiol. **33**(5), 501–516 (1997)
30. Narosky, T., Yzurieta, D.: Aves de Argentina y Uruguay-Birds of Argentina & Uruguay: Guía de Identificación Edición Total-A Field Guide Total Edition. Buenos Aires, 16 edn (2010)
31. Päckert, M., Martens, J., Kosuch, J., Nazarenko, A.A., Veith, M.: Phylogenetic signal in the song of crests and kinglets (Aves: Regulus). Evolution **57**(3), 616–629 (2003)
32. Payne, R.B.: Song traditions in indigo buntings: origin, improvisation, dispersal, and extinction in cultural evolution. Ecol. Evol. Acoust. Commun. Birds 198–220 (1996)
33. Planqué, B., Vellinga, W.P.: Xeno-cano.org. http://www.xeno-canto.org. Accessed 10 July 2015
34. Potamitis, I.: Unsupervised dictionary extraction of bird vocalisations and new tools on assessing and visualising bird activity. Ecol. Inform. **26, Part 3**, 6–17 (2015)
35. Potamitis, I., Ntalampiras, S., Jahn, O., Riede, K.: Automatic bird sound detection in long real-field recordings: applications and tools. Appl. Acoust. **80**, 1–9 (2014)
36. Ptacek, L., Machlica, L., Linhart, P., Jaska, P., Muller, L.: Automatic recognition of bird individuals on an open set using as-is recordings. Bioacoustics **25**(1), 1–19 (2015)
37. Raposo, M.A., Höfling, E.: Overestimation of vocal characters in suboscine taxonomy (Aves: Passeriformes: Tyranni): causes and implications. Lundiana **4**(1), 35–42 (2003)
38. Roch, M.A., Soldevilla, M.S., Burtenshaw, J.C., Henderson, E.E., Hildebrand, J.A.: Gaussian mixture model classification of odontocetes in the Southern California bight and the Gulf of California. J. Acoust. Soc. Am. **121**(3), 1737–1748 (2007)
39. Schuller, B., et al.: The INTERSPEECH 2013 Computational Paralinguistics Challenge: Social Signals, Conflict, Emotion, Autism. Proceedings of Interspeech, ISCA, pp. 148–152 (2013)
40. Stowell, D., Plumbley, M.D.: Segregating event streams and noise with a Markov renewal process model. J. Mach. Learn. Res. **14**, 1891–1916 (2013)
41. Towsey, M., Wimmer, J., Williamson, I., Roe, P.: The use of acoustic indices to determine avian species richness in audio-recordings of the environment. Ecol. Inform. **21**, 110–119 (2014)
42. Ventura, T.M., et al.: Audio parameterization with robust frame selection for improved bird identification. Expert Syst. Appl. **42**(22), 8463–8471 (2015)
43. Weninger, F., Eyben, F., Schuller, B.W., Mortillaro, M., Scherer, K.R.: On the acoustics of emotion in audio: what speech, music, and sound have in common. Front. Emot. Sci. **4**(292), 1–12 (2013)

44. Woolley, S.M., Fremouw, T.E., Hsu, A., Theunissen, F.E.: Tuning for spectro-temporal modulations as a mechanism for auditory discrimination of natural sounds. Nature Neurosc. **8**(10), 1371–1379 (2005)
45. Yang, X., Wang, K., Shamma, S.A.: Auditory representations of acoustic signals. IEEE Trans. Inf. Theory **38**(2), 824–839 (1992)
46. Zimmer, K.J., Whittaker, A.: The rufous cacholote (Furnariidae: Pseudoseisura) is two species. Condor **102**(2), 409–422 (2000)
47. Zollinger, S.A., Brumm, H.: Why birds sing loud songs and why they sometimes don't. Anim. Behav. **105**, 289–295 (2015)

Differential Diagnosis of Dengue and Chikungunya in Colombian Children Using Machine Learning

William Caicedo-Torres[1,2(✉)], Ángel Paternina-Caicedo[3],
Hernando Pinzón-Redondo[3,4], and Jairo Gutiérrez[1]

[1] School of Engineering, Computer and Mathematical Sciences,
Auckland University of Technology, Auckland, New Zealand
william.caicedo@aut.ac.nz
[2] Department of Computer Science, Universidad Tecnológica de Bolívar,
Cartagena, Colombia
[3] Hospital Infantil Napoleón Franco Pareja, Cartagena, Colombia
[4] Facultad de Medicina, Universidad de Cartagena, Cartagena, Colombia

Abstract. Dengue and chikungunya are vector borne diseases endemic in tropical countries around the world, with very similar clinical presentation, which makes it hard for physicians to tell them apart. Here we propose the use of Machine Learning based classifiers to perform differential diagnosis of dengue and chikungunya in pediatric patients, using simple blood test results as predictors instead of symptoms. Three variables (platelet count, white cell count and hematocrit percentage) from 447 pediatric patients from Hospital Infantil Napoleón Franco Pareja were collected to construct a dataset, later partitioned into train and test sets using Stratified Random Sampling. Grid Search with Stratified 5-Fold Cross-Validation was conducted to assess the performance of Logistic Regression, Support Vector Machine, and CART Decision Tree classifiers. Cross-Validation results show a L2 Logistic Regression model with second degree polynomial features outperforming the other models considered, with a cross-validated Receiver Operating Characteristic Area Under the Curve (ROC AUC) score of 0.8694. Subsequent results over the test set showed a 0.8502 ROC AUC score. Despite a reduced sample and a heavily imbalanced data set, ROC AUC score results are promising and support our approach for dengue and chikungunya differential diagnosis.

Keywords: Dengue · Chikungunya · Logistic Regression
Support vector machine · Decision Tree · CART

1 Introduction

Dengue and chikungunya are vector borne diseases endemic in tropical countries around the world [1,22]. In the Caribbean and the Americas both diseases co-circulate sharing the same vector (*Aedes Aegypti* and *Aedes Albopictus*). Colombia has been dengue-endemic for decades with a high number of cases [1,9],

© Springer Nature Switzerland AG 2018
G. R. Simari et al. (Eds.): IBERAMIA 2018, LNAI 11238, pp. 181–192, 2018.
https://doi.org/10.1007/978-3-030-03928-8_15

and chikungunya entered the country in 2014, with the first confirmed cases in September of that year [18]. Dengue and chikungunya can be very similar with respect to their clinical presentation [16], although the care needed for each disease can be very different, since dengue can develop into severe dengue or dengue shock syndrome, which can result in death especially in pediatric patients [14]. This latter possibility makes early diagnostic and subsequent monitoring very important in order to adequately manage any dengue related complication that could arise. On the other hand chikungunya infections tend to be self limiting and fatal outcomes are extremely rare, with chronic joint disease as the most common long-term outcome [3]. Dengue virus and Chikungunya virus are RNA viruses [16], which cause infections that present themselves as acute febrile illnesses, with clinical manifestations that overlap with each other. Both diseases cause fever, headache, myalgia and rash [14]. According to some studies, chikungunya patients exhibit shorter duration of fever, conjunctivitis, acute arthritis and rash more prominently [13]; with leukopenia, thrombocytopenia and abdominal pain more commonly associated with dengue diagnosis [13]. Diagnosis in young children (especially for infants under one year of age) is more difficult since arthralgias and other symptoms are not easily identifiable, nor the patient can refer them to medical staff. And while there suggestive clinical signs that might be helpful to diagnose either disease, there is no clinical feature consistent enough to be regarded as definitive for diagnosis. As a result dengue and chikungunya must be included in the differential diagnosis for suspicious patients, and specialized laboratory tests are needed to confirm it. In some settings, these tests are not readily available, negating the possibility of a reliable early diagnosis; which is in itself problematic and hinders the ability of medical staff to offer appropriate care especially for dengue patients, given that their condition might rapidly worsen. It would be extremely useful to have diagnostic tools that could help perform an early, reliable diagnosis based on readily available data. In this way, medical staff in areas where there is no immediate access to sophisticated laboratory tests could monitor closely those patients with a higher likelihood of dengue, offering better, more timely and more appropriate care.

In this paper we compare some Machine Learning models trained using only simple laboratory test results in order to perform early differential diagnosis between dengue and chikungunya in children. We examined popular models as Logistic Regression, Support Vector Machines, and Classification and Regression Trees (CART) to assess their performance at predicting infection by dengue or chikungunya in a pediatric patient. To overcome difficulties associated with eliciting in infants some symptoms routinely used to perform the differential diagnosis, and in contrast with other approaches found in the relevant literature which rely on symptoms as well [14], in this study only platelet level, white cell count and hematocrit levels are used as predictors. Classifier performance is evaluated in terms of their ROC AUC score.

1.1 Related Work

The use of Machine Learning for the differential diagnosis of hemorrhagic fevers goes back to [4], where an Adaptive Resonance Theory Neural Network was trained on Electronic Medical Records (EMR) to perform differential diagnosis between dengue, leptospirosis and malaria in Colombian children. Regarding the use of Machine Learning in dengue, recent literature include the use of Neural Networks for the classification of dengue patients according to their risk of presenting complications [7]. Fathima et al. [8] use Random Forests to discover significant clinical factors that predict dengue infection prognosis. Khan et al. [12] used traditional statistical techniques to identify the factors that predict severe dengue. Potts et al. [21] show the results of applying traditional statistical models to prediction of dengue severity in Thai children using early lab tests. Caicedo et al. [5] compare the performance of several Machine Learning algorithms for early dengue severity prediction in Colombian Children. In the specific case of dengue-chikungunya discrimination, Lee et al. [15] propose the use of statistical/machine learning models to perform differential diagnosis between dengue and chikungunya, but only use Multivariate Logistic Regression and Decision Trees. Furthermore they employ an adult cohort and include clinical symptoms that are not likely to be well elicited from very young children. Laoprasopwattana et al. [13] conducted a prospective study with a small cohort of children in southern Thailand, in which was found that the standard clinical triad (fever, arthralgia, rash) showed 70.6% and 83.3% positive predictive value (precision) and specificity, respectively; under a standard Logistic Regression model. Paternina-Caicedo et al. [19] used a Decision Tree to perform differential diagnosis on a small dataset of children under 24 months of age, with interesting results. It is worth noting that the work presented in this paper offers a broader comparison of learning models and a larger dataset focused on patients under 18 years of age, making use only of simple, readily-available blood tests.

2 Methods and Materials

2.1 Participants

A case-control study was carried out, in order to construct a data set to learn and test a set of classifiers. Cases were defined as children with confirmed diagnosis of chikungunya and controls as children with a confirmed diagnosis of dengue.

Definition of Cases. Cases were prospectively collected between September 22 and December 14, 2014; corresponding to patients under 18 years of age, arriving to Hospital Napoleón Franco Pareja (HINFP) emergency department in Cartagena, Colombia; with acute febrile illness ≤12 days with no dengue infection. Dengue infection was ruled out via IgM and/or NS1 dengue rapid test. If positive, patients were discarded as cases. Only children admitted to the emergency department because of severity were included. Full work-up was performed to rule out other infectious diseases as well. Chikungunya diagnosis was confirmed using real-time polymerase chain reaction (RT-PCR).

Definition of Controls. Controls were retrospectively collected, corresponding to children admitted to HINFP emergency department between November 15, 2013 and August 17, 2014 with confirmed dengue. Patients under 18 years of age arriving to HINFP with acute febrile illness ≤12 days were considered for inclusion. Diagnostic confirmation was made via SD BIOLINE Dengue Duo© IgM and/or NS1 positive rapid test. Full work-up was performed to rule out other infectious diseases as well.

2.2   Dataset

According to study guidelines, 39 cases and 408 controls were finally collected. Input features were selected according to current literature, with simplicity and availability as additional selection criteria, in order to learn models based on features easily available to medical staff in poor or remote areas. According to this, the predictor variables included were platelet count (cells per mm^3), white blood cell count (cells per mm^3) and hematocrit (percentage). All variables were collected at admission to the emergency department. Median age was 0.24 years (Q1–Q3, 0.09–4.22) in patients with chikungunya, and 7.82 years (Q1–Q3, 4.66–10.78) in patients with dengue. Most children with chikungunya were below 5 years of age (n = 30; 76.2%), this is significantly different in the case of children with dengue (n = 112; 27.5%). We included 7/39 (17.9%) neonates with chikungunya, and no cases of neonatal dengue (Table 1).

Table 1. Collected patient data.

Feature	Negative class (dengue)	Positive class (chikungunya)
Median hematocrit (Q1–Q3), %	37 (36.5–38)	38.35 (37.8–39)
Median platelets (Q1–Q3), *per 1,000* cells/mm^3	136.5 (90–198.5)	248 (203–303)
Median white blood cells (Q1–Q3), *per 1,000* cells/mm^3	6.0 (4.5–8.5)	6.25 (4.5–8.6)

After collection and preliminary analysis, 447 patient charts had complete data for the three variables this study considered, and were included into the dataset. Thirty nine children with confirmed chikungunya were finally included, representing 8.72% of all cases, thus showing heavily imbalanced classes. Data was partitioned into disjoint training and test sets, and the training set was then standardized ($\mu = 0, \sigma = 1$). The relevant transformation parameters were stored to be applied later for test set standardization. Partition was performed before standardization to avoid data leakage. Details of training and test sets are shown in Table 2.

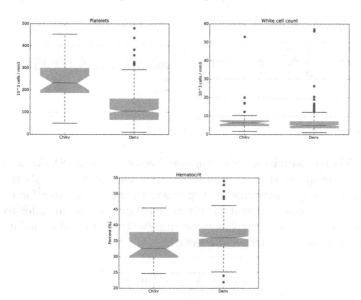

Fig. 1. Box plots by class for platelet count, white cell count, and hematocrit percentage

Table 2. Dataset partition.

Class	Training	Test	Total
Denv	285	123	408
Chikv	27	12	39
Total			**447**

2.3   Learning Models

In this study, several Machine Learning techniques were considered. We used L2 Regularized Logistic Regression with and without polynomial features, Support Vector Machine with Gaussian kernel, and CART Decision Tree classifiers. All models were implemented using the Scikit-Learn Python Machine Learning library [20].

Logistic Regression. Logistic Regression is a classification algorithm [17] that applies a logistic sigmoid function to the output of a linear regression model, restricting it to the interval $(0, 1)$. The output of Logistic Regression can be interpreted as a probability distribution over the classes, i.e. how likely is that the input belongs to the positive class, $p(Y = 1|x; \theta)$. In this study, Logistic Regression was trained by minimizing the negative log-likelihood of the model. L2 regularization is used to account for model complexity and avoid overfitting.

The loss is then

$$min \ -\frac{1}{N} \sum_{i=1}^{N} [y_i logh_\theta(x_i) + (1 - y_i)log(1 - h_\theta(x_i))] + \lambda ||\theta||^2$$

where

$$h_\theta(x) = \frac{1}{1 + e^{-\theta^t x}}$$

Support Vector Machine. The Support Vector Machine (SVM) [6] is a classification model invented in its original form by Vapnik et al. SVMs try to find the maximum margin hyperplane to provide a robust separator for the problem classes while being tolerant of misclassification as well, in order to handle non-linearly separable problems (soft-margin SVM). Its primal formulation minimizes the structural risk to avoid overfitting:

$$min \ \frac{1}{N} \sum_{i=1}^{N} \xi_i + \lambda ||w||^2$$

Subject to:

$$y_i(\boldsymbol{x_i} \cdot w + b) \geq 1 - \xi_i \quad and \quad \xi_i \geq 0, \forall i$$

where

$$\xi_i = max(0, 1 - y_i(w \cdot \boldsymbol{x_i} + b)), \text{ the hinge loss.}$$

The Lagrangian dual of the optimization problem is

$$max_\alpha \ \sum_{i=1}^{N} \alpha_i - \frac{1}{2} \sum_{i=1}^{N} \sum_{j=1}^{N} y_i\alpha_i(\boldsymbol{x_i} \cdot \boldsymbol{x_j})y_j\alpha_j$$

Subject to:

$$\sum_{i=1}^{N} \alpha_i y_i = 0 \quad and \quad 0 \leq \alpha_i \leq \frac{1}{2n\lambda}, \forall i$$

The dual formulation reveals that some inputs have non-zero associated Lagrangian Multipliers (α), meaning that their corresponding constraints are "active", so they lie on the classification margin; hence the name support vectors.

The solution to the dual (optimal multipliers $\{\alpha_{i,o}\}_{i=1}^{l}$) allows us to formulate the maximum margin hyperplane for classification. The optimal weight vector is given by

$$\boldsymbol{w_o} = \sum_{i=1}^{l} \alpha_{i,o} y_i \boldsymbol{x_i}$$

so the hyperplane is then

$$\boldsymbol{w_o^t} \boldsymbol{x} + b_o = \sum_{i=1}^{l} \alpha_{i,o} y_i \boldsymbol{x_i} \cdot \boldsymbol{x} + b_o = 0$$

The SVM formulation can be generalized to handle non-linear decision boundaries, by getting advantage of its structure. The dot product $x_i \cdot x_j$ can be replaced by a dot product of transforms of the original inputs, $\phi(x_i) \cdot \phi(x)$. The Kernel trick [6] provides a way to compute the dot product without computing the transformation ϕ explicitly, via Kernel functions; which by definition represent dot products in high dimensional spaces [6]. In this way, the SVM can handle high dimensional feature transformations with computational efficiency, with good regularization. We used for our experiments the Gaussian Kernel $K(x_i, x_j) = exp(-\frac{||x_i - x_j||^2}{2\sigma^2})$.

CART. Classification And Regression Trees (CART) [2] is a non-parametric Machine Learning technique that learns decision rules from a dataset, and said rules can be arranged in a tree-like structure in order to predict a target variable. CART recursively partitions the data space in rectangular regions, choosing the dimension to split that minimizes the impurity of the resulting regions. To measure such impurity several functions exist, being Entropy and Gini Index some popular ones. Impurity of node t, $i(t) = \phi[p(1|t), p(2|t), \ldots, p(K|t)]$, is a non-negative, symmetric function defined on the set of all K-tuples $[p(1|t), p(2|t), \ldots, p(K|t)]$, where $p(j|t) \geq 0$ is the proportion of training samples which belong to class j in node t. Additionally $\sum_{j=1}^{K} p(j|t) = 1$. The function maximum is achieved when all $p(j|t) = 1/K$, and its minimum when $p(j|t) = 1$ for some j. Specifically, the Gini Index [2] is an impurity function defined as

$$i(t) = 1 - \sum_{j=1}^{K} p^2(j|t)$$

Moreover, the change in impurity after a given split is

$$\Delta i(t) = i(t_p) - P_l i(t_l) - P_r i(t_r)$$

At each node CART will try to solve the following optimization problem

$$\max_{x_j \leq x_j^R, j=1,\ldots,M} [i(t_p) - P_l i(t_l) - P_r i(t_r)]$$

where t_p is the current node (parent), t_l and t_r are respectively the left and right children nodes. P_l and P_r are the fraction of training samples that go to the left and right node, in that order. In other words, CART will search through all values of all dimensions of the data space in order to find the best split rule $x_j \leq x_j^R$ (i.e. if true go to the left node, if not go to the right one) which will maximize the (negative) change in impurity. If we select the Gini Index as our impurity function, the optimization problem for CART will be

$$\max_{x_j \leq x_j^R, j=1,\ldots,M} [-\sum_{j=1}^{K} p^2(j|t_p) + P_l \sum_{j=1}^{K} p^2(j|t_l) + P_r \sum_{j=1}^{K} p^2(j|t_r)]$$

This procedure will recur until certain stopping condition is met. Various conditions as reaching a maximum tree depth or reaching a minimum number of samples in a node, can be employed.

3   Results

Models were learned and performance was cross-validated using the training set, which represents 70% of the original dataset. The model with best performance was then tested on the remaining 30%. Procedures and results are presented next.

3.1   Training and Validation

All learning models were trained using 5-Fold Stratified Cross-Validation. We report ROC AUC results using the whole predictor set. All model hyperparameters were selected via Grid Search. For logistic regression models, we considered the original dataset variables and additional second degree polynomial features, using Grid Search. Best performance was exhibited by a model comprised of all original features plus cross-terms, i.e. a second degree model without the quadratic terms; and a regularization factor (λ) of 990.001. For this study a Gaussian Kernel was selected given it can generate an infinite dimensional transformation of the input, yet it reduces to linear behavior if needed [11]. Our classifier was trained with parameters $\gamma = 0.101019$ and cost $C = 0.02021$. Figure 2 shows results for Logistic Regression and SVM models. Results for a CART decision tree are shown in Fig. 3. Different separation criteria were tested to be used by the algorithm to build trees (gini and entropy), and gini criterion offered best Cross-Validation results.

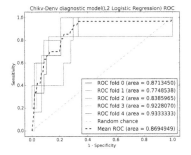 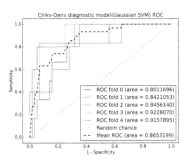

Fig. 2. L2 Regularized Logistic Regression, second degree transform with cross-terms and no quadratic features ($\lambda = 990.001$) and SVM with Gaussian Kernel ($\gamma = 0.101019, C = 0.02021$).

3.2   Test

Table 3 shows Cross-Validation results for each classifier. According to these, Logistic Regression with L2 regularization ($\lambda = 990.001$) outperformed the other models (ROC AUC $= 0.8694$), with the Gaussian SVM very close behind (ROC

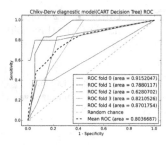

Fig. 3. CART Decision Tree.

AUC = 0.8653). We decided then to assess the Logistic Regression classifier performance on the test set considering that albeit the performance advantage is slight, Logistic Regression is a more interpretable model than the Gaussian SVM, which is a desirable feature in medical diagnostic problems. ROC AUC Results are shown in Fig. 4 and the confusion matrix for thresholds zero can be found in Table 4.

Table 3. 5-Fold Cross-validation results for each model. L2 Logistic Regression with cross-terms comes on top with a 0.8694 ROC AUC.

Model	Parameters	ROC AUC
L2 Logistic Regression	$\lambda = 990.001$	**0.8694**
Gaussian SVM	$\gamma = 0.101019, C = 0.02021$	0.8653
CART	Partition by gini	0.8036

4 Discussion

Cross-Validation results show Logistic Regression offering a slight edge over the Gaussian SVM in terms of ROC AUC score. A CART decision tree came third, and while being a very interpretable model (which is why it tends to be favored by clinical staff), in this case it offered results a bit far from the Logistic Regression and the SVM performance. The Logistic Regression model structure shows platelets as the most single important predictor (higher platelet count pushes the classifier towards predicting chikungunya). White cell count and its interaction with platelet count bias the prediction towards chikungunya as well. On the other hand, hematocrit percentage and its interactions with other features correlate with dengue (Table 5).

It is interesting that test results are very close to the Cross-Validation ones for Logistic Regression. A test ROC AUC of 0.8502 shows a good performance, with 91.66% sensitivity and 64.23% specificity at zero threshold. This despite an imbalanced data set and only considering simple blood test results and no additional clinical features.

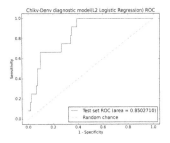

Fig. 4. L2 Logistic Regression test results.

Table 4. L2 Logistic Regression test confusion matrix (zero threshold).

		Predicted	
		Dengue	Chikungunya
Actual	Dengue	79(64.23%)	44(35.77%)
	Chikungunya	1(8.33%)	11(91.66%)

Table 5. Logistic Regression coefficients.

Feature	Coefficient value
Intercept	−0.02261886
Platelets	0.15605011
Hematocrit	−0.04225827
White Cells	0.03496771
Platelets - hematocrit interaction	−0.05628708
Platelets - white cells interaction	0.04335795
Hematocrit - white cells interaction	−0.00753848

4.1 Limitations

This study has some limitations. The dataset is heavily imbalanced, as chikungunya class has low size (8.72%) compared to dengue class (91.28%); which affects the generalization ability of our models. Also, our assumption of missing-at-random data can be erroneous, hence the dataset might be biased and our results would not hold for further validation. The tests used to diagnose patients possess good sensitivity and specificity, reason for which they are standard tools in the practice. However it is possible (however unlikely) that given the error margins of lab tests, we could have wrong labeled instances on our dataset.

5 Conclusions and Future Work

Dengue and chikungunya are endemic diseases in the Caribbean and Americas and their presentation can be very similar in terms of clinical features. In this paper, a Machine Learning based approach to the differential diagnosis of dengue and chikungunya was proposed. Three variables (platelet count, white cell count and hematocrit percentage) from pediatric patients of Hospital Infantil Napoleón Franco Pareja in Cartagena - Colombia were collected and used to train and validate several classification models. Regularization and class weighting were used in order to overcome poor classification results and avoid overfitting. 5-Fold Stratified Cross-Validation results show good prediction capabilities and a model based on a L2 Logistic Regression classifier offered the best results measured by Receiver Operating Characteristic Area Under the Curve score (validation-AUC = 0.8694, test-AUC = 0.8502), with platelet levels being the most significant predictor. Results obtained are promising and support the validity of the approach. Future work could include a multi-centre study to validate our results with a more heterogeneous patient population, and the use of a larger patient population to be able to apply higher variance models as Deep Neural Networks [10].

References

1. Bhatt, S., et al.: The global distribution and burden of dengue. Nature **496**(7446), 504–507 (2013). https://doi.org/10.1038/nature12060, http://www.ncbi.nlm.nih.gov/pmc/articles/PMC3651993/
2. Breiman, L., Friedman, J., Olshen, R., Stone, C.: Classification and Regression Trees. Wadsworth and Brooks, Monterey (1984)
3. Caglioti, C., Lalle, E., Castilletti, C., Carletti, F., Capobianchi, M.R., Bordi, L.: Chikungunya virus infection: an overview. New Microbiologica **36**(3), 211–227 (2013). http://www.newmicrobiologica.org/PUB/allegati_pdf/2013/3/211.pdf
4. Caicedo, W., Quintana, M., Pinzón, H.: Differential diagnosis of hemorrhagic fevers using ARTMAP. In: Pavón, J., Duque-Méndez, N.D., Fuentes-Fernández, R. (eds.) IBERAMIA 2012. LNCS (LNAI), vol. 7637, pp. 221–230. Springer, Heidelberg (2012). https://doi.org/10.1007/978-3-642-34654-5_23
5. Caicedo-Torres, W., Paternina, Á., Pinzón, H.: Machine learning models for early dengue severity prediction. In: Montes-y-Gómez, M., Escalante, H.J., Segura, A., Murillo, J.D. (eds.) IBERAMIA 2016. LNCS (LNAI), vol. 10022, pp. 247–258. Springer, Cham (2016). https://doi.org/10.1007/978-3-319-47955-2_21
6. Cortes, C., Vapnik, V.: Support-vector networks. Mach. Learn. **20**(3), 273–297 (1995). https://doi.org/10.1007/BF00994018
7. Faisal, T., Taib, M.N., Ibrahim, F.: Neural network diagnostic system for dengue patients risk classification. J. Med. Syst. **36**(2), 661–676 (2012). https://doi.org/10.1007/s10916-010-9532-x
8. Shameem Fathima, A., Manimeglai, D.: Analysis of significant factors for dengue infection prognosis using the random forest classifier. Int. J. Adv. Comput. Sci. Appl. (IJACSA) **6**(2) (2015). https://doi.org/10.14569/IJACSA.2015.060235
9. Fullerton, L.M., Dickin, S.K., Schuster-Wallace, C.J.: Mapping global vulnerability to dengue using the water associated disease index. Technical report, United Nations University (2014)
10. Goodfellow, I., Bengio, Y., Courville, A.: Deep Learning. MIT Press, Cambridge (2016). http://www.deeplearningbook.org
11. Keerthi, S.S., Lin, C.J.: Asymptotic behaviors of support vector machines with Gaussian kernel. Neural Comput. **15**(7), 1667–1689 (2003). https://doi.org/10.1162/089976603321891855
12. Khan, M.I.H., et al.: Factors predicting severe dengue in patients with dengue fever. Mediterr. J. Hematol. Infect. Diseases **5**(1) (2013)

13. Laoprasopwattana, K., Kaewjungwad, L., Jarumanokul, R., Geater, A.: Differential diagnosis of chikungunya, dengue viral infection and other acute febrile illnesses in children. Pediatr. Infect. Disease J. **31**(5) (2012). http://journals.lww.com/pidj/ Fulltext/2012/05000/Differential_Diagnosis_of_Chikungunya,_Dengue.8.aspx
14. Lee, V.J., et al.: Simple clinical and laboratory predictors of chikungunya versus dengue infections in adults. PLoS Negl. Trop. Diseases **6**(9), 1–9 (2012). https:// doi.org/10.1371/journal.pntd.0001786
15. Lee, V.J., et al.: Simple clinical and laboratory predictors of chikungunya versus dengue infections in adults. PLoS Negl. Trop. Diseases **6**(9), e1786 (2012). https://doi.org/10.1371/journal.pntd.0001786, http://www.ncbi.nlm.nih. gov/pmc/articles/PMC3459852/
16. Mardekian, S.K., Roberts, A.L.: Diagnostic options and challenges for dengue and chikungunya viruses. BioMed. Res. Int. **2015**, 834371 (2015). https://doi.org/10. 1155/2015/834371. http://www.ncbi.nlm.nih.gov/pmc/articles/PMC4609775/
17. McCullagh, P., Nelder, J.: Generalized Linear Models. Chapman & Hall/CRC Monographs on Statistics & Applied Probability, 2nd edn. Taylor & Francis, Boa Raton (1989). https://books.google.co.uk/books?id=h9kFH2_FfBkC
18. Pan American Health Organization: Chikungunya: Statistical Data (2014). http:// www.paho.org/hq/index.php?option=com_topics&view=readall&cid=5932& Itemid=40931&lang=en. Accessed 29 Feb 2016
19. Paternina-Caicedo, A., et al.: Features of dengue and chikungunya infections of Colombian children under 24 months of age admitted to the emergency department. J. Trop. Pediatr. (2017). https://doi.org/10.1093/tropej/fmx024
20. Pedregosa, F., et al.: Scikit-learn: machine learning in Python. J. Mach. Learn. Res. **12**, 2825–2830 (2011)
21. Potts, J.A., et al.: Prediction of dengue disease severity among pediatric Thai patients using early clinical laboratory indicators. PLoS Negl. Trop. Dis. **4**(8), e769 (2010)
22. World Health Organization: Chikungunya (2015). http://www.who.int/ mediacentre/factsheets/fs327/en/. Accessed 29 Feb 2016

Supervised and Unsupervised Identification of Concept Drifts in Data Streams of Seismic-Volcanic Signals

Paola Alexandra Castro-Cabrera[1]([⊠]), Mauricio Orozco-Alzate[1],
Cesar Germán Castellanos-Domínguez[1], Fernando Huenupán[2],
and Luis Enrique Franco[3]

[1] Universidad Nacional de Colombia - Sede Manizales, Manizales, Colombia
{pacastroc,morozcoa,cgcastellanosd}@unal.edu.co
[2] Universidad de la Frontera (UFRO), Temuco, Chile
[3] Observatorio Vulcanológico de los Andes del Sur, Temuco, Chile

Abstract. The volcanic activity analysis by means of seismic signals is a scenario typically treated by studies in the Artificial Intelligence area under the assumption of invariant probability distribution over time. The literature in geophysics, on the other hand, qualitatively claims that the volcanic phenomenon evolves over long periods of time. This article shows, by three methods, one supervised and two unsupervised, the existence of significant changes in the intrinsic components of the data (*concept drifts*) generated within the volcanic phenomenon. Here it is also shown how the performance of a learning model is considerably affected in a classification task, when concept drifts are not treated in the analysis of a volcanic environment.

Keywords: Data stream · Change detection · Concept drift
Artificial Intelligence · Seismic signal · Volcanology

1 Introduction

The Signal Processing and Artificial Intelligence techniques can rarely be applied in a direct way to data from real-world applications. In dynamic environments, the properties of the generated data are usually time-varying; situation that should be handled with assumptions in order to fit the reality to theoretical frameworks. The most common assumption is that historical data come from the same distribution when actually they tend to change over time, condition known as *concept drift* [5]. Many sensor-based applications generate an increasing volume of data that must be continuously stored and analyzed. In such *data stream* environments, data arrive continuously, and concept drifts cause that patterns and relations in data evolve over time. Then, predictive models designed for either classification or regression tasks in those environments, may become obsolete due to changes in underlying physical processes or in the environment itself [11].

© Springer Nature Switzerland AG 2018
G. R. Simari et al. (Eds.): IBERAMIA 2018, LNAI 11238, pp. 193–205, 2018.
https://doi.org/10.1007/978-3-030-03928-8_16

Volcanic monitoring and the evaluation of the associated risks are issues of continuous study due to the vital importance of risk mitigation related to volcanic unrest. Nowadays, most of the active volcanoes around the world are monitored through different techniques such as geodesy, geochemistry, magnetometry, and specially, through seismological measurements. Seismic signals are the result of particular processes inside the volcano and, therefore, can be used to understand the volcanic phenomenon [1]. Consequently, based on the geophysical literature [1,9,15], the volcanic phenomenon and especially its monitoring by seismology, may be defined as a data stream and changing environment; however, no reference in the engineering area was found where such drifts are quantified or at least identified.

During the last two decades, Machine Learning studies have provided tools and techniques to face the challenge of the volcanic monitoring, by facilitating a time-consuming and repetitive task such as, for instance, the identification of categories and label assignment of registered seismic events. Applications of methods such as Hidden Markov Models, Artificial Neural Networks, Support Vector Machines, among others (see details in [10]), have shown satisfactory results in the state-of-the-art. However, these have been achieved with basic experimental configurations, that is, with small samples sizes taken in a short period of volcanic activity, and without taking into account the chronological order of the examples. Under this arrangement, it is difficult to identify drifts in the volcanic dynamics and, consequently, the classification performance might deteriorate once the learning model is deployed on-line.

This paper is aimed to demonstrate the existence of concept drifts in the volcanic phenomenon, exhibited in its seismic recordings. We maintained the chronological order of the examples to simulate an on-line situation. We use a straightforward supervised method that evaluates the performance of a classifier by its accuracy over time (called DDM). We also tested this hypothesis without the use of class labels through a semi-parametric method of log-likelihood (called SPLL). Additionally, we present a simple but direct method to identify time periods in which there is a change of a so-called *context* (components of an environment with a common dynamics), based on a sum of distances generated with the k nearest neighbor (k-NN) rule. As an illustrative case, this work analyzes the alterations of the dynamics of Villarrica volcano (Chile) over time from its seismic recordings.

2   Concept Drift

In non-stationary environments, the distribution that generates the data can change over time, yielding a phenomenon known as *concept drift*. This scenario requires a different treatment to the traditional one when facing learning tasks. The formal definition of concept drift between times t_0 and t_1 is [5]:

$$\exists \mathbf{x} : p\left(\mathbf{x}, y\right)_{t_0} \neq p\left(\mathbf{x}, y\right)_{t_1} \tag{1}$$

where $p\left(\mathbf{x}, y\right)_{t_0}$ and $p\left(\mathbf{x}, y\right)_{t_1}$ are the joint distributions at times t_0 and t_1, respectively; $\mathbf{x}$ is a vector of input data (an observation or example), and y is the target variable, that for our case is the vector of class labels. In general terms, there is a concept drift if any component of this relation is altered, that is: (1) if the class prior probability $p(y)$ changes, or (2) if the class conditional probability $p(\mathbf{x}|y)$ changes. In consequence, the prediction is affected because the posterior probability of classes $p(y|\mathbf{x})$ may change. In this case, the drift is considered as *real*. Other kinds of concept drifts can be found in [5].

In recent years, the study of change detection in data streams has become more extensive because of its potential applications in real scenarios such as network traffic control, market analysis, fraud detection, medical condition monitoring, among others [5]. This is because most of this contexts may be environments where new sources of data generation arise, and where the new yielded data are detected and react to changes.

3   Methods

3.1   The Drift Detection Method (DDM)

We use the general framework (instead of the experimental one) proposed in [4], denominated drift detection method (DDM). The aim of the proposed method is to detect new *"contexts"*, by understanding them as sequences of examples with a stationary distribution. According to DDM, a change in the data distribution occurs when the error increases until reaching a warning level at observation n_i, and a drift level at observation n_j, where $i < j$, in a sequence of n observations. For each point of the sequence, the error rate (E_i) is the probability of misclassification, with standard deviation defined as $s_i = \sqrt{E_i \left(1 - E_i\right)/i}$. Machine Learning theory assumes that, if the data distribution is stationary, the error of a learning model will reduce when the number of observations grows.

3.2   The Semi-parametric Log-Likelihood Detector (SPLL)

The semi-parametric log-likelihood detector (SPLL), proposed in [7], is a method that comes from joining the benefits of two log-likelihood frameworks, namely, the Kullback-Leibler (K-L) criterion and the Hotelling's t^2 test, but overcoming the weaknesses of both criteria and with a greater computational simplicity.

SPLL assumes that all the data come from the same distribution, generated from a Gaussian mixture $p_1(\mathbf{x})$, corresponding to the number of classes or categories (denoted as c), with the same covariance matrix. Two data windows are defined, W_1 and W_2. In the first one, the parameters of the Gaussian mixture are estimated, while in W_2 the change detection criterion is derived using an upper bound of the log-likelihood, which is one standard deviation of the mean of the criterion value in case the two distributions are the same. The criterion is calculated as follows:

$$SPLL\left(W_1, W_2\right) = \frac{1}{M_2} \sum_{\mathbf{x} \in W_2} \left(\mathbf{x} - \mu_{i*}\right)^{\mathrm{T}} \Sigma^{-1} \left(\mathbf{x} - \mu_{i*}\right) \tag{2}$$

where $i* = \arg\min\limits_{i=1}^{c} \left\{ (\mathbf{x} - \mu_i)^{\mathrm{T}} \Sigma^{-1} (\mathbf{x} - \mu_i) \right\}$ is the index of the component with the smallest squared Mahalanobis distance between $\mathbf{x}$ and its center, and M_2 as the amount of observations in W_2.

3.3   Sum of the Distances to the Nearest Neighbor

We propose to represent the differences between observation sets (or batches) through distances by using the k-NN rule with its simplest case: $k = 1$. We do not developed the k-NN rule as far as the label assignment but only until the storing of the distance measured between each observation of the test set and its nearest neighbor, using the Euclidean distance (d_{L_2}) as metric. Within a more formal definition, let $\mathbf{x}_i$ be one observation from the training set and $\mathbf{x}'_j$ one observation from the test set, with $i = 1, ..., N$ and $j = 1, ..., M$.

The distance $D_{1\text{-}NN_j}$ defined for each $\mathbf{x}'_j$ is $D_{1\text{-}NN_j} = \min \left\{ d_{L_2} \left(\mathbf{x}'_j, \mathbf{x}_i \right) \right\}$, and finally, the batch distance is computed as: $D_{Batch} = \sum\limits_{j=1}^{M} D_{1\text{-}NN_j}$.

In summary, for a batch formed by a sliding window of test data, if we add those distances from each observation $\mathbf{x}'_j$ to the one responsible of assigning the label, we can estimate how far the test points are from the training set.

4   Experimental Setup

4.1   Data Set Description

The data used for the experiments are composed by seismic signals from the Villarrica volcano, Chile. This volcano has a seismological network with eight stations which are monitored by *Observatorio Volcanológico de Los Andes del Sur* (OVDAS), located in Temuco and belonging to the *Servicio Nacional de Geología y Minería* of Chile.

The OVDAS distinguishes 9 types of events, whose class labels are assigned by trained analysts, guided by, among others, the visual definition of parameters on the shape and spectral content of the signal, namely: Volcano-Tectonic (VT), Long Period (LP), Tremor (TR), Hybrid (HB), Ice Quakes (IC), Very Long Period (VLP), "Tornillos" (TO), Volcano Distal (DVT) and Tectonics-Seismic events (non-volcanic earthquakes); see a typical description of them in [9]. Three types of seismic events predominate in the seismic activity of Villarrica volcano: LP, TR and VT events, which are considered the most characteristic ones. Therefore, we considered these three classes of events for the experiments. The employed dataset includes seismic signals recorded during 7.3 years (from January 2010 to April 2017), with a total of $317,648$ labeled events, distributed into the three classes as follows: LP $- 251,123$; TR $- 55,271$ and VT $- 2,081$ records. Each class was divided into two groups, one used for training and the other one for testing, depending on the time stamps of the seismic events, as explained in Sect. 4.3.

4.2 Data Processing

Pre-processing. In this work, only records from the vertical axis (Z) of the reference station (triaxial broadband seismometer) assigned by the OVDAS were considered due to its better signal/noise ratio (SNR), compared to the registers from the other two horizontal axes (N, E). Additionally, a data cleansing was carried out, excluding those registers with a low SNR or because the reference station was out of service, remaining a total of $260, 365$ records. Next, the records were filtered with a Butterworth band-pass filter of order 10 between 0.5 and 15 Hz, because most of the meaningful energy of the events is in this frequency band. After this pre-processing, the number of labeled events per class is: LP $-$ $222, 441$; TR $-$ $37, 735$ and VT $-$ 189 records.

Feature Extraction. In this stage several parameters were computed which, according to the literature, have shown to be beneficial for classification tasks. They can be grouped into three families according to the information that they represent:

1. Morphological and geophysical features: those that provide information about the nature of the events; some of them are used by experts in manual classification: signal impulsiveness, event duration and number of zero crossings (dominant frequency of the signal within the trigger time window) [13].
2. Spectral features: which are obtained by converting the seismic register (considered as a time series) into the frequency domain using the Fourier Transform. They are: dominant frequency, mean of the 5 largest frequency peaks and pitch [2]. Other ones were obtained from the spectrogram: frequency range defined by the spectral contour, frequency of spectral contour centroid and frequency of the energy maximum in the spectrogram [13].
3. Transformed feature spaces: These features are obtained through transformations of either the signal waveform or the characterized signal to a domain different from the original one. The features obtained by transformations are: Wavelet energy from level 1 to 7 [2], 5 linear prediction coefficients (LPCs) [3] and 13 cepstral coefficients [6] (see equations of the features in the cited references).

After dividing the whole set into training and test sets, the extracted features were normalized by subtracting the mean (μ) and dividing by the standard deviation (**s**) of the training set. Next, μ and **s** were used to normalize the test set. The characterized dataset was formed storing data in a matrix of $260, 365$ rows (characterized events) and 34 columns (features).

Feature Selection. In order to find a subset of relevant features that provide greater discrimination in the classification task, we chose a traditional filter-type method called Relief, which uses a criterion independent from the learning algorithm, and provides a feature ranking according to their estimated relevance.

The Relief algorithm defines the quality of a feature (as strongly relevant) according to how well it distinguishes between two examples of different classes and, based on this criterion, it assigns the weight for each feature. However, the original version of Relief is limited because it cannot deal with incomplete data and only works for two-class problems. Its extended version, called ReliefF, is able to solve the aforementioned problems and other additional ones. The ReliefF algorithm searches for a nearest neighbor for each class and finds the feature weights penalizing the ones that give different values to neighbors of the same class, and rewards the features that give different values to neighbors of different classes (see more details in [12]).

Applying the ReliefF algorithm, the initial set of 34 features was reduced to 4, namely: mean of the 5 largest frequency peaks, event duration and wavelet energy at the levels 7 and 2.

4.3   Experiments

Three different methods were applied to demonstrate that the volcanic phenomenon is a changing environment where there are concept drifts, which are observable in the evolution of the seismic data over time.

Definition of Experimental Periods. Authors in geophysics have indicated that alterations in the records of volcanic signals, in relation to other indicators such as geochemical or geodesic parameters (among others), contribute to determine a possible instability period in the dynamics of a volcano, or are even precursors of eruptions [1,15]. In the case of volcanic seismology, the periods of variations in the internal dynamics of a volcano could generate underlying changes, which are evident in indicators such as changes in the number of recorded events, changes in the signal signatures and their intrinsic components (usually the frequency ones), among others [1]. Since the aim of this work is to identify a concept drift in volcanic phenomenon, it was necessary to acquire a priori knowledge about the dynamics of volcanic activity through the records of seismic signals in order to recognize such periods in time series processed with change detection algorithms.

Since the last major eruptions (1984–1985 and 1991 [16]), Villarrica volcano has established a "background" seismic activity, which, in several occasions and for short periods, has increased its levels, but without necessarily ending in an eruptive crisis (the most recent eruption was on March 3, 2015). Such a background activity is permanently studied by the OVDAS. The seismic activity is usually measured by volcanological observatories in terms of Real-Time Seismic Amplitude Measurements (RSAM), Spectral Seismic Amplitude Measurement (SSAM), Reduced Desplacement (RD), Local Magnitude (ML), and number/energy of the events [1]. Since the volcanic activity is dominated by fluid activity (LP and TR), a baseline level measured with the RD could be considered when it is below $10\,cm^2$ and RSAM varies between 8 and 20 units [14].

According to the analysis carried out by the OVDAS experts about the seismic activity recorded in the Villarrica volcano from 2010 onwards, periods of volcanic stability and instability were defined in coherence with a study of records obtained in the geochemical area. These definitions were based on the congruence of either low or high levels of parameters such as number of daily events recorded per class, RSAM, SSAM and RD −in seismology− and levels of SO_2 −in geochemistry. Thus, the defined periods were:

- Stability: January 1, 2013 to December 31, 2013 (hereinafter referred to as the "Stability Period" frame (*SP frame*)), with 13, 857 examples, from which 9, 762 are LP, 4, 065 are TR and 30 are VT.
- Instability: June 1, 2014 to April 21, 2017 (hereinafter referred to as the "Instability Period" frame (*IP frame*)), with 213, 301 examples, from which 195, 941 are LP, 17, 297 are TR and 63 are VT.

Experiment 1. In Machine Learning, concept drifts are often managed either with weighted examples according to their age or with sliding time windows; in this case, we use the last option, with windows W of fixed size. The experimental procedure (see Sect. 3.1) was developed as in [4] and is summarized as follows:

1. As learning model, we use the k-NN classifier, where the optimal number of neighbors was defined heuristically, testing with $k = \{1, 3, 5, 7, 9, 11\}$ and keeping the W size fixed.
2. The examples were chronologically ordered to emulate the data stream context where new examples arrive to be processed consecutively. The observations within the *IP frame* were arranged as the training set, and those belonging to the *SP frame* as test set.
3. The learning model is generated from training data, and the validation is carried out n times with W_n sliding windows that move over the *IP frame* with an overlap of $\alpha\%$ and a window size M, where, $n = \{1, 2, 3, ..., N\}$, with N equals to the number of times that the window W of size M fits within the *IP frame*. For this experiment, we iteratively tested with $\alpha = \{20, 50, 80\}$ and $M = \{100, 200, 300, ..., N_{SP}\}$, where N_{SP} is the maximum number of examples belonging to the *SP frame* that fit in a single window.

Experiment 2. This test demonstrates how the seismic data of volcanic origin suffer changes in their distribution when they evolve over time, moving from a period of stable activity to a period of volcanic crisis that ended up with an eruption. This test is carried out through the SPLL criterion proposed in [7].

The procedure to implement this experiment was the following:

1. Given two (2) sliding data windows $W1$ and $W2$, a clustering is carried out on $W1$ into cl clusters applying the k-Means algorithm, with $k = 3$ as suggested in [8].
2. A weighted intra-cluster covariance matrix S is calculated.

3. The squared Mahalanobis distance is computed for each example in $W2$ with respect to the cluster centroids.
4. Calculate $SPLL(W1, W2)$, by using Eq. 2, as the mean of the minimum distances computed previously.
5. Swap windows $W1$ and $W2$ and repeat from step 1 to 4: $SPLL(W2, W1)$.
6. Take the maximum of the two values calculated in steps 4 and 5, and find out its chi-squared distribution to define the p-value.

The following considerations were taken into account for executing the experiment:

– Windows $W1$ and $W2$ were defined under the assumption that each one comes from two different probability mass functions. For this purpose, $W2$ was located at the beginning of the *IP frame*, and slided with an overlap $\alpha\%$. $W1$ was set to a fixed single window, centered within the *SP frame*. We ran experiments with $\alpha = \{20, 50, 80\}$.
– The size of the windows is a sensitive parameter in the performance of any change detection algorithm [4,7], so we tested exhaustively with different sizes. Proportional sizes were established for $W1$ and $W2$ windows as suggested in [7] and [8], respectively: $|W1| = |W2|$ and $|W1| = 2 * |W2|$.
– We iteratively tried with different window sizes, $M = \{100, 200, 300, ..., N_{SP}\}$, where N_{SP} is the maximum number of examples belonging to the *SP frame* that fit in a single window. We kept $cl = 3$ for the number of clusters, as recommended in [8].

Experiment 3. With this experiment we intend to show the temporal changes that can occur in the data of a recent period with respect to a previous one, making use of a distance (see Sect. 3.3). Given a window of previously unseen data, $W2$, which arrives in chronological order (test set), a sum of the distances is done from each of them to the prototype responsible for the label assignment in a 1-NN rule. This will serve as an estimation of how much the test data differ (proportional to how far they are) from the prototypes belonging to $W1$ (P_{W1}), where $W1$ is a data window assumed coming from the same distribution, and $i = \{1, 2, 3, ..., |W1|\}$.

For the execution of this experiment, the following considerations were taken into account:

1. As $W1$, a fixed window consisting of the data located in the *SP frame* was defined. $W2$ is a sliding window that moves across the *IP frame*, according to an overlap of $\alpha\%$. Here we tested with $\alpha = \{20, 50, 80\}$.
2. Calculate the distance from each point of $W2$ to its nearest neighbor, using the Euclidean distance as a metric: $D_{1\text{-}NN} = \min\left(d_{L_2}(X_{W2}, P_{W1})\right)$.
3. A representative value for each sliding window $W2$ is obtained from the sum of all the distances calculated for each (X_{W2}).

5   Results and Discussion

In this section, we evaluate the dynamics of the seismic volcanic activity in three different ways in order to determine whether or not there is a concept drift in this environment and, therefore, consider the need for a change detection stage in a classification task. It is not the aim of this article to compare the results for defining the best method for change detection, nor distinguishing between gradual or abrupt changes. The objective is just to obtain evidence of the presence of factors that generate changes in the volcano dynamics.

In order to validate the method used in the first experiment, we employed 13, 857 chronologically ordered observations to train the model, which belong to a period of "quietness" in the volcanic activity, and tested with 4, 625 different test sets with 100 observations ($M = 100$ was the chosen window size because it showed the best resolution in the time), which resulted in sliding the time window with an overlap of $\alpha = 50\%$, that is, forgetting 50 observations for each new test set and including 50 new ones, also chronologically ordered. After trying with different values for k in the k-NN rule, we saw that the performance of the classifier did not show much difference. Results for $k = 1$ are shown below.

Figure 1 shows the deterioration of the classifier performance when the data stream grows and facing an atypical period that produces data generated by a different probability density function. The graph illustrates the predictive error curve pointing out episodes of importance in volcano activity. It is observed how the misclassification shows a significant increase centered between January and May of 2015, period in which the last eruptive crisis took place, which led to the eruption of March 3 of the same year. The error rate of the months of "quietness" of the volcanic activity rose from a maximum of 4% to 27% during the months that the critical phase occurred. Between June and August 2014 there was an important rise of the LP type seismicity (these annotations are documented in reports generated by the OVDAS found in [14]); this period requires a further examination. The last statements are based on the statistical theory which indicates that, if the class distribution is stationary, then the error of the decision model will reduce while the examples increase [4]. Therefore, a significant rise of the error rate of the learning algorithm performance suggests a change in the class distribution and that, consequently, the decision model used has become obsolete. Then, this experiment shows the importance of adding a detection change stage and making a concept drift handling within a classification task.

The subsequent two experiments show that such a change in the volcanic seismology dynamics can be dealt through unsupervised ways. According to the method proposed by Kuncheva (Sect. 3.2), a too large value of the SPLL criterion will indicate a change; however, she justifies that setting up a threshold for defining a change or no change is an aside problem not analyzed in her work. The author points out that such a threshold may be specific for each kind of data, and can be tuned according to the desired level of false and true positives.

According to the latest, if we look at the values of the blue line (and more specifically the red line that represents an average envelope of the blue one), we can notice that Fig. 2 shows changes in the region of the graph between

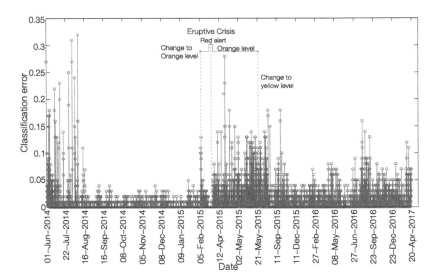

Fig. 1. Deterioration of the classifier accuracy going through different periods of volcano activity. Level of alerts are also indicated (from highest to lowest: red, orange, yellow, green [14])

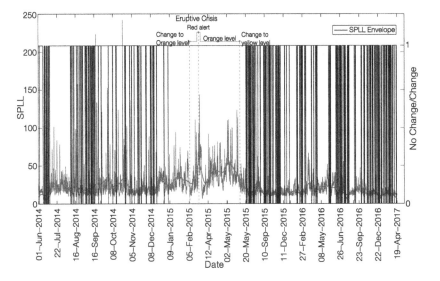

Fig. 2. Definition of a changing environment according to the SPLL criterion on the dynamics of the Villarrica volcano. (Color figure online)

January and May 2015, which coincides with those shown in Fig. 1. The black line indicates the change/no-change criterion. Since we did not make a fine-tuning of the threshold, an alternating variation of such a criterion will be understood as a no change or a small and little significant change.

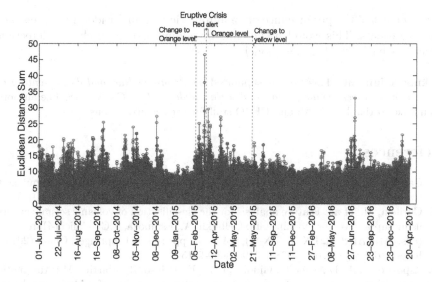

Fig. 3. Identification of significant changes in volcanic activity through the sum of 1-NN distances.

Regarding the third experiment, as shown in Fig. 3, the sum of the distances had the higher values in the region between February and May 2015, in particular, one of them coincides with the eruptive crisis. This is explained as a movement of the points of such period to a region of lower density, which would increase the distance (it can be understood as a mismatch between the compared points) between the events that represents the "future" dynamics of the volcano with respect to the prototypes of the past that within the 1-NN rule would assign the label. If there are changes, then it is presumed that the assignment of the label will be less reliable, and that a decrease in the confidence can be indirectly measured through the distance from the prototype that assigns the label to the test point.

6 Conclusion

Several techniques for the automatic analysis of seismic-volcanic signals have been proposed but they are often limited because of having been designed and trained under assumptions of unchanging data distribution over time. Within a volcanic environment, it was demonstrated how a learning model can increase its error rate up to 23% when the volcano faces a different dynamics, as it happens in phases of eruptive crisis. Additionally, it was demonstrated by two unsupervised methods (one of them very simple and straightforward, proposed by us) that, by setting thresholds, concept drifts can be identified in certain periods that cause changes in contexts. As future work, it is convenient to make a detailed analysis of the deterioration of classification performance by class in order to determine the contributions of each class. Also, the possibilities are open for verifying the improvement of the performance of an automatic system for identifying seismic-volcanic events. This would be possible by adding a stage of change detection which feedbacks the learning model.

Acknowledgment. This work is supported by *Programa Nacional de Fomento a la Formación de Investigadores, Doctorados Nacionales – COLCIENCIAS*. The authors would like to thank OVDAS and UFRO staff for their contributions.

References

1. Carniel, R.: Characterization of volcanic regimes and identification of significant transitions using geophysical data: a review. Bull. Volcanol. **76**(8), 848 (2014)
2. Curilem, M., et al.: Feature analysis for the classification of volcanic seismic events using support vector machines. In: Gelbukh, A., Espinoza, F.C., Galicia-Haro, S.N. (eds.) MICAI 2014. LNCS (LNAI), vol. 8857, pp. 160–171. Springer, Cham (2014). https://doi.org/10.1007/978-3-319-13650-9_15
3. Esposito, A.M., D'Auria, L., Giudicepietro, F., Peluso, R., Martini, M.: Automatic recognition of landslides based on neural network analysis of seismic signals: an application to the monitoring of Stromboli volcano (Southern Italy). Pure Appl. Geophys. **170**(11), 1821–1832 (2013)
4. Gama, J., Medas, P., Castillo, G., Rodrigues, P.: Learning with drift detection. In: Bazzan, A.L.C., Labidi, S. (eds.) SBIA 2004. LNCS (LNAI), vol. 3171, pp. 286–295. Springer, Heidelberg (2004). https://doi.org/10.1007/978-3-540-28645-5_29
5. Gama, J., Žliobaitė, I., Bifet, A., Pechenizkiy, M., Bouchachia, A.: A survey on concept drift adaptation. ACM Comput. Surv. (CSUR) **46**(4), 44 (2014)
6. Ibáñez, J.M., Benítez, C., Gutiérrez, L.A., Cortés, G., García-Yeguas, A., Alguacil, G.: The classification of seismo-volcanic signals using Hidden Markov Models as applied to the Stromboli and Etna volcanoes. J. Volcanol. Geoth. Res. **187**(3–4), 218–226 (2009)
7. Kuncheva, L.I.: Change detection in streaming multivariate data using likelihood detectors. IEEE Trans. Knowl. Data Eng. **25**(5), 1175–1180 (2013)
8. Kuncheva, L.I., Faithfull, W.J.: PCA feature extraction for change detection in multidimensional unlabeled data. IEEE Trans. Neural Netw. Learn. Syst. **25**(1), 69–80 (2014)
9. McNutt, S.R., Roman, D.C.: Volcanic seismicity. In: The Encyclopedia of Volcanoes (Second Edition), pp. 1011–1034. Elsevier (2015)
10. Orozco-Alzate, M., Acosta-Muñoz, C., Londoño-Bonilla, J.M.: The automated identification of volcanic earthquakes: concepts, applications and challenges. In: Earthquake Research and Analysis-Seismology, Seismotectonic and Earthquake Geology. InTech (2012)
11. Pears, R., Sakthithasan, S., Koh, Y.S.: Detecting concept change in dynamic data streams. Mach. Learn. **97**(3), 259–293 (2014)
12. Robnik-Šikonja, M., Kononenko, I.: Theoretical and empirical analysis of ReliefF and RReliefF. Mach. Learn. **53**(1–2), 23–69 (2003)
13. Ibs-von Seht, M.: Detection and identification of seismic signals recorded at Krakatau volcano (Indonesia) using artificial neural networks. J. Volcanol. Geoth. Res. **176**(4), 448–456 (2008)
14. SERNAGEOMIN, RNVV, OVDAS: Reportes de actividad volcánica (2015). http://sitiohistorico.sernageomin.cl/volcan.php?pagina=5&iId=22

15. Tárraga, M., Martí, J., Abella, R., Carniel, R., López, C.: Volcanic tremors: good indicators of change in plumbing systems during volcanic eruptions. J. Volcanol. Geoth. Res. **273**, 33–40 (2014)
16. Van Daele, M., et al.: The 600 yr eruptive history of Villarrica volcano (Chile) revealed by annually laminated lake sediments. GSA Bull. **126**(3–4), 481–498 (2014)

Evaluating Deep Neural Networks for Automatic Fake News Detection in Political Domain

Francis C. Fernández-Reyes and Suraj Shinde[✉]

everis AI digital lab, Mexico City 06600, Mexico
{ffernare,suraj.shinde}@everis.com

Abstract. Fake news has become a hot trending topic after the latest U.S. presidential elections when Donald Trump took office. The political speech during the presidential campaign was plagued with half-truths, falsehoods, and click-baits, creating confusion for the voters. Several algorithms have been designed to tackle the automatic fake news detection problem, but some issues still remain uncovered. Some approaches address the problem from a perspective where the website reputation is used as part of their analysis. Typical algorithms take into account text patterns and statistics for automatic fake news detection. Commonly, the fake news detection problem is treated as a multi-class text classifier. This paper proposes several deep neural architectures to classify fake news in the political domain. Furthermore, we demonstrate that combining statements and credibility patterns of politicians are very important for detecting fake news in a deep neural network classifier. We have found that the information about the politician is very useful for any of the tested architectures.

Keywords: Deep neural network · Fake news detection
Multi-class text classifier

1 Introduction

Concern arose after the 2016 elections related to the dissemination of false news on the internet. The email account of John Podesta (Hillary Clinton's campaign manager) was hacked in a spear-phishing attack, and his emails were made public by WikiLeaks. This incident is known as a conspiracy theory called "Pizzagate" created in october of 2016. The authors of the "Pizzagate" theory falsely claimed that those emails had coded messages referring to human trafficking and connecting several U.S. restaurants and high-ranking officials of the Democratic Party with a child-sex ring. On December of 2016, Edgar Maddison Welch, a 28-year-old man fired three shots in the Comet Ping Pong restaurant with a rifle, nobody was hurt. Welch told police that he had planned to "self-investigate" the conspiracy theory. It was estimated that over one million tweets were related to the fake news Pizzagate theory by the end of the presidential election [14].

© Springer Nature Switzerland AG 2018
G. R. Simari et al. (Eds.): IBERAMIA 2018, LNAI 11238, pp. 206–216, 2018.
https://doi.org/10.1007/978-3-030-03928-8_17

Normally, fake news travel faster than real news on social media[1]. Shu et al. [14] have shown that 62% of U.S. adults read news on social media in 2016, while in 2012, only 49% reported reading news on social media. They also state that social media now outperforms television as the major news source.

The most popular fake news stories are more widely shared on Facebook as compared to the most popular mainstream news stories. Many people, who read fake news stories, reported that they believe them and the most discussed fake news stories tended to be in favor of Donald Trump as compared to Hillary Clinton[2]. In summary, detecting fake news in social media can combat misinformation and violent acts derived from them. Current algorithms mostly use heuristics based on untrusted sites.

The rest of the paper has the following structure. Section 2 is devoted to show the related work associated with our research objectives and Sect. 2.1 is dedicated to define the problem. Section 3 describes the different models tested. Section 4 describes the corpus used and the design of our experiments. It also shows the main results achieved. Finally, Sect. 5 provides some conclusions and directions for future work.

2   Related Work

Distinguishing between truth and falsehood has received important attention from fields as diverse as philosophy, psychology and sociology [10]. Recent studies have proposed stylometric [4], semi-supervised learning [6], and linguistic approaches [12] to detect deceptive text on crowdsourced datasets [18]. The fake news detection problem is more challenging than detecting deceptive reviews. The political language on TV interviews and posts on social media are mostly short statements.

Several proposals are trying to apply deceptive detection algorithms and models to fake news detection problem. One way to approach the problem is checking the credibility of major claims in a news article to decide the news veracity; treating the problem as a binary classifier. Commonly, the techniques applied to hoax detection are: keywords-based methods with logistic regression [9], distance-based methods [7,13], neural network with advanced text processing [17], and evolutionary algorithms [19]. Machine learning techniques, such as SVM, Decision Trees, and Decision Rules have also been used to tackle the problem of automatic fake news detection [1].

Another way to tackle the fake news detection problem is treating it as a multi-class classifier assuming that a statement, or a news article can have some degrees of truth for distinct classes (satire, hoaxes, clickbait, propaganda, etc.). Volkova et al. [16] collected 130 K tweets to propose the use of neural networks that use linguistic and graph features. Their findings show that Recurrent

---

[1] https://www.independent.co.uk/news/science/fake-news-twitter-spreads-further-faster-real-stories-retweets-political-a8247491.html.

[2] https://www.buzzfeed.com/craigsilverman/viral-fake-election-news-outperformed-real-news-on-facebook?utm_term=.rxZwY7J1l#.myza45rGB.

and Convolutional neural networks provide strong performance in distinguishing news for several categories. Wang et al. [18] proposes a dataset that consists of 12.8 K manually annotated short statements obtained from PolitiFact. Besides, they design a Convolutional neural network for fusing linguistic features with metadata. Their proposed model outperforms SVM and Logistic Regression algorithms.

Nevertheless, from our knowledge there is no reported study, about the best way to design deep neural network architectures in order to combine linguistic and metadata features for fake news detection. Our main contribution is the designing and testing of several deep neural network architectures (including preprocessing steps) for combining in the best way possible, the linguistic and metadata features in political domain. At the end, we provide some interesting conclusions and recommendations.

2.1 Research Problem

Let s refers to a statement, and m refers to metadata features. Statement includes a set of linguistically extracted features (based on embeddings) and Metadata includes a set of profile features to describe the original author. We also define truthfulness classes as a set of tuples $\Gamma = \{\gamma_i\}$ where each γ is defined over the possible classes, for instance, for our case { *pants-fire, false, barely-true, half-true, mostly-true* and *true* }. Each γ_i then refers to the specific truthfulness class assigned to a pair s and m. A function $\mathcal{F} : \{s_i, m_i\} \rightarrow \{\gamma_i\}$ is the prediction function learned by a multi-class classifier. We decided to join all textual data inside s and keep credibility as part of m.

3 Proposed Model

Several deep learning models have been proposed to tackle deceptive detection problems. The most interesting architectures proposed include Recurrent and Convolutional Neural Networks, RNNs and CNNs respectively. RNNs are been used in NLP tasks, and CNNs mainly for computer vision tasks. However, CNNs have been used recently for mapping features of n-grams patterns in Natural Language Processing (NLP) tasks. Wang et al. [18] propose a dataset for fake news detection in political domain and also made some experiments with a deep neural network fusion architecture. Their architecture can be found in Fig. 1.

We strongly believe that a deep neural network architecture that combine RNNs or CNNs for embeddings analysis and a fully connected layer for combining the metadata features is one of the best possible combinations for a multi-class classifier. Our intuition is guided by the assumption that n-grams can be discovered by CNNs and word sequences by RNNs. We also expect that patterns on metadata features are based on each of their numerical values instead of n-grams or sequences data, that is the main reason why our models include them at the top of the fully connected layer.

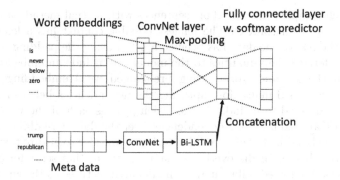

Fig. 1. Hybrid Convolutional Neural Networks framework for integrating text and meta-data [18].

Our main differences from previous approaches is that we occupy the word embeddings and freeze them, as a way of doing transfer learning. In this case, we can keep the learning parameters at minimum. We combine all textual data as part of the statement and keep credibility data as part of metadata. We also propose a framework in order to test several neural network architectures, Fig. 2 shows our main process design.

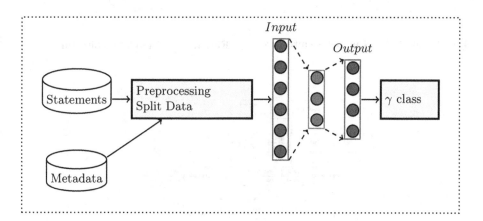

Fig. 2. Main framework for combining RNNs and CNNs architectures for detecting fake news.

Short sentences are difficult for understanding word meanings due to the constrained context. For instance, if we just said "I saw a bat" it is difficult to understand if we are referring to the nocturnal animal or the baseball equipment. The context here is not enough to understand the meaning of the word "bat". The dataset used to train and test our architectures suffer from the same problem. Speaker sentences are too short for modelling the word meanings. However, our approach complements the short sentences with textual metadata to ensure the most meaningful context. The longest possible context has a length of 54 words and the rest of the data has been completed using the padding technique.

For transferring the semantics to the model, we include an embedding layer that was initialized and frozen using pre-trained word embeddings as it is explained in Sect. 4. Finally, for capturing the dependencies between the word meanings we decided to include RNNs, which process each of the word embeddings and are able to find long dependencies over the data. Credibility data was also normalized and included in a different input in order to ensure textual data is modelled by RNNs for discovering semantic patterns that serve for classification purposes. We tested different RNN model architectures as shown in Figs. 3, 4 and 5.

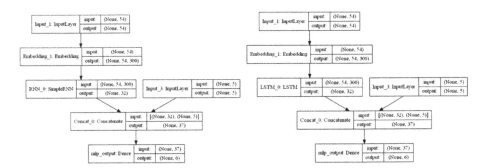

Fig. 3. Simple RNN model architecture   **Fig. 4.** LSTM model architecture

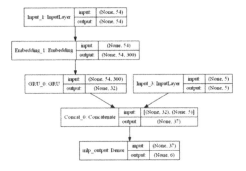

Fig. 5. GRU model architecture

Fixed term dependencies such as n-grams have been used before for language modelling [3,15]. Instead of computing long embedding dependencies with RNNs, we decided to model fixed n-grams with CNNs. We tested for $n = (2, 3, 4, 5)$ which are commonly used values for n-grams. Our best results were obtained

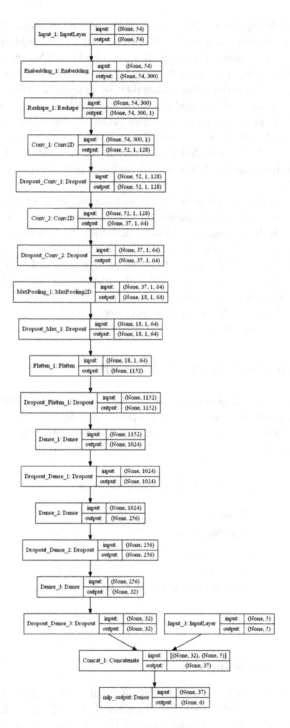

Fig. 6. CNN model architecture

with 3-g. For building the CNNs architecture, we first reshape the embedding data in order to observe 3-g embeddings each time. We add dropout layers as a regularization technique after each layer of the CNNs model. We add a second convolutional layer in order to detect patterns inside the 3-g. We include a MaxPooling layer to reduce dimensionality by conserving the learn patterns. A Flatten layer is inserted to combine all values by computing just one vector of length 1152. Finally, we pass the 1152 vector through an artificial neural network build with a fully connected dense layers. Just as before, credibility data was normalized and included in a different input layer. We tested different parameter combinations for CNN model architectures. In Fig. 6 is shown our best CNN model.

Experiments with the proposed architectures appears in Sect. 4 and some interesting remarks are also included. In preprocessing steps we do the follow actions: all textual data is mapped to word embeddings, this layer of embeddings is frozen and numerical data (credibility) is scaled. Figure 6 shows our main difference to the Wang et al. model [18]: The proposed model uses 2-dimensional convolution layers, instead of 1-dimensional convolutions, which help to find n-g patterns in embeddings for discovering the correct γ class. The CNN model architecture is deeper than the RNNs architecture. However, in our case the RNNs train faster than the Convolution architecture.

4   Experimental Design and Results

In this section, we first describe in Table 1 the dataset used in our experiments. This dataset is publicly available and proposed in [18]. All classes are well balanced. Section 4.1 describes the baselines used to compare our models. Section 4.2 describes our results.

Table 1. Dataset statistics

Dataset	
Training set size	10,269
Validation set size	1,284
Test set size	1,283
Avg. statement length (tokens)	17,9

4.1   Experimental Setup

We used six baselines: a majority baseline, a regularized logistic regression classifier (LR), a support vector machine classifier (SVM) [2], a bi-directional long short-term memory network model (Bi-LSTMs) [5] and a convolutional neural network model (CNNs) [8]. All baselines results found in Table 2 are taken from

Wang et al. [18]. We also used as baseline the top two best models developed by Wang et al. [18]: HybridCNN(Text+Speaker) and HybridCNN(Text+Job). At the end of the table appears our proposed model architecture: SimpleRNN refers to Fig. 3, LSTM refers to Fig. 4, GRU refers to Fig. 5 and StackedCNN refers to Fig. 6.

Table 2. Dataset statistics

Models	Valid. acc.
Majority	0.204
SVMs	0.258
Logistic Regression	0.257
Bi-LSTMs	0.223
CNNs	0.260
HybridCNN (Text+Speaker)	0.277
HybridCNN (Text+Job)	0.270
SimpleRNN	0.462
LSTM	0.468
GRU	0.472
StackedCNN	0.485

Our models used pretrained 300-dimensional word2vec embeddings from Google News [11] and this layer was frozen for text embeddings. Our Stacked-CNN model was configured with 128 filters of $(3, 3)$ kernel size. We add a dropout rate of 0.3 as the regularization technique for all our models. This means that 30% of the neurons are dropped for each of the hidden layers. The batch size for RMSprop optimization was set to 128, and the learning rate was initialized at 0.001. SimpleRNN requires 8 epochs, LSTM requires 6 epochs, GRU requires 6 epochs and StackedCNN requires 25 epochs for training. We also normalized credibility metadata for each speaker.

4.2 Results

First, we compare various models using an approach similar to Wang et al. [18]. Our models outperform all baselines. We have found that using all textual data as input helps the models to increase accuracy, as compared to dividing them into statements and other textual metadata. Also the normalization process of credibility metadata helps improve accuracy.

We observe that read in our RNN models the GRU model performs the best. Figures 7 and 8 shows the accuracy and the loss observed during the training process. After epoch 6, the model begins to overfit as can be observed by increasing the difference between training and testing curves as shown in Fig. 8. Testing accuracy is greater than training accuracy as it can be observed in Fig. 7 due to Dropout regularization technique. Dropout is similar to forcing the neural network to become a very large collection of weak classifiers, like an ensemble. Individual weak classifiers suffer from low classification accuracy, but they become stronger once you put them together. During training, dropout turns off some random collection of these classifiers causing training accuracy to suffer. On the other hand, during testing, dropout turns on all classifiers, which improve testing accuracy.

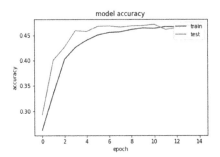
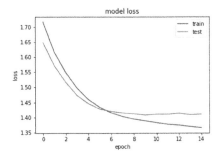

Fig. 7. GRU model accuracy during training.

Fig. 8. GRU model loss during training.

Our StackedCNN model, was trained until 100 epochs. Figures 9 and 10 show the accuracy and loss observed during the training process. Until epoch 100, the training and testing loss became steady around 1.40. The testing accuracy is greater than the training accuracy due to Dropout technique as stated in the previous case.

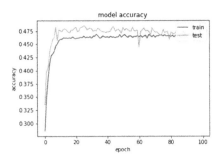
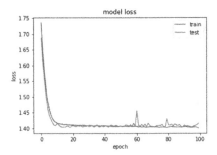

Fig. 9. StackedCNN model accuracy during training.

Fig. 10. StackedCNN model loss during training.

From Figs. 8 and 10 the loss value are around 1.40 which is high and means that we have around 0.4 probability of predicting actual class during testing. This corresponds with the reported model accuracies found in the Table 2.

5 Conclusions

We introduced four new architectures for automatic fake news detection. Compared to prior approaches, our models outperforms by almost twice. Our Stacked-CNN model is the best empirically tested one and shows that a combination of pre-trained embeddings with 2-dimensional convolutional layers helps for discovering patterns in textual data. On the other hands, a normalization process for credibility metadata shows greater benefits when concatenated at the end of the model, but not at the beginning. We also experimented with parallel architectures, combining RNNs with CNNs which did not result in much improvement. Fine-grained fake news detection is still a big challenge from a research perspective.

References

1. Castillo, C., Mendoza, M., Poblete, B.: Information credibility on Twitter. In: Proceedings of the 20th International Conference on World Wide Web, WWW 2011, pp. 675–684. ACM, New York (2011). https://doi.org/10.1145/1963405.1963500
2. Crammer, K., Singer, Y.: On the algorithmic implementation of multi-class kernel-based vector machines. J. Mach. Learn. Res. **2**, 265–292 (2002). http://dl.acm.org/citation.cfm?id=944790.944813
3. Damashek, M.: Gauging similarity with n-grams: language-independent categorization of text. Science **267**(5199), 843–848 (1995)
4. Feng, S., Banerjee, R., Choi, Y.: Syntactic stylometry for deception detection. In: Proceedings of the 50th Annual Meeting of the Association for Computational Linguistics: Short Papers-Volume 2, pp. 171–175. Association for Computational Linguistics (2012)
5. Graves, A., Schmidhuber, J.: Framewise phoneme classification with bidirectional LSTM and other neural network architectures. Neural Netw. **18**(5), 602–610 (2005). iJCNN 2005. http://www.sciencedirect.com/science/article/pii/S0893608005001206
6. Hai, Z., Zhao, P., Cheng, P., Yang, P., Li, X.L., Li, G.: Deceptive review spam detection via exploiting task relatedness and unlabeled data. In: Proceedings of the 2016 Conference on Empirical Methods in Natural Language Processing, pp. 1817–1826 (2016)
7. Ishak, A., Chen, Y., Yong, S.P.: Distance-based hoax detection system. In: 2012 International Conference on Computer and Information Science (ICCIS), vol. 1, pp. 215–220. IEEE (2012)
8. Kim, Y.: Convolutional neural networks for sentence classification. arXiv preprint arXiv:1408.5882 (2014)
9. Mason, J.: Filtering spam with SpamAssassin. In: HEANet Annual Conference, p. 103 (2002)
10. Mihalcea, R., Strapparava, C.: The lie detector: explorations in the automatic recognition of deceptive language. In: Proceedings of the ACL-IJCNLP 2009 Conference Short Papers, pp. 309–312. Association for Computational Linguistics (2009)
11. Mikolov, T., Sutskever, I., Chen, K., Corrado, G.S., Dean, J.: Distributed representations of words and phrases and their compositionality. In: Advances in Neural Information Processing Systems, pp. 3111–3119 (2013)

12. Pérez-Rosas, V., Mihalcea, R.: Experiments in open domain deception detection. In: Proceedings of the 2015 Conference on Empirical Methods in Natural Language Processing, pp. 1120–1125 (2015)
13. Petković, T., Kostanjčar, Z., Pale, P.: E-mail system for automatic hoax recognition. In: MIPRO CIS-Inteligentni sustavi (2005)
14. Shu, K., Sliva, A., Wang, S., Tang, J., Liu, H.: Fake news detection on social media: a data mining perspective. ACM SIGKDD Explor. Newsl. **19**(1), 22–36 (2017)
15. Stolcke, A.: SRILM-an extensible language modeling toolkit. In: Seventh International Conference on Spoken Language Processing (2002)
16. Volkova, S., Shaffer, K., Jang, J.Y., Hodas, N.: Separating facts from fiction: linguistic models to classify suspicious and trusted news posts on Twitter. In: Proceedings of the 55th Annual Meeting of the Association for Computational Linguistics (Volume 2: Short Papers), vol. 2, pp. 647–653 (2017)
17. Vuković, M., Pripužić, K., Belani, H.: An intelligent automatic hoax detection system. In: Velásquez, J.D., Ríos, S.A., Howlett, R.J., Jain, L.C. (eds.) KES 2009. LNCS (LNAI), vol. 5711, pp. 318–325. Springer, Heidelberg (2009). https://doi.org/10.1007/978-3-642-04595-0_39
18. Wang, W.Y.: "Liar, liar pants on fire": a new benchmark dataset for fake news detection. arXiv preprint arXiv:1705.00648 (2017)
19. Yevseyeva, I., Basto-Fernandes, V., Ruano-OrdáS, D., MéNdez, J.R.: Optimising anti-spam filters with evolutionary algorithms. Expert Syst. Appl. **40**(10), 4010–4021 (2013)

A Comparative Study Between Deep Learning and Traditional Machine Learning Techniques for Facial Biometric Recognition

Jonnathann Silva Finizola[✉], Jonas Mendonça Targino[✉],
Felipe Gustavo Silva Teodoro[✉], and Clodoaldo Aparecido de Moraes Lima[✉]

University of Sao Paulo, Sao Paulo, Brazil
{jonnathann.finizola,jonas.mendonca,felipe.teodoro,c.lima}@usp.br

Abstract. There is a growing incentive to use biometric technology to improve and even replace traditional security methods. Biometric modalities are characteristics drawn from the human body, which are unique to each individual and can be used to establish their identity in a population. Among the biometric modalities, the face is the most commonly seen and used in daily life. Several works have been proposed involving Deep Learning, with emphasis on the Convolutional Neural Networks, for facial recognition. However none of these studies perform a detailed comparative study between traditional machine learning techniques and Deep Learning presenting the pros and cons of each one. In this context, the present work aims to conduct a comparative study between traditional machine learning techniques, such as K-Nearest Neighbors, Optimum-Path Forest, Support Vector Machine, Extreme Learning Machine, Artificial Neural Networks and Deep Learning, focusing on Convolutional Neural Networks, for facial recognition.

Keywords: Face recognition · K-Nearest Neighbors
Optimum-Path Forest · Support vector machine
Extreme Learning Machine · Artificial Neural Networks
Deep learning · Convolutional neural networks

1 Introduction

The field of Biometrics (Bio-Life and metrics-measure) refers to a wide variety of technologies used to identify and verify the identity of a person by measuring and analyzing various physical and behavioral aspects of the human being [8]. These systems provide security based on "what you own" rather than "what you know" (password/PIN) or "what you have" (smart-card). Biometric modalities are characteristics drawn from the human body that are unique to each individual and can be used to establish their identity in a population. Among the most used biometric modalities are: fingerprint, face, palm print and iris. The fact

G. R. Simari et al. (Eds.): IBERAMIA 2018, LNAI 11238, pp. 217–228, 2018.
https://doi.org/10.1007/978-3-030-03928-8_18

that biometric modalities are directly related to some of the characteristics of users is an extraordinary possibility to overcome the security gaps caused by traditional recognition strategies.

Among the biometric modalities, the face is the most commonly seen and used in our daily lives. Since the advent of photography, both government agencies and private organizations have maintained photo database of people containing the face (e.g. for personal identification, passports, membership cards). Facial recognition is one of the research topics in the interdisciplinary area of biometrics, pattern recognition, computer vision and machine learning. The face is a universal characteristic, unique to each person and has good acceptability in capture environments.

Advanced machine learning techniques have been applied successfully in facial recognition, obtaining high recognition rate. However, the process of extracting characteristics of the face images and the training of the classifiers makes the recognition process very costly. For this reason, many researchers have investigated strategies to circumvent this problem. Deep Learning is a new machine learning approach composed of multiple layers of processing aimed at learning data representations at multiple levels of abstractions.

Deep Learning has achieved superior results over traditional machine learning techniques in issues related to speech recognition, object detection, and various other domains [9]. However, there are still no studies that make a detailed comparative study that highlights the advantages and disadvantages of Deep Learning, especially the Convolutional Neural Networks, when compared to the traditional machine learning techniques for facial recognition. This paper aims to fill this gap in the literature.

In this work a comparative study will be carried out between Convolutional Neural Networks (CNNs) and traditional machine learning techniques, such as, Artificial Neural Networks (ANN), Support Vector Machine (SVM), K-Nearest Neighbors (KNN), Optimum-Path Forest (OPF) and Extreme Learning Machine (ELM) for facial recognition.

This paper is organized as follows: the Sect. 2 presents some works related to deep learning; the Sect. 3 describes concepts related to deep learning; in Sect. 4 the traditional machine learning techniques are presented. The Sect. 5 describes the configurations of the experiments performed; the Sect. 6 presents and discusses the results obtained. Finally the Sect. 7 brings an overview of the main contributions of this paper and provides some remarks on future work.

2   Related Work

In this section, some works related to convolutional neural networks for biometric facial recognition are presented.

In [11] a cascaded architecture built using CNNs was proposed for face detection. The proposed approach operates in several resolutions, in low resolution, it rejects background regions of the image and in high resolution, it evaluates each part of the regions of the image to identify whether there is face present in those regions. The proposed architecture presents superior results when compared to state-of-the-art methods such as TSM, Shen et al., Structure Models, HeadHunter, DPM.

In [19] was investigated a method of facial recognition based on deep neural networks. The sparse coding neural network and the softmax classifiers were used in this work to construct and train the deep hierarchical network after the preprocessing of the facial image. The method was evaluated in the ORL database, Yale, Yale-B and PERET, respectively. Experimental results show that the deep learning method can express the original data in an abstract way with efficiency and precision, as well as achieving good performance in lighting, expression, posture and low resolution conditions.

In [2], a modified convolutional neural network was proposed, which consists of adding two normalization operations to two of the layers. The normalization operation which is batch normalization provided acceleration of the network. CNN architecture was employed to extract distinctive face features and Softmax classifier was used to classify faces in the fully connected layer of CNN. In the experiment part, the architecture reaches an accuracy rate of 98.4% in the Georgia Tech face database.

3   Deep Learning

Traditional facial biometric systems are composed of the following steps: segmentation, preprocessing, feature extraction and classification. For each of these steps it is necessary to choose the most appropriate technique. This hampers the use of traditional biometric systems, since each technique has different advantages and disadvantages. In contrast, Deep learning can learn hierarchical features directly from raw data for use in specific tasks. As one of deep learning models, Convolutional Neural Networks (CNN) integrates feature extraction and classification, and has achieved noteworthy success with its repeatedly confirmed superiorities in various computer vision tasks.

Convolutional Neural Networks [10] are composed of several layers, which are organized hierarchically. Similar to Artificial Neural Networks, CNNs also have weights and bias that can be adjusted by the gradient algorithm. In general, a CNN has three layers:

1. **Convolutional layer:** this layer performs convolution operations between the image and a kernel or filter in order to find patterns. The kernel or filter can be seen as the weights of the neurons of this layer, which can be adjusted using a supervised learning approach. At each translation of the kernel, on a given region of the image, an activation function, usually of the Relu type, is applied [10].
2. **Subsampling Layer (Pooling):** After a convolution operation we usually perform pooling to reduce the dimensionality of the image. This enables us to reduce the number of parameters, which both shortens the training time and combats overfitting. Pooling layers downsample each feature map independently, reducing the height and width, keeping the depth intact. The most

common type of pooling is max pooling which just takes the max value in the pooling window. It slides a window over its input, and simply takes the max value in the window. Similar to a convolution, we specify the window size and stride.

3. **Fully Connected layer:** This layer performs the classification task. After the convolution and subsampling operations, the last subsampling layer feeds a fully connected neural network. The Fig. 1 shows the architecture of a CNN.

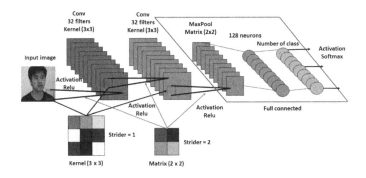

Fig. 1. Architecture of a Convolutional Neural Network (CNN)

4   Traditional Machine Learning Techniques for Face Recognition

In this section, some traditional machine learning techniques for classification task aiming at facial recognition are briefly described.

4.1   K-Nearest Neighbors (KNN)

KNN algorithm is one of the simplest classification algorithm and it is one of the most used learning algorithms. A test instance is classified by a majority vote of its neighbors, with the instance being assigned to the class most common among its k nearest neighbors (k is a positive integer, typically small) [4]. If $k = 1$, then the instance is simply assigned to the class of that single nearest neighbor. One of the weaknesses of this classifier is the definition of the K parameter, which defines the number of neighbors. The value of K controls the shape of the decision boundary. When K is small, the region used to perform the prediction is constrained, forcing the classifier to be "more blind" to the general distribution. A small value for K provides the most flexible adjustment, which will have low bias but high variance. On the other hand, a higher K averages more voters in each prediction and hence is more resilient to outliers. Larger values of K will have smoother decision boundaries which means lower variance but increased bias.

4.2   Support Vector Machine (SVM)

Support vector machines allude to a relatively novel class of non-parametric supervised learning schemes that exhibit properties similar to those presented by neural network models and which are based on theoretical principles borrowed from the statistical learning theory [15]. SVMs have shown remarkably robust performance with respect to sparse and noisy data. As well, the number of free parameters in an SVM does not explicitly depend upon the input dimensionality of the problem at hand, something very interesting when taking into consideration scalability requirements. Another important character of the support vector learning approach is that the underlying optimization problems are inherently convex and have no local minimal, which comes as the result of applying Mercer's conditions on the characterization of kernels.

The SVMs tackle non-trivial classification, regression, and forecasting problems by (non)linearly mapping input data into high-dimensional feature spaces, wherein a linear decision surface is properly designed. In this sense, SVMs comprise an approximate implementation of the structural risk minimization principle, which asserts that the generalization error of a learned hypothesis is delimited by the sum of the training error of the learning machine and a parcel that depends on the Vapnik–Chervonenkis dimension. By minimizing this sum, high generalization performance is theoretically ensured.

4.3   Optimum Path Forest (OPF)

The OPF classifier models the problem of pattern recognition as a graph partition in a given feature space. The nodes represent the patterns and all pairs of nodes are connected by edges, defining a complete graph. This kind of representation is straightforward, given that the graph does not need to be explicitly represented, and has low memory requirements. The partition of the graph is carried out by a competition process between some key nodes (prototypes), which offer optimum paths to the remaining nodes of the graph. Each prototype defines its optimum path tree (OPT), and the collection of all OPT defines the optimum path forest, which gives the name to the classifier. The OPF classifier is composed of two distinct phases: (i) training and (ii) classification. The former step consists, essentially, in finding the prototypes and computing the optimum path forest. In the second step, a pattern is picked from the test sample and labeled with the class of its most strongly connected prototype through the optimum path forest generated in the training phase [16].

4.4   Multilayer Perceptron Neural Networks (MLP)

An Artificial Neural Network (ANN) is a computational model biologically inspired in the functioning of the human brain. This model has been widely used in problems of pattern recognition, signal processing, face recognition, among other applications. In a nutshell, an MLP is a feedforward neural network composed of several layers of perceptrons aiming to solve multiclass problems [6].

In this setting, the output of a neuron of the ith layer feeds the inputs of neurons at the $(i + 1)$th layer. This neural network assigns an feature x to a class q if the qth output neuron achieves the highest value. The backpropagation algorithm is usually employed to train a MLP. This algorithm minimizes the mean squared error between the desired outputs and the obtained outputs of each node of the output layer. Therefore, the idea is to minimize the mean square error.

4.5 Extreme Learning Machine (ELM)

Huang et al. [7] proposed a novel machine learning algorithm called the Extreme Learning Machine (ELM) that has significantly faster learning speed and requires less human intervention than other learning methods. It has been proven that the hidden nodes of the "generalized" single-hidden-layer feedforward networks (SLFNs) can be randomly generated and that the universal approximation capability of such SLFNs can be guaranteed. The ELM can determine analytically all the parameters of SLFNs instead of adjusting parameters iteratively. Thus, it can overcome the demerits of the gradient-based method and of most other learning methods. Compared to the most effective SVM-based method, the latest research [7] also shows that the ELM tends to achieve better generalization performance, less sensitivity to user-specified parameters, and easier implementation than a traditional SVM.

5   Experiment Settings

In what follows, we provide details about the classification task and dataset used in the experiments.

– **AR Face**, this database was created at the Universidad Autonóma de Barcelona [14].
  This database contains 2600 frontal face images of 100 individuals (50 males and 50 females). From each individual, 26 photos were collected, which were captured under significantly different lighting conditions and with varying expressions. Another characteristic is a possible presence of glasses or scarf.
– **YALE**, this database is a collection of 165 grayscale images of 15 different individuals [5]. In this dataset, images to a person present variations in expressions and illumination conditions, and 11 images of each individual are available with different expressions: happy, sad, sleepy, etc, and different lighting sources.
– **SDUMLA-HMT**, this database was collected during the summer of 2010 at Shandong University, Jinan, China [18]. This database consists of the following biometric modality: face, finger vein, gait, iris and fingerprint of 106 individuals (including 61 males and 45 females with age between 17 and 31). In this paper, we use only the images of the face totaling 8904 face images with different pose, facial expressions, accessories (such as glasses and hat) and illuminations.

5.1 Preprocessing Face Images

Aiming at the use of traditional machine learning techniques for facial recognition, the following steps were performed in the preprocessing of face images: (i) conversion to gray scale, (ii) application of the Viola Jones algorithm [17] in order to detect the face region, (iii) rescaled the face image to a resolution of 256×256 pixels, (iv) normalization of face images using z-score.

In the context of Deep Learning the following steps were taken in preprocessing: (i) image conversion to gray scale, (ii) rescaled the face image to a resolution of 256×256 pixels, (iii) normalization of face images for the range of $[-1, 1]$.

5.2 Feature Extraction

After the face region detection and the resizing of all faces, we apply the wavelet transform (WT) [13] to feature extraction. This step was not applied in the context of deep learning.

The Wavelet transform is a time-frequency (or spatial-frequency) analysis tool and its applications is increasingly popular in science and engineering fields [13]. It represents an alternative tool for the short-time Fourier Transform when the analyses of quasi-stationary signals are being considered. The Wavelet coefficients are defined as inner products of the signal being transformed with each base functions. These functions are obtained from translation and dilation operations applied to a single function called mother Wavelet function.

The computation of the Wavelet Coefficients of a signal can be executed by the Mallat's Algorithm [13]. In this approach, a high-pass filter h and a low-pass filter g is applied, that is two Finite Impulse Response Filters, instead of using a Wavelet function. The output is composed by two parts, the first representing the details (from the filter h) and the second is the approximation (from the filter g) coefficients.

There are different ways of applying a 2D-WT to an image. The most commonly used decomposition scheme is the pyramid scheme. At a resolution depth of k, this scheme decomposes an image into $3k + 1$ sub-bands, LL_k, LH_k, HL_k, HH_k, $LH(k - l)$, $HL(k - I)$, $\cdots$, LH_1, HL_I. The sub-band LL of the Wavelet Transform corresponds to the low frequency in vertical and horizontal directions of the original image. The sub-band LH corresponds to the low frequency in the horizontal direction and high frequency in vertical direction, holding its vertical details. Similar interpretation is made on the sub-bands HL and HH.

In this work, the coefficients LL of the level of decomposition 3 were used. The mother functions used were Daubechies of order 2, 4 and Symlets of order 3, 4, 5. The Table 1 shows the amount of coefficients generated by the mother functions used in this work.

5.3 Configuration of the Experiments

In order to evaluate the performance of the traditional techniques of machine learning and deep learning, the repeated hold-out method was used. In the hold-out method, we randomly assign data points to two sets, usually called the

Table 1. Number of features extracted using wavelet transform

Mother functions	Daubechies 2	Daubechies 4	Symlet 3	Symlet 4	Symlet 5
Abbreviation	db2	db4	sym3	sym4	sym5
# features	1156	1444	1296	1444	1521

training set and the test set, respectively. In the repeated hold-out, this process is applied repeatedly (i.e., several times) to produce different training set and the test set. In each iteration, a certain proportion of the entire dataset is randomly selected to construct the training set and test set. The error rates made by the system in these iterations on the test set are averaged to produce the overall error rate.

In this work, we used 70% of the database to compose the training set and 30% for the set of tests. The hold-out method was repeated 10 times and each time an accuracy rate was produced. To ensure that the data were shuffled equally for each classifier, a seed was planted that guaranteed this shuffling so that each classifier received the same data set.

The traditional machine learning techniques discussed in this work were implemented using the Matlab programming language, with the exception of SVM. In this case, the library libsvm [1] was used. The parameters used in each technique are described below:

- KNN - the following values were used for k: 1, 3, 5, 8 and 10.
- SVM - was used the radial base function kernel, the parameter C, that controls the trade off between margin maximization and error minimization, was set at 1000 and for the parameter σ, which denotes the variance, the following values were used [3]: $2e{-}3$, $2e{-}6$, $2e{-}9$, $2e{-}12$ and $2e{-}14$.
- OPF - Euclidean distance was used.
- MLP - sigmoid activation function was used, as stopping criterion was used 2000 epochs, for the number of neurons in the hidden layer the following values were used: 10, 20, 50, 100 and 150.
- ELM - sigmoid activation function was used, the following values were used for the number of neurons in the hidden layer: 200, 500, 1000, 2000 and 4000.

Due to computational cost issues we opted to implement our CNN model to analyze the impact that this architecture would have when compared to traditional models. The Keras library was used to implement a CNN with 5 layers. The CNN architecture implemented has 2 layers of convolution, 1 layer of subsampling and 2 layers of classification. In the convolution layer there are 32 kernels (3×3). In the subsampling layer, a 2×2 mask was used. In each convolution layer the Relu activation function was used. After the convolution and subsampling layers a *dropout* value of 0.25 was applied to avoid overlapping. The first classification layer has 128 neurons with Relu activation function. In the second layer, activation function *softmax* and *dropout* equal to 0.5 were used. In the classification layer 128 neurons were used in the hidden layer and the number of neurons of the output layer was set equal to the number of classes. As criteria of stopping were used 15, 30 and 50 epochs.

All parameters described above were defined through preliminary experiments. The best configurations were chosen for this comparative study.

6 Results and Discussions

Table 2 provide the results obtained in the experiments, in terms of identification error achieved by traditional machine learning techniques, when they were induced with the coefficients generated by different mother Wavelet functions. In the case of CNN, the preprocessed face image was used as the input, instead of using the wavelet coefficients. The accuracy is shown in terms of average and standard deviation error rate. The error rate was calculated as the number of misclassifications divided by the total number of test set.

Table 2. Results obtained using traditional machine learning techniques and convolutional neural networks

Classifier		P	AR		Yale		Sdumla	
			mean ± std	MF	mean ± std	MF	mean ± std	MF
MLP	Neurons	10	38.26 ± 6.07	sym5	92.20 ± 4.04	db2	37.14 ± 2.79	db2
		20	76.58 ± 5.08	db2	94.20 ± 2.39	db2	68.23 ± 2.47	db2
		50	98.66 ± 0.45	db4	95.40 ± 2.83	db2	81.83 ± 0.78	sym3
		100	99.26 ± 0.33	sym3	94.40 ± 3.74	db4	86.17 ± 0.58	db2
		150	99.30 ± 0.41	db2	94.00 ± 4.10	db2	87.95 ± 1.01	db4
ELM	Neurons	200	93.82 ± 1.19	db2	89.60 ± 6.02	db2	63.03 ± 1.15	sym4
		500	97.23 ± 0.69	sym3	95.20 ± 3.01	sym3	73.71 ± 0.98	sym5
		1000	96.64 ± 0.59	sym4	95.60 ± 2.06	db4	80.19 ± 0.84	sym5
		2000	81.89 ± 1.51	db4	96.60 ± 1.89	sym3	84.83 ± 0.90	sym5
		4000	98.25 ± 0.49	sym5	96.80 ± 2.14	db2	84.76 ± 0.50	sym4
KNN	K	1	59.07 ± 2.26	sym3	77.40 ± 5.66	db4	74.83 ± 0.84	sym4
		3	58.98 ± 1.80	db4	77.40 ± 5.66	sym3	74.83 ± 0.84	sym4
		5	56.10 ± 1.73	db4	76.80 ± 4.91	sym3	74.44 ± 0.84	sym5
		8	53.58 ± 1.49	db4	76.20 ± 5.20	db2	74.32 ± 1.03	sym4
		10	49.79 ± 2.66	db4	75.80 ± 5.92	db4	74.83 ± 0.84	sym4
SVM	γ	−3	82.23 ± 1.37	db2	80.00 ± 4.80	db2	86.41 ± 0.64	db2
		−6	98.37 ± 0.34	db4	91.00 ± 4.83	db2	83.32 ± 0.45	sym4
		−9	96.87 ± 0.76	db2	86.00 ± 3.88	db2	75.17 ± 1.02	sym5
		−12	17.84 ± 3.35	sym3	61.79 ± 13.34	db2	6.72 ± 2.87	db2
		−14	19.66 ± 3.87	db4	59.60 ± 11.57	sym3	13.25 ± 1.01	sym4
OPF	D	E	76.08 ± 5.67	sym3	57.19 ± 1.78	sym3	74.17 ± 0.92	sym4
CNN	Epoch	15	63.54 ± 18.94	N/A	88.75 ± 11.41	N/A	95.00 ± 3.70	N/A
		30	88.89 ± 7.51	N/A	95.28 ± 0.70	N/A	95.06 ± 0.60	N/A
		50	94.72 ± 0.79	N/A	96.04 ± 2.11	N/A	97.26 ± 0.79	N/A

P = parameter | D = distance metric | E = Euclidean | MF = Mother Function | N/A = not applicable

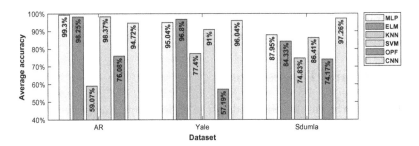

Fig. 2. Results obtained for each database using the best configurations for each technique

By analyzing the results described in the Table 2 it can be observed that MLP with 150 neurons presented the best results for the AR database when compared to the other traditional classifiers and CNN. For the Yale database, the best results were achieved with ELM using 4000 neurons. However, for the Sdumla database the best results were achieved with CNN using 50 epochs. This is due to the fact that the Sdumla database has more images when compared to other databases.

The Fig. 2 presents the best results obtained for each database using the best configurations for each technique. Based on these results it is possible to observe that MLP and ELM presented good results in terms of the recognition rate for the three databases. On the other hand, CNN presented better results for the Sdumla database. This database presents a larger number of images per individual and greater intra-class variability. Therefore, it can be inferred that CNN presents better results for large databases [20].

In this work, we used the Wilcoxon rank sum test [12] to formally check whether the accuracy difference among two classifiers is significant. The Wilcoxon rank sum test is a nonparametric statistical procedure. The null hypothesis attempts to show that no variation exists between classifiers, i.e, the classifiers have the same performance. Whether or not the null hypothesis is rejected depends on the statistical significance of the test, commonly referred to as a p-value. The significance level is commonly set to $\alpha = 0.05$, which represents the threshold at which there is only 5% probability that the null hypothesis is correct. A p-value greater than α means that us cannot reject the null hypothesis. A p-value less than α tells us to reject the null hypothesis and conclude that the two classifiers are drawn from two significantly different distributions.

The accuracy results are complemented with those reported in Table 3, which relates to the application of the Wilcoxon rank sum test over the accuracy samples from the 10 executions of the best classifiers for each database.

Analyzing the Wilcoxon rank sum test result presented in Table 3, it can be noted that MLP with 150 neurons is the best classifier for the AR database. However, for the Yale base the null hypothesis was not rejected when compared to ELM with 4000 neurons with MLP with 50 neurons and with CNN with 50

Table 3. Results of the Wilcoxon rank sum test over the accuracy samples obtained for each database

Best	Dataset	Classifier	Parameter	p-value	Null hypothesis
MLP	AR	OPF	Euclidian	0.0001	Rejected
		KNN	1	0.0001	Rejected
		SVM	−6	0.0005	Rejected
		ELM	4000	0.0005	Rejected
		CNN	50	0.0001	Rejected
ELM	Yale	MLP	50	0.2929	Not rejected
		OPF	Euclidean	0.0001	Rejected
		KNN	1	0.0001	Rejected
		SVM	−6	0.0005	Rejected
		CNN	50	0.1364	Not rejected
CNN	Sdumla	OPF	Euclidian	0.0001	Rejected
		MLP	150	0.0001	Rejected
		KNN	1	0.0001	Rejected
		SVM	−3	0.0001	Rejected
		ELM	4000	0.0001	Rejected

epochs. For the Sdumla Base, the null hypothesis was rejected when compared to CNN with the traditional techniques of machine learning. Therefore, it can be said that CNN is the best classifier for this database.

7   Conclusion

This paper carried out a comparative study between traditional machine learning techniques and Convolutional Neural Networks aiming at facial biometric recognition. In order to adequately evaluate each technique, three databases were used widely in the literature. Based on the results obtained it is possible to notice that CNN presented better results when using the Sdumla database. This database contains more face images per individual when compared to the other databases.

On the other hand, CNN presented lower results for the AR and Yale database when compared to the traditional machine learning techniques. Therefore, it can be noticed that for databases with a small amount of face images per individual, it is more interesting to use traditional machine learning techniques. As future works, we intend to use other CNNs and perform a comparative study involving other traditional machine learning techniques and other techniques of feature extraction.

References

1. Chang, C.C., Lin, C.J.: LIBSVM: a library for support vector machines. ACM Trans. Intell. Syst. Technol. (TIST) **2**(3), 27 (2011)
2. Coşkun, M., Uçar, A., Yıldırım, Ö., Demir, Y.: Face recognition based on convolutional neural network. In: 2017 International Conference on Modern Electrical and Energy Systems, MEES, pp. 376–379. IEEE (2017)
3. Costa, D.M.M.D.: Ensemble baseado em métodos de Kernel para reconhecimento biométrico multimodal. Ph.D. thesis. Universidade de São Paulo (2011)
4. Cover, T., Hart, P.: Nearest neighbor pattern classification. IEEE Trans. Inf. Theory **13**(1), 21–27 (2006)
5. Georghiades, A., Belhumeur, P., Kriegman, D.: Yale face database, vol. 2. Center for computational Vision and Control at Yale University (1997). http://cvc.yale.edu/projects/yalefaces/yalefa
6. Haykin, S.S., Haykin, S.S., Haykin, S.S., Haykin, S.S.: Neural Networks and Learning Machines, vol. 3. Pearson, Upper Saddle River (2009)
7. Huang, G.B., Zhu, Q.Y., Siew, C.K.: Extreme learning machine: a new learning scheme of feedforward neural networks. In: Proceedings of the 2004 IEEE International Joint Conference on Neural Networks, vol. 2, pp. 985–990. IEEE (2004)
8. Jain, A., Flynn, P., Ross, A.A.: Handbook of Biometrics. Springer, Heidelberg (2007). https://doi.org/10.1007/978-0-387-71041-9
9. LeCun, Y., Bengio, Y., Hinton, G.: Deep learning. Nature **521**, 436–444 (2015)
10. LeCun, Y., Bottou, L., Bengio, Y., Haffner, P.: Gradient-based learning applied to document recognition. Proc. IEEE **86**(11), 2278–2324 (1998)
11. Li, H., Lin, Z., Shen, X., Brandt, J., Hua, G.: A convolutional neural network cascade for face detection. In: Proceedings of the IEEE Conference on Computer Vision and Pattern Recognition, pp. 5325–5334 (2015)
12. Litchfield, J., Wilcoxon, F.: A simplified method of evaluating dose-effect experiments. J. Pharmacol. **96**(2), 99–113 (1949)
13. Mallat, S.G.: A theory for multiresolution signal decomposition: the wavelet representation. IEEE Trans. Pattern Anal. Mach. Intell. **11**(7), 674–693 (1989)
14. Martinez, A.M.: The AR face database. CVC technical report 24 (1998)
15. Müller, K.-R., Smola, A.J., Rätsch, G., Schölkopf, B., Kohlmorgen, J., Vapnik, V.: Predicting time series with support vector machines. In: Gerstner, W., Germond, A., Hasler, M., Nicoud, J.-D. (eds.) ICANN 1997. LNCS, vol. 1327, pp. 999–1004. Springer, Heidelberg (1997). https://doi.org/10.1007/BFb0020283
16. Papa, J.P., Falcao, A.X., Suzuki, C.T.: Supervised pattern classification based on optimum-path forest. Int. J. Imag. Syst. Technol. **19**(2), 120–131 (2009)
17. Viola, P., Jones, M.J.: Robust real-time face detection. Int. J. Comput. Vis. **57**(2), 137–154 (2004)
18. Yin, Y., Liu, L., Sun, X.: SDUMLA-HMT: a multimodal biometric database. In: Sun, Z., Lai, J., Chen, X., Tan, T. (eds.) CCBR 2011. LNCS, vol. 7098, pp. 260–268. Springer, Heidelberg (2011). https://doi.org/10.1007/978-3-642-25449-9_33
19. Zhang, Z., Li, J., Zhu, R.: Deep neural network for face recognition based on sparse autoencoder. In: 2015 8th International Congress on Image and Signal Processing, CISP, pp. 594–598. IEEE (2015)
20. Zhao, W.: Research on the deep learning of the small sample data based on transfer learning. In: Proceedings of the AIP Conference, vol. 1864, p. 020018. AIP Publishing (2017)

Using Fuzzy Neural Networks to the Prediction of Improvement in Expert Systems for Treatment of Immunotherapy

Augusto Junio Guimarães[2] ⓘ, Vinicius Jonathan Silva Araujo[2] ⓘ,
Paulo Vitor de Campos Souza[1,2(✉)] ⓘ, Vanessa Souza Araujo[2] ⓘ,
and Thiago Silva Rezende[2] ⓘ

[1] Secretariat of Information Governance-CEFET-MG, Avenue Amazonas 5253,
Belo Horizonte, Minas Gerais 30421-169, Brazil
goldenpaul@informatica.esp.ufmg.br
[2] Information Systems Course, Faculdade Una de Betim, Av. Gov. Valadares,
640 - Center, Betim, Minas Gerais 32510-010, Brazil
augustojunioguimaraes@gmail.com,
vinicius.j.s.a22@hotmail.com,
v.souzaaraujo@yahoo.com.br,
silvarezendethiago@gmail.com

Abstract. Warts and condylomas are benign skin proliferation caused by HPV (human papillomavirus), which can appear anywhere in the body, including the genital regions. One of the treatments used to combat this type of tumor is immunotherapy, a technique that advances the stimulation of the immune system through the use of substances that modify the biological response in human beings. Immunological reactions may be the result of the antigen-antibody interaction or the mechanisms involved in cell-mediated immunity. Health professionals working with these techniques can use specialist systems to assist in the diagnosis of treatment effectiveness in patients. A system based on fuzzy logic was developed with data from medical research. This system can predict the adaptability of a patient to the treatment with 83.33% accuracy. This article proposes the use of a hybrid model of artificial intelligence and fuzzy logic to improve the predictive results of the expert system through the creation of fuzzy rules to construct a more interpretative expert system. Based on the tests performed, we can infer that the proposed model kept the results statistically equal in the prediction of efficiency in the immunotherapeutic treatment, besides making possible the creation of fuzzy rules based on the data of the research on the medication.

Keywords: Immunotherapy · Fuzzy neural networks · Fuzzy rules

1 Introduction

Warts present in the human body can generate annoyances and other types of damages, principally for being benign tumors. They can be caused by the human papillomavirus, which can grow in many parts of humans, causing disorders that can reduce a person's

G. R. Simari et al. (Eds.): IBERAMIA 2018, LNAI 11238, pp. 229–240, 2018.
https://doi.org/10.1007/978-3-030-03928-8_19

quality of life and even in more extreme cases to become factors that contribute to cancer of the cervix uterus in women. Many instances of this type of cancer can be prevented by the efficient monitoring of the growth of these warts. If quality, coverage, and follow-up with a physician are high, the incidence of cervical cancer can be reduced by as much as 80% [1]. In addition to screening, the effectiveness of treatments based on chemical composites is present to prevent women from suffering from this type of virus. But this is not an illness that attacks only women. Men may also suffer from these genital warts [2], resulting in severe damage to situations such as the anus and penis, especially if they become malignant tumors.

A widely used technique for the removal of warts in humans is based on the application of a superficial vaccine to the skin, in a predetermined period, composed of an inactivated bacterium that will stimulate the immune system. Immunotherapy allows warts to be combated more naturally as this treatment allows the immune system of each person to recognize the HPV viruses present in moles, as well as promote proper healing of the skin. But this technique is not sufficient for all people due to various immunological or environmental factors [1].

Recent studies have allowed the creation of expert systems based on fuzzy rules [3] for the prediction of efficiency and impacts of treatments in human wart removal. This system acts with a knowledge base that can generate fuzzy rules to classify whether the patient will perform well or not in eliminating the wart with the treatment applied on their skin. This system can reach 83.1% accuracy in responding to the efficiency of the procedure in a patient. It system responds whether or not immunotherapy is appropriate to the patient's treatment. The algorithm that obtained the best prediction results in [3] uses concepts of neural networks based on fuzzy decision trees. A disadvantage that this model has is the need to update whenever knowledge base characteristics change on a large scale, in addition to being an algorithm that makes it difficult to interpret its results by non-specialists. However, this type of system has several benefits, highlighting the ease and accuracy of physicians' diagnoses, reducing the waiting time of patients who undergo a treatment that will not have efficiency for the problem, extinguishing eventualities with the use of anesthetics and anesthetics, scarring and the high costs associated with treatment.

This work proposes the use of a hybrid structure, also based on fuzzy rules systems, but which has faster and simpler responses than a decision tree, to improve the accuracy of the predictive method of immunotherapy for patients with benign tumors proposed by [3]. The use of fuzzy neural networks has been used in several areas, such as economy [4], in the field of phoneme recognition [5], prediction of cardiac arrhythmia characteristics [6], selection of features [7], time series prediction [8], rain forecast [9] and pulsar selection [10]. The training of the fuzzy neural network proposed by [11] and improved in [12] seeks to perform binary classification tests with the database of characteristics related to the treatment of immunotherapy [3] used to create the rules of knowledge of the prediction system for immunotherapeutic treatments. The use of the extreme learning machine [14] facilitates the creation and updating of weights and parameters of the system, allowing the prediction of the intelligent network to happen faster, more precise and adaptive.

The article is organized as follows: Sect. 2 presents concepts related to the theoretical structure that is involved in the resolution and improvement of the intelligent system. Section 3 shows the characteristics of the neural network model used in this article, with emphasis on its architecture, nebula rules creation and training for parameter adjustments. In Sect. 4 we present the tests that try to verify if the approach of the neural network can improve the prediction of the expert system, and finally, in Sect. 5, the conclusions of this work are presented.

2 Literature Review

2.1 Concepts of Immunotherapy and HPV

For [15], human papillomavirus (HPV) infection is the leading cause of cervical cancer, but the risk associated with various types of HPV has not been adequately assessed. It is a disease that has been growing and worrying about the medical society. HPV is characterized by the induction of genital and extra-genital warts (conjunctiva, nasal mucosa, oral and laryngeal). Persistent HPV infection represents an essential role in the development of cervical cancer and men, especially in the anus and penis [16].

For the treatment of warts in humans, several procedures have been proposed, among which the most relevant are immunotherapy and cryotherapy. The choice of therapy should be based on the number, size of warts, morphology, the location of the lesions, their clinical status regarding the assessment of their immunity, as well as the financial relevance of the treatment and patient aspects [16].

Many immunotherapy methods were used. In an example, the patient is subjected to the application of a product in the wart to which it has been identified as being a chemical compound that the patient is allergic to. A reaction occurs around the wart, and it ends up disappearing. Interferon can also be injected to stimulate the immune response and cause the rejection of moles and consequently their destruction [3]. In Fig. 1 it can be seen how the immunotherapy procedure is performed.

It is found that this procedure is quite invasive for the patient, so the more advanced it is known about the acceptance or not of this procedure in a person, the better is the way to avoid slow and inefficient treatments.

2.2 Related Works

Several papers are presented in the literature on the use of immunotherapy for various purposes. The work of [18] used immunotherapy for the treatment of allergic persons, where it has long-term efficacy and can prevent the progression of the allergic disease, in addition to improving the quality of life of patients. Already in [19] used immunotherapy for studies in the treatment of Alzheimer's. In the work of [3], a specialist system was developed that can make predictions about the acceptance or not of immune therapy treatment. In [13], a comparison between the results obtained in immunotherapy and cryotherapy treatments in the elimination of warts is performed, and finally, in the work of [20], a comparison between the efficacy of the cryotherapy treatments and immunotherapy for the treatment of Candida has proceeded.

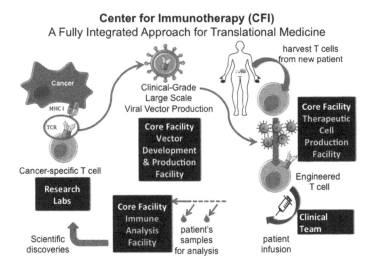

Fig. 1. Immunotherapy procedure in humans [17].

2.3 Artificial Neural Networks

Artificial neural networks are models that use in their structures the logical neuron, seeking to simulate the processing of information of the human brain through a system of several interconnected artificial neurons that are attached employing synaptic connections. In a simplified procedure, an artificial neural network can be seen as a graph where the nodes are the neurons, and the links make the function of the synapses. Artificial neural networks are distinguished by their architecture and the way the weights associated with the connections are adjusted during the learning process. Learning is the way in which the neural network captures the information provided by the inputs and through the links and the synaptic weights make decisions about the central theme of the database. The architecture of a neural network restricts the type of problem in which the system can be used, and is defined by the number of layers (single layer or multiple layers), number of nodes in each layer, type of connection between nodes (feedforward or feedback) and its topology [21]. Figure 2 shows the structure of a neural network with multiple layers. It also highlights the neurons and their synaptic relationships.

2.4 Fuzzy Systems

For [23] the use of fuzzy systems is necessary in cases where the classical approach becomes unfeasible for the resolution of a problem due to the nature of its complexity. The best-known methods are capable of abrupt changes to solve problems due to the simplification of the real model, but the fuzzy systems have resources (membership functions, rules, and aggregation operators) that allow a more accurate approximation to the actual model, avoiding that the solution generated by the fuzzy system is considerably different from the real model. Figure 3 presents the main elements of fuzzy

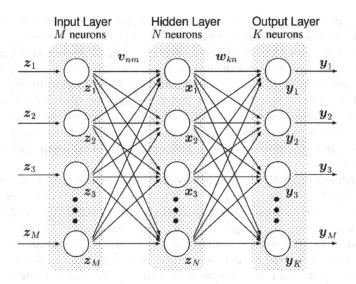

Fig. 2. Example of an artificial neural network of multiple layers and multiple outputs [22].

logic: its inputs, the process of converting data into fuzzy components, the creation of input fuzzy sets, the set of rules and inferences, the obtaining of fuzzy acknowledgment sets, which is to make the values obtained according to the inputs of the system and the outputs as required.

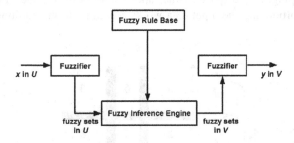

Fig. 3. Fuzzy inference system [24].

3 Fuzzy Neural Network for the Prediction on the Efficiency of Immunotherapy Treatment in Patients with Warts

3.1 Fuzzy Neural Network Architecture and Training for Binary Classification Problems

The computational knowledge area presents considerable improvements in the development of techniques and models that simulate human behavior acting in processes and systems, with importance on artificial neural networks, fuzzy systems, and their hybrid models, with a significant number of new applications being proposed in the literature.

One of the primary purposes of computational intelligence research is to create and model systems that emulate distinct human characteristics, such as learning, intuition, logical reasoning, classification and regression [21]. One of the mathematical models used to perform human behavior simulations is fuzzy neural networks, which are neural networks composed in their fuzzy neuron structure. These models diverge from the traditional models of neural networks and fuzzy systems due to the cooperation between the concepts of neural networks and the ideas derived from the theory of fuzzy sets, generating a model able to use the learning capacity of the neural networks together the efficiency of the I deal with the imprecision and the interpretation of fuzzy systems [25].

The architecture of the fuzzy neural network used in this work is the same one described in [12]. Therefore, the fuzzy neural network to be used in this paper practices in the first layer the division of input space in grid format called ANFIS [26], that is, does the fuzzification process reported in Fig. 3 using the space division of entry into a number M of fuzzy relevance functions of the Gaussian type equally spaced and centered at 0.5. This type of division through membership functions with the same characteristics can assist in semantic interpretation. The Fuzzy Inference System (FIS) is a computational structure based on the concepts of fuzzy set theory, fuzzy rules of the IF … THEN style and fuzzy thought where its structure has three conceptual layers: a rule base, a database and a base of reasoning [26]. In [26] explains that the FIS can perform a non-linear mapping from its input space to the output space. This mapping is accompanied by many fuzzy rules IF … THEN, where each one describes the local operation of the mapping. The antecedents in the rules of a fuzzy inference system implement a multidimensional neural partition that can be in the grid, decision tree or by grouping, in the space of the input variables of a model. Figure 4 below explains how partitioning the input data works according to the partition used.

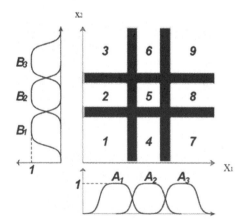

Fig. 4. Division of input space performed by Gaussian membership functions [26].

Considering x1 and x2 as two characteristics present in the data collected from patients, we can infer linguistic rules of the type: If x1 is small and x2 is small, so y is 1, just as if x1 and x2 were significant, the class of y is 9. However, as described in [11] and [12] grid division can become a great approach since it trades with an exponential relation between the number of membership functions determined to partition the input space and number of characteristics of the problem. In this paper, an evaluation was used to filter the neurons that will leave the first layer: If the number of attributes of the problem is less than six and the number of pertinence functions chosen is less than or equal to three, then this approach is based on several previous tests that found that the ability to create fuzzy rules made the problem much more complicated than was necessary. If the premise is not satisfied, the number of neurons in the first layer is defined using a modified proposal by [23], where there is a limiting filter of random creation of 500 fuzzy neurons based on the input space. The number 500 was arbitrated after several algorithm performance tests using cross-validation concepts with various combinations of feature numbers and membership functions.

In the second layer, there are fuzzy logic neurons that use unineuron concepts introduced in [27] that perform the aggregation of the weights and activation functions of the fuzzy neurons of the first layer. In this paper it was decided to evaluate the regularized approaches that use the bolasso [28] and unregulated model of [12], to confirm if the quantity of neurons affects the accuracy of the model. The second layer weights are defined using the concepts of extreme learning machine [14] that act efficiently in the fast generation of weights, unlike methods that work with back propagation to update the net architecture. In models that work with large data mass, this approach becomes feasible due to its more straightforward nature of generating the weights using pseudo inverse concepts. The model uses a simple artificial neuron, which can be seen as a singleton. The architecture of the fuzzy neural network applied in the paper is presented in Fig. 5.

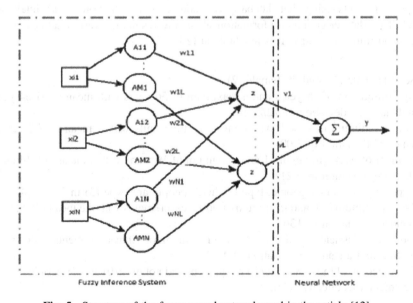

Fig. 5. Structure of the fuzzy neural network used in the article [12].

4 Classification Tests of Patients Using the Fuzzy Neural Network

4.1 Tests Configuration

In the tests conducted out in the database, the regularized version of the model [12] was used. The membership functions are of the Gaussian type, the weights of the first and second layers were estimated randomly in the interval of $[-3, 3]$. The model response is determined by comparing the network output with the expected classification value. The sum of these values is divided by the total of samples used in the training and test steps to determine the accuracy of training and test, respectively. More information can be seen in [11, 12, 27]. 30 replicates were performed with the randomized entries in each of them to avoid tendencies in the model. The percentage allocated to training is 70% and 30% for testing. When the regularized model was used, the replication value was 8, and the decision consensus on the neurons was used 50%. These two values were obtained after previous tests using cross-validation with values between 8, 16, 32 bootstrap replications and 50%, 60%, 70% decision consensus. The outputs of the model were normalized to -1 and 1 to facilitate the accurate calculations. Accuracy results are evaluated by summing the correct answers in the comparison of the expected result, dividing the sum by the total of the samples used in the training and the test. The results are presented in, and the standard deviation of the 30 replicates is presented in parentheses.

4.2 General Characteristics of the Patient Base

The database was provided by [13] and was used in [3] to select the best treatment for groups of patients using that database as a source of information for an intelligent model. This dataset contains information about the results of warts treatment of 90 patients on immunotherapy. It is available at [29].

Its dimensions are:

- Sex (41 male (1), and 49 female (2));
- Age (minimum of 15 years and a maximum of 56 years with mean in 31.04 years and standard deviation of 12.23);
- Time (minimum of 1 and maximum of 12-time units with a mean of 7.23 and a standard deviation of 3.09);
- Number of warts (minimum 1 and maximum of 19 warts with a mean of 6.14 and a standard deviation of 4.21);
- Type (type (1) in 47 people, type (2) in 22 people and type (3) in 21 people);
- Area (minimum of 6 and maximum of 900 measurements with the mean of 95.7 and standard deviation of 136.61);
- Induration diameter (minimum of 2 and maximum of 70 measurements with a mean of 14.3 and a standard deviation of 17.21);
- The outcome of the treatment (19 people who did not give (0) and 71 people that the treatment was effective (1)).

4.3 Classification Tests of Patients

All the results of the tests presented below developed from the regularized model using the bolasso [28]. To perform the pattern classification tests for immunotherapy patients, it's played several tests with various configurations of the [12]. Table 1 shows the most significant results from the tests conducted. All values of the test precision, the accuracy of training and the number of neurons used in this table, demonstrate in mean values after 30 repetitions and the amounts indicated in parentheses are the averages of the standard deviations for the experiment.

Table 1. Fuzzy neural network test performance with regularization use.

M. Functions	Training accuracy	Neurons used	Test accuracy
6	95.23 (5.69)	17.66 (7.16)	79.22 (7.05)
6	93.12 (6.48)	19.2 (22.39)	78.71 (6.07)
6	**85.82 (4.71)**	**7.4 (22.45)**	**81.03 (7.4)**
4	91.43 (6.82)	23.36 (35.49)	80.27 (7.45)

We can verify that the model presented proper pattern classification for the immunotherapy base. However, it can be observed that it did not reach the percentage of 83.1% of [3] we can also analyze the high Test Accuracy index and its high standard deviation. Through the t-student test we can verify with a p-value of 0.08 performed in the statistical software R, us can state that for a level of 95% confidence that we can accept that the models proposed in this paper have the same statistical performance for the classification of treatment for patients than the one proposed in [3]. Thus, to demonstrate the effectiveness and performance of the tests, Table 2 shows the results using algorithms known in the neural network literature found in the same database of immunotherapy submitted in the [30] to the following models described in it. To understand the values suggested in the test, its parameters and configurations, see [30].

Table 2. Performance of tests performed by [30].

N	σ	LSVC	SVC	RF	XGB	KNN	CG	FTCG
10	0.4	55.3	45.5	57.8	55	56.3	57.9	57.8
50	0.4	53.6	64.1	67.4	67.4	66.8	68.2	67.8

4.4 Fuzzy Rules for Assistance to Specialists

Fuzzy rules can be extracted from the system to assist specialists. In immunotherapy treatments to be predicted with more interpretability on fuzzy neural network responses. The best answers were obtained with six pertinence functions, so this grid division can receive textual values to help in the interpretation of the contexts in a more straightforward and more usual way to professionals who do not act directly with computational intelligence. Consider that each of the six Gaussian membership functions can have the following denominations: minimal, small, medium, high, very high, extremely high. The resulting fuzzy rules were extracted from the system.

Rule1: If *Age* is s*mall* with certainty 0.5432
and *Time* is *very small* with certainty *0.2561*
   then treatment is -1
Rule2: If Number of warts is very high with certainty *0.7654*
and *Age* is *Medium* with certainty *0.3245*   (1)
   then treatment é 1
Rule3: If Area is extremely high with certainty *0.6789*
and Induration diameter *is high* with certainty *0.8765*
   then treatment is 1

5 Conclusion

We can conclude from the experiments carried out that the fuzzy neural networks to maintain the interpretability through their fuzzy rules, of the diagnoses made based on the intelligent system proposed by [3], thus obtained a great income equating to him, taking in the t-student test result. At its best conclusion, we can get 81.03% (7.4) of accuracy test percent. Also, the model showed better accuracy than the studies performed by [30], which used several approaches of neural networks to play the classification of patients. Because it is an expensive treatment that gives patients hope of getting rid of warts, this increases the chances of more patients getting rid of warts than saving the money spent to treat people who have warts probability of cure. As future work the application of the database to also act and improve the classification of patients undergoing treatment with other diseases. To further enhance the accuracy of accuracy, fuzzy neural network accuracy testing is proposed in future with other pertinence function values, with different amounts of the number of replications and decision coefficient and, finally, other types of pertinence functions, for example, the triangular one.

References

1. Mandelblatt, J.S., et al.: Benefits and costs of using HPV testing to screen for cervical cancer. Jama **287**(18), 2372–2381 (2002)
2. Marianelli, R., Nadal, S.R.: Utilidade da citologia anal no rastreamento dos homens heterossexuais portadores do HPV genital Anal cytology for screening heterosexual men harboring genital HPV infection. Rev. Bras. Coloproctol. **30**(3), 365–367 (2010)
3. Khozeimeh, F., Alizadehsani, R., Roshanzamir, M., Khosravi, A., Layegh, P., Nahavandi, S.: An expert system for selecting wart treatment method. Comput. Biol. Med. **81**, 167–175 (2017)
4. Bakirtzis, A.G., Theocharis, J.B., Kiartzis, S.J., Satsios, K.J.: Short term load forecasting using fuzzy neural networks. IEEE Trans. Power Syst. **10**(3), 1518–1524 (1995)

5. Kasabov, N.: Evolving fuzzy neural networks-algorithms, applications and biological motivation. Methodol. Concept. Des. Appl. Soft Comput. World Sci. **1**, 271–274 (1998)
6. Özbay, Y., Ceylan, R., Karlik, B.: A fuzzy clustering neural network architecture for classification of ECG arrhythmias. Comput. Biol. Med. **36**(4), 376–388 (2006)
7. Silva, A.M., Caminhas, W.M., Lemos, A.P., Gomide, F.: Evolving neo-fuzzy neural network with adaptive feature selection. In: 2013 BRICS Congress on Computational Intelligence and 11th Brazilian Congress on Computational Intelligence (BRICS-CCI & CBIC), pp. 341–349. IEEE, September 2013
8. Souza, P.V.C., Torres, L.C.B.: Regularized fuzzy neural network based on or neuron for time series forecasting. In: Proceedings of 37th North American Fuzzy Information Processing Society Annual Conference (NAFIPS 2018), Fortaleza (2018)
9. Ballini, R., Soares, S., Andrade, M.G.: Previsão de vazões médias mensais usando redes neurais nebulosas. SBA: Controle Automação Sociedade Brasileira de Automatica **14**(3), 680–693 (2003)
10. Souza, P.V.C.: Detecção de pulsares utilizando redes neurais nebulosas baseadas em uninormas. In: Quinto Congresso Brasileiro de Sistemas Fuzzy? V CBSF, 2018, Fortaleza. Anais do Quinto Congresso Brasileiro de Sistemas Fuzzy. V CBSF (2018)
11. Souza, P.V.C.: Regularized fuzzy neural networks for pattern classification problems. Int. J. Appl. Eng. Res. **13**(5), 2985–2991 (2018)
12. Souza, P.V.C., Silva, G.R.L., Torres, L.C.B.: Uninorm based regularized fuzzy neural network. In: IEEE Technical Committee on Evolving and Adaptive Intelligent Systems, Proceedings 2018 IEEE Conference on Evolving and Adaptive Intelligent Systems (EAIS 2018) 2018. SMC Society and the IEEE Computation, Rhodes/Greece, Greece (2018)
13. Khozeimeh, F., et al.: Intralesional immunotherapy compared to cryotherapy in the treatment of warts. Int. J. Dermatol. **56**(4), 474–478 (2017)
14. Huang, G.B., Zhu, Q.Y., Siew, C.K.: Extreme learning machine: theory and applications. Neurocomputing **70**(1–3), 489–501 (2006)
15. Muñoz, N., et al.: Epidemiologic classification of human papillomavirus types associated with cervical cancer. N. Engl. J. Med. **348**(6), 518–527 (2003)
16. Scheinfeld, N., Lehman, D.S.: An evidence-based review of medical and surgical treatments of genital warts. Dermatol. Online J. **12**(3), 5 (2006)
17. How Does Immunotherapy Work? https://www.roswellpark.org/immunotherapy/about-immunotherapy/how-does-immunotherapy-work. Accessed 31 May 2018
18. Alvarez-Cuesta, E., Bousquet, J., Canonica, G.W., Durham, S.R., Malling, H.J., Valovirta, E.: Standards for practical allergen-specific immunotherapy. Allergy **61**, 1–3 (2006)
19. Panza, F., et al.: Immunotherapy for Alzheimer's disease: from anti-β-amyloid to tau-based immunization strategies. Immunotherapy **4**(2), 213–238 (2012)
20. Majid, I., Imran, S.: Immunotherapy with intralesional Candida albicans antigen in resistant or recurrent warts: a study. Indian J. Dermatol. **58**(5), 360 (2013)
21. Haykin, S., Network, N.: A comprehensive foundation. Neural Netw. **2**(2004), 41 (2004)
22. de Oliveira, A.C.S., de Souza, A.A., Lacerda, W.S., Gonçalves, L.R.: Aplicação de redes neurais artificiais na previsão da produção de álcool (2010)
23. Calvo, R.: Arquitetura híbrida inteligente para navegação autônoma de robôs (Doctoral dissertation, Universidade de São Paulo) (2007)
24. https://www.researchgate.net/publication/221908927_Development_of_Fuzzy-Logic-Based_Self_Tuning_PI_Controller_for_Servomotor/figures?lo=1&utm_source=google&utm_medium=organic. Accessed 31 May 2018
25. Pedrycz, W.: Processing in relational structures: fuzzy relational equations. Fuzzy Sets Syst. **40**(1), 77–106 (1991)

26. Jang, J.S.: ANFIS: adaptive-network-based fuzzy inference system. IEEE Trans. Syst. Man Cybern. **23**(3), 665–685 (1993)
27. Lemos, A., Caminhas, W., Gomide, F.: New uninorm-based neuron model and fuzzy neural networks. In: Fuzzy Information Processing Society (NAFIPS), 2010 Annual Meeting of the North American, pp. 1–6. IEEE, July 2010
28. Bach, F.R.: Bolasso: model consistent lasso estimation through the bootstrap. In: Proceedings of the 25th international conference on Machine learning, pp. 33–40. ACM, July 2008
29. UCI Machine Learning- Immunotherapy Dataset Data Set https://archive.ics.uci.edu/ml/datasets/Immunotherapy+Dataset#. Accessed 31 May 2018
30. Guttenberg, N., Kanai, R.: Learning to generate classifiers. arXiv preprint arXiv:1803.11373 (2018)

Stakeholders Classification System Based on Clustering Techniques

Yasiel Pérez Vera[1]([⊠]) [iD] and Anié Bermudez Peña[2] [iD]

[1] La Salle University, Arequipa, Peru
yasielpv@gmail.com
[2] University of Informatics Science, Havana, Cuba
abp@uci.cu

Abstract. Stakeholder classification is carried out by project managers using methods such as interviews with experts, brainstorming and checklists. These methods are carried out manually and present a subjective character as they depend on the appreciation of the interviewees. It affects the accuracy of the classification and the making-decisions. The objective of this research is to propose a fuzzy inference system for the classification of stakeholders, which will improve the quality of such classification in the projects. The proposal performs the automatic learning and the adjustment of the fuzzy inference system to classify the stakeholders executing two clustering algorithms: SBC and DENFIS. It examines the results of applying them in 10 iterations by calculating the measures: accuracy, false positive cases, false negative cases, mean square error and symmetric mean absolute percentage error. The best results are shown by the SBC algorithm. The fuzzy inference system for stakeholder's classification generated improves the quality of this classification as well as the tools to support decision-making in organizations oriented to projects.

Keywords: Clustering algorithms · Fuzzy inference system
Project management · Stakeholders classification

1 Introduction

The success or failure of a project is related to the perception that stakeholders have of its value and the type of relationships established between the involved parts. In [1] a study is made regarding the success and failure of the projects, as well as their causes. The number of software projects that do not complete successfully is significant, only 29% are considered satisfactory. This study analyzes the elements that are considered relevant to achieve a successful project and a large part is directly related to the management of stakeholders [2].

The management of stakeholders in a project includes the necessary processes to identify them, analyze their expectations and impact on the project and achieve their effective participation in decision-making. A correct identification and classification of those involved helps the project manager to concentrate on the necessary relationships to ensure the success of the project [3].

© Springer Nature Switzerland AG 2018
G. R. Simari et al. (Eds.): IBERAMIA 2018, LNAI 11238, pp. 241–252, 2018.
https://doi.org/10.1007/978-3-030-03928-8_20

Stakeholder classification process is usually carried out by the project manager using techniques such as interview with experts, brainstorming and checklists [4]. There are several methods that make use of different attributes to characterize the stakeholders. These methods are carried out manually and present a subjective nature on the part of the specialists linked to the projects, which introduces delays, vagueness and imprecision in the classification process.

An alternative solution to the aforementioned problems is the application of machine learning and soft computing techniques. These techniques bring to the computer tools a human reasoning approach, through the use of knowledge and accumulated experience [5]. These techniques are robust in environments where the data have inaccurate values; they allow to develop solutions of low cost and greater capacity of modeling [6].

Among these techniques are the clustering algorithms, which focus on partitioning a set of entries in n-dimensional space where the elements of a same partition are more similar to each other than with the elements of another partition. These techniques are widely used in unsupervised learning because they allow working with data not classified a priori [7].

The inadequacies in the manual classification of stakeholders affect its accuracy and the project managers do not have more detailed information when making decisions about stakeholders. The objective of this work is to propose a system for the classification of stakeholders, which allows improving the quality of the classification with respect to that carried out manually by the project managers.

2   Related Works

As part of the research, a study is made about the stakeholder classification process. Following, the fundamental elements of fuzzy inference systems and clustering algorithms are analyzed. Then the application of two clustering algorithms in the generation and optimization of fuzzy inference systems is described.

2.1   Stakeholders Classification

The objective of the stakeholder classification process is to group them according to their characteristics, functions, expectations, interests and influence on the project. Once they have identified and collected their information, the stakeholders are classified in order to guarantee the efficient use of the effort to communicate and manage their expectations. This allows the project manager to concentrate on the necessary relationships to ensure the success of the project [8].

There are several techniques for the classification of stakeholders, among which is the Mitchell prominence model [9]. This model defines the classification of stakeholders based on a diagram in which relate the variables: power, legitimacy and urgency. The power is the ability of the stakeholder to influence the project; legitimacy refers to the relationship and actions of the interested parts with the project in terms of desirability, property or convenience; and the urgency refers to the immediate attention to the stakeholder's requirements by the project. According to several investigations [10–14], this model is one of the most discussed and used in the world.

In [9], power variable is associated with the disposition or possibility of obtaining coercive resources (physical force, weapons), utilitarian resources (technology, money, knowledge, logistics, raw materials) and symbolic resources (prestige, esteem, charisma) that allow a stakeholder to impose his will on others in the organization. So, the Mitchell model defines the following attributes to measure power:

- Coercive Power: is that which involves the use of weapons or physical punishment. In this way, the stakeholder's control is based on applications of physical meaning.
- Utilitarian power: comes from the use of material rewards such as goods and services. The granting of symbols such as money that allow the acquisition of goods and services is classified as material since the final effect is similar. In this way, the use of material means to control a relationship constitutes the utilitarian power.
- Normative-social power: it is the one that is transmitted through symbols, whose use does not constitute a physical treatment or a claim of material rewards. Thus, these symbols include normative (prestige and esteem) and social (love and acceptance).

Legitimacy is considered as the presumption or generalized perception that the actions of a stakeholder are desirable or appropriate within certain socially constructed systems of norms, values, beliefs and definitions [9]. Legitimacy can be measured based on the attributes: organizational legitimacy and social legitimacy. Where the first expresses the attribution of a degree of desirability of the actions of the stakeholder at the organizational level and the second at the social level.

The urgency variable is defined as the degree to which stakeholders consider their claims to the project important [9]. In this context, they differentiate the degree of emergency possession according to the possession of two attributes:

- Temporal sensitivity: it shows when a relationship or issue has a nature sensitive to time, that is, the degree of unacceptability on the part of the stakeholder in the delay of the manager in addressing their claims.
- Criticism: manifests itself in the importance that stakeholders consider having their claims or issues and, therefore, when a matter is considered critical for the stakeholder.

For each of these described attributes, the experts value the degree of possession of the stakeholders. This classification given by experts contains inaccuracies and vagueness; problem to be solved in this investigation with the application of fuzzy inference systems and clustering techniques, described in the following sections.

2.2 Fuzzy Inference Systems

A fuzzy inference system imitates the form of human reasoning, allowing to correctly handle the uncertainty, ambiguity and vagueness of information such as those used in everyday life. These systems are considered expert systems with approximate reasoning to transform an input vector to a single output based on fuzzy logic [15]. They use a knowledge base expressed in conditional rules and are responsible for manipulating fuzzy sets. There are three main models of fuzzy inference defined in the literature as: Mamdani [16], Sugeno [17] and Tsukamoto [18].

The model proposed by Mamdani has been the most widely accepted, being considered more intuitive and adaptable to human language, in addition to being able to be converted to the Sugeno type [19]. The model proposed by Sugeno is better adapted to mathematical analysis and does not need a concretion process since each rule has an exact output value, to which an average or weighted sum is applied to obtain the final result [20]. Tsukamoto proposes a model where the conclusion of the defined fuzzy rules is represented through a fuzzy set. It defines an exact value for each rule, which implies not carrying out a concretion process [21].

The basis of rules of a fuzzy inference system can be defined statically from the knowledge and experience of experts in the intended scope. This way does not allow the adaptation of the system to changes in the organization and completely depends on the expertise of the people in the subject. It is convenient to use optimization techniques that allow rules to be adjusted automatically according to the development of the application environment.

For the automatic learning of fuzzy rules different methods are used, one of the strategies focuses on generating a base of candidate rules and then refining them. A variant within this strategy is the construction of fuzzy rules based on the formation of groups using supervised or unsupervised learning. In this approach, learning based on the application of clustering has a proven efficiency [22].

2.3   Clustering Algorithms

In general, the clustering techniques are responsible for the following: given several elements in n-dimensional space, they are partitioned into k clusters such that the elements within the same group are more similar to each other than to each one of the other groups. This similarity is measured according to a certain distance function.

For example, the K-means [23] is one of the simplest and best-known clustering algorithms. This follows a simple way to divide a database into k groups set a priori. The main idea is to define k centroids (one for each group) and then take each point of the database and place it in the class of its closest centroid. The next step is to recalculate the centroid of each group and redistribute all objects according to the nearest centroid. The process is repeated until, from one step to the next, there is no change in the groups.

In [24] a neuro-fuzzy system is proposed for classification, which uses dynamic adaptive clustering to determine the cluster number for each attribute. Then the optimal amount of Gaussian membership functions is created and rules are constructed from them. Other works employing clustering are presented in [25, 26]. In these variants, the rules generated from the base of candidate rules are consistent and can be exploited.

The application of clustering in the generation of rules greatly improves the need to previously define the fuzzy sets, which would require the intervention of experts prior to the application. Next, a characterization of the clustering algorithms used in the field of the optimization of the parameters of the fuzzy inference system for stakeholder's classification is carried out.

Subtractive and K-Means Fuzzy Clustering Method (SBC). In [27] the SBC hybrid algorithm (subtractive clustering) is presented, which is based on the methods of subtractive clustering [28] and fuzzy K-means [29]. Subtractive clustering is a partition method that divides cases into groups according to the degree of membership. In the generation of the rules in the learning phase, the subtractive clustering method is used to obtain the cluster centers. Subsequently, the parameters of the rules are optimized by means of an efficient algorithm of descending gradient.

SBC considers each case as a potential cluster center; determines the potential of a case based on its distances to all other cases. A case has a high potential value if it has many close neighbors. The highest potential is chosen as the center of the cluster and then the potential of each case is updated.

The process of determining new groups and updating potentials is repeated until the remaining potential for all cases falls below a fraction of the potential of the first cluster center. After obtaining all the cluster centers of the subtractive clustering, these are optimized according to fuzzy k-means.

Dynamic Evolutionary Neuro-Fuzzy Inference System (DENFIS). In [30] DENFIS is presented, this allows learning to be done online and offline. DENFIS evolves incrementally and hybrid (supervised/unsupervised), learning and accommodating new input data (including new features and classes) through the adjustment of local elements.

During the operation of the system, new fuzzy rules are created and updated. At each moment, the output of DENFIS is calculated through a fuzzy inference system based on the m most active rules, which are dynamically chosen from a set of fuzzy rules.

The original model proposes two approaches: online DENFIS model that is based on the dynamic creation of a set of fuzzy rules of type Takagi-Sugeno first-order [31]; and offline DENFIS model that creates a set of fuzzy rules of type Takagi-Sugeno first-order or one of higher order expanded.

There are some steps in DENFIS that determine the cluster centers using Evolutionary Clustering Method (ECM) [32], to divide the input space and find optimal parameters in the consequent part of the fuzzy rule using a least squares estimator.

ECM is a distance-based clustering method that is determined by a threshold value. This parameter influences the number of created clusters. At the beginning of the clustering process, the first instance of the training data is chosen to be a grouping center, and the determination radius is set to zero. Then, using the next instance, the cluster centers and the radius are changed. The radius grows as more clusters are assigned to the cluster, but without exceeding the threshold. The definitive cluster centers are obtained after evaluating all the training data.

The next step in DENFIS is to update the parameters in the consequent part assuming that the background part given by ECM is fixed. DENFIS allows you to insert a set of fuzzy rules before or during your learning process. Similarly, fuzzy rules can also be extracted during or after the learning process.

3 Stakeholders Classification System Based on Clustering Techniques

Below are the bases of the development environment used for learning the stakeholder classification system. Next, the parameters of the algorithms and the characteristics of the data sets used in the training and validation of the system are shown.

3.1 Working Environment and the Parameters of the Algorithms

The R language and the object-oriented relational database management system PostgreSQL are used at the application of clustering algorithms to adjust the parameters of the fuzzy inference system. R is an environment and programming language with a focus on statistical analysis, being also very popular in the field of data mining.

The integration between R and PostgreSQL is done through the PL/R extension that facilitates the use of R-Cran[1] packages for exploitation and testing in experimental projects. Among these packages is FRBS[2], published in [33]. FRBS is based on the concept of fuzzy logic proposed in [15] and represents fuzzy systems to handle various problems through the implementation of soft computing techniques. The *frbs.learn* functionality is used to perform the learning of the fuzzy inference system, with the parameters shown in Table 1.

3.2 Training and Test Data

In the learning process, a base of previously classified stakeholders is used. The base of cases contains the values of the attributes of 137 interested, as well as their classification offered by experts (with values of 1, 2 and 3 for stakeholders classified as Not prioritized, Less prioritized and Highly prioritized respectively). The attributes of each stakeholder collected in the base of cases coincide with the attributes of the Mitchell model, these are: coercive power, utilitarian power, normative-social power, organizational legitimacy, legitimacy social, temporal sensitivity and criticality.

The base of cases used has the following distribution: 62 classified stakeholders of Very prioritized (45%), 53 of Less prioritized (39%) and 22 Not prioritized (16%); it does not contain null or out of range values. It is divided randomly into 10 different partitions. Each partition has 110 cases (80%) to train and 27 cases (20%) to validate the training. These partitions of the dataset are used in the cross-validation procedure of the experiments, performing 10 executions of each clustering algorithm.

---

[1] Repository of packages with algorithms implemented in R for its application in different domains. Available in: http://cran.r-project.org/web/packages/.

[2] Systems based on fuzzy rules for classification and regression tasks. Available in: https://cran.r-project.org/web/packages/frbs/.

Table 1. Parameter values by algorithms.

Algorithm	Parameter	Description	Value
SBC	r.a	Radius value defining a neighborhood	0.5
	eps.high	An upper threshold value, between 0 and 1	0.5
	eps.low	A lower threshold value, between 0 and 1	0.15
DENFIS	Dthr	The threshold value for the Evolving Clustering Method (ECM), between 0 and 1	0.3
	max.iter	The maximal number of iterations	150
	step.size	The step size of the least squares method, between 0 and 1	0.1
	d	The width of the triangular membership function	2

4 Evaluation and Results

Next, the results obtained after applying the fuzzy inference system for the classification of stakeholders are shown. In this application, the two clustering algorithms are combined, using metrics and statistical rigor tests. The results obtained with the execution of the system in the 10 data combinations allow to compare the performance of the generated system with respect to the different algorithms used.

The following metrics are taken into account to validate the training of the fuzzy inference system: accuracy, number of false negatives, number of false positives, mean square error and percentage error of the symmetric absolute mean. Next, the results of each of these metrics are analyzed in the validation of the training.

The accuracy (percentage of correct classifications) is the index that specifies the percentage of stakeholders correctly classified by the system. Figure 1 shows a comparison between the SBC and DENFIS algorithms for the 10 data partitions. As can be seen, the SBC algorithm obtained results superior to 88.88% of accuracy, reaching 100% while the DENFIS algorithm had a hit rate between 44.44% and 85.19%.

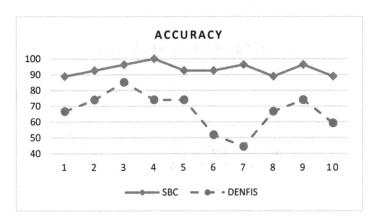

Fig. 1. Accuracy of the algorithms.

The number of false positives (FP) is the index that indicates the number of stakeholders classified in a category higher than the category that actually belongs. This index refers to how many stakeholders have less priority than the one determined by the system. Figure 2 shows a comparison between the clustering algorithms analyzed for the 10 data partitions. As can be seen, the number of false positives in the SBC ranges from 0 to 2, while the DENFIS algorithm has higher values (between 1 and 15) in the different partitions.

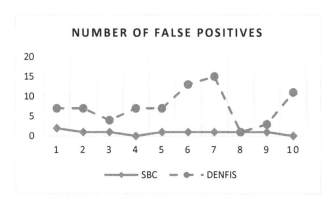

Fig. 2. Number of false positives by algorithm.

The number of false negatives (FN) is the index that refers to the number of interested people classified in a category lower than the category that actually belongs. This index indicates how many stakeholders have more priority than the one determined by the system. Figure 3 shows a comparison between the algorithms implemented for the 10 data partitions. Although DENFIS did not have false negatives in 70% of the partitions of the data, in partition 8 it reached a peak of eight times higher to the average reached by SBC. This indicates that the SBC algorithm is more stable in terms of the number of false negatives.

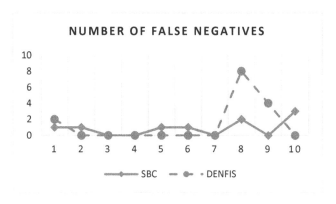

Fig. 3. Number of false negatives cases by algorithm.

The Mean Square Error (MSE) is the dispersion measure that calculates the difference between each classification and the general average. Figure 4 shows a comparison between the clustering algorithms implemented by the fuzzy inference system for the 10 data partitions. As is evident, for all data partitions, the SBC algorithm had an error lower than DENFIS. In addition, DENFFIS had error peaks at partitions 7 and 10.

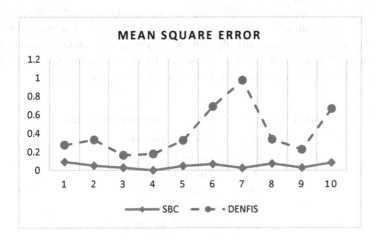

Fig. 4. Mean Square Error by algorithm.

The Symmetric Mean Absolute Percentage Error (SMAPE) is the dispersion measure that calculates the size of the classification error in percentage terms. Figure 5 shows a comparison between the algorithms analyzed for the 10 data partitions. In each of the analyzed partitions, the DENFIS algorithm error exceeds the SBC error by more than three times, thus demonstrates the effectiveness of SBC.

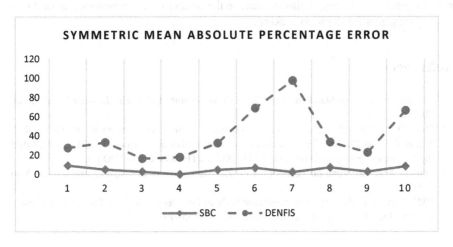

Fig. 5. Symmetric Mean Absolute Percentage Error by algorithm.

To validate the results, the Shapiro-Wilk test is applied to check the normality of data with less than 2000 samples. This verifies that the data of the metrics analyzed above, do not follow a normal distribution. Taking this into account, for each of the metrics analyzed, the non-parametric Friedman test for K related samples is applied. The results showed that there are significant differences between both algorithms, so the Wilcoxon test is applied.

The objective of applying the Wilcoxon test is to group, if possible, the algorithms that do not have significant differences in the same group. Table 2 shows the result of this non-parametric test where the algorithms are grouped ascending, presenting the best results in "Group 1" per metric. These results show that the SBC algorithm is superior to DENFIS with the parameters and the case base used.

Table 2. Wilcoxon tests result of each validation metric.

Metric	SBC	DENFIS
Accuracy	Group 1	Group 2
FP	Group 1	Group 2
FN	Group 1	Group 2
MSE	Group 1	Group 2
SMAPE	Group 1	Group 2

5 Conclusions

The use of machine learning methods for project stakeholder classification increases the accuracy of the result. The uncertainty provided for the information is adequately handled by these methods. The SBC clustering algorithm implemented in the fuzzy inference system provides better results in stakeholder classification than the DENFIS algorithm. The clustering algorithms application in informatics tools represents a significant contribution since it allows increase the quality of the information available to project managers for decision-making.

References

1. The Standish Group: Standish Group 2015 Chaos Report - Q&A with Jennifer Lynch. InfoQ (2015)
2. Pico, Ó.: Los stakeholders como actores estratégico-instrumentales en los proyectos de la Nueva Gestión Pública. Tesis de maestría, Universidad de Oviedo, España (2016). http://digibuo.uniovi.es/dspace/bitstream/10651/38421/4/TFMOscarPicoRUO.pdf
3. Schwalbe, K.: Information Technology Project Management. Cengage Learning, New York (2015)
4. PMI: A guide to the project management body of knowledge, 5th edn. Project Management Institute Inc., Pennsylvania (2013). ISBN 978-1-935589-67-9

5. Bello, R., Verdegay, J.L.: Los conjuntos aproximados en el contexto de la soft computing. Revista Cubana de Ciencias Informáticas **4**(1–2) (2011). http://rcci.uci.cu/?journal=rcci&page=article&op=view&path%5B%5D=103
6. Piñero, P.Y., García, M.M.: Un modelo para el aprendizaje y la clasificación automática basado en técnicas de softcomputing. Tesis de doctorado. Universidad Central de las Villas, Santa Clara (2005)
7. Kanungo, T., et al.: An efficient k-means clustering algorithm: analysis and implementation. IEEE Trans. Pattern Anal. Mach. Intell. **24**(7), 881–892 (2002). https://www.cs.umd.edu/~mount/Projects/KMeans/pami02.pdf, https://doi.org/10.1109/TPAMI.2002.1017616
8. Mainardes, E.W., Alves, H., Raposo, M.: A model for stakeholder classification and stakeholder relationships. Manag. Decis. **50**(10), 1861–1879 (2012). https://doi.org/10.1108/00251741211279648
9. Mitchell, R.K., Agle, B.R., Wood, D.J.: Toward a theory of stakeholder identification and salience: defining the principle of who and what really counts. Acad. Manag. Rev. **22**(4), 853 (1997). https://doi.org/10.5465/AMR.1997.9711022105
10. Poplawska, J., Labib, A., Reed, D.M., Ishizaka, A.: Stakeholder profile definition and salience measurement with fuzzy logic and visual analytics applied to corporate social responsibility case study. J. Clean. Prod. **105**, 103–115 (2015). https://doi.org/10.1016/j.jclepro.2014.10.095
11. Samboni, A.P., Blanco, J.G.: Herramientas de gestión de interesados utilizadas en las etapas de planeación y control de proyectos. Tesis de especialidad, Universidad de San Buenaventura, Santiago de Cali (2015). http://bibliotecadigital.usb.edu.co/bitstream/10819/2549/1/Herramientas_Interesados_Gestion_Etapas_Control_Proyectos_Samboni_2015.pdf
12. Arévalo, A.U., Requena, R.: Considerations of the stakeholder approach. Punto de Vista **4**(7), 31–50 (2013)
13. Bernal, A., Rivas, L.A.: Modelos para la identificación de stakeholders y su aplicación a la gestión de los pequeños abastecimientos comunitarios de agua. Revista Lebret **4**(4), 251–273 (2012). https://doi.org/10.15332/rl.v4i4.337
14. Acuña, A.P.: La gestión de los stakeholders. Análisis de los diferentes modelos. Grupo de Investigación RSE y Sistemas de Información de la Universidad Nacional del Sur, pp. 1–12 (2012). http://www.adenag.org.ar/uploads/congresos/regionales/Ponencia_Acu%C3%B1a.pdf
15. Zadeh, L.A.: Fuzzy logic, neural networks, and soft computing. Commun. ACM **37**(3), 77–85 (1994). https://doi.org/10.1145/175247.175255
16. Mamdani, E.H.: Application of fuzzy logic to approximate reasoning using linguistic synthesis. In: International Symposium on Multiple-valued logic, pp. 196–202. IEEE Computer Society Press (1976). https://doi.org/10.1109/TC.1977.1674779
17. Sugeno, M.: Fuzzy measure and fuzzy integral. Trans. Soc. Instrum. Control Eng. **8**(2), 218–226 (1972). https://doi.org/10.9746/sicetr1965.8.218
18. Tsukamoto, Y.: An Approach to Fuzzy Reasoning Method. North-Holland Publishing Company, Amsterdam, New York (1979)
19. Lugo, J.A., Piñero, P.Y., Bello, R., Delgado, R.: Modelo para el control de la ejecución de proyectos basado en soft computing. Tesis de doctorado, Universidad de las Ciencias Informáticas, La Habana (2016). https://doi.org/10.13140/RG.2.1.4270.8565
20. Lugo, J.A., Delgado, R.: Modelo para el control de la ejecución de proyectos basado en indicadores y lógica borrosa. Tesis de maestría. Universidad de las Ciencias Informáticas, La Habana (2013). https://doi.org/10.13140/2.1.1523.5362
21. Soria, L., Verdecia, P.: Estimación del esfuerzo en proyectos a partir de puntos de función y técnicas de soft computing. Tesis de maestría. Universidad de las Ciencias Informáticas, La Habana (2015)

22. Herrera, F.: Genetic fuzzy systems: taxonomy, current research trends and prospects. J. Evol. Intell. **1**(1), 27–46 (2008). https://doi.org/10.1007/s12065-007-0001-5. ISSN 1864-5917

23. MacQueen, J.B.: Some methods for classification and analysis of multivariate observations. In: Proceedings of 5th Berkeley Symposium on Mathematical Statistics and Probability, pp. 281–297. University of California Press (1967)

24. Napook, P., Eiamkanitchat, N.: The adaptive dynamic clustering neuro-fuzzy system for classification. In: Kim, K.J. (ed.) Information Science and Applications. LNEE, vol. 339, pp. 721–728. Springer, Heidelberg (2015). https://doi.org/10.1007/978-3-662-46578-3_85

25. Prasad, M., et al.: Collaborative fuzzy rule learning for Mamdani type fuzzy inference system with mapping of cluster centers. In: 2014 IEEE Symposium on Computational Intelligence in Control and Automation, CICA, Orlando, Florida, pp. 1–6 (2014). https://doi.org/10.1109/CICA.2014.7013227

26. Chou, K.P., et al.: Takagi-Sugeno-Kang type collaborative fuzzy rule based system. In: IEEE Symposium on Computational Intelligence and Data Mining, CIDM, Orlando, Florida, pp. 315–320 (2014). https://doi.org/10.1109/cidm.2014.7008684

27. Chiu, S.: Method and software for extracting fuzzy classification rules by subtractive clustering. In: Fuzzy Information Processing Society, NAFIPS, pp. 461–465 (1996). https://doi.org/10.1109/NAFIPS.1996.534778

28. Yager, R., Filev, D.: Generation of fuzzy rules by mountain clustering. J. Intell. Fuzzy Syst. **2**(3), 209–219 (1994). https://doi.org/10.3233/IFS-1994-2301

29. Bezdek, J.C., Ehrlich, R., Full, W.: FCM: the fuzzy c-means clustering algorithm. Comput. Geosci. **10**(2–3), 191–203 (1984). https://doi.org/10.1016/0098-3004(84)90020-7

30. Kasabov, N.K., Song, Q.: DENFIS: dynamic evolving neural-fuzzy inference system and its application for time-series prediction. IEEE Trans. Fuzzy Syst. **10**(2), 144–154 (2002). https://doi.org/10.1109/91.995117

31. Takagi, T., Sugeno, M.: Fuzzy identification of systems and its application to modeling and control. IEEE Trans. Syst. Man Cybern. **15**, 116–132 (1985). https://doi.org/10.1109/TSMC.1985.6313399

32. Song, Q., Kasabov, N.: ECM - a novel on-line evolving clustering method and its applications. In: Posner, M.I. (ed.) Foundations of Cognitive Science, pp. 631–682. The MIT Press, Cambridge (2001)

33. Riza, L.S., Christoph, B., Herrera, F., Benítez, J.M.: Frbs: fuzzy rule-based systems for classification and regression in R. J. Stat. Softw. **65**(6), 130 (2015). https://doi.org/10.18637/jss.v065.i06

Investigation of Surface EMG and Acceleration Signals of Limbs' Tremor in Parkinson's Disease Patients Using the Method of Electrical Activity Analysis Based on Wave Trains

Olga S. Sushkova[1(✉)], Alexei A. Morozov[1], Alexandra V. Gabova[2], and Alexei V. Karabanov[3]

[1] Kotel'nikov Institute of Radio Engineering and Electronics of RAS, Mokhovaya 11-7, Moscow 125009, Russia
o.sushkova@mail.ru, morozov@cplire.ru
[2] Institute of Higher Nervous Activity and Neurophysiology of RAS, Butlerova 5A, Moscow 117485, Russia
agabova@yandex.ru
[3] FSBI "Research Center of Neurology", Volokolamskoe shosse 80, Moscow 125367, Russia
doctor.karabanov@mail.ru
http://www.fullvision.ru/

Abstract. In recent years, spindle-shaped electrical activity became interesting for researchers looking for new methods of time-frequency analysis of electromyograms (EMG) and acceleration (ACC) signals. We call signals of this type as wave trains; a wave train (a wave packet) is an electrical signal that is localized in space, frequency, and time. Examples of wave trains in electroencephalograms (EEG) are alpha spindles, beta spindles, and sleep spindles. We analyze all kinds of wave train electrical activity of the muscles in a wide frequency range. We have developed a new method for analyzing wave train electrical activity of muscles based on wavelet analysis and ROC analysis that enables to study the time-frequency features of EMG and ACC in limbs' tremor in patients with neurodegenerative diseases such as Parkinson's disease (PD).

The idea of the method is to find local maxima in the wavelet spectrogram and to calculate various characteristics describing these maxima (called wave trains): the leading frequency, the duration in periods (the full-width on the square root of 1/2 of the peak in the spectrogram), the bandwidth (the full-width on the square root of 1/2 of the peak in the spectrogram), the number of wave trains per second. Then we conduct a statistical analysis of these characteristics. In our previous papers, frequency ranges (based on EEG features) were found where the quantity of wave trains per second differs between a group of patients of the early stage of PD and a group of healthy volunteers. In this paper, we search similar frequency ranges based on time-frequency features of EMG and ACC.

© Springer Nature Switzerland AG 2018
G. R. Simari et al. (Eds.): IBERAMIA 2018, LNAI 11238, pp. 253–264, 2018.
https://doi.org/10.1007/978-3-030-03928-8_21

Keywords: Exploratory data analysis · Pattern recognition
Wavelet spectrogram · ROC analysis · Wave train
Muscle electrical activity · Signal processing · Electromyography
EMG · Acceleration · Parkinson's disease

1   Introduction

The pre-clinical diagnostics is very important for the management of PD. Although PD has been studied intensively in the last decades, the pre-clinical indicators of this motor disorder have yet to be established. Several approaches were proposed but the definitive method is still lacking [8].

EMG and ACC investigations would be objective methods to assess neuromuscular function in PD. Surface EMG signals are often analyzed using amplitude and spectral based methods. These methods are used to measure the degree of muscle activation and fatigue. The neuromuscular function can be also measured indirectly by measuring limb tremor controlled by it. This can be done by using movement sensors such as accelerometers [14]. The mathematical approaches used for EMG and ACC analysis in PD include spectral based methods (mean frequency, proportion of power at particular frequency bands) [2,17], analysis of EMG burst characteristics (counts, magnitudes, durations, and frequencies) [3,12,15,16], analysis of EMG signal morphology [13], and methods of nonlinear EMG analysis [2].

Studies, where both EMG and ACC signals have been analyzed, have concentrated on analyzing the regularity of arm tremor and their low-frequency coherence in PD [14]. It has been shown that the PD patients' tremor is more regular (i.e., lower entropy) than the physiological tremor measured in neurologically healthy subjects [22]. In addition, it has been shown that the regularity of PD patients' tremor reduces due to the treatment of the disease by medication and deep brain stimulation [18]. The coherence studies on ACC and EMG have shown that the low-frequency coherence between these signals is higher for patients with PD than for the healthy persons [22].

Measurements of EMG and limb tremor can be used in the objective and quantitative assessment of the neuromuscular system function and motor disorders in PD. In the future, they may help in the diagnosis and follow-up of treatment in PD. In addition, neurophysiologic measurements may improve the understanding of the disease neurological mechanisms [23]. However, these measurements are still rarely used in the assessment of PD. Because EMG is a spiky, impulse-like waveform, the nonlinear and morphological methods can be more effective in analyzing EMG than the methods that are traditionally used in the EMG analysis (amplitudes and mean/median frequencies).

Earlier, the authors have developed a method for analyzing the wave train electrical activity of the cerebral cortex, based on wavelet analysis and ROC analysis [19,20]. The idea of this method of EEG analysis is in that the EEG signal is considered as a set of wave trains [21]. Unlike works devoted to the detection of wave train electrical activity of one or two specific types, such as alpha spindles [6] and sleep spindles [1,4,5,9–11], we analyze all kinds of wave train electrical activity in the brain cortex in a wide frequency range. Moreover, we considered the wave train as a typical component of EEG, but not as a special kind of EEG signals. This method of analysis is based on a statistical analysis of wavelet spectrograms, a new method of visualization of the neurophysiological data, and a new algorithm for detection of the wave trains.

Earlier, in the papers [19,20], one has already found differences between patients with PD and healthy volunteers in the C3 and C4 cortex areas. It was found that patients with the left arm tremor demonstrated increased quantity of the wave trains in the lower alpha range and reduced quantity of the wave trains in the upper alpha range and in the beta range. In patients with the right arm tremor, the areas of increased quantity of wave trains are much bigger and differ in values. In this paper, we check how our method works on other biomedical signals, namely, EMG and ACC signals.

The purpose of this work is to study an advanced method for feature extraction and investigation of EMG and ACC signals on the basis of the analysis of the wave train electrical activity. To investigate it, a new imaging technique based on AUC values (the area under the ROC curve) was used. Therefore, the first task of our study is to check the presence of wave train electrical activity in EMG and ACC signals in PD and the second task is to study the properties of the wave train electrical activity that can be useful for the diagnosis of PD. The third task is to investigate the possibility of using wave train electrical activity for early PD diagnosis.

The message of this paper is in that the wave train approach to biomedical signal analysis is applicable for analyzing EMG and ACC signals and yields new interesting regularities in the area of Parkinson's disease diagnosis.

2   Experimental Setting

The EMG and ACC signals of arms tremor in untreated (that is, not taking special medications earlier) patients with PD at early stages of PD are compared with EMG and ACC signals in healthy volunteers. The group of PD patients included patients with the left arm tremor (15 persons) and patients with the right arm tremor (18 persons), 33 patients in total. The number of healthy volunteers was 18 people. All patients and healthy volunteers were right-handed. There were no statistically significant differences between the ages of the patients and healthy volunteers.

A standard EMG acquisition schema was used. Electrodes were placed from the outside of the arms. Accelerometer sensors were placed on the back side of the hand. EMG and ACC signals were recorded in standard conditions. The examined person sat in an armchair, arms laid on armrests of an armchair, palms were straightened. The eyes were closed during the recordings. A 41-channel digital EEG and EMG system Neuron-Spectrum-5 (Neurosoft Ltd.) and special accelerometer device were used. The sampling rate of EMG was 500 Hz and the sampling rate of ACC was 1378.125 Hz. The 0.5 Hz high-pass filter and the 50 Hz notch filter were used for EMG and ACC records, also Butterworth filter from 60 to 240 Hz and Hilbert transform for envelope detection were used for EMG signals. The duration of every record was about 2 min. The record was analyzed as is, without a selection of areas in the signal.

To analyze the EMG and ACC signals, the developed algorithm [20] was modified, namely, an additional stage of smoothing the wavelet spectrograms was added. Smoothing is required because the standard fast algorithms for calculating wavelets have the following drawback: wavelet spectrograms (when processing signals of a complex shape) are inevitably contaminated with artifacts (ejections and high-frequency oscillations). These artifacts can be mistakenly recognized as "wave trains". To solve this problem, the smoothing of the spectrograms by the Gaussian window with specially selected parameters developed by the authors was applied to remove the "jags" in the spectrograms. The parameters of the smoothing window (width in the time and frequency planes) are changed adaptively depending on the wavelet scaling. Besides, the threshold used for the initial selection of the wave trains was decreased; currently, the duration of the wave train is to be more or equal to 1 period. The duration of the wave train is measured on the square root of 1/2 of the high of the peak.

3   Methods

Let's compare spectra of the patients with the right side tremor, spectra of the patients with the left side tremor, and spectra of the control group of healthy volunteers. See examples of EMG spectrum of the left arms on Fig. 1 (on the left side) and ACC spectrum of the left arms on Fig. 1 (on the right side). The abscissa is the frequency. The ordinate is the power spectral density in the logarithmic scale. The thin lines around the spectra are 2 sigma confidence intervals. Three lines under the figure indicate results of the following statistical tests: the lower line corresponds to the Mann-Whitney statistical test (alpha level is 0.05), the middle line corresponds to the Mann-Whitney statistical test with the Bonferroni correction on the number of frequencies in the spectra (31), and the upper line corresponds to the Mann-Whitney statistical test with Bonferroni correction on the number of frequencies in the spectra (31) and the number of figures (there are 2 figures in this case).

Typical spectra contain characteristic features of EMG and ACC signals in PD described in the literature [7]. Namely, in the frequency range from 3 to 7 Hz, there is a statistically significant increase in the amplitude of signals in PD patients in comparison with the control group of volunteers. Theoretically speaking, it is possible to diagnose PD at an early stage using the EMG and ACC spectra. A characteristic feature of PD is in that at an early stage only one limb (arm or leg) trembles in patients. We will call the arm of the patient where an increase in the amplitude in the spectrum is observed in the range from 3 to 7 Hz as the "tremor arm". And we will call the arm where such increase in amplitude is absent as the "conditionally healthy arm". It is interesting that some differences in the spectra are observed not only in the tremor arms but also in conditionally

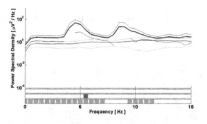 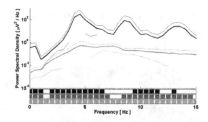

Fig. 1. On the left side: the upper line is the average EMG spectrum of the left arms of the patients with the left side tremor. The lower line is the average EMG spectrum of the left arms of the healthy volunteers. On the right side: the upper line is the average ACC spectrum of the left arms of the patients with the left side tremor. The lower line is the average ACC spectrum of the left arms of the healthy volunteers.

healthy ones. Note that in Fig. 1 EMG and ACC spectra are different. One of the reasons for this difference is in that EMG electrodes and accelerometer sensors are located on different parts of the arms (see the experimental settings section). Thus, these devices register information of different types. The EMG receiver registers an electrical activity of the muscles. The accelerometer registers an acceleration of the arm.

Our idea is in that a conditionally healthy arm can be used as a model for the early diagnosis of PD. That is, we will study the tremor in the conditionally healthy arm of patients with PD to discover pre-clinical features of PD.

We have calculated wave trains in the frequency interval from 1 to 10 Hz on EMG and ACC signals in each patient with PD (the left arm tremor patients and the right arm tremor patients were investigated separately) and in each healthy volunteers. For these data, the AUC values for various frequency ranges from 1 to 10 Hz were calculated.

Figure 2 (the first column, the first row) demonstrates the AUC values of EMG for the left tremor arms for the patients with PD with the left side tremor and for the healthy volunteers. Figure 2 (the second column, the first row) demonstrates the AUC values of EMG for the left healthy arms for the patients with PD with the right side tremor and for the healthy volunteers. Figure 2 (the first column, the second row) demonstrates the AUC values of EMG for the right healthy arms for the patients with PD with the left side tremor and for the healthy volunteers. Figure 2 (the second column, the second row) demonstrates the AUC values of EMG for the right tremor arms for the patients with PD with the right side tremor and for the healthy volunteers. Frequencies from 1 to 10 Hz in 0.01 Hz step were calculated in all these figures.

The frequency diagrams (Fig. 2) demonstrate that there are differences in EMG in the tremor arms in the 1–3 Hz range (AUC = 0.11 for the right tremor arms for the patients with the right side tremor and AUC = 0.04 for the left tremor arms for the patients with the left side tremor) and in the 3–7 Hz range (AUC = 0.75 for the right tremor arms for the patients with the right side tremor and AUC = 0.90 for the left tremor arms for the patients with the left side tremor).

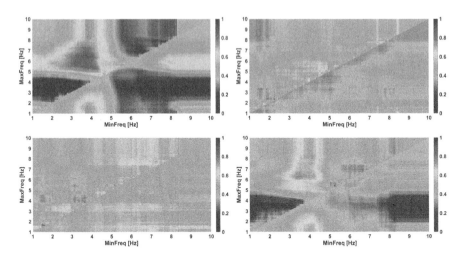

Fig. 2. Diagrams of AUC values calculated for various frequency bands. In the left column: the left arm tremor patients; in the right column: the right arm tremor patients. The first row corresponds to the EMG electrode on the left arm and the second row corresponds to the EMG electrode on the right arm. Frequencies from 1 to 10 Hz in 0.01 Hz step were calculated.

Figure 3 (the first column, the first row) demonstrates the AUC values of ACC for the left tremor arms for the patients with PD with the left side tremor and for the healthy volunteers. Figure 3 (the second column, the first row) demonstrates the AUC values of ACC for the left healthy arms for the patients with PD with the right side tremor and for the healthy volunteers. Figure 3 (the first column, the second row) demonstrates the AUC values of ACC for the right healthy arms for the patients with PD with the left side tremor and for the healthy volunteers. Figure 3 (the second column, the second row) demonstrates the AUC values of ACC for the right tremor arms for the patients with PD with the right side tremor and for the healthy volunteers. Frequencies from 1 to 10 Hz in 0.01 Hz step were calculated in all these figures.

The frequency diagrams indicate that there are no differences in ACC signals in the 3–7 Hz range both in the tremor arms and in the healthy arms. But in the 1–3 Hz range there are differences both in the tremor arms (AUC = 0.24 for right tremor arm for the patients with the right side tremor and AUC = 0.01 for the left tremor arms for the patients with the left side tremor) and in the healthy arms (AUC = 0.12 for the left healthy arms for the patients with the right side tremor and AUC = 0.17 for the right healthy arms for the patients with the left side tremor) in ACC signals (see Fig. 3).

We observe regularities that were never described in the literature in the 1–3 Hz region on EMG and ACC. At the same time, in EMG we observe differences

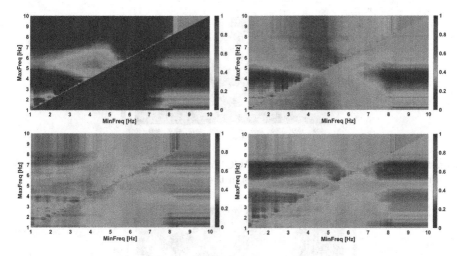

Fig. 3. Diagrams of AUC values calculated for various frequency bands. In the left column: the left arm tremor patients; in the right column: the right arm tremor patients. The first row corresponds to the ACC electrode on the left arm and the second row corresponds to the ACC electrode on the right arm. Frequencies from 1 to 10 Hz in 0.01 Hz step were calculated.

in this range only on the tremor arms. In ACC we observe differences both in the healthy arms and in the tremor arms. In this paper, we confine ourselves to the study of only the 3–7 Hz frequency range; the 1–3 Hz frequency range is to be investigated separately.

Note that there are no differences in the frequency diagrams in the tremor arms in the range of 3 to 7 Hz in ACC, though one can see such differences in EMG. Let us investigate the reasons for this difference. We have calculated the amplitude, periods, and bandwidth diagrams for this frequency range. Using these diagrams we will demonstrate that the differences in the frequency diagram became visible not only in the tremor arms, but also in the healthy arms in both EMG and ACC signals, when we consider only wave trains corresponding to certain amplitude, period, and bandwidth thresholds.

Let us consider the amplitude diagram for the frequency range from 3 to 7 Hz. The diagrams for both EMG and ACC signals were approximately the same. See an example of the amplitude diagram for an ACC for the left tremor arms of patients with the left side tremor (Fig. 4). One can see that the 50 μV threshold can be selected (AUC = 0.97) to separate the wave trains that are characteristic of PD patients, but not of the healthy volunteers.

Let us consider the period diagram for the 3 to 7 Hz frequency band. The diagrams for both EMG and ACC were approximately the same. See an example of periods diagram for ACC in the left tremor arm of patients with the left side tremor (Fig. 5). One can see that the 1-period threshold can be selected in the diagram to separate the wave trains that are characteristic of PD patients, but not of the healthy volunteers (AUC = 0.99).

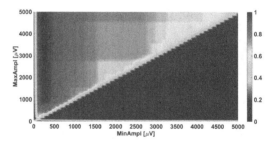

Fig. 4. The amplitude diagram for an ACC for the left tremor arms of the patients with the left side tremor. The amplitudes in the range 0–5000 μV are considered.

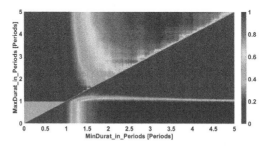

Fig. 5. The periods diagram for ACC in the left tremor arm of patients with the left side tremor. Various durations in the range of 0–5 periods are considered.

Let us consider the bandwidth diagram for the 3–7 Hz frequency band. The diagrams for EMG and ACC are approximately the same. See an example of the bandwidth diagram for ACC in the left tremor arm of patients with the left side tremor (Fig. 6). One can see that the 1 Hz threshold can be selected in the diagram to separate the wave trains that are characteristic of PD patients, but not of the healthy volunteers (AUC = 0.09).

One can see strong differences between the PD patients and healthy volunteers in both EMG and ACC when the set of selected thresholds (the amplitude of the wave trains is from 50 μV to infinity, the full width on the square root of 1/2 of the wave trains is from 1 to 5 periods, and the bandwidth of the wave trains is from 1 to 5 Hz) are applied (Figs. 7, 8).

The regularities in EMG are visible in the tremor arms (both for the patients with the right side tremor (AUC = 0.83) and the patients with the left side tremor (AUC = 0.83)) and in the healthy arms (for the patients with the right side tremor only (AUC = 0.73)). Differences in the healthy arms of the patients with the left side tremor are almost invisible (AUC = 0.61). In ACC, the regularities are visible both in the tremor arms (AUC = 0.74 for the right tremor arm for the patients with the right side tremor and AUC = 0.95 for the left tremor arm for the patients with the left side tremor) and in the healthy arms (AUC = 0.70 for the left healthy arm for the patients with the right side tremor and AUC = 0.82 for the right healthy arm for the patients with the left side tremor). Note that

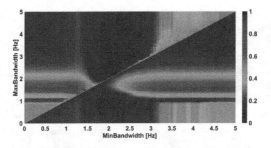

Fig. 6. The bandwidth diagram for ACC in the left tremor arm of patients with the left side tremor. The bandwidths in the range 0–5 Hz are considered.

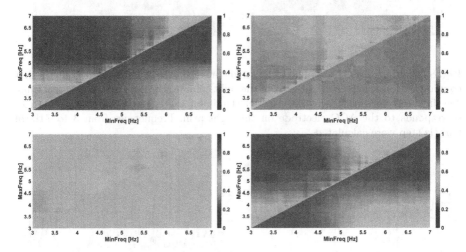

Fig. 7. Diagrams of AUC values calculated for various frequency bands. In the left column: the left arm tremor patients; in the right column: the right arm tremor patients. The first row corresponds to the EMG electrode on the left arm and the second row corresponds to the EMG electrode on the right arm. Frequencies from 3 to 7 Hz in 0.01 Hz step were calculated.

the differences between the right healthy arms of the patients with the left side tremor and healthy volunteers are present in ACC (AUC = 0.82), but not in EMG. The differences in the left healthy arms in the patients with the right side tremor are observed both in EMG (AUC = 0.73) and ACC (AUC = 0.70).

Let us consider an example of wave trains detected by our method in EMG in the healthy right arm of the patient with the left side tremor. An example of EMG signal is demonstrated in Fig. 9 (on the left side) and the envelope of the signal is demonstrated in Fig. 9 (on the right side). The first wave train consists of 2 periods (the duration is 0.24 s. and the bandwidth is 1.64 Hz) and the second one consists of 3 periods (the duration is 0.26 s and the bandwidth is 1.65 Hz).

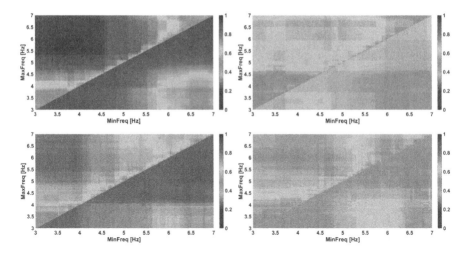

Fig. 8. Diagrams of AUC values calculated for various frequency bands. In the left column: the left arm tremor patients; in the right column: the right arm tremor patients. The first row corresponds to the ACC electrode on the left arm and the second row corresponds to the ACC electrode on the right arm. Frequencies from 3 to 7 Hz in 0.01 Hz step were calculated.

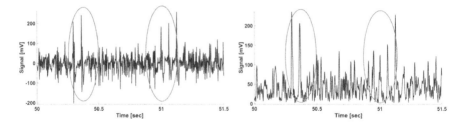

Fig. 9. On the left side: an example of EMG signal. On the right side: the envelope of the signal. There are two wave trains in the signal. The first one consists of 2 periods and the second one consists of 3 periods.

4   Conclusions

The method of wave trains analysis and special statistical diagrams are developed. One can consider these means as universal instruments for exploratory data analysis. We have approved them on the example of biomedical signal analysis and have revealed new regularities in EMG and ACC signals in PD patients. In comparison with spectra, the wave train analysis enables investigation of the detailed time-frequency structure of EMG and ACC signals, that can provide additional information for clinical neurology. Namely, the method reveals new regularities in the 1–3 Hz and 3–7 Hz frequency bands that are promising for early PD diagnosis. The 1–3 Hz and the 10–50 Hz frequency bands are to be investigated in the future. We have demonstrated that the wave trains in the 3–7 Hz frequency band have the following characteristics: the differences between the PD patients and the healthy volunteers are observed in the healthy arms both in EMG and ACC (ACC demonstrates much better differences), if one applies a set of constraints to the set of wave trains to be considered (the frequency range from 3 to 7 Hz, the amplitude range from 50 μV to infinity, the duration range from 1 to 5 periods, and the bandwidth range from 1 to 5 Hz). Thus, the investigation of ACC is probably more promising for the purposes of the early PD diagnosis. Investigation of EMG and ACC gives qualitatively different results. A possible reason for this difference is in that the accelerometer is a more sensitive device. However, even when leveling the sensitivity of the devices, we see that these devices give similar but different results, namely: EMG is less suitable for the analysis of the tremor on the healthy arms of the patients with the left side tremor. Accelerometer, on the contrary, is less suitable for the analysis of the tremor on the healthy arms of the patients with the right side tremor, but ACC gives qualitatively better results than EMG in the healthy arms in the patients with the left side tremor.

The experiments with the developed method of EMG and ACC analysis based on the wave trains demonstrate that the method is promising for looking for group statistical regularities in the early stages of Parkinson's disease and can give a new basic knowledge about this disease. Discovered EMG and ACC features can be useful for diagnostics of early stages of Parkinson's disease.

Acknowledgment. The work is supported by the Ministry of Science and Higher Education of Russian Federation, project No. 0030-2015-0189; the Scholarship of the President of the Russian Federation to Young Scientists and Post-graduate Students, grant No. $C\Pi$-5247.2018.4; and Russian Academy of Sciences.

References

1. Camilleri, T.A., Camilleri, K.P., Fabri, S.G.: Automatic detection of spindles and K-complexes in sleep EEG using switching multiple models. Biomed. Signal Process. Control **10**, 117–127 (2014)
2. Fattorini, L., Felici, F., Filligoi, G., Traballesi, M., Farina, D.: Influence of high motor unit synchronization levels on non-linear and spectral variables of the surface EMG. J. Neurosci. Methods **143**(2), 133–139 (2005)
3. Flament, D., Vaillancourt, D., Kempf, T., Shannon, K., Corcos, D.: EMG remains fractionated in Parkinson's disease, despite practice-related improvements in performance. Clin. Neurophysiol. **114**(12), 2385–2396 (2003)
4. Huupponen, E., et al.: Determination of dominant simulated spindle frequency with different methods. J. Neurosci. Methods **156**, 275–283 (2006)
5. Jaleel, A., Ahmed, B., Tafreshi, R., Boivin, D.B., Streletz, L., Haddad, N.: Improved spindle detection through intuitive pre-processing of electroencephalogram. J. Neurosci. Methods **233**, 1–12 (2014)
6. Lawhern, V., Kerick, S., Robbins, K.A.: Detecting alpha spindle events in EEG time series using adaptive autoregressive models. BMC Neurosci. **14**, 101 (2013). http://www.biomedcentral.com/1471-2202/14/101
7. Meigal, A.Y., et al.: Linear and nonlinear tremor acceleration characteristics in patients with Parkinson's disease. Physiol. Meas. **33**(3), 395 (2012)

8. Meigal, A.Y., Rissanen, S.M., Tarvainen, M.P., Airaksinen, O., Kankaanp, M., Karjalainen, P.A.: Non-linear EMG parameters for differential and early diagnostics of Parkinson's disease. Front. Neurol. **4**, 135 (2013)

9. Nonclercq, A., Urbain, C., Verheulpen, D., Decaestecker, C., Bogaert, P.V., Peigneux, P.: Sleep spindle detection through amplitude-frequency normal modelling. J. Neurosci. Methods **214**, 192–203 (2013)

10. O'Reilly, C., Nielsen, T.: Automatic sleep spindle detection: benchmarking with fine temporal resolution using open science tools. Front. Hum. Neurosci. **9**, 353 (2015). https://doi.org/10.3389/fnhum.2015.00353

11. Parekh, A., Selesnick, I., Rapoport, D., Ayappa, I.: Sleep spindle detection using time-frequency sparsity. In: IEEE Signal Processing in Medicine and Biology Symposium, pp. 1–6. IEEE, Philadelphia (2014)

12. Pfann, K.D., Buchman, A.S., Comella, C.L., Corcos, D.M.: Control of movement distance in Parkinson's disease. Mov. Disord. **16**(6), 1048–1065 (2001)

13. Rissanen, S., et al.: Analysis of surface EMG signal morphology in Parkinson's disease. Physiol. Meas. **28**(12), 1507 (2007)

14. Rissanen, S.M., et al.: Surface EMG and acceleration signals in Parkinson's disease: feature extraction and cluster analysis. Med. Biol. Eng. Comput. **46**(9), 849–858 (2008)

15. Robichaud, J.A., Pfann, K.D., Comella, C.L., Brandabur, M., Corcos, D.M.: Greater impairment of extension movements as compared to flexion movements in Parkinson's disease. Exp. Brain Res. **156**(2), 240–254 (2004)

16. Robichaud, J.A., Pfann, K.D., Comella, C.L., Corcos, D.M.: Effect of medication on EMG patterns in individuals with Parkinson's disease. Mov. Disord. **17**(5), 950–960 (2002)

17. Robichaud, J.A., Pfann, K.D., Vaillancourt, D.E., Comella, C.L., Corcos, D.M.: Force control and disease severity in Parkinson's disease. Mov. Disord. **20**(4), 441–450 (2005)

18. Sturman, M.M., Vaillancourt, D.E., Metman, L.V., Bakay, R.A., Corcos, D.M.: Effects of subthalamic nucleus stimulation and medication on resting and postural tremor in Parkinson's disease. Brain **127**(9), 2131–2143 (2004)

19. Sushkova, O., Morozov, A., Gabova, A.: A method of analysis of EEG wave trains in early stages of Parkinson's disease. In: International Conference on Bioinformatics and Systems Biology (BSB-2016), pp. 1–4. IEEE (2016)

20. Sushkova, O.S., Morozov, A.A., Gabova, A.V.: Data mining in EEG wave trains in early stages of Parkinson's disease. In: Pichardo-Lagunas, O., Miranda-Jiménez, S. (eds.) MICAI 2016. LNCS (LNAI), vol. 10062, pp. 403–412. Springer, Cham (2017). https://doi.org/10.1007/978-3-319-62428-0_32

21. Sushkova, O., Morozov, A., Gabova, A., Karabanov, A.: Data mining in EEG wave trains in early stages of Parkinson's disease. Proceedings of the 12th Russian-German Conference on Biomedical Engineering, pp. 80–84 (2016)

22. Vaillancourt, D.E., Newell, K.M.: The dynamics of resting and postural tremor in Parkinson's disease. Clin. Neurophysiol. **111**(11), 2046–2056 (2000)

23. Valls-Solé, J., Valldeoriola, F.: Neurophysiological correlate of clinical signs in Parkinson's disease. Clin. Neurophysiol. **113**(6), 792–805 (2002)

Neural Network Pruning Using Discriminative Information for Emotion Recognition

Máximo Sánchez-Gutiérrez[1] and Enrique Marcelo Albornoz[2(✉)]

[1] Departamento de Matemáticas Aplicadas y Sistemas,
Universidad Autónoma Metropolitana, Mexico City, Mexico
edmax86@gmail.com

[2] Instituto sinc(i), Universidad Nacional del Litoral - CONICET, Santa Fe, Argentina
emalbornoz@sinc.unl.edu.ar

Abstract. In the last years, the effort devoted by the scientific community to develop better emotion recognition systems has been increased, mainly impulsed by the potential applications. The Boltzmann restricted machines (RBM) and the deep machines of Boltzmann (DBM) are models that, in recent years, have received much attention due to their good performance for different issues. However, it is usually difficult to measure their predictive capacity and, specifically, the individual importance of hidden units. In this work, some measures are computed in the hidden units in order to rank their discriminative ability among multiple classes. Then, this information is used to prune those units that seem less relevant. The results show a significant decrease in the number of units used in the classification at the same time that the error rate is improved.

Keywords: RBM · DBM · Pruning · Entropy · Divergence
Feature selection · Emotions

1 Introduction

While humans can differentiate most of the natural emotions expressed in almost all environmental conditions, machine learning systems still present difficulties in this task. In recent years, a series of systems for automatic emotion recognition have been developed with varying degrees of success [21]. In the case of artificial neural networks, there are several criteria used to evaluate a network's quality e.g. training time, scalability, and generalisation ability, among others. One common approach to determine an appropriate network size for a specific task is by using heuristics and/or trial-and-error, usually looking for good performance and generalisation ability on a validation set. Another approach considers ways of 'growing' an artificial neural network until satisfactory performance is achieved [7,22]. A different technique uses 'pruning' methods [4,14,24]. In general, these methods begin by training an artificial neural network, which is large enough

© Springer Nature Switzerland AG 2018
G. R. Simari et al. (Eds.): IBERAMIA 2018, LNAI 11238, pp. 265–273, 2018.
https://doi.org/10.1007/978-3-030-03928-8_22

to ensure a satisfactory performance. Afterwards, neurons are removed from the trained net (for example, the ones with the smallest weights) and then the network is often fine-tuned or retrained. This procedure could also be repeated until some convergence criterion is achieved, otherwise the smallest network that performed adequately is assumed to have the most suitable topology for the given data set. This type of pruning was called post–training pruning (PTP) [4].

Networks size is especially relevant and recent works show that larger or deeper nets can solve the tasks using a more appropriate space [8,13,15]. In consequence, new complications associated with complex and computationally demanding training algorithms must be addressed [3,12,23]. In this context, optimise a feed–forward artificial neural network has proven to be a difficult task. The best results obtained on supervised learning tasks involve an unsupervised learning component, usually in an unsupervised greedy pre–training phase [6,11].

In this work, the standard DBM-RBM configuration is considered, where a RBM is training (unsupervised) at the first step and then, a posterior classifier is feeding with its outputs. However, instead of using the last layer of the RBM to feed the classifier, the more discriminative hidden units are used based on a post-training ranking. In order to measure the discriminative capability two criterion were used and the multi-class emotion classification task was addressed. A binary approach was presented in [18].

In the next section, the material and methods are introduced. Section 3 deals with experiments and results and finally, the discussions are presented.

2   Materials and Methods

As it was mentioned, the multi-class emotion classification task is addressed using two emotional speech corpora and well-known parameterisations.

2.1   Speech Corpora and Feature Extraction

Both databases have been extendly used and they are labeled using seven emotions with a distribution showed in Table 1. From the INTERFACE project which involves four languages: English, French, Slovenian and Spanish, the last one was used here. This corpus was created by the Center for Language and Speech Technologies and Applications (TALP) of the Polytechnic University of Catalonia (UPC) with the purpose of investigating emotional discourse. Two professional actors, a man and a woman, elicited 5113 spoken sentences. The other corpus was developed at the Communication Science Institute, in the Berlin Technical University [2]. The corpus has 535 utterances, and the same sentences were recorded in German by 10 actors: 5 females and 5 males. In a first step, 10 utterances for each emotion type (from 1 to 7 s) were elicited and then, a perception test with 20 individuals was carried out to ensure the emotional quality and naturalness of the utterances and the most confusing were eliminated.

Although there is no a definitive consensus about the best characteristics for emotional speech recognition [5], the research community considers some

Table 1. Emotional corpora distribution.

	Neutral	Anger	Disgust	Fear	Joy	Surprise boredom[*]	Sadness
INTERFACE	734	724	731	735	731	728	730
EmoDB	79	127	46	69	71	81[*]	62

suitable attributes to define baselines [20,25]. In this work, a well-known set computed over the whole sentences was used: the means of the {first 12 MFCCs, F_0, energy} and the zero-crossing rate; in addition, the means of their first derivatives. Consequently, each audio file is represented by a 30–dimensional vector.

2.2 Classifiers: Restricted Boltzmann Machines

The RBM is an artificial neural network with two layers (Fig. 1): the input (visible) layer and the hidden (output) layer [6,8]. There is no connections between the units in the same layer [10], and the RBM represents the joint distribution between the input vector and hidden layers (random variables).

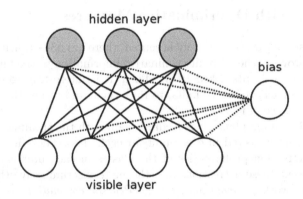

Fig. 1. Restricted Boltzmann machine

As it is a generative stochastic network, it can learn the probability distribution over the data using an energy function E defined as:

$$E(v, h) = -a^\top v - b^\top h - v^\top W h \tag{1}$$

where v and h are the input and the hidden state vectors respectively, W is a symmetric matrix of the connection weights, and $\{a, b\}$ are bias vectors for the layers. The joint probability $(p(v, h))$ assigns a probability to each configuration (v, h) using:

$$p(v,h) = \frac{e^{-E(v,h)}}{Z} \qquad (2)$$

where $Z = \sum_{v,h} e^{-E(v,h)}$ is a normalisation constant. Then, the probability assigned by the network to the visible vector v is:

$$p(v) = \frac{1}{Z} \sum_h e^{-E(v,h)} \qquad (3)$$

As there is no connections in the same layer, the visible variables are conditionally independent, given the hidden variables, and vice versa. Then, the conditional probabilities are: $p(v_j = 1|h) = \sigma(a_i + \sum_j h_j w_{i,j})$ and $p(h_j = 1|v) = \sigma(b_j + \sum_i v_i w_{i,j})$, where $\sigma(x) = \frac{1}{1+e^{-x}}$.

In order to find the parameters $\{W, a, b\}$, the contrastive divergence algorithm is applied [9].

The standard configuration of a deep RBM is a pipeline that includes a RBM (it may have multiple stacked RBMs) and, connected to its output a final classifier. The last can be a standard classifier as K-nearest neighbors (KNN), decision trees or multilayer perceptrons (MLP), among others [1,5]. After training the RBM, the outputs from the hidden neurons feed the final classifier.

3   Pruning with Discriminative Measures

Although the standard way is widely accepted, there are not explicit proofs that the last layer provides the more discriminative information to the final classifier, and much less in a deep stacked RBM. Then, it is interesting to evaluate the discriminative capacity of every units, to rank them and to use the best to feed the final classifier (see Fig. 2).

After RBM training phase, it is feeding again with the training samples and the activations are collected in every unit for each class. Then, it is possible to think about activation probabilities of the classes in each unit. Consequently, the more different these activations are, the more discriminative that the unit could be. In this work, *information gain* and *Pearson correlation* are proposed to measure this in order to rank the units. The general steps used in the multi–class approach are described in Algorithm 1.

3.1   Information Gain

The information gain is used to measure about the 'information gained' in the classification task, in presence or absence of a neuron, by the decrease of global entropy. Entropy is considered as a measure of the unpredictability of the system, then, if the randomness of the given variable is known, the amount of information provided by an event can be estimated. For a random variable X with probability mass function p, it is computed as $H(X) = -\sum_x p(x) \log_2 p(x)$.

Then, a more probable event is less informative and it is possible to define the information for a particular event as $I(x) = -\log_2 p(x)$, and its expected value

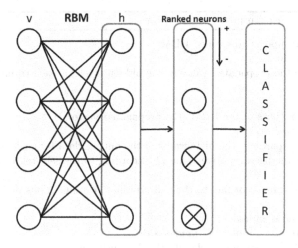

Fig. 2. Proposed DBM.

over all possible values of x leads to the Shannon's entropy. From Shannon's entropy we can define the conditional entropy of a random variable X given the random variable Y by:

$$H(X|Y) = \sum_{x,y} p(x,y) \log_2 p(x|y) \tag{4}$$

where $p(x,y)$ is the joint probability that $X = x$ and $Y = y$. Using that, the information gain of a class for a unit is defined as:

$$IG\,(Class, Attribute) = H\,(Class) - H\,(Class|Attribute) \tag{5}$$

In this context, the hidden unit is an attribute.

3.2   Pearson Correlation

In this work, the Pearson correlation coefficient (PCC) [16] is computed as the normalized covariance: 1 means direct correlation, -1 means inverse correlation and 0 denoting the absence of any relationship. The idea is that the correlation of the samples within a class is expected to be greater than the correlation between classes [26], in this way, the ranking of neurons uses the correlation values. This coefficient can be expressed as:

$$r = r_{xy} = \frac{cov\,(x,y)}{\sigma_x \sigma_y} = \frac{\sum x_i y_i - n\bar{x}\bar{y}}{\sqrt{(\sum x_i^2 - n\bar{x}^2)}\,\sqrt{(\sum y_i^2 - n\bar{y}^2)}} \tag{6}$$

where σ is the standard deviation, n is the sample size and $\bar{x}, \bar{y}$ are the means. When x and y come from the same class, this coefficient is interpreted as the intra–class correlation while, when they come from different classes, as the inter–class correlation. It means, for each neuron, the correlation is obtained using the

---

Algorithm 1. Discriminative evaluation

Require: An unsupervised trained RBM
 1: **for all** class **do**
 2:     calculate the propagated value in the hidden layer for each training vector
 3: **end for**

Require: The outputs of the RBM (the propagated vectors)
 4: **for all** neuron i **do**
 5:     estimate separately the histograms of the output data for each class.
 6:     calculate i's discriminative value D_i according to the selected measure.
 7: **end for**
 8: Rank the neurons according to their discriminative value in descending order.

Require: Ranked neurons
 9: **for** $i \leftarrow 1$ **to** *total number of neurons* **do**
10:     use the first i neurons to classify the data using Knn.
11: **end for**

---

neuron's output values for the samples of the classes. Then the ranking is carried out as described in Algorithm 1.

4   Experiments and Results

The baseline was defined as a standard DBM using a 10–fold cross-validation (CV)[17], and a confidence interval (CI) with 0.05 level of significance was computed. Then, the pruning performance was evaluated on the final classifier with 10–fold CV. For each pruning, a new final classifier is trained an tested. The experiments were performed using an RBM with 30 visible and 1920 hidden units for the Interface corpus, for the EmoDB database 30 visible and 960 hidden neurons were used. The number of hidden units were set based on the number of audio samples [19]. The baseline is represented with a solid-line and the confidence interval (CI) with a dashed-line in the Fig. 3. The pruning was done with the best 200 units and then, adding 200 successively for Interface, and using 100 and an increment of 100 for EmoDB. When the performance of the pruned networks crosses the baseline CI, it is a good point to stop the searching. However, it is possible to see the better performances reached by the pruned networks.

5   Discussion

Results show that the two proposed measures are useful to achieve an acceptable error rate with fewer neurons. As can be seen, the pruned networks use less units than the full RBM and reach better classification rates. This may keep the advantages in classification using a big net and to improve the results using a standard DBM.

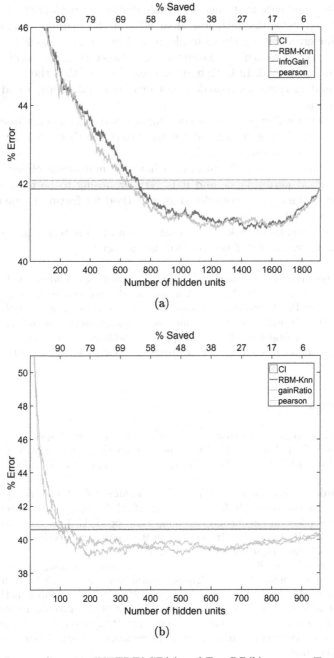

Fig. 3. Pruning results using INTERFACE(a) and EmoDB(b) corpora. Test were performed using different RBM configurations.

The results indicate that once a suitable number of initial neurons has been chosen, pruned networks with less than 50% of the neurons produce better-than-baseline error results. For example in the Fig. 3(a), around 40% of the total neurons are needed to achieve the same performance than the baseline while in (b), only 10% is needed. In both figures, it can be seen that the error decreases until that adding more neurons does not give more information and make the net more complex.

In the post-training pruning method for restricted Boltzmann machines presented in this work, the hidden units were ranked and then pruned using *information gain* and *Pearson correlation*.

In this work, we used the pruning scheme in multi-class classification and it obtain a good performance and it is very promising to be applied in other tasks. Finally, this can be considered as a method for feature extraction (from the hidden units of a RBM).

In future work, more task will be evaluated and more techniques to measure the discriminative ability of neurons will be explored.

Acknowledgements. The authors wish to thank to *Universidad Autónoma Metropolitana* from México; *Agencia Nacional de Promoción Científica y Tecnológica* (ANPCyT)(with PICT-2015-977), *Universidad Nacional del Litoral* (with CAID-PJ-50020150100055LI) and *Consejo Nacional de Investigaciones Científicas y Técnicas* (CONICET), from Argentina, for their support. In addition, they want to thank ELRA for supplying the emotional speech synthesis database, catalogue reference: ELRA-S0329.

References

1. Batliner, A., et al.: The automatic recognition of emotions in speech. In: Cowie, R., Pelachaud, C., Petta, P. (eds.) Emotion-Oriented Systems. Cognitive Technologies, pp. 71–99. Springer, Heidelberg (2011). https://doi.org/10.1007/978-3-642-15184-2_6
2. Burkhardt, F., Paeschke, A., Rolfes, M., Sendlmeier, W., Weiss, B.: A database of German emotional speech. In: Proceedings of 9th European Conference on Speech Communication and Technology (Interspeech), pp. 1517–1520, September 2005
3. Cao, F., Liu, B., Park, D.S.: Image classification based on effective extreme learning machine. Neurocomputing **102**, 90–97 (2013)
4. Castellano, G., Fanelli, A.M., Pelillo, M.: An iterative pruning algorithm for feed-forward neural networks. IEEE Trans. Neural Netw. **8**(3), 519–531 (1997)
5. Cen, L., Li, H., Yu, Z.L., Dong, M., Chan, P.: Machine learning methods in the application of speech emotion recognition. INTECH Open Access Publisher (2010)
6. Erhan, D., Bengio, Y., Courville, A., Manzagol, P.A., Vincent, P., Bengio, S.: Why does unsupervised pre-training help deep learning? J. Mach. Learn. Res. **11**(Feb), 625–660 (2010)
7. Guo, X.L., Wang, H.Y., Glass, D.H.: A growing Bayesian self-organizing map for data clustering. In: 2012 International Conference on Machine Learning and Cybernetics, vol. 2, pp. 708–713, July 2012
8. Hinton, G.E., Salakhutdinov, R.R.: Reducing the dimensionality of data with neural networks. Science **313**(5786), 504–507 (2006)

9. Hinton, G.E.: Training products of experts by minimizing contrastive divergence. Neural Comput. **14**(8), 1771–1800 (2002)
10. Hinton, G.E.: A practical guide to training restricted Boltzmann machines. Department of Computer Science, University of Toronto (2010)
11. Hinton, G.E.: A practical guide to training restricted boltzmann machines. In: Montavon, G., Orr, G.B., Müller, K.-R. (eds.) Neural Networks: Tricks of the Trade. LNCS, vol. 7700, pp. 599–619. Springer, Heidelberg (2012). https://doi.org/10.1007/978-3-642-35289-8_32
12. Huang, F.J., Boureau, Y.L., LeCun, Y., et al.: Unsupervised learning of invariant feature hierarchies with applications to object recognition. In: 2007 IEEE Conference on Computer Vision and Pattern Recognition, pp. 1–8. IEEE (2007)
13. Huang, G.B., Wang, D.H., Lan, Y.: Extreme learning machines: a survey. Int. J. Mach. Learn. Cybern. **2**(2), 107–122 (2011)
14. Hussain, S., Alili, A.A.: A pruning approach to optimize synaptic connections and select relevant input parameters for neural network modelling of solar radiation. Appl. Soft Comput. **52**, 898–908 (2016)
15. Lee, H., Grosse, R., Ranganath, R., Ng, A.Y.: Convolutional deep belief networks for scalable unsupervised learning of hierarchical representations. In: Proceedings of the 26th Annual International Conference on Machine Learning, ICML 2009, pp. 609–616. ACM, New York (2009)
16. Lee Rodgers, J., Nicewander, W.A.: Thirteen ways to look at the correlation coefficient. Am. Stat. **42**(1), 59–66 (1988)
17. Michie, D., Spiegelhalter, D., Taylor, C.: Machine Learning, Neural and Statistical Classification. Ellis Horwood, University College, London (1994)
18. Sánchez-Gutiérrez, M., Albornoz, E.M., Rufiner, H.L., Close, J.G.: Post-training discriminative pruning for RBMs. Soft Comput. **2017**, 1–15 (2017). https://doi.org/10.1007/s00500-017-2784-3
19. Sánchez-Gutiérrez, M.E., Albornoz, E.M., Martinez-Licona, F., Rufiner, H.L., Goddard, J.: Deep learning for emotional speech recognition. In: Martínez-Trinidad, J.F., Carrasco-Ochoa, J.A., Olvera-Lopez, J.A., Salas-Rodríguez, J., Suen, C.Y. (eds.) MCPR 2014. LNCS, vol. 8495, pp. 311–320. Springer, Cham (2014). https://doi.org/10.1007/978-3-319-07491-7_32
20. Schuller, B., et al.: The INTERSPEECH 2013 computational paralinguistics challenge: social signals, conflict, emotion, autism. In: Proceedings of Interspeech, pp. 148–152. ISCA, August 2013
21. Soleymani, M., Garcia, D., Jou, B., Schuller, B., Chang, S.F., Pantic, M.: A survey of multimodal sentiment analysis. Image Vis. Comput. **65**, 3–14 (2017). https://doi.org/10.1016/j.imavis.2017.08.003. Multimodal Sentiment Analysis and Mining in the Wild Image and Vision Computing
22. Stanley, K.O., Miikkulainen, R.: Evolving neural networks through augmenting topologies. Evol. Comput. **10**(2), 99–127 (2002)
23. Sutskever, I., Hinton, G.E.: Learning multilevel distributed representations for high-dimensional sequences. In: AISTATS, vol. 2, pp. 548–555 (2007)
24. Suzuki, K., Horiba, I., Sugie, N.: A simple neural network pruning algorithm with application to filter synthesis. Neural Process. Lett. **13**(1), 43–53 (2001)
25. Tao, J., Kang, Y.: Features importance analysis for emotional speech classification. In: Tao, J., Tan, T., Picard, R.W. (eds.) ACII 2005. LNCS, vol. 3784, pp. 449–457. Springer, Heidelberg (2005). https://doi.org/10.1007/11573548_58
26. Wei, X., Li, K.C.: Exploring the within-and between-class correlation distributions for tumor classification. Proc. Natl. Acad. Sci. **107**(15), 6737–6742 (2010)

Planning and Scheduling, Robotics, Vision

When a Robot Reaches Out for Human Help

Ignasi Andrés[1(✉)], Leliane Nunes de Barros[1], Denis D. Mauá[1],
and Thiago D. Simão[2]

[1] University of São Paulo, São Paulo, Brazil
{ignasi,leliane,ddm}@ime.usp.br
[2] Delft University of Technology, Delft, The Netherlands
T.DiasSimao@tudelft.nl

Abstract. In many realistic planning situations, any policy has a non-zero probability of reaching a dead-end. In such cases, a popular approach is to plan to maximize the probability of reaching the goal. While this strategy increases the robustness and expected autonomy of the robot, it considers that the robot gives up on the task whenever a dead-end is encountered. In this work, we consider planning for agents that pro-actively and autonomously resort to human help when an unavoidable dead-end is encountered (the so-called symbiotic agents). To this end, we develop a new class of Goal-Oriented Markov Decision Process that includes a set of human actions that ensures the existence of a proper policy, one that possibly resorts to human help. We discuss two different optimization criteria: *minimizing the probability to use human help* and *minimizing the expected cumulative cost with a finite penalty for using human help for the first time*. We show that for a large enough penalty both criteria are equivalent. We report on experiments with standard probabilistic planning domains for reasonably large problems.

Keywords: Probabilistic planning · Shortest stochastic path
Human-robot collaboration

1 Introduction

The next generation of robots will arguably operate surrounded and in symbiosis with humans. Autonomous robots are expected to perform tasks like driving a car, cleaning the floor, delivering products and caring for elders in the presence and under the guidance of humans. This proximity to humans provides new opportunities for building robots that are robust to failures [13].

Goal-oriented Markov Decision Processes (GMDP) are the standard framework for building mission guided planning robots [3,11,17,18]. The typical strategy in this framework is to maximize the probability of reaching the goal while minimizing the expected cumulative cost. Although this generates policies that

© Springer Nature Switzerland AG 2018
G. R. Simari et al. (Eds.): IBERAMIA 2018, LNAI 11238, pp. 277–289, 2018.
https://doi.org/10.1007/978-3-030-03928-8_23

are robust and cost-effective, it assumes that the robot aborts the mission whenever a dead-end (a state from which the goal cannot be attained) is encountered. An arguably better approach is to reach out for human help.

In complex environments as the ones mentioned above, it is often difficult to model all human help actions available. For example, a domestic robot designed for elder care cannot rely on the elder action of opening the door to the kitchen; nevertheless, it might still be preferable to expect that some human help is available than to simply refuse to grabbing an item from the kitchen.

In this work, we consider the problem of goal-oriented probabilistic planning with unknown human help actions. We propose a generalization of Goal-Oriented Markov Decision Processes (GMDP), called **GMDP augmented with Human Help (GMDP-HH)**, where the robot can infer from the model a distinguished set of human help actions, i.e., it can modify a single fluent (a predicate from the state description) with an uniform cost (Sect. 3). These somehow artificial actions enable robots to plan beyond dead-ends, and allow to introduce human actions into any given GMDP.

In order to increase the robustness of robots, we assume that human help actions are a scarce resource to be used only if necessary. We thus seek for a proper policy (one that reaches the goal with certainty, eventually relying on human actions) but that minimizes the probability of using human help. We call this criterion **MinHProb** (*minimizing the human-help probability*). While appealing, this criterion is difficult to obtain, as the corresponding Bellman equation has multiple non-optimal fixed points, and heuristics for probability estimation are usually inefficient [18].

We then consider an alternative class of decision problems, called **GMDPs with a Penalty on Human Help (GMDP-PHH)**, where a finite penalty is incurred only the first time a human help is used (Sect. 4). This can be seen as modeling a situation where requesting the presence of a human is expensive, but once the human is available subsequent calls for human help are cheap. An optimal policy minimizes then the expected cumulative cost (which includes the penalty for using a human help for the first time); we call this criterion **MinPCost**.

The one-time penalty leads to optimal policies that are non-Markovian. To avoid dealing with such policies, we instead operate over an augmented state space (where states are augmented with a fluent h indicating whether they were reached with the help of human); This allows us to formulate the problem as a standard Stochastic Shortest Path MDP (SSP) making the assumption that there is a proper policy from every state and all improper policies have infinite cost, and employ any of the state-of-the-art SSP solvers.

We connect both classes of problems by proving that, for a large enough penalty, the MinPCost criterion finds policies with *minimum probability of using human help*, that is, which are also optimal under the MinHProb criterion. While there is no known strategy for finding a "large enough" penalty, our empirical results show that it is often possible to efficiently find one by linear search (that

is, by solving MinPCost problems with increasingly large penalty values until
the optimal policy converges).

We present experiments with extended versions of three standard planning
domains (Doors, Tire World and Navigation) that suggest that solutions for the
proposed models can be effectively found (Sect. 5).

2 Notation and Background

A **Goal-Oriented Markov Decision Process** (GMDP) consists of a finite
set of states S, an initial state $s_0 \in S$, a set of absorbing goal states $G \subset S$,
a finite set of actions A, the probabilistic transition function $T(s, a, s') \in [0, 1]$
that returns the probability of moving from s to s' after executing action a, and
a cost function $C(s, a) \in \mathbb{R}_0^+$ that specifies the cost of applying action a in state
s. The cost function is assumed to satisfy $C(s, a) = 0$ for all $a \in A$ and $s \in G$,
and $C(s, a) > 0$ for all $a \in A, s \notin G$.

A **policy** $\pi : S \to A$ is a mapping from states to actions that prescribes the
agent behavior.[1] A **history** $\sigma = \langle s_1, s_2, \ldots, s_{|\sigma|} \rangle$ is a finite sequence of non-goal
states ending in a goal state $s_{|\sigma|} \in G$. We say that σ starts at s if $s_1 = s$, and
write $\sigma \sim s$. The **probability of reaching the goal** when executing policy π
from state s is

$$P_G^\pi(s) = \sum_{\sigma \sim s} \prod_{i=1}^{|\sigma|-1} T(s_i, \pi(s_i), s_{i+1}). \tag{1}$$

We say that a policy π is **proper** for s if $P_G^\pi(s) = 1$. The **expected cumulative
cost** of a policy π in state s is

$$V^\pi(s) = \sum_{\sigma \sim s} \prod_{i=1}^{|\sigma|-1} T(s_i, \pi(s_i), s_{i+1}) \sum_{i=1}^{|\sigma|} C(s_i, \pi(s_i)), \tag{2}$$

if π is proper, else $V^\pi(s) = \infty$. We assume that a **Stochastic Shortest Path
MDP** (SSP) is a GMDP such that: (Assumption I) there exists at least one proper
policy π for any $s \in S$ and (Assumption II) all improper policies have infinite
cost. Thus, the minimum expected cumulative cost of a policy in an SSP is the
unique fixed-point solution for the following Bellman equations [2,12]:

$$V^*(s) = \begin{cases} 0, & \text{if } s \in G; \\ \min_{a \in A} C(s, a) + \sum_{s' \in S} T(s, a, s') V^*(s'), & \text{otherwise.} \end{cases} \tag{3}$$

The corresponding optimal policy π^* is any greedy policy w.r.t. V^* (i.e., one
obtained by applying *argmin* instead of min in the equation above). A Value
Iteration (VI) algorithm solves an SSP by applying Eq. 3 from some initialization
$V^*(s)$ until a fixed-point is found [12]. To speed up convergence, the values $V^*(s)$
are usually initialized with a heuristic function, and updated asynchronously
[4,5,11].

---

[1] We implicitly assume that every state has at least one applicable action.

A GMDP can be more concisely and conveniently specified using a **planning domain description language**, where states are described in terms of **fluents** that represent properties of the world whose truth value can be modified by the actions. So let F be a finite set of fluents. By making a Closed World Assumption (CWA), we identify any state $s \in S$ with the set of fluents that hold true in that state.

3   Goal-Oriented MDP Augmented with Human Help

For GMDPs with no proper policy, Eq. 3 might not converge, and policies might have unbounded expected cumulative cost and hence be incomparable. While several alternative optimization criteria have been proposed to cope with this issue [11,17,18], none of them have addressed the behavior of an agent that meets a dead-end, or have considered human assistance in the process.

In this work we allow the agent (e.g. a robot) to be equipped with a special set of operations called **human help actions** that can modify the truth value of any fluent at any state, thus ensuring the existence of proper policies from any state $s \in S$.

So let $\mathcal{M} = \langle S, s_0, G, A, T, C \rangle$ be a GMDP described in a planning domain description language with fluents F (so $s \subseteq F$, due to the CWA). To model unknown human help actions we introduce for every fluent $f \in F$ a pair of human help actions a_f and $a_{\neg f}$ that deterministically determine the value of fluent f at an uniform cost $C_H > 0$, that is

$$T(s, a_f, s \cup \{h, f\}) = 1 \,, \quad T(s, a_{\neg f}, s \cup \{h\} \setminus \{f\}) = 1 \,,$$

and $C(s, a_f, s') = C(s, a_{\neg f}, s') = C_H$, where h is a fluent (not yet in F) indicating that human help was used. Note that this definition is equivalent to allowing non-atomic human actions (that modify several fluents at once) at a cost proportional to the number of fluents they modify. To allow for Markovian policies while distinguishing the use of human help, we augment the state space so that for every state $s \in S$ there is a state $s_h = s \cup \{h\}$ representing that s was reached using some human help action in the past (while s now represents that it was reached without human help), and modify the transition function accordingly (i.e., we set $T(s, a, s') = 0$ if $h \in s$ and $h \notin s'$). Call S_H the set of all states reached with human help. We also distinguish goal states reached through human help as $G_H = \{s \cup \{h\} : s \in G\}$. We call the tuple $\mathcal{M}_{HH} = \langle S \cup S_H, s_0, G \cup G_H, A \cup A_H, T, C, C_H \rangle$ a GMDP **augmented with human help** (GMDP-HH), where T and C are extended to account for human actions.

Now, we can decompose the expected cumulative cost of any policy π as the sum of expected cumulative cost of the robot actions $V_{\pi,R}(s)$ and the expected cumulative cost of the human actions $V_{\pi,H}(s), \forall s \in S \cup S_H$:

$$V^\pi(s) = V_R^\pi(s) + V_H^\pi(s), \tag{4}$$

where

$$V_R^\pi(s) = \sum_{\sigma \sim s} \prod_{i=1}^{|\sigma|-1} T(s_i, \pi(s_i), s_{i+1}) \sum_{i=1}^{|\sigma|} \left\{ C(s_i, \pi(s_i)) : \pi(s_i) \in A \right\} \qquad (5)$$

and

$$V_H^\pi(s) = \sum_{\sigma \sim s} \prod_{i=1}^{|\sigma|-1} T(s_i, \pi(s_i), s_{i+1}) \sum_{i=1}^{|\sigma|} \left\{ C(s_i, \pi(s_i)) : \pi(s_i) \in A_H \right\}. \qquad (6)$$

The human actions allow any goal state to be reached from any state with certainty. At the same time, improper policies remain having infinite expected costs. Hence:

Theorem 1. *A Goal-Oriented Markov Decision Process augmented with human help actions is an SSP with Assumption I and II.*

Our definition of GMDP-HH might lead to trivial solutions in domains where the goals have a distinguished fluent that can be modified from any state by the human. In order to avoid such trivial solutions, we remove human actions that modify fluents appearing in the goal, whenever this does not remove the existence of proper policies. This preprocessing step can be accomplished efficiently by analyzing the *causal graph* [8] of a determinized version of a planning domain description. We omit the details of this transformation due to space limitation.

3.1   Minimizing the Probability of Human Help (MinHProb)

Given that the human help is a costly resource, an intuitive criterion for solving a GMDP-HH is to find a proper policy that minimizes the probability of using human help. To this end, we define the **probability of reaching a goal using human help** when executing a policy π as:

$$P_{G_H}^\pi(s) = \sum_{\sigma \sim s : s_{|\sigma|} \in G_H} \prod_{i=1}^{|\sigma|-1} T(s_i, \pi(s_i), s_{i+1}), \qquad (7)$$

where the sum is over all histories that end up in some $s_{|\sigma|} \in G_H$. The optimal policy under the **minimum human help probability** criterion, called **MinHProb**, is π_{MinHProb} such that:

$$P_{G_H}^{\pi_{\text{MinHProb}}}(s_0) = \min_\pi P_{G_H}^\pi(s_0) \text{ subject to } P_{G \cup G_H}^\pi(s_0) = 1. \qquad (8)$$

In words, the optimal policy is a proper policy that minimizes the probability of using human help. The requirement of being a proper policy is necessary to avoid improper policies that e.g. do not use human help (hence have probability zero of reaching the goal with human help). This criterion has the following interesting properties:

Proposition 1. *If the original* GMDP $\mathcal{M}$ *has a proper policy* π^* *for* s_0 *then* $\pi^* \in \arg\min_\pi P^\pi_{G_H}(s_0)$. *Conversely, if* $P^{\pi_{MinHProb}}_{G_H}(s_0) = 0$ *then the original* MDP *has a proper policy* $\pi_{MinHProb}$ *for* s_0.

Proof. Note that $P^\pi_{G \cup G_H}(s_0) = P^\pi_G(s_0) + P^\pi_{G_H}(s_0) = 1$. Hence, a proper policy π for s_0 in the original GMDP $\mathcal{M}$ satisfies $P^G_\pi(s_0) = 1$, which implies that $P^\pi_{G_H}(s_0) = 0$. Conversely, any policy π with $P^\pi_{G_H}(s_0) = 0$ must satisfy $P^\pi_G(s_0) = 1$, and hence be proper for s_0 in the original problem.   □

According to the proposition above, the MinHProb criterion finds a policy that uses human help only if necessary, that is, only when the robot finds itself in a dead-end.

3.2   Bellman Equation for MinHProb

One can show that $P^*_{G_H} = P^{\pi_{MinHProb}}_{G_H}$ is a fixed-point of the following Bellman equation:

$$
P^*_{G_H}(s) = \begin{cases} 0, & \text{if } s \in G; \\ 1, & \text{if } s \in G_H; \\ \min_{a \in A} \sum_{s' \in S \cup S_H} T(s, a, s') P^*_{G_H}(s'), & \text{otherwise.} \end{cases} \tag{9}
$$

However, not every fixed-point of the Eq. (9) is equal to $P^{\pi_{MinHProb}}_{G_H}$. To see this, consider the GMDP-HH in Fig. 1 (left) for which $P^{\pi_{MinHProb}}_{G_H}(x) = 0.5$ and $P^{\pi_{MinHProb}}_{G_H}(y) = P^{\pi_{MinHProb}}_{G_H}(y, z) = 1$. Any solution such that $P^*_{G_H}(y) = P^*_{G_H}(y, z) < 1$ is also a fixed-point.

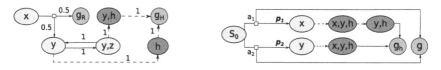

Fig. 1. Examples of GMDP-HH with fluents $F = \{x, y, z, h\}$: nodes, solid edges and dotted edges represent, resp., states, agent actions and human help actions; the numbers denote transition probability; g_H (resp., g_R) is the goal reached using (not using) human actions. Left: a GMDP-HH with multiple fixed-point solutions. Right: two actions are applicable at s_0, resulting in four different histories starting at s_0, all of them with the same $P^{\pi_{MinHProb}}_{G_H}(s_0)$.

As usual we can apply Value Iteration based algorithms to solve Eq. 9. However, since this equation has multiple fixed-points not every initialization leads to an optimal fixed-point. In particular, admissible heuristics for $P^*_{G_H}$ do not ensure convergence and hence cannot be used. One possible solution is to adapt algorithms for SSPs such as FRET and FRET-π that find and remove problematic cycles [10,16], ensuring convergence from any initialization. Another possible approach is to use linear programming reformulations of the problem as in [18].

Another issue with the MinHProb is that two policies might achieve the same probability $P^\pi_{G_H}(s_0)$ while executing a very different number of human actions. For example, take the GMDP-HH in Fig. 1 (right), and assume that $p_1 = p_2 = p$. Then, selecting either action at s_0 leads to an optimal policy π_{MinHProb} with $P^{\pi_{\text{MinHProb}}}_{G_H}(s_0) = p$, while executing a different number of human actions (and obtaining different cumulative costs). Situations like these can be remedied by additionally minimizing the expected cumulative cost among policies π_{MinHProb}, that is, by adopting a lexicographic criterion that first minimizes $P^\pi_{G_h}(s_0)$ then minimizes $V^\pi(s_0)$. We show in the next Section how this two-step criterion can be more efficiently computed using a surrogate criterion that introduces a finite penalty on the first time a human action is used.

4 Goal-Oriented MDP with a Penalty on Human Help

An alternative criterion to find a policy that minimizes human help is to minimize the expected cumulative cost while severely penalizing any history that uses a human help. Intuitively, this criterion assumes that the cost of human help is amortized if used repeatedly. This is a realistic scenario when there is a high cost of requesting human presence, but a small cost for actually using human help. Thus, we define the **Goal-Oriented MDP with a Penalty on Human Help** (**GMDP-PHH**) as the tuple $M_{HP} = \langle S \cup S_H, s_0, G \cup G_H, A \cup A_H, T, C, D_H \rangle$, where all terms are defined as in a GMDP-HH, and $D_H > 0$ is a finite value denoting the penalty incurred the first time a human action is used.

4.1 Minimizing Expected Cumulative Cost with a Penalty on Human Action

Solving a GMDP-PHH is akin to solving GMDPs with a give-up action that takes the agent from any state directly into a goal state and incurs a (usually large) finite penalty [11]. Conceptually however a GMPDP-PHH differs from a GMPD with a give-up action (a.k.a. fSSPUDE) since in the former the agent resumes planning after paying the penalty D_H.

We can solve a GMDP-PHH efficiently by using any off-the-shelf SSP solver by modifying the cost function $C(s,a)$ so that it returns $C_H + D_H$ if $s \in S$ and $a \in A_H$, and otherwise remains unchanged. We call this criterion of minimizing the expected cumulative cost increased with the penalty D_H the **MinPCost** criterion. It is easy to prove that a GMDP-PHH with this modified cost function is still an SSP.

4.2 MinHProb Versus MinPCost

Theorem 2 shows that one can use MinPCost as a solution to MinHProb.

Theorem 2. *There exists a value* $D_{MinHProb}$ *such that for all* $D_H >$ $D_{MinHProb}$ *a* $\pi_{MinPCost}$ *policy with* D_H *is also a* $\pi_{MinHProb}$ *policy. Additionally, any* $\pi_{MinPCost}$ *policy with* D_H *minimizes the unpenalized expected cumulative cost among all* $\pi_{MinHProb}$ *policies (i.e., it optimizes the two-step criterion),*

Proof. Given a policy π, we can decompose $V^\pi(s)$ as the sum of expected cumulative costs of robot actions, human actions and the one-time penalty:

$$V^\pi(s) = V_R^\pi(s) + V_H^\pi(s) + P_{G_H}^\pi(s) \cdot D_H, \tag{10}$$

where $P_{G_H}^\pi(s)$ is given by Eq. 7. For large enough D_H, a policy that uses a human help action in a given state has a higher expected cumulative cost than a policy that differs only by the choice of agent action in that same state. Hence, an optimal policy will use a human action only if no agent action can lead the agent out of a dead-end. The same argument shows that MinPCost breaks ties by selecting a policy that minimizes the expected cost of robot and human actions, thus satisfying the lexicographic criterion.   □

According to Theorem 2, for large enough D_H the optimal policy π_{MinPCost} also optimizes MinHProb while minimizing the unpenalized expected cumulative cost, that is, $P_{G_H}^{\pi_{\text{MinPCost}}}(s_0) = P_{G_H}^{\pi_{\text{MinHProb}}}(s_0)$ and π_{MinPCost} minimizes $V_R^\pi(s) + V_H^\pi(s)$. However, there is no known procedure for finding the value D_{MinHProb} or even for verifying if a given value satisfies the condition on the Theorem 2. In our experiments we observed that by guessing a sufficiently large value D_H and verifying whether increasing this value changes the optimal policy provides an effective means for finding D_{MinHProb} in practice.

5   Empirical Analysis

We performed experiments with the objective to: (i) *analyze the soundness and performance time of solving* GMDP-HH *problems under the MinPCost criterion using state-of-the-art* SSP *planners*, and (ii) **investigate the effectiveness of finding the** $\pi_{MinHProb}$ **by solving GMDP-HH problems under the MinPCost criterion with increasingly large penalties**. Our tests show that directly solving GMDP-HH problems under the MinHProb criterion using state-of-the-art SSP planners was highly inefficient in nearly all instances; for this reason we omit this analysis here.

We find optimal policies under the *MinPCost* criterion using a modified version of the LRTDP algorithm [4] implemented on the mGPT Framework [6]. This modification was done to deal with the augmented state space and includes a function to verify if a state s satisfies the fluent h. All experiments were performed in a Linux machine with a 2.4 GHz processor and 213 GB RAM, with a time limit of 1 h per instance.

To perform our tests, we considered several instances of the following modified versions of three standard planning domains:

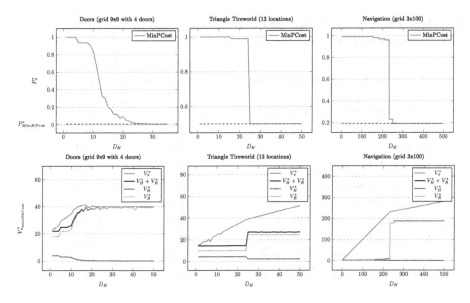

Fig. 2. Characteristics of the optimal policy for three large instances of the tested domains. Top: $P^*(s_0) = P_{G_H}^{\pi \mathrm{MinPCost}}(s_0)$ for increasing values of the penalty D_H; $P^*(s_0) = P_{MinHProb}(s_0)$ is the minimal probability. Bottom: $V_{MinPcost}(s_0)$, $V_R^*(s_0)$, $V_H^*(s_0)$ and $V_R^*(s_0) + V_H^*(s_0)$ for increasing values of the penalty D_H.

- **Doors**, where a robot must navigate in a grid world to reach a goal location, while passing through a sequence of locked doors; and for each door the robot needs to find the key in order to open it; in each step there is a 0.5 probability of finding the key to the next door in the current cell; alternatively, the robot can ask for a human to open the door;
- **Navigation**, where a robot navigates in a grid world to reach a goal location; in every cell there is a certain probability that the robot gets stuck (and thus reaches a dead-end). A human can take the robot to any location (other than the goal) and thus escape dead-ends; and
- **Triangle Tireworld**, where a car moves through connected locations and has to reach a goal location; in each movement between locations the car can have a flat tire with non-zero probability; some locations contain a spare; the agent would be in a dead-end if it has a flat tire and no spare; a human can deliver a spare tire or take the car to any location.

As discussed in the introduction, the large number of human actions leads to a large branching factor in the search, which makes heuristic search less efficient. To overcome this issue, we select a subset $A_H' \subseteq A_H$ involving only the set of *relevant* fluents [7,8], that is, the fluents that are relevant to lead the agent to the goal which was automatically extracted from the domains description in PDDL [19]. For the largest Triangle Tireworld instance, from a total of 92 fluents, we only used 46 relevant fluents to create the set of human help actions; for the largest Navigation instance, from a total of 309 fluents, only 154 were the relevant fluents; for the largest Doors instance, from the total of 417 fluents, we only consider 146 relevant fluents.

Table 1. Optimal values and exec. time in secs for a given D_H.

Problem instance	D_H	$P_{G_H}^{\pi_{MinPCost}}(s_0)$	$V^{\pi_{MinPCost}}(s_0)$	Time (sec)
Doors-7	30	0.03	31.6	3.4
Doors-9	30	0.01	39.4	5.4
Triangle Tireworld-4	50	0.50	49.6	0.6
Triangle Tireworld-5	50	0.50	57.6	3.0
Triangle Tireworld-6	70	0.50	74.0	65.4
Triangle Tireworld-7	90	0.50	90.5	757.0
Navigation 3 × 103	500	0.19	321.3	15.4
Navigation 4 × 103	500	0.27	381.9	19.5
Navigation 5 × 103	500	0.34	435.7	32.7

Solving GMDP-HH *Problems Under the MinPCost Criterion.* Table 1 shows the values of $P_{G_H}^{\pi_{MinPCost}}(s_0)$ and $V_{G_H}^{\pi_{MinPCost}}(s_0)$ for large enough values of D_H that allow convergence to MinHProb policies; and time in seconds for finding the optimal policies for 9 instances of the tested domains. For each instance, the $P_{G_H}^{\pi_{MinPCost}}(s_0)$ and $V_{G_H}^{\pi_{MinPCost}}(s_0)$ values were confirmed to be equal to the analytically computed value proving the soundness of our solution. We also see from Table 1, that for all Doors instances and the two small Triangle Tireworld instances, the optimal solution was found in few seconds; while for the Navigation domain and the larger instances of the Triangle Tireworld domain the time was one order of magnitude larger, with the exceptions being the largest Triangle Tireworld instance, which are considerably larger than the other instances.

Finding $P^*(s_0)$ with Increasingly Large Penalties D_H. Figure 2 shows the results of our experiments using the *MinPCost* criterion on large instances of selected domains (a 9×9 grid with 4 doors for the Doors, a triangle with 11 locations at each side for the Triangle Tireworld, and a 3×100 grid for Navigation). In all domains the probability of using human actions to reach the goal from s_0 decreases as the penalty increases until it reaches the minimal probability $P_{G_H}^*(s_0)$ (analytically computed as 0.0078 for Doors, 0.5 for Triangle Tireworld and 0.19 for Navigation). This decreasing is smoother for the Doors instance (as the probability of using human help is very small) and somewhat abrupt for the other two domains, showing that the optimal policies are very sensitive to the penalty value. We also see that as predicted, the optimal expected cumulative cost $V^*(s_0)$ increases as the penalty D_H increases, with an inflection point near the steepest descent of the probability (note however that the cost $V_\pi^*(s_0)$ still grows linear with D_H even after the policy has converged). We also see a similar behavior to the probability $P_{G_H}^\pi(s_0)$ in the factors V_H* and V_R*, that is, they have a clear inflection point when the policy converges to the MinHProb, and eventually converge to their values (again, this change is smoother for Doors and more abrupt for the other domains). These experiment suggest that a reasonable value for the penalty can often be found with some experimentation and analysis of the domain which proves that this is a reliable solutions to find an optimal policy for GMDP-HHs problems under the criteria proposed in this paper.

6   Related Work

Most of the work on human-robot interaction is based on POMDPs (*Partially Observable Markov Decision Process*) [1,9,14,15], augmented with a set of given human observations and actions, with negative reward and whose objective is to find a policy that maximizes the expected reward over a given horizon, not explicitly treating goal and dead-end states. In this work we consider GMDP with fully observability and the presence of dead-ends.

In all previous approaches, the human observations are known a priori, while in our work we automatically generate human actions from the GMDP problem description. The goal of this work is to maximize agent autonomy in domains where assessing the cost and specially the type of human intervention is difficult, costly or simply undesirable.

7   Conclusions

Algorithms that solve GMDPs assume that when an agent encounters a dead-end its only action is abort the mission. However, robots operating in the presence and under the guidance of humans can often reach out for help in order to resume its mission. Still, in many complex environments, it is unrealistic to assume that the available human help actions are known a priori.

In this work we develop two new classes of Goal-Oriented Markov Decision Processes that allow for planning in uncertain environments and with unknown human actions. The first class, called goal-oriented Markov Decision Problem augmented with Human Help (GMDP-HH), assumes that human actions can modify the state of any fluent, and thus ensure that a goal is reached from any state. To avoid trivializing the problem, we then seek for the optimal policy that reaches the goal with certainty while minimizing the probability of using human help. While this criterion is appealing as it uses human help only if necessary, it leads to inefficient optimization problems.

Our second class of problems, called Goal-Oriented Markov Decision Problems with a Penalty on Human Help (GMDP-PHH), assumes that an additional finite penalty is incurred the first time a human action is used. An optimal policy simply minimizes the expected cumulative cost (including the finite penalty) and can take advantage of standard solvers. Importantly, we show that for a large enough penalty, the optimal policy also minimizes the probability of using human help, thus providing an efficient solution to the first class of problems but also guaranteeing minimal costs.

The atomic human actions that we considered in this work can be interpreted as possible explanations for a mission failure in a standard Goal-Oriented Markov Decision Process, as in [7]; it also can be used to provide some guidance in modifying the domain so as to ensure that the goal is always met (i.e., to transform the problem into an Stochastic Shortest Path MDP).

An open question is how to find the minimum value of the finite penalty that ensures that the probability of reaching the goal using human help is minimized.

As future work we intend to compute the minimum human help probability by adapting the algorithm FRET for the *MinHProb* criterion [10] and using linear programming reformulations of a GMDP-HH problem as in [18].

Acknowledgments. Authors received financial support from CAPES, FAPESP (grants #2015/01587-0 and #2016/01055-1) and CNPq (grants #303920/2016-5 and #420669/2016-7).

References

1. Armstrong Crews, N., Veloso, M.: Oracular partially observable markov decision processes: a very special case. In: Proceedings of the IEEE ICRA (2007)
2. Bellman, R.: Dynamic Programming. Princeton University Press, Princeton (1957)
3. Bertsekas, D.P., Tsitsiklis, J.N.: An analysis of stochastic shortest path problems. Math. Oper. Res. **16**(3), 580–595 (1991). INFORMS
4. Bonet, B.: Labeled RTDP: improving the convergence of real-time dynamic programming. In: Proceedings ICAPS-03 (2003)
5. Bonet, B., Geffner, H.: Faster heuristic search algorithms for planning with uncertainty and full feedback. In: Proceedings of the IJCAI (2003)
6. Bonet, B., Geffner, H.: mGPT: a probabilistic planner based on heuristic search. J. Artif. Intell. Res. **24**, 933–944 (2005)
7. Göbelbecker, M., Keller, T., Eyerich, P., Brenner, M., Nebel, B.: Coming up with good excuses: what to do when no plan can be found. In: ICAPS (2010)
8. Helmert, M.: The fast downward planning system. J. Artif. Intell. Res. **26**, 191–246 (2006)
9. Karami, A.B., Jeanpierre, L., Mouaddib, A.I.: Partially observable markov decision process for managing robot collaboration with human. In: Proceedings of the 21st IEEE ICTAI (2009)
10. Kolobov, A., Daniel, M., Weld, S., Geffner, H.: Heuristic search for generalized stochastic shortest path MDPs. In: Proceedings of the ICAPS (2011)
11. Kolobov, A., Mausam, M., Weld, D.: A theory of goal-oriented MDPs with dead ends. In: Proceedings of the 28th Conference on UAI (2012)
12. Puterman, M.L.: Markov Decision Processes: Discrete Stochastic Dynamic Programming. Wiley (2014)
13. Rosenthal, S., Biswas, J., Veloso, M.: An effective personal mobile robot agent through symbiotic human-robot interaction. In: Proceedings of the AAMAS (2010)
14. Rosenthal, S., Veloso, M., Dey, A.K.: Learning accuracy and availability of humans who help mobile robots. In: Proceedings of the AAAI (2011)
15. Schmidt-Rohr, S.R., Knoop, S., Lösch, M., Dillmann, R.: Reasoning for a multi-modal service robot considering uncertainty in human-robot interaction. In: Proceedings of the 3rd HRI (2008)

16. Steinmetz, M., Hoffmann, J., Buffet, O.: Revisiting goal probability analysis in probabilistic planning. In: Proceedings of the 26th ICAPS (2016)
17. Teichteil-Königsbuch, F.: Stochastic safest and shortest path problems. In: Proceedings of the NCAI (2012)
18. Trevizan, F., Teichteil-Königsbuch, F., Thiébaux, S.: Efficient solutions for stochastic shortest path problems with dead ends. In: Proceedings of 33rd Conference on UAI (2017)
19. Younes, H.L., Littman, M.L.: PPDDL1.0: an extension to PDDL for expressing planning domains with probabilistic effects. Technical report CMU-CS-04-162 (2004)

Multi-agent Path Finding on Real Robots: First Experience with Ozobots

Roman Barták[(✉)], Jiří Švancara, Věra Škopková, and David Nohejl

Faculty of Mathematics and Physics, Charles University, Prague, Czech Republic
bartak@ktiml.mff.cuni.cz

Abstract. The problem of Multi-Agent Path Finding (MAPF) is to find paths for a fixed set of agents from their current locations to some desired locations in such a way that the agents do not collide with each other. This problem has been extensively theoretically studied, frequently using an abstract model, that expects uniform durations of moving primitives and perfect synchronization of agents/robots. In this paper we study the question of how the abstract plans generated by existing MAPF algorithms perform in practice when executed on real robots, namely Ozobots. In particular, we use several abstract models of MAPF, including a robust version and a version that assumes turning of a robot, we translate the abstract plans to sequences of motion primitives executable on Ozobots, and we empirically compare the quality of plan execution (real makespan, the number of collisions).

Keywords: Path planning · Multi-agent systems · Real robots

1 Introduction

Multi-agent path finding (MAPF) recently attracted a lot of attention of AI research community. It is a hard problem with practical applicability in areas such as warehousing and games. Frequently, an abstract version of the problem is solved, where a graph defines possible locations (vertices) and movements (edges) of agents and agents move synchronously. At any time, no two agents can stay in the same vertex to prevent collisions so the obtained plans are collision free and hence blindly executable. The plan of each agent consists of move (to a neighboring vertex) and wait (in the same vertex) actions. Makespan and sum-of-cost (plan lengths) are two frequently studied objectives.

In this paper, we focus on answering two questions: how to execute abstract plans obtained from existing MAPF algorithms and models on real robots and how the quality of abstract plans is reflected in the quality of executed plans. The goal is to verify if the abstract plans are practically relevant and, if the answer is no (as expected), to provide feedback to improve abstract models to be closer to reality. We use a fleet of Ozobot Evo robots to perform the plans. These robots provide motion primitives, for example, they can turn left/right, follow a line, and recognize line junction, so it is not necessary to solve classical

© Springer Nature Switzerland AG 2018
G. R. Simari et al. (Eds.): IBERAMIA 2018, LNAI 11238, pp. 290–301, 2018.
https://doi.org/10.1007/978-3-030-03928-8_24

robotics tasks such as localization. Though the robots have proximity sensors, the plans are executed blindly based on the MAPF setting as the plans should already be collision free.

Specifically, we explore the very classical MAPF setting as described above, the k-robust setting [1], where a gap is required between the robots to compensate possible delays during execution, and finally a model that directly encodes turning operations (the classical setting does not assume direction of movement). The abstract plans are then translated to motion primitives, which consist of forward movement, turning left/right, and waiting. We explore different durations of these primitives to see their effect on robot synchronization. As far as we know this is the first study of practical quality of plans obtained from abstract MAPF models.

The paper is organized as follows. We will first introduce the abstract MAPF problem formally and survey approaches for its solving. Then we will give more details on why it is important to look at the execution of abstract plans on real robots. After that, we will describe all the models used in this study and how they are translated to executable primitives of Ozobot Evo robots. Finally, we will describe our experimental setting and give results of an empirical evaluation.

2   The MAPF Problem

Formally, the MAPF problem is defined by a graph $G = (V, E)$ and a set of agents $a_1, \ldots, a_k$, where each agent a_i is associated with starting location $s_i \in V$ and goal location $g_i \in V$. The time is discrete and in every time step each agent can either move from its location to a neighboring location or wait in its current location. A grid map with a unit length of each edge is often used to represent the environment [10]. We will also be using this type of maps in this paper.

Let $\pi_i[t]$ denote the location (vertex of graph G) of agent a_i at time step t. Plan π_i is the sequence of locations for agent a_i. The MAPF task is to find a valid plan π that is a union of plans of all agents. We say that π is valid if (i) each agent starts and ends in its starting and goal location respectively, (ii) no two agents occupy the same vertex at the same time, and (iii) no two agents move along the same edge at the same time in opposite directions (they do not swap their positions). Formally this can be written as:

(i) $\forall i : \pi_i[0] = s_i \wedge \pi_i[T] = g_i$, where T is the last time step.
(ii) $\forall t, i \neq j : \pi_i[t] \neq \pi_j[t]$
(iii) $\forall t, i \neq j : \pi_i[t] \neq \pi_j[t + 1] \vee \pi_i[t + 1] \neq \pi_j[t]$.

We denote $|\pi_i|$ as the length of plan for agent a_i. Then we can define an objective function that measures the quality of the found valid plan π.

$$Makespan(\pi) = \max_i |\pi_i|$$

The makespan objective function is well known and often studied in the literature [15]. It can be shown that when we require the solution to be makespan optimal (i.e. a solution with minimal makespan), the problem is NP-hard [17].

To solve MAPF optimally, one can generally use algorithms from one of the following categories:

1. **Reduction-based solvers** are solvers that reduce MAPF to another known problem such as SAT [14], integer linear programming [16], and answer set programming [6]. These approaches are based on using fast solvers for given formalism and consist mainly of translating MAPF to that formalism.
2. **Search-based solvers** include variants of A* over a global search space – all possibilities how to place agents into the nodes of the graph [13]. Other make use of novel search trees [4,11,12] that search over some constraints put on the agents.

Though the plans obtained by different MAPF solvers might be different, the optimal plans are frequently similar and tight (no superfluous steps are used). As solving MAPF is not the topic of this paper (we focus on evaluating the practical relevance of obtained plans), any optimal MAPF solver can be used. We decided for the reduction-based solver implemented in the Picat programming language [3] that uses translation to SAT. This solver has performance comparable to state-of-the-art solvers and has the advantage of easy modification and extension of the core model, for example adding further constraints or using numerical constraints.

The Picat solver (like other reduction-based solvers) follows the planning-as-satisfiability framework [8], where a layered graph is used to encode the plans of a given length. Each layer describes positions of all agents in a given time step. As the plan length is unknown, the number of layers is incrementally increased until a solvable model is obtained. A Boolean variable B_{tav} indicates if agent a ($a = 1, 2, \ldots, k$) occupies vertex v ($v = 1, 2, \ldots, n$) at time t ($t = 0, 1, \ldots, m$). The following constraints ensure the validity of every state and every transition:

(1) Each agent occupies exactly one vertex at each time.

$\Sigma_{v=1}^{n} B_{tav} = 1$ for $t = 0, \ldots, m$, and $a = 1, \ldots, k$.

(2) No two agents occupy the same vertex at any time.

$\Sigma_{a=1}^{k} B_{tav} \leq 1$ for $t = 0, \ldots, m$, and $v = 1, \ldots, n$.

(3) If agent a occupies vertex v at time t, then a occupies a neighboring vertex at time $t + 1$.

$B_{tav} = 1 \Rightarrow \Sigma_{u \in neibs(v)}(B_{(t+1)au}) \geq 1$
for $t = 0, \ldots, m - 1$, $a = 1, \ldots, k$, and $v = 1, \ldots, n$.

The model consists of $k \times (m + 1) \times n$ Boolean variables, where k is the number of agents, m is the makespan, and n is the number of vertices in the graph. Further constraints can be added easily, for example, to prevent swaps or to introduce robustness. Figure 1 shows the executable Picat code with the core model to demonstrate how close the program is to the abstract model.

```
import sat.

path(N,As) =>
    K = len(As),
    lower_upper_bounds(As,LB,UB),
    between(LB,UB,M),
    B = new_array(M+1,K,N),
    B :: 0..1,

    % Initialize the first and last states
    foreach (A in 1..K)
        (V,FV) = As[A],
        B[1,A,V] = 1,
        B[M+1,A,FV] = 1
    end,

    % Each agent occupies exactly one vertex
    foreach (T in 1..M+1, A in 1..K)
        sum([B[T,A,V] : V in 1..N]) #= 1
    end,

    % No two agents occupy the same vertex
    foreach (T in 1..M+1, V in 1..N)
        sum([B[T,A,V] : A in 1..K]) #=< 1
    end,

    % Every transition is valid
    foreach (T in 1..M, A in 1..K, V in 1..N)
        neibs(V,Neibs),
        B[T,A,V] #=>
            sum([B[T+1,A,U] : U in Neibs]) #>= 1
    end,

    solve(B),
    output_plan(B).
```

Fig. 1. A program in Picat for MAPF.

3   Motivation and Contribution

The abstract plan outputted by MAPF solvers is, as defined, a sequence of locations that the agents visit. However, a physical agent has to translate these locations to a series of actions that the agent can perform. We assume that the agent can turn left and right and move forward. By concatenating these actions, the agent can perform all the required steps from the abstract plan (recall, that we are working with grid worlds). This translates to five possible actions at each time step - (1) wait, (2) move forward, (3, 4) turn left/right and move, and (5) turn back and move. As the mobile robot cannot move backward directly, turning back is implemented as two turns right (or left). For example, an agent with starting location in v_1 and goal location in v_7 in Fig. 2 has an abstract plan of seven locations. However, the physical agent has to perform four additional turning actions that the classical MAPF solvers do not take into consideration.

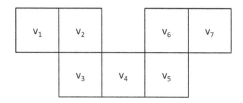

Fig. 2. Example of graph where an agent has to perform turning actions.

As the abstract steps may have durations different from the physical steps, the abstract plans, which are perfectly synchronized, may desynchronize when being executed, which may further lead to collisions. This is even more probable in dense and optimal plans, where agents often move close to each other.

The intuition says that such desynchronization will indeed happen. In the paper, we will empirically verify this hypothesis and we will explore several abstract models for MAPF and the output transformations to robot actions. These models not only try to keep the agent synchronous during the execution of the plan but also to avoid collisions caused by some small unforeseen flaw in the execution. We then compare and evaluate these models on an example grid using real robots. Note that the real robots only blindly follow the computed plan and cannot intervene if, for example, an obstacle is detected.

4   Models

In this section, we describe the studied abstract MAPF models and possible transformations of abstract plans to executable sequences of physical actions. Let t_t be the time needed by the robot to turn by 90° to either side and t_f be the time to move forward to the neighboring vertex in the grid. Both t_t and t_f are nonzero. The time spend while the agent is performing the wait operation t_w will depend on each model.

4.1   Classical Model

The first and most straightforward model is a direct translation of the abstract plan to the action sequence. We shall call this a *classic* model. At the end of each timestep, an agent is facing in a direction. Based on the next location, the agent picks one of the five actions described above and performs it. This means that all move actions consist of possible turning and then going forward. There are no independent turning moves. As the two most common actions in abstract plans are (2) and (3, 4), we suggest to set the time t_w of waiting actions to be $t_f + 1/2 * t_t$ as the average of durations of actions (2) and (3, 4).

One can easily see that this simple model can be prone to desynchronization, as turning adds time over agents that just move forward. Recall Fig. 2 and suppose there is another agent with the same number of steps, but all of the actions are moving forward. This agent will reach its goal $4 * t_t$ sooner than the agent from the example.

To fix this synchronization issue, we introduce a *classic + wait* model. The basic idea is that each abstract action takes the same time, which is realized by adding some wait time to "fast" actions. The longest action is (5), therefore each action now takes $2 * t_t + t_f$ including the waiting action. The consequence is that plan execution takes longer time, which may not be desirable.

Note that both of these models do not require the MAPF algorithm and model to change. They only use different durations of abstract actions which are implemented in the translation of abstract plans to executable actions.

4.2 Robust Model

Another way to fix the synchronization problem is to create a plan π that is robust to possible delays during execution. The k-robust plan is a valid MAPF plan that in addition requires for each vertex of the graph to be unoccupied for at least k time steps before another agent can enter it [1]. In our experiments, we choose k to be 1. We presume that this is a good balance between keeping the agents from colliding with each other while not prolonging the plan too much. The 1-robust plan is then translated to executable actions using the same principle as the *classic* model. This yields a *1-robust* model.

The synchronization issue is not fixed in a guaranteed way, but hopefully, collisions are avoided as the agents tend to not move close to each other.

4.3 Split Actions Model

One may assume that executable actions might be directly represented in the abstract model. In particular, the need to turn can be represented by an abstract turning action. In the reduction-based solvers, this can be done by splitting each vertex v_i from the original graph G into four new vertices $v_i^{up}, v_i^{right}, v_i^{down}, v_i^{left}$ indicating directions where the agent is facing to. The new edges now represent the turn actions, while the original edges correspond to move only actions, see Fig. 3. Note that when an agent leaves a vertex facing some direction, it will arrive to the neighboring vertex also facing that direction. This change to the input graph also requires a change in the MAPF solver (constraints), because the split vertices need to be treated as one to avoid collisions of type (ii). This means that at any time there can be at most one agent in those four vertices representing a given location. The abstract plan is then translated to an executable plan in a direct way as the agent is given a sequence of individual actions wait, turn left/right, and move forward. The waiting time t_w is set as the bigger time of the remaining actions: $t_w = \max(t_t, t_f)$. We shall call this a *split* model.

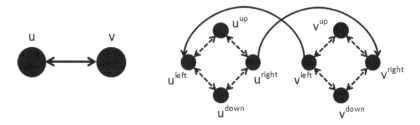

Fig. 3. Example of how two horizontally connected vertices (left) are split into new vertices (right) describing possible agent's orientations. The dotted edges correspond to turning actions.

A synchronization issue is still present in the *split* model, if the times t_t and t_f are not the same. Recall that the solvers assume equal durations of all actions. To fix this, we will use a notion from weighted MAPF [2]. Each edge in the graph is assigned an integer value that denotes its length. The weighted MAPF solver finds a plan that takes these lengths into account. Formally this can cause gaps in the plan of an agent as the agent may not be present in any vertex in the next step because the agent is still moving over an edge. This indeed does not break our definitions and the time is still discrete, only more finely divided. The lengths of turning edges are assigned a length of t_t and the other edges are assigned a length of t_f (or its scaled value to integers). The waiting time t_w is set as the smaller time of the remaining actions: $t_w = \min(t_t, t_f)$. We shall call this a *weighted-split* model or *w-split* for short.

A final enhancement to the *weighted-split* model is to introduce k-robustness there. This will again ensure that the agents do not tend to move close to each other to avoid undesirable collisions. In this case, however, it is not enough to use 1-robustness, as the plan is split into more time steps. Instead, we use $\max(t_t, t_f)$-robustness. We shall call this *robust-weighted-split* model or *rw-split* for short.

5   Experiments

The proposed models for MAPF were empirically evaluated on real robots and in this chapter we will present the obtained results. We shall first give some details on robots, that we used, and on the problem instance.

5.1   Ozobots

The robots used were Ozobot Evo from company Evollve [9]. These are small robots (about 3 cm in diameter) shown in Fig. 4. We have chosen them because their built-in actions are close to actions needed in the MAPF problems so there is no need to do low–level robotic programming. The robots are programmable through a programming language Ozoblockly [7] which is primarily meant as a teaching tool for children. The program is uploaded to the robot and then the robot executes it. Most importantly, the robots have sensors underneath that allow the robot to follow a line and to detect intersection. An intersection is defined as at least two lines crossing each other. The robots also have forward and backward facing proximity sensors allowing them to detect obstacles. We used them to synchronize the start of robots (see further), but we did not exploit sensors further during plan execution. In addition, the robots have LED diodes and speakers that act as the robots output. We use them to indicate some states of the robot such as a finished plan. The moving speed and turning speed can be adjusted up to a speed limit of the robot.

Fig. 4. Ozobot Evo from Evollve used for the experiments. Picture is taken from [9].

There are some drawbacks in the simplicity of the robots. The main one is that there is currently no communication between multiple robots and therefore starting an instance of MAPF for all of the present robots at the same time is difficult. To solve this problem, we used the proximity sensors and forbid the agents to start performing the computed plan if an obstacle is present in front of them. An obstacle was placed in front of all of the agents and once they were ready to start executing the plan, all of the obstacles were removed. This ensured that the start time was identical and any desynchronization at the end of the plan was caused during the execution and not at the start.

5.2   Problem Instance

An instance was created to test the described models. It is a 5 by 8 grid map that was obtained by randomly removing vertices and edges in such a way that the rest of the graph still remained connected. This yielded map shown in Fig. 5. As opposed to the usual representation, where agents reside in the cells in between lines, here the agents follow the line and the vertex is represented as the crossing of two lines. This map was then printed on A3 paper in a scale such that each edge is 5 cm long and the line is 5 mm thick as per Ozobots recommended specification. The edge length was chosen to allow two robots to safely stay in neighboring nodes and to observe even minor desynchronization due to turning (if the edges are longer than the duration of moving is much bigger than the duration of turning and hence the effect of extra turning actions is less visible).

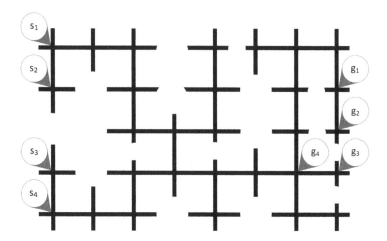

Fig. 5. Instance map for Ozobots. Ozobots follow the black line, the gray circles indicate starting and goal locations. They were not actually printed.

We used four robots; their initial and goal locations are also indicated in Fig. 5. These locations were chosen to ensure several bottlenecks in the map that will force the agents to navigate close to each other.

The speed of the robots was set in such a way that moving along a line takes 1600 ms and turning takes 800 ms. This means that $t_f = 1600$ and $t_t = 800$, however since the numbers are both divisible by 800, we can simplify the times for the MAPF solver to $t_f = 2$ and $t_t = 1$. This then gives us all required times for the models as described in the previous section.

5.3   Results

We generated plans using each MAPF model for the problem instance described above and then we executed the plans five times in total for each model. Several properties were measured with results shown in Table 1.

Table 1. Measured performance of Ozobots using each proposed model.

	Computed makespan	Failed runs	Number of collisions	Total time [s]	Max Δ time [s]
classic	17	5	4	NA	5
classic + wait	17	0	4.2	53	0
1-robust	19	0	0	41	4
split	27	0	2	36	3
w-split	45	0	2.6	39	0
rw-split	47	0	0	39	0

Computed makespan is the makespan of the plan returned by the MAPF solver. It is measured by the (weighted) number of abstract actions. Note that the *split* models have larger makespan than the rest because the *split* models use a finer resolution of actions, namely turning actions are included in the makespan calculation. This is even more noticeable with *w-split* and *rw-split*, where the moving-forward action has a duration (weight) of two.

The number of failed runs is also shown. The only model that did not finish any run is the *classic* model while the rest managed to finish all of the runs. A run fails if there is a collision that throws any of the robots off the track so the plan cannot be finished. The average number of collisions per run shows how many collisions that did not ruin the plan occurred. These collisions can range from small one, where the robots only touched each other and did not affect the execution of the plan, to big collisions, where the agent was slightly delayed in their individual plan, but still managed to finish the plan. For the *classic* model, where no execution finished, we present the number of collisions occurring before the major collision that stopped the plan.

Since we are using the makespan objective function, all of the plans can have their length equal to the longest plan without worsening the objective function. Even if the agents reached their destinations sooner, their plans were prolonged by waiting actions to match the length of the longest plan. To visually observe this behavior, we used the LEDs on the robots. The LEDs were turned on during the execution of the whole plan (including wait actions) and they were turned off once the plan was finished. This helped us to measure the overall time of the plan execution as the time from start to the last robot turning LEDs off. For the *classic* model, there is no total time, since the agents did not finish at all.

Each individual agent was let to execute the plan without interference with other agents to measure the difference between the fastest and slowest agent as Max Δ time. If the agents are perfectly synchronized then this Δ should be zero. All of the times are rounded to seconds because the measurements were conducted by hand.

From the number of collisions and times, we can conclude some properties of the models. Indeed, models *classic + wait*, *w-split*, and *rw-split* keep the agents synchronous, while the other models do not (there is a gap between finishing the plans by different agents). From all models, the *classic + wait* model is the slowest one to perform the plan. This is expected as this model uses longest durations of actions. Further, we can see that even if the agents are synchronous, some collisions may appear, since the agents have a nonzero diameter and are moving close to each other. This issue is solved by making a k-robust plan, however, the simple *1-robust* model was not synchronous and this desynchronization could cause a collision eventually if the plan was long enough.

In general, the *split* models provide the fastest execution of plans. This is expected because these models optimize the makespan that is closer to the real makespan. From the results, we can also see that introduction of robustness and weighted edges to the classical MAPF is of practical use if we plan to use the computed plan for real robots.

6 Conclusion

In this paper, we studied the behavior of MAPF plans when executed on real robots. We defined several models that either take the classical plan and translate it into a sequence of robot actions or create a plan that already consists of the robot actions. This mainly included the need for turning of the robot.

In the experiments, we concluded that the classical plan produced by MAPF solvers is not suitable to be performed on robots. The introduction of splitting the position of the robot to include orientation proved to be useful as well as using weighted edges to correspond with travel time. Furthermore, introducing k-robustness forbid the agents to travel close to each other to prevent collisions.

Acknowledgement. Roman Barták is supported by the Czech Science Foundation under the project P202/12/G061 and together with Jiří Švancara by the Czech-Israeli Cooperative Scientific Research Project 8G15027. This research was also partially supported by SVV project number 260 453.

References

1. Atzmon, D., Felner, A., Stern, R., Wagner, G., Barták, R., Zhou, N.: k-robust multi-agent path finding. In: Fukunaga, A., Kishimoto, A. (eds.) Proceedings of the Tenth International Symposium on Combinatorial Search, 16–17 June 2017, Pittsburgh, Pennsylvania, USA, pp. 157–158. AAAI Press (2017). https://aaai.org/ocs/index.php/SOCS/SOCS17/paper/view/15797
2. Barták, R., Švancara, J., Vlk, M.: A scheduling-based approach to multi-agent path finding with weighted and capacitated arcs. In: Proceedings of the 17th International Conference on Autonomous Agents and MultiAgent Systems, AAMAS 2018, Stockholm, Sweden, 11–13 July 2018, pp. 748–756. International Foundation for Autonomous Agents and Multiagent Systems, Richland, SC (2018). http://dl.acm.org/citation.cfm?id=3237383.3237494
3. Barták, R., Zhou, N.F., Stern, R., Boyarski, E., Surynek, P.: Modeling and solving the multi-agent pathfinding problem in picat. In: 29th IEEE International Conference on Tools with Artificial Intelligence (ICTAI), pp. 959–966. IEEE Computer Society (2017). https://doi.org/10.1109/ICTAI.2017.00147
4. Boyarski, E., et al.: ICBS: the improved conflict-based search algorithm for multi-agent pathfinding. In: Lelis, L., Stern, R. (eds.) Proceedings of the Eighth Annual Symposium on Combinatorial Search, SOCS 2015, Ein Gedi, the Dead Sea, Israel, 11–13 June 2015, pp. 223–225. AAAI Press (2015). http://www.aaai.org/ocs/index.php/SOCS/SOCS15/paper/view/10974
5. desJardins, M., Littman, M.L. (eds.): Proceedings of the Twenty-Seventh AAAI Conference on Artificial Intelligence, Bellevue, Washington, USA, 14–18 July 2013. AAAI Press (2013). http://www.aaai.org/Library/AAAI/aaai13contents.php
6. Erdem, E., Kisa, D.G., Öztok, U., Schüller, P.: A general formal framework for pathfinding problems with multiple agents. In: desJardins, Littman [5]. http://www.aaai.org/ocs/index.php/AAAI/AAAI13/paper/view/6293
7. Evollve Inc., Ozobot & OzoBlockly: Welcome to OzoBlockly (2015). https://ozoblockly.com/

8. Kautz, H.A., Selman, B.: Planning as satisfiability. In: ECAI, pp. 359–363 (1992). https://dl.acm.org/citation.cfm?id=146725

9. Ozobot & Evollve Inc.: Ozobot—Robots to code, create, and connect with (2018). https://ozobot.com/

10. Ryan, M.R.K.: Exploiting subgraph structure in multi-robot path planning. J. Artif. Intell. Res. **31**, 497–542 (2008). https://doi.org/10.1613/jair.2408

11. Sharon, G., Stern, R., Felner, A., Sturtevant, N.R.: Conflict-based search for optimal multi-agent pathfinding. Artif. Intell. **219**, 40–66 (2015). https://doi.org/10.1016/j.artint.2014.11.006

12. Sharon, G., Stern, R., Goldenberg, M., Felner, A.: The increasing cost tree search for optimal multi-agent pathfinding. Artif. Intell. **195**, 470–495 (2013). https://doi.org/10.1016/j.artint.2012.11.006

13. Standley, T.S.: Finding optimal solutions to cooperative pathfinding problems. In: Fox, M., Poole, D. (eds.) Proceedings of the Twenty-Fourth AAAI Conference on Artificial Intelligence, AAAI 2010, Atlanta, Georgia, USA, 11–15 July 2010. AAAI Press (2010). http://www.aaai.org/ocs/index.php/AAAI/AAAI10/paper/view/1926

14. Surynek, P.: On propositional encodings of cooperative path-finding. In: IEEE 24th International Conference on Tools with Artificial Intelligence, ICTAI 2012, Athens, Greece, 7–9 November 2012, pp. 524–531. IEEE Computer Society (2012). https://doi.org/10.1109/ICTAI.2012.77

15. Surynek, P.: Compact representations of cooperative path-finding as SAT based on matchings in bipartite graphs. In: 26th IEEE International Conference on Tools with Artificial Intelligence, ICTAI 2014, Limassol, Cyprus, 10–12 November 2014, pp. 875–882. IEEE Computer Society (2014). https://doi.org/10.1109/ICTAI.2014.134

16. Yu, J., LaValle, S.M.: Planning optimal paths for multiple robots on graphs. In: 2013 IEEE International Conference on Robotics and Automation, ICRA 2013, pp. 3612–3617, May 2013. https://doi.org/10.1109/ICRA.2013.6631084

17. Yu, J., LaValle, S.M.: Structure and intractability of optimal multi-robot path planning on graphs. In: desJardins, Littman [5]. http://www.aaai.org/ocs/index.php/AAAI/AAAI13/paper/view/6111

A Fully Fuzzy Linear Programming Model for Berth Allocation and Quay Crane Assignment

Flabio Gutierrez[1]([✉]), Edwar Lujan[2], Rafael Asmat[3], and Edmundo Vergara[3]

[1] Department of Mathematics, National University of Piura, Piura, Peru
flabio@unp.edu.pe
[2] Department of Informatics, National University of Trujillo, Trujillo, Peru
elujans@unitru.edu.pe
[3] Department of Mathematics, National University of Trujillo, Trujillo, Peru
{rasmat,evergara}@unitru.edu.pe

Abstract. In this work, we develop a model of fully fuzzy linear programming (FFLP) for the continuous and dynamic Berth Allocation and Quay Crane Assignment (BAP+QCAP). We assume that the arrival time of vessels is imprecise, meaning that vessels can be late or early up to a threshold allowed. Triangular fuzzy numbers represent the imprecision of the arrivals. The model proposed has been implemented in MIP solver and evaluated to a study case composed of 10 vessels. The model allows us to obtain a fuzzy berthing plan assigning likewise an adequate number of cranes to each vessel. The plan is adaptable to incidences that may occur in the vessel arrivals.

1 Introduction

The Berth Allocation Problem (BAP) is a NP-Hard problem [4], which assign a position and a berthing time at the quay, to each vessel arriving to the Maritime Container Terminal (MCT). The Quay Crane Assignment Problem (QCAP) is another problem NP-hard which assign a certain number of cranes for the operations of loading and unloading in containers for every vessel.

The actual times of arrivals for each vessel are highly uncertain and this uncertainty depends on the weather conditions (rains, storms), technical problems, other terminals that vessels have to visit, etc. The vessels can arrive before or after their scheduled arrival time [1,3]. This situation affects the operations of loading and unloading, other activities at the terminal and the services required by costumers.

The administrators of MCT change or review the plans, but the frequent review of a berthing plan is not desirable from the point of view of resource planning. Therefore, is important to have in mind the capacity of adaptation of the berthing plan to obtain a good system performance that a MCT manages. As a result, it is desirable to have a robust model providing a berthing plan

© Springer Nature Switzerland AG 2018
G. R. Simari et al. (Eds.): IBERAMIA 2018, LNAI 11238, pp. 302–313, 2018.
https://doi.org/10.1007/978-3-030-03928-8_25

easily adaptable and supporting possible early or lateness (imprecision) in the arrival time of vessels. Fuzzy sets are specially designed to deal with imprecision.

The problem of BAP+QCAP has been used with mathematical models and models based on metaheuristics.

In [5], the author propose a combination of genetic algorithms with heuristics to minimize the service time, the waiting time and delay time of each vessel. A robust model to the BAP+QCAP based in genetic algorithm is presented in [7], the robustness is inserted in the model by buffer times allowing to absorb possible incidences. The jobs above mentioned do not consider imprecision in the arrival of vessels, that is, the possibility or earliness or delays.

In [12], the authors make an exhaustive review of the current existing literature about BAP+QCAP. To our knowledge, there are very few studies dealing with BAP+QCAP and with imprecise (fuzzy) data.

A fuzzy MILP (Mixed Integer Linear Programming) model for the discrete and dynamic BAP+QCAP was proposed in [10], triangular fuzzy numbers represent the arrival times of vessels, they do not address the continuous problem. According to Bierwith [12], to design a continuous model, the planning of berthing is more complicated than for a discrete one, but the advantage is a better use of the space available at the quay.

A Fully Fuzzy Linear Programming (FFLP) model to the continuous and dynamical BAP is proposed in [2]. In this model, the arrival of vessel is assumed to be imprecise (fuzzy). The results show that the berthing plans obtained support earliness or delays, but do not consider the problem of crane assignment to the vessels at the quay.

In this work, we study the dynamical and continuous BAP+QCAP with imprecision in the arrival of vessels. The simulation is done in the MCT of the port of Valencia.

This paper is structured as follows: In Sect. 2, we describe the basic concepts of fuzzy arithmetic operation necessary for the development of the present work. The Sect. 3, presents the notation, the assumptions and restrictions of the problem. In Sect. 4, we show the solution and the evaluation of the FFLP model for the BAP+QCAP. Finally, conclusions and future lines of research are presented in Sect. 5.

2   Fuzzy Arithmetic

The fuzzy sets and fuzzy arithmetic, offer a flexible environment to optimize complex systems. The concepts about fuzzy arithmetic are taken from [11].

Definition 1. A fuzzy number is a normal and convex fuzzy set in R.

Definition 2. A triangular fuzzy number is represented by $\widetilde{A} = (a_1, a_2, a_3)$.

If we have the nonnegative triangular fuzzy numbers $\widetilde{a} = (a1, a2, a3)$ y $\widetilde{b} = (b1, b2, b3)$, the operations of sum and difference are defined as follows:

Sum:
$$\widetilde{a} + \widetilde{b} = (a1 + b1, a2 + b2, a3 + b3) \tag{1}$$

Difference:
$$\widetilde{a} - \widetilde{b} = (a1 - b3, a2 - b2, a3 - b1) \tag{2}$$

Comparison of fuzzy numbers allows us to infer between two fuzzy numbers $\widetilde{a}$ and $\widetilde{b}$ to indicate the greatest one. However, fuzzy numbers do not always provide an ordered set as the real numbers do. All methods for ordering fuzzy numbers have advantages and disadvantages. Different properties have been applied to justify comparison of fuzzy numbers, such as: preference, rationality, and robustness [8].

In this work, we use the method called First Index of Yagger [9]. This method uses the ordering function

$$\mathscr{R}(A) = \frac{a1 + a2 + a3}{3} \tag{3}$$

As a result, $A \leq B$, when $\mathscr{R}(A) \leq \mathscr{R}(B)$, that is,

$$a1 + a2 + a3 \leq b1 + b2 + b3.$$

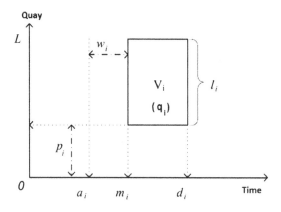

Fig. 1. Representation of a vessel according to the time and position

3   Problem Description

Among the many attributes commonly desired to classify the models related to the BAP+QCAP [12], the spatial and temporal attributes are the most important. The spatial attribute can be discrete or continuous. In the discrete case, the quay is considered as a finite set of berths, where segments of finite length describe every berth and usually a berth just works for one vessel at a time, whereas in for the continuous case, the vessels can berth at any position within the limits of the quay. On the other hand, the temporal attribute can be static or dynamic. In the static case, all the vessels are assumed to be at the port before performing the berthing plan while for the dynamical case, the vessels can arrive to the port at different times during the planning horizon.

In this work, we study the dynamical and continuous BAP+QCAP.

The BAP+QCAP can be represented in a bidimensional way, as shown in Fig. 1, the horizontal axis (Time) represents the time horizon and the vertical axis (Quay) the length of the quay. The notation to be used in the formulation of the problem is showed in Fig. 1 and Table 1.

Table 1. Notation of variables and parameters of the problem

Variables and parameters	Description
V	The set of incoming vessel
QC	Available quay cranes (QCs) in the MCT
L	Total length of the quay at the MCT
H	Planning horizon
a_i	Arrival time at port, $i \in V$
l_i	Vessel length, $i \in V$
c_i	Number of required movements to load and unload containers, $i \in V$
h_i	Loading and unloading time at quay (handling time), $i \in V$
m_i	Berthing time of vessel, $i \in V$
p_i	Berthing position, where the vessel will moor, $i \in V$
w_i	Waiting time of vessel since the arrival to the berthing, $i \in V$
d_i	Departure Time, $i \in V$
q_i	Number of assigned QCs, $i \in V$
u_{ik}	Indicates whether the QC k works (1) or not (0), $i \in V$
t_{ik}	Working time of the QC k that is assigned to vessel $i \in V$
s_i, e_i	Index for the first and last QC used in vessel $i \in V$, respectively

The decision variables are: m_i, $w_i = m_i - a_i$, p_i, u_{ik}.

The variables derived from the previous ones are: $h_i = \frac{c_i}{q_i * movsQC}$, t_{ik}, $d_{iq} = m_{iq} + h_i$, s_i, e_i.

We consider the next assumptions:

All the information related to the waiting vessels is known in advance (arrival, moves and length), every vessel has a draft lower or equal to the draft of the quay, the berthing and departures are not time consuming, simultaneous berthing is allowed, safety distance between vessels is not considered.

The number of QCs assigned to a vessel do not vary along the moored time. Once a QC starts to work with a vessel, it must continue without any pause or changes (non-preemptive tasks). Thus, all QCs assigned to the same vessel have the same working time $t_{ik} = h_i, \forall k \in QC, u_{ik} = 1$.

All QCs carry out the same number of movements per time unit (movsQC), given by the container terminal.

H is calculated as the last departure when the first-come, first-served (FCFS) policy is applied to the incoming vessels.

The arrival times, berthing times, handling time and departure times of vessels are considered of fuzzy nature (imprecise) and denoted by $\tilde{a}$, $\tilde{m}$, $\tilde{h}$ and $\tilde{d}$, respectively.

Constraints:

The length of the quay is 700 m, The number of cranes available is 7. The maximum number of cranes allocated to the vessels depend of its length. There is a distance of security that must be respected (35 m between cranes). The maximum number of cranes to be allocated is 5. The number of movement performed for a crane in a certain time is 2.5.

4   FFLP Model for the BAP+QCAP

The objective is to allocate all vessels and quay cranes according to several constraints, minimizing the sum of the waiting and handling times for all vessels.

Based on the deterministic model to the BAP+QCAP [7], the FFLP model to the BAP [2]; and assuming the imprecision of some parameters and decision variables, we propose the following fuzzy model optimization to the BAP+QCAP.

$$\min \sum_{i \in V} (\tilde{w}_i + \tilde{h}_i) \tag{4}$$

Subject to:

$$\tilde{m}_i \geq \tilde{a}_i \quad \forall i \in V \tag{5}$$

$$\tilde{w}_i = \tilde{m}_i - \tilde{a}_i \quad \forall i \in V \tag{6}$$

$$\tilde{d}_i = \tilde{m}_i + \tilde{h}_i \quad \forall i \in V \tag{7}$$

$$p_i + l_i \leq L \quad \forall i \in V \tag{8}$$

$$q_i = \sum_{k \in QC} u_{ik} \quad \forall i \in V \tag{9}$$

$$1 \leq q_i \leq QC_i^+ \quad \forall i \in V \tag{10}$$

$$1 \leq s_i, e_i \leq |QC| \quad \forall i \in V \tag{11}$$

$$s_i \geq e_i \quad \forall i \in V \tag{12}$$

$$q_i = e_i - s_i + 1 \quad \forall i \in V \tag{13}$$

$$\sum_{k \in QC} t_{ik} \, movsQC \geq c_i \quad \forall i \in V \tag{14}$$

$$\tilde{h}_i = max_{k \in QC} \, t_{ik} \quad \forall i \in V \tag{15}$$

$$t_{ik} - M u_{ik} \leq 0 \quad \forall i \in V, \forall k \in QC \tag{16}$$

$$\tilde{h}_i - M(1 - u_{ik}) - t_{ik} \leq 0 \quad \forall i \in V, \forall k \in QC \tag{17}$$

$$u_{ik} + u_{jk} + z_{ij}^x \leq 2 \quad \forall i, j \in V, \forall k \in QC \tag{18}$$

$$M(1 - u_{ik}) + (e_i - k) \geq 0 \quad \forall i \in V, \forall k \in QC \tag{19}$$

$$M(1 - u_{ik}) + (k - s_i) \geq 0 \quad \forall i \in V, \forall k \in QC \tag{20}$$

$$p_i + l_i \leq p_j + M(1 - z_{ij}^x) \quad \forall i, j \in V, \ i \neq j \tag{21}$$

$$e_i + 1 \leq s_j + M(1 - z_{ij}^x) \quad \forall i, j \in V, \ i \neq j \tag{22}$$

$$\widetilde{d}_i \leq \widetilde{m}_j + M(1 - z_{ij}^y) \quad \forall i, j \in V, \ i \neq j \tag{23}$$

$$z_{ij}^x + z_{ji}^x + z_{ij}^y + z_{ji}^y \geq 1 \quad \forall i, j \in V, \ i \neq j \tag{24}$$

$$z_{ij}^x, z_{ij}^y, u_{ik} \in \{0, 1\} \quad \forall i, j \in V, \ i \neq j, \forall k \in QC \tag{25}$$

The constraint 5 ensures that vessels must moor once they arrive to the terminal. Constraint 8 guarantees that a moored vessel does not exceed the length of the quay. Constraints 6 and 7 establish the waiting and departure times according to m_i. Constraints 9, 10, 11, 12 and 13 assign the number of QCs to the vessel i. Constraint 14 establishes the minimum handling time needed to load and unload the containers according to the number of assigned QCs. Constraint 15 assigns the handling time for vessel i. Constraint 16 ensures that QCs are not assigned to vessel i have $t_{ik} = 0$. Constraint 17 forces all assigned QCs to vessel i working the same number of hours. Constraint 18 avoids that one QC is assigned to two different vessels at the time, constraints 19 and 20 force the QCs to be contiguously assigned (from s_i up to e_i). Constraint 21 takes into account the safety distance between vessels. Constraint 22 avoids that one vessel uses QC which should cross through the others QCs. Constraint 23 avoids that vessel j moors while the previous vessel i is still at the quay q. Finally, constraint 24 establishes the relationship between each pair of vessels. There are two auxiliary variables: z_{ijq}^x is a decision variable that indicates if vessels i is located to the left of vessels j on the berth ($z_{ijq}^x = 1$), and ($z_{ijq}^y = 1$) indicates that vessel i is moored before vessel j in time (constraint 25).

4.1 Solution of the Model

We assume that all parameters and decision variables are linear and some of them are fuzzy. Thus, we have a fully fuzzy linear programming problem (FFLP).

We assume that the arrival times of vessels are imprecise and it is necessary to request the time interval of possible arrival of each vessel, as well as the more possible time when the arrival will occur. This information could be given by vessel expert.

The arrival of each vessel is represented by a triangular possibility distribution $\widetilde{a} = (a1, a2, a3)$.

In a similar way, the berthing time is represented by $\widetilde{m} = (m1, m1, m3)$, $\widetilde{h} = (h1, h2, h3)$ is considered a singleton, $\widetilde{d} = (d1, d2, d3)$.

When representing parameters and variables by triangular fuzzy numbers, we obtain a solution to the fuzzy model proposed applying the methodology proposed by Nasseri (see [6]).

To apply this methodology, we use the operation of the fuzzy sum on the constraints and the objective function; the First Index of Yagger as an ordering function on the objective function (see Sect. 2), obtaining the next auxiliary MILP model.

$$\min \sum_{i \in V} \frac{1}{3}((m1_i + h1_i) + (m2_i + h2_i) + (m3_i + h3_i)) \tag{26}$$

Subject to:

$$m1_{iq} \geq a1_i, m2_{iq} \geq a2_i, m3_{iq} \geq a3_i \quad \forall i \in V \tag{27}$$

$$m2_{iq} > m1_{iq}, m3_{iq} > m2_{iq} \quad \forall i \in V \tag{28}$$

$$w1_i = m1_i - a1_i, w2_i = m2_i - a2_i, w3_i = m3_i - a3_i \quad \forall i \in V \tag{29}$$

$$d1_i = m1_i + h1_i, d2_i = m2_i + h2_i, d3_i = m3_i + h3_i \quad \forall i \in V \tag{30}$$

$$p_i + l_i \leq L \quad \forall i \in V \tag{31}$$

$$q_i = \sum_{k \in QC} u_{ik} \quad \forall i \in V \tag{32}$$

$$1 \leq q_i \leq QC_i^+ \quad \forall i \in V \tag{33}$$

$$1 \leq s_i, e_i \leq |QC|, s_i \geq e_i \quad \forall i \in V \tag{34}$$

$$s_i \geq e_i \quad \forall i \in V \tag{35}$$

$$q_i = e_i - s_i + 1 \quad \forall i \in V \tag{36}$$

$$\sum_{k \in QC} t_{ik} * movsQC \geq c_i \quad \forall i \in V \tag{37}$$

$$h1_i = max_{k \in QC} - t_{ik}, h2_i = max_{k \in QC} - t_{ik}, h3_i = max_{k \in QC} - t_{ik} \quad \forall i \in V \tag{38}$$

$$t_{ik} - M * ul_i \leq 0 \quad \forall i \in V, \forall k \in QC \tag{39}$$

$$h1_i - M(1 - u_{ik}) - t_{ik} \leq 0 \quad \forall i \in V, \forall k \in QC \tag{40}$$

$$h2_i - M(1 - u_{ik}) - t_{ik} \leq 0 \quad \forall i \in V, \forall k \in QC \tag{41}$$

$$h3_i - M(1 - u_{ik}) - t_{ik} \leq 0 \quad \forall i \in V, \forall k \in QC \tag{42}$$

$$u_{ik} + u_{jk} + z_{ij}^x \leq 2 \quad \forall i, j \in V, \forall k \in QC \tag{43}$$

$$M(1 - u_{ik}) + (e_i - k) \geq 0 \quad \forall i \in V, \forall k \in QC \tag{44}$$

$$M(1 - u_{ik}) + (k - s_i) \geq 0 \quad \forall i \in V, \forall k \in QC \tag{45}$$

$$p_i + l_i \leq p_j + M(1 - z_{ij}^x) \quad \forall i, j \in V, \ i \neq j \tag{46}$$

$$e_i + 1 \leq s_j + M(1 - z_{ij}^x) \quad \forall i, j \in V, \ i \neq j \tag{47}$$

$$d1_i \leq m1_j + M(1 - z_{ij}^y) \quad \forall i, j \in V, \ i \neq j \tag{48}$$

$$d2_i \leq m2_j + M(1 - z_{ij}^y) \quad \forall i, j \in V, \ i \neq j \tag{49}$$

$$d3_i \leq m3_j + M(1 - z_{ij}^y) \quad \forall i, j \in V, \ i \neq j \tag{50}$$

$$z_{ij}^x + z_{ji}^x + z_{ij}^y + z_{ji}^y \geq 1 \quad \forall i, j \in V, \ i \neq j \tag{51}$$

$$z_{ij}^x, z_{ij}^y, u_{ik} \in \{0, 1\} \quad \forall i, j \in V, \ i \neq j, \forall k \in QC \tag{52}$$

4.2   Evaluation

To the evaluation a personal computer equipped with a Core (TM) i3 CPU M370 @ 2.4 GHz with 4.00 Gb RAM was used. The experiment was performed within a timeout of 60 min.

The model has been coded and solved by using CPLEX. To the study case presented in this work, for the timeout a total waiting time (objective function) of 1429 time units was obtained.

We use as a study case one instance consisting of 10 vessels (see Table 2).

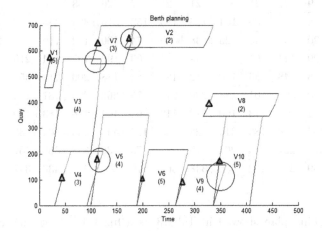

Fig. 2. Fuzzy berthing plan in polygonal-shape (Color figure online)

Table 2. Instance with 10 vessels

Vessel	a1	a2	a3	l	c
V1	9	21	21	242	2050
V2	12	24	39	87	7600
V3	20	33	45	359	7330
V4	29	44	61	210	4700
V5	48	48	53	351	8750
V6	90	96	101	216	9290
V7	92	99	113	150	4740
V8	164	168	183	86	6340
V9	226	227	244	157	7290
V10	239	243	262	347	8720

For example, to the vessel V2, the most possible arrival is at 24 units of time, but it could be early or late up to 12 and 39 units of time, respectively;

the length of vessel is 232 and the number of required movements to load and unload containers is 7600.

The berthing plan obtained with the model is showed in Table 3, and the polygonal-shaped is showed in Fig. 2.

Table 3. Fuzzy berthing plan obtained to the study case

Vessel	a1	a2	a3	m1	m2	m3	h	d1	d2	d3	l	p	q
V1	9	21	21	9	21	21	17	26	38	38	242	458	5
V2	12	24	39	164	176	183	152	316	328	335	87	613	2
V3	20	33	45	26	38	45	74	100	112	119	359	210	4
V4	29	44	61	29	44	61	63	92	107	124	210	0	3
V5	48	48	53	100	112	124	88	188	200	212	351	0	4
V6	90	96	101	188	200	212	75	263	275	287	216	0	5
V7	92	99	113	100	112	119	64	164	176	183	150	550	3
V8	164	168	183	316	328	335	127	443	455	462	86	347	2
V9	226	227	244	263	275	287	73	336	348	360	157	0	4
V10	239	243	262	336	348	360	70	406	418	430	347	0	5

The berthing plan showed in Table 3, is a fuzzy berthing one, e.g., to the vessel V2 the most possible berthing time is at 176 units of time, but it could berth between 164 and 183 units of time; the most possible departure time is at 328 units of time, but it could departure between 316 and 335 units of time; the berthing is in position 613 of the quay; it has assigned 2 cranes.

An appropriate way to observe the robustness of the fuzzy berthing plan is the polygonal-shape representation (Fig. 2). The red line represents the possible Berthing time of earliness; the green line, the possible berthing time of delay, the small triangle represents the optimum berthing time (with a greater possibility of occurrence) and the blue line represents the time that vessel will stay at the quay. At the center of each vessel we can see the number of the vessel and in parenthesis the number of cranes assigned.

In the circle of Fig. 2, we observe an apparent conflict between the departure time of vessel $V4$ and the berthing time of vessel $V5$ in the quay one. The conflict is not such, if the vessel $V4$ is late, the vessel V5 has slack times supporting delays. For example, assume that vessel $V4$ is late 8 units of time; according the Table 3, the berthing occurs at $m = 44 + 8 = 52$ units of time and its departure occurs at $d = 107 + 8 = 115$ units of time. The vessel V5 can berth during this space of time, since according to Table 3, its berthing can occurs between 100 and 124 units of time. This fact is observed in Fig. 3. The same happens for $V3 - V7, V7 - V2$ and $V9 - V10$.

In order to analyze the robustness of the fuzzy berthing plan, we simulate the incidences showed in Table 4.

Table 4. Incidences in the vessel arrival times

Vessel	Time	Incidence
V1	10	Earliness
V2	6	Delay
V3	·10	Delay
V4	14	Earliness
V5	9	Earliness
V6	9	Earliness
V7	5	Delay
V8	12	Earliness
V9	7	Delay
V10	8	Delay

With the incidences of Table 4, a feasible berthing plan can be obtained as showing in Table 5. In Fig. 4, we observe that the berthing plan obtained, is a part of the fuzzy plan obtained initially.

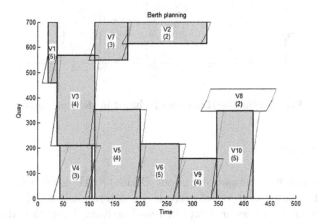

Fig. 3. Delayed berthing of vessel V5 and V6

Table 5. Final berthing plan including incidents

Vessel	m	h	d	l	p	q
V1	11	17	28	242	458	5
V2	182	152	334	87	613	2
V3	28	74	102	359	210	4
V4	30	63	93	210	0	3
V5	103	88	191	351	0	4
V6	191	75	266	216	0	5
V7	117	64	181	150	550	3
V8	316	127	443	86	347	2
V9	282	73	355	157	0	4
V10	356	70	426	347	0	5

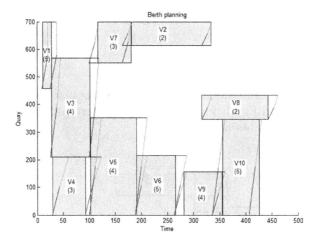

Fig. 4. Final berthing plan included in the fuzzy plan

5   Conclusion

Even though many investigations about BAP+QCAP have been carried out, most of them assume that vessel arrivals are deterministic. This is not real, in practice there are earliness or delays in vessel arrivals. Thus, the adaptability of a berthing plan is important for the global performance of the system in a MCT.

The results obtained show that the FFLP model presented in this work solve the continuous and dynamical BAP+QCAP with imprecision in the arrival of vessels. The fuzzy berthing plan obtained can be adapted to possible incidences in the vessel arrivals.

The model has been evaluated for a study case of 10 vessels and solved optimally by CPLEX. The number of vessel is for illustrative purposes only, the model works in the same way for a large number of vessels.

Finally, because of this research, we have open problems for future researches: To extend the model that considers multiples quays. The use of meta-heuristics to solve the fuzzy BAP+QCAP model more efficiently, when the number of vessels is greater.

Acknowledgements. This work was supported by INNOVATE-PERU, Project N° PIBA-2-P-069-14.

References

1. Bruggeling, M., Verbraeck, A., Honig, H.: Decision support for container terminal berth planning: integration and visualization of terminal information. In: Proceedings of Van de Vervoers logistieke Werkdagen, VLW 2011, pp. 263–283. University Press, Zelzate (2011)
2. Gutierrez, F., Lujan, E., Vergara, E., Asmat, R.: A fully fuzzy linear programming model to the berth allocation problem. Ann. Comput. Sci. Inf. Syst. **11**, 453–458 (2017)
3. Laumanns, M., et al.: Robust adaptive resource allocation in container terminals. In: Proceedings of 25th Mini-EURO Conference Uncertainty and Robustness in Planning and Decision Making, Coimbra, Portugal, pp. 501–517 (2010)
4. Lim, A.: The berth planning problem. Oper. Res. Lett. **22**(2), 105–110 (1998)
5. Meisel, F., Bierwirth, C.: A unified approach for the evaluation of quay crane scheduling models and algorithms. Comput. Oper. Res. **38**, 683–693 (2010)
6. Nasseri, S.H., Behmanesh, E., Taleshian, F., Abdolalipoor, M., Taghi-Nezhad, N.A.: Fully fuzzy linear programming with inequality constraints. Int. J. Ind. Math. **5**(4), 309–316 (2013)
7. Rodriguez-Molins, M., Ingolotti, L., Barber, F., Salido, M.A., Sierra, M.R., Puente, J.: A genetic algorithm for robust berth allocation and quay crane assignment. Prog. Artif. Intell. **2**(4), 177–192 (2014)
8. Wang, X., Kerre, E.: Reasonable properties for the ordering of fuzzy quantities (I). Fuzzy Sets Syst. **118**(3), 375–385 (2001)
9. Yager, R.R.: A procedure for ordering fuzzy subsets of the unit interval. Inf. Sci. **24**(2), 143–161 (1981)
10. Expósito-Izquiero, C., Lalla-Ruiz, E., Lamata, T., Melián-Batista, B., Moreno-Vega, J.M.: Fuzzy optimization models for seaside port logistics: berthing and quay crane scheduling. In: Madani, K., Dourado, A., Rosa, A., Filipe, J., Kacprzyk, J. (eds.) Computational Intelligence. SCI, vol. 613, pp. 323–343. Springer, Cham (2016). https://doi.org/10.1007/978-3-319-23392-5_18
11. Lai, Y.-J., Hwang, C.-L.: Fuzzy Mathematical Programming: Methods and Applications, vol. 394. Springer, Heidelberg (1992)
12. Bierwirth, C., Meisel, F.: A survey of berth allocation and quay crane scheduling problems in container terminals. Eur. J. Oper. Res. **202**(3), 615–627 (2010)

Design of a Bio-Inspired Controller to Operate a Modular Robot Autonomously

Henry Hernández[1]($\boxtimes$), Rodrigo Moreno[1], Andres Faina[2], and Jonatan Gomez[1]

[1] Faculty of Engineering, Department of Computer and Industrial Engineering, National University of Colombia, 110811 Bogotá D.C., Colombia
{heahernandezma,rmorenoga,jgomezpe}@unal.edu.co
[2] Department of Computer Science, IT University of Copenhagen, 2300 Copenhagen, Denmark
anfv@itu.dk

Abstract. A modular robot can be reconfigured and reorganized to perform different tasks. Due to the large number of configurations that this type of robot can have, several types of techniques have been developed to generate locomotion tasks in an adaptive manner. One of these techniques transfers sets of parameters to the robot controller from a simulation. However, in most cases the simulated approach is not appropriate, since it does not take into account all physical interactions between the robot and the environment. This paper shows the design of a flexible controller that adapts to the different configurations of a modular chain-type robot, which coordinates the movements of the robot using a Central Pattern Generator (CPG). The CPG is integrated with an optimization algorithm to estimate sets of movements, which allow the robot to navigate in its environment autonomously from the information of sensors and in real time.

Keywords: Genetic algorithm · Autonomous operation
Modular robot

1 Introduction

The environmental or terrain conditions limit the access that people have to certain areas, since they can convert the activity to be developed into a high-risk one. Consequently, various robots have been proposed to reduce the accident rate, because it is possible that they adapt to unknown environments and communicate with the operator.

Some proposed robotic prototypes have been adjusted according to the terrain variability [15]. This variability of the terrain has allowed the authors to fabricate mechanisms that allow the robot to have stability in diverse environments. Among the mechanisms manufactured are the; legs, tracks or wheels. However, they still have limitations. For example, robots with caterpillars or smooth wheels cannot recover their orientation in case of capsizing [2,16].

© Springer Nature Switzerland AG 2018
G. R. Simari et al. (Eds.): IBERAMIA 2018, LNAI 11238, pp. 314–325, 2018.
https://doi.org/10.1007/978-3-030-03928-8_26

A partial solution to this limitation has been the development of modular robots, which have been used to reproduce patterns of animal locomotion from body movements. A modular robot is a set of two or more coupled structures called modules. The modules can be grouped in different configurations and generate movement patterns such as: rolling, walking or crawling [13,14,23].

The movements generated by a modular robot have been estimated using several techniques, among which the Central Pattern Generators (CPG) stand out. An advantage of the CPG is that it allows generating movement sets in modular robots with arbitrary structures easily, since they can be represented by simple mathematical expressions [8,17,24].

These approaches have allowed us to estimate the movements of a modular robot using simulators, which emulate certain features of the terrain or the robot [7]. In addition, in some cases interfaces are designed that establish a link with the real robot, to transfer to the robot sets of parameters that allow it to coordinate its modules and thus generate different sets of movements [9,11].

These sets of movements depend on the amount of degrees of freedom that the robot can have. Consequently, the dimensions of the search space do not have a certain size, increasing the difficulty in designing control mechanisms [4,10,19–21]. However, different control techniques have been proposed that allow this type of robot to perform tasks in unimpeded environments [1,5].

The control techniques have certain limitations, one of them is that the robot cannot adapt to irregular terrains or obstacles, from the information of sensory perception reducing its autonomy. This article proposes a partial solution to this limitation, through the development of a centralized controller that allows a modular robot to generate coordinated movements in an autonomous and adaptive way. These movements are generated by modulating the parameters of a CPG with a Genetic Algorithm (GA), which is updated from the information of the robot's sensors.

The controller was implemented in the EMeRGE (Easy Modular Embodied Robot Generator) modular robot, which is described in Sect. 2. The adapting strategy and the control system are shown in Sect. 3. The experimental configuration and the results are presented in Sect. 4 and, finally, the discussion in Sect. 5.

2   The EMeRGE Modular Robot

The EMeRGE modular robot was used to perform experimental tests [12]. The structures are assembled with homogeneous modules (Fig. 1a), which are connected using magnets in mating connectors. The connectors are on the four (4) sides of the module, of which three (3) of them have a female connector and the remaining has a male connector.

In addition, each module has a local driver that allows it; communicate with other modules or devices using the CAN (Controller Area Network) protocol, control the angular position of the motor and detect obstacles with four (4) proximity sensors located on each side of the module. These actions are performed

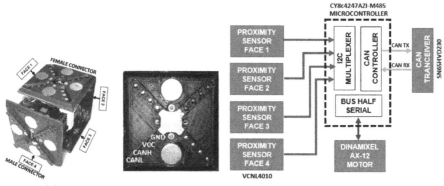

(a) The EMeRGE module   (b) Diagram of the electronic circuit of each module.

Fig. 1. Structure of an EMeRGE modular robot module

by different electronic elements, which are connected by a printed circuit to a micro-controller (Fig. 1b).

The printed circuit is divided into four (4) parts that are connected to each other (Fig. 1a), which are under each face of the module to allow its connection with other modules through spring pins and pads. When connecting the modules, a four (4) wire bus is established, of which two (2) are used to transmit information using the CAN protocol and the remaining two (2) are used to energize the local controller with an external source 12 V.

Each pin of the four (4) wire bus is flexible and allows connecting other devices to the robot that interact with it. This feature allowed coupling two accessories to the robot (Fig. 2); the first is an XBEE communication module that functions as a CAN sniffer and sends all the data shared by the modules to a computer. The second is an ultrasound sensor that allows you to measure the distance between the robot and an obstacle. In addition, this accessory works as a centralized controller that modulates the movement parameters generated by the local controllers.

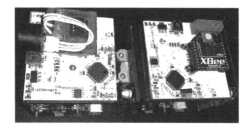

Fig. 2. Modular robot accessories EMeRGE

The link between the local controllers of the robot and the centralized controller is stable once each module has executed an initialization routine. This routine has the following functions: assign a different address to each module, detect the status of the electronic components and assign initial conditions to the movement parameters. In case the link is not established, the centralized controller will not initiate the optimization routine, which will not allow the movement parameters of the robot to be modulated.

3   CPG Model Used

A CPG is a model that resembles the behavior of a set of specialized neurons and one of its functions is to imitate rhythmic movements [3]. In this project, the CPG model based on coupled oscillators was implemented, which establishes a way to couple the independent outputs of the Eqs. 1, 2 and 3 [4,6,9].

$$\ddot{r}_i = a_r\left(\frac{a_r}{4}(R_i - r_i) - \dot{r}_i\right) \tag{1}$$

$$\ddot{x}_i = a_x\left(\frac{a_x}{4}(X_i - x_i) - \dot{x}_i\right) \tag{2}$$

$$\theta_i = x_i + r_i cos(\phi_i) \tag{3}$$

These equations are used to estimate an approximate value of the angular position of each module (θ_i), which depends on the parameters; amplitude (r_i), phase (x_i) and offset (ϕ_i). Each independent output (θ_i) is shared with the neighboring modules and linked to its output value by means of the coupling Eqs. 4 and 5.

The Eq. 4 ensures that the movement of the modules converges to a phase difference (φ_{ij}), where ϕ_i is the independent output of the module whose intrinsic oscillation depends on the value w_{ij} and ϕ_j represents the output of the neighbor module. This equation expands from the current module i to the number of neighbors j.

$$\dot{\phi}_i = w_i + \sum_i^j (w_{ij} Sin(\phi_j - \phi_i + \varphi_{ij}) \tag{4}$$

$$\theta_i^{\text{inf}} = X_i + R_i * cos(w_i t + i\varphi_{ij} + \phi_0) \tag{5}$$

The Eq. 5 is a representation of the output of all the modules of the robot when they converge to an oscillating and stable state, whose amplitude R_i, phase ϕ_0 and offset X_i parameters are given by the centralized controller. Finally, the Eqs. 1, 2, 3 and 4 are solved in each local controller using the Euler method with a step time of 300 mS once the parameters of the Eq. 5 have been established.

3.1 CPG Optimization

An optimization technique is a method that is responsible for finding the best value in a set of solutions. Some of these techniques are based on iterative methods that evaluate the fitness value of different individuals and thus select the best. Taking into account that the fitness value is a measure, which indicates the performance of an individual when trying to solve a problem.

In this work a comparison of three optimization techniques is made, which were implemented in a centralized controller and generate sets of movements that allow a modular robot to move in its environment in an adaptive way. The characteristics of the fitness function, the individuals and the techniques implemented are described below.

Characteristics of Fitness Function: The function to be optimized in this case is the distance traveled (F) by the robot (Fig. 3a), which is shown in the Eq. 6. From this equation the values X_a and X_b are the measurements made by the ultrasound sensor before and after modifying the parameters of the CPG. Each time the centralized controller will perform a measurement, the robot remains motionless for five (5) seconds for the sensor to stabilize.

$$F = |X_a - X_b| \tag{6}$$

The execution of the parameters of the CPG last 30 s, that is to say, each individual is executed during 40 s. In this case, the parameters of the CPG are the individuals to be evaluated and are composed of 5 different parameters, which are: Amplitude and offset of the modules according to their orientation and phase. The modules have two possible orientations, which are determined by the proximity sensor of the third face. When the sensor is active during robot initialization this module will have horizontal orientation, otherwise it will be vertical orientation.

When generating an individual, its components are limited according to their orientation and depend on a randomly generated number. If The generated number is greater than 0.5, the ranges of the components are; $0 < r_v < 1.0$, $0 < r_h < 0.2$, $0 < \phi < 2\pi$, $-0.2 < x_v < 0.2$ and $x_h = 0.0$. In another case they will be; $0 < r_v < 0.2$, $0 < r_h < 1.0$, $0 < \phi < 2\pi$, $x_v = 0.0$ and $-0.2 < x_h < 0.2$ (the subscript indicates orientation). Finally, each component is generated randomly within the aforementioned ranges and when an individual is sent to the robot each module has a filter, to classify the information and thus determine which components of the individual correspond to their CPG parameters.

Mutation of an Individual: A mutation is a change that occurs in an individual, to modify their fitness value. In this work, the mutation operator depends on the activation of the proximity sensors in various combinations (Fig. 3b), since, when activated, they allow the selected individual to be changed to a new one. In another case, one of the individual parameters is selected randomly and a random value is added between -0.1 and 0.1, as shown in the Algorithm 1. This

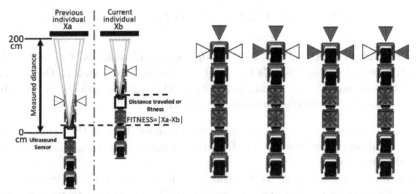

(a) Fitness value measured with the ultrasound sensor

(b) Combinations of proximity sensors

Fig. 3. Sensors available in the EMeRGE robot

mutation operator is used in all the optimization techniques implemented in this work.

> P: Population
> a: Individual
> $a \leftarrow$ Select individual(P);
> **if** *Active proximity sensor* **then**
> | $\quad a \leftarrow$ New individual();
> **end**
> **else**
> | $\quad$ M $\leftarrow$ Select parameter(a);
> | $\quad$ S $\leftarrow$ Random $(-0.1, 0.1)$;
> | $\quad$ M $\leftarrow$ M+S;
> | $\quad a \leftarrow$ Replace parameter(M);
> **end**

Algorithm 1. Mutation function

Hill Climbing and Simulated Annealing: These optimization algorithms are used to solve optimization problems iteratively. In both cases, the best known individual is temporarily stored and used to generate a new one by applying a mutation. When applying the mutation, the individual generated is evaluated and each technique has an acceptance parameter, which are: in the case of hill climbing [22], the best known individual is replaced by the one generated if it is better. Similarly, the Simulated annealing technique accepts a new individual, if this is better than the known one. In addition, it adds a condition of acceptance of a new individual, which depends on a temperature value determined by the Eqs. 7, 8 and a random number [18] (F_1 = current individual, F_2 = Best individual).

$$\triangle F = F_1 - F_2 \tag{7}$$

$$P(\triangle f, \tau) = e^{-} \triangle f / \tau \tag{8}$$

Genetic Algorithm (GA): It is a population optimization technique, that is, optimizes sets of individuals to find a solution to a problem. In this work, a population of ten (10) individuals was optimized using the parameters described below, following the scheme proposed in Algorithm 2.

1. *Initial population:* The way to generate the individuals is the same as mentioned above, each generated individual is temporarily stored in the centralized controller.
2. *Selection:* The selection mechanism used is based on the roulette method and its objective is to select the most suitable individuals to form the next generation. Initially the centralized controller evaluates each individual and then selects them.
3. *Cross:* The crossing of two individuals allows combining their characteristics to form similar ones and incorporate them into the population. In this work, a cross-over by combination of linear factors was implemented, which consists of adding and multiplying ordered pairs of the components of the selected individuals.
4. *Mutation:* The mutation of a randomly selected individual is performed in the manner described above.
5. *Generational replacement:* The generational replacement is carried out directly, that is, the population saved is replaced by the population to which the operations have been applied; selection, crossing and mutation.

d: distance traveled
$P_0 \leftarrow$ New population(10);
while *Stop condition not active* **do**
    $d \leftarrow$ Evaluate(P_0);
    $P_1 \leftarrow$ Select individuals(P_0);
    if *Random(0,1)<0.7* **then**
        | $P_1 \leftarrow$ Cross-over(P_1);
    end
    if *Random(0,1)<0.1* **then**
        | $P_1 \leftarrow$ Mutation(P_1);
    end
    $P_0 \leftarrow P_1$;
end

Algorithm 2. Genetic algorithm structure implemented.

4   Experimental Result

The different configuration parameters of the robot and the fitness value were stored automatically in a computer, using the CAN sniffer that was incorporated into the robot. The sniffer was linked to an application that allows to export the information in plain text format[1].

The first test performed on the robot consisted of; connect three modules of the structure in vertical orientation and modulate the parameters of the CPG using the three optimization techniques in an environment without obstacles. The results obtained are presented in a graph (Fig. 4) with three different lines, which show the behavior of the best individual found during 150 iterations of each technique. In the case of the genetic algorithm, it is the value of the best individual in each generation.

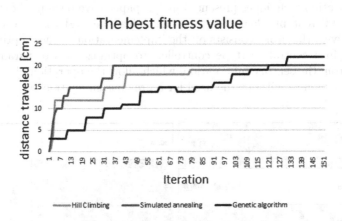

Fig. 4. Trend of the best value found using the three optimization techniques.

The second test performed consists of; propose two scenarios (Fig. 6) to determine if the robot adapts to different environments. On stage one (Fig. 6a), 150 fitness assessments were made and on stage two (Fig. 6b), 250 fitness assessments were made. The results obtained correspond to 5 executions of each optimization technique and are presented graphically in two box diagrams (Fig. 6c and d), which show the behavior of the best individuals found.

Finally, a genetic algorithm test was performed to determine if there were sets of movements that would allow a robot to evade an obstacle above. The staircase has two steps; The first step is 3 cm high and the second is 6 cm. To avoid this obstacle, 50 generations of the genetic algorithm were executed, as shown in the frames (Fig. 5).

---

[1] The graphical user interface, the programs and steps necessary to assemble the robot are available at the following link: https://sites.google.com/view/emergemodular.

Fig. 5. Frames of the EMeRGE robot evading an obstacle in the form of a ladder.

5 Discussion

The optimization techniques presented in this paper have been used extensively in solving different problems. Despite this, it can be said that the contribution made with this work consists of; the implementation of these optimization techniques in a centralized type controller, to optimize sets of parameters of the CPG from the sensory information, which allow the operation of a modular robot autonomously without the need for a previous simulation.

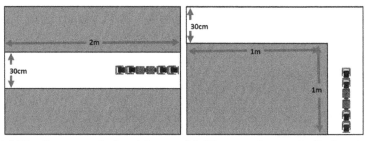

(a) The first scenario (straight cor- (b) The second scenario (L shape)
ridor)

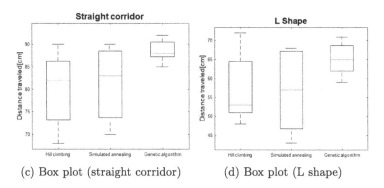

(c) Box plot (straight corridor)   (d) Box plot (L shape)

Fig. 6. Outline of the two proposed scenarios and the behavior of the best individuals found for each optimization technique.

Of the results presented as shown in the Fig. 4, the genetic algorithm showed a higher performance, since it found sets of movements that allow a robot with three modules to travel a distance of 22 cm. In addition, as shown in the box diagrams, GA is a technique that finds repeatable movements, that is, it allows the robot to generate the same movement schemes to solve a problem if it is on the right track. However, as observed in a segment of the executions made using the hill climbing algorithm (Fig. 7), There are sudden bursts of fitness that allow the robot to evade obstacles, this is because the fitness calculation is based the difference of two points and a high fitness value is assigned to a turning movement so that the robot does not move.

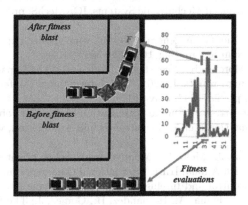

Fig. 7. Fitness explosion.

Future work is based on decentralized control strategies that allow the incorporation of optimization algorithms that work in parallel. That is, each robot can operate autonomously and synchronize with them forming a structure with other modules. However, a partial problem may arise because fitness is estimated locally. One way to improve the measurement of physical shape is to implement an artificial vision system that allows the robot to have a better perception of the environment. The idea is to maintain autonomy, therefore, a minicomputer will be implemented in the robot to avoid the incorporation of an external controller.

References

1. Brunete, A., Hernando, M., Gambao, E.: Offline GA-based optimization for heterogeneous modular multiconfigurable chained microrobots. IEEE/ASME Trans. Mech. **18**(2), 578–585 (2013)
2. Chand, P.: Fuzzy reactive control for wheeled mobile robots. In: 2015 6th International Conference on Automation, Robotics and Applications, ICARA, pp. 167–172, February 2015
3. Cohen, A.H., Holmes, P.J., Rand, R.H.: The nature of the coupling between segmental oscillators of the lamprey spinal generator for locomotion: a mathematical model. J. Math. Biol. **13**(3), 345–369 (1982)

4. Crespi, A., Ijspeert, A.J.: Online optimization of swimming and crawling in an amphibious snake robot. IEEE Trans. Robot. **24**(1), 75–87 (2008)
5. Kernbach, S., et al.: Symbiotic robot organisms: REPLICATOR and SYMBRION projects, January 2008
6. Lachat, D., Crespi, A., Ijspeert, A.J.: BoxyBot: a swimming and crawling fish robot controlled by a central pattern generator. In: The First IEEE/RAS-EMBS International Conference on Biomedical Robotics and Biomechatronics, BioRob 2006, pp. 643–648, February 2006
7. Li, G., Urbina, R., Zhang, H., Gomez, J.G.: Concept design and simulation of a water proofing modular robot for amphibious locomotion. In: 2017 International Conference on Advanced Mechatronic Systems, ICAMechS, pp. 145–150, December 2017
8. Li, L., Wang, C., Xie, G.: A general CPG network and its implementation on the microcontroller. Neurocomputing **167**, 299–305 (2015)
9. Liu, C., Liu, J., Moreno, R., Veenstra, F., Faina, A.: The impact of module morphologies on modular robots. In: 2017 18th International Conference on Advanced Robotics, ICAR, pp. 237–243, July 2017
10. Marbach, D., Ijspeert, A.J.: Online optimization of modular robot locomotion. In: IEEE International Conference Mechatronics and Automation, vol. 1, pp. 248–253, July 2005
11. Monsalve, J., Leon, J., Melo, K.: Modular snake robot oriented open simulation software. In: The 4th Annual IEEE International Conference on Cyber Technology in Automation, Control and Intelligent, pp. 546–550, June 2014
12. Moreno, R., Liu, C., Faina, A., Hernandez, H., Gomez, J.: The EMeRGE modular robot, an open platform for quick testing of evolved robot morphologies. In: Proceedings of the Genetic and Evolutionary Computation Conference Companion, GECCO 2017, pp. 71–72. ACM, New York (2017)
13. Murata, S., Kurokawa, H.: Self-reconfigurable robots. IEEE Robot. Autom. Mag. **14**(1), 71–78 (2007)
14. Ben-Tzvi, P., Moubarak, P.: Modular and reconfigurable mobile robotics. Robot. Auton. Syst. **1**(60), 1648–1663 (2012)
15. Suzuki, H., Lee, J.H., Okamoto, S.: Development of semi-passive biped walking robot embedded with CPG-based locomotion control. In: 2017 14th International Conference on Ubiquitous Robots and Ambient Intelligence, URAI, pp. 75–78, June 2017
16. Tavakoli, M., Viegas, C., Marques, L., Pires, J.N., de Almeida, A.T.: Magnetic omnidirectional wheels for climbing robots. In: 2013 IEEE/RSJ International Conference on Intelligent Robots and Systems, pp. 266–271, November 2013
17. Tian, Y., Gomez, V., Ma, S.: Influence of two SLAM algorithms using serpentine locomotion in a featureless environment. In: 2015 IEEE International Conference on Robotics and Biomimetics, ROBIO, pp. 182–187, December 2015
18. van Laarhoven, P.J., Aarts, E.H.: Simulated Annealing: Theory and Applications. Mathematics and Its Applications. Springer, Dordrecht (1987). https://doi.org/10.1007/978-94-015-7744-1
19. Vonásek, V., Faigl, J.: Evolution of multiple gaits for modular robots. In: 2016 IEEE Symposium Series on Computational Intelligence, SSCI, pp. 1–8, December 2016
20. Vonásek, V., Neumann, S., Oertel, D., Wörn, H.: Online motion planning for failure recovery of modular robotic systems. In: 2015 IEEE International Conference on Robotics and Automation, ICRA, pp. 1905–1910, May 2015

21. Wu, W., Guan, Y., Yang, Y., Dong, B.: Multi-objective configuration optimization of assembly-level reconfigurable modular robots. In: 2016 IEEE International Conference on Information and Automation, ICIA, pp. 528–533, August 2016
22. Xi, B., Liu, Z., Raghavachari, M., Xia, C.H., Zhang, L.: A smart hill-climbing algorithm for application server configuration. In: Proceedings of the 13th International Conference on World Wide Web, WWW 2004, pp. 287–296. ACM, New York (2004)
23. Yim, M., et al.: Modular self-reconfigurable robot systems [grand challenges of robotics]. IEEE Robot. Autom. Mag. 14(1), 43–52 (2007)
24. Zhao, W., Hu, Y., Zhang, L., Wang, L.: Design and CPG-based control of biomimetic robotic fish. IET Control Theory Appl. 3(3), 281–293 (2009)

Using Communication for the Evolution of Scalable Role Allocation in Collective Robotics

Gustavo Martins[1,3]($\boxtimes$), Paulo Urbano[1], and Anders Lyhne Christensen[2,3]

[1] BioISI, Faculdade de Ciências da Universidade de Lisboa, Lisbon, Portugal
`pub@di.fc.ul.pt`
[2] Instituto Universitário de Lisboa (ISCTE-IUL), Lisbon, Portugal
`anders.christensen@iscte.pt`
[3] Instituto de Telecomunicações, Lisbon, Portugal

Abstract. In evolutionary robotics role allocation studies, it is common that the role assumed by each robot is strongly associated with specific local conditions, which may compromise scalability and robustness because of the dependency on those conditions. To increase scalability, communication has been proposed as a means for robots to exchange signals that represent roles. This idea was successfully applied to evolve communication-based role allocation for a two-role task. However, it was necessary to reward signal differentiation in the fitness function, which is a serious limitation as it does not generalize to tasks where the number of roles is unknown a priori. In this paper, we show that rewarding signal differentiation is not necessary to evolve communication-based role allocation strategies for the given task, and we improve reported scalability, while requiring less a priori knowledge. Our approach puts fewer constrains on the evolutionary process and enhances the potential of evolving communication-based role allocation for more complex tasks.

Keywords: Role allocation · Collective robotics · Swarm · NEAT
Fitness function · Artificial evolution · Evolutionary robotics

1 Introduction

Research on evolutionary collective robotics [2,16,19] for homogeneous robots suggests that role differentiation, which is fundamental for cooperation in natural and artificial systems, is triggered by differences in local physical interactions. In [2], a group of four robots was evolved to collectively navigate toward a light. In the most successful strategy, the robot in the front right position assumed the guide role, setting the path, while the robots in other positions followed. This strategy clearly depended on the specific positions of the robots in the group. In [16], a team of three robots was evolved for the ability to navigate as a group. The most successful strategy relied on two phases: (i) robots negotiate their positions until they reach a line formation; (ii) the first robot moves backwards

© Springer Nature Switzerland AG 2018
G. R. Simari et al. (Eds.): IBERAMIA 2018, LNAI 11238, pp. 326–337, 2018.
https://doi.org/10.1007/978-3-030-03928-8_27

while the others move forward following the first robot. If any robot is removed, the remaining robots cease motion. In [19], a group of five robots was evolved to guard a nest and forage simultaneously. The environment had two variations that required different behaviors to maximize fitness: (i) most robots stayed in the nest while others foraged; or (ii) fewer robots stayed in the nest while others foraged. Each variation had a corresponding nest color that robots could detect. The nest was divided into six sectors and each robot was randomly placed in a sector. The study concluded that the role each robot assumed depended on the nest color and the robot's position at the nest. For the above studies, the role assumed by a robot depends directly on very specific local conditions potentially decreasing robustness and scalability of the evolved strategies.

To evolve scalable and robust solutions for role allocation, two studies [8], [9], proposed the introduction of explicit communication. Communication allowed robots to emit a signal with a numeric value in the range [0, 1]. In [8], the goal was to have one robot emitting a high value, and the others a low value. Although scalable solutions were evolved, there was no actual behavioral task for the robots to execute. The second study [9] introduced a two-role, double patrolling task (Fig. 1), which we replicate in this study.

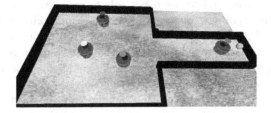

Fig. 1. The double patrolling task environment. One robot must enter the corridor to find a light source while all others keep away. Reprinted with permission.

To evolve suitable controllers for the double patrolling task, Gigliotta et al. [9] rewarded signal differentiation in the fitness function. This reward constitutes a priori knowledge, which is knowledge that is included by the system designer, to favor the evolution of a desired behavior but also constrain the evolutionary process [10]. Including less a priori knowledge imposes fewer restrictions on evolution, which can lead to more adaptive behaviors [13]. Furthermore, the authors [9] used a fixed-topology neuroevolution algorithm. However, different topologies result in different evolved behaviors and scalability for the same task [7]. Thus, we pose the hypothesis: rewarding signal differentiation was required because evolution was tied to a fixed-topology neural network. To test our hypothesis, we substitute the fixed-topology neuroevolution algorithm by NEAT [18], a well known and widely applied, neuroevolution algorithm, that combines the search for appropriate network weights with a search for appropriate network topology, and thus avoids the shortcomings of manual design [17].

Our goal is to evolve controllers with less dependency on a priori knowledge than required in previous research [9]. We aim to attain more robust and general solutions for the evolution of communication-based role allocation. We replicate the double patrolling task, and conduct experiments with a novel fitness function that does not reward signal differentiation. To determine the impact of the number of robots used during evolution on the scalability of the evolved solutions, we vary the number of robots used during evolution. Although communication-based role allocation was evolved in [9], the relevance of communication for performing the task and for evolving scalable strategies was not fully determined, because no control experiment without communication ability was conducted. In order to assess the relevance of communication for the task, we also conduct experiments with no communication ability.

2   Related Work

Gigliota et al. [8] proposed the ability of robots to communicate their adopted roles by means of a numeric signal, to increase scalability of role allocation strategies. This approach facilitated the evolution of scalable strategies for the double patrolling task [9], where a group of robots has to allocate a sole robot to move to a light source while the other robots must stay away from light. In the most successful strategy, one robot emits a signal with a high value and assumes the role of exploring the environment to find the light while the other robots emit low values and avoid moving. Although evolution was conducted for groups of four robots, the evolved strategy was scalable for groups of 2–8 robots. The robots' controllers were neural networks evolved by means of an artificial evolutionary process. Artificial evolution depends on, amongst other factors, a fitness function to measure the quality of the evolved behaviors. Fitness function design is known to be a critical aspect of evolutionary robotics [3,6,14,15].

Two fitness functions were used in the referred study [9], BF and CRF. The first, BF (Eq. 1), rewards a closer distance between light and the closest robot, while rewarding a long distance between light and all other robots.

$$BF = 0.75 \times BFC1 + 0.25 \times BFC2 \qquad (1)$$

Component $BFC1$ (Eq. 2) rewards controllers able to have one robot close to light while $BFC2$ (Eq. 3) rewards controllers able to have all other robots away from light. These components are computed as follows:

$$BFC1 = \frac{1}{T} \times \sum_{t}^{T} \frac{\max(0, (M - d_t(L, light)))}{M} \qquad (2)$$

$$BFC2 = \frac{1}{T \times (N-1)} \times \sum_{t}^{T} \sum_{i}^{F} \frac{\min(M, d_t(F_i, light))}{M} \qquad (3)$$

where $M = 0.9$ m is a maximal distance, $d_t(L, light)$ is the distance between light and its closest robot at instant t, T is the number of total time steps of a trial, F_i is robot i – excluding the closest robot to light, $d_t(F_i, light)$ is the distance between light and robot F_i at instant t and N is the number of robots.

The second fitness function, CRF (Eq. 5), extends BF to include a reward for signal differentiation, CFC: one robot emits a high signal and all other robots emit low signals.

$$CRF = 0.8 \times BF + 0.2 \times CFC \qquad (4)$$

where CFC (Eq. 5) is computed as follows:

$$CFC = \frac{\sum_t^T \sum_i^N O_{t,max} - O_{t,i}}{T \times (N - 1)} \qquad (5)$$

where $O_{t,max}$ is the highest value emitted at instant t, $O_{t,i}$ is the value emitted by robot i at instant t, and N is the number of robots in the group.

To illustrate how these functions behave, let us assume one robot at 0.0 m from light, a second robot inside the corridor at 0.25 m from light and all other robots in the home area at 0.75 m from light. One robot emits a 1.0 signal and all others emit 0.0. Table 1 shows fitness values according to BF and CRF, for such a situation, with different numbers of robots.

Table 1. BF and CRF fitness values for different numbers of robots.

Robots	BFC1	BFC2	BF	CFC	CRF
2	1	0.28	0.82	1	0.86
4	1	0.65	0.91	1	0.93
6	1	0.72	0.93	1	0.94
10	1	0.77	0.94	1	0.95

As the number of robots increases, fitness increases, with no performance improvement, because the second robot inside the corridor weights less in the group of robots supposed to be in the home area. The higher the number of robots, the lower the negative impact on fitness of a second robot in the corridor and the less effective BF becomes to evolve suitable controllers. Furthermore, BF is inadequate to measure performance when the number of robots in a group may vary, because variation in the number of robots has an impact on the fitness value, without any change in performance. The CRF fitness function shares the above limitations because BF is a component of CRF.

In [9], with BF the authors were not able to evolve communication use or any strategy to perform the task. Only with CRF were they able to evolve communication use and a scalable strategy, suggesting that communication is a potential solution to support scalability for role allocation strategies. However, CRF rewards signal differentiation, which is undesirable because it forces a specific communicational scheme – one robot emitting a high signal and all other robots emitting low signals – hindering the system's ability to find other potentially suitable communicational schemes. We avoid such reward with the introduction of a novel fitness function presented in the next section (Eq. 6).

3   Evolving Role Allocation with Less a Priori Knowledge

To evolve scalable strategies for the two-role task in [9], it was necessary to reward a signal differentiation scheme – one robot emits a high signal and all other robots emit low signals – in the fitness function, CRF. This approach, which resulted in the evolution of controllers able to perform the given two-role task, was possible because the authors were able to find, a priori, the above signal differentiation scheme which suits the two roles required for the task: one robot near the light and all other robots far away. However, as the number of roles needed to perform more complex tasks increases it is likely that the complexity of the required communicative behavior also increases. Therefore, it is unclear how rewarding signal differentiation could be used when a signal differentiation scheme that suits the roles required to perform the task can not be found a priori. As the task complexity increases, it becomes increasingly challenging to determine the specific signal differentiation scheme a priori to reward in the fitness function.

To avoid the reward for signal differentiation used in CRF and the dependency of BF on the number of robots, we introduce the TCD fitness function (Eq. 6). This function accounts for the existence of a sole robot in the corridor and the distance between light and the closest robot to light. TCD does not account for the number of robots as BF nor the communicative behavior as CRF.

$$TCD = \frac{1}{T} \times \sum_t^T \begin{cases} D_{t,light} & r = 1 \\ -D_{t,light} & r > 1 \\ 0 & r = 0 \end{cases} \tag{6}$$

where T is the number of time steps, r is the number of robots in the corridor (a robot is inside the corridor when its body center is inside the corridor) and $Dt, light$ is determined as shown in Eq. 7.

$$D_{t,light} = \frac{\max(0, (Range - d_t(L, light)))}{Range} \tag{7}$$

where $Range$ is the light sensor range and $d_t(L, light)$ is the distance between light and its closest robot, at instant t. The closer to light this robot is, the higher $Dt, light$ is in range [0,1]. Fitness is $Dt, light$ if there is only one robot in the corridor and $-Dt, light$ when two or more robots are in the corridor. Otherwise, fitness is zero. If the trial's final fitness is less than zero, the fitness is set to zero.

4   Experimental Setup

We use simulated e-puck [11] robots, that have a body diameter of 7.4 cm and distance between wheels of 5.2 cm. Robots have two independent wheel actuators to set the speed of each wheel, in [−0.1, 0.1] m/s, and a role actuator to emit a signal containing a decimal number in [0, 1]. Robots have eight obstacle sensors, equally spaced on the perimeter of the circular body, which measure the proximity of another robot or a wall, within 0.2 m; eight light sensors, also placed on the perimeter of the body, which measure the proximity to light, within 0.3 m; one non-directional role sensor with a range of 1.2 m which perceives the highest signal emitted by any other robot from any position; and a sensor to perceive the signal emitted by the robot itself in the previous time step. Each robot in the group is controlled by a copy of the same neural network and each input neuron receives values from one sensor and each output neuron sends values to one actuator. To simulate noise, each of these values is multiplied by a random number in range [0.95, 1.05]. Values coming from the sensors into the network are normalized in [0, 1] where closer proximity is represented by a higher value. Neural network output values are also normalized in [0, 1].

The experimental environment we replicated is composed of a 0.6 × 0.6 m area – the home – with an opening to a 0.2 m wide and 0.5 m long corridor (see Fig. 1). At the end of the corridor, there is a light source that robots cannot perceive from the home area. At the beginning of each experimental trial, robots emit a random signal and are placed in random positions and orientations in the home area, ensuring that no robots are colliding. Our experiments were run in the JBotEvolver [5] simulation platform.

In each experiment, we conducted 30 evolutionary runs of 1000 generations. The population has 100 individuals. In every generation, 15 trials with random initial conditions are generated and every individual in a generation faces the same set of trials. The fitness of an individual – a neural network – is the average fitness obtained in all those trials. A trial has a maximum duration of 2000 time steps. However, if a collision occurs the trial is terminated immediately to promote solutions that do not rely on or cause collisions. The NEAT implementation we used is Neat4J [12] with standard parameters.

In our experiments, we use the two fitness functions described above, BF (Eq. 1) and CRF (Eq. 4), as well as a new fitness function, TCD (Eq. 6). We conducted separate evolutions for groups of four robots, six robots, and ten and two robots where the numbers two and ten were randomly chosen by the simulator for each trial. In some experiments, we removed the robots' ability to communicate by removing the role sensor, as control – in the results section below, these experiments' names have the prefix "noRole".

5   Results

We post-evaluated the evolved controllers following the methodology used in [9] to allow for a direct comparison: only the controller that achieved the highest fitness during evolution is post-evaluated; the number of robots in the group varies between two and ten (we extended to twelve); each group with a different number of robots is post-evaluated in 100 trials; the post-evaluation function measures the percentage of time steps, within the last 100, when there is a sole robot in the corridor; satisfactory performance is one that shows a minimum post-evaluation fitness of 80%.

5.1   Evolution with Four Robots

In Fig. 2, we show the post-evaluation results for groups evolved with four robots.

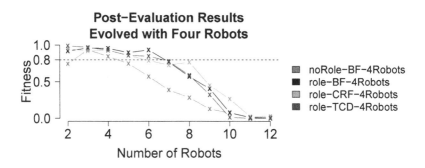

Fig. 2. Post-evaluation results when evolved with four robots

With No Communication Ability. For the noRole-BF-4Robots controller, performance is above 80% for groups of three and four robots, showing that communication is not strictly necessary to perform the task. Robots move in straight paths from corner to corner. To avoid collisions, robots change paths and eventually one robot enters the corridor and moves to the light. With fewer robots in the home area, there is also less interference and thus, it is less probable that another robot enters the corridor. If another robot enters the corridor, it moves towards the light, perceives another robot at the light and leaves the corridor. This strategy does not scale because the higher the number of robots, the higher the probability that interference occurs causing robots to enter the corridor.

With Communication Ability. Controllers role-BF-4Robots and role-TCD-4Robots, show a common strategy and a similar performance (Friedman $p = 0.179$), scaling for groups of two to six robots. Robots move in random directions emitting a 0.0 signal, until a robot finds the light and emits a 1.0 signal. All other robots continue to emit 0.0, leaving the corridor if inside, and change their motion pattern to small orbits in place, decreasing the probability of entering the corridor. However, a robot might enter the corridor to avoid a collision. In such case, the robot moves to the light, detects another robot nearby and leaves. The higher the number of robots, the more challenging it is for robots to maintain an orbital path in the home area while avoiding collisions, and the higher the probability of extra robots entering the corridor.

The role-CRF-4Robots controller scales for groups of two to five robots and shows a different strategy: before any robot enters the corridor one robot emits a 1.0 signal – the leader – and all other robots – the followers – emit a 0.0 signal. The leader moves along the wall while the followers orbit in place. If the leader detects another robot in the way, it relays the leadership to the detected robot and becomes a follower. Eventually, the leader enters the corridor and finds the light. Exceptionally, a follower enters the corridor to avoid a collision, moves to the light and becomes a leader. The previous leader, still in the home area, becomes a follower. A similar relay strategy was evolved in [7], with CRF, where different topologies where manually chosen and evaluated. Interestingly, for the other top controllers, a different strategy was evolved. Robots move in random directions in the home area; a robot enters the corridor to avoid a collision, finds the light and emits a 1.0 signal. The other robots maintain their behavior but avoid the corridor entrance. As the number of robots increases, the ability to avoid the corridor entrance decreases due to path interferences between robots.

The strategy evolved with the BF fitness function is scalable for 2–6 robots while in the previous work [9], no strategy that performs the task was evolved with BF. This improvement over previous work, where a fixed-topology neuroevolutionary algorithm was used, illustrates how a non fixed-topology neuroevolutionary algorithm may be more powerful when it comes to explore the solutions space. Furthermore, scalability is observed only in the communicative controllers, which suggest that communication is a relevant factor to the evolution of scalable role allocation strategies.

5.2   Evolution with Six Robots

In Fig. 3, we show the post-evaluation results for groups evolved with six robots.

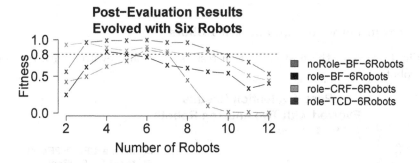

Fig. 3. Post-evaluation results when evolved with six robots

With No Communication Ability. Controller noRole-BF-6Robots shows satisfactory performance for six and seven robots but does not scale. Robots describe small elliptical paths in place, avoiding other robots within the obstacles sensor range. In this process, one of the robots enters the corridor and moves to the light. If another robot enters the corridor, it detects the first robot and leaves.

With Communication Ability. Controller role-BF-6Robots shows poor performance. When a robot finds the light and emits 1.0 all other robots also emit 1.0 and spin in place, even if that place is inside the corridor. This is a crucial difference to the previous communicative strategies evolved, where extra robots inside the corridor would leave. This strategy attained the highest fitness during evolution because the BF fitness function allows high fitness when more than one robot is inside the corridor, in spite of that behavior being the opposite of the desired.

For the role-CRF-6Robots and role-TCD-6Robots controllers, performance improved for seven, eight and nine robots, when compared to the 4-Robots experiments. For both controllers, the evolved strategy is similar to the main communicative strategy described earlier: robots explore the environment until one robot finds the light and emits a 1.0 signal; if another robot is in the corridor, it leaves; all robots in the home area change their behavior to avoid entering the corridor, but if another robot enters the corridor, it detects the robot at the light and leaves.

Exceptionally, controller role-TCD-6Robots shows poor performance for two robots, because robots follow the walls instead of moving in random directions, when exploring the environment. Robots cannot distinguish walls from fellow robots and when the group is composed of two robots and both robots are distant from any wall, they follow each other in a circle as if they were following a wall, entering into a deadlock. Nevertheless, the strategy evolved with the TCD fitness function shows a higher post-evaluation fitness when compared to the strategy evolved with CRF (Friedman $p = 7.78 \times 10^{-5}$ for the null hypothesis of a similar performance for CRF and TCD).

5.3   Evolution with Two and ten Robots

In Fig. 4, we show the post-evaluation results for groups evolved with two and ten robots.

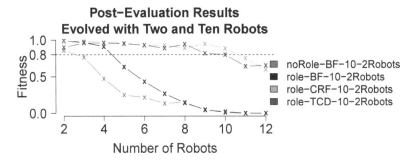

Fig. 4. Post-evaluation results when evolved with two and ten robots

With No Communication Ability. For the noRole-BF-10-2Robots controller, robots follow the wall, in the home area. The first robot entering the corridor, moves to the light. The other robots always enter the corridor but leave after detecting the robot at the light. This strategy works well for two robots because the second robot spends more time exploring the home area before reentering the corridor than inside the corridor, thus minimizing the time an extra robot spends inside the corridor. As the number of robots increases, though, the time extra robots spend inside the corridor, increases as well, resulting in a lower post-evaluation fitness.

With Communication Ability. For the role-BF-10-2Robots controller, an alternative communication use has evolved. Robots explore the environment, emitting a 1.0 signal, instead of 0.0. When a robot moves to the light emits a 0.0 signal. If the group is composed of only two robots, the remaining robot in the home area changes the motion pattern to small orbits in place and the task is accomplished. However, if the group is composed of more than two robots, the robots in the home area do not change the motion pattern, for two reasons: (i) robots can only perceive the highest signal being emitted and, (ii) robots in the home area are emitting 1.0, the highest possible signal. Thus, the 0.0 signal being emitted by the robot at the light is not perceived by any robot. This instance illustrates how the desired solution was so deeply hardwired in the robots' design: by having a role sensor that only detects the highest signal being emitted, the system designers forced the robot at the light to use the highest possible signal, to inform it has found the light, in order to assure that the signal is perceived by the other robots. The communicational scheme evolved in this experiment was possible because the BF fitness function attains higher fitness for larger groups of robots, as illustrated in Table 1. In this experiment, the evolved communicational scheme attains high BF fitness for two and ten robots because it allows the task to be performed with precisely two robots and also because a group of ten robots is large enough to attain high fitness. In other words, according to BF, the evolved strategy is adequate for two robots and not so inadequate for ten robots. However, post-evaluation results show that, after all, the behavior is not advantageous for a high number of robots.

For the role-CRF-10-2Robots controller, the evolved strategy is the main communicative strategy described earlier because the CRF fitness function forces the desired communicational scheme. For the role-TCD-10-2Robots controller, when the robots at the home area receive the 1.0 signal emitted by the robot at the light, they spin in place and avoid the corridor, as seen before. Controllers role-TCD-10-2Robots and role-CRF-10-2Robots show no statistically significant difference in performance (Friedman $p = 0.062$) and the highest post-evaluation performance of all experiments, increasing previously reported scalability in [9] of 2–8 robots to 2–10 robots. TCD requires less a priori knowledge and is thus preferable over CRF.

6 Discussion and Future Work

We showed how to evolve communication-based scalable role allocation strategies without rewarding signal differentiation. We introduced a novel fitness function that does not reward signal differentiation, and demonstrated that it is simple to co-evolve the necessary communicative and non-communicative behavioral aspects, contrary to previous findings [9]. Furthermore, our fitness function is more adequate to measure the quality of the evolved strategies, as it does not suffer from the limitations identified in fitness functions used in earlier research [9].

Evolving communication is not trivial because evolution must produce both appropriate signals and corresponding reactions [1]. In our research, however, we evolved a communicative system without explicit selective pressure for communication use in the fitness function. We showed that although communication is not strictly necessary to perform the task, it is a relevant factor to evolve scalable solutions. The number of robots used in evolution is also important because it has an impact on the scalability of the evolved solutions, and achieving maximum scalability depends on choosing an adequate number of robots.

We also substituted the fixed-topology neuroevolution algorithm, previously used [9], by NEAT, which is a neuroevolution algorithm that evolves both topology and weights, and we were able to evolve scalable strategies where previously had not been possible, confirming our research hypothesis. Our results suggest that future research should avoid fixed-topology neuroevolution algorithms as well as rewarding signal differentiation, to allow evolution to find adequate communication schemes. Instead, focus should be on defining fitness functions that accurately measure the quality of the evolved strategies and not how communication is used. Advances in the field of evolutionary robotics are achieved, amongst other ways, by designing systems able to perform increasingly complex tasks while minimizing the amount of a priori knowledge from the designer [4,13]. Our goal is to find a generalizable evolutionary setup to evolve scalable and robust communication-based role allocation. Therefore, we will expand this line of research to evolve strategies for more general and complex tasks, where more than two roles are necessary and larger groups of robots are included, without rewarding communication use. Communication-based role allocation is a research path worth pursuing because it might offer scalability and robustness for cooperative multi robot systems.

Acknowledgements. Fundação para a Ciência e Tecnologia grant SFRH/BD/ 94432/2013

References

1. Ampatzis, C., Tuci, E., Trianni, V., Dorigo, M.: Evolution of signaling in a multi-robot system: categorization and communication. Adapt. Behav. **16**(1), 5–26 (2008)
2. Baldassarre, G., Nolfi, S., Parisi, D.: Evolving mobile robots able to display collective behaviors. Artif. Life **9**(3), 255–267 (2003)

3. Divband Soorati, M., Hamann, H.: The effect of fitness function design on performance in evolutionary robotics: the influence of a priori knowledge. In: Proceedings of the 2015 Annual Conference on Genetic and Evolutionary Computation,
   GECCO 2015, pp. 153–160. ACM, New York (2015)
4. Doncieux, S., Mouret, J.B.: Beyond black-box optimization: a review of selective
   pressures for evolutionary robotics. Evol. Intell. **7**(2), 71–93 (2014)
5. Duarte, M., Silva, F., Rodrigues, T., Oliveira, S.M., Christensen, A.L.: JBotE-
   volver: a versatile simulation platform for evolutionary robotics. In: 14th International Conference on the Synthesis and Simulation of Living Systems-ALIFE, pp.
   1–8. MIT Press, Cambridge (2014)
6. Floreano, D., Urzelai, J.: Evolutionary robots with on-line self-organization and
   behavioral fitness. Neural Netw. **13**(4–5), 431–443 (2000)
7. Gigliotta, O.: Task allocation in evolved communicating homogeneous robots: the
   importance of being different. Trends in Practical Applications of Scalable Multi-
   Agent Systems, the PAAMS Collection. AISC, vol. 473, pp. 181–190. Springer,
   Cham (2016). https://doi.org/10.1007/978-3-319-40159-1_15
8. Gigliotta, O., Mirolli, M., Nolfi, S.: Who is the leader? Dynamic role allocation
   through communication in a population of homogeneous robots. In: Artificial Life
   and Evolutionary Computation, pp. 167–177 (2010)
9. Gigliotta, O., Mirolli, M., Nolfi, S.: Communication based dynamic role allocation
   in a group of homogeneous robots. Nat. Comput. **13**(3), 391–402 (2014)
10. König, L.: Complex Behavior in Evolutionary Robotics. Walter de Gruyter GmbH
    & Co KG, Berlin (2015)
11. Mondada, F., et al.: The e-puck, a robot designed for education in engineering,
    vol. 1, pp. 59–65. IPCB: Instituto Politécnico de Castelo Branco, Portugal (2009)
12. NEAT4J: Neat4j Java framework (2006). http://neat4j.sourceforge.net
13. Nelson, A.L., Barlow, G.J., Doitsidis, L.: Fitness functions in evolutionary robotics:
    a survey and analysis. Robot. Auton. Syst. **57**(4), 345–370 (2009)
14. Nolfi, S.: Evolutionary robotics: exploiting the full power of self-organization. Con-
    nect. Sci. **10**, 167–183 (1998)
15. Nolfi, S., Floreano, D.: Evolutionary Robotics: The Biology, Intelligence, and Tech-
    nology. MIT Press, Cambridge (2000)
16. Quinn, M., Smith, L., Mayley, G., Husbands, P.: Evolving controllers for a homo-
    geneous system of physical robots: structured cooperation with minimal sensors.
    Philos. Trans. R. Soc. Lond. A: Math. Phys. Eng. Sci. **361**(1811), 2321–2343 (2003)
17. Stanley, K.O., Miikkulainen, R.: Efficient reinforcement learning through evolv-
    ing neural network topologies. In: Proceedings of the Genetic and Evolutionary
    Computation Conference (GECCO-2002), p. 9. Morgan Kaufmann, San Francisco
    (2002)
18. Stanley, K.O., Miikkulainen, R.: Evolving neural networks through augmenting
    topologies. Evol. Comput. **10**(2), 99–127 (2002)
19. Tuci, E., Mitavskiy, B., Francesca, G.: On the evolution of self-organised role-
    allocation and role-switching behaviour in swarm robotics: a case study. In: Pro-
    ceedings of the European Conference on Artificial Life (ECAL 2013), pp. 379–386
    (2013)

Natural Language Processing, Human-Computer Interaction, AI in Education, NLP and Knowledge Representation, NLP and Machine Learning, NLP and Text Mining, Humans and AI,Human-Aware AI

A Rule-Based AMR Parser
for Portuguese

Rafael Torres Anchiêta[(✉)][iD] and Thiago Alexandre Salgueiro Pardo[iD]

Interinstitutional Center for Computational Linguistics (NILC),
Institute of Mathematical and Computer Sciences, University of São Paulo,
São Carlos, Brazil
rta@usp.br, taspardo@icmc.usp.br

Abstract. Semantic parsers help to better understand a language and may produce better computer systems. They map natural language statements into meaning representations. Abstract Meaning Representation (AMR) is a new semantic representation designed to capture the meaning of a sentence, representing it as a single rooted acyclic directed graph with labeled nodes (concepts) and edged (relations) among them. Although it is receiving growing attention in the Natural Language Processing community, most of the works have focused on the English language due to the lack of large annotated corpora for other languages. Thus, the task of developing parsers becomes difficult, producing a gap between English and other languages. In this paper, we introduce an approach for a rule-based parser with generic rules in order to overcome this gap. We evaluate the parser on a manually annotated corpus in Portuguese, achieving promising results and outperforming one of the current parser development strategies in the area.

Keywords: Abstract Meaning Representation · Semantic parsing
Portuguese language

1 Introduction

Computational semantics is the area in charge of studying possible semantic representations for human language expressions [14]. A semantic analyzer, also known as a semantic parser, may automatically perform such analysis, and it is responsible for mapping natural language statements into meaning representations, abstracting away from syntactic phenomena and identifying, for example, word senses to eliminate ambiguous interpretations [12]. It aims to understand and translate natural language into a formal meaning representation on which a machine may act, subsidizing more informed and better Natural Language Processing (NLP) systems.

There are several formal meaning representations, as the traditional first-order logic detailed in [14], semantic networks [16], Universal Networking Language [28], and, more recently proposed, the Abstract Meaning Representation

© Springer Nature Switzerland AG 2018
G. R. Simari et al. (Eds.): IBERAMIA 2018, LNAI 11238, pp. 341–353, 2018.
https://doi.org/10.1007/978-3-030-03928-8_28

(AMR) [3], among several others. In special, AMR got the attention of the scientific community due to its relatively simpler structure, showing the relations among concepts and making them easy to read. Moreover, AMR structures are arguably easier to produce than traditional formal meaning representations [6]. At last, AMRs may be evaluated in a standard way by computing precision, recall, and f-measure over gold-standard annotations by the Smatch metric [8].

According to Banarescu et al. [3], AMR was motivated by the need of providing to the research community corpora with embedded annotations related to traditional tasks of NLP, as named entity recognition, semantic role labeling, word sense disambiguation, coreference, and others. From the available corpora, a variety of semantic parsers emerged [10–12, 24, 32, 33], and, with the available parsers, some applications were developed and/or improved: automatic summarization [17], text generation [25, 26], entity linking [7, 23], and question answering systems [20], for instance.

Most of the parsers are for the English language. However, it is important to develop semantic parsers for other languages in order to support the production of more effective NLP applications. Taking into account the lack of large annotated corpora for non-English languages and the high cost of annotation, semantic parsers based on machine learning approaches become less suitable. Two works tried to overcome these difficulties for non-English languages. Vanderwende et al. [30] developed a set of rules to convert logical forms into AMR representations, and Damonte and Cohen [9] adopted a cross-linguistic approach for creating AMR representations.

In this context, inspired by the above initiatives, in order to create an AMR parser for Portuguese, we developed a rule-based parser. Our parser incorporates a Semantic Role Labeling (SRL) system and a syntactic parser, aiming to preprocess the sentences of interest and producing the respective part of speech tags, dependency trees, named entities, and predicate-argument structures. We then apply a set of manually designed rules on the preprocessed sentences to generate an AMR representation. In addition to the rule-based approach, we adapted for Portuguese the cross-lingual approach of Damonte and Cohen [9] in order to create a baseline system and to compare the results with the rule-based parser. To evaluate these approaches, we adopted a fine-grained strategy introduced by Damonte et al. [10] and we extended it. We noted that the rule-based approach achieved an overall Smatch F-score of 53.5% on the test set, outperforming the cross-lingual approach, which reached 37% of F-score. To the best of our knowledge, this is the first initiative to create an AMR parser for Portuguese.

The remaining of this paper is organized as follows. Section 2 describes the main related work. In Sect. 3, we briefly introduce AMR fundamentals. Section 4 details our rule-based parser. In Sect. 5, we report the experiments and the obtained results. Finally, Sect. 6 presents some conclusions and future directions.

2   Related Work

AMR parsing is a relatively new task, as the AMR language is also new. Several advances have been achieved, but, as the literature review shows us, there is still a long way to go.

Flanigan et al. [11] developed the first AMR parser for English, called JAMR. The authors addressed the problem in two stages: concept identification and relation identification. They handled concept identification as a sequence labeling task and utilized a semi-Markov model to map spans of words in a sentence to concept graph fragments. In the relation identification task, they adopted graph-based techniques of McDonald et al. [19] for non-projective dependency parsing. Instead of finding maximum-scoring trees over words, they proposed an algorithm to find the maximum spanning connected subgraph (MSCG) over concept fragments obtained from the first stage. With this approach, the authors reached a Smatch F-score of 58%.

Wang et al. [32] described a transitional-based parser, named CAMR, that also involves two stages. In the first step, they parse an input sentence into a dependency tree. The second step transforms the dependency tree into an AMR graph by performing a series of manually projected actions. One of the main advantages of this approach is the use of a dependency parser, which may be trained in a large dataset. The CAMR parser obtained a Smatch F-score of 63%. In a posterior work [31], they added a new action to infer abstract concepts and incorporated richer features produced by auxiliary analyzers such as a semantic role labeler and a coreference solver. They reported an improvement of 7% in Smatch F-score.

Peng et al. [24] formalized the AMR parsing as a machine translation problem by learning string-graph/string-tree rules from the annotated data. They applied Markov Chain Monte Carlo (MCMC) algorithms to learn Synchronous Hyperedge Replacement Grammar (SHRG) rules from a forest that represent likely derivations that are consistent with a fixed string-to-graph alignment. They achieved a Smatch F-score of 58%.

Goodman et al. [12] improved the transitional-based parser proposed by Wang et al. [32], applying imitation learning algorithms in order to reduce noise. They achieved a similar performance as that of Wang et al. [31].

Damonte et al. [10] introduced a parser inspired by the ArcEager dependency transition system of Nivre [21]. The main difference between them is that Damonte et al. [10] consider the mapping from word tokens to AMR nodes, non-projectivity of AMR structures and re-entrant nodes (multiple incoming edges). They pointed that dependency parsing algorithms with some modifications may be used for AMR parsing. Their parser reached a Smatch F-score of 64%.

The majority of current AMR parsers are for the English language, using some form of supervised machine learning technique that exploits existing AMR corpora. The lack of large annotated corpora for other languages makes the task of developing parsers difficult. To the best of our knowledge, only two works tried to automatically build AMR graphs for non-English sentences. In the first one, Vanderwende et al. [30] produced a parser that may generate AMR graphs for sentences in French, German, Spanish, and Japanese, where AMR annotations were not available. For this end, they converted logical forms from an existing semantic analyzer [29] into AMR graphs, using a set of rules. In the second approach, Damonte and Cohen [9] proposed a method based on annotation projection, which involves exploiting annotations in a source language and a parallel corpus of the source language and a target language. Using English as the source language, the authors produced AMR graphs in Italian, Spanish, German, and Chinese target languages. Overall, the obtained results are still far from the parsers for English.

3   AMR Fundamentals

Abstract Meaning Representation (AMR) is a semantic representation language designed to capture the meaning of a sentence, abstracting away from elements of the surface syntactic structure such as morphosyntactic information and word ordering [3]. Besides, words that do not contribute to the meaning of a sentence are left out of the annotation. This representation focuses on the predicate-argument structure of a sentence, as defined by the PropBank resource [15,22], and it may be represented as a single-rooted acyclic directed graph with labeled nodes (concepts) and edges (relations) among them. Nodes represent the main events and entities mentioned in a sentence, and edges represent the semantic relationships among nodes.

AMR concepts are either words in their lexicalized forms (e.g., "girl"), PropBank framesets ("adjust-01"), or special keywords such as "date-entity", "distance-quantity", and "and", among others. PropBank framesets are essentially verbs linked to lists of possible arguments and their semantic roles. Figure 1 presents a PropBank frameset example. The frameset "edge.01", whose sense is "move slightly", has six arguments (Arg 0 to 5).

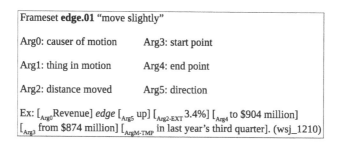

Fig. 1. A PropBank frameset [22]

For the semantic relationships, besides the PropBank semantic roles, AMR adopts approximately 100 additional relations. We list below some of them. For more details, we suggest consulting the original paper [3].

- **General semantic relations.** :mod, :location, :manner, :name, :polarity
- **Relations for quantities.** :quant, :unit, :scale
- **Relations for date-entity.** :day, :month, :year, :weekday, :dayperiod
- **Relations for list.** :op1, :op2, :op3, and so on.

In addition to the graph structure, AMR may be represented in two different notations: traditionally, in first-order logic; or in the PENMAN notation [18], for easier human reading and writing. For example, Figs. 2 and 3 present the canonical form in PENMAN and its corresponding graph notation, respectively, for the sentences with similar senses in Table 1.

Table 1. Sentences with similar meaning

Sentences
The girl made adjustment to the machine
The girl adjusted the machine
The machine was adjusted by the girls

```
(a / adjust-01
    :ARG0 (g / girl)
    :ARG1 (m / machine))
```

Fig. 2. PENMAN notation

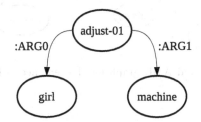

Fig. 3. AMR graph notation

As it is possible to see, AMR assigns the same representation to sentences with the same basic meaning. In the example, the concepts are "adjust-01", "girl", and "machine", and the relations are :ARG0 and :ARG1, represented by labeled and directed edges in the graph. In Fig. 2, the symbols "a", "g", and "m" are variables and may be re-used in the annotation, corresponding to reentrancies (multiple incoming edges) in the graph.

To evaluate AMR structures, Cai and Knight [8] introduced the Smatch metric to asses both inter-annotator agreement and automatic parsing accuracy. This metric computes the degree of overlap between two AMR structures, computing precision, recall, and f-score over AMR annotation triples.

4   A Rule-Based AMR Parser

In order to develop an AMR parser for Portuguese without a large annotated corpus, we designed a set of rules based on dependency links and predicate-argument structures produced by a syntactic parser and a Semantic Role Labeling (SRL) system, respectively.

We proposed a pipeline organized in three steps: (i) to run a syntactic parser in order to identify the dependency links between the words, morphosyntactic categories, named entities, and the main verb in the sentence; (ii) to execute a SRL tool to extract the predicate-argument structure, and (iii) to apply rules to generate the final AMR. We used the "PALAVRAS" parser [4] and the Brazilis SRL [13], which are state-of-the-art systems for Portuguese.

The syntactic parser produces a dependency structure that has some resemblance with the intended AMR graph. Figure 4 illustrates the similarity between the dependency tree (left) and the AMR graph (right).

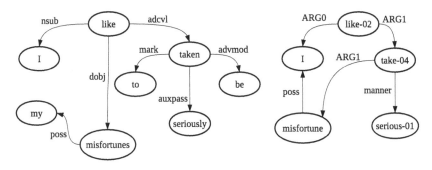

Fig. 4. Dependency tree and AMR graph for the sentence "I like my misfortunes to be taken seriously."

According to Wang et al. [32], in linguistic terms, there are many similarities between the dependency structure of a sentence and an AMR structure. Both describe relations as holding between a parent and its child, or between a head and its dependent. AMR concepts and relations abstract away from actual tokens, but there are regularities in their mappings. Content words generally become concepts, while function words and some relations either become relations or get omitted if they do not contribute to the meaning of a sentence. For instance, 'to', 'be', and 'my' in the dependency tree are omitted from the AMR, and the *advmod* (adverbial modifier) in the dependency tree becomes a *manner* relation in the AMR graph. Furthermore, in AMR, the *poss* relation indicates a reentrancy, used to represent coreference.

After parsing, following the pipeline, the SRL is used to obtain the predicate-argument structure, extensively used by AMR [3]. For the previous sentence, SRL returns the predicates 'like' and 'take' with their respective arguments.

We finally apply a set of rules that were manually developed for the task. Although the AMR has approximately 100 relations, some of them occur more frequently than others and may be produced by our rules. We defined six rules, described below, for the most frequent relations.

- **Named Entity rule.** This rule identifies the named entities indicated by the parser[1] and assigns a concept **name** and their **opn** children. Figure 5 shows the AMR graph for the sentence "At a glance I can distinguish China from Arizona". The parser does not distinguish among country, state, city and other places. It has a unique tag for this, named *<civ>*. Hence, we used ConceptNet [27] to distinguish them.
- **:mod relation rule.** This rule creates a *:mod* relation when an adjective follows a noun[2]. In Fig. 6, we show an AMR example for the sentence "The little prince".
- **:manner relation rule.** This rule applies a *:manner* relation for *advmod* relations of the dependency tree (see Fig. 4).
- **:degree relation rule.** This rule creates a *:degree* relation when the parser produces a relation of adverbial modifier. Figure 7 illustrates this for the sentence "When a mystery is too overpowering".
- **Negative polarity rule.** This rule applies the '−' symbol with the *:polarity* relation when the SRL returns the *AM-NEG* argument. In Fig. 8, we show an example for the sentence "That does not matter".

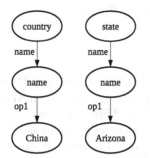

Fig. 5. Rule for named entity

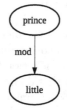

Fig. 6. Rule for :mod relation

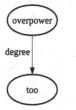

Fig. 7. Rule for :degree relation

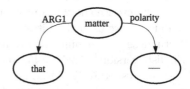

Fig. 8. Rule for negative polarity relation

---

[1] Although PALAVRAS is a typical syntactical parser, it also produces some shallow semantic annotation.

[2] It is important to notice that this rule was designed for Portuguese, in which the noun-adjective order is the most common ordering.

– **:time relation rule.** This rule creates a *:time* relation when the SRL returns an *AM-TMP* argument. Figure 9 shows an example for the sentence "The little prince said to me later on".

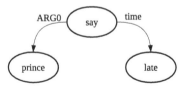

Fig. 9. Rule for :time relation

We designed these rules to be generic, using resources that are common in several languages. For example, the *AM-NEG* and *AM-TMP* arguments are obtained from PropBank, and the *advmod* relation is common in dependency parsers. Thus, we believe that the rules may be reused (with some minor adaptations, if necessary) for other languages without large annotated corpora.

In what follows, we evaluate our semantic parsing strategy.

5   Evaluation

Smatch score [8] is the metric used to evaluate AMR parsers in the area. However, AMR parsing involves many subtasks, as concept identification, named-entity recognition, and negation treatment, among others, and Smatch score consists of single numbers that do not individually assess the quality of each subtask. Therefore, we adopted a fine-grained evaluation introduced by Damonte et al. [10]. More than this, we extended it, analyzing the subtasks by sentence length, as this shows to be an important factor for semantic parsing (the longer the sentence is, the more difficult the semantic parsing is). A fine-grained evaluation shows us the strong points of a semantic parser and, especially, its weaknesses, indicating where we should improve in future work.

As dataset, we used the Little Prince corpus, which was manually annotated for Portuguese [2], keeping the original training/dev/test division proposed for the English version[3]: 1,274, 145, and 143 sentences for training, development, and testing, respectively. Although it may look strange at the first moment, it has been common to use the Little Prince book for AMR processing purposes, as the book went into public domain and had already been adopted by other semantic parsing initiatives that handled different semantic languages.

We computed the average sentence length in the corpus and obtained the 10.46 value. Hence, we organized our evaluation in two ways: for sentences shorter than the average and sentences longer than the average.

---

[3] https://amr.isi.edu/download.html.

Table 2. F-score results for sentences longer than the average on the test set

Metric	CL (%)	RB (%)
Smatch	29	46
Unlabeled smatch	44	60.5
Concepts	38	61.5
Named entities	43	49
Negations	35	85
# Sentences	80	

Table 3. F-score results for sentences shorter than the average on the test set

Metric	CL (%)	RB (%)
Smatch	45	61
Unlabeled smatch	60	65
Concepts	42	66
Named entities	45	60
Negations	50	88
# Sentences	63	

Table 4. Evaluation for all sentences on the test set

Metric	CL (%)	RB (%)	CL-WA (%)	RB-WA (%)
Smatch	37	53.5	36	52.2
Unlabeled smatch	52	62.7	51	62
Concepts	40	63.7	40	63
Named entities	44	54.5	44	54
Negations	42.5	86.5	42	86
# Sentences	143			

Furthermore, we compared the results of our parser with those of a cross-lingual approach proposed in Damonte et al. [9]. This method is based on word-alignment between two parallel corpora, projecting the AMR structure from the source language (English) to the target (Portuguese) language.

In Tables 2 and 3, we present the F-score results for the test set of the corpus, for longer and shorter sentences, respectively. Table 4 shows the overall average for all sentences and also a weighted average (WA) (as the corpus has different sentence sizes). We show the results for both approaches - the Cross-Lingual (CL) and our Rule-Based (RB) one.

We reported the general results of Smatch and an unlabeled version of it, as well as the fine-grained results for the identification of concepts, named entities and negations. In the unlabeled metric, we only assess the node labels, i.e., we removed all edge labels from the AMR graph. This metric is useful to determine whether two entities are related to each other, not considering the specific type of relationship between them. Concept identification is a critical component of the parsing process: if a concept is incorrectly identified, it is impossible to retrieve any edge involving that concept. We also report results for named entities, which are also related to the concepts and are important to retrieve their related edges. At last, we computed negation detection since it gets researchers special attention [5].

One may see that our rule-based approach achieved better results than the cross-lingual one in all the situations. Specially for shorter sentences, we achieved the best results, as expected (as longer sentences are more prone to error propagation of the syntactic parser and SRL system). Moreover, as AMR is closer to English than other languages, it is less cross-linguistically applicable [1], which may explain the poor results of the cross-lingual approach. As discussed in [2], the Portuguese language shows some differences in relation to the English version of our corpus, as the higher occurrence of hidden subjects, indeterminate subjects, and modifications in part of speech, among others.

We believe that our results are promising given the simplicity of our method, providing a strong baseline for Portuguese. For comparisons purposes, the first AMR parser for English (with better tools and resources than Portuguese) reached a Smatch F-score of 58% and it is used as the baseline for the well-known SemEval tasks, while our first AMR parser for Portuguese presented an overall Smatch F-score of 53.5%. On the other side, one may see that there is a lot of room for improvement. We still have very limited results for identifying concepts, for instance. An error that may be solved by improving the rules is related to the linking verbs. In the sentence "The marble is small", the syntactic parser returns the verb 'to be' as the main verb. However, the verb 'to be' is not used in AMR. In these cases, the root of the graph must be the adjective 'small' instead of the verb 'to be'. Another problem is the generation of duplicate concepts due to the errors of the syntactic parser. For this, pruning methods may be applied to remove duplicate concepts. These improvements may produce better parsing results.

6   Conclusion and Future Work

In this paper, we presented a rule-based AMR parser for Portuguese, trying to overcome the lack of large annotated corpora for system training. We defined a set of generic rules based on the dependency tree relations and the predicate-argument structures from PropBank. We adopted a fine-grained evaluation to verify the performance of the parser and we compared it with a cross-lingual approach. Our parser achieved a Smatch F-score of 53.5%, outperforming the cross-lingual one. To the best of our knowledge, this is the first AMR parsing investigation for Portuguese.

As future work, we intend to improve the set of rules and to test other methods for Portuguese.

Acknowledgments. The authors are grateful to FAPESP and IFPI for supporting this work.

References

1. Abend, O., Rappoport, A.: The state of the art in semantic representation. In: Proceedings of the 55th Annual Meeting of the Association for Computational Linguistics (Volume 1: Long Papers), pp. 77–89 (2017)

2. Anchiêta, R.T., Pardo, T.A.S.: Towards AMR-BR: a semBank for Brazilian Portuguese. In: Proceedings of the 11th Edition of the Language Resources and Evaluation Conference, pp. 974–979 (2018)
3. Banarescu, L., et al.: Abstract meaning representation for sembanking. In: Proceedings of the 7th Linguistic Annotation Workshop and Interoperability with Discourse, pp. 178–186 (2013)
4. Bick, E.: The Parsing System "Palavras": Automatic Grammatical Analysis of Portuguese in a Constraint Grammar Framework. Aarhus Universitetsforlag, Aarhus (2000)
5. Blanco, E., Moldovan, D.: Semantic representation of negation using focus detection. In: Proceedings of the 49th Annual Meeting of the Association for Computational Linguistics: Human Language Technologies, vol. 1, pp. 581–589. Association for Computational Linguistics (2011)
6. Bos, J.: Expressive power of abstract meaning representations. Comput. Linguist. **42**, 527–535 (2016)
7. Burns, G.A., Hermjakob, U., Ambite, J.L.: Abstract meaning representations as linked data. In: Groth, P., Simperl, E., Gray, A., Sabou, M., Krötzsch, M., Lecue, F., Flöck, F., Gil, Y. (eds.) ISWC 2016. LNCS, vol. 9982, pp. 12–20. Springer, Cham (2016). https://doi.org/10.1007/978-3-319-46547-0_2
8. Cai, S., Knight, K.: Smatch: an evaluation metric for semantic feature structures. In: Proceedings of the 51st Annual Meeting of the Association for Computational Linguistics (Volume 2: Short Papers), pp. 748–752 (2013)
9. Damonte, M., Cohen, S.B.: Cross-lingual abstract meaning representation parsing. In: Proceedings of the 16th Annual Conference of the North American Chapter of the Association for Computational Linguistics - Human Language Technologies, pp. 1146–1155 (2018)
10. Damonte, M., Cohen, S.B., Satta, G.: An incremental parser for abstract meaning representation. In: Proceedings of the 15th Conference of the European Chapter of the Association for Computational Linguistics: Volume 1, Long Papers, pp. 536–546 (2017)
11. Flanigan, J., Thomson, S., Carbonell, J.G., Dyer, C., Smith, N.A.: A discriminative graph-based parser for the abstract meaning representation. In: Proceedings of the 52nd Annual Meeting of the Association for Computational Linguistics, pp. 1426–1436 (2014)
12. Goodman, J., Vlachos, A., Naradowsky, J.: Noise reduction and targeted exploration in imitation learning for abstract meaning representation parsing. In: Proceedings of the 54th Annual Meeting of the Association for Computational Linguistics (Volume 1: Long Papers), vol. 1, pp. 1–11 (2016)
13. Hartmann, N.S., Duran, M.S., Aluísio, S.M.: Automatic semantic role labeling on non-revised syntactic trees of journalistic texts. In: Silva, J., Ribeiro, R., Quaresma, P., Adami, A., Branco, A. (eds.) PROPOR 2016. LNCS (LNAI), vol. 9727, pp. 202–212. Springer, Cham (2016). https://doi.org/10.1007/978-3-319-41552-9_20
14. Jurafsky, D., Martin, J.: Speech and Language Processing: An Introduction to Natural Language Processing, Computational Linguistics and Speech Recognition. Prentice Hall, Upper Saddle River (2009)
15. Kingsbury, P., Palmer, M.: From Treebank to Propbank. In: Proceedings of the 3rd International Conference on Language Resources and Evaluation, pp. 1989–1993 (2002)
16. Lehmann, F.: Semantic Networks in Artificial Intelligence. Elsevier Science Inc., Amsterdam (1992)

17. Liu, F., Flanigan, J., Thomson, S., Sadeh, N., Smith, N.A.: Toward abstractive summarization using semantic representations. In: Proceedings of the 2015 Conference of the North American Chapter of the Association for Computational Linguistics: Human Language Technologies, pp. 1077–1086 (2015)

18. Matthiessen, C., Bateman, J.A.: Text Generation and Systemic-functional Linguistics: Experiences from English and Japanese. Pinter Publishers, London (1991)

19. McDonald, R., Pereira, F., Ribarov, K., Hajič, J.: Non-projective dependency parsing using spanning tree algorithms. In: Proceedings of the Conference on Human Language Technology and Empirical Methods in Natural Language Processing, pp. 523–530 (2005)

20. Mitra, A., Baral, C.: Addressing a question answering challenge by combining statistical methods with inductive rule learning and reasoning. In: Proceedings of the 30th Conference on Artificial Intelligence, pp. 2779–2785 (2016)

21. Nivre, J.: Incrementality in deterministic dependency parsing. In: Proceedings of the Workshop on Incremental Parsing: Bringing Engineering and Cognition Together, pp. 50–57 (2004)

22. Palmer, M., Gildea, D., Kingsbury, P.: The proposition bank: an annotated corpus of semantic roles. Comput. Linguist. **31**(1), 71–106 (2005)

23. Pan, X., Cassidy, T., Hermjakob, U., Ji, H., Knight, K.: Unsupervised entity linking with abstract meaning representation. In: Proceedings of the 2015 Conference of the North American Chapter of the Association for Computational Linguistics: Human Language Technologies, pp. 1130–1139 (2015)

24. Peng, X., Song, L., Gildea, D.: A synchronous hyperedge replacement grammar based approach for AMR parsing. In: Conference on Computational Language Learning, pp. 32–41 (2015)

25. Pourdamghani, N., Knight, K., Hermjakob, U.: Generating English from abstract meaning representations. In: International Conference on Natural Language Generation, pp. 21–25 (2016)

26. Song, L., Peng, X., Zhang, Y., Wang, Z., Gildea, D.: AMR-to-text generation with synchronous node replacement grammar. In: Proceedings of the 55th Annual Meeting of the Association for Computational Linguistics (Volume 2: Short Papers), pp. 7–13 (2017)

27. Speer, R., Havasi, C.: Representing general relational knowledge in ConceptNet 5. In: Proceedings of the 8th International Conference on Language Resources and Evaluation, pp. 3679–3686 (2012)

28. Uchida, H., Zhu, M., Della Senta, T.: UNL: Universal Networking Language-an Electronic Language for Communication, Understanding, and Collaboration. UNU/IAS/UNL Center, Tokyo (1996)

29. Vanderwende, L.: NLPwin-an introduction. Technical report, Microsoft Research tech report no. MSR-TR-2015-23 (2015)

30. Vanderwende, L., Menezes, A., Quirk, C.: An AMR parser for English, French, German, Spanish and Japanese and a new AMR-annotated corpus. In: Proceedings of the 2015 Meeting of the North American Chapter of the Association for Computational Linguistics - Human Language Technologies, pp. 26–30 (2015)

31. Wang, C., Xue, N., Pradhan, S.: Boosting transition-based AMR parsing with refined actions and auxiliary analyzers. In: Proceedings of the 53rd Annual Meeting of the Association for Computational Linguistics and the 7th International Joint Conference on Natural Language Processing (Volume 2: Short Papers), pp. 857–862 (2015)

32. Wang, C., Xue, N., Pradhan, S., Pradhan, S.: A transition-based algorithm for AMR parsing. In: Proceedings of the 2015 Conference of the North American Chapter of the Association for Computational Linguistics: Human Language Technologies, pp. 366–375 (2015)
33. Zhou, J., Xu, F., Uszkoreit, H., Qu, W., Li, R., Gu, Y.: AMR parsing with an incremental joint model. In: Proceedings of the 2016 Conference on Empirical Methods in Natural Language Processing, pp. 680–689 (2016)

On the Automatic Analysis of Rules Governing Online Communities

Adan Beltran[1,2(✉)], Nardine Osman[1], Lourdes Aguilar[2], and Carles Sierra[1]

[1] Artificial Intelligence Research Institute (IIIA-CSIC), Barcelona, Spain
{adan.beltran,nardine,sierra}@iiia.csic.es
[2] Universitat Autònoma de Barcelona, Barcelona, Spain
lourdes.aguilar@uab.cat

Abstract. The automatic translation of rules or legal text from natural language into formal language has gained interest in the natural language processing domain, especially in the field of law and AI. Our research goal is to be able to automatically extract, from rules in natural language, the necessary elements that define these rules, such as the action in question, its modality (duty, right, privilege, ...), the first person the rule addresses, the second person affected by the rule, and the condition (if the rule was a conditional rule). As a first step toward identifying these elements, we start by identifying the semantic subjects, verbs, and objects in sentences of online normative texts. This paper presents the SVO+ model that achieves this, and our evaluation illustrates the model's high precision when tested with the terms of use from websites like Facebook and Twitter.

Keywords: Text analysis · Normative texts · Semantic subjects
Verbs · Objects

1 Introduction

The automatic translation of natural language into formal language has gained some interest in the natural language processing domain. For example, [19] illustrates and discusses the use of existing state-of-the-art techniques in the automatic translation of regulatory rules in natural language into a machine readable formal representation. [15] translates a complete set of paediatric guideline recommendations into a controlled language (Attempto Controlled English, ACE). [18] adopts and applies a controlled natural language to constrain the domain of discourse in an on-line discussion forum for e-government policy-making. Each of the policy statements is then automatically translated into first-order logic. [20] presents a linguistically-oriented, rule-based approach, for extracting conditional and deontic rules from regulations specified in natural language. Finally, [3] presents approaches for the logical representation of regulations.

In this paper, however, we are interested in the translation of the normative texts governing our online communities, such as the Twitter rules, Facebook's

© Springer Nature Switzerland AG 2018
G. R. Simari et al. (Eds.): IBERAMIA 2018, LNAI 11238, pp. 354–366, 2018.
https://doi.org/10.1007/978-3-030-03928-8_29

terms of service, or Wikipedia's terms of use. This interest is motivated by our belief that the future will be for humans and machines working together, where the machines should automatically understand the rules setup by the humans and mediate our interactions accordingly. This paper presents our initial work on the automatic analysis of such normative texts. We are inspired by the A-Hohfeld language, which is claimed to be expressive enough to specify any legal statement [2]. When formalised, the A-Hohfeld language may be viewed as a deontic logic that is extended with operators on power and disability, which are used as meta-rules that help edit/maintain existing rules. The A-Hohfeld language is based on the 8 basic Hohfeldian constructs: right, duty, no right, privilege, power, liability, disability and immunity. The parameters of these constructs are usually[1] the person the rule applies to, the action that this rule is concerned with, and the second person with respect to whom the rule applies. For example, if we say "the government has a duty to provide basic education to its citizens", then the first person would be 'the government', the second person would be 'the citizens', and the action is 'providing basic education'.

We argue that if the A-Hohfeld language is sufficient for specifying any legal statement, then rules governing online interactions should be easily translated into A-Hohfeld. Our goal is to automatically extract, from rules in natural language, the first person, the second person, the action, the modality (such as duty, right, privilege, ...), and the condition (when applicable) of each rule.

To identify the first person, we argue that this usually is the subject of the sentence specifying the rule. The second person is usually the indirect object. The action is the extended verb, that is, the verb with additional information such as location, time, direct object, etc. As such, our initial work focuses on extracting the subjects, verbs, and objects in sentences of online normative texts.

The rest of this paper is divided as follows. Section 2 opens with an overview of related work. Section 3 presents our proposed algorithm, SVO+ which identifies the semantic subject, verb and object in sentences. Section 4 evaluates the SVO+ algorithm with a set of normative texts from Twitter, Facebook, and Wikipedia. Finally, Sect. 5 closes with concluding remarks.

2   Background

The issue of automatically translating legal text into a formal language is a difficult yet important issue in the field of artificial intelligence and law. Some work has been developed on the formalisation of legal texts, but it usually depends on manual effort. For example, the LegalRuleML language is an annotation language that has been used in [14] to annotate legal instruments provided by the Scottish Government's Parliamentary Counsel Office and bearing on Scottish smoking legislation and regulation. In our case, however, we are interested in the *automatic* translation of normative text from natural language into a formal one, as opposed to the manual annotation of normative text.

---

[1] Power-based Hohfeldian constructs are a bit different. For example, the second person is not present for these constructs in the A-Hohfeld language.

Other approaches have used machine learning to classify documents or sentences [12], without annotating the different parts of a norm. In [6], a combination of machine learning with hand coded approaches is used. In [9] a combination of machine learning and NLP is used to classify norms and extract their elements. The work of [20] is more similar to ours, where the GATE platform is used to develop new JAPE rules, for example for exception clauses, conditional sentences, and deontic rules. In a deontic rule, they identify the deontic operator, the main verb, the semantic roles that noun phrases play, and exceptions. [4] also uses similar syntactic parsing to us to classify norms and extract their elements. In [7], syntactic analysis is used not only to extract verbs and their corresponding subjects and objects, but also attributes, and prepositional phrases referring to locations, instrumentals, manners, causes, etc.

In our approach, we intend to translate normative text into a formal language based on the A-Hohfeldian language. That is, we need to identify the modality (Hohfeldian construct), the first person that the norm addresses, the second person affected by the norm, the main action of the norm, and sometimes, the condition [1]. For this, we need to *semantically* understand the sentence. For example, the first person is usually the subject (though it may sometimes be the agent). The second person is usually the indirect object. The extended verb is usually the verb with all necessary information that specifies the details of the action in question (such as direct object, time, location, etc.). As such, we start with a syntactic dependency tree (generated by the spaCy library, https://spacy.io/), and we use the dependency information between words to recognise the extended subject, the extended verb, and the extended object. Future work will use this annotation to obtain the required A-Hohfeldian elements of a norm.

Another novelty of this work is dividing a sentence with more than one main verb into multiple norms. For example, the sentence 'You will not facilitate or encourage any violations of this Statement' can be written as two norms: (1) 'You will not facilitate any violations of this Statement', and (2) 'You will not encourage any violations of this Statement'. This is useful when we expect the machine to be the one enforcing norms, or verifying the adherence to norms.

3   The SVO+ Model

This section describes our proposal, the SVO+ model, for analysing the semantic subjects, verbs, and objects in normative texts. Section 3.1 presents the linguistic analysis that motivates our approach, along with a description of the corpus used for evaluating our work. Section 3.2 presents the SVO+ model and its algorithms.

3.1   Linguistic Analysis

To our knowledge, there is no specific linguistic analysis of normative texts governing online communities, but they can be considered as representative of written legal language. Legal language has recognisable patterns in the deployment of the linguistic resources. The most common features of legal texts are: long and complex sentences, technical vocabulary, archaic words, unusual sentence structure, unusual prepositional phrases, nominalisations and passives, multiple negation and impersonal constructions and redundancy or doublets [10,16,17]. Complex prepositions are also mentioned as characteristic of legal vocabulary, though no comprehensive study on the occurrence and distribution of complex prepositions in legal texts has been conducted yet [5].

Norms (and laws) are usually written as classical definitions, comprised of a list of elements all of which must obtain for the norm to apply to a given situation. Each element is necessary, and together they are sufficient to define what is proscribed. The elements, in turn, are presented either conjunctively or as part of a list of which at least one member must obtain [11].

These characteristics imply that to translate rules into the A-Hohfeld language, a deep syntactic analysis is not sufficient, since there is no one-to-one correspondence between the parameters of the Hohfeldian constructs and the syntactic constituents. For instance, in the sentence 'You will not transfer any of your rights or obligations under this Statement to anyone else without our consent', our proposed model is expected to identify 'You' as the subject, 'will not transfer' as the predicate, and 'any of your rights or obligations under this Statement to anyone else without our consent' as the object, or semantic object. We can see here that following syntactic criteria, the semantic object is composed of three parts: (1) the direct object, 'any of your rights or obligations', (2) the indirect object, 'to anyone else', and (3) the object of preposition, 'without our consent'. These three constituents are merged into the tag "object" because the final aim of the parsing is to connect the stretch of words with the A-Hohfeld language, where a taxonomy of fundamental legal relations are established [2].

The basis of building sentences is the notion of predication, defined as the process and the result of assignment of properties to objects or circumstances. From this point of view, predication is the foundation of any form of enunciation and its linguistic realisation is the predicate. According to this, a sentence is built around a predicative element, usually the verb. The nature of the verb determines what nouns will accompany it, its relation to these nouns and how will these nouns be semantically specified. This modern understanding of predicates is compatible with the dependency grammar approach to sentence structure, as in the Syntactic Dependency Parsing. In this model, a syntactic dependency is semantically defined as a binary operation that takes as arguments the denotations of the two related words (both the head and the dependent), and gives as a result a more elaborate arrangement of their denotations [8].

For our analysis of normative text, we have selected a subset of dependency categories depending on their incidence in the detection of subject, main verb(s) and object. The main verb in a clause determines whether and what objects are present. Transitive verbs require the presence of a direct object, whereas intransitive verbs block the appearance of a direct object; and any of them can have a prepositional object. The label, 'conj', is selected to identify those sentences with more than one main verb: that is, cases of coordinate and subordinate clauses. To discard the identification of auxiliary verbs as main verbs, the labels 'aux', 'auxpass', and (due to the high occurrence of norms written in a negative form, such as prohibitions) 'neg' is used. The forms that the constituent 'subject' can be realised, in their active or passive form, and in different type of clauses are identified through the labels 'nsub', 'csubj', 'nsubjpass', 'csubjpass'. As for objects, various types are commonly acknowledged: direct (entity acted upon), indirect (entity indirectly affected by the action), and prepositional (object introduced by a preposition). Direct and indirect objects can be realised by means of noun phrases or clauses (identified through the labels 'dobj', 'dative', 'oprd', 'xcomp', 'attr','ccomp', 'acomp'), whereas prepositional objects are introduced by a preposition (identified by the labels 'prep' and 'npadvmod'). Table 1 provides a summary of the labels used in our SVO+ model. How these labels are used by our SVO+ algorithms to identify the different main verbs and their corresponding semantics subjects and objects is described next in more detail.

Table 1. Selected dependency labels

Category	Selected labels (Universal dependency labels [13])
Main Verbs	'conj' (conjunct)
Auxiliary information	'aux' (auxiliary), 'auxpass' (passive auxiliary), 'neg' (negation modifier)
Subject	'nsub' (nominal subject), 'csubj' (clausal subject), 'nsubjpass' (nominal passive subject), 'csubjpass' (clausal passive subject)
Object	'dobj' (direct object), 'dative' (dative), 'oprd' (object predicate), 'xcomp' (open clausal complement), 'attr' (attribute), 'ccomp' (clausal complement), 'acomp' (adjectival complement)
Complement object	'prep' (prepositional modifier), 'npadvmod' (noun phrase as adverbial modifier)

3.2 The SVO+ Algorithms

The main objective of our work is to identify the main verbs in a sentence, along with their corresponding semantic subjects and objects. To do so, the proposed SVO+ model relies on Syntactic Dependency Parsing, whose output is a Syntactic Dependency Tree (SDT). Specifically, we make use of the spaCy representation of the SDT (https://spacy.io/). An SDT is specified as a vector of 'tokens' (with tokens representing the words and punctuation marks in a sentence), where the tokens are ordered by their appearance in a sentence. Each token is specified as a tuple of six attributes, where the first specifies the word or punctuation mark ('text'), the second specifies the syntactic parent ('head'), the third specifies the part of speech ('pos'), the fourth specifies the syntactic dependency relation with the parent ('dep'), the fifth specifies the list of immediate children (dependent) tokens ('children'), and the sixth specifies the list of all the descendent tokens ('subtree'), that is not just the children but their subtrees. As the SDT becomes too large very quickly, we provide a graphical presentation of the dependencies between words in Fig. 1.

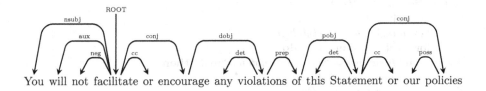

Fig. 1. Sample tree dependency

Given an SDT, we next illustrate how main verbs are identified (Algorithm 1), and how their corresponding information is identified/predicted (Algorithms 2/3).

Identifying Main Verbs. The identification of the main verb is one of the most important tasks in the analysis of norms. The action that a norm addresses (and the modality of the norm) are usually described by the main verb. Additionally, as mentioned earlier (Sect. 3.1), sentences are built around main verbs, and other parts of a sentence (such as the subject and the object) are connected to those main verbs and can only be identified after identifying their corresponding main verb. We note that a sentence may contain a number of verbs. We refer to the verbs that a sentence is built around as the main verbs. For example, in the sentence 'Ads must not promote products or items that facilitate or encourage unauthorised access to digital media', there are three verbs ('promote', 'facilitate', and 'encourage') but only one of them is a main verb ('promote').

Algorithm 1 identifies the main verbs in an SDT. First (Lines 4–6), the algorithm iterates over the vector of tokens of the dependency tree looking for the token representing the root node. The root is expected to be a verb, and is marked as the main verb. However, if the root is not a verb, then the main verb remains empty (this usually happens when the sentence is not a complete sentence in English). Once this node is identified, the function *findMoreMainVerbs* is called to find other main verbs (Line 8). The input of this function is the main verb found above and the current vector of main verbs (which would simply contain the main verb found above until now). This function is needed because sometimes the sentence may contain more than one action that the norm addresses, such as 'You will not facilitate or encourage any violations of this Statement'. In this case, there are two main verbs: 'facilitate' and 'encourage'.

The *findMoreMainVerbs* function checks the children nodes of the received token, and if any of those is a verb (has the 'pos', or part of speech, marked as 'verb') and is connected to its parent node (an already recognised main verb) through 'conj', then it is considered as another main verb. As such, it is added to the vector of main verbs (MV). Then, we recursively call the

---

Algorithm 1. Identifying Main Verbs

Require: SDT ▷ This is the syntactic depdendency tree
Require: $MV : (n)T\ Vector$ ▷ MV is a vector of n tokens (T)
Require: $emptytoken$ ▷ This is an empty token, i.e. a token with empty attributes.
1. **function** MAIN(SDT)
2.   Let $MV = T\langle\rangle$
3.   Let $mainVerb = emptytoken$
4.   **for** each $token$ in SDT **do**
5.   **if** $token.pos =$ "verb" $\wedge token.dep =$ "root" **then**
6. $mainVerb \leftarrow token$
7.   add $token$ to MV
8. $MV \leftarrow findMoreMainVerbs(mainVerb, MV)$
       return MV
9. **function** $findMoreMainVerbs(tokenVerb, MV)$
10.   **for** each $token$ in $tokenVerb.children$ **do**
11.   **if** $token.dep =$ "conj" $\wedge token.pos =$ "verb" **then**
12.   add $token$ to MV
13. $findMoreMainVerbs(token, MV)$
       return MV

$findMoreMainVerbs$ function again, to check for other main verbs that are connected to the newly identified main verb. This process is repeated until all main verbs are identified.

Identifying Subjects, Objects, and Suxiliary Information of Main Verbs. Once the main verbs are identified (Algorithm 1), the next step is to identify their subjects, objects, and what we refer to as auxiliary information. We define auxiliary information as information that helps complete the verb. For example, in 'will not be removed', the syntactic dependency parser recognises 'removed' as the main verb, and the rest are connected to the verb through different dependency relations (the dependency label of 'will' with the main verb is 'aux', the dependency label of 'not' with the main verb is 'neg', and the dependency label of 'be' with the main verb is 'auxpass').

Finding the subject, object, and auxiliary information is achieved by Algorithm 2. For each verb of the main verbs in MV (Lines 4–5), the 'children' nodes are obtained, and for each child, its dependency with its parent is checked (the 'dep' label) (Lines 7–8). The child is then categorised as being part of the subject, object, or auxiliary information based on this dependency:

- If the dependency is one of the labels in {'neg', 'aux', 'auxpass'}, then the child is considered to be part of the auxiliary information that completes the main verb (Lines 9–14). We note that one verb may have more than child labelled as auxiliary information, and in such cases, we append these children together (Line 23), as in the example 'will not be removed'.
- If the dependency is one of the labels in {'nsubj', 'csubj', 'nsubjpass', 'csubjpass'}, then the child is considered to be part of the subject (Lines 15–16).
- If the dependency is one of the labels {'dobj', 'dative', 'oprd', 'xcomp', 'attr', 'ccomp','acomp'}, the child is considered part of the object (Lines 17–18).

- If the dependency label is in {'npavmod', 'prep'}, then the child is considered as information that completes the object (Lines 19–20). But this information is appended to the object only if the object exists (Lines 21–22).

All this information is then saved in a matrix MVM (Lines 23–26), which constitutes the algorithm's output. The rows in the matrix represent the main verbs and their corresponding information. The columns of the matrix represent the auxiliary information of a main verb, the main verb itself, the main verb's subject, and the main verb's object, respectively.

Algorithm 2. Identifying Subjects, Objects, & Auxiliary Information

---

Require: $MV : (n)T$ $Vector$ $\triangleright$ MV is the input for this algorithm, and it is a vector of n tokens (T), where $MV[i]$ represents token number i

Require: $MVM : (n \times 4)String\ Matrix$ $\triangleright$ MVM represents a matrix with n rows (for n main verbs) and 4 columns (for the verb and its corresponding auxiliary info, subject, and object).

Require: T $\triangleright$ T represents a token with 6 attributes, where $T.text$ refers to the token's text, $T.dep$ refers to the token's dependency with its parent node, $T.children$ refers to the tokens list of children, and $subtree$ refers to the token's subtree.

1. Let $verb = T$
2. Let $aux = neg = auxpass = subject = object = objectComp =$ ""
3. Let $MVM = String\ Matrix[n \times 4]$
4. **for** $i = 1$ up to $i = n$ **do**
5. $verb \leftarrow MV[i]$
6. $aux = neg = auxpass = subject = object = objectComp =$ ""
7.   **for** each token in $verb.children$ **do**
8.   **switch** $token.dep$ **do**
9.   **case** "neg"
10. $neg \leftarrow token.subtree$
11.   **case** "aux"
12. $aux \leftarrow token.subtree$
13.   **case** "auxpass"
14. $auxPass \leftarrow token.subtree$
15.   **case** in { "nsubj","csubj","nsubjpass","csubjpass" }
16. $subject \leftarrow token.subtree$
17.   **case** in { "dobj","dative","oprd","xcomp","attr","ccomp","acomp"}
18. $object \leftarrow token.subtree$
19.   **case** in { "npavmod","prep" }
20. $objectComp \leftarrow token.subtree$
21.   **if** $object \neq$ "" $\wedge$ $objectComp \neq$ "" **then:**
22. $object \leftarrow object + objectComp$
23. $MVM[i,1] \leftarrow aux + neg + auxpass$
24. $MVM[i,2] \leftarrow verb.text$
25. $MVM[i,3] \leftarrow subject$
26. $MVM[i,4] \leftarrow object$

Completing Missing Information. When using ellipsis, the matrix MVM obtained by Algorithm 2 may contain gaps, for instance missing subjects or objects. Algorithm 3 fills gaps in this matrix (noted as MVM) by looking into the info of other main verbs in the same sentence. For any verb in the matrix (row i) it completes the missing gaps as follows. If the object is missing, the verb gets the object of the nearest verb towards the end of sentence (lines 2–4). If the auxiliary or subject information is missing, the verb gets them from the nearest verb towards the beginning of the sentence (lines 5–9).

Algorithm 3. Completing Missing Information

Require: $MVM : (n \times 4)String\ Matrix$ ▷ MVM is the input of this algorithm, and it is a matrix with n rows (for n main verbs) and 4 columns (for the verb and its corresponding auxiliary info, subject, and object).

1. **for** $i = 1$ up to $i = n$ **do**
2.   **for** $j = i + 1$ up to $j = n$ **do**
3.   **if** $MVM[i,4] = $ "" **then**
4. $MVM[i,4] \leftarrow MVM[j,4]$
5.   **for** $j = i - 1$ down to $j = 1$ **do**
6.   **if** $MVM[i,3] = $ "" **then**
7. $MVM[i,3] \leftarrow MVM[j,3]$
8.   **if** $MVM[i,1] = $ "" **then**
9. $MVM[i,1] \leftarrow MVM[j,1]$
10. return MVM

For example, in the sentence 'You will not facilitate or encourage any violations of this Statement' the main verbs are: $\langle$ *"facilitate"*, *"encourage"* $\rangle$, generated by Algorithm 1. Then, Algorithm 2 finds the auxiliary information, the subject, and the object of the main verbs to complete their descriptions:

$\langle\langle$ " will not ", " facilitate   ", " You ", "   "$\rangle$,
$\langle$ "   ", " encourage ", "   ", " any violations of this Statement "$\rangle\rangle$

In this case the verb "facilitate" has no specified object, and the verb "encourage" has no information neither of the auxiliary nor of the subject. Algorithm 3 is responsible for completing as much as possible the verb descriptions. The output in this particular case would be:

$\langle\langle$ " will not ", " facilitate   ", " You ", " any violations of this Statement "$\rangle$,
$\langle$ " will not ", " encourage ", " You ", " any violations of this Statement "$\rangle\rangle$

4   Evaluation

To evaluate SVO+, we first constructed the corpus of normative text and manually annotated the semantic subjects, verbs, and objects. This was used as the gold-standard for evaluating SVO+. We then carried out our evaluation using the spaCy, with the 'en-core-web-lg' model (https://spacy.io/).

We note, however, that to evaluate the accuracy of the proposed SVO+ algorithm, we must first separate between the errors of the Syntactic Dependency Parsing (SDP) and our proposal. This is because errors in the SDP will naturally result in errors in SVO+'s identification of the main verbs, subject and object.

In what follows, we first describe the process for constructing our gold standard corpus, followed by an evaluation of the SDP performance, and then an evaluation of the proposed SVO+ performance.

Construction of the Annotated Gold Standard Corpus. To construct our corpus, we looked into the rules (usually labelled as terms and conditions) of the following online communities: Facebook, Twitter, Wikipedia, and some online time bank communities. As illustrated earlier, normative text usually uses long and complex sentences, unusual sentence structure, references, and is context dependent. As such, from those rules, we have selected those that are simple. And in very few cases, we have slightly modified the punctuation without changing the meaning, such as replacing a semicolon with a fullstop or a comma (depending on the context). The result was a set if 138 normative sentences.

Next a linguist and a computer scientist helped labelling the semantic subjects, verbs, and objects. This is needed to generate the gold-standard that our algorithms results need to be verified against.

Evaluating the SDP Performance. Although the accuracy of the SDP has already been widely evaluated (https://spacy.io/models/en/), in what follows we analyse the SDP errors with respect to our corpus. Our results show that the SDP fails with 22 of our norms, that is 84% precision (see Table 2). Some of the most common errors due to the *SDP* are:

- Failing to find the main verb, as a non-main verb was marked as root.
- Failing to find a main verb, as it was not labelled as a verb (but a noun).
- Failing to find the object as the object was not directly connected to the main verb, but indirectly connected through the 'prep' dependency.

Table 2. Results of SDP's precision

	Correctly labelled	Incorrectly labelled	Precision
109 Sentences with 1 main verb	95	14	87.2%
29 Sentences with more than 1 main verb	21	8	72.4%
138 Sentences in total	116	22	84%

Evaluating the SVO+ Performance. The input of our proposed SVO+ algorithm is the SDP tree. As such, all 22 sentences that the parser parses incorrectly result in errors with our SVO+ algorithms. For this reason, to analyse the errors of the SVO+ algorithms, we first remove those 22 sentences from our corpus, leaving us with 116 sentences to analyse. The results are shown in Table 3. Notice that with a correct SDP tree, the SVO+ algorithms are 100% accurate when it comes to identifying the main verbs (and their auxiliary information) and the subjects. The problem is with identifying the objects. The precision is 99% when it comes to sentences with only one main verb. This, however, drops to 95.7% for sentences with more than one verb. The reasons for failure are described below.

- **Marking the subtree of an object as being part of the extended object.** The SVO+ model marks the subtree of a recognised object as being part of that object. However, in some cases, the subtree contains other information, such as conditions. For example, in the sentence 'If you select a username or similar identifier for your account or page, we reserve the right to remove or reclaim it if we believe it is appropriate', the second condition 'if we believe it is appropriate' was incorrectly considered to be part of the object. This is because the condition, to 'believe it is appropriate' is dependent on the verb 'remove', which consists part of the extended object.
- **With more than one verb, we fill in the missing objects by looking for the objects of subsequent verbs.** This works in the majority of cases, such as 'You will not facilitate or encourage any violations of this Statement'. However, there are exceptions to this rules (2 in our corpus). For example, in the sentence 'Ads must not discriminate or encourage discrimination', the object 'discrimination' of the second main verb 'encourage' cannot also be considered the object of the first main verb 'discriminate'.

Table 3. Results of precision of sentence with one main verb

	Correctly identified	Not identified	Precision
95 Sentences with 1 main verb			
95 Verbs with it auxiliary information	95	0	100%
95 Subjects	95	0	100%
95 Objects	94	1	99%
21 Sentences with more than 1 main verb			
46 Verbs with auxiliary information	46	0	100%
46 Subjects	46	0	100%
46 Objects	44	2	95.7%

5   Conclusions

This paper has presented the SVO+ model for the automatic analysis of norms governing online communities. The model identifies the semantic subject, verb, and object with very high precision. Future work will test our model on other existing data sets. We also plan to publish our own data set for other to benefit from. We will then focus on identifying additional information that would allow us to fulfil our vision of automatically translating normative text specified in natural language into norms specified in a formal language. This will include identifying conditions, identifying the modality of the norm (obligation, permission, prohibition), as well as identifying the first and second person involved in a norm. Our ultimate objective is to be able to automatically translate norms governing online communities into a formal A-Hohfeld language.

References

1. Allen, L.E.: Some examples of using the legal relations language in the legal domain: applied deontic logic. Notre Dame L. Rev. **73**, 535 (1997)
2. Allen, L.E., Saxon, C.S.: Better language, better thought, better communication: the A-Hohfeld language for legal analysis. In: Proceedings of ICAIL 1995. ACM (1995)
3. Athan, T., Boley, H., Governatori, G., Palmirani, M., Paschke, A., Wyner, A.: OASIS LegalRuleML. In: Proceedings of ICAIL 2013, pp. 3–12. ACM (2013)
4. Azzopardi, S., Gatt, A., Pace, G.J.: Integrating natural language and formal analysis for legal documents. In: 10th Conference on Language Technologies and Digital Humanities (2016)
5. Coulthard, M., Johnson, A.: The Routledge Handbook of Forensic Linguistics. Routledge, Abingdon (2010)
6. Curtotti, M., Mccreath, E.: Corpus based classification of text in Australian contracts. In: Proceedings of Australasian Language Technology Association Workshop (2010)
7. Gamallo, P., Garcia, M.: Multilingual open information extraction. In: Pereira, F., Machado, P., Costa, E., Cardoso, A. (eds.) EPIA 2015. LNCS (LNAI), vol. 9273, pp. 711–722. Springer, Cham (2015). https://doi.org/10.1007/978-3-319-23485-4_72
8. Gamallo Otero, P.: The meaning of syntactic dependencies. Linguist. Online **35**(3), 33–53 (2008)
9. Gao, X., Singh, M.P.: Extracting normative relationships from business contracts. In: Proceedings of AAMAS 2014, pp. 101–108. IFAAMAS (2014)
10. Gibbons, J.: Forensic Linguistics: An Introduction to Language in the Justice System. Wiley-Blackwell, Hoboken (2003)
11. Hobbs, P.: Not semantics but just results: the use of linguistic analysis in constitutional interpretation. J. Pragmat. **44**(6–7), 815–828 (2012)
12. de Maat, E., Winkels, R.: Automated classification of norms in sources of law. In: Francesconi, E., Montemagni, S., Peters, W., Tiscornia, D. (eds.) Semantic Processing of Legal Texts. LNCS (LNAI), vol. 6036, pp. 170–191. Springer, Heidelberg (2010). https://doi.org/10.1007/978-3-642-12837-0_10
13. McDonald, R., et al.: Universal dependency annotation for multilingual parsing. In: Proceedings of the 51st Annual Meeting of the Association for Computational Linguistics, vol. 2, pp. 92–97 (2013)
14. Palmirani, M., Governatori, G., Rotolo, A., Tabet, S., Boley, H., Paschke, A.: LegalRuleML: XML-based rules and norms. In: Olken, F., Palmirani, M., Sottara, D. (eds.) RuleML 2011. LNCS, vol. 7018, pp. 298–312. Springer, Heidelberg (2011). https://doi.org/10.1007/978-3-642-24908-2_30

15. Shiffman, R.N., Michel, G., Krauthammer, M., Fuchs, N.E., Kaljurand, K., Kuhn, T.: Writing clinical practice guidelines in controlled natural language. In: Fuchs, N.E. (ed.) CNL 2009. LNCS (LNAI), vol. 5972, pp. 265–280. Springer, Heidelberg (2010). https://doi.org/10.1007/978-3-642-14418-9_16
16. Tiersma, P.M.: Legal Language. University of Chicago Press, Chicago (1999)
17. Trosborg, A.: Rhetorical Strategies in Legal Language: Discourse Analysis of Statutes and Contracts, vol. 424. Gunter Narr Verlag, T übingen (1997)
18. Wyner, A., van Engers, T., Bahreini, K.: From policy-making statements to first-order logic. In: Andersen, K.N., Francesconi, E., Grönlund, Å., van Engers, T.M. (eds.) EGOVIS 2010. LNCS, vol. 6267, pp. 47–61. Springer, Heidelberg (2010). https://doi.org/10.1007/978-3-642-15172-9_5
19. Wyner, A., Governatori, G.: A study on translating regulatory rules from natural language to defeasible logic. In: RuleML 2013, pp. 16.1–16.8, July 2013
20. Wyner, A., Peters, W.: On rule extraction from regulations. In: Proceedings of JURIX 2011, vol. 235, pp. 113–122. IOS Press (2011)

Free Tools and Resources for HMM-Based Brazilian Portuguese Speech Synthesis

Ericson Costa[(✉)] [iD] and Nelson Neto[(✉)] [iD]

Institute of Exact and Natural Sciences, Federal University of Pará,
Augusto Correa. 1, Belém, PA 66075-110, Brazil
{ericson,nelsonneto}@ufpa.br
http://labvis.ufpa.br/falabrasil/

Abstract. Text-to-speech (TTS) is currently a mature technology used
in many areas such as education and accessibility. Some modules of a
TTS system depend on the language and, while there are many public
materials for some languages (e.g., English and Japanese), the resources
for Brazilian Portuguese (BP) are still limited. This work describes the
development of a complete hidden Markov model (HMM) based TTS
system for BP which can be applied to the desktop environment. It
also releases a set of natural language processing tools for BP, which
expands the already publicly available resources, supporting the development of new researches for academic or industrial purposes. Subjective
and objective performance tests are presented, comparing the proposed
TTS system with other softwares currently available for BP.

Keywords: Speech synthesis · Hidden Markov models
Natural language processing · Brazilian Portuguese
Speech-based applications

1 Introduction

Speech processing includes several technologies, among which automatic speech
recognition (ASR) and text-to-speech (TTS) are the most prominent, with a
large number of applications for users with and without disabilities. Speech synthesis technology has made great improvement during the last years. In the
90's, the technique which employs unit selection and concatenation of waveform segments was the most popular approach. In the academy, some TTS systems were developed for BP using the concatenative method [17], however, for
this technique, the obtainment of high quality itself requires the availability of
large corpora. A worldwide collaborative initiative is the MBROLA project [12].
MBROLA is a concatenative speech synthesizer distributed at no financial cost
but in binary form only. Note that the MBROLA software is not a complete
TTS system for BP, since a natural language processing (NLP) module, which
is the front-end of a TTS system, is not available for this Portuguese dialect.

© Springer Nature Switzerland AG 2018
G. R. Simari et al. (Eds.): IBERAMIA 2018, LNAI 11238, pp. 367–379, 2018.
https://doi.org/10.1007/978-3-030-03928-8_30

More recently, a probabilistic approach in which the speech waveform is synthesized from parameters directly derived from hidden Markov models (HMMs) [25] has shown good results for several languages. When compared with other methods, the HMM-based synthesis technique can be competitive in quality with small databases (about one hour of speech) and the voice features could be easier modified in order to produce voices with different styles and emotions. In [15], the authors describe the characteristics of an HMM-based BP speech synthesizer, which is part of the HTS project [3], as well as its training process. The results obtained by [15] were very relevant, considering the BP language, and have encouraged other researchers to use and expand the knowledge and the set of tools that were proposed.

Microsoft's initial efforts to develop an HMM-based BP synthetic voice interfaces are shown in [7]. The system was trained with a total of 11,500 prompts (nearly 13 h of speech) subjected to a recording quality control. It used the HTS technology in the back-end and its own language processing set of tools. Comprehension tests were conducted by seven native listeners who were exposed to a set of 410 prompts divided by six domains: addresses, date and time, proper nouns, phone numbers, single e-mail/news sentences, and e-mail/news paragraphs. As result, the overall intelligibility rate was 98.91%.

In [14], two BP voices were developed and tested using the HTS training script and engine. The voices analysis acquired pertinent results compared with a commercial synthesizer. In [22], the same research group again created two HMM-based voices for BP but now the authors used the MARY TTS system [18], which is an open-source framework written in Java that supports both concatenative and HMM-based synthesis in a client-server architecture. Finally, the main objective of evaluating the ability of the MARY TTS portability for the Android environment was satisfactorily met. As usual, both works did not described (or made available) the employed NLP module and, considering the habitual problems of connectivity services that occur in Brazil, the authors believe that a offline architecture is more suitable.

Since nowadays the digital signal processing (or the back-end block) is a stable module, to make a TTS system robust, efficient, and reliable, it is crucial to have a good language dependent front-end module and, as far as we know, none is publicly available for BP. In response to this need, this work aims at developing and deploying resources for BP language processing. The implemented system establishes a baseline, enables the comparison of results among research groups, and promotes the development of speech-enabled software via the proposed application programming interface (API). In summary, the contributions of this work are:

– Resources for the training and test stages of an HMM-based TTS system: a speech corpus corresponding to approximately 1.6 h of audio; and a label generator following the contextual factors defined in [15].
– A grapheme-to-phone (G2P) converter with stress mark.
– A rule-based syllabification tool.

– An API that hides from the user the low level details of the engine operation. The proposed API was designed to be multi-platform and localhost.

The tools and resources listed above represent the evolution of our research in this topic [10,11]. Basically, a more recent version of the HTS software package was adopted to train the acoustic model, the G2P converter with stress mark was improved, and our own syllabification tool was used.

This paper is organized as follows. Section 2 presents a description of HMM-based speech synthesis. Section 3 describes the linguistic resources for BP developed and used in this work. Section 4 describes the API to operate the TTS engine. In Sect. 5, objective and subjective tests were conducted in order to compare the proposed synthetic voice with two BP synthesizers. Finally, Sect. 6 summarizes our conclusions and addresses future works.

2 HMM-Based Speech Synthesis

HMM-based speech synthesis is classified as a statistical parametric approach [23]. Compared to unit selection speech synthesis, which concatenates sub-word units automatically selected from large databases of natural speech, HMM-based synthesis can be understood as generating the average of similar sounding speech units in the database [26]. Figure 1 shows a block diagram of an HMM-based speech synthesis system. It consists of two steps: the training part and the synthesis part. The training script (or software *recipe*) used in this work was developed by [15], within the HTS project [3].

In the training stage, excitation parameters (fundamental frequency logarithm, $log(F0)$, and aperiodic features), including voicing decision information (if $F0 = 0$ the frame is considered unvoiced), and spectral parameters (mel-cepstral coefficients) are extracted from a speech database. In the next step, the NLP module generates utterance information for all the sentences of the training database and converts them into contextual labels. In speech synthesis, some factors are usually necessary to be taken into account in order to provide a natural reproduction of the prosody. These factors might include context dependent terms, such as preceding/succeeding phone, syllable, word, phrase, etc., and are referred to as contextual factors [15]. The determination of contextual factors for a particular language is based on prosodic characteristics of the referred language and consequently linguistic assumptions should be considered. Then, both spectrum and excitation parameters are modeled by a set of multi-stream context-dependent HMMs.

In the synthesis stage, the utterance information of a given sentence is converted into contextual labels. Then, the context-dependent HMMs are concatenated according to that labels and an HMM sequence is constructed. In the sequel, the speech parameter generation algorithm outputs the spectral and excitation parameters from the HMM sequence with state durations. Finally, according to these parameters, a synthesis filter module generates a speech waveform. This work uses the hts-engine software package [4] in order to synthesize speech waveform from HMMs.

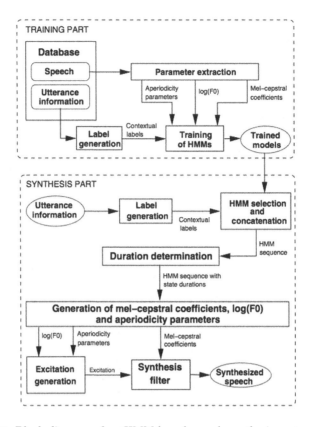

Fig. 1. Block diagram of an HMM-based speech synthesis system [15].

3   Linguistic Resources for BP

In order to increase the number of TTS resources for BP, a speech database and some specific language processing tools were built, namely: grapheme-to-phone converter, syllabification tool, and contextual label generator. All of them are publicly available [2].

3.1   Grapheme-to-Phone Module

An essential building block for services involving speech processing techniques is the correspondence between the orthography and the pronunciation. This mapping can be done by invoking a grapheme-to-phone (G2P) module. In this context, this work presents a G2P converter with stress determination for BP that is based on a set of rules described in [19]. The original conversion rules were improved and they did not focus in any BP dialect.

The proposed conversion is based on phonological pre-established criteria, its architecture does not rely on intermediate stages, i.e., other algorithms such as syllabic division or plural identification. There is a set of rules for each grapheme and a specific order of application is assumed. First, the more specific rules are considered until a general case rule is reached, which ends the process. The rules are specified in a set of regular expressions using the Java programming language. Regular expressions are also allowed in the definition of non-terminals symbols (e.g. #abacaxi#). The rules of the G2P converter are organized in three phases. Each phase has the following function: (i) a simple procedure that inserts the non-terminal symbol # before and after each word; (ii) the stress phase consists of 29 rules that mark the stressed vowel of the word; (iii) the bulk of the system, which consists of 140 rules, that convert the graphemes (including the stressed vowel brand) to 38 phones represented using the SAMPA alphabet.

The following example illustrates the regular expression specification used to analyze the word: "abacaxi", which identifies i as the stressed vowel. First, the "Regex" object is created with the pattern to be found within the word analyzed. After that, the "Match" object receives the response pattern comparison with the word presented. Being true, the stressed vowel is determined, otherwise, other rules are tested until they run out the possibilities and the general case is applied. An example is shown below:

```
Regex rule_8 = new Regex("[^aeiou][iu][#]");
Match m8 = rule_8.Match(word);
if(m8.Success) {
    index_strVw = m8.Index+1;
    strVw = word.Substring(index_strVw,1);
    break;
}
```

The code presented above describes the rule 8 applied for the determination of the stressed vowel [19] and can be explained as follows. The end of the word is indicated by the symbol #. So, the grapheme <i> or <u> is the last character of the word and the next to the last character can not be a vowel. The "Match" object index is a pointer for the first component of the pattern analysis, in this case, the character that is not a vowel. Finally, the last character is defined as the stressed vowel. For example, considering the last syllable <xi> in the word "abacaxi", since this case falls into rule 8 the stressed vowel is the letter <i>. Based on this information, the next phase is the G2P conversion, which follows the sequential order of the word (left-right). The following example presents one of the rules applied for the transcription, where the letter <x> is converted into the corresponding phone [S].

```
letter = word.Substring(index,1);
Regex idX = new Regex("x");
Match gX = idX.Match(letter);
if(gX.Success) {
    phone[index] = "S";
    index++;
}
```

The conversion is temporarily stored in an array of strings until the last G2P converter step, which removes the graphemes in order to produce a sequence of phones. Finally, the word and its corresponding G2P conversion are written in the form:

```
abacaxi a b a k a S i
```

therefore the developed G2P converter deals only with single words and does not implement co-articulation analysis between words. During the research, some rules proposed by [19] were improved and others were added. A summary of the added or modified rules can be seen in [21].

3.2 Syllabification Tool

The proposed syllabification algorithm for BP is implemented by means of Java program language and is based on the 20 rules designed in [20], plus the two rules added by [16] to treat specific diphthongs, including the stressed vowel brand, as well as some improvements. All the rules are based on orthography and do not focus in any BP dialect. In fact, phonological criteria are also considered in this work, but only the classical ones, where the grapheme sequence is admittedly represented by a single phoneme, for example, the sequences <ss> and <rr>.

Each linguistic rule of the algorithm is basically composed of a condition to be evaluated and actions to be executed, considering that every syllable must have a vowel as a nucleus[1]. Each condition evaluates all the graphemes that surround the syllable nucleus (the vowel currently under analysis). If it is fulfilled, then the algorithm calls the method that executes the action associated to such rule to perform the required syllabification.

The algorithms on [20] and [16] were subject to a baseline evaluation process with 150,000 words (and their respective syllabification) extracted from the Dicio database [1]. During this phase, the analysis of the problems gave the input for some improvements on the rules proposed by [20]. First of all, the group composed by the Rules 1 to 5 was analyzed. This initial set of rules deals with syllables that begin with vowels.

It was added the check of liquid consonants to the conditional loop of Rule 2, besides the original presence of stop consonants. This addition corrected the syllabification of few words, such as "adpresso" <ad-pre-sso> and "ecplexia" <ec-ple-xi-a>, which are not treated by the reference algorithm [20].

---

[1] The syllable is a unit relatively easy to identify and segmental if the splitting rules stipulated by the language orthography are followed. However, as a phonological unit, there is no consensus about its basic structure, as discussed in [9]. For most authors, a syllable is defined so that its nucleus, canonically a vowel, constitutes a peak in the curve of audibility that is preceded (onset) and/or followed (coda) by a sequence of segments (none or more consonants), with progressively decreasing sonority values. The nucleus and coda are sometimes lumped together to form what is called the rhyme. By applying these principles, the syllable is a speech unit of rhythmic organization, although other authors disagree, stating that the syllable should not be seen in parts but as a whole.

The modification made to the Rule 3 reached words like "exceto", which the original syllabification follows the orthography (<ex-ce-to>). The letter <x> represents the most variable consonant sound in Portuguese. Its pronunciation depends on the letters before and after it. In this context, [13] suggested that the phonology conditional statement: <xc> → [s] is needed for the <xc> combination, to prevent other rules from forming a doubled sound [ss]. Therefore, the Rule 3 was modified to keep the consonantal sequence <xc> in the same syllable (<e-xce-to>).

The Rule 4 is a discussion of consonants not followed by vowel (or voiceless consonants). On the original rule, the voiceless consonant is joined to the next syllable (e.g. "advogar" <a-dvo-gar>). Although the existence of an empty nucleus is hypothesized [13] (i.e. the word is in actually pronounced with an additional syllable, like "adivogar"), this work chose to follow the orthography and other studies [6], and kept the voiceless consonant in the same syllable (e.g. "advogar" <ad-vo-gar>).

The group formed by the Rules 6 to 20 treats the syllables that begin with consonants. Initially, it was observed that uncommon words were not correctly separated by the Rule 13 (e.g. "acampsia" <a-campsia>). Thus, the nasal consonants were added to the original condition in order to solve these faults. As consequence, the exemplified syllabic splitting was updated to <a-camp-si-a>. A conditional statement was also added to treat hiatus formed by the grapheme sequence <ui>, like in the verb "fluir" <flu-ir>). The proposed Rule 15 follows the same logic applied to the Rule 4 with respect to the voiceless consonants. For instance, the syllabic splitting defined for the word "captar" is <cap-tar>, instead of <ca-ptar>, as presented in [20].

Finally, the Rule 19 was improved to treat specific hiatus (vowel + vowel) not considered in the analyses made by [20] and [16]. This rule correctly handled the hiatus present in the words 'campeonato' <cam-pe-o-na-to>, 'joelho' <jo-e-lho>, and 'israelense' <is-ra-e-len-se>, for example. In turn, [16,20] assumed these hiatus as diphthongs and mistakenly maintained them in the same syllable. Since this kind of vocalic sequence has a strong presence in the Portuguese lexicon, this modified rule is an important contribution of this work.

Regarding the algorithm for determining the stressed vowel, it is based on the set of rules cited in Sect. 3.1. The 29 rules were implemented in hierarchical order (the general case rule was the last one) and the output character (i.e. the stressed vowel) is used as input to the splitting rules.

3.3   Label Generator

In order to convert the utterance information of a given sentence into contextual labels, a label generator script was implemented in Java. The utterance information corresponds to the basic text knowledge (i.e. G2P conversion; syllabication; stress determination; and part-of-speech) which is input by the system in order to train acoustic models and generate speech.

The contextual factors employed by this work were derived from those used in the HMM-based BP TTS system developed by [15]. They contain phone, syllable, word, and phrase level features, such as position of current phone in current syllable, whether or not current syllable is stressed, number of syllables and words in the phrase, etc. The contextual labels include all this information in a phone-by-phone basis. In other words, for each phone of the input utterance information the whole set of features related to the respective phone is included into the corresponding label. The idea is the same for the other levels. However, the script offered by [15] does not contain a tool to convert utterance information into contextual labels. Therefore, a label generator was implemented.

3.4   Speech Corpus

The developed speech corpus employed to train the models has data from an adult male speaker with 1,000 phonetically balanced sentences described in [8]. It corresponds to 1.6 h of audio, where the average duration of each sentence is approximately five seconds. None manual phonetic alignment of the database was carried out. The used sampling rate was 16 kHz and each sample was represented with 16 bits. The recordings were performed on computers using common (cheap) desktop microphones and the acoustic environment was not controlled.

4   Application Programming Interface

While trying to promote the widespread development of applications based on speech technologies, the authors noted that it was not enough to make available resources such as statistical models. These resources are useful for speech scientists but most programmers demand an easy-to-use API. Hence, it was necessary to complement the documentation and code that is part of the hts-engine software package [4], which has been implemented under the HTS project to synthesize speech waveform from HMMs. The hts-engine software has its own API, which is for C/C++ programming. However, in order to gain flexibility with respect to the operating system, a simple API was proposed to allow the real-time control of the hts-engine component, via Java Native Interface (JNI), as well as the language processing module and the audio interface. As shown in Fig. 2, the application interacts with the synthesizer through the API.

The proposed API [2] consists of a Java archive referred to as *UFPAT2S.jar*. This file exposes to the application a set of methods that are described in Table 1. The *UFPAT2S* class converts the utterance information of a given sentence into contextual labels [15], using the developed NLP tools. It also enables the application to control aspects of the synthesizer. First, the application initializes the engine and loads the trained models to be used from files using a given directory path. Then, the *convertTextToSpeechFile* method receives the sentence to be synthesized and performs the procedure of synthesis of the built label string into the correspondent speech waveform (array of short integers). Finally, the *speakAudioFile* method is employed to play the audio.

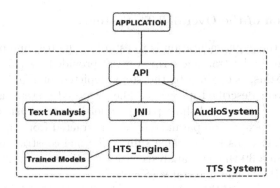

Fig. 2. In the designed architecture, the API is used for easing the task of driving hts-engine on a Java-based desktop runtime environment.

Table 1. Main API methods.

Method	Basic description
initializeTts()	Initialize engine
convertTextToSpeechFile()	Synthesize speech from strings
speakAudioFile()	Play the audio file generated
finalizeTts()	Free engine

5 Experimental Results

5.1 Evaluation Metrics

The quality of synthetic speech can be measured by using two factors: intelligibility and pleasantness [24]. Intelligibility is an objective metric that indicates how accurately spoken sentences have been received by the user, and was measured by comparing transcription and reference messages. In other words, the subject listens to a set of synthetic phrases and speaks what he/she heard. Then, the so-called word error rate (WER) is calculated by:

$$WER = \frac{D + S + A}{P} \times 100\%, \tag{1}$$

where D, S, and A mean the number of deleted, substituted, and added words extracted from the speech of the subject, respectively, and P corresponds to the number of words in the reference message. Pleasantness was measured by collecting user opinions. In this sense, the mean opinion score (MOS) was used to measure subjectively the quality of the generated speech. It gives a numerical indication of the perceived quality of the media received ranging from 1 to 5, 1 being the worst.

5.2   Evaluation of the Overall TTS System

The purpose of the experimentation is to establish the baseline performance. A modified version of the training script rev.2.2 provided by [15] was employed to train the HMMs, according to the steps depicted in Fig. 1 and using the linguistic resources described in Sect. 3. The proposed system uses a set of 40 phones (including silence and short pause models), as the basic acoustic units. The spectrum and excitation parameters were extracted from the speech corpus at every 5 ms (i.e. 5 ms is the frame shift). The mel-cepstral coefficients were obtained through a 39-th order analysis with the utilization of 25 ms Blackman windows. Each HMM had five states ($S = 5$).

After training the HMMs, objective and subjective evaluations were conducted in order to compare the current synthetic voice with two publicly available BP synthesizers: SVOX (com.svox.classic - Luciana Voice v.3.1.4) and Google Text-to-Speech female voice (com.google.android.tts). For speech synthesis, this work adopted the hts-engine rev.1.05 (br.ufpa.ufpat2s). To perform the test, a total of ten phonetically balanced sentences which were not used to train the referred system were extracted from the first subset of phrases listed in [5].

In parallel, a web form was developed in order to streamline the evaluation procedure. In this form, the subject listens the ten test sentences one at a time and gives a score for the speech quality, from bad (1) to excellent (5), according to the MOS. The subject also has to type the sentence he/she heard. These data are used to calculate the WER. A total of 30 subjects (native speakers of BP) were selected to fill out the form. Since the intention was to evaluate the overall quality of the voices from the viewpoint of the general user, the chosen listeners had no training and were not familiarized with the speech processing area.

Each test sentence was played for the subject only once being synthesized by one of the softwares. The order of the sentences was randomly chosen for each participant as well as the software that synthesizes each phrase. However, the equal sharing of sentences among them was guaranteed (i.e. considering all the

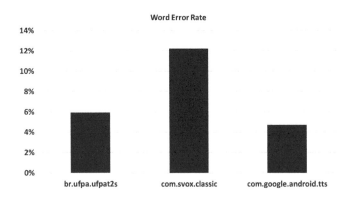

Fig. 3. Overall result of the WER test comparing the proposed BP voice with two other TTS systems.

interviews, the phrase #1 was played 30 times - ten times per software - and so on). The WER and MOS results are showed in Figs. 3 and 4, respectively.

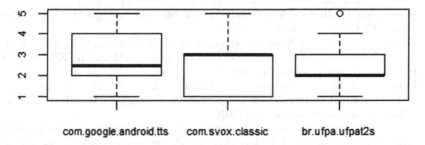

Fig. 4. Overall result of the MOS test comparing the proposed BP voice with two other TTS systems

6   Conclusion

Even still remain many limitations for the adoption of TTS systems in large scale on BP, especially in the academy, this work showed that the development of the HMM-based system can be very useful because requiring less effort for the development of acoustic models with a good quality, using a training approach semi-supervised and semi-automated. By other hands, this technique can also improve variability of speakers available since it can use poor recording databases and a more limited number of sentences for training. Besides the developed NLP tools and resources, a Java implementation example using the API and the scripts employed to train the HMM-based acoustic model are publicly available [2]. Future work includes the use of the deep neural networks (DNNs) to perform speech synthesis in the Portuguese language.

References

1. Dicionário Online de Português. (2018). http://www.dicio.com.br/
2. Grupo falabrasil (2018). https://goo.gl/EWcfdg
3. HTS (2018). http://hts.sp.nitech.ac.jp/
4. HTS Engine (2018). http://hts-engine.sourceforge.net/
5. Alcaim, A., Solewicz, J.A., de Morais, J.A.: Frequência de ocorrência dos fones e listas de frases foneticamente balanceadas para o português falado no Rio de Janeiro. Revista da Sociedade Brasileira de Telecomunicacoes **7**(1), 23–41 (1992)
6. Braga, D., Coelho, L., Resende Jr., F.G.V.: A rule-based grapheme-to-phone converter for TTS systems in European Portuguese, pp. 141–156 (2007)
7. Braga, D., Silva, P., Ribeiro, M., Dias, M.S., Campillo, F., Garc'a-Mateo, C.: Hélia, Heloisa and Helena: new HTS systems in European Portuguese, Brazilian Portuguese and Galician. In: International Conference on Computational Processing of the Portuguese Language, PROPOR 2010 (2010)

8. Cirigliano, R.J.R., Monteiro, C., Barbosa, F.L., Resende Jr., F.G.V.R., Couto, L.R., de Morais, J.A.: Um conjunto de 1000 frases foneticamente balanceadas para o português brasileiro obtido utilizando e a abordagem de algoritmos genéticos. Anais do Simpósio Brasileiro de Telecomunicações (SBrT) (2005)
9. Collischonn, G.: Introdução a Estudos de Fonologia do Português Brasileiro. Porto Alegre: EDIPUCRS, pp. 95–126 (2005)
10. Costa, E., Monte, A., Neto, N., Klautau, A.: Um Framework para Desenvolvimento de Sistemas TTS Personalizados no Português do Brasil. In: XXX Simpósio Brasileiro de Telecomunicações (2012)
11. Couto, I., Neto, N., Tadaiesky, V., Klautau, A., Maia, R.: An open source HMM-based text-to-speech system for Brazilian Portuguese. In: 7th International Telecommunications Symposium (2010)
12. Dutoit, T., Pagel, V., Pierret, N., Bataille, F., Vrecken, O.V.D.: The MBROLA project: towards a set of high-quality speech synthesizers free of use for noncommercial purposes. In: Proceedings of ICSLP 1996, Philadelphia, vol. 3, pp. 1393–1396 (1996)
13. Faria, A.: Applied Phonetics: Portuguese Text-to-Speech. Technical report, University of California (2003)
14. Maciel, A., Carvalho, E.: Integration and evaluation of an HMM-based text-to-speech system to FIVE. In: 19th International Conference on Systems, Signals and Image Processing, IWSSIP 2012 (2012)
15. Maia, R., Zen, H., Tokuda, K., Kitamura, T., Resende, F.: An HMM-based Brazilian Portuguese speech synthetiser and its characteristics. J. Commun. Inf. Syst. **21**, 58–71 (2006)
16. Monte, A., Ribeiro, D., Neto, N., Cruz, R., Klautau, A.: A rule-based syllabification algorithm with stress determination for Brazilian Portuguese natural language processing. In: 17th International Congress of Phonetic Sciences, pp. 1418–1421 (2011)
17. Barbosa, P., et al.: Aiuruete: a high-quality concatenative text-to-speech system for Brazilian Portuguese with demisyllabic analysis-based units and hierarchical model of rhythm production. In: Proceedings of the Eurospeech 1999, pp. 2059–2062 (1999)
18. Schröder, M., Trouvain, J.: The German text-to-speech synthesis system MARY: a tool for research, development and teaching. Int. J. Speech Technol. **6**, 365–377 (2001)
19. Silva, D., de Lima, A., Maia, R., Braga, D., de Moraes, J.F., de Moraes, J.A., Resende Jr., F.G.: A rule-based grapheme-phone converter and stress determination for Brazilian Portuguese natural language processing. In: VI International Telecommunications Symposium (2006)
20. Silva, D.C., Braga, D., Resende Jr., F.G.V.: Separação das Silabas e Determinação da Tonicidade no Português Brasileiro. In: XXVI Simpósio Brasileiro de Telecomunicações, SBrT 2008 (2008)
21. Siravenha, A., Neto, N., Macedo, V., Klautau, A.: Uso de Regras Fonológicas com de terminação de Vogal Tônica para Conversão Grafema-Fone em Português Brasileiro. In: 7th International Information and Telecommunication Technologies Symposium (2008)
22. Souza, D., Saturnino, L., Maciel, A.: A portability evaluation of Brazilian Portuguese voice produced with MARY TTS. In: 2014 International Conference on Systems, Signals and Image Processing (IWSSIP) (2014)
23. Taylor, P.: Text-To-Speech Synthesis. Cambridge University Press, Cambridge (2009)

24. Turunen, M.: Speech application design and development. Technical report (2004)
25. Yoshimura, T., Tokuda, K., Masuko, T., Kobayashi, T., Kitamura, T.: Simultaneous modeling of spectrum, pitch and duration in HMM-based speech synthesis. In: Proceedings of EUROSPEECH, vol. 5, no. 98, pp. 2347–2350 (1999)
26. Zen, H., Tokuda, K., Black, A.W.: Statistical parametric speech synthesis. Speech Commun. **51**(11), 1039–1064 (2009)

Machine Learning Approach
for Automatic Short Answer Grading:
A Systematic Review

Lucas Busatta Galhardi$^{(\boxtimes)}$ (iD) and Jacques Duílio Brancher (iD)

Computer Science Department, State University of Londrina, Londrina, PR, Brazil
{lucasbgalhardi,jacques}@uel.br

Abstract. In this systematic review, we investigate the automatic short answer grading (ASAG) field, which focuses on assessing short natural language responses to questions in an automatic way. Short answers have been recognized as a tool to perform a deeper assessment of the student's knowledge than, for example, multiple choice questions. Automatically scoring short responses can be used as an important resource to the educational field, where the student's answers can be easily, fairly and quickly evaluated for feedback purposes in, for instance, massive open online courses, in which precision and agility are required. We conducted the research by including only works that employed machine learning methods in order to solve the problem. The final selection considering all criteria selected 44 papers reporting different ASAG systems. Those studies were analyzed by answering the proposed research questions, extracting: the nature of datasets, used natural language processing and machine learning techniques, features selected to create the models and the results obtained from their systems' evaluation.

Keywords: Automatic grading · Short answers · Machine learning
Systematic review

1 Introduction

Different tools as VLEs (Virtual Learning Environments), MOOCs (Massive Open Online Courses) and CBA (Computer-Based Assessment) have recently improved their popularity as they provide a new resource for teachers so they can define and manage their didactic resources and expose multimedia contents to help students in their learning process. In addition, these environments can have assessment systems that can support teachers in evaluating many students.

In their learning process, students will have to experience evaluations to demonstrate their acquired knowledge. However, teachers usually find the task of assessing respondents' answers very time-consuming. Also, students may have to wait for a long time to receive feedback on their responses and, when they finally get it, the grade can be different from another classmate's, who has given a very similar answer [13,16].

© Springer Nature Switzerland AG 2018
G. R. Simari et al. (Eds.): IBERAMIA 2018, LNAI 11238, pp. 380–391, 2018.
https://doi.org/10.1007/978-3-030-03928-8_31

Computer-based assessment came to address these issues and improve other aspects of learning by automating the evaluation process. Some of the benefits of automatic assessments are: criteria is formalized, can provide faster feedback to both teacher and student, can save professors' time so they can use it to work better, and allows teachers to easily follow the class performance [1, 7].

There are many different types of questions used to evaluate students. In this work, the focus of interest is in short answers. In addition to the answer length, short answers are written in some natural language and recalls to external knowledge outside the question statement. Important to state that short answers differ from essays as the last can have from two paragraphs to several pages, the evaluation focus is on the writing style and it has a more open scope [1].

To the best of our knowledge, there are six literature reviews in the automatic short answer field. However, two of them [14, 18] have essay systems along with the short answer ones. [3] reviews only studies that used an Information Extraction approach for ASAG. The other three [1, 15, 20] reviews only automatic short answer grading systems and without restrictions on the approach, especially [1] that has the most recent and comprehensive review. Despite all these reviews, this work proposes a systematic approach for conducting the literature review based on [4] guidelines. Also, this paper is limited to review only studies that used machine learning (ML) approaches to solve ASAG, as ML is indicated to be the new trend for ASAG [1].

This paper is organized following the steps of a systematic review [4]. In Sect. 2 the methodology of the research is presented, alongside with its planning and conduction. Section 3 shows the results obtained, answering the research questions. Finally, the conclusions of the work can be seen in Sect. 4.

2   Methodology

According to [4], systematic reviews can identify, evaluate and interpret all available research concerning a specific research question or topic area. It can present a fair review of the research topic by using a rigorous, trustworthy and auditable methodology. The process defines a research protocol which researchers have to follow when conducting the research. The detailed and replicable aspects of systematic reviews are their main advantage since other researchers can follow the conducted process and even repeat the research obtaining the same results (considering same period). Common steps in this kind of reviews are: Planning, Conducting and Reporting.

2.1   Planning

The planning stage of a systematic review creates the review protocol, which specifies the methods that will be used before starting the review. Such early definition helps researchers avoid a biased process [4].

This systematic review seeks to study, explore and understand the current state-of-the-art of automatic short answer grading with focus on works that used machine learning approaches to handle ASAG. The elaborated research questions to address the review objective are: **RQ1:** "What is the nature of datasets?", **RQ2:** "Which natural language processing and machine learning techniques are used?", **RQ3:** "What are the selected features?" and **RQ4:** "What are the achieved results?".

The sources of this systematic review are the following nine online databases: *LearnTechLib, Microsoft Research, ScienceDirect, IEEE Xplore Digital Library, ACM Digital Library, Scopus, Springer, Semantic Scholar* and *Keele University Library.*

Some preliminary research was made to determine the most used words for the subject matter. Similar words were grouped and a search string using boolean operators was created and refined using one of the online databases until it was considered good despite all the possibilities that those keywords creates. The search string composed by the keywords and synonyms is:

("automatic assessment" OR "automatic scoring" OR "automatic marking" OR "automatic grading") AND (short OR "short answer" OR "free text" OR free OR text) AND (response OR question OR answer)

The Inclusion (I), Exclusion (E) and Quality (Q) criteria applied to each reviewed work is detailed in Table 1. Filtering of papers were performed strictly considering these criteria.

Table 1. Criteria

Type	Criteria	Type	Criteria
I	Studies written in English	E	Studies written in another language than English
I	Article, Conference or Methodology papers	E	Studies that do not match the research questions
I	Studies relevant to the subject matter	E	Papers about the same study or system
E	Secondary studies	Q	Are most of the research questions answered?
E	Semi automatic approaches	Q	Is the research methodology properly exposed?
E	Studies that assess essay length answers	Q	Are all the used techniques properly described?

2.2   Conducting

In this stage, the defined search string was used to perform the search in the nine online databases. The results were exported from the databases in some bibliography reference format like bibtex, RIS or CSV. The sum of the retrieved results from the nine databases was 6789. From those papers, 1562 consisted of duplicated papers due to papers that are in more than one online database. The large initial number of results is due to the broad range that the string creates. The search string fits good for getting wanted results, but it also gets other areas of research like medicine. For instance, one possible form that the search string can assume is "automatic scoring short response" which can refer to analyses about the performance of medical tools for measuring short body responses like stimulus or impulses.

In sight of the 5227 remaining papers, we applied the inclusion, exclusion and quality criteria in three levels. First, the inclusion and exclusion criteria were applied only in the title and keywords (and abstract if necessary), which returned 182 papers. These were related with the research area but not necessarily addressing all criteria. In the second stage, the title, keywords and abstract were carefully read to identify relevant studies. That stage left 112 remaining papers, which were all downloaded with the exception of papers that we did not have access to (five). These 107 papers were read using a skimming approach, passing by the title, abstract, introduction and section and sub-section headings. The results, figures and references were also glanced through to determine if the paper would pass to the next step, which resulted in 75 remaining papers.

Among the 75 studies, we selected only the papers that used a machine learning approach to handle ASAG. We did so by looking at each paper's abstract and introduction and searching for keywords like *"machine learning"*, *feature*, *classifier*, *regression* and similar, which left us with 18 papers.

Knowing that due to the nature of the field a variety of keywords could be used in the studies even though not being present in those 18 papers, we looked up for studies using the machine learning keywords in the six identified review papers mentioned in the introduction (Sect. 1). We gathered 26 more papers by looking in their references and 14 more looking at papers that cite those reviews in Google Scholar or in the references of the 14 recently acquired papers (from 2014 to 2016), which left us with 58 papers. Then, the remaining 58 papers were fully read in order to apply the quality criteria and at the same time do the data extraction step. After the quality filter, the number of papers was finally established in 44 as seen in Table 2. From these 44 studies, the answers of the research questions were obtained, the data was summarized and the results created.

Table 2. Selected Papers (IDs and References)

ID	Reference	ID	Reference	ID	Reference
1	[Rosé et al. 2003]	16	[Peters and Jankiewicz 2012]	31	[Higgins et al. 2014]
2	[Pulman and Sukkarieh 2005]	17	[Sil et al. 2012]	32	[Aldabe et al. 2015]
3	[Makatchev and VanLehn 2007]	18	[Dzikovska et al. 2012]	33	[Sakaguchi et al. 2015]
4	[Nielsen et al. 2008]	19	[Madnani et al. 2013]	34	[Nye et al. 2015]
5	[Wang et al. 2008]	20	[Levy et al. 2013]	35	[Luo et al. 2015]
6	[Lee et al. 2009]	21	[Heilman and Madnani 2013]	36	[Sorour et al. 2015]
7	[Sukkarieh 2010]	22	[Jimenez et al. 2013]	37	[Ramachandran et al. 2015]
8	[HOU and TSAO 2011]	23	[Bicici and van Genabith 2013]	38	[Zesch and Heilman 2015]
9	[Mohler et al. 2011]	24	[Gleize and Grau 2013]	39	[Zhang et al. 2016]
10	[Meurers et al. 2011a]	25	[Ott et al. 2013]	40	[Magooda et al. 2016]
11	[Meurers et al. 2011b]	26	[Kouylekov et al. 2013]	41	[Sultan et al. 2016b]
12	[Zbontar 2012]	27	[Horbach et al. 2013]	42	[Roy et al. 2016]
13	[Tandalla 2012]	28	[Leeman-Munk et al. 2014]	43	[Liu et al. 2016]
14	[Conort 2012]	29	[Gomaa and Fahmy 2014]	44	[Sultan et al. 2016a]
15	[Jesensky 2012]	30	[Moharreri et al. 2014]		

3   Results

In this section, the results of the systematic review are presented. The next subsections answers to the research questions defined in Sect. 2.1. In the remainder of this work, references to works from Table 2 are made by the following way: (ID) (e.g. (16) or (20, 21, 22)). When referring to the number of papers that used a specific technique, they are presented in this way: technique {Number}.

3.1   RQ1: Nature of Datasets

There is a great variety in the nature of datasets used by each reviewed paper. They vary in many aspects such as in the topic of the questions, language, student characteristics, grading scale, answers average size and the number of questions, answers and reference answers.

We identified 28 different datasets among the 44 reviewed papers. Some works evaluates in more than one dataset and some evaluates in one of the six publicly available datasets, released to stimulate new researches in the ASAG field. In 2011, three datasets were published: the Texas [12][1] and the CREE and CREG from the CoMic project [9,10][2]. In 2012 and 2013, two ASAG competitions took place, highly increasing the number of researches on the field. They were the 2012 Automated Student Assessment Prize (ASAP) from the Kaggle website[3] and the SemEval 2013 Task 7, the Joint Student Response Analysis and Eighth Recognizing Textual Entailment Challenge, who released two datasets, Beetle and SciEntsBank [2][4].

Regarding the subject matter of the questions, science related topics are the most common (57%) in the studies. Some studies only reports generic science (D6) whereas some specify like Scientific Inquiry (43), Biology (30), Physics (39) and Electronics (D5). Another greatly used kind of question is the reading comprehension type, present in 21% of the datasets (19, 33, D2). Computer Science related topics are also present (11%) in some works dealing with programming basic concepts, introductory and formal language content (8, 35, D1). Other topics comprise of Philosophy (29), US citizenship test (38) and interdisciplinary content (D4).

Concerning the language of the datasets, 75% of them are in English. The other 25% are distributed between Chinese (5, 6), Arabic (29, 40), Japanese (35), Hindi (42) and German (D3).

The respondents' educational level is reported in 89% of the papers. From those, 56% are in school as some report being in "middle school", "high school", "grade x to y" or the students' age. The other large group (36%) is in college, usually without specified age or year. Two works also deal with Second (Foreign) Language Studies (in English and German, (D2, D3)).

---

[1] http://web.eecs.umich.edu/~mihalcea/downloads.html.

[2] www.uni-tuebingen.de/en/research/core-research/collaborative-research-centers/sfb -833/section-a-context/a4-meurers/software-resources-and-corpora.html.

[3] www.kaggle.com/c/asap-sas.

[4] www.cs.york.ac.uk/semeval-2013/task7/index.php%3Fid=data.html.

The number of questions present in the 28 datasets varies between 1 (1, 6) and 482 (39) prompts. Usually works with less questions have more answers and works with more questions have less answers. The number of answers per question is distributed in this way: 18% have up to 12 answers, 32% have between 12 and 99 (dozens), the greater part (36%) have hundreds of answers and 14% of the works have more than 1000 answers (the maximum being 2295 (D4)).

The number of reference answers is not reported in one third of the works. Most studies used 1 (sometimes more) reference answers for comparisons with the students' ones. Some works does not make use of reference answers and some describe the use of concepts (a very short sentence (1, 3, 5, 7, 33)).

The grading scale is reported in three possible formats: number of matches, a range of points or the number of classes. Some datasets have more than one grading scale for the same questions. Two, three, four and five points or classes correspond to the majority of works (D1, D2, D3, D4, D5, D6). Some have a 10 point scale (6,29) and one isolated work has a 30 point range scale (5).

Only half the studies reports the responses' length. They are presented in terms of average number of words, sentences, tokens, lines or a written estimate (like "from short verb phrases to several sentences", "from a couple of words to several sentences", "up to around five lines" and "one to few sentences" (2, 4, 28, D3)). The number of sentences varies from 1 to 7 and the number of words from 7 to 63 in average.

3.2 RQ2: Natural Language Processing Techniques

In order to model answers in easier ways for the computer to interpret them, some Natural Language Processing (NLP) techniques are used. They are employed in the prepossessing stage to prepare the answers for the feature extraction. A reasonable number of different techniques are used in the reviewed studies to perform this step.

Not all works describe using NLP for preprocessing and we can assume that either they did not use these techniques or considered them not sufficiently relevant to report. We found the use of more than 10 different techniques among the 44 works. The basic and self-explained are: punctuation, numbers and other symbols removal, acronym expansion, sentence segmentation, case normalization and tokenization.

Besides these essential techniques, we have some more that aggregates value to the answer by acting in the lexical, syntactical or semantic level. Techniques applied considering only the words by themselves are stopword removal (to not account for too common words {12}), spelling correction (to increase the chances of matches with another words {14}) and stemming and lemmatization (two processes to shorten words by reducing their morphological variance in order to increase matches between words {17 and 10}).

Syntactically, part-of-speech is usually {18} performed to account for the syntactic role of each word in the sentence. To improve this technique, entities with more than one word can be tagged together as a single word, using chuncking, present in {6} works. Also, chuncking helps this process by identifying structures inside the sentence that can be grouped. Simple part-of-speech tagging would tag "the man" as an article and a noun. Chuncking could identify them as a single entity to be tagged. Also, the reviewed works performs syntactic parsing {16} to identify important structural aspects of sentences.

Finally, in the semantic level, the reviewed works uses mainly two techniques. The first is Semantic Role Labeling (17, 33), a process that assigns labels to the roles that words represent in sentences considering their semantic aspect. The another technique is to use WordNet (9, 25, 27, 37), a semantic network, to retrieve semantic synonyms for the words in the answers, improving their capabilities to match with other answers.

3.3   RQ2: Machine Learning Algorithms

A specific kind of task addressed by machine learning algorithms is the supervised learning, where the computer is presented with a set of example inputs and outputs and the challenge of the algorithm is to discover a general rule that models the maximum number of world samples. Real world problems are not easily classified and thus the goal is to reach as close to 100% accuracy as possible.

In ASAG, machine learning is used to solve a classification or regression problem, usually using supervised learning. The model is built upon the answers of students and the correspondent grades assigned by a teacher. The objective is to predict which score should be assigned to a new answer. By collecting the data and building and evaluating the model, an automatic short answer grading system can be built and be ready to use with some specific degree of confidence.

Four different approaches were identified in the selected papers. Firstly, three works used Artificial Neural Networks (15, 35, 39) and one used Deep Belief Networks (40), algorithms inspired by the neural connexions of the human brain. Secondly, one work (36) approached the ASAG task as an unsupervised learning, using K-Means to find clusters of answers.

Then, the most common approach found was to used a classification or regression algorithm to build the model. The ones used were the following: Support Vector Machine {24}, Decision Tree {9}, Logistic Regression {7}, Ridge Regression {6}, Naive Bayes {5}, K-Nearest Neighbors {5} and Linear Regression {2}. Finally, in order to boost the results, several papers reported the use of ensemble learning algorithms: Stacked Generalization {7}, Random Forests {6}, Gradient Boosting Machine {6}, Bagging {3} and Adaptive Boosting {1}.

3.4   RQ3: Features

In ASAG, a large number of different features have been used in the literature to improve the results. They can be grouped in three categories: Lexical, Syntactic and Semantic. Each subsequent subsection will explore each of them and present some of the most used and representative features.

Lexical. The most common model used in the reviewed works is Ngrams, with the basic model present in more than 70% of the reviewed studies. This model takes the input text and groups n words together. Considering the phrase "The man fishes on the lake", a bigram would produce: "The man", "man fishes", "fishes on", "on the" and "the lake". Ngrams are not restricted to words but can also be used with letters. In the literature the n of ngrams varies from one to six. A special case of the word ngrams is when n equals 1, which is commonly known as Bag-of-Words (BoW).

Ngrams can use three approaches to be represented as document-term matrices. One will use the simple binary presence (1) or absence (0) of the ngram. Another approach is to count the number of times that the word appears (the term frequency). Finally, the weight of a word can be given by the Term Frequency-Inverse Document Frequency (TF-IDF), a metric of frequency used to penalize general words by decreasing their value.

Some studies use established metrics that have ngrams underneath like BLEU (19, 21, 31, 33) and ROUGE (19). Another growing representation of words as vectors in recent studies is Word2Vec (33, 35, 42, 44). One of its main difference from simple ngrams is in the concept of word embeddings, employed as a dense alternative to ngrams sparse models.

Another group of features are those who uses some metric to measure the lexical similarity between answers. These string similarities measures are created using Cosine, Overlap, Sorensen, Levenshtein, Hamming and similar. Another similarities used in the reviewed works can be seen in [19] survey.

Other greatly used features are text statistics like response's length, count of words, count of unique words, verb counts, number of characters, sentences, word average length and similar.

Syntactic. Representing the syntactical features, reviewed studies uses phrase and dependency ngrams. Phrase ngrams are the combination of the main verb and their noun phrase. Dependency ngrams are made of the syntactical relations between words. These dependencies can be obtained from a natural language parser like Stanford Parser [5]. The usual format is a triple containing two words and their relation dependency. These triples are used as features in 23% of the reviewed works.

Another important syntactic feature is the similarity between student's and reference's answer's part-of-speech tags. PoS tags represent the words' class and what is the behavior of that group in syntactic terms. Therefore, if two answers share many PoS tags they have a similar structure and more likely to be meaning the same.

Semantic. A greatly used approach in the semantic level are knowledge-based features. Present in 25% of the reviewed studies, it is used to calculate similarity between words using a knowledge source. The similarity in this case means the

---

[5] https://nlp.stanford.edu/software/lex-parser.shtml.

semantic properties of the words [8]. The most used source of knowledge similarity is WordNet [11]. WordNet is a lexical database of English words and their part-of-speeches. WordNet also models semantics by grouping and linking words with similar meanings in Synsets. Some similarities measures that can be used in WordNet are Resnik, Lin, Jiang-Conrath, Leacock-Chodorow, Hirst-St.Onge, Wu-Palmer, Banerjee-Pedersen and Patwardhan-Pedersen.

Another group of semantic features is composed by textual entailment (TE). TE consists of judging if one text can be inferred by another text. Some of the reviewed works interpret the ASAG problem as a textual entailment recognition problem (like [17]). One of them is the study of [6] that uses a TE recognition engine: BIUTEE. This tool tries to convert one text to another by applying a series of transformations. This is used in ASAG by making the student answers the test instance and the reference answer the hypothesis. As output, BIUTEE will return numerical entailment confidence values that are used as features. In [5], the EDITS system is used to generate these features.

The last group of semantic information features are the corpus-based similarity measures. They use large corpus to obtain statistical information that can later be used to calculate a relation value between words and documents. Three different similarity measures of this kind were identified in the reviewed works: Latent Semantic Analysis (LSA) (34, 36, 39, 42), Explicit Semantic Analysis (ESA) (9, 20) and "Extracting DIStributionally similar words using CO-occurrences" (DISCO) (29, 40).

3.5   RQ4: Systems' Evaluation

This research question deals with the evaluation of the proposed systems. Each of the 44 reviewed papers describing a specific ASAG methodology was evaluated by the authors on the datasets presented in Subsect. 3.1. Some studies evaluate in only one dataset while others report experiments in more than one. An important difference between researches is the use of private or public datasets.

Different datasets, evaluation metrics and number of classes preclude fair and direct comparisons. In this work, the evaluations of all systems were analyzed, but due to available space, only works that evaluated on public datasets are reported. From the six publicly available datasets presented in this work, only CREE and CREG were left behind due the fact that only one more work evaluates on CREG (with worst results) and none in CREE (only considering the reviewed papers) regarding the original work that introduced the dataset.

In Table 3, the evaluations from systems on public datasets are presented. It is composed with an ID column that refers to the analyzed work from Table 2 and with the evaluation score obtained. The table is divided by dataset and it is in chronological order. Scores of the same dataset uses the same metric, but each dataset has a different metric, presented as follows.

First, we have results for the Texas dataset [12] presented in terms of Pearson's correlation coefficient. The work from Mohler (9) was the first published as the releasing research and in the following years four more works filling our criteria were found and reported comparable results. It is possible to notice that

Table 3. Systems' evaluations

Texas		ASAP-SAS		Beetle UA 5-way		SciEntsBank UA 5-way	
ID	Score	ID	Score	ID	Score	ID	Score
9-Mohler2011	0,518	12-Zbontar2012	0,7711	20-Levy2013	0,448	21-Heilman2013	0,625
37-Ramachandran2015	0,610	13-Tandalla2012	0,7717	21-Heilman2013	0,705	22-Jimenez2013	0,537
40-Magooda2016	0,550	16-Peters2012	0,7653	22-Jimenez2013	0,558	25-Ott2013	0,598
41-Sultan2016	0,630	31-Higgins2014	0,7680	23-Bicici2013	0,547	40-Magooda2016	0,470
44-Roy2016	0,564	37-Ramachandran2015	0,7800	24-Gleize2013	0,505	41-Sultan2016	0,582
		38-Zesch2015	0,6700	25-Ott2013	0,675	44-Roy2016	0,672

a great improvement has been done, with the work of Sultan (41) exceeding the original work by 0,112.

Then, in 2012 the ASAP-SAS competition from Kaggle released a new dataset and the five winners reported methodology papers. In Table 3, the top three performers from the competition are compared to three more works, using mean quadratically weighted Kappa statistics. Higgins (31) suggests that his work did not perform as good as the winner Tandalla (13) because he did not performed any optimizations, especially of the question-specific type, in order to present a more generalized model. Ramachandran (37) recognizes that Tandalla's performance was greatly helped by manually crafted regular expressions to match simple patterns expected by each question. Thus, Ramachandran proposed a technique to automatically generate these regular expressions in order to fully automate the process and compare results, which showed to be a good strategy as it obtained better results.

In 2013, the SemEval Task 7 competition took place as the Joint Student Response Analysis [2], releasing two more public datasets, Beetle and SciEntsBank. In Table 3 weighted averaged F1 scores achieved in the Beetle dataset are presented, considering the five-way task and the Unseen Answers scenario (more details in [2]). Papers from ID 20 to 25 are from the competition itself and only one more work was found evaluating on the Beetle dataset. However, it did not reported their results in a comparable setting. The best results were obtained by Heilman and Ott, far surpassing the others.

Finally, following the SemEval competition, we report results for the SciEntsBank dataset, also in the five-way task, for the Unseen Answers scenario and with weighted averaged F1 scores. In Table 3, the three top performers in the competition are compared to three more recent works. Magooda (40) did not obtained better results from the three best performers, whereas Sultan (41) obtained similar scores. However, Roy (44) obtained a much higher score, using an ensemble technique that combines bag-of-words modeling with similarity measures extracted from answers, in a similar but improved approach from Heilman (21).

4 Conclusions

This work's objective was to perform a systematic review in the research field of automatic short answer grading with works using a ML approach. We began by exposing the ASAG scenario and its importance on the educational field and specially in virtual environments. Then, the research was planned and conducted following systematic review's guidelines. The final selection resulted in 44 papers and four research questions were answered based on them.

We first explored the data used in ASAG research, considering many aspects from the language to number of questions, answers, etc. Then, we looked at which natural language processing and machine learning techniques are the most used in the field. After that, we presented the core of the research, how answers are modeled in order to extract features that can predict their scores. And finally, we showed how researchers evaluated their systems and how they can (or can not) be compared to each other.

All presented results shows the essence and evolution of ASAG research using machine learning methods. Public datasets are available for not too long ago, and research in the field is open to new techniques, datasets and specially to deep learning, that has been recently contributing to a lot of different areas and still very underexplored in ASAG.

References

1. Burrows, S., Gurevych, I., Stein, B.: The eras and trends of automatic short answer grading. Int. J. Artif. Intell. Educ. **25**, 60–117 (2015)
2. Dzikovska, M., et al.: SemEval-2013 task 7: the joint student response analysis and 8th recognizing textual entailment challenge. In: Seventh International Workshop on Semantic Evaluation, pp. 263–274 (2013)
3. Hasanah, U., Permanasari, A.E., Kusumawardani, S.S., Pribadi, F.S.: A review of an information extraction technique approach for automatic short answer grading. In: International Conference on Information Technology, Information Systems and Electrical Engineering (ICITISEE), pp. 192–196. IEEE (2016)
4. Kitchenham, B.: Procedures for performing systematic reviews. Keele, UK, Keele Univ. **33**(2004), 1–26 (2004)
5. Kouylekov, M., Dini, L., Bosca, A., Trevisan, M.: Celi: EDITS and generic text pair classification. In: Second Joint Conference on Lexical and Computational Semantics (*SEM), Volume 2: Proceedings of the Seventh International Workshop on Semantic Evaluation (SemEval 2013), vol. 2, pp. 592–597 (2013)
6. Levy, O., Zesch, T., Dagan, I., Gurevych, I.: UKP-BIU: similarity and entailment metrics for student response analysis. In: Second Joint Conference on Lexical and Computational Semantics, Volume 2: Proceedings of the Seventh International Workshop on Semantic Evaluation (SemEval 2013), vol. 2, pp. 285–289 (2013)
7. Liu, O.L., Rios, J.A., Heilman, M., Gerard, L., Linn, M.C.: Validation of automated scoring of science assessments. J. Res. Sci. Teach. **53**(2), 215–233 (2016). https://doi.org/10.1002/tea.21299
8. Magooda, A., Zahran, M.A., Rashwan, M., Raafat, H., Fayek, M.B.: Vector based techniques for short answer grading. In: International Florida Artificial Intelligence Research Society Conference Ahmed, pp. 238–243 (2016)

9. Meurers, D., Ziai, R., Ott, N., Bailey, S.M.: Integrating parallel analysis modules to evaluate the meaning of answers to reading comprehension questions. Int. J. Continuing Eng. Educ. Life-Long Learn. **21**(4), 355 (2011). https://doi.org/10. 1504/IJCEELL.2011.042793

10. Meurers, D., Ziai, R., Ott, N., Kopp, J.: Evaluating answers to reading comprehension questions in context: results for German and the role of information structure. In: Proceedings of the TextInfer 2011 Workshop on Textual Entailment, pp. 1–9 (2011)

11. Miller, G.A.: Wordnet: a lexical database for English. Commun. ACM **38**(11), 39–41 (1995)

12. Mohler, M., Bunescu, R., Mihalcea, R.: Learning to grade short answer questions using semantic similarity measures and dependency graph alignments. In: Proceedings of the 49th Annual Meeting of the Association for Computational Linguistics: Human Language Technologies, pp. 752–762 (2011)

13. Passero, G., Haendchen Filho, A., Dazzi, R.: Avaliação do uso de métodos baseados em lsa e wordnet para correção de questões discursivas. In: Brazilian Symposium on Computers in Education (Simpósio Brasileiro de Informática na Educação-SBIE), vol. 27, p. 1136 (2016)

14. Pérez-Marín, D., Pascual-Nieto, I., Rodríguez, P.: Computer-assisted assessment of free-text answers. Knowl. Eng. Rev. **24**(04), 353–374 (2009)

15. Roy, S., Narahari, Y., Deshmukh, O.D.: A perspective on computer assisted assessment techniques for short free-text answers. In: Ras, E., Joosten-ten Brinke, D. (eds.) CAA 2015. CCIS, vol. 571, pp. 96–109. Springer, Cham (2015). https://doi. org/10.1007/978-3-319-27704-2_10

16. Santos, J.C.A.D., et al.: Avaliação automática de questões discursivas usando lsa. Universidade Federal do Pará (2016)

17. Sukkarieh, J.Z.: Using a MaxEnt classifier for the automatic content scoring of free-text responses. In: American Institute of Physics Conference Proceedings, pp. 41–48 (2010). https://doi.org/10.1063/1.3573647

18. Valenti, S., Neri, F., Cucchiarelli, A.: An overview of current research on automated essay grading. J. Inf. Technol. Educ. **2**, 319–330 (2003)

19. Vijaymeena, M., Kavitha, K.: A survey on similarity measures in text mining. Mach. Learn. Appl.: Int. J. **3**(2), 19–28 (2016)

20. Ziai, R., Ott, N., Meurers, D.: Short answer assessment: establishing links between research strands. In: Proceedings of the Seventh Workshop on Building Educational Applications Using NLP, pp. 190–200 (2012)

LAR-WordNet: A Machine-Translated, Pan-Hispanic and Regional WordNet for Spanish

Sergio Jimenez$^{(\boxtimes)}$ and George Dueñas

Instituto Caro y Cuervo, Bogotá D.C., Colombia
{sergio.jimenez,george.duenas}@caroycuervo.gov.co
http://www.caroycuervo.gov.co

Abstract. WordNet is one of the most used resources in Natural Language Processing (NLP). However, the only WordNet available for Spanish is mainly representative of Spain and its size is approximately 50 % compared to Princeton's WordNet in English. To address these issues, we automatically translate the Princeton version using lemmas and sentences from all the available corpora annotated with WordNet senses (LAS-WordNet). In addition, we enrich the translated version using lexicons that contain Pan-Hispanic regionalisms extracted from Twitter (LAR-WordNet). The proposed resources were evaluated in the task of Semantic Textual Similarity in Spanish and cross-lingual between Spanish and English. The results showed that LAS-WordNet significantly outperformed the current Spanish WordNet and that the regionalisms added to LAR-WordNet do not hinder its performance. Although the proposed resources are noisier than the current WordNet in Spanish, their size and representativeness make them suitable for many NLP applications.

Keywords: Spanish WordNet · Machine-translated WordNet
WordNet · Semantic textual similarity · Cross-lingual textual similarity

1 Introduction

Princeton's WordNet (PWN) is a free, machine-readable, and large lexical graph in English useful for research and development in Natural Language Processing and Computational Linguistics [9,15]. The construction of such a resource is expensive, involving considerable resources in professional labor, mainly by lexicographers. Similar efforts have been made for other languages under commercial (e.g. EuroWordNet [30]) and open licences (e.g. Open Mutilingual WordNet [5]). The Multilingual Central Repository (MCR) [11] is an open Iberian initiative that includes a Spanish version of approximately half the size of PWN 3.0. That version was preceded by a smaller WordNet in Spanish aligned with PWN 1.6 included in the MultiWordNet initiative [25] and by an even smaller manually

---

Supported by the Asociación de Amigos del Instituto Caro y Cuervo.

G. R. Simari et al. (Eds.): IBERAMIA 2018, LNAI 11238, pp. 392–403, 2018.
https://doi.org/10.1007/978-3-030-03928-8_32

translation attempt [10]. Alternatively, Navigli and Ponzetto (2012) proposed BabelNet [21], a large lexical database similar in structure to WordNet, built by automatic means for more than 250 languages. BabelNet is open for research (prior approval), but not open for modifications, redistribution or business. In this work, we propose a free machine-translated version of PWN for Spanish and an extended version that includes regional words of the Hispanic world.

Oliver and Climent (2012) compared two alternative methodologies for automatic WordNet translation from PWN to another language L [23]. The necessary resources for that are a parallel corpus (in English and L), and WordNet's synset annotations on the English side of the corpus. When these resources are available, the task is reduced to a problem of bilingual text alignment [22], because annotations on the English side can be assigned to words in Spanish through the alignment. The first methodology consist in obtaining the parallel corpus by translating into L an English corpus with synset annotations made by humans using Statistical Machine Translation. The second methodology is to use a parallel corpus and to annotate words on the English side using a Word Sense Disambiguation system. They found that the former methodology is significantly better than the later. Following these results, we gathered all available English corpora with annotations from [27] (and the Princeton's Glosstag corpus) and translated it into Spanish using Google Translate.

In this paper, we describe the methodology used to translate PWN into Spanish and to add regional words. In addition, we propose an experimental evaluation to compare the current Spanish WordNet with the proposed ones. That evaluation aims to provide insights on the trade-off between the correctness and the coverage represented by WordNet of the MCR and ours. As test bed, we used the task of Semantic Textual Similarity (STS)in Spanish and the cross-lingual variation between Spanish and English. In addition, this evaluation provides some ideas about the effect of regional words on the performance of the proposed resources in the STS task.

The rest of the paper is organized as follows. In Sect. 2, we provide the necessary context for understanding this work. In Sect. 3 the proposed method and used data are presented. In Sect. 4, the experimental validation and results are presented. Finally, the results are discussed in Sect. 5 and some concluding remarks are provided in Sect. 6.

2   Background

2.1   WordNet

The key components in WordNet are: the *synsets*, which represent concepts; *lemmas*, which are English words that lexicalize the synsets; and *pointers*, which are semantical relationships either between pairs of synsets or lemmas. The lemmas linked to a synset are synonymous and the polysemous lemmas are linked to several synsets. These elements make up a large graph of hundreds of thousands of nodes (synsets and lemmas) linked by pointers. This graph covers the four types of content words, namely: nouns, verbs, adjectives and adverbs. There are more than 20 types of pointers for semantic relationships like hypernymy (is-a), meronymy (is-part-of), antonymy, etc. WordNet is one of the most used resources for research and development in NLP and several versions and translations to other languages have been proposed [5,11,21,30]. Probably, the success of WordNet is found in psycholinguistic theories stating that human memory exhibits a structure similar to that used in WordNet [16].

2.2   Statistical Machine Translation and Alignment

Statistical Machine Translation (SMT) is a method that provides translations between two languages (source and target) that exploits parallel corpora to translate a given text in a target language. This approach aims to identify patterns in the alignment of the corpus, which serve to produce an approximate translation of a text combining these patterns. Next, this translation is refined by making use of the corpus in the target language. This approach contrasts with the classic approach of the last century of making a deep analysis of the text in the source language, and then, to make a reverse synthesis on the target language. In addition, this approach contrast with the WordNet-based methods used in NLP to address other tasks. These are considered knowledge-based approaches, whereas SMT is essentially a corpus-based approach.

An important component in SMT is alignment, which consist in providing a mapping between words and phrases in the parallel corpus. This mapping is constructed by analyzing token co-occurrence patterns in the two text sequences. Giza++ is one of the most popular tools for this purpose [22].

Recently, Google Translate, probably the most used SMT system, migrated to Neural MT adopting the new deep learning paradigm to produce translations of complete sentences at a time instead of translations based on words and phrases from previous SMT systems [31].

2.3   Regionalism Detection and Meaning Mapping

The identification of regional words (i.e. regionalisms) can be achieved by analyzing the frequency of use of words in a large corpus, whose texts are labeled with the geographical locations where they were produced [6]. In that way, words that show greater use in a few locations are characterized as regionalisms. This approach was broadened by analyzing the geographical distributions of the locations using spatial-autocorrelation [13]. In this approach, the meaning of regionalisms is determined by relating them to their semantically related words in a neural word embedding model [14] obtained from a large corpus in Spanish.

3   Proposed Method

The aim of the method described in the following subsections is to obtain a translation for the PWN in English into Spanish. Basically, we seek to provide

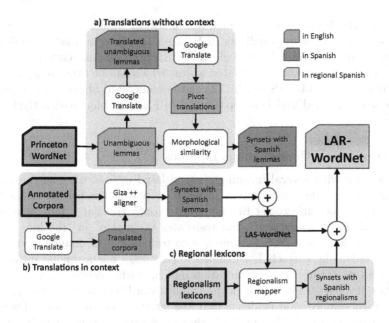

Fig. 1. Block diagram of the process to obtain a translated-regional WordNet from the Princeton's WordNet

translations for the largest possible number of lemmas in English, while preserving the semantic structure of PWN. After that, we want to enrich this translated WordNet with additional lemmas representative of the different dialects of Spanish in the Hispanic world. Figure 1 illustrates the general architecture of the proposed method.

3.1   The Data

The main resource for this study is the PWN version 3.0 [9, 15], whose content we aim to translate into Spanish. That version contains 117,659 synsets lexicalized by 377,592 lemmas in English.

The second necessary resource is annotated corpora, whose words and multi-word expressions have annotations linked to the synsets in PWN 3.0. For that, we used the data collected by Raganato et al. (2017) [27]. That collection contains the SemCor corpus [17] and the OMSTI corpus [29]. In addition, it contains labeled sentences from the following evaluation campaigns: Senseval-2 [8], Senseval-3 task 1 [28], SemEval-07 task 17 [26], SemEval-13 task 12 [20], and SemEval-15 task 13 [19]. We added to that collection the "Princeton Annotated Gloss Corpus" (GlossTag[1]), which provides annotations to the words in the 135,871 definitions and 48,436 examples in PWN.

---

[1] https://github.com/sgjimenezv/wordnet_3_0_glosstag.

Finally, the lexicons of regional words made by Jimenez et al. (2018) [13] were used to provide regionalisms in Spanish for 21 countries[2]. The lexicon for each country contains 5,000 regional words, each one associated to a set of approximately 30 semantically related words, which can be other regionalism or words from the standard Spanish. The data enumerated above is the input for the proposed method and it is represented in Fig. 1 as blocks with thick black borders.

3.2   Translating Unambiguous Lemmas

When a word with several meanings is translated into another language, it is necessary to provide some context in order to obtain the correct translation. For example, the ambiguous English word *"lead"* translates into Spanish as *"leadership"* in *"the race lead"*, but translates as *"plomo"* in *"the lead toy soldier"*. Unlike ambiguous words, context-free translations of unambiguous words are expected to be correct. For example, *"mattress"* has a unique meaning in English, so its out-of-context translation into Spanish, *"colchón"*, is correct. In WordNet, if a particular lemma (word or multi-word) is associated with a single synset, then that is good evidence that the word is not ambiguous. There are 122,262 lemmas (of 377,592) in PWN that meet this condition, which could be translated without the need of contexts. We translated these lemmas into Spanish with the function =GOOGLETRANSLATE(w_1,w_2, "en", "es") in a spreadsheet in Drive[3] during June 2017. To evaluate the quality of these translations we used Spanish as a pivotal language, so they were translated back into English with the same method and compared with the original lemma. In the case of verbs, the preposition "to" was added before the lemma to promote Google Translate to produce translations for their infinitive form.

The method for comparing the original lemmas with the doubly translated lemmas was to represent the lemmas as sets of bigrams of characters. Next, the pair of sets was compared using the Jaccard coefficient. Thus, a lemma whose double translation through Spanish produced the same original lemma in English gets the maximum score of 1. At the other extreme, if two lemmas do not share at least two consecutive characters (bigrams), then they get the minimum score of 0. For example, suppose that the word *"week"* is translated into Spanish and back into English as *"weeks"*. The two lemmas are represented as $A=\{we,ee,ek\}$ and $B=\{we,ee,ek,ks\}$, so $A \cap B=\{we,ee,ek\}$ and $A \cup B=\{we,ee,ek,ks\}$. The Jaccard score is $\frac{|A \cap B|}{|A \cup B|} = 0.75$. Intuitively, we established a filtering threshold of 0.6 for that score obtaining 83,698 translations to their corresponding synset identifiers in WordNet. The component described above is illustrated in Fig. 1(a).

3.3   Translating Lemmas in Context

The context helps to provide correct translations for ambiguous words. For instance, the phrases *"the chair of the conference"* and *"the leg of the chair"*

---

[2] Available at https://www.datos.gov.co/browse?q=regionalismos%20ejemplos.

[3] https://www.google.com/drive/.

provide evidence to determine that the correct translation for *"chair"* in the first sentence is *"presidente"* (position of a person) and *"silla"* (a furniture) in the second. If these phrases contain annotations indicating the associated synset for *"chair"* in both cases, then *"presidente"* and *"silla"* should be suitable translations for these synsets. Basically, this is the approach to obtain translations for lemmas using sentences whose words are annotated with WordNet synsets.

Again, we translated into Spanish all the sentences in the corpora considered (1,040,418 sentences) using Google Translate. Next, the English and Spanish-translated corpora were aligned at word level using Giza++ [22]. Finally, we took the 1,647,712 synset annotations on the English side and obtained their Spanish translations by following the alignments provided by Giza++. This process produced 1,491,592 Spanish translations for 67,583 different synsets. These translations were merged with the translations obtained from the unambiguous lemmas producing a total of 279,314 distinct Spanish translations to 97,960 synsets. This translated WordNet, which we called LAS-WordNet, can be compared with PWN, obtaining 74% of its size with respect to the number of lemmas and 83% of the synsets. The component described above is illustrated in Fig. 1(b).

3.4 Adding Regionalisms

The geographical representativeness of the proposed machine-translated LAS-WordNet depends to a large extent on the English-Spanish parallel corpora used by Google Translate. It is probable that these corpora are not totally representative of the different dialectal variations of Spanish in the Americas due to the underrepresentation of Internet content in many countries of the region. To remedy this situation, we incorporated regional words in Spanish from 21 countries to LAS-WordNet, producing an extended version that we called LAR-WordNet. The regionalisms used came from the lexicons created recently by Jimenez et al. (2018) [13], which were extracted from a large corpus of Twitter. The resource used to associate these regional words to the synsets in LAS-WordNet is based on the sets of semantically-close words associated with each regionalism provided by the lexicons.

The method to make such associations is as follows. First, only the regional words that were not already included in LAS-WordNet were considered. Next, for each of the remaining regionalisms, their sets of semantically related words (approximately 30 words for each regionalism) were compared against the sets of lemmas associated to all synsets in LAS-WordNet. When we found two or more common words in such comparisons, the regionalisms are added as lemmas to their corresponding synsets. Using this method, the number of lemmas in LAR-WordNet reaches to 300,732 compared to the 279,314 lemmas in LAS-WordNet[4]. The component described above is illustrated in Fig. 1(c). Table 1 shows some synsets in PWN represented by their most common English lemma,

---

[4] LAS-WordNet and LAR-WordNet are available at https://www.datos.gov.co/browse?q=wordnet.

some examples of the lemmas included in LAS-WordNet, and the additions made in LAR-WordNet. As expected, a Spanish speaker could recognize that the lemmas of LAS-WordNet correspond to words from the "standard" language, and those of LAR-WordNet reflect different regional variations of the Spanish of the Americas.

Table 1. Examples of the translated lemmas in LAS-WordNet and the added regionalisms in LAR-WordNet

POS	PWN	LAS-WordNet	LAR-WordNet
noun	coat	capa, túnica, abrigo	ruana, casaca, chomba
noun	boy	niño, jóvenes, muchachos	chiquillo, pelaito, pibito, chavo, chaval
noun	girl	niña, muchacha, chica	princesita, chibola, pibita, tipa, chava
noun	bus	bus, autobús, autobuses	pesero, transmilenio, bondi, charabanc
adj.	boring	tedioso, aburrido	infumable, ladillado, cansadora, fome
adj.	fastidious	exigente, fastidioso	cargoso, ñoña, cansón, mierdoso, cansino
verb	work	trabajar, colaborar	brete, labura, chambea, curra
verb	irritate	irritar, molestar	encojona, enerva, encabrona, enfade
adv.	awfully	terriblemente	arrechamente, jodidamente, cabronamente
adv.	suddenly	repentinamente	enseguida, pum, paf

4   Experimental Validation

Since the methods used to build LAS-WordNet and LAR-WordNet are completely automatic, they contain more errors than a human-curated version of WordNet. However, we showed that the sizes of the proposed WordNets are comparable to that of PWN, being considerably larger than the current Spanish WordNet [11]. That greater coverage of the language must be weighed against the higher error rate. This experimental validation aims to determine if the balance between these two factors produce whether a positive, negative, or null combined effect.

To measure the general suitability of a WordNet, we evaluate it through an NLP task where such WordNet plays a central role. If that task has an established and generally accepted method for evaluation, then variations in the resulting performance due to the exchange of different versions of WordNet would reflect the convenience of each version. The NLP task selected for that purpose is Semantic Textual Similarity (STS). This task has been proposed uninterruptedly in the International Workshops on Semantic Evaluation (SemEval)[5] since 2012 to 2017. Those campaigns have produced a large test bed for evaluation and a consensus on the methods to measure performance in STS systems[6].

---

[5] https://en.wikipedia.org/wiki/SemEval.
[6] STS Benchmark http://ixa2.si.ehu.es/stswiki/index.php/STSbenchmark.

To do this, we formatted LAS-WordNet and LAR-WordNet with the same structure used by WordNets included in the Open Multilingual WordNet [5]. This, also means that the proposed WordNets can be used in the popular Natural Language Toolkit (NLTK) [4], easing the construction and evaluation of STS systems based on different WordNets.

4.1 Benchmarks

The STS task is to compare a pair of short texts and determine their degree of semantic equivalence quantitatively. Therefore, no matter what lexical, syntactic or semantic structures are used in the texts, if their meaning is similar, then an STS system would provide a high numerical score. At the other extreme, two unrelated texts in meaning should get a low score.

The gold standards used to evaluate STS systems come from the aggregation of judgments provided by humans for the same task. We collected all the text pairs involving Spanish proposed in SemEval along with their corresponding gold-standard scores of similarity. That is, data from the Spanish-Spanish monolingual and Spanish-English cross-lingual versions. The first five columns in Table 2 provide some details and references of the datasets used.

4.2 The Baseline WordNet for Comparison

The WordNet used to compare the proposed automatically created WordNets is the Spanish WordNet included in the *Multilingual Central Repository* v3.0 [11][7]. The development of this resource involved a considerable and expensive manual effort of hundreds of person-years. This initiative reached coverage on PWN synsets of 50% for Spanish, 39% for Catalan, 26% for Basque, and 8% for Galician. In our results, we identify that version as SPA-WordNet.

4.3 A Simple STS System Based on WordNet for Evaluation

Competitive STS systems are built using a plethora of resources and algorithmic approaches that may include: WordNet, neural embeddings, word alignments, word-sense disambiguation, dependency analysis, part-of-speech tagging, morphological similarity, among many others [1–3,7]. Since our goal is to measure the contribution of a particular WordNet to the task, we build an STS system based solely on WordNet. Basically, we use the simplest lexical similarity function (i.e. *path* [24]), which is combined with the Monge-Elkan formula [12,18] to provide a textual similarity function.

The *path* function is the inverse of the number of nodes in the shortest path between two synsets, ss_1 and ss_2, in the *is-a* hierarchy in WordNet:

$$path(ss_1, ss_b) = \frac{1}{path\_length(ss_1, ss_2) + 1}. \tag{1}$$

---

[7] http://adimen.si.ehu.es/web/mcr/.

This function must be adapted to compare pairs of words instead of pairs of synsets. Let a be a word and SS_a the set of all synsets having a in their lemmas. The lexical similarity between two words is given by:

$$SIM_{LEX}(a,b) = \max_{(i,j) \in SS_a \times SS_b} path(i,j).$$

Let A and B two short texts represented by their corresponding lists of content words (i.e. not stop-words). The textual similarity between A and B can be determined by leveraging the lexical-similarity function SIM_{LEX} using the Monge-Elkan method:

$$SIM_{TEX}(A,B) = \sqrt{\frac{1}{|A|} \sum_{i=1}^{|A|} \left(\max_{j=1}^{|B|} \{SIM_{LEX}(a_i, b_j)\} \right)^2}.$$

Here, $|A|$ is the number of words in A. Note that the SIM_{TEX} function is not symmetrical. Therefore, the final STS function is obtained by symmetrizing SIM_{TEX} as follows:

$$STS(A,B) = SIM_{LEX}(A,B) + SIM_{LEX}(B,A). \tag{2}$$

4.4 Experimental Setup

The proposed experiment consists in testing three STS systems based on Eq. 2 using three different versions of the *path* function (Eq. 1). The difference between these instances of *path* is the version of the WordNet used to determine the path lengths between synsets. These systems are identified as SPA (using the baseline WordNet presented in Subsect. 4.2), LAS (using LAS-WordNet), and LAR (using LAR-WordNet). When the STS is cross-lingual, English words are mapped to synsets using PWN. Each STS system, produced predictions of semantic similarity for each of the 2,650 text pairs in the benchmarks described in Subsect. 4.1. Then, the predictions for each of the 7 datasets are evaluated with their corresponding gold-standard scores using Pearson's correlation r. Finally, the values of r obtained for each dataset are aggregated into a single global score using the weighted average by the number of pairs on each dataset. This weighted average is known to the STS research community as the measure "*mean*". This measure reflects the extent to which an STS system approximates similarity judgments given by humans across several datasets. The scores of *mean* vary between 1 (perfect correlation) to 0 (no correlation).

4.5 Results

Table 2 shows the results of the experiment. The scores for each combination of dataset and STS system corresponds to the Pearson correlation r measured between the predictions made by the systems and the gold standard from the benchmarks. The last row reports the measure *mean* for the three STS systems.

Boldface is used to highlight the best results for each dataset and for the global *mean*.

The first observation is that LAS and LAR exceeded SPA in all datasets. The relative improvements of LAS and LAR with respect to SPA are 16.9% and 17.5%, respectively, which is very significant for a sample size of 2,650. The second observation is that LAR obtained the best results in 6 out of 8 datasets and in the measure *mean*. However, the overall difference between LAS and LAR is negligible.

Table 2. Results obtained by the systems SPA, LAS y LAR in the task of Semantic Textual Similarity. The results correspond to the Pearson correlations between the systems predictions and the gold-standard scores.

Dataset	SemEval	lang.1	lang.2	# pairs	SPA	LAS	LAR
Wikipedia [2]	2014	ES	ES	324	0.5570	0.5738	**0.5883**
News [2]	2014	ES	ES	480	0.7162	0.7231	**0.7272**
Wikipedia [1]	2015	ES	ES	251	0.3569	0.4430	**0.4505**
Newswire [1]	2015	ES	ES	500	0.2915	0.3281	**0.3376**
Track3 [7]	2017	ES	ES	250	0.5061	0.7068	**0.7070**
Track4a [7]	2017	ES	**EN**	250	0.3912	0.6092	**0.6110**
News [3]	2016	ES	**EN**	301	0.6877	**0.7748**	0.7738
Multisource [3]	2016	ES	**EN**	294	0.3895	**0.5286**	0.5075
Total/weighted average (*mean* measure)				2650	0.4926	0.5758	**0.5785**

5 Discussion

The results clearly indicate that both LAS and LAR are better STS systems than SPA for the task. Given the simplicity of these STS systems, it is reasonable to assume that there is no other intervening factor other than the WordNet used that could favor LAS and LAR over SPA. Therefore, we can conclude that the underlying resources of LAS and LAR (i.e. LAS-WordNet and LAR-WordNet) are also preferable for the task compared to SPA-WordNet. In addition, it is reasonable to expect that the difference in performance will occur in other similar NLP tasks such as textual entailment, paraphrase detection, MT evaluation and others.

Regarding the comparison between LAS and LAR, the results show that although LAR outperformed LAS, the difference is not significant. This may be a consequence of the fact that the journalistic and encyclopedic written style used in the texts of the benchmarks is not particularly influenced by regional dialects. However, the small superiority of LAR over LAS allows us conclude that the additional regional words included in LAR do not harm LAS performance.

6   Conclusion

We built two WordNet versions freely available for Pan-Hispanic Spanish using automatic means. Although these resources are subject to inaccuracy, they are preferable to a Spanish WordNet of better quality, manually constructed, but smaller. According to our experimental results, this conclusion applies to the Semantic Textual Similarity (STS) task and possibly to other similar tasks.

Perspectives of future work include strategies to reduce the noise level in automatically built WordNets and the evaluation of other NLP tasks.

References

1. Agirre, E., et al.: Semeval-2015 task 2: Semantic textual similarity, English, Spanish and pilot on interpretability. In: Proceedings of SemEval 2015, pp. 252–263. ACL (2015)
2. Agirre, E., et al.: Semeval-2014 task 10: Multilingual semantic textual similarity. In: Proceedings of SemEval 2014, pp. 81–91. ACL and Dublin City University (2014)
3. Agirre, E., et al.: Semeval-2016 task 1: Semantic textual similarity, monolingual and cross-lingual evaluation. In: Proceedings of SemEval-2016, pp. 497–511. ACL (2016)
4. Bird, S., Loper, E.: NLTK: the natural language toolkit. In: Proceedings of the ACL 2004 on Interactive Poster and Demonstration Sessions, p. 31. ACL (2004)
5. Bond, F., et al.: Open multilingual wordnet. Web page of the resource and project (2013). http://compling.hss.ntu.edu.sg/omw/
6. Calvo, H.: Simple TF·IDF is not the best you can get for regionalism classification. In: Gelbukh, A. (ed.) CICLing 2014. LNCS, vol. 8403, pp. 92–101. Springer, Heidelberg (2014). https://doi.org/10.1007/978-3-642-54906-9_8
7. Cer, D., Diab, M., Agirre, E., Lopez-Gazpio, I., Specia, L.: Semeval-2017 task 1: Semantic textual similarity multilingual and crosslingual focused evaluation. In: Proceedings of SemEval-2017, pp. 1–14. ACL (2017)
8. Edmonds, P., Cotton, S.: Senseval-2: overview. In: The Proceedings of the Second International Workshop on Evaluating Word Sense Disambiguation Systems, pp. 1–5. ACL (2001)
9. Fellbaum, C.: WordNet. Wiley, Hoboken (1998)
10. Fernández-Montraveta, A., Vázquez, G., Fellbaum, C.: The Spanish version of WordNet 3.0. Mouton de Gruyter, Berlin
11. Gonzalez-Agirre, A., Laparra, E., Rigau, G.: Multilingual central repository version 3.0. In: LREC, pp. 2525–2529 (2012)
12. Jimenez, S., Becerra, C., Gelbukh, A., Gonzalez, F.: Generalized Mongue-Elkan method for approximate text string comparison. In: Gelbukh, A. (ed.) CICLing 2009. LNCS, vol. 5449, pp. 559–570. Springer, Heidelberg (2009). https://doi.org/10.1007/978-3-642-00382-0_45
13. Jimenez, S., Dueñas, G., Gelbukh, A., Rodriguez-Diaz, C.A., Mancera, S.: Automatic detection of regional words from twitter for the Pan-Hispanic Spanish (2018, to appear)
14. Mikolov, T., Sutskever, I., Chen, K., Corrado, G.S., Dean, J.: Distributed representations of words and phrases and their compositionality. In: Advances in Neural Information Processing Systems, pp. 3111–3119 (2013)

15. Miller, G.A.: Wordnet: a lexical database for english. Commun. ACM **38**(11), 39–41 (1995)
16. Miller, G.A., Charles, W.G.: Contextual correlates of semantic similarity. Lang. Cogn. Processes **6**(1), 1–28 (1991)
17. Miller, G.A., Chodorow, M., Landes, S., Leacock, C., Thomas, R.G.: Using a semantic concordance for sense identification. In: Proceedings of the workshop on Human Language Technology, pp. 240–243. ACL (1994)
18. Monge, A.E., Elkan, C., et al.: The field matching problem: algorithms and applications. In: KDD, pp. 267–270 (1996)
19. Moro, A., Navigli, R.: Semeval-2015 task 13: multilingual all-words sense disambiguation and entity linking. In: Proceedings of SemEval 2015, pp. 288–297. ACL (2015)
20. Navigli, R., Jurgens, D., Vannella, D.: Semeval-2013 task 12: multilingual word sense disambiguation. In: Proceedings of SemEval 2013. vol. 2, pp. 222–231. ACL (2013)
21. Navigli, R., Ponzetto, S.P.: Babelnet: the automatic construction, evaluation and application of a wide-coverage multilingual semantic network. Artif. Intell. **193**, 217–250 (2012)
22. Och, F.J., Ney, H.: A systematic comparison of various statistical alignment models. Comput. Linguist. **29**(1), 19–51 (2003)
23. Oliver, A., Climent, S.: Parallel corpora for wordnet construction: machine translation vs. automatic sense tagging. In: Gelbukh, A. (ed.) CICLing 2012. LNCS, vol. 7182, pp. 110–121. Springer, Heidelberg (2012). https://doi.org/10.1007/978-3-642-28601-8_10
24. Pedersen, T., Pakhomov, S.V., Patwardhan, S., Chute, C.G.: Measures of semantic similarity and relatedness in the biomedical domain. J. Biomed. Inform. **40**(3), 288–299 (2007)
25. Pianta, E., Bentivogli, L., Girardi, C.: Multiwordnet: developing an aligned multilingual database. 1st GWC. In: Proceedings of the First International Conference on Global WordNet, Mysore, India, pp. 293–302 (2002)
26. Pradhan, S.S., Loper, E., Dligach, D., Palmer, M.: Semeval-2007 task 17: English lexical sample, SRL and all words. In: Proceedings of the 4th International Workshop on Semantic Evaluations, pp. 87–92. ACL (2007)
27. Raganato, A., Camacho-Collados, J., Navigli, R.: Word sense disambiguation: a unified evaluation framework and empirical comparison. In: Proceedings of the 15th Conference of the European Chapter of the ACL. vol. 1, pp. 99–110 (2017)
28. Snyder, B., Palmer, M.: The English all-words task. In: Proceedings of SENSEVAL-3, the Third International Workshop on the Evaluation of Systems for the Semantic Analysis of Text (2004)
29. Taghipour, K., Ng, H.T.: One million sense-tagged instances for word sense disambiguation and induction. In: Proceedings of the Nineteenth Conference on Computational Natural Language Learning, pp. 338–344 (2015)
30. Vossen, P.: Eurowordnet: a multilingual database of autonomous and language-specific wordnets connected via an inter-lingualindex. Int. J. Lexicography **17**(2), 161–173 (2004)
31. Wu, Y., et al.: Google's neural machine translation system: Bridging the gap between human and machine translation. arXiv preprint arXiv:1609.08144 (2016)

Automatic Detection of Regional Words for Pan-Hispanic Spanish on Twitter

Sergio Jimenez[1(✉)], George Dueñas[1], Alexander Gelbukh[2],
Carlos A. Rodriguez-Diaz[1], and Sergio Mancera[1,2]

[1] Instituto Caro y Cuervo, Bogotá D.C., Colombia
{sergio.jimenez,george.duenas,carlos.rodriguez}@caroycuervo.gov.co
[2] Centro de Investigación en Computación, Instituto Politécnico Nacional,
Mexico City, Mexico
gelbukh@gelbukh.com, sergiomanceranom@gmail.com
http://www.caroycuervo.gov.co, http://www.cic.ipn.mx/

Abstract. Languages, such as Spanish, spoken by hundreds of millions of people in large geographic areas are subject to a high degree of regional variation. Regional words are frequently used in informal contexts, but their meaning is shared only by a relatively small group of people. Dealing with these regionalisms is a challenge for most applications in the field of Natural Language Processing. We propose a novel method to identify regional words and provide their meaning based on a large corpus of geolocated 'tweets'. The method combines the notions of specificity (tf-idf), space correlation (HSIC) and neural word embedding (word2vec) to produce a list of words ranked by their degree of regionalism along with their meaning represented by a set of words semantically related and examples of use. The method was evaluated against lists of regional words taken from regional dictionaries produced by lexicographers and from collaborative websites where users contribute freely with regional words. We tested the effectiveness of the proposed method and produced a new resource for 21 Spanish-speaking countries composed of 5,000 regional words per country along with similar words and example 'tweets'.

Keywords: Spanish regionalisms
Automatic regional words detection · Regionalisms meaning
HSIC · TF-IDF · Word2vec

1 Introduction

Most NLP applications for a particular language assume that the language is homogeneous in the geographical territory where it is used. This situation worsens when that language, like Spanish, is spoken in a very extensive and diverse territory. This situation is probably due to the lack of an updated, representative

Supported by Asociación de Amigos del Instituto Caro y Cuervo. S. Mancera was supported by a scholarship given by CONACYT, Mexico.

G. R. Simari et al. (Eds.): IBERAMIA 2018, LNAI 11238, pp. 404–416, 2018.
https://doi.org/10.1007/978-3-030-03928-8_33

and machine-readable source of linguistic differences in the language's territory. In corpus linguistics, a regionalism can be considered as a word that meets two conditions: comparatively, it is more used in a region than in the rest of the territory where the same language is spoken (specificity) and its frequency of use in different places is related to a continuous geographical distribution (spatial correlation). The automatic detection of such regionalisms and their meanings could improve the performance of other NLP tasks, such as word sense disambiguation, language understanding, automatic translation, among others. We can expect that improvement at least in these scenarios: (a) when a common concept like "a bus" is lexicalized in particular regions with different regional words (e.g. *micro* in Peru, *bondi* in Argentina, etc.); (b) when a word refers to concepts that varies from one region to another[1]; and (c) when a word was created in a specific region to define a local concept that is unknown in the rest of the language's territory[2].

As an antecedent to this problem, Calvo (2014) [2] implemented the concept of specificity using the measure *tf-idf* to classify regionalisms in Spanish. He used the snippets returned by the Google search results to expand an initial list of regionalisms using the country code in the URL to determine the country of origin of the text snippets. This approach has two drawbacks. First, the country code in the URL does not guarantee that the text was produced in that country. Second, the geographical distribution of the countries was ignored. This work aims to remedy these problems by collecting a geolocated Twitter corpus, following the trend of current practices in the field of dialectometry [3,7,11]. Unlike the Google search results used by Calvo, Twitter data can be considered as an information source updated, representative, close to oral language, geographically accurate, and large enough to detect regionalisms.

The proposed approach extends Calvo's work by combining the measure *tf-idf* with the HSIC spatial autocorrelation test [6,10] avoiding the need for an initial list of regionalisms. In addition to the detection of regional words, we provide their meanings by associating them with other regional and non-regional words, and also providing a set of sample tweets for each regionalism found. The proposed method was evaluated with different dictionaries of regionalisms and lists of regional words compiled collaboratively in asihablamos.com and diccionariolibre.com. The proposed method produced a new resource that includes the regional words detected together with their semantically closed words, and examples of use, for 21 countries in the Pan-Hispanic world.

The rest of the paper is organized as follows. In Sect. 2, we present the concepts used to construct the proposed approach. Section 3 provides a detailed description of the methods and data used. In Sect. 4, we present the experimental validation. Finally, in Sects. 5 and 6, the results are discussed and some concluding remarks are provided.

---

[1] For example, in some regions of Colombia, the word *galería* refers to a marketplace, but in general Spanish, that word means an art gallery or a covered path.

[2] For example, in Colombia, *ajiaco* refer to a type of soup particular of that country.

2 Background

2.1 Inverse Document Frequency, IDF

IDF is a measure of the specificity of a word in a document collection [13]. In this way, a word that appears in all the documents obtains the minimum value of the measure (that is, zero). In contrast, a word that appears in a single document among n gets the maximum (that is, $\log n$). In our scenario, a document means the corpus compiled for each geographic location. Thus, the IDF of a word w is defined by:

$$IDF(L_w) = \log \frac{n}{df(L_w)}$$

where, $L_w = \{l_1, \cdots l_n\}$ is the list of frequencies of w in the n locations and $df(L_w)$ is the number of locations where w occurred. In an attempt to make the measure robust against noise and given that the number of words in the corpus of each location is considerable, we consider that w occurred in the i-th location only if $l_i > 3$.

2.2 Hilbert-Schmidt Independence Criterion, HSIC

HSIC is a measure capable of evaluating the correlation between two multidimensional and non-linear variables [4]. These non-linearities of the variables are admissible because HSIC is a kernel-based method [6]. Since the representation of each variable in the kernel methods is a square matrix that contains pairwise distances between samples (the Gram matrix), the dimensionality and the original coordinates of the variables become irrelevant. Support for nonlinearities is provided by the so-called "kernel trick", which projects the data from the original input space to a feature space with a greater dimensionality by applying a simple transformation to the inputs of the Gram matrix (for example, raising its inputs to a power). Once the two input variables to be tested are converted into Gram matrices and projected to a feature space, the covariance between the two resulting matrices is the value of the HSIC measure.

Recently, Nguyen and Eisenstein [10] used HSIC to measure the auto-spatial correlation of the geographical coordinates of a set of locations and a linguistic variable associated with each location (for example, the frequency of a word). HSIC proved to be a better alternative for this task compared to traditional approaches such as Moran's I [5], join count analysis [8], and the Mantel Test [12]. A linguistic variable that obtains a high value of HSIC with a set of geographic locations means that it exhibits a regional pattern. It also means that the linguistic variable is a good predictor of the geographical location, that is, a regional word. In practice, the measurement of HSIC between a geographic variable G ($g_1 \ldots g_n$ longitude-latitude pairs) and a linguistic variable L ($l_1 \ldots l_n$ word frequencies paired to the g_i coordinates) is calculated by:

$$\mathrm{HSIC}(G, L) = \frac{\mathbf{tr}(K_G \times H \times K_L \times H)}{n^2}$$

where K_G and K_L are, respectively, the Gram matrices for G and L. H is a centering matrix defined by $H = \mathbb{I}_n - \frac{1}{n}\mathbf{11}_n$, where $\mathbb{I}_n$ is the identity matrix and $\mathbf{11}_n$ is a matrix filled with ones, both of dimensions $n \times n$. Finally, $\mathbf{tr}(\cdot)$ is the trace of the resulting matrix, that is. the sum of the elements in the diagonal (covariance). The Gram matrix K_G is obtained by projecting the pairwise Euclidean distances, $dist(\cdot,\cdot)$, between the n locations with a Gaussian transformation. K_L is obtained analogously. The expressions are:

$$K_G(g_i, g_j) = e^{-\gamma_g dist(g_i, g_j)^2}; \ K_L(l_i, l_j) = e^{-\gamma_l (l_i - l_j)^2}; \ i, j \in 1 \ldots n.$$

In essence, HSIC is a nonparametric test that does not require assumptions about the data. The only parameter is γ_g that can be determined heuristically by the median of the squared pairwise distances, $dist(g_i, g_j)^2$. Similarly, γ_l is the median of the squared differences $(l_i - l_j)^2$. The schematic process for calculating HSIC is depicted in Fig. 1.

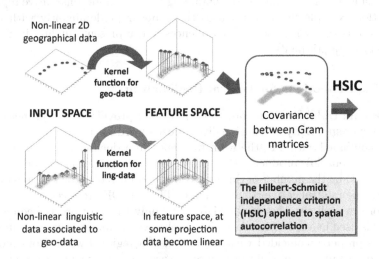

Fig. 1. The Hilbert-Schmidt independence criterion applied to spatial autocorrelation with frequencies of words obtained from a corpus.

2.3 Word2vec Word Embedding

Word2vec is a popular method based on a neural network to obtain a geometric model for the meaning of words from a large corpus [9]. In that model, words are represented as points in a high-dimensional space, usually from 100 to 1000 dimensions. There, the distances between pairs of words reflect their semantic similarity and those distances combined with the direction of the differences reflect semantic relations. Another property, which is still not fully understood, is that the relative positions of the words represent semantic relationships that give the model the ability to make compositional and analogical reasoning.

3   Data and Proposed Method

3.1   Data

The data for this study was collected semi-automatically from the web search interface of Twitter respectfully of their access quotas. We selected 333 cities with more than 100,000 inhabitants in the Pan-Hispanic world. In those locations, a query by the official geographical coordinates of each city specifying a 15 miles radius and Spanish language. When two cities overlapped their query areas, the small one was discarded. The collected tweets were preprocessed by removing URLs, hashtags, references to user names and non-alphabetical words. The size and other features of collected corpus are presented in Table 1. From that corpus we obtained a large database with the number of occurrences of each word for each city. Although by Twitter policies, the corpus can not be published publicly, we made available the word frequencies database[3]. In addition, for the analysis of regionalisms, we ignored any word containing three or more consecutive repeated letters (for example 'holaaaa'), words that appear predominantly with initial capital letters (proper names), and sequences that represent laughter in Spanish (for example 'jajajajjaa').

3.2   Rank Functions for Lexical Regionalism

The IDF and HSIC functions presented in Sect. 2 provide a general measure of the degree of specificity and regionalism of each word in the corpus. The IDF is usually combined with TF, the term frequency in a document (the corpus of a city in our scenario), producing the well-known term weighting scheme TF.IDF. Let $TF(w, i)$ be the number of times the word w occurred at the i-th location. In this way, the multiplicative combination of TF and IDF produces a measure for each word in each city that yields high scores only when a word is frequent in a city and is used in a few cities. As Calvo [2] observed in an intuitive and empirical way, this property coincided with the notion of a regional word. However, IDF can not discriminate regional words in some cases, depending on the geographical distribution of occurrences. For example, a word that appears in half of cities can be considered regional only if those cities are grouped in a region. In the event that these cities were sparsely distributed throughout the geographical area, the word could not be considered a regionalism. In contrast, HSIC can effectively discriminate these geographic patterns. To exemplify HSIC, Table 2 shows the words with the highest HSIC values in the corpus. The majority of these words are Mexican regionalisms that occur almost in all 74 Mexican cities among all 333 cities in the corpus (i.e. low specificity). However, HSIC does not identify regionalisms with maximum specificity. That is, when a word occurs only in a city, the HSIC measure gets its minimum score.

Given that neither IDF nor HSIC seem to adequately model our notion of regionalism based on specificity and geographic association, we propose several

---

[3]   https://www.datos.gov.co/browse?q=F-TWITTER.

Table 1. Statistics of the Spanish corpus collected from Twitter

Country	ISO	Cities	Words	Tweets	Vocabulary	Users
Argentina	ar	26	254,982,258	26,933,107	5,264,160	859,197
Bolivia	bo	8	3,136,167	289,683	206,944	24,508
Chile	cl	24	155,791,513	15,291,490	3,679,096	599,059
Colombia	co	31	209,085,865	19,875,419	4,575,636	871,247
Costa Rica	cr	5	43,905,034	4,272,517	674,130	97,211
Cuba	cu	1	122,595	13,246	14,044	5,354
Ecuador	ec	10	49,016,999	4,483,875	1,257,676	197,544
El Salvador	sv	3	19,898,193	1,835,850	453,030	65,543
Guatemala	gt	7	31,753,056	3,131,936	827,927	147,460
Honduras	hn	7	18,282,159	1,710,399	579,025	65,786
Mexico	mx	74	453,724,537	43,544,549	10,187,200	1,983,207
Nicaragua	ni	4	10,982,904	1,222,135	321,567	25,862
Panama	pa	5	33,237,123	3,078,389	855,235	114,062
Paraguay	py	6	39,753,880	3,968,928	765,886	113,243
Peru	pe	14	35,355,182	3,329,937	973,957	181,880
Puerto Rico	pr	3	35,230,113	3,863,552	666,343	94,589
Dominican Rep.	do	5	86,657,210	8,608,484	1,603,572	245,348
Spain	es	36	499,630,471	45,276,446	10,771,631	1,646,083
USA	us	35	59,974,018	6,172,521	2,759,849	956,255
Uruguay	uy	7	37,121,241	4,252,022	896,557	102,350
Venezuela	ve	22	194,073,318	16,773,933	4,343,584	764,215
Total	21	333	2,271,713,836	217,928,418	51,677,049	9,160,003

multiplicative combinations of the TF, IDF and HSIC factors. A fourth factor
identified as HSIC1 is equivalent to HSIC but it filters small values of the measure, which could be produced by the effect of randomness. In our experiments,
we observed that a convenient value for the filtering threshold is $\theta = 0.009$.
Therefore, the four classification functions used to determine the degree of regionalism of a word w in the i-th location are:

$$\text{TF.HSIC}(w, i) = TF(w, i) \times (HSIC(G, L_w) + 1)$$
$$\text{TF.IDF}(w, i) = TF(w, i) \times IDF(L_w)$$
$$\text{TF.IDF.HSIC}(w, i) = TF(w, i \times IDF(L_w) \times (HSIC(G, L_w) + 1)$$
$$\text{TF.IDF.HSIC1}(w, i) = TF(w, i) \times IDF(L_w) \times (HSIC1(G, L_w) + 1)$$

3.3 Determining the Meaning of Regional Words

Once the k words with the highest regional score for each location are determined
using one of the proposed ranking functions, the meaning of these words must

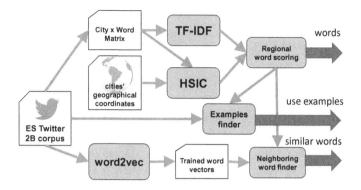

Fig. 2. Process for regional word detection, exemplification and meaning determination from a large corpus

Table 2. The 24 words with the highest scores of the HSIC measure for the corpus.

word	HSIC	word	HSIC	word	HSIC	word	HSIC
mexicanos	0.0464	chingar	0.0426	cabrona	0.0417	pelu	0.0404
tamales	0.0451	mexico	0.0426	pinche	0.0417	chivas	0.0403
frijoles	0.0450	chicharito	0.0425	mero	0.0416	yolo	0.0401
cabron	0.0448	orale	0.0419	culero	0.0408	impresentable	0.0400
cabrones	0.0440	fam	0.0419	chingaderas	0.0406	tortillas	0.0399
corridos	0.0430	chingada	0.0418	chicharo	0.0404	azteca	0.0397

be determined to make that list useful. For that, we provided two mechanisms to determine the meaning of the regionalisms. First, we trained a *word2vec*[4] model with the corpus using the following parameters: CBOW algorithm, 100 dimensions, window size of 5 words, and a learning rate of 0.025. Next, we obtained the nearest c neighbors to each regionalism. Second, we look for tweets where each regional word is used in context. Then, we calculate the average regionalism score for each example tweet and report the best t tweets with the lowest regionalism score for each regional word. In this way, the selected tweets illustrate the regional word surrounded by non-regional words thus facilitating the inference of its meaning. Finally, the 333 cities were added in their 21 corresponding countries and the lists were produced by establishing $k = 5,000$, $c = 30$, and $t = 30$. We published the 21 list of regional words with their nearest neighbors[5] and with their example tweets[6]. Table 3 contains a small sample of the created resource.

Figure 2 shows a summary in a block diagram of the architecture of the proposed method.

---

[4] https://www.datos.gov.co/browse?q=word2vec.

[5] https://www.datos.gov.co/browse?q=regionalismos%20cercanas.

[6] https://www.datos.gov.co/browse?q=regionalismos%20ejemplos.

Table 3. Examples for four countries of their top-regional words found (in bold face) along with their closest neighboring words in meaning and a sample tweet.

ARGENTINA	
lpm	lrpm, lcdsm, lptm, lpmmm, lcdll, lpmm, ptm, lpmmmm, laputamadre, jodeeeer,csm, lpmqlp, jodeer, lpmqlp, puff, jodeeeer, lpmqlrp *"me duelen los cortes en la mano lpm no doy mas"*
pelotuda	boluda, pajera, pendeja, tarada, forra, boba, tonta, mogolica, gila, payasa, weona, retrasada, estupida, cabrona, maricona, conchuda *"Me tendrían que regalar un premio por ser tan pelotuda"*
chabon	pibito, vato, pibe, bato, waso, chaval, muchacho, chamo, weon, wn, tipito, wey, pive, vaguito, maje, chaboncito, chavalo, chabón *"Ya me pone de mal humor este chabon loco ..."*
COLOMBIA	
hpta	hpt, hp, hijueputa, hijuemadre, ijueputa, hptaa, hptaaa, hijueputaa, hijodeputa, wn, csm, hijoeputa, hijueputaaa, weon, conchesumadre *"Por mas hpta que sea no lo voy a dejar."*
vallenato	rap, folclore, ballenato, regueton, malianteo, reggae, folklor,flocklore, regaeton, mariachi, reggeaton, reggueton, reggeton, folklore, mayimbe *"Que vivan las mujeres hermosas que interpretan el vallenato"*
chimba	gonorrea, chimbita, chimbaa, chimbaaaaa, chimbaa, chiva, depinga, pinga, chimbo, chingon, tuanis, bacan, chevere, guay, chido, bacano *"Que chimba es ir a la nevera y encontrar algo de comer."*
nojoda	njd, njda, nojodas, nojodaaaa, nojodaa, nojodaaaaaa, nojodaaa, coñoooo, coñooo, coñooooo, coñoooooo, vergacion, nojodaaaaaa *"Hoy tengo más ganas de beber que de vivir, nojoda"*
MEXICO	
neta	enserio, vdd, encerio, esque, alchile, sinceramente, acho, env, puñeta, netaaaa, pucha, verga, verdad, posta, marico, netaaaaa, netaaaa *"Ganamos y neta a como jugamos no merecíamos ganar"*
peda	borrachera, farra, pedota, fiesta, juerga, pedita, pisteada, pedocha, guarapeta, peduki, parranda, bebeta, fiestota, pedaaaa, verguera *"Un brindis por esos amigos que te cuidan en la peda"*
hueva	weba, flojera, weva, pereza, paja, flojerita, ladilla, wueba, wueva, caligueva, arrechera, flogera, fiaca, webita, bronca, hueba, jartera *"A mi mamá y a mi nos dio hueva cocinar"*
PERU	
chamba	ofi, oficina, faena, peguita, uni, mudanza, facu, talacha, ofis, chambita, uní, biblio, vagancia, vacavión, pachanga, pelu, pegita, farra, maleta *"Un día más de chamba para cerrar una buena semana! xD"*
csm	ctm, ptm, conchesumadre, conchesumare, conchasumadre, hpta, csmmmm, csmr, cdsm, jueputa, ptmr, hpt, conchetumare, hp, ptmre *"Quiero llegar temprano y hay un trafico de la csm"*
huevadas	webadas, babosadas, tonteras, giladas, pelotudeces, pavadas, chorradas, idioteces, pendejadas, wevadas, muladas, boludeces *"Ya, mejor me voy a dormir antes de seguir pensando huevadas."*

4   Experimental Validation

The experimental validation proposed in this section is aimed to determine to what extent the proposed ranking functions for the detection of regionalisms coincide with the notion and definition of "regional word" given by the Spanish speakers and by professional lexicographers.

4.1   Benchmarks

The benchmarks used for evaluation were two collaborative edited websites in which users contribute freely with regional words and expressions of their countries of origin, namely 'AsiHablamos' and 'DiccionarioLibre'. A third benchmark ('Diccionarios') was built by merging sources such as the "Diccionario de Colombianismos" (2018) from the Instituto Caro y Cuervo, the "Diccionario breve de mexicanismos" de Guido Gómez de Silva (2001), and others. From all these sources we removed all multi-word expressions and definitions[7]. The number of words included on each benchmark for each country is reported in Table 4.

Table 4. Number of regional words on each one of the evaluation benchmarks for each country.

Benchmark	ar	bo	cl	co	cr	cu	ec	sv	gt	hn	mx
AsiHablamos	309	27	150	226	106	12	98	51	77	47	245
DiccionarioLibre	1,321	860	320	1,042	86	94	158	70	105	80	-
Diccionarios	905	529	672	5,893	347	-	228	52	-	2,407	6,153
Benchmark	**ni**	**pa**	**py**	**pe**	**pr**	**do**	**es**	**us**	**uy**	**ve**	**Total**
AsiHablamos	40	75	36	38	102	69	109	94	-	173	2,084
DiccionarioLibre	77	909	33	1,219	339	2,667	1,777	-	124	1,853	13,134
Diccionarios	699	225	-	332	-	469	-	-	-	-	18,911

4.2   Evaluation Measures

The objective of the evaluation measures is to quantitatively assess the degree of agreement between a list of regionalisms obtained from one of the ranking functions proposed in Subsect. 3.2 and a benchmark list. For that, we used two popular measures of the *Information Retrieval* field [1], that is *Mean Average Precision* (MAP) and *Precision at 100* (P@100). P@100 measures the percentage of common words between a ranked list and a benchmark list in the first 100 positions. MAP measures the average of the P@n only for positions n in the ranked list that contains a word in the benchmark. Figure 3 illustrates four examples of calculation of these measures in our particular setting.

---

[7] https://github.com/sgjimenezv/spanish_regional_words_benchmark.

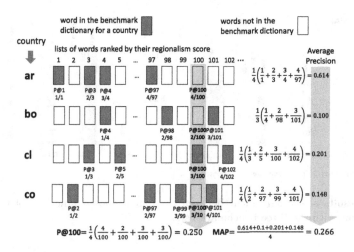

Fig. 3. Calculation examples of the evaluation measures MAP and P@100.

4.3 Experimental Setup

The procedure to obtain a list of words ranked by their degree of regionalism is as follows. First, we processed the complete corpus by collecting word occurrences for each of the 333 cities and the global word frequency. Then, the IDFs and HSICs scores were obtained for the 100,000 most frequent words in the corpus. Next, these scores were used to calculate each of the proposed ranking functions for each city (see Subsect. 3.2). Then, the rankings were merged to produce a ranking for each one of the 21 countries and for each function taking the top-5,000 words. Finally, the country rankings were compared with the three benchmarks by measuring MAP and P@100 for each possible combination of ranking function, country and benchmark.

4.4 Results

Figure 4 shows the results of the averages obtained in all countries for each benchmark for MAP and P@100 measures. That figure clearly shows that the TF.HSIC measure performed considerably worse than the other measures. The second observation is that, both in MAP and in P@100, TF.IDF performed practically identically as TF.IDF.HSIC. However, there is a difference in the performance between TF.IDF and TF.IDF.HSIC1. The average for the two measures throughout the 52 evaluations (that is, 20 countries for AsiHablamos, 19 for DiccionarioLibre, and 13 for Diccionarios) reveals a difference of 7.46% in MAP and of 1.36% in P@100. To evaluate the statistical significance of these differences, we used the Wilcoxon signed rank test obtaining $p = 0.0025$ for MAP (highly significant) and $p = 0.5656$ for P@10 (non-significant).

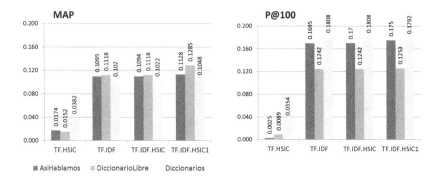

Fig. 4. Results of the agreement between the four proposed functions of ranking of regionalisms with the three benchmark lists.

5   Discussion

The results clearly indicate that spatial correlation is a weaker signal for the detection of regionalisms compared to specificity. In addition, the HSIC measure does not seem to contribute in the top-100 regionalisms compared to any of the three benchmarks. However, the HSIC1 factor managed to improve the results for the MAP measure. This lead us to the conclusion that the HSIC scores lower than the threshold established in HSIC1 ($\theta = 0.009$) seems to be noisy producing a decrease in performance equivalent to the benefit of using the scores above that threshold, yielding zero effect consolidation when comparing TF.IDF versus TF.IDF.HSIC. In fact, the value for the threshold θ was obtained by optimizing the MAP measurement. In addition, the results reveal that the HSIC1 factor benefits mainly in positions beyond the word 100th in the ranked list of regionalisms. Given this result, the 21 datasets were obtained using the TF-IDF.HSIC1 ranking function. Regarding the performance differences between benchmarks, it is clear the variations are considerable for the leadership positions in the ranking (P@100), while the performance becomes a tie when the full ranking is evaluated (MAP).

Being the authors of this paper native speakers of Spanish, we manually evaluated the first 100 regionalism produced for our country of origin, Colombia. In that list we recognized 71 regional words associated to global concepts, 13 names of regional entities, 3 names for local concepts, 11 standard Spanish words with a noticeable increase in use in our country, and 2 errors. This result contrasts with the fact that, on average, only 16 of every 100 words in the top positions of the ranking were also included in one of the benchmark lists. This comparison reveals that the proposed method is effective for the identification of regionalisms and that the benchmarks obtained from compilations made by speakers or professional lexicographers have a very low coverage of the real regional patterns of the Spanish language.

6 Conclusion

A corpus-based and language-independent method was proposed to build a new resource containing the most representative regional words and their meanings for 21 countries in the Pan-Hispanic world. This resource has the potential to benefit NLP applications that deal with utterances produced in informal environments, where the use of regional words is frequent. The constructed resource was evaluated in comparison with a benchmark composed of contributions of speakers and professional lexicographers. This evaluation leads us to conclude that, for the detection of regional words, the specificity of a word in a corpus (measured by tf-idf) is a stronger signal than the geographic correlation of its use (measured by HSIC). However, the combination of tf-idf and HSIC produce the best results. In addition, a manual inspection of the results for a country showed that the proposed benchmarks suffer from lack of representativeness and that the list produced by our methods reflects the regional jargon quite well. As future work, we hope to extend this work by addressing the more challenging task of identifying regional expressions of multiple words and their meanings.

References

1. Baeza-Yates, R., et al.: Modern Information Retrieval, vol. 463. ACM press, New York (1999)
2. Calvo, H.: Simple TF· IDF is not the best you can get for regionalism classification. In: Gelbukh, A. (ed.) CICLing 2014. LNCS, vol. 8403, pp. 92–101. Springer, Heidelberg (2014). https://doi.org/10.1007/978-3-642-54906-9_8
3. Donoso, G., Sanchez, D.: Dialectometric analysis of language variation in twitter. In: Proceedings of the Fourth Workshop on NLP for Similar Languages, Varieties and Dialects (VarDial), pp. 16–25. Association for Computational Linguistics, Valencia, Spain (April 2017)
4. Gretton, A., Fukumizu, K., Teo, C.H., Song, L., Schölkopf, B., Smola, A.J.: A kernel statistical test of independence. In: Advances in Neural Information Processing Systems, pp. 585–592 (2008)
5. Grieve, J., Speelman, D., Geeraerts, D.: A statistical method for the identification and aggregation of regional linguistic variation. Lang. Var. Change **23**(2), 193–221 (2011)
6. Hofmann, T., Schölkopf, B., Smola, A.J.: Kernel methods in machine learning. Ann. Stat., pp. 1171–1220 (2008)
7. Huang, Y., Guo, D., Kasakoff, A., Grieve, J.: Understanding us regional linguistic variation with twitter data analysis. Comput. Environ. Urban Syst. **59**, 244–255 (2016)
8. Lee, J., Kretzschmar Jr., W.A.: Spatial analysis of linguistic data with GIS functions. Int. J. Geogr. Inf. Sci. **7**(6), 541–560 (1993)
9. Mikolov, T., Sutskever, I., Chen, K., Corrado, G.S., Dean, J.: Distributed representations of words and phrases and their compositionality. In: Advances in Neural Information Processing Systems, pp. 3111–3119 (2013)
10. Nguyen, D., Eisenstein, J.: A kernel independence test for geographical language variation. Comput. Linguist. **43**(3), 567–592 (2017)

11. Rodriguez-Diaz, C.A., Jimenez, S., Dueñas, G., Bonilla, J.E., Gelbukh, A.: Dialectones: Finding statistically significant dialectal boundaries using twitter data. In: International Conference on Intelligent Text Processing and Computational Linguistics Springer (2018). (in press)
12. Scherrer, Y.: Recovering dialect geography from an unaligned comparable corpus. In: Proceedings of the EACL 2012 Joint Workshop of LINGVIS & UNCLH, pp. 63–71. Association for Computational Linguistics (2012)
13. Spärck Jones, K.: IDF term weighting and IR research lessons. J. Doc. **60**(5), 521–523 (2004)

Exploring the Relevance of Bilingual Morph-Units in Automatic Induction of Translation Templates

Kavitha Karimbi Mahesh[1,2]([✉]), Luís Gomes[1], and José Gabriel Pereira Lopes[1]

[1] NOVA Laboratory for Computer Science and Informatics (NOVA LINCS),
Faculdade de Ciências e Tecnologia, Universidade Nova de Lisboa, Lisbon, Portugal
kavithakmahesh@gmail.com, luismsgomes@gmail.com, gpl@fct.unl.pt
[2] Department of Computer Science and Engineering, St Joseph Engineering College
Vamanjoor, Mangaluru 575 028, India

Abstract. To tackle the problem of out-of-vocabulary (OOV) words and improve bilingual lexicon coverage, the relevance of bilingual morph-units is explored in inducing translation patterns considering unigram to n-gram and n-gram to unigram translations. The approach relies on induction of translation templates using bilingual stems learnt from automatically acquired bilingual translation lexicons. By generalising the templates using bilingual suffix clusters, new translations are automatically suggested.

1 Introduction

Numerous investigations have been reported on learning suffixes and suffixation operations using a lexicon or corpus of a language, for tackling out-of-vocabulary (OOV) words [1–3]. Beyond mere words or word forms, morphological similarities between known word to word translation forms have also been explored as a means to generalise the existing examples for automatic induction of word-to-word translations [4]. Learning approaches such as these employ available bilingual examples in inducing new translations that are infrequent or have never been encountered in the corpus used for lexicon acquisition. Approaches that allow simultaneous learning of morphology from multiple languages work well in inducing morphological segmentation by exploiting cross-lingual morpheme patterns [5]. The underlying benefit is that morphological structure ambiguous in one language is explicitly marked in another language. Along similar lines, is the bilingual learning approach [6] that works in improving the coverage of available bilingual lexica by employing bilingual stems, suffixes and their clusters, thereby generating those OOV word to word translations that remain missing.

To further enhance the coverage of existing bilingual lexicon beyond word level, a generative approach based on translation templates induced from existing bilingual lexicon augmented with bilingual stems, and bilingual stem and suffix clusters is discussed in this paper. In our previous work [6] we addressed

© Springer Nature Switzerland AG 2018
G. R. Simari et al. (Eds.): IBERAMIA 2018, LNAI 11238, pp. 417–429, 2018.
https://doi.org/10.1007/978-3-030-03928-8_34

the extraction of word to word translations and here we extend our method to generate word to n-gram translations through the use of translation templates. Translation templates are composed of one or more template tokens on each language side. Each template token is responsible for generating a token in the resulting translation pairs. In this paper we restrict ourselves to word to n-gram templates, but in principle the procedure can be generalised to n-gram to n-gram translations. Induction of translation templates might be further viewed as an application of bilingual morph-units, previously learnt [6] from a specific corpora of linguistically validated bilingual translations. Identifying the correspondence between units in a bilingual pair of phrases is essential for inducing translation templates and is determined by using a dictionary of bilingual stems acquired using the bilingual learning approach [6]. Induced templates serve in generating new[1] translations.

2   Related Work

Güvenir et al. [7] use analogical reasoning between translation pairs to learn structural correspondences between two languages from a corpus of translated sentence pairs.

Hu's approach [8] relies on extracting semantic groups and phrase structure groups from the language pairs under consideration. The phrase structure groups upon alignment are post-processed to yield translation templates.

Another approach for generating generalised templates is based on finding common patterns in a bilingual corpus [9]. Combination of commonly used approaches such as, identifying similar or dissimilar portions of text in groups of sentence pairs, finding semantically similar words, finding syntactic correspondences employing dictionaries and parsers, are used in identifying common patterns. Upon grouping the semantically related phrase-pairs based on the contexts, templates are induced by replacing clustered phrase-pairs by their class labels.

The bilingual stems [6] induced from similar bilingual pairs (translations), employed in template induction, is in line with the aspects related to the identification of common and different parts proposed by Gangadharaiah et al. [9]. While this identification relies on sentence pairs in their approach, word-to-word translation pairs form the source of our study. The common parts, referred to as bilingual stems, correspond to semantically similar morph-units and these bilingual segments conflates the meaning conveyed by similar translation pairs. The different parts represent their bilingual morphological extensions, referred to as bilingual suffixes. Our work loosely coincides with the approach proposed by Gangadharaiah et al. [9] in the use of clusters. Nevertheless, in our approach, clusters of bilingual stems aid in suggesting new translations after the induction of translation templates.

---

[1] Translations not present in the existing lexicon.

3   Background

In the current section we provide a brief overview of the bilingual resources, the validated lexicon of translations augmented with bilingual stems, suffixes, and their clusters, employed in template induction. Also, a brief overview of the approaches employed in acquiring those resources is presented.

3.1   Validated Bilingual Lexicons

We used English-Portuguese (EN-PT) bilingual lexicon acquired automatically employing various extraction techniques [10–13,15] applied on aligned parallel corpora[2]. Methods proposed by Brown et al. [10] and Lardilleux and Lepage [11] were employed for initial extractions. The former provides an alignment for every word in the corpus based on corpus-wide frequency counts, while the latter follows random sub-corpus sampling. In a different strategy, a bilingual lexicon was used to initially align parallel texts [14,15]. New[3] term-pairs were then extracted from those aligned texts. In this setting, the extraction method proposed by Aires et al. [12] employs the alignments [14,15] as anchors to further infer alignments for neighbouring unaligned words, based on co-occurrence statistics. The extracted term-pairs were manually verified and the correct ones were added to the bilingual lexicon, marked as *'accepted'*, with the incorrect ones marked as *'rejected'*. Remaining extractions were done following two different approaches proposed by Gomes and Lopes [13,15], one of which is based on combining the co-occurrence statistics with SpSim - a spelling similarity score for estimating the similarity between words, and the other based on translation templates. It is to be noted that, unlike the templates induced using the approach proposed in this paper, the templates used for extraction [15] were handwritten. Using the handwritten templates enabled extraction of translation equivalents with very high precision. 16 most productive EN-PT patterns extracted 228,645 translation equivalents with precision as high as 98.63% and 2,631 EN-PT patterns extracted 217,775 translation equivalents with precision 97.21% [15]. These results further motivated us to research on the use of human validated bilingual lexicon in automatic template induction for generating missing translations.

Entries in the lexicon were classified as *'accepted'* or *'rejected'* automatically using SVM based classifiers [16] and were later validated by linguists making use of a bilingual concordancer [17]. The translation lexicon thus obtained, being sufficiently large with enough near word and phrase translation forms, was used in a bilingual morphology learning framework for lexicon augmentation, yielding bilingual stems, suffixes and their clusters (further discussed in Sect. 3.2).

---

[2] DGT-TM - https://open-data.europa.eu/en/data/dataset/dgt-translation-memory
Europarl - http://www.statmt.org/europarl/
OPUS (EUconst, EMEA) - http://opus.lingfil.uu.se/.
[3] Not in the bilingual lexicon that was used for aligning the parallel texts.

3.2   Bilingual Resources

The bilingual lexicon discussed in the previous section augmented with bilingual stems, suffixes and their clusters learnt from EN-PT lexicon of unigram translations[4] serve as fundamental resources in inducing translation templates. Throughout this paper, the term bilingual morph-units is alternatively used to collectively refer to bilingual stems and suffixes. As the bilingual morph units, primarily the bilingual stems form the basis of translation template induction process, a brief overview of the approach employed in learning them is presented for the language pair EN-PT.

Bingual Stems and Suffixes. The induction of bilingual stems and suffixes follows the bilingual learning approach [6] applied to the EN-PT lexicon of unigram translations. The approach involves identification and extraction of orthographically and semantically similar bilingual segments, as for instance, 'ensur' ⇔ 'assegur', occurring in known translation examples, such as, 'ensuring' ⇔ 'assegurando', 'ensured' ⇔ 'assegurou', 'ensure' ⇔ 'assegurar', 'ensured' ⇔ 'assegurado', 'ensured' ⇔ 'assegurados', 'ensured' ⇔ 'asseguradas', 'ensures' ⇔ 'assegure', 'ensures' ⇔ 'assegura', 'ensure' ⇔ 'asseguram', 'ensure' ⇔ 'assegurem', and 'ensured' ⇔ 'asseguraram' together with their bilingual extensions constituting dissimilar bilingual segments (bilingual suffixes), ('e', 'ar'), ('e', 'arem'), ('e', 'am'), ('e', 'em'), ('es', 'e'), ('es', 'a'), ('ed', 'ada'), ('ed', 'adas'), ('ed', 'ado'), ('ed', 'ados'), ('ed', 'aram'), ('ed', 'ou'), ('ing', 'ando'), ('ing', 'ar'). The common part of translations that conflates all its bilingual variants[5] represents a bilingual stem ('ensur' ⇔ 'assegur'). The different parts of the translations contributing to various surface forms represent bilingual suffixes ((('e', 'ar'), ('e', 'arem'), and so forth)).

Clusters of Bilingual Stems and Suffixes. A set of bilingual suffixes representing bilingual extensions for a set of bilingual stems together form bilingual suffix clusters[6]. In other words, bilingual stems undergoing same suffix transformations form a cluster.

Table 1 illustrates bilingual stems, suffixes and 2 largest verb clusters[7] learnt for the data set size presented in Table 3 (refer to Sect. 5). The bilingual stem 'declar' ⇔ 'declar' shares same morphological extension as the bilinguals stem 'ensur' ⇔ 'ensur' and hence forms a cluster [6].

In our experiments, bilingual stems are employed in inducing translation templates. Further, clusters are used in generating new translations via generalisation of translation templates.

---

[4] Word-to-word translations taken from the lexicon discussed in Sect. 3.1.

[5] Translations that are lexically similar.

[6] A *suffix cluster* may or may not correspond to Part-of-Speech such as noun or adjective but there are cases where the same suffix cluster aggregates nouns, adjectives and adverbs.

[7] Verb - ('','ar') and ('e','ar').

Table 1. Clusters of bilingual stems sharing same morphological extensions

Cluster number	Suffix pairs	Stem pairs
17	(", er), (", erem), (", am), (", em), (s, e), (s, a), (ed, ida), (ed, idas), (ed, ido), (ed, idos), (ed, eram), (ed, eu), (ing, endo), (ing, er)	answer ⇔ respond, reply ⇔ respond, spend ⇔ dispend
32	(e, ar), (e, arem), (e, am), (e, em), (es, e), (es, a), (ed, ada), (ed, adas), (ed, ado), (ed, ados), (ed, aram), (ed, ou), (ing, ando), (ing, ar)	**declar ⇔ declar**, encourag ⇔ estimul, **ensur ⇔ assegur**, argu ⇔ afirm

4 Approach

The current section presents the approach for automatic induction of translation templates using the automatically learnt bilingual morph-units [6] consisting of stem pairs. Using the clusters of bilingual stems and suffixes learnt [6], new surface translation forms are automatically suggested as discussed in Sect. 4.4.

4.1 Definitions

Let L be a Bilingual Lexicon consisting of unique word pairs.

Let P be a validated bilingual lexicon of unigram to n-gram, n-gram to unigram translations.

Let L1, L2 be languages with alphabet set Σ_1, Σ_2.

Let (p_i, p_j) be any bilingual pair (translation) in P, $1 \leq i \leq m$, $1 \leq j \leq n$, m and n are the number of unique phrases in language L1 and L2.

Let (s_a, s_b) represent a bilingual stem in the set of bilingual stems, S, induced by bilingual learning approach; where $a \leq m$ and $b \leq n$.

If S_{L1} and S_{L2} represents the set of stems in languages L1 and L2, then $s_a \in S_{L1}$ and $s_b \in S_{L2}$.

$\$_a$ and $\$T_{a\#b}$ respectively represent wildcard symbols for stem in first language and its translation in second language, where a represents the identifier for the stem in first language and $a\#b$ represents the identifier for its translation in second language. It should be noted that a stem in first language may have multiple translations in second language. Thus, $\$T_{a\#b}$ and $\$T_{a\#c}$ represents different translations (with identifiers $a\#b$ and $a\#c$) for the same stem, $\$_a$, in first language.

4.2 Inputs

Bilingual/Translation Lexicon (P). The Translation lexicon used for template induction consists of unigrams (taken as a single word - any contiguous sequence of characters) in the first language cross-listed with their corresponding translations consisting of n-grams (contiguous sequence of n words, $2 \leq n \leq 4$) in second language or vice-versa, such that they share the same meaning or are usable in equivalent contexts. Examples illustrating bilingual variants are shown in Table 2.

Table 2. Translation examples

Translation forms	EN	PT
Verb	Involving	que envolva
	Involving	que envolvam
	Involving	que envolvem
Noun	Forwarding agent	expedidor
	Watermark	marca de água
Adjective	Lower	mais pequena
	Quickest	mais rápidos
Adverb	Indirectly	de modo inderecto
	Comprehensively	de forma aprofundada
	Scientifically	a nível de a ciência

List of Bilingual Stems. These are orthographically and semantically similar bilingual segments shared by similar surface translation forms and are induced by applying the bilingual learning mechanism [6] on the translation lexicon L containing only word-to-word translations. Column 3 of Table 1 lists various bilingual stems with their respective morphological extensions in column 2.

4.3 Automatic Induction of Translation Templates

The steps involved in translation template induction are as outlined in Algorithm 1. The approach employs a lexicon of translations P (consisting of unigram to n-gram and n-gram to unigram translations), and a dictionary of bilingual stems, S. We begin by building separate keyword trees (Trie) of all stems in S_{L1} (say, T_{L1}) and S_{L2} (say, T_{L2}). We extend the keyword tree into an automaton to allow $O(k)$ lookup time, where k is the size of the key. The Aho-Corasick set matching algorithm [18] is then applied to look for all occurrences of matching bilingual stems in each of the translations under consideration. Specifically, this involves for each bilingual pair (p_i, p_j) in P, traversing the phrase p_i over the built automaton T_{L1} and similarly traversing p_j over T_{L1} to find all matching stems. If the matching stems happen to be the translations of each other (i.e., a bilingual stem existing in S), we generalise the stem in first linguage with a wildcard symbol $\$_a$ and with $\$T_{a\#b}$ in second language, where a and $a\#b$ represent the identifiers of the matched stems in L1 and L2, respectively.

4.4 Automatic Generation of New Translations

Upon induction of preliminary translation templates as specified in Algorithm 1, new translations are automatically suggested by employing clusters of bilingual stems and suffixes. Generation of new translations involves the following steps:

1. Identify the bilingual stem employed in template induction.

Algorithm 1. Induction of Translation Templates

```
 1: procedure TRANSLATIONTEMPLATEINDUCTION
 2:     Construct separate keyword trees $T_{L1}$, $T_{L2}$ for stems in $S_{L1}$ and $S_{L2}$ respectively
 3:     for each translation $(p_i, p_j)$ ∊ P do
 4:         Traverse $p_i$ over $T_{L1}$ and $p_j$ over $T_{L2}$ to find matching stems.
 5:         for each pattern $s_a$ found in $p_i$ and $s_b$ found in $p_j$ do
 6:             if $(s_a, s_b)$ ∊ S then
 7:                 Replace $s_a$ by $\$_a$ and $s_b$ by $\$T_{a\#b}$
 8:             end if
 9:         end for
10:     end for
11: end procedure
```

2. Identify the cluster to which the bilingual stem employed in a particular template induction belongs.
3. Identify all other bilingual stems that belong to the identified cluster.
4. For each bilingual stem in the cluster (different from that used in template induction), replace the string representing the bilingual stem used in template induction ($\$_a$ and with $\$T_{a\#b}$) with the remaining bilingual stems in the cluster.

4.5 Illustration

As an example, consider a translation with two words in first language and a word in second language (as in the bilingual pair 'we declare' ↔ 'declaramos'). To extract translation pattern, a set matching is performed using the previously learnt bilingual stems, represented as a Trie. For the example considered, this enables the induction of translation templates, 'we $\$_{2511}$e' ↔ '$\$T_{2511\#8}$amos'[8], as the lexicon of bilingual stems contains the bilingual pair 'declar' ↔ 'declar'. By identifying all the stem pairs that associate with this particular template (refer Table 1), using the bilingual suffix clusters [19], new translations are suggested. We may see that, the bilingual stem 'declar' ↔ 'declar' belongs to the cluster 32. Thus, a possible translation suggestion in this case would be, 'we *argue*' ↔ '*afirm*amos', obtained by replacing 'declar' on the left hand side with 'argu' and 'declar' on the right hand side with 'afirm' (translation of 'argu' is 'afirm'), in the bilingual pair 'we *declare*' ↔ '*declar*amos'. Likewise, other suggestions proposed are, 'we *encourage*' ↔ '*estimula*mos', 'we *toggle*' ↔ '*comuta*mos' and so forth, all of which are instances of correct translations missing in the existing lexicon.

---

[8] $\$_{2511}$ represents the stem 'declar' in English and $\$T_{2511\#8}$ represents its translation in Portuguese, which is 'declar' as well.

5 Experimental Setup and Evaluation

5.1 Data Sets

The translations used for template induction were acquired using various extraction techniques [10–13, 15] applied on a (sub-)sentence aligned parallel corpora introduced in Sect. 3.

Table 3. Statistics of EN-PT datasets used in bilingual learning and template induction

Description	Bilingual pairs	Bilingual stems	Bilingual suffixes
Bilingual Learning	209,739	24,223	232
Template Induction	1,476	24,223	-

The dataset used for bilingual learning (column 2) and the associated statistics of unique bilingual segments identified using the bilingual learning approach (columns 3 and 4) [6] are shown in the first row of Table 3. The last row shows the statistics of bilingual pairs used as input in inducing translation templates. A subset of bilingual stems used in translation template induction are shown in the Table 4.

Table 4. Selected list of indexed bilingual stems employed in newly induced translation templates shown in Table 6

ID_EN - EN	ID_PT - PT	ID_EN - EN	ID_PT - PT
18618 involv	18618#5 interess	1 provid	1#21 facult
18618 involv	18618#6 envolv	681 provid	681#18 conced
5621 precipit	5621#2 precipit	17882 meteor	17882#2 meteor
18758 analys	18758#4 analis	701 mass	701#4 mass
18758 analys	18758#6 examin	718 affect	718#22 afect
1996 plat	1996#2 prat	1 provid	1#33 fornec
435 cycl	435#6 cicl	1393 organ	1393#9 organ
1605 estimat	1605#6 estimat	3416 regular	3416#2 regular
18897 establish	18897#18 estabelec	800 past	800#5 passad
18897 establish	18897#19 afix	1078 introduc	1078#3 introduz
16585 digit	16585#6 digit	16585 digit	16585#1 númer

Table 5. Statistics of newly induced translation templates

Description	Statistics
Total templates induced	958
Templates occurring once	587
Templates occurring more than once	82
Unigram to bigram templates induced	580

5.2   Results and Discussion

The statistics of translation templates learnt from EN-PT bilingual lexicon using the dataset described in Sect. 5.1 are presented in Table 5.

Table 6 presents few of the randomly chosen templates that were automatically induced from unigram to n-gram and n-gram to unigram translations.

Table 6. Unigram to bigram and bigram to unigram translation templates

Description	EN	PT
Verb forms	$\$_{18618}$ing	que $\$T_{18618\#6}$a
	$\$_{18618}$ing	que $\$T_{18618\#6}$em
	$\$_{18618}$ing	que $\$T_{18618\#6}$am
	$\$_{5621}$ated	o $\$T_{5621\#2}$ado
	was $\$_1$ing	$\$T_{1\#21}$ava
	to $\$_{1078}$e	$\$T_{1078\#3}$ir
Noun forms	$\$_{18758}$er	o $\$T_{18758\#4}$ador
	$\$_{1996}$es	as $\$T_{1996\#9}$as
	$\$_{435}$ists	os $\$T_{435\#6}$istas
	$\$_{1393}$ism	o $\$T_{1393\#9}$ismo
	$\$_{1605}$es	uma $\$T_{1605\#6}$iva
	ir$\$_{3416}$ity	a ir$\$T_{3416\#2}$idade
	$\$_{17882}$ology	a $\$T_{17882\#2}$ologia
	$\$_{18897}$ments	os $\$T_{18897\#18}$imentos
Adjective forms	$\$_{16585}$al	a $\$T_{16585\#6}$al

Manual evaluation of a subset of induced templates showed that few of the templates induced were too specific and were less productive. Translation templates presented in Table 7, for instance, are unproductive as they do not contribute to any new translation forms.

Generalising each of the induced templates by replacing the initial representations (indicating specific stem pairs such as $\$_{9800} \leftrightarrow \$T_{9800\#4}$) with $\$ \leftrightarrow \$T$ and

Table 7. Less productive translation templates

EN	PT	Bilingual stem (EN↔PT)
$\$_{9800}$ol	a $\$T_{9800\#4}$ol	9800 europ ↔ 9800#4 europ
some$\$_{9805}$s	por $\$T_{9805\#6}$s	9805 time ↔ 9805#6 veze
de$\$_{659}$ees	os de$\$T_{659\#10}$ados	659 sign ↔ 659#10 sign
to take ac$\$_{2347}$ of	a fim de ter em $\$T_{2347\#9}$	2347 count ↔ 2347#9 conta

counting the occurrence frequency of the resulting templates, we observed that the templates shown in Table 7 appeared only once. Thus, by generalising and filtering the induced translation templates based on the occurrence frequency we were able to discard templates that are unproductive. Alternatively, to avoid over-generations, templates sharing same contexts were further grouped together yielding generalised templates. In other words, after the stems were generalised to a wildcard symbol of the form $\$_a \leftrightarrow \$T_{a\#b}$ as explained in the Sect. 4, the preliminary set of induced templates were clustered by finding stems that shared common contexts, where the context comprised of the suffix and other surrounding words. These clustered templates are used to suggest new translation forms that remain missing from the lexicon.

Templates such as $\$_{13830}$s ↔ os $\$T_{13830\#3}$s, $\$_{13830}$s ↔ os $\$T_{13830\#2}$tos and $\$_{13830}$s ↔ os $\$T_{13830\#1}$s[9] lead to the generation of entries longer than necessary, containing articles[10] that may or may not occur in English.

In our earlier work, we had learnt bilingual morphology from word to word translations [6] and now with the newly induced bigram to unigram templates, we infer those other pair of suffixes that were not learnt in our earlier experiments. For instance, 'shall consider ↔ considerará' includes the suffix 'ará' in the Portuguese side, which was not learnt previously. As it co-occurs with stems such as 815 consider ↔ 815#5 analis, 815 consider ↔ 815#1 consider, 815 consider ↔ 815#4 ponder and so forth in the Portuguese side, the suffix belongs to the same class of suffixes for bigram to unigram as the suffix pairs and other Portuguese verbs belonging to the cluster characterised by suffix pairs: (ed, ada), (ed, adas), (ed, ado), (ing ando), (ing, ar) etc. Here, we have a gapped pattern 'shall $\$_a \leftrightarrow \$T_{a\#b}$arão'.

Further, knowing 14815 affect ↔ 14815#22 afect, 14815 affect ↔ 14815#18 influenci, 14815 affect ↔ 14815#13 prejudic, 14815 affect ↔ 14815#6 consider, 14815 affect ↔ 14815#5 interess, 14815 affect ↔ 14815#4 afet, 14815 affect ↔ 14815#3 implic and the templates learnt employing these stem pairs $\$_{14815}$ing ↔ que $\$T_{14815\#22}$em, $\$_{14815}$ing ↔ que $\$T_{14815\#22}$a, $\$_{14815}$ing ↔ que $\$T_{14815\#22}$am, different future forms 'shall affect ↔ afectará' or 'shall affect ↔ afectarão', can be generated as we also know that the suffixes 'ará' or 'arão' for those patterns apply to verbs of first conjugation ending in 'a'.

---

[9] 13830 contract ↔ 13830#2 contra, 13830 contract ↔ 13830#1 contrat and 13831 buyout ↔ 13831#3 compra.

[10] masculine plural.

Unlike the hand-written templates proposed by Gomes [15] that are highly precise and productive in extracting translation equivalents, the templates induced using the approach proposed in this paper are particularly suitable for automatic translation generation. While the hand-written templates generated are intended for aligning and extraction of translation equivalents from parallel corpora [15], the templates generated lack information about the suffixes and hence is not adequate for translation generation, which is addressed in this study.

6 Conclusion

We have presented a method for automatic induction of translation templates from a lexicon of unigram to n-gram, n-gram to unigram translations using bilingual stems, suffixes and their clusters. By generalising the induced templates using clusters of bilingual stems and suffixes, new translations can be automatically suggested. The contributions of the study can be summarised as follows:

1. Automatic induction of translation templates from a bilingual corpus of translations by employing the bilingual morph-units such as bilingual stems.
2. Continual accommodation of the newly acquired knowledge in enhancing the learning process. Human validation of newly generated translations (or templates) prevent learning from incorrectly generated or extracted translation pairs (or templates).

As future work, we intend to focus exclusively on generation of lexical entries considering the templates induced using the approach proposed in this paper and taking into account those stem pairs that belong to a cluster [6]. Further, the inflection-based method could be generalised so as to make it applicable to any morphological phenomenon representing grammatical information, rather than just verb forms. Learning bilingual prefixes using the previously proposed algorithm [6] could be explored in future.

Acknowledgements. K. M. Kavitha and Luís Gomes acknowledge the Research Fellowship by FCT/MCTES with Ref. nos., SFRH/BD/64371/2009 and SFRH/BD/65059/2009, respectively, and the funded research project ISTRION (Ref. PTDC/EIA-EIA/114521/2009) that provided other means for the research carried out. The authors thank NOVA LINCS, FCT/UNL for the support and SJEC for the partial financial assistance provided.

References

1. Yang, M., Kirchhoff, K.: Phrase-based backoff models for machine translation of highly inflected languages. In: Proceedings of EACL, pp. 41–48 (2006)
2. de Gispert, A., Mariño, J.B. Crego, J.M.: Improving statistical machine translation by classifying and generalizing inflected verb forms. In: Proceedings of 9th European Conference on Speech Communication and Technology, Lisboa, Portugal , pp. 3193–3196 (2005)

3. Poon, H., Cherry, C., Toutanova, K.: Unsupervised morphological segmentation with log-linear models. In: Proceedings of Human Language Technologies: The 2009 Annual Conference of the North American Chapter of the Association for Computational Linguistics, pp. 209–217. ACL (2009)
4. Momouchi, H.S.K.A.Y., Tochinai, K.: Prediction method of word for translation of unknown word. In: Proceedings of the IASTED International Conference, Artificial Intelligence and Soft Computing, 27 July–1 August 1997, Banff, Canada, p. 228. Acta Pr. (1997)
5. Snyder, B., Barzilay, R.: Unsupervised multilingual learning for morphological segmentation. In: Proceedings of ACL 2008: HLT, pp. 737–745. ACL (2008)
6. Karimbi Mahesh, K., Gomes, L., Lopes, J.G.P.: Identification of bilingual segments for translation generation. In: Blockeel, H., van Leeuwen, M., Vinciotti, V. (eds.) IDA 2014. LNCS, vol. 8819, pp. 167–178. Springer, Cham (2014). https://doi.org/10.1007/978-3-319-12571-8_15
7. Cicekli, I., Güvenir, H.A.: Learning translation templates from bilingual translation examples. In: Carl, M., Way, A. (eds.) Recent Advances in Example-Based Machine Translation. TLTB, vol. 21, pp. 255–286. Springer, Dordrecht (2003). https://doi.org/10.1007/978-94-010-0181-6_9
8. Rile, H., Zong, C., Bo, X.: An approach to automatic acquisition of translation templates based on phrase structure extraction and alignment. IEEE Trans. Audio Speech Lang. Process. **14**(5), 1656–1663 (2006)
9. Gangadharaiah, R., Brown, R.D., Carbonell, J.: Phrasal equivalence classes for generalized corpus-based machine translation. In: Gelbukh, A. (ed.) CICLing 2011. LNCS, vol. 6609, pp. 13–28. Springer, Heidelberg (2011). https://doi.org/10.1007/978-3-642-19437-5_2
10. Brown, P.F., Pietra, V.J.D., Pietra, S.A.D., Mercer, R.L.: The mathematics of statistical machine translation: parameter estimation. Comput. Linguist. **19**(2), 263–311 (1993)
11. Lardilleux, A., Lepage, Y.: Sampling-based multilingual alignment. In: Proceedings of Recent Advances in Natural Language Processing, pp. 214–218 (2009)
12. Aires, J., Lopes, G.P., Gomes, L.: Phrase translation extraction from aligned parallel corpora using suffix arrays and related structures. In: Lopes, L.S., Lau, N., Mariano, P., Rocha, L.M. (eds.) EPIA 2009. LNCS (LNAI), vol. 5816, pp. 587–597. Springer, Heidelberg (2009). https://doi.org/10.1007/978-3-642-04686-5_48
13. Gomes, L., Pereira Lopes, J.G.: Measuring spelling similarity for cognate identification. In: Antunes, L., Pinto, H.S. (eds.) EPIA 2011. LNCS (LNAI), vol. 7026, pp. 624–633. Springer, Heidelberg (2011). https://doi.org/10.1007/978-3-642-24769-9_45
14. Gomes, L.. Lopes, G.P.: Parallel texts alignment. In: New Trends in Artificial Intelligence, 14th Portuguese Conference in Artificial Intelligence, EPIA 2009, Aveiro, pp. 513–524, October 2009
15. Gomes, L.: Translation alignment and extraction within a lexica-centered iterative workflow. Ph.D. thesis, Lisboa, Portugal, December 2017
16. Kavitha, K.M., Gomes, L., Aires, J., Lopes, J.G.P.: Classification and selection of translation candidates for parallel corpora alignment. In: Pereira, F., Machado, P., Costa, E., Cardoso, A. (eds.) EPIA 2015. LNCS (LNAI), vol. 9273, pp. 723–734. Springer, Cham (2015). https://doi.org/10.1007/978-3-319-23485-4_73
17. Costa, J., Gomes, L., Lopes, G.P., Russo, L.M.S.: Improving bilingual search performance using compact full-text indices. In: Gelbukh, A. (ed.) CICLing 2015. LNCS, vol. 9041, pp. 582–595. Springer, Cham (2015). https://doi.org/10.1007/978-3-319-18111-0_44

18. Gusfield, D.: Algorithms on Strings, Trees, and Sequences: Computer Science and Computational Biology, pp. 52–61. Cambridge University Press, Cambridge (1997)

19. Kavitha, K.M., Gomes, L., Lopes, J.G.P.: Learning clusters of bilingual suffixes using bilingual translation lexicon. In: Prasath, R., Vuppala, A.K., Kathirvalavakumar, T. (eds.) MIKE 2015. LNCS (LNAI), vol. 9468, pp. 607–615. Springer, Cham (2015). https://doi.org/10.1007/978-3-319-26832-3_57

Deep Neural Network Approaches
for Spanish Sentiment Analysis
of Short Texts

José Ochoa-Luna[1(✉)] ⓘ and Disraeli Ari[2]

[1] Department of Computer Science, Universidad Católica San Pablo, Arequipa, Peru
jeochoa@ucsp.edu.pe
[2] Universidad Nacional de San Agustin, Arequipa, Peru
disraely.ar.m@gmail.com

Abstract. Sentiment Analysis has been extensively researched in the last years. While important theoretical and practical results have been obtained, there is still room for improvement. In particular, when short sentences and low resources languages are considered. Thus, in this work we focus on sentiment analysis for Spanish Twitter messages. We explore the combination of several word representations (Word2Vec, Glove, Fastext) and Deep Neural Networks models in order to classify short texts. Previous Deep Learning approaches were unable to obtain optimal results for Spanish Twitter sentence classification. Conversely, we show promising results in that direction. Our best setting combines data augmentation, three word embeddings representations, Convolutional Neural Networks and Recurrent Neural Networks. This setup allows us to obtain state-of-the-art results on the TASS/SEPLN Spanish benchmark dataset, in terms of accuracy.

Keywords: Deep neural networks · Sentiment analysis
Twitter sentences

1 Introduction

Spanish is the third language most used on the Internet[1]. However, the development of Natural Language Processing (NLP) techniques for this language did not follow the same trend. In particular, this research gap can be observed in Spanish *sentiment analysis*. Sentiment analysis allows us to perform an automated analysis of millions of reviews. Its basic task, called polarity detection, targets at determining whether a given opinion is positive, negative or neutral. This area has been widely researched since 2002 [16]. In fact, it is one of the most active research areas in NLP, data mining and social media analytics [27].

Polarity detection has been addressed as a text classification problem thus, can be approached by supervised and unsupervised learning methods [29]. In

---

[1] http://www.internetworldstats.com/stats7.htm.

G. R. Simari et al. (Eds.): IBERAMIA 2018, LNAI 11238, pp. 430–441, 2018.
https://doi.org/10.1007/978-3-030-03928-8_35

the unsupervised approach, a vocabulary of positive and negative words is constructed so as to polarity is inferred according to the similarity between vocabulary and opinionated words. The second approach is based on machine learning, training data and labelled reviews are used to define a classifier [16]. This last approach relies heavily on feature engineering. However, recent learning representation paradigms perform these tasks automatically [15]. In this context, Machine Learning has recently become the dominant approach for sentiment analysis, due to availability of data, better models and hardware resources [28].

In this paper we adopt a Deep Learning approach for sentiment analysis. In particular we aim at performing automated classification of short texts in Spanish. This is challenging because of the limited contextual information that they normally contain.

To do so, sentence words are mapped to word embeddings. Distributional approaches such as word embeddings have proven useful to model context in several NLP tasks [18]. Three kinds of word representations (Word2vec [18], Glove [24], Fastext [3]) have been considered. This setting, which is novel for Spanish sentiment analysis, can be useful in several domains.

The Deep Learning architecture proposed is composed by a Convolutional Neural Network [14], a Recurrent Neural Network [12] and a final dense layer. In order to avoid overfitting, besides traditional dropout schemes, we rely on data augmentation. Data augmentation is useful for low resources languages such as Spanish.

Those design choices allow us to obtain results comparable to state-of-the-art approaches over the InterTASS 2017 dataset, in terms of accuracy. The dataset was proposed in the TASS workshop at SEPLN. In the last six years, this workshop has been the main source for Spanish sentiment analysis datasets and proposals [17].

The remainder of the paper is organized as follows. Section 2 reviews preliminaries on sentiment analysis and neural networks. Our proposal is presented in Sect. 3. Results are described in Sect. 4. Related work is presented in Sect. 5. Finally, Sect. 6 concludes the paper.

2   Preliminary

2.1   Sentiment Analysis

Sentiment analysis (also known as opinion mining) is an active research area in natural language processing [28]. Sentiment classification is a fundamental and extensively studied area in sentiment analysis. It targets at determining the sentiment polarity (positive or negative) of a sentence (or a document) based on its textual content [27]. Polarity classification tasks have usually based on two main approaches [4]: a supervised approach, which applies machine learning algorithms in order to train a polarity classifier using a labelled corpus; an unsupervised approach, semantic lexicon-based, which integrates linguistic resources in a model in order to identify the polarity of the opinions.

Since the performance of a machine learner heavily depends on the choices of data representation, many studies devote to building powerful feature extractor with domain expert and careful engineering [20].

As stated by Liu [16], sentiment analysis has been researched at three levels: (i) Document level: The task at this level is to classify whether a whole opinion document expresses a positive or negative sentiment [22]; (ii) Sentence level: The task at this level goes to the sentences and determines whether each sentence expressed a positive, negative, or neutral opinion. Neutral usually means no opinion; (iii) Entity and Aspect level [22]: Both the document level and the sentence level analyses do not discover what exactly people liked and did not like. Aspect level performs finer-grained analysis.

2.2   Deep Neural Networks

Several deep neural network approaches have been successfully applied to sentiment analysis in the last years [31]. However, these results have been mostly obtained for English Language [17]. The related work section further describes, several attempts to apply deep learning algorithms for Spanish sentiment analysis. In this section we only focus on word representations, Convolutional Neural Networks (CNNs) and Recurrent Neural Networks (RNNs), which are the main building blocks of our proposal.

Word Representations (Word2vec, Glove, Fastext). Nowadays, word representations are paramount for sentiment analysis [31]. In order to model text words as features within a machine learning framework, a common approach is to encode words as discrete atomic symbols. These encodings are arbitrary and provide no useful information to the system regarding the relationships that may exist between the individual symbols [28]. The discrete representation has some problems such as missing new words. This representation also requires human labor to create and adapt. It is also hard to compute accurate word similarity and is quite subjective. To cope with these problems, the distributional similarity based representations propose to represent a word by means of its neighbors, its context [27].

Word2vec [18] is a particularly computationally-efficient predictive model for learning word embeddings from raw text. Take a vector with several hundred dimensions where each word is represented by a distribution of weights across those elements [2,7]. Thus, instead of a one-to-one mapping between an element in the vector and a word, the representation of a word is spread across all the elements in the vector.

In contrast to Word2vec, Glove [24] seeks to make explicit what Word2vec does implicitly: encoding meaning as vector offsets in an embedding space. In Glove, it is stated that the ratio of the co-occurrence probabilities of two words (rather than their co-occurrence probabilities themselves) is what contains information and so look to encode this information as vector differences.

In Fastext [3] instead of directly learning a vector representation for a word, a representation for each character n-gram is learned. In this sense, each word is represented as a bag of character n-grams, thus the overall word embedding is a sum of these characters n-grams. The advantage of Fastext is that generates better embeddings for rare and out-of-corpus words. By using different n-grams Fastext explores key structural components of words.

Convolutional Neural Networks. While Convolutional Neural Networks (CNN) have been primarily applied to image processing, they have also been used for NLP tasks [14].

In the image context [15], given a raw input (2D arrays of pixel intensities) several *convolutional* layers allow us to capture features images at several abstraction levels. In this context, a discrete convolution takes a filter matrix and multiply its values element-wise with the original matrix, then sum them up. To get the full convolution we do this for each element by sliding the filter over the whole matrix.

The convolved map feature denotes a level of abstraction obtained after the convolution operations (there are also ReLU activation, Pooling and Softmax layers). CNN exploits the property that many natural signals are compositional hierarchies: higher-level features are obtained by composing lower-level ones. In images, local combinations of edges form motifs, motifs assemble into parts, and parts from objects [15]. All this learning representation is performed in an unsupervised manner. The amount of filters and convolutional layers denote how rich features and abstraction levels we wish to obtain from images.

Conversely, if we wish to apply CNNs in natural language tasks several changes are needed [14]. Texts are tokenized and must be encoded as numbers — input numerical variables are usual in neural networks algorithms. In the last five years, word embeddings representations (but also character and paragraph) have been preferred. This is due to semantical/syntactical similarity is better expressed in a distributed manner [18].

A sentence can be represented as a matrix. Thus, the sentence length denotes the number of rows and the word embedding dimension denotes the number of columns. This allows us to perform discrete convolutions as in the image case (2D input matrix). However, one must be careful when defining filter sizes, which usually have the same width as word embeddings [14].

Instead of working with 2D representation, we may also work with 1D representation, i.e., to concatenate several word embeddings in a long vector and then apply several convolution layers.

Recurrent Neural Networks. Recurrent Neural Networks (RNN) [8] are a kind of neural network that makes it possible to model long-distance dependencies among variables. Therefore, RNN are best suited for tasks that involve sequential inputs such as speech and language [15]. RNNs process an input sequence one element at a time, maintaining in their hidden units a state vector that implicitly contains information about the history of all the past elements of the sequence. To do so, a connection is added that references the previously hidden states h_{t-1} when computing hidden state h, formally [21]:

$$h_t = tanh(W_{xh}x_t + W_{hh}h_{t-1} + b_h)$$

$h_t = 0$ when the initial step is $t = 0$. The only difference from the hidden layer in a standard neural network is the addition of the connection $W_{hh}h_{t-1}$ from the hidden state at time step $t - 1$ connecting to that at time step t. As this is a recursive equation that use h_{t-1} from the previous time step.

In the context of Sentiment Analysis, an opinionated sentence is a sequence of words. Thus, RNNs are suitable for modeling this input [12]. Similar to CNNs, input is given as words (character) embeddings which can be learned during training or may also be pre-trained (Glove, Word2vec, Fastext).

Each word is mapped to a word embedding which is the input at every time step of the RNN. The maximum sequence length denotes the length of the recurrent neural network. Rach hidden state models the dependence among a current word and all the precedent words. Usually, the final hidden state, which ideally denotes all the encoded sentence, is connected to a dense layer so as to perform sentiment classification [12].

RNNs are very powerful dynamic systems, but training them has proved to be problematic because the backpropagated gradients either grow or shrink at each time step. Thus, over many time steps they typical explode or vanish. A sequence of words comprise a sequence of RNNs cells. This cells can have some gate mechanism in order to avoid gradient vanishing longer sequences. In this setting Long Short Term Memory Cells (LSTM) or Gated Recurrent Units (GRU) are common choices [21].

3   Proposal

The aim of this paper is to explore several Deep Learning algorithms possibilities in order to perform sentiment analysis. The focus is to tackle polarity detection in Spanish Tweets. In this sense, some models were tested. Details of these experiments are given in Sect. 4.

In this section, we present our best pipeline for Spanish sentiment analysis of short texts. Basically, it is composed by Word embeddings, CNN and RNN models. The pipeline is showed in Fig. 1. A concise description is given as follows.

(i) Basic pre-processing is performed as the focus is given to data augmentation; (ii) The input is a sequence of words — a short opinionated sentence. These words are mapped to three pre-trained Spanish word embeddings (Word2vec, Glove, Fastext); (iii) The three channels are the input to a 3D Convolutional Neural Network. After several convolutional and max pooling layers we obtain a feature vector of a given length; (iv)The feature vector obtained from the CNN is mapped to a sequence and passed to a RNN. It is a simple RNN model, with LSTM cells; (v) The final hidden state of the RNN is completely connected to a dense layer.

Further details about these design choices are given as follows.

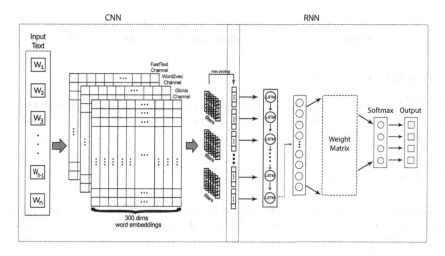

Fig. 1. Pipeline of our proposal: Word Embeddings+CNN+RNN.

3.1 Data Augmentation

In general a few pre-processing steps are performed over raw data. Since we have few training examples in Spanish and Deep Learning techniques are susceptible to overfitting, we would rather focus on data augmentation. We propose a novel approach for data augmentation. Basically, we identify nouns, adjectives and verbs on sentences by performing Part-Of-Speech tagging[2]. By doing so, we emphasize tokens that are prone to be opinionated words. Then, more examples are created by combining bigrams and trigrams from the former tokens. In addition, we augment data based on word synonyms [31]. Opinionated words are replaced by synonyms. Overall, this process allowed us to obtain better generalization results.

3.2 Word Embeddings Choice

One of the main contributions of this paper was to find the best word embedding setting. We have trained Word2vec and Glove embedding on Spanish corpus and we have used a pre-trained Fastext embedding. At the end, empirical tests allowed us to decide for using these three mappings as channels in our CNN building block. None of the previous works for Spanish Sentiment Analysis had used three embedding channels in CNNs before.

3.3 CNN Architecture

Our CNN architecture is based on Kim's work [14]. Since three word embeddings are used, then the first convolutional layer receives a 3D input. Filters have the

---

[2] The following tool was used to perform POS tagging: http://www.cis.uni-muenchen.de/~schmid/tools/TreeTagger/.

same width as embeddings dimension, and we perform convolutions from 1 to 5 words. The pooling layer allows us control the desired feature vector obtained.

3.4   RNN Architecture

The RNN receives a CNN vector as input, and LSTMs cells are defined accordingly. The last hidden state is fully connected to a dense layer which allows us to define a classifier [12].

4   Experiments

Experiments were performed using Deep Learning algorithms. CNNs and RNNs were tested separately. Our best result was obtained by composing word embeddings, CNNs and RNNs. We first describe the benchmark dataset used. Then, accuracy results are showed.

4.1   Dataset

The dataset used to perform comparisons was InterTASS, which is a collection of Spanish Tweets, used in TASS at SEPLN workshop in 2017 [17]. We have used this dataset since it is the most recent benchmark that allows us to compare among Deep Learning approaches for Spanish sentiment analysis. The dataset is further detailed in Table 1.

Table 1. InterTASS dataset (TASS 2017)

Corpus	Tweets
Training	1,008
Development	506
Test	1,899
Total	3,413

4.2   Results

We have implemented several deep neural networks models and the dataset Inter-TASS 2017 was used for training. For this implementation we use Tensorflow[3]. In order to find the best hyper parameters, we have used a ten-fold cross validation process. The test set has only been used to report results. In Table 2 we report results in terms of accuracy.

A first attempt was to test several RNNs models (*many-to-one architecture*, single layer, multilayer, bidirectional). The reported model, RNN in Table 2, has

---

[3] https://www.tensorflow.org/.

a many-to-one architecture. The input is a sequence of words and the output is the resulting polarity. There is only a hidden layer, and the input is a pre-trained sequence of Word2vec embeddings. A second attempt was to test several CNN models, i.e., 1D CNN, 2D CNN and 3D CNNs, until 4 convolutional/pooling layers. The reported model, CNN in Table 2, is a 3D CNN. Thus, the input received three channels of pre-trained word embeddings. It had only three layers: a convolutional, a pooling and a dense layer. It is worth noting that our best result was obtained by the model described in Sect. 3 (CNN+RNN in Table 2). This is a combination of a 3D CNN and a many-to-one RNN. A 3D CNN architecture whose outputs where mapped to a sequence of LSTM cells. Our data augmentation scheme was also used in order to avoid overfitting.

Table 2. Deep Learning approaches results on InterTASS dataset (TASS 2017)

Our DL attempts	Accuracy
CNN+RNN	**0.609**
CNN	0.5552
RNN	0.4972

In Table 3, we compare our best model (CNN+RNN) with the state-of-the-art InterTASS 2017 results, in terms of accuracy. It is worth noting that our approach is comparable to the other approaches. In addition, our proposal is the only top result using a Deep Learning approach.

Table 3. State-of-the-art results on InterTASS dataset (TASS 2017)

System	Accuracy
CNN+RNN (our approach)	**0.609**
jacerong-run1 [6]	0.608
ELiRF-UPV-run1 [13]	0.607
RETUYT-svm cnn [25]	0.596
tecnolenguasent [19]	0.595

5 Related Work

There is a plethora of related works for sentiment analysis but, we are only interested in contributions for the Spanish language. Arguably one of the most complete Spanish sentiment analysis systems was proposed by Brooke et al. [5], which had a linguistically approach. That approach integrated linguistic resources in a model to decide about polarity opinions [29]. However, recent successful approaches for Spanish polarity classification have been mostly based on machine learning [9].

In the last six years, the TASS at SEPLN Workshop has been the main source for Spanish sentiment analysis datasets and proposals [10,17]. Benchmarks for both the polarity detection task and aspect-based sentiment analysis task have been proposed in several editions of this Workshop (Spanish Tweets have been emphasized).

Recently, deep learning approaches emerge as powerful computational models that discover intricate semantic representations of texts automatically from data without feature engineering. These approaches have improved the state-of-the-art in many sentiment analysis tasks including sentiment classification of sentences/documents, sentiment extraction and sentiment lexicon learning [27]. However, these results have been mostly obtained for English Language. Due to our proposal is based on Deep Learning, the related work that follows emphasizes these kinds of algorithms.

Arguably, the first approach using Deep Learning techniques for Spanish Sentiment Analysis was proposed in the TASS at SEPLN workshop in 2015 [30]. The authors presented one architecture that was composed by a RNN layer (LSTMs cells), a dense layer and a Sigmoid function as output. The performance over the general dataset was poor, 0.60 in terms of accuracy (the best result was 0.69 in TASS 2015).

The first Convolutional Neural Network approach for Spanish Sentiment Analysis was described in [26]. However, the CNN model proposed for sentiment analysis was mostly based on Kim's work [14]. It was comprised by only a single convolutional layer, followed by a max-pooling layer and a Softmax classifier as final layer. Word embeddings were used in three ways: a learned word embedding from scratch, and two pre-trained Word2vec models. In terms of accuracy they obtained 0.64, which was far from the best result (0.72 was the best result in TASS 2016 [10]).

Another CNN approach for Spanish Sentiment Analysis was presented by Paredes et al. [23]. First, a preprocessing step (tokenization and normalization) was performed which was followed by a Word2vec embedding. Then, the model was comprised of a 2D convolutional layer, a max pooling and a final Softmax layer, i.e., it is also similar to Kim's work [14]. It was reported an F-measure of 0.887 over a non public Twitter corpus of 10000 tweets.

Most of the Deep Learning approaches for Spanish sentiment analysis have been presented in TASS 2017 [17]. For instance, Rosa et al. [25] used word embeddings within two approaches, SVM (with manually crafted features) and Convolutional Neural Networks. Pre-trained Word2vec, Glove and fastext embeddings were used. Unlike our approach, these embeddings were used separately. In fact, the best results of this paper were obtained using Word2vec. When CNN was employed, unidimensional convolutions were performed. Several convolutional layers were tested. The best model had three convolutional layers, using 2, 3 and 4 word filters. However, their best results were obtained when combined with SVM and CNN, using simply a decision rule based on both probability results. Interesting results were obtained, 0.596 in terms of accuracy, for the InterTASS dataset (the best accuracy result was 0.608 for TASS 2017 [17]).

Garcia-Vega et al. [11] used word embeddings with shallow classifiers. Recurrent neural networks with LSTM nodes and a dense layer were also tested. Two kinds of experiments were performed using word embeddings and TFIDF values as inputs. Both experiments obtained poor results (0.333 and 0.404 in terms of accuracy for the InterTASS dataset in 2017).

Araque et al. [1] explored recurrent neural networks in two ways (i) a set of LSTM cells whose input were word embeddings, (ii) a combination of input word vector and polarity values obtained from a sentiment lexicon. As usual, a last dense layer with a Softmax function was used as final output. While interesting, experimental results showed that the best performance was obtained by the second model, LSTM + Lexicon + dense. In terms of accuracy they obtained 0.562. This value is far from the TASS 2017 top results.

In the last years, the best results were obtained for the group ELiRF [13]. In TASS 2017, they obtained the second best result for the InterTSS task, 0.607, in terms of accuracy (The first place presented an ensemble approach [6]). It is worth noting that ELiRF best results were obtained using a Multilayer perceptron with word embeddings as inputs. This MLP had two layers with ReLu activation functions. A Second approach used a stack of CNN and LSTM models, using pre-trained word embeddings. The architecture was composed by one convolutional layer, 64 LSTM cel and a fully connected MLP, with ReLU activation functions. This last architecture had a poor performance (0.436 in terms of Accuracy).

6 Conclusion

Despite being one of the three most used languages at Internet, Spanish has had few resources developed for natural language processing tasks. For instance, unlike English sentiment analysis, Deep Learning approaches were unable to obtain state-of-the-art results on Spanish benchmark datasets in the past. The aim of this work was to demonstrate that Deep Learning is the best choice for Spanish Twitter sentiment analysis. Our experimental results have showed that a combination of data augmentation, at least three kinds of word embeddings, a 3D Convolutional Neural Network, followed by a Recurrent Neural Network allows us to obtain results comparable to state-of-the-art approaches over the InterTASS 2017 benchmark. In addition, this setup could be easily adapted to other domains.

References

1. Araque, O., Barbado, R., Sanchez-Rada, J.F., Iglesias, C.A.: Applying recurrent neural networks to sentiment analysis of spanish tweets. In: Proceedings of TASS 2017: Workshop on Sentiment Analysis at SEPLN, pp. 71–76 (2017)
2. Bengio, Y., Ducharme, R., Vincent, P., Janvin, C.: A neural probabilistic language model. J. Mach. Learn. Res. **3**, 1137–1155 (2003)
3. Bojanowski, P., Grave, E., Joulin, A., Mikolov, T.: Enriching word vectors with subword information. Trans. Assoc. Comput. Linguist. **5**, 135–146 (2017)

4. Brody, S., Elhadad, N.: An unsupervised aspect-sentiment model for online reviews. In: Human Language Technologies: The 2010 Annual Conference of the North American Chapter of the Association for Computational Linguistics, HLT 2010, pp. 804–812. Association for Computational Linguistics, Stroudsburg, PA, USA (2010)
5. Brooke, J., Tofiloski, M., Taboada, M.: Cross-linguistic sentiment analysis: from English to Spanish. Proc. RANLP **2009**, 50–54 (2009)
6. Ceron-Guzman, J.A.: Classier ensembles that push the state-of-the-art in sentiment analysis of Spanish tweets. In: Proceedings of TASS 2017: Workshop on Sentiment Analysis at SEPLN, pp. 59–64 (2017)
7. Collobert, R., Weston, J., Bottou, L., Karlen, M., Kavukcuoglu, K., Kuksa, P.P.: Natural language processing (almost) from scratch. CoRR abs/1103.0398 (2011)
8. Elman, J.L.: Finding structure in time. Cogn. Sci. **14**(2), 179–211 (1990)
9. Garcia, M., Martinez, E., Villena, J., Garcia, J.: Tass 2015 - the evolution of the spanish opinion mining systems. Procesamiento de Lenguaje Natural **56**, 33–40 (2016)
10. Garcia-Cumbreras, M.A., Villena-Roman, J., Martinez-Camara, E., Diaz-Galiano, M., Martin-Valdivia, T., Ureña Lopez, A.: Overview of TASS 2016. In: Proceedings of TASS 2016: Workshop on Sentiment Analysis at SEPLN, pp. 13–21 (2016)
11. Garcia-Vega, M., Montejo-Raez, A., Diaz-Galiano, M.C., Jimenez-Zafra, S.M.: SINAI in TASS 2017: tweet polarity classification integrating user information. In: Proceedings of TASS 2017: Workshop on Sentiment Analysis at SEPLN, pp. 91–96 (2017)
12. Graves, A.: Supervised Sequence Labelling with Recurrent Neural Networks. SCI. Springer, Heidelberg (2012). https://doi.org/10.1007/978-3-642-24797-2. https://cds.cern.ch/record/1503877
13. Hurtado, L.F., Pla, F., Gonzalez, J.A.: ELiRF-UPV at TASS 2017: Sentiment analysis in twitter based on deep learning. In: Proceedings of TASS 2017: Workshop on Sentiment Analysis at SEPLN, pp. 29–34 (2017)
14. Kim, Y.: Convolutional neural networks for sentence classification. In: Proceedings of the 2014 Conference on Empirical Methods in Natural Language Processing, EMNLP 2014, 25–29 October 2014, Doha, Qatar, A meeting of SIGDAT, A Special Interest Group of the ACL, pp. 1746–1751 (2014). http://aclweb.org/anthology/D/D14/D14-1181.pdf
15. LeCun, Y., Bengio, Y., Hinton, G.: Deep learning. Nature **521**(7553), 436–444 (2015)
16. Liu, B.: Sentiment Analysis and Opinion Mining. Morgan and Claypool Publishers, San Rafael (2012)
17. Martinez-Camara, E., Diaz-Galiano, M., Garcia-Cumbreras, M.A., Garcia-Vega, M., Villena-Roman, J.: Overview of Tass 2017. In: Proceedings of TASS 2017: Workshop on Sentiment Analysis at SEPLN, pp. 13–21 (2017)
18. Mikolov, T., Sutskever, I., Chen, K., Corrado, G.S., Dean, J.: Distributed representations of words and phrases and their compositionality. In: Burges, C.J.C., Bottou, L., Welling, M., Ghahramani, Z., Weinberger, K.Q. (eds.) Advances in Neural Information Processing Systems 26, pp. 3111–3119. Curran Associates, Inc. (2013). http://papers.nips.cc/paper/5021-distributed-representations-of-words-and-phrases-and-their-compositionality.pdf
19. Moreno-Ortiz, A., Perez-Hernendez, C.: Tecnolengua lingmotif at TASS 2017: Spanish twitter dataset classification combining wide-coverage lexical resources and text features. In: Proceedings of TASS 2017: Workshop on Sentiment Analysis at SEPLN, pp. 35–42 (2017)

20. Narayanan, V., Arora, I., Bhatia, A.: Fast and accurate sentiment classification using an enhanced Naive Bayes model. In: Yin, H., et al. (eds.) IDEAL 2013. LNCS, vol. 8206, pp. 194–201. Springer, Heidelberg (2013). https://doi.org/10.1007/978-3-642-41278-3_24
21. Neubig, G.: Neural machine translation and sequence-to-sequence models: a tutorial. CoRR abs/1703.01619 (2017). http://arxiv.org/abs/1703.01619
22. Pang, B., Lee, L.: Opinion mining and sentiment analysis. Found. Trends Inf. Retr. **2**(1–2), 1–135 (2008). http://dx.doi.org/10.1561/1500000011
23. Paredes-Valverde, M.A., Colomo-Palacios, R., Salas-Zarate, M.D.P., Valencia-Garcia, R.: Sentiment analysis in Spanish for improvement of products and services: a deep learning approach. Sci. Program. **6**, 1–6 (2017)
24. Pennington, J., Socher, R., Manning, C.D.: Glove: global vectors for word representation. In: Empirical Methods in Natural Language Processing (EMNLP), pp. 1532–1543 (2014)
25. Rosa, A., Chiruzzo, L., Etcheverry, M., Castro, S.: RETUYT in TASS 2017: Sentiment analysis for Spanish tweets using SVM and CNN. In: Proceedings of TASS 2017: Workshop on Sentiment Analysis at SEPLN, pp. 77–83 (2017)
26. Segura-Bedmar, I., Quiros, A., Martínez, P.: Exploring convolutional neural networks for sentiment analysis of spanish tweets. In: Proceedings of the 15th Conference of the European Chapter of the Association for Computational Linguistics, Long Papers, vol. 1, pp. 1014–1022. Association for Computational Linguistics (2017). http://aclweb.org/anthology/E17-1095
27. Tang, D., Wei, F., Qin, B., Yang, N., Liu, T., Zhou, M.: Sentiment embeddings with applications to sentiment analysis. IEEE Trans. Knowl. Data Eng. **28**(2), 496–509 (2016)
28. Tang, D., Qin, B., Liu, T.: Deep learning for sentiment analysis: successful approaches and future challenges. Wiley Interdisc. Rev.: Data Min. Knowl. Disc. **5**(6), 292–303 (2015)
29. Turney, P.D.: Thumbs up or thumbs down?: semantic orientation applied to unsupervised classification of reviews. In: Proceedings of the 40th Annual Meeting on Association for Computational Linguistics, ACL 2002, pp. 417–424. Association for Computational Linguistics, Stroudsburg, PA, USA (2002)
30. Vilares, D., Doval, Y., Alonso, M.A., Gomez-Rodriguez, C.: LyS at TASS 2015: Deep learning experiments for sentiment analysis on Spanish tweets. In: Proceedings of TASS 2015: Workshop on Sentiment Analysis at SEPLN, pp. 47–52 (2015)
31. Zhang, L., Wang, S., Liu, B.: Deep learning for sentiment analysis : a survey. CoRR abs/1801.07883 (2018). http://arxiv.org/abs/1801.07883

Calculating the Upper Bounds for Portuguese Automatic Text Summarization Using Genetic Algorithm

Jonathan Rojas-Simón[✉], Yulia Ledeneva[✉],
and René Arnulfo García-Hernández[✉]

Autonomous University of the State of Mexico, Instituto Literario no. 100,
50000 Toluca, State of Mexico, Mexico
ids_jonathan_rojas@hotmail.com, yledeneva@yahoo.com,
renearnulfo@hotmail.com

Abstract. Over the last years, Automatic Text Summarization (ATS) has been considered as one of the main tasks in Natural Language Processing (NLP) that generates summaries in several languages (e.g., English, Portuguese, Spanish, etc.). One of the most significant advances in ATS is developed for Portuguese reflected with the proposals of various state-of-art methods. It is essential to know the performance of different state-of-the-art methods with respect to the upper bounds (*Topline*), lower bounds (*Baseline-random*), and other heuristics (*Baseline-first*). In recent works, the significance and upper bounds for Single-Document Summarization (SDS) and Multi-Document Summarization (MDS) using corpora from Document Understanding Conferences (DUC) were calculated. In this paper, a calculus of upper bounds for SDS in Portuguese using Genetic Algorithms (GA) is performed. Moreover, we present a comparison of some state-of-the-art methods with respect to the upper bounds, lower bounds, and heuristics to determinate their level of significance.

Keywords: *Topline* · Single-document summarization · Portuguese
Genetic algorithms · State-of-the-art methods

1 Introduction

Automatic Text Summarization (ATS) has been considered one of the most critical tasks in Natural Language Processing (NLP) that continues to be open. In the last three decades, a great variety of advances has been presented over the Document Understanding Conferences (DUC) and Text Analysis Conferences (TAC) workshops,[1] organized by the National Institute of Standards and Technology (NIST). These workshops have been focused in generate summaries in English. However, other organizations have been reported several advances in the state-of-the-art. One of the primary organization of this area is the Interinstitutional Center for Computational

---

[1] DUC website: https://www-nlpir.nist.gov/projects/duc/, TAC website: https://tac.nist.gov/.

© Springer Nature Switzerland AG 2018
G. R. Simari et al. (Eds.): IBERAMIA 2018, LNAI 11238, pp. 442–454, 2018.
https://doi.org/10.1007/978-3-030-03928-8_36

Linguistics[2] (NILC, abbreviation in Portuguese) has been performed several advances and resources for NLP in Portuguese.

Since 1993, the researchers of NILC and others have been performed several applications for Portuguese ATS. Some of them include the use of supervised and unsupervised machine learning methods [1, 2], discursive knowledge models [3–5], identification of "gist sentence" from the source documents to generate extractive summaries [6], Text Simplification (TS) [7], complex networks and graph-based methods to text analysis [8–11]. On the other hand, some ATS systems have been proposed to generate extractive summaries through optimization-based methods [12–15]. In the most of these works have been presented ATS systems for Single-Document Summarization (SDS) and Multi-Document Summarization (MDS) using corpora like TeMario and CSTNews respectively [16–18].

In [19, 20] has been mentioned that the primary challenge of ATS is to generate extractive summaries of better similarity in comparison to the summaries created by humans (gold-standard summaries). However, for several domains, the gold-standard summaries are made by substituting some terms (words and phrases) from the source documents. This case is happened with DUC, TeMario and CSTNews corpus [16, 18, 21]. Consequently, the level of maximum similarity will be less than 100%, and therefore the upper bounds will be lower for any method. To determine the maximum similarity to the gold-standard summaries involves the search and evaluation of several numbers of possible sentence combinations from a document to generate the best extractive summary.

Currently, some heuristics have been used to compare the performance of several state-of-the-art methods to know their level of advance. These heuristics are known as *Baseline-first* and *Baseline-random* that reflects the standard and lower bounds respectively [19]. On the other hand, the use of *Topline* heuristic has been introduced in recent works, with the purpose of reflecting the upper bounds [22]. These one have been used to calculate the significance of SDS and MDS tasks [19, 20]. However, for Portuguese SDS has not performed a significant analysis to compare the best state-of-the-art methods due to that *Topline* was unknown.

The use of optimization-based methods for SDS and MDS have been represented a viable solution to generate extractive summaries of superior performance. These ones include the use of Genetic Algorithms [13]. Therefore, the use of optimization-based methods represents a viable solution to obtain extractive summaries closest to the human-written summaries. In this paper, a GA is used with some adjustment of parameters of [19] to get the sentence combinations of best similarity to the sentences selected by humans in Portuguese, using some evaluation measures of the ROUGE system. Moreover, different lengths of summaries and sentence segmentations as constraints were considered to calculate the upper bounds.

The rest of the paper is organized as follows: Sect. 2 presents some related works and previous works that have used techniques based on exhaustive searches and optimized based techniques to determine the best sentence combinations to calculate the significance for SDS and MDS methods. Section 3 describes the structure and

---

[2] http://www.nilc.icmc.usp.br/nilc/index.php.

development of proposed GA. Section 4 shows the experimental configuration of GA to determine the *Topline* for TeMario corpus. Moreover, a significant analysis to identify the best state-of-the-art methods with the use of *Baseline-first*, *Baseline-random*, and *Topline* heuristics. Finally, Sect. 5 describes the conclusions and future work.

2   Related Works

Over of the last two decades, many problems have been treated around the ATS (e.g., automatic evaluation of summaries [23, 24], sentence boundary detection, language analysis, etc.). However, few studies have been performed to determine the best extractive summaries. Some related works use techniques based on exhaustive searches to represent the summaries made by humans [25, 26].

In the work of Ceylan [25], an exhaustive search-based method was presented to obtain the best combinations of sentences. Unlike of Lin and Hovy [26], this method employs a probability density function to reduce the number of all possible combinations of sentences in different domains (literary, scientific, journalistic and legal). Each sequence is evaluated with some metrics of the ROUGE system. A similar approach has been performed in [27]. Nevertheless, the main problem of this method involves the partial processing of several source document subsets to reduce their handling [19, 20]. Therefore, the use of this strategy can generate biased results.

In the work of [28], nine heuristic methods to reduce and assign scores to the sentence combinations for SDS and MDS have been presented. First, the redundant sentences are removed. Subsequently, the remaining sentences are introduced into eight methods to assign them a score according to the gold-standard summaries, with the purpose of eliminating the low scoring sentences. However, the use of several heuristics to determine the best combinations of sentences in different domains and different entries allows the increase of computational cost to find the best sentence combinations. Furthermore, for SDS only a single gold-standard summary was used. In the case of MDS, only 533 documents of 567 on DUC02 were used, generating more biased results.

Finally, a calculus of significance and upper bounds for SDS and MDS using GAs were presented in [19, 20]. Using three different heuristics (*Baseline-random*, *Baseline-first*, and *Topline*) that represent the lower, standard and upper bounds it has been calculated the percentage of advance of several state-of-the-art methods for SDS and MDS, using DUC01 and DUC02 as test datasets. Unlike the previous works, all sentences were considered as candidates to construct the best extractive summaries and calculate the upper bounds using GAs. In this paper, we propose the calculus of upper bounds in Portuguese using GAs to find the best combinations of sentences that can be generated from the single-document summaries of TeMario corpus and rank the best SDS methods for Portuguese.

3   Calculating Upper Bounds

To calculate the upper bounds for SDS in Portuguese, we propose the use of typical steps and procedures of basic GA described in [29], to evaluate several combinations of sentences in an optimized search space. In this section, the main stages and descriptions of the proposed GA to calculate the upper bounds are shown.

Solution Representation. In previous works [19, 20], the solution is presented using a coding of individuals considering the order of sentences that can appear in the extractive summary. Therefore, each individual X_i (a candidate of best extractive summary) is represented in a vector of n positions $[P_1, P_2, \ldots, P_n]$, where each position includes a sentence $\{S_1, S_2, \ldots, S_n\}$ of original document D. For each coding to be considered like an extractive summary, the first sentences are considered according to a limit of words.

Fitness Function. The evaluation of individuals is an essential stage of GA where each candidate summary X_i is evaluated according to the F-measure score from ROUGE system metrics [30]. The maximum F-measure score of summary X_k obtained from g generations determine the best combination of sentences found by GA. This maximization is shown in Eq. (1), where n is the length of n-grams for evaluation of candidate summaries.

$$Max(F(X_k(g))) = \frac{\sum_{S \in S_{ref}} \sum_{gram_n \in S} Count_{match}(gram_n)}{\sum_{S \in S_{ref}} \sum_{gram_n \in S} Count(gram_n)}, g = \{0, \ldots, G\} \quad (1)$$

In this case, we have focused in optimize through ROUGE-1 and ROUGE-2 metrics (evaluation based on bag-of-words and bigrams respectively) due to that these metrics have been obtained the maximum correlations with respect to human judgments [30]. F is the F-measure score of the ROUGE system, and $Count_{match}(gram_n)$ is the number of co-occurrent n-grams between a candidate summary X_i and gold-standard summary. If the candidate summary $X_k(g)$ has the highest co-occurrence of n-grams from all populations $X_i(g)$, then it will have the best combination of sentences due to that it has the most substantial of retrieved n-grams.

Initialization of Individuals. To initialize the population of individuals (when $g = 0$) must be generated with codifications of random real numbers for signature each sentence of source document $D = \{S_1, S_2, \ldots, S_n\}$ in each position P_i of $[P_1, P_2, \ldots, P_n]$. Therefore, the first generation of individuals will be according to Eq. (2), where a_s represents a real integer number $\{1, 2, \ldots, n\}$ that corresponds to the number of the selected sentence in document D, $c = 1, 2, \ldots, N_{pop}$, $s = 1, 2, \ldots, n$, n is the number of the n-th sentence from the source document.

$$X_c(0) = [X_{c,1}(0), X_{c,2}(0), \ldots, X_{c,n}(0)], X_{c,s} = a_s \quad (2)$$

Therefore, each sentence has the same probability of being included as part of an extractive summary according to a number W of requested words (see Eq. (3)).

$$\sum\nolimits_{S_i \in Summary} l_i \leq W \qquad (3)$$

where l_i is the length of the sentence S_i (measured in words) and W is the maximum number of words allowed to generate an extractive summary. In this case, we considered the use of several numbers of words per document as a constraint, due to that the lengths of each document of TeMario (gold-standard summaries and source documents) are made up of different compression rates.

Selection. In the selection stage, we propose the use of two selection operators to obtain the best subsets of individuals for each population of individuals. The first one consists in selecting a small subset of individuals through the elitism operator, which has the feature to choose minimal subgroups of individuals of best aptitude from generation g to pass the next generation $(g + 1)$. To select the remaining individuals from each generation, we propose several select of individuals from the tournament selection operator. This operator generates several subsets of N_{Tor} randomly picked individuals to retrieve the individual with the best fitness value, as shown in Eq. (4), where $X_b(g)$ is the individual with the best fitness value and F is the F-measure score of ROUGE metric.

$$X_b(g) = argmax(F(X_1(g)), F(X_2(g)), \ldots, F(X_{N_{Tor}}(g))) \qquad (4)$$

To integrate the selection stage, we propose to use the elitism operator to choose the best individuals of each population, using a percentage of them. Finally, the remaining individuals are obtained from the tournament selection operator, using samples of two randomly obtained individuals.

Crossover. For the crossing of individuals, we use the cycle crossover algorithm (CX) to interchange a subset of genes according to a start point (initial gene). For the CX operator to be started, it is necessary considering a crossover probability P to determine the subset of individuals who will perform the genetic exchange. Therefore, if b_{rand} (a random number) is between 0 and P, then the operator must select a starting point to perform the genetic exchange of parents $X_{p1}(g)$ and $X_{p2}(g)$ to generate an offspring $Y_i(g)$, otherwise, the first parent $(X_{p1}(g))$ will be $Y_i(g)$. To produce the second offspring, the roles of $X_{p1}(g)$ and $X_{p2}(g)$ are exchanged.

Mutation. For the mutation stage, we propose taking a set of individuals $Y_i(g)$ to generate individuals $Z_i(g)$ modifying some genes of each population of individuals. To the mutation of individuals, we used the insertion mutation operator to select a pair of genes of the individual $Y_{i,t}(g)$ and $Y_{i,r}(g)$ randomly to insert the gene $Y_{i,t}(g)$ in the gene $Y_{i,r}(g)$, as shown in Eq. (5), where r is the variable that relates the gene to be inserted, the variable t represents the target gene to be inserted, which are an element of subset $s = \{1, 2, \ldots, n\}$, and n is the number of the sentence S_i from the source document D.

$$Z_{i,s}(g) = \begin{cases} Y_{i,t}(g) = Y_{i,r}(g), Y_{i,t\pm1}(g) = Y_{i,t}(g), \ldots, Y_{i,r}(g) = Y_{i,r\pm1}(g); & \text{if } 0 < rand \leq P \\ Y_{i,s}(g) & \text{otherwise} \end{cases}$$

$$(5)$$

Therefore, if *rand* (a random number) is between 0 and P, then the mutation of individuals is performed by insertion operator, otherwise, the individual is not modified.

Replacement of Individuals. Taking as reference the previous works [19, 20], the replacement of individuals step, we propose to integrate the set of individuals generated by elitist selection $(E(g + 1))$ and the set of individuals $Z_i(g)$ from the mutation stage, to integrate the population of the next generation $(X_i(g + 1) = X_i(g + 1) \cup Z_i(g))$.

Termination Criterion. The termination criterion used to halt the GA iterations is determined by the number of G generations established as a constraint of stop. In the experimentation stage, 50 generations were used for each document of TeMario due to that was the best parameter found.

4   Experimental Results

In this section, we describe TeMario corpus and the experiments performed to generate the best extractive summaries. Moreover, the performance of some state-of-the-art methods and heuristics are presented to determine which methods of the state-of-the-art are more significant.

4.1   TeMario Corpus

TeMario (derived from "TExtos com suMÁRIOs") is a corpus of 100 newspaper articles written in Brazilian Portuguese. 60 documents were written by the online Brazilian newspaper *Folha de São Paulo*, and 40 documents were written by the newspaper *Journal do Brasil* (Brazilian Newspaper) [16]. The TeMario documents are distributed into equitably five sections (Special, World, Opinion, International, and Politics).[3] Moreover, a gold-standard summary was generated for each document of TeMario by a professional writer. Table 1 shows some features of TeMario corpus.

Unlike DUC datasets, TeMario was not created with specific constraints to indicate the comparison of the performance of the state-of-the-art methods. One of the main problems is derived from the lack of explicit identification of sentences or phrases to generate summaries because it was not determined the sentence labeling. Due to this, we present the segmentation of sentences in three different cases.[4] The first segmentation consists in divide the documents by paragraph, the second segmentation includes in split the source documents into several sentences manually (Tagged), and finally, the third division consists in divide the documents into sentences through an automatic sentence boundary detection tool (SENTER) developed by the same author of TeMario.[5] Table 2 shows the number of sentences of each segmentation.

---

[3] https://www.linguateca.pt/Repositorio/TeMario/.

[4] Each segmentation can be downloaded from https://gitlab.com/JohnRojas/Corpus-TeMario.

[5] http://conteudo.icmc.usp.br/pessoas/taspardo/SENTER_Por.zip.

Table 1. TeMario corpus description [16].

Journal	Section	Number of documents	Number of words	Mean of words per document
Folha de São Paulo	Special	20	12340	617
	World	20	13739	686
	Opinion	20	10438	521
Journal do Brazil	International	20	12098	604
	Politics	20	12797	439
	Total	100	61412	
	Mean		12282	613

Table 2. Number of sentences obtained from TeMario corpus using different segmentations.

	Paragraph	Tagged	SENTER
Total	1275	2896	2899
Mean	12.75	28.96	28.99
Std	6.20	9.08	9.22

According to the number of sentences obtained from different segmentations (see Table 2), the use of varying segmentations of terms generates different sequences to construct extractive summaries, and therefore the performance of SDS methods can be affected. The division by paragraphs presents fewer sentences to combine. Tagged and SENTER segmentations presents a similar number of sentences. However, these segmentations capture different sequences of terms due to that Std indicator is different between segmentations.

4.2   Parameters of GA

With respect to the GA, different parameters were carried out; however, the best parameters performed are presented in Table 3. Unlike the previous works [19, 20], the *Topline* was calculated considering different segmentations of sentences described above. Moreover, the gold-standard summaries were written with different lengths and therefore were not possible to determine the upper bounds. Considering this constraint, the *Topline* was calculated for different lengths. These are: 1. Summaries with a compression rate of 30% (parameter proposed in [1, 10]). 2. Summaries with 100 words. 3. Summaries according to the length of words to the gold-standard summaries.

4.3   State-of-the-Art Methods and Heuristics

In this paper, we determine the level of advance with respect to other heuristics (*Baseline-first*, *Baseline-random*, and *Topline*). The methods and heuristics taken into consideration for this comparison are the following:

Table 3. GA parameters to calculate the upper bounds of TeMario corpus.

N_{pop}	Selection				Crossover		Mutation	
200	Operator	e	Operator	N_{Tor}	Operator	P	Operator	P
	Elitism	1%	Tournament	2	CX	85%	Insertion	0.012%

Baseline-first: This heuristic uses the first sentences from the source text to generate an extractive summary, according to a length of words. The performance of this heuristic has been generated good results in SDS and MDS [19]. However, this heuristic must be overcome by state-of-the-art methods.

Baseline-random: This heuristic consists in selecting a random number of sentences according to a length of words to generate an extractive summary. This heuristic allows us to determine how significant is the performance of the state-of-the-art methods [29].

Topline: It is an heuristic that allows to obtain the upper bounds for SDS and MDS that any state-of-the-art method can achieve, due to the lack of concordance between evaluators [22].

GA-Summarization: The method presented in [13] uses a GA to generate extractive independent-language summaries. This method evaluates the quality of each candidate summary considering three features: 1. Frequency of terms in sentence. 2. Frequency of terms in summary. 3. Importance of sentences according to the position from the source document.

GistSumm: The method presented in [6] uses a gist-sentence approach to generate extractive summaries. First, the identification of the "gist-sentence" is performed through simple statistical measures. Then, the gist sentence is used as a guideline to identify and select other sentences to integrate the extractive summary. This method can generate extractive summaries in three different forms: 1. Intrasentential Summarization (*GistSumm-1*). 2. Query-based summarization (*GistSumm-2*). 3. Average keywords ranking (*GistSumm-3*).

Shvoong: It is an online tool founded by Avi Shaked and Avner Avrahami to generate extractive summaries in 21 different languages.[6] Some of them include the English, French, German, Portuguese, and others.

Open Text Summarizer (OTS): It is an open-source application to generate multilingual extractive summaries that can be downloaded online.[7] This tool allows constructing extractive summaries based on the detection of the main ideas from the source document, considering the reduction of redundant information.

To compare the performance of heuristics and the state-of-the-art methods previously described, the evaluation based on the statistical co-occurrence of bag-of-words and bigrams (ROUGE-1 and ROUGE-2) from the ROUGE system was performed [30]. ROUGE-1 and ROUGE-2 use the ROUGE-N evaluation method, based on the

---

[6] http://www.shvoong.com/summarizer/. (URL viewed May 7th, 2017).

[7] https://github.com/neopunisher/Open-Text-Summarizer/ (URL viewed February 10th, 2018).

statistical co-occurrence of terms included between a candidate summary and the gold-standard summaries (see Eq. (6)).

$$ROUGE - N = \frac{\sum_{S \in Summ_{ref}} \sum_{gram_n \in S} Count_{match}(gram_n)}{\sum_{S \in Summ_{ref}} \sum_{gram_n \in S} Count(gram_n)} \tag{6}$$

Tables 4, 5 and 6 show the average results of ROUGE-1 and ROUGE-2 (R1 and R2) scores of *Baseline-first*, *Baseline-random*, and *Topline* heuristics considering different segmentations of TeMario. As we can see, the performance of *Baseline-random* and *Topline* was affected, due to that the selection of sentences was obtained from different criteria (paragraph, automatic and manual form). On the other hand, the performance of *Baseline-first* was not affected significantly, due to this heuristic only uses the length of words to construct extractive summaries. However, each segmentation of sentences generated a higher number of words (some words were split), and therefore, the evaluation step generates different results (but it is not significant). Moreover, the use of different compression rates (100 words, 30% of the source text and according to the length of gold-standard summaries) affects the performance of all heuristics, due to the gold-standard summaries has different lengths of words and therefore must be evaluated with varying rates of compression.

To compare the state-of-the-art methods and heuristics previously described, we generated summaries according to human segmentation (Tagged) with a compression rate of 30% from the source documents (see Table 7). Table 7 shows the performance of GA-Summarization method (48.791) is better than other state-of-the-art methods in ROUGE-1. However, the performance of GistSumm-2 method (18.375) is better than other state-of-the-art methods in ROUGE-2. On the other hand, the performance of *Baseline-first* outperforms all state-of-the-art methods in ROUGE-1 (48.986) and ROUGE-2 (18.948). Furthermore, some methods have been obtained worse performance than *Baseline-random* heuristic (Gist-Summ-3 and *GistSumm-1*).

To unify the performance of the state-of-the-art methods in ROUGE-1 and ROUGE-2, the Eq. (7) was used to rank the best ones according to the position of each method (See Table 7).

$$Ran(method) = \sum_{r=1}^{6} \frac{(6 - r + 1)R_r}{6} \tag{7}$$

where R_r refers the number of times the method occurs in the *r-th* rank. The number 6 represents the total number of methods involved in this comparison.

Table 8 shows the result rank of each state-of-the-art method. As we can see, the performance of *GA-Summarization* (1.833) and *GistSumm-2* (1.833) methods show the best positions in the method rankings. However, *GA-Summarization* performs some independent-language features, while the performance of *GistSumm-2* depends on some language features. On the other hand, the methods *Shvoong*, *OTS*, *GistSumm-3* and *GistSumm-1* present the same positions across ROUGE metrics.

Table 4. Results of heuristics considering the segmentation by paragraph.

	100 words		30% of source text		Gold-standard summary	
	R1	R2	R1	R2	R1	R2
Topline	54.653	27.808	58.253	28.693	58.848	28.647
Baseline-first	46.448	19.881	49.001	18.952	49.514	18.883
Baseline-random	37.605	10.497	46.242	15.540	47.952	16.669

Table 5. Results of heuristics considering the tagged segmentation.

	100 words		30% of source text		Gold-standard summary	
	R1	R2	R1	R2	R1	R2
Topline	59.986	32.401	62.342	32.558	63.223	32.870
Baseline-first	46.452	19.881	48.986	18.948	49.493	18.866
Baseline-random	38.324	10.731	45.721	14.616	48.527	16.515

Table 6. Results of heuristics considering the segmentation of SENTER.

	100 words		30% of source text		Gold-standard summary	
	R1	R2	R1	R2	R1	R2
Topline	59.765	32.437	62.282	32.598	63.155	32.779
Baseline-first	46.448	19.881	49.005	18.953	49.515	18.883
Baseline-random	38.009	10.507	45.743	15.126	47.657	16.227

Table 7. Results of the state-of-the-art methods and heuristics considering a tagged segmentation of sentences with a compression rate of 30%.

	ROUGE-1	ROUGE-2
Topline	**62.342**	**32.558**
Baseline-first	**48.986**	**18.948**
GA-Summarization	48.791 (1)	18.375 (2)
GistSumm-2	48.552 (2)	18.862 (1)
Shvoong	47.819 (3)	17.923 (3)
OTS	47.199 (4)	17.401 (4)
Baseline-random	**45.721**	**14.616**
GistSumm-3	45.021 (5)	15.651 (5)
GistSumm-1	35.864 (6)	11.563 (6)

Table 8. Ranking of the state-of-the-art methods.

Method	R_r						Resultant rank
	1	2	3	4	5	6	
GA-Summarization	1	1	0	0	0	0	1.833
GistSumm – 2	1	1	0	0	0	0	1.833
Shvoong	0	0	2	0	0	0	1.333
OTS	0	0	0	2	0	0	1.000
GistSumm – 3	0	0	0	0	2	0	0.666
GistSumm – 1	0	0	0	0	0	2	0.333

5   Conclusions and Future Work

In several works have been presented several ATS methods for SDS and MDS tasks to generate extractive summaries in Portuguese. However, the calculus of upper bounds was unknown. In this paper, a calculus of upper bounds for SDS in Portuguese was presented. Furthermore, it was possible to generate a general ranking of the state-of-the-art methods according to their position.

In the process of calculating the upper bounds, it was necessary the use of different segmentation of sentences to obtain the best extractive summaries in Portuguese, due to that TeMario has not a specific delimitation of items to generate extractive summaries. Nevertheless, in this work, we proposed the use of three different segmentation of sequences (Paragraph, Tagged and Automatic Segmentation of sentences) to generate extractive summaries in TeMario.

The length of gold-standard summaries affects the performance of lower bounds and upper bounds (*Topline* and *Baseline-random* respectively) (see Tables 4, 5 and 6), due to that these summaries were not written with a specific compression rate. The use of different segmentations of sentences with different compression rates affects the performance of all state-of-the-art methods and heuristics, therefore, it is necessary consider these constraints to generate and evaluate summaries.

The performance of *Baseline-first* was not affected significantly by the segmentation of sentences, because this heuristic employs the number of the first words to generate an extractive summary. Moreover, the performance of this heuristic it was better with respect to all state-of-the-art methods (see Table 7).

In Table 7 it is observed that *Baseline-first* heuristic outperforms all state-of-the-art methods involved in this comparison, therefore to generate summaries with better performance we propose the use of other methods (or combinations of them) to generate summaries to outperform this heuristic. Finally, we propose the generation and evaluation of summaries in TeMario considering the constraints mentioned above to generate a comparison with respect the upper bounds and lower bounds.

Acknowledgements. Work done under partial support of Mexican Government CONACyT Thematic Network program (Language Technologies Thematic Network project 295022). We also thank UAEMex for their support.

References

1. Pardo, T.A.S., Rino, L.H.M., Nunes, M.G.V.: NeuralSumm: Uma Abordagem Conexionista para a Sumarização Automática de Textos. An. do IV Encontro Nac. Inteligência Artif., no. 1 (2003)
2. Orrú, T., Rosa, J.L.G., de Andrade Netto, M.L.: SABio: an automatic portuguese text summarizer through artificial neural networks in a more biologically plausible model. In: Vieira, R., et al. (eds.) PROPOR 2006. LNCS (LNAI), vol. 3960, pp. 11–20. Springer, Heidelberg (2006). https://doi.org/10.1007/11751984_2
3. Pardo, T.A.S., Rino, L.H.M.: DMSumm: review and assessment. In: Ranchhod, E., Mamede, N.J. (eds.) PorTAL 2002. LNCS (LNAI), vol. 2389, pp. 263–273. Springer, Heidelberg (2002). https://doi.org/10.1007/3-540-45433-0_36
4. Cardoso, P.C.F.: Exploração de métodos de sumarização automática multidocumento com base em conhecimento semântico- discursivo. USP (2014)
5. Nunes, M.D.G.V., Aluisio, S.M., Pardo, T.A.S.: Um panorama do Núcleo Interinstitucional de Linguística Computacional às vésperas de sua maioridade. Linguamática **2**(2), 13–27 (2010)
6. Pardo, T.A.S., Rino, L.H.M., Nunes, M.D.G.V.: GistSumm: a summarization tool based on a new extractive method. In: Mamede, N.J., Trancoso, I., Baptista, J., das Graças Volpe Nunes, M. (eds.) PROPOR 2003. LNCS (LNAI), vol. 2721, pp. 210–218. Springer, Heidelberg (2003). https://doi.org/10.1007/3-540-45011-4_34
7. Margarido, P.R., et al.: Automatic summarization for text simplification. In: Companion Proceedings of the XIV Brazilian Symposium on Multimedia and the Web, pp. 310–315 (2008)
8. Pardo, T.A.S., Antiqueira, L., Nunes, M.D.G.V., Oliveira, O.N., Costa, L.D.F.: Using complex networks for language processing: the case of summary evaluation. In: International Conference on Communications, Circuits and Systems, pp. 2678–2682 (2006)
9. Antiqueira, L.: Desenvolvimento de técnicas baseadas em redes complexas para sumarização extrativa de textos. USP – São Carlos (2007)
10. Amancio, D.R., Nunes, M.G., Oliveira, O.N., Costa, L.D.F.: Extractive summarization using complex networks and syntactic dependency. Physica A: Stat. Mech. Appl. **391**(4), 1855–1864 (2012)
11. Mihalcea, R., Tarau, P.: A language independent algorithm for single and multiple document summarization. Department of Computer Science and Engineering, vol. 5, pp. 19–24 (2005)
12. Leite, D., Rino, L.: A genetic fuzzy automatic text summarizer. In: CSBC 2009. Inf. UFRGS, Brazil, vol. 2007, pp. 779–788 (2009)
13. Matías, G.A.: Generación Automática de Resúmenes Independientes del Lenguaje. Universidad Autónoma del Estado de México (2016)
14. Oliveira, M.A.D., Guelpeli, M.V.: BLMSumm – Métodos de Busca Local e Metaheurísticas na Sumarização de Textos. In: Proceedings of ENIA - VIII Encontro Nac. Inteligência Artif., vol. 1, no. 1, pp. 287–298 (2011)
15. Oliveira, M.A., Guelpeli, M.V.C.: The performance of BLMSumm: distinct languages with antagonistic domains and varied compressions. In: Information Science and Technology, ICIST 2012, pp. 609–614 (2012)
16. Pardo, T., Rino, L.: TeMário: Um Corpus para Sumarização Automática de Textos. NILC - ICMC-USP, São Carlos (2003)
17. Maziero, E.G., Volpe, G.: TeMário 2006 : Estendendo o Córpus TeMário (2007)

18. Aleixo, P., Pardo, T.A.S.: CSTNews: um Córpus de Textos Jornalísticos Anotados segundo a Teoria Discursiva Multidocumento CST (cross-document structure theory), Structure, pp. 1–12 (2008)
19. Rojas-Simón, J., Ledeneva, Y., García-Hernández, R.A.: Calculating the significance of automatic extractive text summarization using a genetic algorithm. J. of Intell. Fuzzy Syst. **35**(1), 293–304 (2018)
20. Rojas Simón, J., Ledeneva, Y., García Hernández, R.A.: Calculating the upper bounds for multi-document summarization using genetic algorithms. Comput. y Sist. **22**(1), 11–26 (2018)
21. Verma, R., Lee, D.: Extractive summarization: limits, compression, generalized model and heuristics, p. 19 (2017)
22. Sidorov, G.: Non-linear construction of n-grams in computational linguistics, 1st edn. Sociedad Mexicana de Inteligencia Artificial, México (2013)
23. Louis, A., Nenkova, A.: Automatically evaluating content selection in summarization without human models. In: Proceedings of the 2009 Conference on Empirical Methods in Natural Language Processing, no. August, pp. 306–314 (2009)
24. Torres-Moreno, J.M., Saggion, H., Cunha, I.D., SanJuan, E., Velázquez-Morales, P.: Summary evaluation with and without references. Polibits Res. J. Comput. Sci. Comput. Eng. Appl. **42**, 13–20 (2010)
25. Ceylan, H., Mihalcea, R., Özertem, U., Lloret, E., Palomar, M.: Quantifying the limits and success of extractive summarization systems across domains. In: Human Language Technologies, no. June, pp. 903–911 (2010)
26. Lin, C.-Y., Hovy, E.: The potential and limitations of automatic sentence extraction for summarization. In: Proceedings of the HLT-NAACL 2003 on Text Summarization Workshop, vol. 5, pp. 73–80 (2003)
27. Hong, K., Marcus, M., Nenkova, A.: System combination for multi-document summarization, pp. 107–117, September 2015
28. Wang, W.M., Li, Z., Wang, J.W., Zheng, Z.H.: How far we can go with extractive text summarization? Heuristic methods to obtain near upper bounds. Expert Syst. Appl. **90**, 439–463 (2017)
29. Ledeneva, Y., García-Hernández, R.A.: Generación automática de resúmenes Retos, propuestas y experimentos (2017)
30. Lin, C.: Rouge: a package for automatic evaluation of summaries. In: Proceedings of the Workshop on Text Summarization Branches Out (WAS 2004), no. 1, pp. 25–26 (2004)

Feature Set Optimisation for Infant Cry Classification

Leandro D. Vignolo[1,2](✉), Enrique Marcelo Albornoz[1,2], and César Ernesto Martínez[1,3]

[1] Research Institute for Signals, Systems and Computational Intelligence (sinc(i)), Facultad de Ingeniería y Cs. Hídricas, Universidad Nacional del Litoral CC217, Ciudad Universitaria, Paraje El Pozo, S3000 Santa Fe, Argentina
{ldvignolo,emalbornoz,cmartinez}@sinc.unl.edu.ar
[2] Consejo Nacional de Investigaciones Científicas y Técnicas (CONICET), Buenos Aires, Argentina
[3] Laboratorio de Cibernética, Facultad de Ingeniería, Universidad Nacional de Entre Ríos, Entre Ríos, Argentina

Abstract. This work deals with the development of features for the automatic classification of infant cry, considering three categories: neutral, fussing and crying vocalisations. Mel-frequency cepstral coefficients, together with standard functional obtained from these, have long been the most widely used features for all kind of speech-related tasks, including infant cry classification. However, recent works have introduced alternative filter banks leading to performance improvements and increased robustness. In this work, the optimisation of a filter bank is proposed for feature extraction and two other spectrum-based feature sets are compared. The first set of features is obtained through the optimisation of filter banks, by means of an evolutionary algorithm, in order to find a more suitable speech representation for the infant cry classification. Moreover, the classification performance of the optimised representation combined with other spectral features based on the mean log-spectrum and auditory spectrum is evaluated. The results show that these feature sets are able to improve the performance for the cry classification task.

Keywords: Evolutionary algorithms · Features optimization
Crying classification

1 Introduction

Crying is an important communication tool for infants to express their emotional states and psychological needs [10]. Since infant may cry for a variety of reasons, parents and childcare specialists need to be able to distinguish between different types of cries through their auditive perceptions. However, this requires experience and this can be subjective from one person to another. Also, it has been demonstrated that the experienced subjects are often not able to explain the basis of such skills [10]. This motivates the work on the development of

© Springer Nature Switzerland AG 2018
G. R. Simari et al. (Eds.): IBERAMIA 2018, LNAI 11238, pp. 455–466, 2018.
https://doi.org/10.1007/978-3-030-03928-8_37

automatic tools for the analysis and recognition of infant cry applicable to real life.

Many approaches have been proposed to deal with the problem of feature extraction from audio signals, and many of them are focused on aspects like human auditory perception. Among them, the MFCC are the most widespread features for any kind of sound signals [9]. Since their use is not limited to voice signals [27], as in speaker identification [3], emotional state recognition [17], or spoken language classification [7]. These features have also been used for tasks involving other sound signals such as music information retrieval [26] and the detection of acoustic events [33]. The MFCC features have also been used for the recognition of pathologies in recently born babies through their crying [21], for the analysis of infant cry with hypothyroidism [37] and for classification of normal and pathological cry [12]. Also, the use of MFCC features was proposed for cry signal segmentation and boundary detection of expiratory and inspiratory episodes [1].

The MFCC features are based on the mel filter bank, which mimics the frequency response in the human ear. However, since the physiology of human perception is not yet fully understood, the parameters for the optimal filter bank are not known. Moreover, what is the relevant information contained in a signal spectrum depends on the application. Thus, it is doubtful that only one filter bank would be able to enhance the information that is relevant for any particular task. This has motivated the development of many approaches for tuning the filter bank in order to obtain better representations [2,15,16]. The use of a weighting function based on the harmonic structure was also proposed for improving the robustness of MFCC [13]. Similarly, other tuning to the parameters of the mel filter bank have been introduced [34,36]. Although, to our knowledge, an evolutionary strategy for the optimisation of a filter bank for cry recognition has not yet been proposed.

A common approach that has been used for many different machine learning problems is to introduce learning in the pre-processing step for producing optimised features [19,28]. That is the case in [25], where a deep learning approach was used to optimise the features used in an end-to-end approach. The versatility of genetic algorithms has motivated many approaches for feature selection [20,30], like the optimisation of wavelet decompositions for speech recognition [29]. Also, many other strategies for developing optimised representation for speech related tasks have been presented [31,32]. Evolutionary approaches have also shown success for the development of new features for stressed speech classification [6]. Although, the evolutionary optimisation of representations for the cry recognition task has not been explored.

This work tackles the automatic classification of crying vocalisations to allow automatic mood monitoring of babies for clinical or home applications [24]. Particularly, an approach based on an evolutionary algorithm (EA) for the optimisation of a filter bank for feature extraction is presented. The approach relies on an EA and introduces a scheme for parameter encoding based on spline interpolation, with the goal of finding an optimised filter bank which takes part in the extraction of cepstral features. In this proposal the EA is designed to evolve a filter bank that is part of the process for computing cepstral features, using a classifier to assess the fitness in the evaluation of the evolved individuals. This approach provides an alternative representation to improve the performance of cry recognition.

In this work, the use of a set of features based on a bio-inspired model is also proposed. These features, which were first introduced for emotion recognition [5], are based on an auditory model to mimic the human perception [35]. Since these features have not yet been used for cry recognition, it is interesting to inquire if the properties provided by the auditory model are useful for this purpose.

2   Materials and Methods

2.1   Speech Corpus and Baseline Systems

For the experiments the Cry Recognition In Early Development (CRIED) corpus was used, which is composed of 5587 utterances [24]. The vocalisations were produced by 20 healthy infants (10 male and 10 female), each of which was recorded 7 times. The corpus consists of audio-video recordings, though only audio is considered in this work. The original audio is sampled at 44.1 kHz and was down-sampled to 8 kHz in this work for the filter bank optimisation. This database was made available for the Crying Sub-Challenge of the Interspeech 2018 Computational Paralinguistics ChallengE (ComParE) [24].

The database is split into training and test partitions. The utterances were classified into the following three categories: (i) neutral/positive mood vocalisations, (ii) fussing vocalisations, and (iii) crying vocalisations. The categorisation process was done on the basis of audio-video clips by two experts in the field of early speech-language development [18]. In the experiments only audio recordings were considered and, since the labels for the instances of the test partition are not available, cross validation was performed using the training data.

In order to compare the proposed features with a well known representation, a set of features based on the MFCCs [9] was considered as a baseline. The first 17 MFCCs were computed on a time frame basis, using a 20-ms window with 10-ms step. Then, the feature set was obtained by applying a number of functionals (listed on Table 1) on the MFCCs, resulting in 531 attributes. These features are considered because they are widely used in many speaker state recognition tasks.

2.2   Evolutionary Filter Bank Optimisation

In order to analyse the appropriateness of the mel filter bank for infant cry recognition, the mean log-spectrum was computed along the frames (30 ms long) for all the training utterances in each class of the CRIED corpus. As it can be observed on top of Fig. 1, the plots corresponding to different classes show different peaks at different frequency bands, suggesting that the relevant information is not mainly at low frequency bands.

Table 1. Functionals applied to MFCCs [11,23].

Quartiles 1–3	Mean value of peaks - arithmetic mean
3 inter-quartile ranges	Linear regression slope and quadratic error
1% percentile ($\approx$ min)	Quadratic regression a and b and quadratic error
99% percentile ($\approx$ max)	Arithmetic mean, standard deviation
Percentile range 1%–99%	Standard deviation of peak distances
Simple moving average	Contour is below 25% range
Skewness, kurtosis	Contour is above 90% range
Mean of peak distances	Contour is rising/falling
Mean value of peaks	Linear prediction of MFCC contour (coefficients 1–5)
Contour centroid	Gain of linear prediction

Also, the first-order difference of the mean log-spectrums were computed, which are shown at the bottom of Fig. 1. These plots present peaks at high frequency bands showing different relative energy and shape, which could be useful for classification. Since the mel filter bank (shown on top of Fig. 3) prioritizes low frequencies with higher resolution and amplitude, all these remarks suggest that it is not entirely appropriate for this task. This motivates the work in a methodology useful for finding an optimal filter bank for the task at hand.

The proposed optimisation approach, referred to as *Evolutionary Spline Cepstral Coefficients* (ESCCs), is based on an EA to search for the optimal filter bank parameters. In this approach, instead of encoding the filter bank parameters directly, the candidate solutions in the EA use spline functions to shape the filter banks. In this way, the chromosomes (candidate solutions) in the population of the EA hold spline parameters instead of filter bank parameters, which reduces the chromosome size and the search space. With this encoding, the chromosomes within the EA population contain spline parameters instead of filter bank parameters, reducing the size and complexity of the search space. The spline mapping was defined as $y = c(x)$, with $y \in [0, 1]$, and x taking n_f equally spaced values in $(0, 1)$. Then, for a filter bank with n_f filters, value x_i was assigned to filter i, with $i = 1, ..., n_f$. For a given chromosome, the y_i values were computed for each x_i by means of cubic spline interpolation. The chromosomes encoded two splines: one to determine the frequency values corresponding to the position of each triangular filter and another to set the amplitude of each filter.

Optimisation of Filter Frequency Locations. A monotonically increasing spline is used here, which is constrained to $c(0) = 0$ and $c(1) = 1$. Four parameters are set to define the spline I: y_1^I and y_2^I corresponding to fixed values x_1^I and x_2^I, and the derivatives, σ and ρ, at the fixed points $(x = 0, y = 0)$ and $(x = 1, y = 1)$. Then, parameter y_2^I was obtained as $y_2^I = y_1^I + \delta_{y_2}$, and the parameters actually coded in the chromosomes were y_1^I, δ_{y_2}, σ and ρ. Given a particular chromosome, which set the values for these parameters, the $y[i]$ corresponding to the $x[i] \ \forall \ i = 1, ..., n_f$ were obtained by spline interpolation.

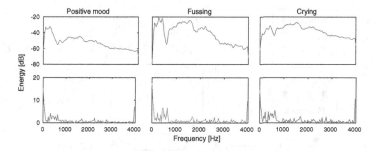

Fig. 1. Mean log-spectrums (top) and first-order difference of mean log-spectrums (bottom) for each of the three classes in the Cry Recognition In Early Development (CRIED) database.

The $y[i]$ values obtained through the spline were then mapped to the frequency range from 0 Hz to $f_s/2$, so the frequency values for the maximum of each of the n_f filters, f_i^c, were obtained as

$$f_i^c = \frac{(y[i] - y_m)f_s}{y_M - y_m}, \tag{1}$$

where y_m and y_M are the spline minimum and maximum values, respectively. Then, the filter spacing was controlled by the slopes of the corresponding points in the spline.

Also a parameter $0 < a < 1$ was defined to limit the range of y_1^I and y_2^I to $[a, 1 - a]$, with the purpose of keeping the splines within $[0, 1]$.

Optimisation of Filter Amplitudes. The spline used for optimising filter amplitudes were restricted to the range $[0, 1]$, but y was free at $x = 0$ and $x = 1$. Therefore, the parameters to be optimised here were the y values y_1^{II}, y_2^{II}, y_3^{II} and y_4^{II}, corresponding to the fixed x values x_1^{II}, x_2^{II}, x_3^{II} and x_4^{II}. These four y_j^{II} were limited to $[0, 1]$. In this manner, n_f interpolation values were obtained to set the amplitude of each filter. This is shown in Fig. 2, where the gain of each filter was set according to the value given by spline II at the corresponding points.

2.3   ESCC Optimisation Process

Every chromosome in the EA the contains a set of spline parameters that encode a particular filter bank. The search performed by the EA is guided by the classification performance, which is evaluated for each candidate solution. In order to evaluate a candidate solution, the ESCC feature extraction process was performed on the corpus based on the corresponding filter bank (Fig. 2). Then, the classifier is trained and tested using the features obtained through this process in order to assign the fitness to the corresponding individual.

The spline codification scheme allowed to reduce the chromosome length from $2n_f$ to the number of spline parameters. Since 26 filters were used, the

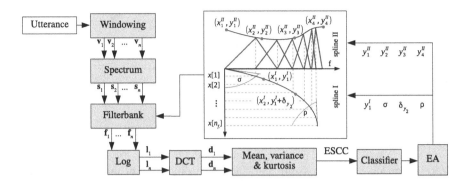

Fig. 2. Schematisation of the optimisation strategy. The output vectors of each block, s_i, f_i, l_i and d_i, indicate that each window v_i is processed isolated and, finally, the mean and variance for each coefficient is computed from the d_i vectors in order to feed the classifier.

number of free parameters in the optimisation was reduced from 46 to 8 (4 parameters for each spline). The spline parameters were randomly initialized in the chromosomes using uniform distribution.

Based on previous works, the population size was set to 30 individuals, while crossover and mutation probabilities were set to 0.9 and 0.12, respectively [31,32]. In this EA, tournament selection and standard one-point crossover methods were used, while the mutation operator was designed to modify splines parameters. The parameters were randomly chosen by the operator and the modifications were performed using a uniform random distribution.

2.4 Log-Spectrum and Auditory-Spectrum Based Coefficients

A set of features obtained from the mean of the log-spectrum (MLS) was also considered. The MLS is defined as

$$S(k) = \frac{1}{N} \sum_{n=1}^{N} \log |f(n,k)|, \tag{2}$$

where k corresponding to the frequency band, N is the total number of frames in the utterance, and $f(n,k)$ is the discrete Fourier transform of the signal in frame n. The spectrograms were computed using from non-overlapped Hamming windows of 25 ms. For 16 kHz sampled signals, in this way 200 coefficients corresponding to equally spaced frequency bands are obtained. This processing was successfully applied for different speech related tasks [4].

Another set of features is used as well, which is based on the auditory spectrogram and the neurophysiological model proposed by Yang et al. [35]. This model consists in two stages, though only the first one is used here, which corresponds to the early auditory spectrogram. In this spectrogram the frequency bands are not uniformly distributed and 128 coefficients are thus obtained.

The mean of the auditory spectrogram (MLSa) is computed as

$$S_a(k) = \frac{1}{N} \sum_{n=1}^{N} \log |a(n,k)|, \tag{3}$$

where k is a frequency band, N is the number of frames in the utterance and $a(n,k)$ is the k-th coefficient obtained by applying the auditory filter bank to the signal in frame n. The MLSa was computed using auditory spectrograms calculated for windows of 25 ms without overlapping. In order to obtain the representation of sound in the auditory model, a Matlab implementation of the Neural System Lab auditory model was used[1].

All MLS and MLSa features were computed on a frame by frame basis in order to compute statistics (mean and standard deviation) for each utterance.

In order to reduce the number of features obtained with MLS and MLSa, maintaining the most relevant for this classification problem, a ranking feature selection procedure was performed based on the F-Score measure [8]. The F-Score rates the features based on their discriminative capacity. Given a feature vector FV_k, this score was computed considering the True instances (N_T) and the False instances (N_F) as follows:

$$F(i) = \frac{\left(\bar{x}_i^{(T)} - \bar{x}_i\right)^2 + \left(\bar{x}_i^{(F)} - \bar{x}_i\right)^2}{\frac{1}{N_T-1}\sum_{j=1}^{N_T}\left(x_{j,i}^{(T)} - \bar{x}_i^{(T)}\right)^2 + \frac{1}{N_F-1}\sum_{j=1}^{N_F}\left(x_{j,i}^{(F)} - \bar{x}_i^{(F)}\right)^2} \tag{4}$$

where $\bar{x}_i$ is the average of the ith feature, $\bar{x}_i^{(F)}$ and $\bar{x}_i^{(T)}$ are the average False and True instances respectively, and $x_{j,i}$ is the ith feature in the jth instance.

This work proposes the use of MLS and MLSa features separately and also both sets combined. In order to combine the feature sets two approaches were considered. In the first approach the features in each set are ranked separately according to F-Score, and the higher ranked features are kept for each set. In the second approach all the MLS and MLSa features are ranked together by F-Score, in order to select the higher ranked features.

2.5 Classifier

Extreme Learning Machines (ELM) [14] are proposed to learn on the non-linear feature set. The primary implementation of ELM theory is a type of artificial neural network with one hidden layer. The main differences with classical models are in the training algorithm. The hidden units are randomly generated, thus the parameter tuning of this layer is avoided. As a direct consequence, the training time is reduced significantly compared with other training methods that have to use more complex optimisation techniques.

---

[1] Neural Systems Lab., Institutes for Systems Research, UMCP. http://www.isr.umd.edu/Labs/NSL/.

Table 2. Summary of the best results on training.

Features	FV size	UAR[%]	ACC[%]
Baseline (MFCC & functionals)	531	62.15	79.84
MLS	110	65.88	85.73
MLSa	110	68.61	87.88
ESCC	45	68.67	86.05
all MLS + MLSa	328	67.37	85.73
MLS + MLSa (Added)	230	68.76	87.74
MLS + MLSa (Combined)	230	68.94	86.82
ESCC + MLS	155	68.30	85.16
ESCC + MLSa	155	**69.60**	**87.95**
ESCC + MLS + MLSa	265	69.04	87.91

3   Results and Discussion

Since the examples composing the test set of the CRIED database are not labelled, for the experiments the train set consisting on 2838 instances was used in this work. Each of the instances in the train set is labelled as one of three categories: *Positive Mood* (2292), *Fussing* (368) or *Crying* (178). The experiments were carried out with a stratified cross-validation schemed in 10 folds and the best results for different configurations of the ELM classifier are presented. Since the dataset is not balanced, in order to evaluate the performance appropriately the Unweighted Average Recall (UAR) [22] measure was considered, in addition to the classification accuracy.

Table 2 shows the results obtained in the evaluation of the different feature sets. The described feature sets (MLS, MLSa and ESCC) were evaluated separately and combined together. In Table 2, "all MLS + MLSa" refers to the feature set composed of all the MLS and MLSa coefficients, without reducing dimensionality with F-Score. Also, the MLS and MLSa feature set were combined to apply F-Score for dimensionality reduction.

When reducing dimensionality with F-Score, in order to select the appropriate number of features to maintain, the classification performance is evaluated for incremental feature subsets containing the top ranked features. The subset of the top 10 features is evaluated first, then the top 20 and so on. Then the subset that provides the best performance is kept. In this manner, it was determined that for both MLS and MLSa the best feature subset consists of the first 110 features in the rank. The MLS and MLSa were combined applying F-Score first to keep the 110 best features from each set (Added), and were also combined all together to apply F-Score keeping the 230 best features from the complete set (Combined). As the table shows MLS and MLS where also combined, together and separately, with the ESCC features.

As it can be seen in Table 2, the MLS, MLSa and ESCC feature sets significantly outperform the Baseline in both UAR and Accuracy (ACC). Moreover, different combinations of these feature sets are able to provide even better performance. Also, it is important to note that all of these representations have lower dimensionality than the Baseline. For instance, the ESCC features provides an improvement of 6.52% of UAR with less than 10% of the attributes of the Baseline, showing that this representation is much more convenient for this task. The combination of MLS and MLSa also improves their individual performances when the F-Score measure is applied to keep the most discriminative attributes. Finally, the best result is provided by the combination of ESCC and MLSa, in both UAR and Accuracy, with a relatively small feature set.

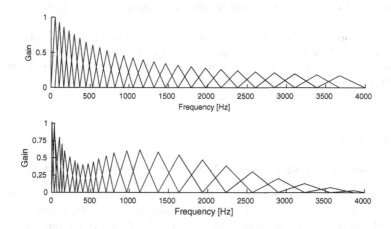

Fig. 3. Mel filter bank (top) and optimised filter bank (bottom).

Figure 3 shows the filter bank that was obtained by the optimisation process for the ESCC features. As it can be seen, the information on frequency band from 500 Hz to 2500 Hz, approximately, is enhanced with higher amplitudes in this filter bank. This corresponds to the frequency bands that show more inter class variance in the corpus (as seen in Fig. 1). Also, at low frequencies (below 1000 Hz) it shows higher resolution to capture the information related to the peaks in the mean log-spectrums of Fig. 1. These remarks, together with results obtained, show that the optimisation provided a filter bank that is much more appropriate for this task.

4   Conclusions

In this work spectrum-based feature sets were proposed to improve the performance in infant cry classification, which is a challenging and relevant problem to be tackled by the affective computing community.

The proposal relies on three different feature sets: the first one based on the mean log-spectrum, a second feature set based on an auditory spectrum and the third one is optimised for this task by means of an evolutionary algorithm. The performance obtained through cross validation outperforms the baseline, showing significantly improved results with reduced sets of features.

The results show that the proposed features are useful as improved speech representations for cry recognition system, suggesting that there is further room for improvement over the classical mel filter bank for specific tasks.

It is important to note that this study was limited to clean signals, though it would be interesting to evaluate the impact of noise on the shape of the filter banks. Thus, further experiments will include noisy signals, as well as other types of cry and recording conditions. Also, other parameters regarding filter banks, such as the filter bandwidth could be also optimised in future work.

Acknowledgements. The authors wish to thank the support of the *Agencia Nacional de Promoción Científica y Tecnológica* (with PICT 2015-0977), the *Universidad Nacional de Litoral* (with CAI+D 50020150100055LI, CAI+D 50020150100059LI, CAI+D 50020150100042LI), and the *Consejo Nacional de Investigaciones Científicas y Técnicas* (CONICET) from Argentina.

References

1. Abou-Abbas, L., Tadj, C., Fersaie, H.A.: A fully automated approach for baby cry signal segmentation and boundary detection of expiratory and inspiratory episodes. J. Acoust. Soc. Am. **142**(3), 1318–1331 (2017). https://doi.org/10.1121/1.5001491
2. Aggarwal, R.K., Dave, M.: Filterbank optimization for robust ASR using GA and PSO. Int. J. Speech Technol. **15**(2), 191–201 (2012). https://doi.org/10.1007/s10772-012-9133-9
3. Ahmad, K.S., Thosar, A.S., Nirmal, J.H., Pande, V.S.: A unique approach in text independent speaker recognition using MFCC feature sets and probabilistic neural network. In: 2015 Eighth International Conference on Advances in Pattern Recognition (ICAPR), pp. 1–6, January 2015. https://doi.org/10.1109/ICAPR.2015.7050669
4. Albornoz, E.M., Milone, D.H., Rufiner, H.L.: Spoken emotion recognition using hierarchical classifiers. Comput. Speech Lang. **25**(3), 556–570 (2011). https://doi.org/10.1016/j.csl.2010.10.001
5. Albornoz, E.M., Milone, D.H., Rufiner, H.L.: Feature extraction based on bio-inspired model for robust emotion recognition. Soft Comput. **21**(17), 5145–5158 (2017). https://doi.org/10.1007/s00500-016-2110-5
6. Anagnostopoulos, C.N., Iliou, T., Giannoukos, I.: Features and classifiers for emotion recognition from speech: a survey from 2000 to 2011. Artif. Intell. Rev. **43**(2), 155–177 (2015). https://doi.org/10.1007/s10462-012-9368-5
7. Arora, V., Sood, P., Keshari, K.U.: A stacked sparse autoencoder based architecture for Punjabi and English spoken language classification using MFCC features. In: 2016 3rd International Conference on Computing for Sustainable Global Development (INDIACom), pp. 269–272, March 2016

8. Chen, Y.W., Lin, C.J.: Combining SVMs with various feature selection strategies. In: Guyon, I., Nikravesh, M., Gunn, S., Zadeh, L.A. (eds.) Feature Extraction, pp. 315–324. Springer, Heidelberg (2006). https://doi.org/10.1007/978-3-540-35488-8_13

9. Davis, S.V., Mermelstein, P.: Comparison of parametric representations for monosyllabic word recognition in continuously spoken sentences. IEEE Trans. Acoust. Speech Signal Process. **28**, 57–366 (1980)

10. Drummond, J.E., McBride, M.L., Wiebe, C.F.: The development of mothers' understanding of infant crying. Clin. Nurs. Res. **2**(4), 396–410 (1993). https://doi.org/10.1177/105477389300200403. pMID: 8220195

11. Eyben, F.: Real-time Speech and Music Classification by Large Audio Feature Space Extraction. Springer theses. Springer, Heidelberg (2015). https://doi.org/10.1007/978-3-319-27299-3. https://books.google.com.ar/books?id=AFBECwAAQBAJ

12. Garcia, J.O., Garcia, C.A.R.: Mel-frequency cepstrum coefficients extraction from infant cry for classification of normal and pathological cry with feed-forward neural networks. In: Proceedings of the International Joint Conference on Neural Networks, vol. 4, pp. 3140–3145, July 2003. https://doi.org/10.1109/IJCNN.2003.1224074

13. Gu, L., Rose, K.: Perceptual harmonic cepstral coefficients for speech recognition in noisy environment. In: 2001 IEEE International Conference on Acoustics, Speech, and Signal Processing. Proceedings (Cat. No. 01CH37221), vol. 1, pp. 125–128 (2001). https://doi.org/10.1109/ICASSP.2001.940783

14. Huang, G.B., Zhu, Q.Y., Siew, C.K.: Extreme learning machine: a new learning scheme of feedforward neural networks. In: 2004 IEEE International Joint Conference on Neural Networks (IEEE Cat. No. 04CH37541), vol. 2, pp. 985–990, July 2004. https://doi.org/10.1109/IJCNN.2004.1380068

15. Hung, J.: Optimization of filter-bank to improve the extraction of MFCC features in speech recognition. In: Proceedings of 2004 International Symposium on Intelligent Multimedia, Video and Speech Processing, 2004, pp. 675–678, October 2004

16. Lee, S., Fang, S., Hung, J., Lee, L.: Improved MFCC feature extraction by PCA-optimized filter-bank for speech recognition. In: IEEE Workshop on Automatic Speech Recognition and Understanding, 2001. ASRU 2001, pp. 49–52 (2001). https://doi.org/10.1109/ASRU.2001.1034586

17. Likitha, M.S., Gupta, S.R.R., Hasitha, K., Raju, A.U.: Speech based human emotion recognition using MFCC. In: 2017 International Conference on Wireless Communications, Signal Processing and Networking (WiSPNET), pp. 2257–2260, March 2017. https://doi.org/10.1109/WiSPNET.2017.8300161

18. Marschik, P.B., et al.: A novel way to measure and predict development: a heuristic approach to facilitate the early detection of neurodevelopmental disorders. Curr. Neurol. Neurosci. Rep. **17**(5), 43 (2017)

19. Oliveira, A.L., Braga, P.L., Lima, R.M., Cornélio, M.L.: GA-based method for feature selection and parameters optimization for machine learning regression applied to software effort estimation. Inf. Softw. Technol. **52**(11), 1155–1166 (2010). https://doi.org/10.1016/j.infsof.2010.05.009

20. Paul, S., Das, S.: Simultaneous feature selection and weighting - an evolutionary multi-objective optimization approach. Pattern Recognit. Lett. **65**, 51–59 (2015). https://doi.org/10.1016/j.patrec.2015.07.007

21. Reyes-Galaviz, O.F., Reyes-Garcia, C.A.: A system for the processing of infant cry to recognize pathologies in recently born babies with neural networks. In: 9th Conference Speech and Computer, SPECOM-2004 (2004)

22. Rosenberg, A.: Classifying skewed data: importance weighting to optimize average recall. In: INTERSPEECH 2012, Portland, USA (2012)
23. Schuller, B., Steidl, S., Batliner, A., Schiel, F., Krajewski, J.: The interspeech 2011 speaker state challenge. In: Proceedings of the Interspeech, ISCA, pp. 3201–3204, March 2011
24. Schuller, B., Steidl, S., Batliner, A., Baumeister, et al.: The interspeech 2018 computational paralinguistics challenge: atypical & self-assessed affect, crying & heart beats. In: Computational Paralinguistics Challenge, Interspeech 2018 (2018)
25. Trigeorgis, G., et al.: Adieu features? End-to-end speech emotion recognition using a deep convolutional recurrent network. In: 2016 IEEE International Conference on Acoustics, Speech and Signal Processing (ICASSP), pp. 5200–5204, March 2016. https://doi.org/10.1109/ICASSP.2016.7472669
26. Tzanetakis, G., Cook, P.: Musical genre classification of audio signals. IEEE Trans. Speech Audio Process. **10**(5), 293–302 (2002). https://doi.org/10.1109/TSA.2002.800560
27. Upadhyaya, P., Farooq, O., Abidi, M.R., Varshney, Y.V.: Continuous Hindi speech recognition model based on Kaldi ASR toolkit. In: 2017 International Conference on Wireless Communications, Signal Processing and Networking (WiSPNET), pp. 786–789, March 2017. https://doi.org/10.1109/WiSPNET.2017.8299868
28. Veer, K., Sharma, T.: A novel feature extraction for robust EMG pattern recognition. J. Med. Eng. Technol. **40**(4), 149–154 (2016). https://doi.org/10.3109/03091902.2016.1153739
29. Vignolo, L.D., Milone, D.H., Rufiner, H.L.: Genetic wavelet packets for speech recognition. Expert Syst. Appl. **40**(6), 2350–2359 (2013). https://doi.org/10.1016/j.eswa.2012.10.050
30. Vignolo, L.D., Milone, D.H., Scharcanski, J.: Feature selection for face recognition based on multi-objective evolutionary wrappers. Expert Syst. Appl. **40**(13), 5077–5084 (2013). https://doi.org/10.1016/j.eswa.2013.03.032
31. Vignolo, L.D., Rufiner, H.L., Milone, D.H., Goddard, J.C.: Evolutionary cepstral coefficients. Appl. Soft Comput. **11**(4), 3419–3428 (2011). https://doi.org/10.1016/j.asoc.2011.01.012
32. Vignolo, L.D., Rufiner, H.L., Milone, D.H., Goddard, J.C.: Evolutionary splines for cepstral filterbank optimization in phoneme classification. EURASIP J. Adv. Signal Proc. **2011**, 8:1–8:14 (2011)
33. Vozáriková, E., Juhár, J., Čižmár, A.: Acoustic events detection using MFCC and MPEG-7 descriptors. In: Dziech, A., Czyżewski, A. (eds.) Multimedia Communications, Services and Security, pp. 191–197. Springer, Heidelberg (2011). https://doi.org/10.1007/978-3-642-21512-4_23
34. Wu, Z., Cao, Z.: Improved MFCC-based feature for robust speaker identification. Tsinghua Sci. Technol. **10**(2), 158–161 (2005)
35. Yang, X., Wang, K., Shamma, S.A.: Auditory representations of acoustic signals. IEEE Trans. Inf. Theory **38**(2), 824–839 (1992)
36. Zão, L., Cavalcante, D., Coelho, R.: Time-frequency feature and AMS-GMM mask for acoustic emotion classification. Signal Process. Lett. **21**(5), 620–624 (2014). https://doi.org/10.1109/LSP.2014.2311435
37. Zabidi, A., Mansor, W., Khuan, L.Y., Sahak, R., Rahman, F.Y.A.: Mel-frequency cepstrum coefficient analysis of infant cry with hypothyroidism. In: 2009 5th International Colloquium on Signal Processing its Applications, pp. 204–208, March 2009. https://doi.org/10.1109/CSPA.2009.5069217

Feature Selection Using Sampling with Replacement, Covering Arrays and Rule-Induction Techniques to Aid Polarity Detection in Twitter Sentiment Analysis

Jorge Villegas[1(✉)], Carlos Cobos[1], Martha Mendoza[1], and Enrique Herrera-Viedma[2]

[1] Information Technology Research Group (GTI) members, Universidad del Cauca, Sector Tulcán Office 422 FIET, Popayán, Colombia
javillegas162@gmail.com,
{ccobos,mmendoza}@unicauca.edu.co
[2] Department of Computer Science and Artificial Intelligence, University of Granada, Granada, Spain
viedma@decsai.ugr.es

Abstract. One of the main tasks in analyzing sentiment on Twitter is polarity detection – i.e. the classification of 'tweets' in terms of feelings, opinions and attitudes expressed. Polarity detection on Twitter by means of machine learning methods is generally affected by the use of irrelevant, redundant, noisy or correlated features, especially when a high-dimensional representation is used in the feature set. There is thus a need for a selection method that removes those features that render the classification algorithm inefficient. In this work, we propose a feature selection method based on the concept of bagging, with two important modifications: (i) the use of covering arrays to support the process of building bootstrap samples; and (ii) the use of the results of rule-induction techniques (JRIP, C4.5, CART or others) to generate the reduced representation of tweets with the features selected. The experimental results show that on using the method proposed, we obtain similar or better results than those obtained with the original representation (this comprising a set of 91 features used in research related to polarity detection in Twitter), bringing the possibility of simpler and faster process models. A subset of features is thereby identified that can facilitate improvements in future polarity detection proposals on Twitter.

Keywords: Sentiment analysis · Polarity detection · Covering arrays
Feature selection · Twitter

1 Introduction

Web 2.0 provides everyone with the possibility of expressing and sharing opinions about different day-to-day activities [1]. Because of this, messages posted on social networking sites have helped to improve business and influence public opinion, profoundly affecting the social and political life of people in general [2]. Such a situation gives rise to research into sentiment analysis, responsible for the detection, extraction

© Springer Nature Switzerland AG 2018
G. R. Simari et al. (Eds.): IBERAMIA 2018, LNAI 11238, pp. 467–480, 2018.
https://doi.org/10.1007/978-3-030-03928-8_38

and classification of opinions, feelings and attitudes in relation to different issues, the observation of the public mood in relation to the political movement, market intelligence, measurement of customer satisfaction and the prediction of movie sales among others [2, 3].

Because of the growing popularity of Twitter, a sub-area of research has emerged, called Twitter Sentiment Analysis (TSA). TSA addresses the problem of analyzing 'tweets' (messages posted on Twitter) in terms of the sentiments they express. Twitter is a new domain for sentiment analysis and poses unique challenges, due to its limitation in message size (140 characters, or more recently 280), informal language (or jargon) and the use of emoticons and hashtags to express and emphasize feelings [4].

One of the tasks of TSA is polarity detection, a very complex problem since a word that expresses sentiment may have quite the opposite orientation or polarity in a different domain or context. By orientation or polarity, a feeling or opinion is said to be positive, negative, or neutral. For example, "suck" usually indicates a negative feeling, e.g. "This camera sucks", but it can also imply a positive feeling, e.g. "This vacuum cleaner really sucks" [1, 2].

Automatic learning is one of the approaches through which polarity detection is addressed, treating the problem as a classification problem and, due to the high dimensionality of the feature set, requiring a prior selection process to obtain more accurate results with simpler models that reduce the preprocessing of tweets [1, 4, 5].

In this article we propose a method of feature selection based on the concept of bagging, involving two new concepts. First, the use of covering arrays [6] to support the process of sampling and feature selection; and secondly, union of the features present in the trees/rules such as the feature set selected to represent the tweets. The experimental results show that on using the method proposed, we obtain similar or better results than those obtained with the original representation (this includes a set of 91 features used in research related to polarity detection in Twitter), bringing the possibility of simpler and faster process models.

The rest of the article is organized as follows: Sect. 2 presents the state of the art. Section 3 presents the proposed method of feature selection in detail. Section 4 then presents the results of the experiments carried out. Finally, in Sect. 5, we present the conclusions of the work to date and some ideas that the research group hopes to work on in the near future.

2   State of the Art

As already mentioned, one of the most notable problems associated with supervised learning is the task of feature selection, focused on determining those features that contribute most value in training the model. Features selected, and their combination, play an important role in detecting the sentiment of a text. Twitter comprises four different kinds of textual features: (1) semantic, (2) syntactic, (3) stylistic, and (4) specific to Twitter. In the processing of tweets, well-known features are included and used in the existing literature of analysis of other genres, such as reviews, blogs and forums [7]. Those most used for the TSA [4] are presented below.

Semantic features include the terms that reveal the negative or positive sentiment of a word or phrase. Among the most used are words of opinion, words of feeling, semantic concepts, and negation [8].

Syntactic features frequently applied include unigrams, bigrams, n-grams, term frequencies, parts-of-speech (POS), dependency trees, and coreference resolution. To explore the impact of different terms in sentiment analysis, a series of studies assign a binary score (presence/absence) to the terms, while others use a more advanced weighting scheme considering term frequency [4, 9].

Stylistic features refer to the non-standard writing style used in Twitter. Some examples are emoticons, intensifiers (they emphasize writing and include repeated characters, emphatic lengthening, and emphatic capitals), abbreviations, slang terms and punctuation marks (e.g. exclamation marks, etc.). An important feature is the presence of emoticons, whose usefulness has been widely examined in the literature [10].

Among the **specific (unique) features** of tweets [1, 4] are retweets, hashtags, responses, mentions, user names, followers and URLs [4, 5, 7].

Feature selection is not a simple process. It requires a detailed and meticulous analysis to detect the most useful features in each domain. In [10], a set of experiments were carried out to examine the usefulness of a number of features, including POS and lexical features, concluding that the most useful combination are the POS features and the polarity of the words. Similarly, in [11] a study was made of the impact of different semantic and stylistic features, including emoticons, abbreviations and the presence of intensifiers; this study concludes that the combination of polarity of terms with n-grams achieves the best performance.

The most typical feature selection process consists in isolating words and other features such as negations, emoticons, hashtags, and intensifiers and applying different techniques to identify the most informative ones. To use this approach, a strategy is needed in order to handle negation or detect sarcasm, but it should be borne in mind that if the number of features is very large, finding the best combination of features is not always feasible [4].

3 The Proposed Method

The method proposed is based on the following steps that are explained below: (1) Preprocessing and definition of initial features; (2) sampling of rows with replacement and of columns based on covering arrays. (3) rule-induction and feature selection.

3.1 Preprocessing and Definition of Initial Features

Due to the use of slang and abbreviations, a specific preprocessing was implemented to appropriately carry out the counts of the features that each tweet represents. The tasks performed include: (1) Remove URLs and mentions and canonicalize jargon and abbreviations (similar to [12]). (2) Divide hashtags into words. (3) Record the number of times the positive, negative, and neutral emoticons are repeated and remove them from the tweet. (4) Remove elongated words (e.g.: wooooooow by wow) and record the number of elongations found in the tweet. (5) Determine the POS tags in the resulting canonicalized text using the Stanford tagger [13]. And (6) Remove any inconsistent punctuation or token that does not belong to the English language. To perform the counting of certain words and emoticons that belong to each tweet, the following lexicons were used: (1) **Words that convey opinion**, i.e. words with positive or negative meaning taken from the lexicon used by Liu in [14]. (2) **SentiWordNet** [15] was used to extract the polarity of words that make sense of opinion, as well as their associated POS tags. We also recorded the count of the number of nouns, verbs, adjectives, and adverbs by tweet. (3) **NRC Hashtag Lexicon** [16] was used to take into account the 78 seed words with positive and negative hashtags, such as #good, #excellent, #bad and #terrible, in such a way that it is useful as an indicator of the polarity of the tweet. And (4) **Lexicon of Wikipedia emoticons**, with 81 emoticons that express positive and negative feelings [12].

Table 1 presents a general description of the 91 features initially extracted for tweets [17].

In [18] it is stated that the final result of a classification algorithm can be affected by negation and the use of specific parts of the language. Therefore, this paper uses a series of rules that can play a key role in the semantic classification of sentences. Table 1 considers the frequency of appearance of these rules in the tweet. The 15 rules mentioned in [18] are described as features 49 to 63.

The result of the representation of the set of tweets with the extracted features according to Table 1 is like that presented in Fig. 1. This representation is called the features matrix (FM) and has a size M × k where M is the number of tweets and k is the number of columns or features (originally 91).

3.2   Sampling of Rows with Replacement and of Columns Based on CAs

As in bagging, a number M of bootstrap samples is created, that is, M samples of randomly selected rows from the training dataset (features matrix, FM), where M is defined based on the number of rows in a covering array, CA [6] previously selected.

A Covering Array (CA) is a mathematical object, which can be described as a matrix of $M \times P$ elements, such that each $M \times t$ subarray contains all the combinations of v^t symbols at least once. It is represented by the equation: $CA(M; P, v, t)$, where M represents the rows of the matrix, P is the number of parameters (columns of the matrix), v the alphabet that indicates the number of possible values that can take each component or cell, and t represents the strength or degree of interaction of the columns or parameters of the CA [6].

In this case we used a binary covering array denoted by CA (M = 206; P = 91, v = 2, t = 5), which is a matrix of M rows and P columns, where M, the number of bootstrap samples and rows in the CA is 206, P is the number of factors or features of MC, 91 in this case for the original FM, v is the number of symbols of the CA that in this case is binary - where 0 implies that the characteristic (attribute) will not be taken into account in the sample and 1 that it will be included in it - and t is the degree of interaction between the parameters, a parameter called strength in the CA. In [21] and [22] the properties of the CAs and their use in the design of experiments and in

Table 1. Description of extracted features (Types (T): W = word count, H = hashtag, E = emoticons, P = Polarity, PT = POS tag, S = Semantic rules, TP = Trigrams polarity and DV = Doc2Vec)

Id	Features	Description	T
1	startle	Number of words before preprocessing	W
2	punct	Number of occurrences of the following characters '!', '??', '!?', '?!'	W
3	avg_len	Average number of words per sentence	W
4	has_ht	Indicates if the tweet contains at least one hashtag	H
5	neutral_emojis	Counts the neutral, negative, and positive emoticons, which are used to intensify the tweets. The intensifier increases or decreases according to the emoticon. Positive ones are added, negatives are subtracted. If it gives zero the last emoticon is observed and if this is positive it is assigned 1.01, if it is negative or neutral it is assigned −1.01	E
6	negative emojis		E
7	positive_emojis		E
8	intensify_emoji		E
9	count_elongated	Number of elongated words	W
10	count_uppercase	Number of words that start in uppercase	W
11	end_len	Counts the number of words at the end of the preprocessing	W
12	neg_words_ht	Number of negative, neutral, and positive hashtags considering factors such as: neighbors, capitals, negations, intensifiers, elongations, among others	H
13	neu_words_ht		H
14	pos_words_ht		H
15	neg_words_ht_sum		H
16	neu_words_ht_sum		H
17	pos_words_ht_sum		H
18	neg_ht	Number of sentiments of the hashtags based on 'NRC Emotion and Sentiment Lexicons' [16]	H
19	pos_ht		H
20	neu_ht		H
21	pol_words_ht		H
22	neg_words_tweet	Number of negative, neutral, and positive words in the tweet, according to the Bing Liu lists	P
23	neu_words_tweet		P
24	pos_words_tweet		P
25	negat_words_ht	Number of negation words in the tweet and hashtags, based on list of negations	H, P
26	negat_words_tweet		P
27	adj_frac	Number of adjectives, adverbs, verbs, and nouns based on NLTK pos tagger English	PT
28	adv_frac		PT
29	v_frac		PT
30	nn_frac		PT
31	neg	All the values of the words that have polarity are imported using SentiWordNet in the hashtags. **neg**: Accumulated negative polarity in the tweet. **neu**: Accumulated neutral polarity in the tweet.	P
32	neu		P
33	pos		P
34	neg_words		P

(continued)

Table 1. (*continued*)

Id	Features	Description	T
35	neu_words	**pos**: Accumulated positive polarity in the tweet.	P
36	pos_words	**neg_words**: Number of negative words.	P
37	neg_words_sum	**neu_words**: Number of objective words.	P
38	neu_words_sum	**pos_words**: Number of positive words.	P
39	pos_words_sum	**neg_words_sum**: Sum of the negative sentiment according to SentiWordNet. **neu_words_sum**:	P
40	pol_words	Sum of the objective sentiment according to	P
41	negat_words	SentiWordNet. **pos_words_sum**: Sum of the positive sentiment according to SentiWordNet. A word is considered objective, if its objective score is $> = 0.8$. **pol_words**: Number of polarity words (not all words have a polarity value in SentiWordNet). **negat_words**: Number of negation words. Negation word is a word whose negative score is $> = 0.8$	P
42	neg_words_ht_lists	Number of negative, neutral, and positive words	H
43	neu_words_ht_lists	of the hashtags belonging to a tweet, according to	H
44	pos_words_ht_lists	the Bing Liu lists	H
45	neg_ht_NRC	Number of sentiment words in the hashtags,	H
46	pos_ht_NRC	based on the list of NRC Emotion and Sentiment	H
47	pol_words_ht_NRC	Lexicons	H
48	neu_ht_NRC		H
49	r1	R1: There is a negation in the tweet. E.g.: 'not bad'. Number of times that rule R1 is met in the tweet	SR
50	r2	R2: There is "of" in the middle of two nouns or pronouns. E.g.: 'Lack of crime in rural areas'. Number of times rule R2 is met in the tweet	SR
51	r3	R3: There is a verb after a noun. E.g.: 'Crime has decreased'. Number of times rule R3 is fulfilled in the tweet	SR
52	r4	R4: There is a noun followed by the verb 'to be', followed by an adjective. E.g.: 'Damage is minimal'. Number of times the rule R4 is met	SR
53	r5	R5: There is a noun, followed by 'of', followed by a verb. E.g.: 'Lack of killing in rural areas'. Number of times rule R5 is met in the tweet	SR
54	r6	R6: There is an adjective followed by 'to', followed by a verb. E.g.: 'Unlikely to destroy the planet'. Number of times rule R6 is met	SR
55	r7	R7: There is a verb followed by a noun. E.g.: 'Destroyed terrorism'. Number of times rule R7 in the tweet is met	SR

(*continued*)

Table 1. (*continued*)

Id	Features	Description	T
56	r8	R8: There is a 'to' in the middle of two verbs. E. g.: 'Refused to deceive the man'. Number of times rule R8 in the tweet is met	SR
57	r9	R9: There is 'as' followed by an adjective, followed by 'as' and then a noun or noun phrase. E.g.: 'As ugly as a rock'. Number of times rule R9 is met in the tweet	SR
58	r10	R10: There is a negation, followed by 'as', followed by an adjective, followed by 'as' and then a noun or noun phrase. E.g.: 'That was not as bad as the original'. Number of times rule R10 in the tweet is met	SR
59	r11	R11: Contains "but" E.g.: 'And I've never liked that director, but I loved this movie'. Number of times rule R11 is met in the tweet	SR
60	r12	R12: Contains "despite" E.g.: 'I love the movie, despite the fact that I hate that director'. Number of times the rule R12 is met in the tweet	SR
61	r13	R13: Contains "unless" E.g.: 'Everyone likes the video unless he is a sociopath'. Number of times rule R13 is met in the tweet	SR
62	r14	R14: Contains "while." E.g.: "While they did their best, the team played a horrible game". Number of times rule R14 is met in the tweet	SR
63	r15	R15: Contains "however." E.g.: 'The film was blessed with good actors. However, the plot was very poor'. Number of times rule R15 is met	SR
64 to 90	Trigrams formed by the polarity of three consecutive words.	A representation of the tweet is added consisting of 27 values, where each represents the frequency of appearance of the polarity of three consecutive words. For example: "*i love you lucy*" would obtain two occurrences, one in neu_pos_neu (i, love, you) and another in pos_neu_neu (love, you, lucy). The other trigrams would have a frequency 0	TP
91	Doc2Vec	Representation of 300 dimensions of each tweet using the Doc2Vec model pre-trained in [19] with documents from Wikipedia [20] and available at https://github.com/jhlau/doc2vec#pre-trained-doc2vec-models. The objective of doc2vec is to create a numerical representation of a document, regardless of its length. While the word vectors represent the concept of a word, the vector of the document represents the complete concept of a document [19]	DV

	1	2	3		k = 91	
	start_len	punct	avg_len	...	Doc2Vec	Class
1	18	2	9	...	1.3 ... 0.5	Positive
2	21	3	7	...	1.4 ... 0.6	Negative
...	...	...	...	...	...	...
M	5	1	5		0.8 ... 0.7	Neutral

Fig. 1. Example of the representation of the tweets, original features matrix (FM)

software and hardware black box tests are described in detail. As an example, Table 2 shows the CA (6; 10, 2, 2). The strength of this covering array is 2 (t = 2), with 10 factors (P = 10) and a binary alphabet (v = 2) represented by the symbols (0 and 1). In the proposed method, this CA indicates that six bootstrap samples must be generated for a FM of ten (10) features and each row of the CA defines which of the ten features is included in each bootstrap sample. Thus in the first sample (first row of the CA) all the features are included, in the second sample/row only features 4, 5, 6 and 7 are included, and so on with the other rows of the CA.

Table 2. Example of CA (6; 10, 2, 2).

1	1	1	1	1	1	1	1	1	1
0	0	0	1	1	1	1	0	0	0
0	1	0	1	0	0	0	0	1	1
1	1	1	0	0	1	0	0	0	0
0	0	1	0	0	0	1	1	1	0
1	0	0	0	1	0	0	1	0	1

3.3 Rule-Induction and Feature Selection

The process of sample creation, rule-induction and feature selection is summarized in Fig. 2. In this step of the proposed method the M bootstrap samples (MB_1, MB_2, ... MB_M) previously constructed are taken. Using rule-induction algorithms (C4.5, CART and JRIP) two trees (one n-ary and another binary) and a list of rules for each bootstrap sample are created. Next, the different features included in the M trees or M rules generated are gathered (controlling a minimum number of instances per leaf in the trees, to perform a pruning that makes it possible to find the minimum number of features necessary for their classification, which provide more information) and these are taken as the final features of the feature selection process. In the middle and lower part of the figure the resulting matrix FM is shown, which corresponds to the matrix (or dataset) of representation of the tweets, but only with the selected p (p < < k) features, which can be used as the training dataset of any classifier, among them Naive Bayes, Linear Regression, Random Forest, C4.5. Support Vector Machines and Multi-Layer Perceptron.

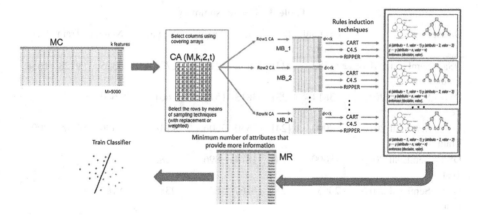

Fig. 2. Proposal for feature selection in tweets

Determining the most appropriate features for the classification (polarity detection) of tweets makes it possible to reduce their preprocessing, decrease the building time of classification models and obtain results that are more readable. In addition, according to the results of the experimentation, these models deliver a quality of classification that is similar or superior to that obtained using the original 91 features.

4 Experimental Results

The experiments carried out sought in each test dataset, first to determine the effectiveness of the feature selection process when the training and test data are obtained from the same dataset (66% and 34% respectively), that is, when the same distribution of the data is used. An experiment was then conducted in which the training and test datasets are different, with which the aim is to evaluate the quality of the training datasets and their effect on the feature selection process.

4.1 Description of Data Sets and Evaluation Measures

Table 3 summarizes the datasets used for experimentation. The "Original total" column shows the number of tweets originally reported in the reference according to the "Ref" column; the "Total" column shows the number of tweets that could be downloaded due to twitter policies; the number of positive, negative, and neutral tweets is then shown. If the dataset was originally formulated for training and development, it shows the number of tweets that could be downloaded in each task. The datasets in bold face were used for evaluation and comparison. Precision (or percentage of correctly classified instances, ICC) and F-measure (F1) are used as measures of evaluation and comparison.

Table 3. Dataset summary

Dataset	Original total	Ref	Total	Positives	Negatives	Neutral	Train	Dev
DSa - SemEval 2013-Train + dev	11382	[23]	11338	4215	1798	5325	9728	1654
DSb - SemEval 2013 Test	3814	[23]	3813	1572	601	1640		
DSc - SemEval 2016-Train + dev	8000	[24]	7350	3606	1148	2596	6000	2000
DSd - SemEval 2016 Test	2000	[24]	1814	896	288	630		
DSe - SemEval 2016 Eval	20632	[25]	16167	5620	2383	8164		
DSf - Sentiment140 Test	498	[26]	498	182	177	139		

4.2   Experimental Results and Discussion

Table 4 presents the main results of the experimentation in the SemEval 2013 Test dataset. This table shows in the first line the result of the percentage of instances correctly classified (ICC) and of F-measure (F1) taking the dataset with the 91 features originally defined in Table 1 and the classifiers Linear Regression (LR), Simple Linear Regression (Simple LR), Naive Bayes, an implementation of Support Vector Machines (Sequential minimal optimization, SMO) and Multi-Layer Perceptron (MLP). Other classifiers were used, such as Random Forest, JRIP, C4.5, CART and SVM, but due to space restrictions in the article, these results are not presented. The results of the second line show that in general the process of feature selection (F.S.) obtains similar results in quality (measured in ICC and F1) but reducing the features from 91 to 21 (column k). Lines 3 and 4 of the table show the same analysis by changing the dataset used to support the feature selection process. In this case, the same previous situation is observed: the quality decreases very little, but there is a notable reduction in the number of features (from 91 to 22). Comparing the results of the two experiments, it is observed that although the dataset of the second experiment is much larger, the quality of the results does not improve significantly. Table 4 also shows that the highest precision achieved with all the features is 66.8% and when making the selection its value is 65.3%, in this case 1.5% precision is being lost, but with a 77% reduction in features. It can be stated that, for this dataset, the proposal obtains a simpler representation that maintains a level of quality like that which can be achieved with all the features. Likewise, it can be said that the dataset used in the second test (SemEval 2013-Train + dev) has a very similar distribution because its highest precision value with all the features is the same (66.8%) and its result when using the selection is comparable to that obtained when validating it with 34%, its precision being 65.5% and achieving a similar reduction of 76%.

Table 4. Results of experimentation in SemEval 2013 Test (best results in bold)

SemEval 2013 Test (DSb)	LR		Simple LR		Naive Bayes		SMO		MLP		k
	ICC	F1	ICC	F1	ICC	F1	ICC	F1	ICC	F1	
Original (66%/34%)	65.0	65.0	**66.8**	66.7	63.1	62.9	**66.1**	66.2	60.0	59.1	91
FS (66%/34%)	64.4	64.5	**65.3**	65.1	61.7	61.9	**64.2**	64.3	61.7	61.6	21
Training: DSa	**66.2**	65.7	**66.8**	66.2	58.5	57.1	**65.0**	64.4	63.4	62.3	91
FS base line	**65.4**	64.8	**65.5**	64.8	60.0	60.0	**65.1**	64.6	59.1	58.8	22
F1 reported state of the art	**69.02** [16] with a SVM classifier trained with two corpus. one of positive and negative tweets that had as hashtags words from 'NRC Hashtag Sentiment Lexicon' [17] with 775.000 tweets. 54.129 unigrams and 316.531 bigrams and another of tweets with emoticons that contains 1.6 million tweets [26]. 62.468 unigrams and 677.698 bigrams.										

The results on the SemEval 2016 Test dataset are presented in Table 5. In the first experiment. unlike with the previous dataset. there is a slight improvement in the quality of the classification when the set of 25 features selected with the proposed method is used. Then. in the second experiment it is observed that the method slightly reduces in quality. but it is much simpler (only 15 features of the 91).

Table 5. Results of the experimentation in SemEval 2016 Test (best results in bold).

SemEval 2016 Test (DSd)	LR		Simple LR		Naive Bayes		SMO		MLP		k
	ICC	F1	ICC	F1	ICC	F1	ICC	F1	ICC	F1	
Original (66%/34%)	50.2	50.7	**55.9**	**54.0**	46.2	47.6	54.9	54.4	53.2	52.5	91
F.S. (66%/34%)	50.1	50.5	**58.5**	**57.1**	52.0	52.7	53.2	52.3	50.9	50.1	25
Base line: DSc	**57.2**	56.2	**56.6**	**55.4**	46.9	48.2	56.4	55.0	48.3	48.7	91
F.S. Base Line	**56.7**	55.5	**57.6**	**56.3**	51.0	51.1	55.8	54.1	52.5	52.7	15
F1 reported state of the art	**63.3** [27] using a convolutional phrase embedding approach. They take advantage of large amounts of data to train a set of two-layer convolutional neural networks whose predictions are combined using Random Forest.										

In addition, it can be noted that although the dataset is much larger there is no corresponding substantial improvement in quality, either in the baseline or with the selection process, which shows that an active process of selection of instances may be required. In the same way, with the proposed method a better quality was obtained, approximately 2.6% and a 72% reduction, having a direct relationship with the training dataset, with which we can obtain a 1.0% improvement and an overall feature reduction of 83%, the results being very comparable.

The results on the SemEval 2016 Eval dataset are presented in Table 6. In the first experiment, like the first dataset, a slight loss in the quality of the classification is obtained when the set of 19 selected characteristics is used with the proposed method. Then, in the second experiment the method is also seen to reduce slightly its quality, but it is simpler (28 characteristics from the 91). It should also be noted that although the dataset is much larger, the quality does not improve either in the baseline or in the selection process, showing that the union of datasets (DSa + DSb + DSc + DSd) does not have a distribution like the test dataset, so it loses between 2% and 3% of quality. The above suggests that an active process of instance selection is required.

Table 6. Results of the experiment in SemEval 2016 Eval (best results in bold).

SemEval 2016 Eval (DSe)	LR		Simple LR		Naive Bayes		SMO		MLP		k
	ICC	F1	ICC	F1	ICC	F1	ICC	F1	ICC	F1	
Original (66%/34%)	62.4	61.7	**63.2**	**62.3**	58.0	58.0	62.3	61.2	58.8	58.4	91
FS (66%/34%)	61.9	61.1	**62.6**	**61.5**	56.7	57.2	61.9	60.7	55.9	55.6	19
Baseline: (DSa + DSb + DSc + DSd)	60.2	60.2	**60.7**	**60.7**	53.5	53.1	60.3	60.3	58.0	58.2	91
FS baseline	59.6	59.6	**59.7**	**59.8**	53.3	54.3	59.9	59.9	52.2	52.5	28
F1 reported state of the art	63.3 [27] using two convolutional neural networks combined with Random Forest.										

The results on the Sentiment140 Test dataset are presented in Table 7. In the first experiment, there is a slight improvement in the quality of the classification when the set of 36 selected features is taken with the proposed method. Then, in the second experiment it is observed that the method slightly reduces its quality, but it is much simpler (28 features of the 91, a 69% reduction). In addition, it is appreciated that with the larger dataset the quality improves both the baseline and the selection process, indicating that its distribution provides more information for classification.

Table 7. Results of the experiment in Sentiment140 Test (best results in bold).

Sentiment140 Test (DSf)	LR		Simple LR		Naive Bayes		SMO		MLP		k
	ICC	F1	ICC	F1	ICC	F1	ICC	F1	ICC	F1	
Original (66%/34%)	44.4	43.5	66.2	66.2	**68.0**	**67.3**	60.4	60.1	63.3	63.1	91
FS (66%/34%)	42.6	42.7	65.6	65.5	**70.4**	**69.9**	61.5	61.3	64.5	64.3	36
Base line: (DSa + DSb + DSc + DSd)	**73.1**	**72.7**	71.1	70.4	63.2	63.4	**73.1**	**73.0**	67.5	67.7	91
FS base Line	**71.5**	**71.1**	69.1	68.2	67.6	3232.0	**71.9**	**71.8**	62.7	62.5	28
F1 reported state of the art	80.0 [17] with Naive Bayes, MaxEnt, and SVM, using a training dataset of 1.6 million tweets with emoticons for distant supervised learning.										

Following experimentation with the four datasets, the features that had most relevance were 21; from the word count group we have 2, punct and count_uppercase; from the 'POS tag' group we have 2, adv_frac and nn_frac; from the polarity group the most recurrent were 13, neg, neg_words_tweet, neu_words_tweet, pos_words_tweet, negat_words_tweet, neu. pos. neg_words, neu_words, pos_words, neg_words_sum, pos_words_sum, negat_words; from semantic rules only 1 characteristic was selected, r1; from the polarity trigrams, only 3 of the 27 were most important, neu_neu_neg, pos_neu_neu, neu_neu_neu; the Doc2Vec representation was fundamental in all the experiments; no feature was selected from the hashtag and emoticons group.

5 Conclusions and Future Work

A new method was proposed for feature selection based on the concept of bagging using covering arrays to support the bootstrap sample building process and rule-induction techniques to obtain the features that provide more information in TSA. With this method it was possible to reduce total features by up to 83% without significantly diminishing precision or F-measure. Furthermore, in one experiment it was possible to increase these measures. It is expected that the results of this research will allow us to improve the results of other polarity detection systems of the state of the art, since most of the classification algorithms are sensitive to the use of features that do not add value and would benefit from training with the optimal features.

The use of covering arrays allows covering all the combinations (in this case of interaction 2) between the features with the least possible effort, making it possible to guarantee the evaluation of many subsets and variations of features with a minimum number of test cases or experiments compared to those required when using other approaches, for example with metaheuristic algorithms. The Doc2Vec feature allowed adding a very important representation of the tweet that, unlike a terms-by-tweet matrix, improves performance by detecting the polarity in all the experiments performed.

As future work it is expected: (1) to evaluate the method of feature selection proposed in contexts other than Twitter sentiment analysis; (2) to implement a deep neural network for TSA using the proposed method; (3) to use a method other than sampling by row replacement that enables selection of the most useful instances for training; (4) to evaluate covering arrays of greater strength; (5) to select a higher quality training data and evaluate the quality of the results with the proposed method; and to use a Doc2Vec model pre-trained only with tweets.

References

1. Ravi, K., Ravi, V.: A survey on opinion mining and sentiment analysis: tasks, approaches and applications. Knowl.-Based Syst. **89**, 14–46 (2015)
2. Liu, B.: Sentiment Analysis: Mining Opinions, Sentiments, and Emotions. Cambridge University Press, Cambridge (2015)
3. Medhat, W., Hassan, A., Korashy, H.: Sentiment analysis algorithms and applications: a survey. Ain Shams Eng. J. **5**, 1093–1113 (2014)
4. Giachanou, A., Crestani, F.: Like it or not: a survey of Twitter sentiment analysis methods. ACM Comput. Surv. **49**(2), 28 (2016)

5. Da Silva, N.F.F., Coletta, L.F.S., Hruschka, E.R.: A survey and comparative study of tweet sentiment analysis via semi-supervised learning. ACM Comput. Surv. **49**(1), 15 (2016)

6. Cohen, M.B., Colbourn, C.J., Ling, A.C.H.: Constructing strength three covering arrays with augmented annealing. Discret. Math. **308**(13), 2709–2722 (2008)

7. Amolik, A., Jivane, N., Bhandari, M., Venkatesan, M.: Twitter sentiment analysis of movie reviews using machine learning techniques. Int. J. Eng. Technol. **7**(6), 2038–2044 (2016). ISSN 0975-4024. http://www.enggjournals.com/ijet/docs/IJET15-07-06-027.pdf

8. Esuli, A., Sebastiani, F., Fernández, A.M.: Distributional correspondence indexing for cross-lingual and cross-domain sentiment classification. J. Artif. Intell. Res. **55**, 131–163 (2016)

9. Zhang, L., Ghosh, R., Dekhil, M., Hsu, M., Liu, B.: Combining lexicon-based and learning-based methods for Twitter sentiment analysis. In: HP Laboratories Technical Report, 89th edn. (2011). http://www.hpl.hp.com/techreports/2011/HPL-2011-89.pdf

10. Agarwal, A., et al.: Sentiment analysis of Twitter data. In: Proceedings of the Workshop on Languages in Social Media. Association for Computational Linguistics (2011)

11. Kouloumpis, E., Wilson, T., Moore, J.D.: Twitter sentiment analysis: the good the bad and the OMG! In: ICWSM, vol. 11, pp. 538–541 (2011)

12. Räbigera, S., et al.: SteM at SemEval-2016 task 4: applying active learning to improve sentiment classification. In: Proceedings of SemEval, pp. 64–70 (2016)

13. Manning, C.D., et al.: The Stanford CoreNLP natural language processing toolkit. In: ACL (System Demonstrations) (2014)

14. Hu, M., Liu, B.: Mining and summarizing customer reviews. In: Proceedings of the Tenth ACM SIGKDD International Conference on Knowledge Discovery and Data Mining. ACM (2004)

15. Baccianella, S., Esuli, A., Sebastiani, F.: SENTIWORDNET 3.0: an enhanced lexical resource for sentiment analysis and opinion mining. In: LREC (2010)

16. Mohammad, S.M., Kiritchenko, S., Zhu, X.: NRC-Canada: building the state-of-the-art in sentiment analysis of tweets. arXiv preprint arXiv:1308.6242 (2013)

17. Mohammad, S.M.: # Emotional tweets. Association for Computational Linguistics (2012)

18. Appel, O., Chiclana, F., Carter, J., Fujita, H.: Successes and challenges in developing a hybrid approach to sentiment analysis. Appl. Intell. **48**(5), 1176–1188 (2018). ISSN 0924-669X. https://doi.org/10.1007/s10489-017-0966-4

19. Le, Q., Mikolov, T.: Distributed representations of sentences and documents. In: International Conference on Machine Learning (2014)

20. Lau, J.H., Baldwin, T.: An empirical evaluation of doc2vec with practical insights into document embedding generation. arXiv preprint arXiv:1607.05368 (2016)

21. George, H.A., Jiménez, J.T., García, V.H.: Verificación de Covering Arrays. Lambert Academic Publishing, Saarbrücken (2010)

22. Jun, Y.: Backtracking algorithms and search heuristics to generate test suites for combinatorial testing (2006)

23. Nakov, P., et al.: SemEval-2013 task 2: sentiment analysis in Twitter, Atlanta, Georgia, USA, p. 312 (2013)

24. Nakov, P., et al.: SemEval-2016 task 4: sentiment analysis in Twitter. In: Proceedings of the 10th International Workshop on Semantic Evaluation (SemEval 2016), San Diego, US (2016, forthcoming)

25. Rosenthal, S., Farra, N., Nakov, P.: SemEval-2017 task 4: sentiment analysis in Twitter. In: Proceedings of the 11th International Workshop on Semantic Evaluation (SemEval-2017) (2017)

26. Go, A., Bhayani, R., Huang, L.: Twitter sentiment classification using distant supervision (2009)

27. Deriu, J., et al.: SwissCheese at SemEval-2016 task 4: sentiment classification using an ensemble of convolutional neural networks with distant supervision. In: Proceedings of SemEval, pp. 1124–1128 (2016)

General AI, Knowledge Engineering, AI and the Web Applications, Computational Sustainability and AI, Heuristic Search and Optimization

ESIA Expert System for Systems Audit Risk-Based

Néstor Darío Duque-Méndez$^{(\boxtimes)}$, Valentina Tabares-Morales, and Hector González

Universidad Nacional de Colombia, Manizales, Colombia
ndduqueme@unal.edu.co

Abstract. Software and hardware resources of the organizations are dynamic and with this the associated risks. In this situation an audit active approach based on the changing risks analysis is required, and not only on existent controls verification. On the institutions that base big part of their activity in informatics technologies a relevant administration component is systems audit, play an important role to guarantee the availability, confidentiality and reliability of the information. This paper introduces an expert system (ESIA) that supports systems auditor in risks evaluation and the choice of controls that reasonably protect the organization. Knowledge base represents the facts given and the actions of the systems audit expert under the methodology of risks analysis. The Expert System is implemented with free software in an Web environment, searching for a better access of beneficiary community. From a technology point of view integrates server and web application with logic server Prolog.

Keywords: Expert system · Risks analysis · Systems audit

1 Introduction

Collecting various authors in [8] informatics audit is defined as a holistic approach to identify and evaluate information resources of the organization and informatics flow, with the objective of searching effective and efficient informatics systems. Audit supply 'an invaluable knowledge structure' in the organizational information strategy formulation and influence on management, technology, systems and content which is well establish on foundational literature. Continue proposing, that on its fuller form, informatics audit covers all methods and necessary tools to schedule, to model, evaluate, to control quality and analyze information assets of an organization and management of them. Systems Audit can be understood as a review and evaluation of controls, systems, procedures, hardware, software and human resources involve on process, looking for signaling alternative curses that accomplish a more efficient and safe information utilization that will be useful for an optimal decision making [6]. Systems Audit

© Springer Nature Switzerland AG 2018
G. R. Simari et al. (Eds.): IBERAMIA 2018, LNAI 11238, pp. 483–494, 2018.
https://doi.org/10.1007/978-3-030-03928-8_39

is a relative new field, where there is a barely methodologies formulation, which must be adjusted to concrete conditions of each installation. The expert labor takes a preponderant role.

Generally, technology incursion on Audit takes place to increase resources efficiency, but is often perceived as a tool to solve data quality problems, instead of a strategically align technology. Principal impacts include a change of corrective controls to preventive and detective controls and an increase on data management trust [19]. To say about [5] intern controls matters are important for entities to assure accuracy, reliability and opportunity of financial informs and propose a design of systems to help managers on detecting weaknesses in intern control in their organizations, besides of benefits and difficulties analysis on the implantation, based on a study in empirical test and manager perceptions.

In [8] it's shown a revision work oriented to revitalize the theory and the practice of informatics audit and connect the powerful practice of information management, the methods and audit applications. The research concludes in the needing of moving forward on the theory and practice expanding the relationship between audit and information management, taking up studies about methodologies and techniques that integrate the approaches.

Referring to risks analysis, in the presented proposal on [9] it is posed that such in the working environment like in the academic environment one of the main difficulties that are found at the time of developing an informatics application is the risks identification; whereby its posed *P.L Risk identification System*, which has a primordial objective to offer to the user a quick, efficient and intuitive way to be able to detect, inform and individualize risks in the developing process of software through a series of questions, that turns out to be a powerful and 'very easy' to use tool.

Artificial intelligence, as in all areas of human society, has a space that gains greater relevance every day. "It is hard to avoid the buzz in the industry around artificial intelligence (AI) and associated technologies. Yet suddenly we are starting to see it being applied more broadly and more enthusiastically by companies as tools in the fight in an increasingly challenging cyberwar" [13].

Saha et al. proposes a knowledge driven automated compliance auditing scheme for the processing of loans by banks. By incorporating experts' opinion along with data mining techniques, the model automates the prediction of risk level, risk impact and ease of detection of fraudulent cases that deal with loan processing. The knowledge based method has the potential to save time and expensive human resources by automating the risk analysis [22].

In [14] it is study and models a financial resources assignation system to commissions companies of stock-market, with the purpose that those resources can be invested with the name of the company (investor), in such way that the risk of non-payment assigned capital can be decrease. The planted model based on Fuzzy Expert Systems allows the supporting of these financial resources assignment decisions. The help that represents for the decisions makers to count with systems tools that incorporate their specific problems become more important every time on a society where the information speed and the time that it's given to take decisions decreases more each time.

At [18] it has been achieved to design and develop an expert system to automatize the process evaluation of annual control planes approval and execution of the same institutional control organs, achieving to obtain the predicted and normed results on the corresponded directives; in addition of obtaining the approval process performance indicator and annual control planes execution. The developed prototype has shown a total functionality with integrated systems, reason why the expert systems utilization to monitoring, control and evaluation of OCI performance, is an adequate way to focus the information systems developing, is a field of governmental control. At [4] it is presented the developing of a teaching support tool of financial states audit, using artificial intelligence techniques and expert systems for non-structured audit activities (dictum, intern control evaluation, planning, risks evaluation, etc.). The striking approach takes the intern control evaluation questionnaire and its weighing and turns it into a rules system. In [17] the purpose of intelligent system is to identify irregular permissions on an informatics system. Lee presents a system denominated construction quality management audit (CMQA) that evaluates the performance of a quality management system (QMS) implemented on a construction company. CMQA Expert is programmed using MATLAB's GUI components and its fuzzy logic tools box. The base rules of CQMA Expert are built using obtained information from QMS auditors [11].

An important work that searches to collect some approaches about the use of artificial intelligent systems from the side of the auditors, with goals to predict some future research directions based on TIC are doing achievements on the modern organizational world with a bigger pressure on auditors that performed a more effective role on governability and the control of corporative entities.

The work in [16] shows the main research efforts and current debates on auditors' use of artificial intelligent systems, with a view to predicting future directions of research and software development in the area. The synthesis of these previous studies revealed certain research vacuum which future studies in the area could fill. Such areas include assessing the impact and benefits of adopting artificial intelligence on internal control systems, implications of using such systems for small and medium audit firms, audit education, public sector organisations' audit, and other.

Finally, in [23] is presents research what painstakingly collected and analysed the content of 311 ES case studies dating from 1984 through 2016. Most of the ES applications were from business- oriented organizations in particular in operations, finance, management and accounting, but very few in audit.

Main contribution this works is to provide professionals of systems auditing with a tool that allows to incorporate the knowledge of experts in the area, supported in the methodology of risk analysis. The rest of the present document is organized in the next way: Numeral 2 outlines the concepts that support the proposed system; numeral 3 it is posed the develop model and its application, then finishes with conclusions.

2   Previous Concepts

2.1   Expert Systems (ES)

Expert Systems as a area of Artificial Intelligence (AI) with its focus on emulating human intelligence, in the way in which a human expert in a thematic acts in the resolution of problems and in the decision making.

Expert Systems are the simplest form of artificial intelligence, which uses rules as the representation for encoding knowledge from a fairly narrow area into an automated system. Mimic the reasoning procedure of a human expert when solving a knowledge-intensive problem and consists of a set of IF-THEN rules, a set of facts and an interpreter controlling the application of the rules, given the facts. Rule-based systems are very simple models and can be adapted and applied to a wide set of different problems, whenever the domain of knowledge can be expressed in the form of IF-THEN rules [20].

ES can be defined as software that simulates the learning process of memorization, reasoning, communication and action of a human expert on a certain dominated area, becoming on a consultant who can replace him and/or supporting on a correct decision making. For an ES construction to make sense it must count with real experts (o their knowledge) and that they can express their solution methods to transfer this knowledge; but at the same time that the multiplication of this experience is necessary for the absence of a big number of these experts. The systems audit with new approaches reunites those requirements [1].

In this systems is very important the validation. In a setng where objectivity is sought and variance is avoided, validation ascertains what a system knows, knows incorrectly or does not know. Validation ascertains the system's level of expertise and investigates the theoretical basis on which the system is based. It evaluates the reliability of decisions made by the system [15].

2.2   Risks Analysis Methodology

Systems audit has like an object to determinate the exposed risks of informatics resources on an organization, o part of it, and evaluate the protection degree looking for operations continuity, confidentiality, exactitude of results thrown and physical security.

Risks Analysis methodology was chosen, because it fits the proposed vision, searching previous actions to the threads impacts, constantly evaluating vulnerabilities that can be presented on the system, which without doubt have a dynamic behavior.

An important previous concept is the definition of the term risk, understood as something persistent that can happen but it hasn't yet; nevertheless, can be identified and act on its causes, and of this way decrease or eliminate its consequences. Another definition a little more technique but that it does not have a distance on the one previously exposed is: The risk is the probability that a certain event can hit a determinate intensity and on a determinate moment [7,10].

A traditional formula that is able to rate risks is the next one:

$$Risk = Occurrence\ Probability * Impact$$

The methodological steps to develop a systems audit, in general terms are:

1. Risks Stages Definition (RSD), defined as the group of services o resources of the application, system or service and that can be located independently of the others.
2. Determinate activities subject to control (ASC), understood as the group of tasks or associated subdivisions to the risks stages and that are allowed to be analyze like an all.
3. Establish Risks. For each activity subject to control it must be establishing all the threads that are exposed.
4. Determinate Controls. For each risk of the previous group it must be establish all the controls that minimize them, making a matrix of risk-control, which constitute a confrontation to risk-control variables, in which each of the intersections rates the activation degree and covering of the control to risk minimization.

   The previous appointed can be translated on a risk-control matrix, similar to the presented on Table 1.

Table 1. Risk-control matrix

	C1	C2	C4	C7	C8	C9	C13	C15
R4	G			R			B	R
R8	B		G	G	B			
R9	G		B	G	R			
R23					G	G		

Taking as criteria the next conventions, G the control has a good cover of the risk, R the control covers of a regular way the risk and B the control has a very little cover of the risk.

5. Selection of minimal controls. This phase is fundamental and represents the design of controls process and operates under the sentence 'Maximal controls aren't optimal controls'. It is proceeding to the selection of minimal control characterizing the risk, according to the previous formula and putting especial attention to the ones defined as critical risks.

   Inside of the criteria for controls selection, according to the risks it has to:
   - Preselect the control if it is the only one that acts well on a critical risk.
   - Preselect the control that acts well to many critical risks.
   - Evaluate the non-existence of incompatible o redundant controls.
   - Verify that any critical risk has been left without enough protection. If there are unprotected risks, choose the quality controls like R or search new ones.

The Fig. 1 shows the process to follow using risks analysis methodology:

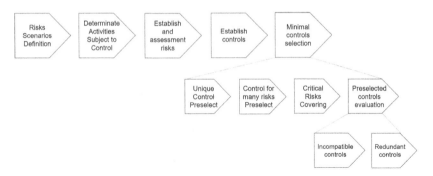

Fig. 1. Risks analysis methodology

2.3 Expert System Developing

The importance of design and build Expert Systems lies on the possibility of multiply the acting way of the experts, in occasions very limited and make the system work as a support for the user with a minor experience. The ES keeps knowledge of the expert for a determinate field and proposes solutions through the logic inference that puts the reasoning that guides the performance of this specialist on the field. This has special importance when it is recognizing that human experience cannot be able and is widely required for problems solutions. The Expert systems are one of the points that refit the researches on the artificial intelligence field. A computers System that works with AI techniques must be in situation of combining information in a 'smart' way, reaching conclusions and justifying them, just like the final result. The Expert Systems are the expression of Systems based of knowledge. With the application of artificial intelligence techniques, the transition of data processing to knowledge processing is specified [3].

Rolston pose that the application of expert systems would be adequate where the experts are provided of complex knowledge on a much delimitated area, where there is not an existence of algorithms already establish o where the existent ones cannot solve some problems. Another application field is where there are theories where is impossible to analyze all the cases theoretically imaginable through algorithms and in a space of time relatively short and reasonable [21].

A point of huge importance is the rigor in the methodology of system development. The Fig. 2 shows the development cycle of an expert system, taken of [12].

3   Intelligent System for a Systems Audit (ESIA)

Like an objective of the experts systems, in this proposal it tends to move the knowledge and experience to different spaces where there can't permanently be the auditor generates a time and resources saving, since an audit can take several

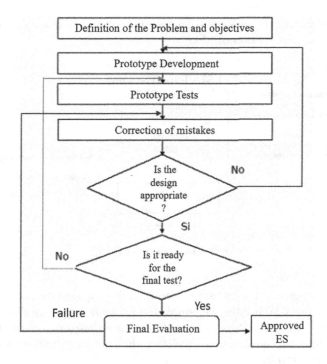

Fig. 2. Development cycle of an ES

days and this system is possible to feed on a working day and immediately make the process to deliver recommendations.

ESIA was developed a few years ago and it has been adjusting works on the frame of projects of the Research Group of adaptive intelligent environments GAIA, of Universidad Nacional de Colombia, sede Manizales.

ESIA has become in an experimental platform and teacher support.

3.1 Development of ESIA

The project development involves three stages:

- The definition of audit program
- The Expert System Design
- Application implementation

The first stage consists on the development of risks analysis methodology applicable to different audit topics (Production systems, applications development, data base systems, internet environment, etc.), defining the involved elements specifics in terms of *RS* or *ASC*.

The second stage consists on design and set in an expert system the processes (rules) and the information (knowledge) that requires the risks analysis methodology and controls design to face a systems audit.

Figure 3 shows the components of a generic expert system and how they were suitable for the construction of ESIA.

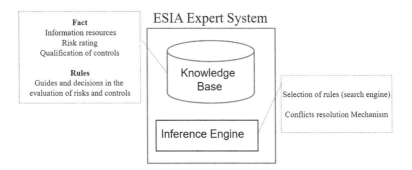

Fig. 3. Components of ESIA

The third stage and the last stage consist in the implementation of the application that gives a Web interface, stores the information of the different audit projects, keeps the knowledge base and besides it integrates with the expert system to apply the methodology realizing the necessary inferences to obtain recommended controls.

For controls rating the values between 0 and 100 were taken as a possible range for the probability of occurrence and the impact of the risk. And as a value of reference is take that a critical risk is the one that exceed a R score, that for practical cases has been defined preliminary in 3600, although this value is subjective it is considerate viable since it corresponds to a risk that has an occurrence probability of 60% and an impact of 60% that would represent compromising situations.

After the risks characterizing it must take into account the criteria for the minimal control selection, exposed on the previous section. Later on the preselection it must be evaluated these controls to guarantee that there is a not incompatible control and there is a not redundant control.

3.2   ESIA Implementation

Knowledge Base for the design of the knowledge base it must be taken into account the knowledge and the rules that form the problem to solve. After the development process of risks analysis methodology for systems audit, the knowledge and rules must have the knowledge base can be translated to the next concepts:

Knowledge

– Risks-Control Matrix. Represents a cell of the risk-control matrix which expresses the intersection of a risk with a control, valued with the form as the control acts on the risk.

- Inconsistent o incompatible controls. Express the incompatibility o redundancy between controls.
- Risks rating. Express the rating that the user of the system gives to the risk, quantified by the factors risks multiplication, occurrence of probability and application impact.

Rules

- Critical Risk Selection. Selection of all risks which rating is mayor or equal to 3600.
- Selection of controls that covers critical risks up. Over the critical risk select the o those controls that have a good performance on the risk. If some critical risk is not cover for any kind of control, it must be selected a control that can cover it up on a safely way.
- Preselect the unique control that performs well on the totality of the critical risks or select the control that covers well to the totality of the critical risks previously selected.
- Preselect a control that acts well for many critical risks. Take two controls and the list of risks that they cover up. Analyze the risks lists, to the selection of optimal controls, on the next way: If a risk of a list is a member of another, that risk is deleted of the list of a minor size; in addition, if a list it is empty, the control it belongs is taken out of the list of optimal installation controls.
- Evaluate the non-existence of incompatible controls. Take two incompatible controls (Inconsistent) and delete of the knowledge base that control which whose risks are cover up for another control.

The used language for the construction of the knowledge base is PROLOG which translates all the syntax to the predicate definition, next is posed some of those:

1. Risk-Control Matrix. This matrix represents the form *(F)* in performance on a control *(C)* facing a risk *(R)*. As a starting point of the system this matrix must be represented on the knowledge base and it will be in the next way:

$$matrix(R, C, F).$$

2. Risks characterization. The System must do an emphasis in the critical risks, which are rated and inserted as a new knowledge in the system, for that the next predicate is used:

$$Rate(R, Cal)$$

3. Rules for optimal controls selection. For the system to make this task is necessary to perfectly imitate the tasks that a human expert would do to achieve this goal, which will be enunciated and analyze below.

Select the controls that have a good cover in the critical risks. For that it is realized the next predicate, which inserts in the knowledge base predicates that show the risk and the control that cover it:

$$Rate(R, V)$$
$$V \geq 3600,$$
$$Matrix(R, C, b)$$
$$assert(cover(R, C))$$

If there's a critical risk without being cover it must be chosen the controls rate as regulars. With the purpose to achieve that certain task a transformation of the previous predicate is done in the next way:

$$rate(R, V)$$
$$v \geq 3600, not(cover(R, \_))$$
$$matrix(R, C, \sigma)$$
$$assert(regularCover(R, C))$$

The rest of the elements are implemented of similar way. This system can be applied to any kind of company; just a previous job has to be done to define the fields that will use the system and the characteristics of the company. Certain rates have to be done and with the data the system throws the recommended controls to protect it.

3.3   Implementation of the Application in an Internet Environment

This implementation was supported on the UML methodology, for software development. There are three defined stages, the analysis, the design and the implementation [2]. The architecture of the system is client-server of 3 layers, using three types of servers, all of them of free use, acceding to those through a web navigator.

1. Web Navigator. Client, which shows the interfaces of the user system and through WWW requests, sends data to the web server to be processed.
2. Web server (Apache Tomcat). Platform server for the execution and later data sent from server applicative of the system, that acceding to the other servers give answers to the sent requests for the client, through the sending of the HTML code, to the navigator through the web server.
3. Data base Server (PostgreSQL). Server with the task of receiving SQL commands of the server applicative and return them the request information.
4. Logic Server (Prolog). Server that has the task of the inference realization in the system according to the logic requests, sent by the applications. The connection between java and the expert system it's done in the next way: The java class invokes the connection API with the prolog, this API rise the expert system, lifting the knowledge base, after and during the execution are aggregated the facts to the memory work and in the precise moment that the class asks for the inference delivering the controls that cover the critical risks. The prolog server performs for request and raises the compile archive that has the knowledge base of the expert system.

4 Conclusions and Future Work

The proposal presents an expert system for system audit supported in the risk analysis methodology. Due its consistence allows the automation in an knowledge-based system. This proposal shows that the expert systems are viable for the problems solution when it is required a big amount of knowledge (empirical or not) of a human expert, like is the case of a systems audit.

The main contribution of this work is providing professionals of systems auditing with a tool that allows to incorporate the knowledge of experts in the area and facilitates the development of audits with a high level of coherence, based on a methodology of consolidated risk analysis. The versatility of the expert system allows it to adapt to the different conditions of the organization.

The evaluation, tests and refinement of the system facing it to real environments has allow the construction of a good tool of support for the systems auditors. The use of the expert system for academicals jobs realization and the university extension us a good support for the involve students on that task, because they count with 'an expert' that guides their actions.

The group has been working in the implementation of other proposals of risks valoration and extending the knowledge base with new stages on specific topics. Besides, it pretend to include a learning module for rating of risks and controls.

References

1. Badaro, S., Ibañez, L., Agüero, M.: Sistemas Expertos: Fundamentos, Metodologías y Aplicaciones. Ciencia y Tecnología, no 13 (2013)
2. Booch, G.: Software Architecture and the UML (1998). http://www.rational.com/uml.
3. Criado, B., Mario, J.: Sistemas Expertos. http://home.worldonline.es/jmariocr/index.htm
4. Cuéllar, M., Controlint, G.: Sistema De Inteligencia Artificial Aplicado A La Enseñanza De La Auditoría De Estados Financieros. Research on Computing Science, vol. 2 (2003)
5. Changchit, C., Holsapple, C.W., Madden, D.L.: Supporting managers' internal control evaluations: an expert system and experimental results. Decis. Support Syst. **30**(4), 437–449 (2001)
6. Néstor, D.M., Alonso, T.A.: La importancia de la auditoria en la seguridad de los sistemas, Revista Decisión Administrativa. Numero 5, Manizales (2000)
7. Echenique, J.A.: Auditoria en informática. Mc Graw Hill, New York (1990)
8. Frost, R., Wei Choo, C.: Revisiting the information audit: a systematic literature review and synthesis. Int. J. Inf. Manag. **37**(1), 1380–1390 (2017)
9. García-Martínez, R., Merlino, H.: Sistema Experto para la Identificación de Riesgos en el Desarrollo de Software: P.L. Risk Identification System (RIS) (2010)
10. ISACA: Normas y estándares de Auditoria. www.isaca.org
11. Lee, D.E., Lim, T.K., Arditi, D.: An expert system for auditing quality management systems in construction. Comput. Aided Civ. Infrastruct. Eng. **26**(8), 612–631 (2011)
12. López Takeyas, B.: Fases de Administración de Proyectos de Sistemas Expertos. www.itnuevolaredo.edu.mx/takeyas

13. Maher, D.: Can artificial intelligence help in the war on cybercrime? Comput. Fraud Secur. **2017**, 7–9 (2017)
14. Medina Hurtado, S., Manco, O.: Diseño de un sistema experto difuso: evaluación de riesgo crediticio en firmas comisionistas de bolsa para el otorgamiento de recursos financieros. Estudios Gerenciales **23**(104), 101–131 (2007)
15. O'Leary, D.E.: Validation of expert systems with applications to auditing and accounting expert systems. Decis. Sci. **18**, 168–186 (1987)
16. Omoteso, K.: The application of artificial intelligence in auditing: looking back to the future. Expert Syst. Appl. **39**(9), 8490–8495 (2012)
17. Parkinson, S., Somaraki, V., Ward, R.: Auditing file system permissions using association rule mining. Expert Syst. Appl. **55**, 274–283 (2016)
18. Rojas, J., Mauricio, D.: Sistema experto para el control de los procesos de monitoreo, control y evaluación de desempeño de los órganos de control institucional del Perú. Revista de investigación de sistemas e informática. RISI **9**(1), 45–55 (2012)
19. Rikhardssona, P., Dullb, R.: An exploratory study of the adoption, application and impacts of continuous auditing technologies in small businesses. Int. J. Acc. Inf. Syst. **20**, 26–37 (2016)
20. del Mar Roldán-García, M., García-Nieto, J., Aldana-Montes, J.F.: Enhancing semantic consistency in anti-fraud rule-based expert systems. Expert Syst. Appl. **90**, 332–343 (2017)
21. Rolston, D.W.: Principios de Inteligencia Artificial y Sistemas Expertos. Mc Graw Hill, New York (1992)
22. Saha, P., Bose, I., Mahanti, A.: A knowledge based scheme for risk assessment in loan processing by banks. Decis. Support Syst. **84**, 78–88 (2016)
23. Wagner, W.P.: Trends in expert system development a longitudinal content analysis of over thirty years of expert system case studies. Expert Syst. Appl. **76**, 85–96 (2017)

Design of a Computational Model for Organizational Learning in Research and Development Centers (R&D)

Marco Javier Suárez Barón[1], José Fdo. López[2],
Carlos Enrique Montenegro-Marin[3,4(✉)],
and Paulo Alonso Gaona García[3]

[1] Faculty of Systems and Computing, Unitec University Corporation,
Bogota, Colombia
marcosuarez@unitec.edu.co
[2] Faculty of Engineering, UNAD, Bogotá, Colombia
fernando.lopez@unad.edu.co
[3] Universidad Distrital Francisco José de Caldas, Bogotá, Colombia
{cemontenegrom, pagaonag}@udistrital.edu.co
[4] Universidad Cooperativa de Colombia, Medellín, Colombia
carlos.montenegrom@campusucc.edu.co

Abstract. This article presents a proposal for a computational model for organizational learning in R&D centers. We explained the first stage of this architecture that enables extracting, retrieval and integrating of lessons learned in the areas of innovation and technological development that have been registered by R&D researchers and personnel in social networks corporative focused to research. In addition, this article provides details about the design and construction of organizational memory as a computational learning mechanism within an organization. The end result of the process is purged information on lessons learned that can serve to support decision-making or strategic analysis to establish patterns, trends, and behaviors with respect to the roadmaps of the R&D center's strategic and operational plans.

Keywords: Computational architecture · Strategic knowledge management
Social networks

1 Introduction

The goal of the science and technology system in any country is to design strategies for the generation of new knowledge, technological development, and social ownership of knowledge. Once these strategies are implemented they should help to resolve real problems in the field. One of these strategies consists of establishing research, technological development, and innovation centers, also known as R&D Centres [1].

R&D centres are considered the most strategic important for resolving the country's main problems and are grounded in the integration of academic and research spheres with the state and the productive sector. The trajectory of each R&D centre reflects its own unique history; this history, in turn, reflects the compilation of experiences and

© Springer Nature Switzerland AG 2018
G. R. Simari et al. (Eds.): IBERAMIA 2018, LNAI 11238, pp. 495–506, 2018.
https://doi.org/10.1007/978-3-030-03928-8_40

best practices, and of successes and failures in the achievement of its objectives and goals or in the implementation of its technological development and research projects [2]. At the core of those experiences and knowledge are the human resources present in the university research groups and the research groups within the R&D centers.

In this research will be taken from lessons learnt contained in specialized social networks driven to research and academic subjects such as Research gate, academy and blogs. Nevertheless, the most part of this specialized experiences and knowledge are not stored and used. Neither information stored in these social academic nor research networks has been exploited [1].

This article presents a proposal for a computational model for organizational learning in R&D centers. This paper is structured as follows: Sect. 2 describes the theoretical background, which involves Knowledge Management (KM) process and methods, the models to manage knowledge on social systems and learning technologies and organizational strategies for exchange knowledge. Section 3 details the proposal to development and the methodology. Section 4 presents a foundations and discussion on the main components and phases of this computational model design. Finally, we present conclusions remarks and outlines further future works.

2 Background

Social media has increased interest in our daily activities, and the user profile of each individual is considered a significant source of information [3]. Both web sites and social networks are potential tools for the management, updating, and exchange of information and knowledge in fields that are interested in knowing the interests, thoughts, ideas, relationships and activities of each individual in their environment, such as marketing [4]. According to [5], as KM theory evolved, different models were proposed for innovation management in companies from multiple sectors in France and Germany, which have led us to focus our work primarily on the concept of Personal Knowledge Management (PKM), one of the most recent lines of work in this field.

Works like the one by [6] at the Edinburgh University information and knowledge sciences research department, in Scotland, have found that knowledge management (KM) is a line of work that complements and reframes the dynamics of research, technological development, and innovation with a view to the formalization of individual-based learning models within organizations.

In the search for and analysis of information, we can conclude that social networks have had an important impact on the world, that many people, societies and organizations have felt obliged to join them, and that the information they handle is so important that many companies around the world are willing to adopt these technologies in order to be a part of this impact [7]. Thus, companies view social networks as an easy channel to grow as a business, improve their commercial relationships, and give better publicity to their products [8]. However, the first time these companies enter this communication medium, they do not usually find what they expected; they obtain too much information that is not very useful, like illogical comments and even impossible suggestions.

Based on the understanding of social capital in knowledge exchange within an organization through social networks, [9] conducted research to develop tools and models to measure organizational learning by applying a combination of the three social capital factors (social network, social trust, and shared goals) and the theory of reasoned action. The study concluded that the application of each factor converges with knowledge creation and transfer. Scenarios such as the one described above lead us to conclude that knowledge that can be formalized and explicitly described is characterized as "know how" [10] also known as "tacit knowledge", and that knowledge expressed through a tangible medium becomes what is known as "explicit knowledge".

Initial attempts to formalize models to manage knowledge on social systems and learning have focused primarily on establishing integrated organizational systems at the level of organizational memories, as demonstrated by [11] of the CNR (Institute for High Performance Computing and Networking) and the University of Calabria in Italia. The research shows that in many cases the basic parameters for "the individual" -who is at the center of knowledge generation- to register, organize, and collaborate on the generation of new knowledge on the basis of lessons learned, have been forgotten, as [11].

Today, the mechanism most frequently used for online knowledge exchange is the well-known social network or web 2.0 approach. Studies, such as the one by [12–14], have demonstrated that individuals share tacit and explicit knowledge within virtual communities in the hopes of enriching their knowledge, seeking support, sharing experiences, and even doing business. However, this tacit and explicit knowledge on R&D that is shared by virtual communities and groups in R&D centers is critical to the success of organizational strategies and activities and, thus, should be strategically reused [15].

Some studies [16], [11] have applied ontology-based vocabularies to analyze this type of data, classifying programs with greater impact on user profiles in conventional social networks. Other studies do not focus exclusively on the quantitative identification of terms, but instead analyze systems of understanding at the machine and semantic enrichment levels [17].

3 Methodology

The process of designing the proposed architecture revealed two methodological perspectives in the existing technologies to support knowledge administration systems, which correspond to two discrete dimensions of knowledge management, according to [18] and to [19]. These two perspectives were used as the methodology for producing this paper and are explained below.

Firstly, the proposed knowledge management system is based on the process-centered perspective, understanding knowledge management as primarily a social communication process that can be improved by considering aspects of support to collaborative group work [14].

In the computational architecture, the process-centered approach focuses on individuals, as the most significant source of knowledge within an organization, and upholds the idea of resolving the cooperation problems amongst them through a process to achieve their social commitment to transfer and share knowledge.

The second approach is known as the product centric perspective [19], which in this project is directed at the creation, storage, and reuse of knowledge documents in the organizational memory, grounded in computer sciences. This approach was at the core of this research project, primarily because it is based on the idea of explicitly stating, documenting, and formalizing knowledge for use as a tangible resource, and attempts to present correct sources of information to the final users at the appropriate time.

This article discusses the management of the extraction and retrieval of information as a technological knowledge management mechanism with the goal of consolidating the Organizational Memory.

Organizational memory should provide mechanisms for storage and use of all formal and informal knowledge that exists within the organization [2]. Organizational memory derives from documents, good practice guides, manuals, and books that help improve the performance of the members of the organization.

Through this approach, we noted the importance that knowledge management has gained, even from a strictly economic perspective, which has led to the rise of numerous information technology-based tools. These tools provide mechanisms for shaping the individual knowledge of employees into the collective knowledge of the community [20]. Table 1 shows how the proposed architecture differs from other learning models, given the lack of consensus on the definition of many of the concepts and terms used in the organizational learning [21] and knowledge management fields.

Table 1. Contributions to scientific knowledge in research.

Component	Functional features and original scientific contributions
Metamodel	Integrates three levels of tasks (processing, knowledge, and learning), while the current models do not integrate these three functional levels
Ontology	Ontology groups join several terms around a set of concepts, and then maps and analyses them
Social analysis	Facilitates the necessary changes and transformations in R&D centers, by requiring structural and cultural configurations that foster innovation and flexible creativity
Extraction and retrieval of lessons learned	Applied in syntactic/morphological analysis of the grammatical structure in texts that contain lessons learned
Semantic analysis of lessons learned	Assists in self-correlation and establishing relationships of similarity and contrast between the strategies to resolve problem situations arising from the vocabulary of the ontology
Organizational memory (OM)	Real time creation of the OM or ranges defined by the user based on a model of creation of semantically analyzed packets of information. Unlike other metamodels, OM combines professional memory, management memory, individual memory, and project memory
Machine learning	Application of information analysis models and application of algorithms and methods for text analysis

Source: Authors

4   Foundations and Discussion

4.1   Framework Design

The framework, as the application will be identified ahead, was generated from the same conception of the model of lessons learnt within a social network environment. For its design, software has been developed to permit registering the lessons learnt by each user with a structure defined in three levels: Profile, Categories, and Subcategories. These can be established in personalized and flexible manner by each user. Given the vast amount of contributions expected, a non-relational database. The model can be seen in Fig. 2 with its explicit components: (1) lessons learnt acquisition, (2) retrieval and indexing Information, and (3) information management.

This framework also includes the promotion of new forms of knowledge capture, based on sources of information, such as lessons learned, that circulate in social networks. The generation of new knowledge is used for decision making in non-simulated and simulated environments within the learning process in the network.

The framework objectives described above are summarized in the functional components set out in Fig. 1. Our approach focuses on four elements of learning. The function and description of each component of the proposed architecture is explained below:

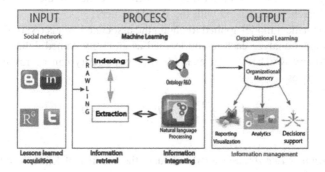

Fig. 1. Learning and organizational knowledge framework. Source: Authors

Lessons Learnt Acquisition

In order to register information, we propose individual knowledge management (from tacit Knowledge to Explicit Knowledge). In this paper the information stored is called as lessons learned through social networks. Therefore, creating profiles for each individual or group of people is imperative for knowledge generation. On the basis of real time information retrieval (IR) algorithms, textual information is acquired and analyzed for lessons learned in the ranges or periods of time established by the users.

The acquisition of a lesson learnt, in the architecture represents the relationship between the result of a process, project, indicators, conditions or causes that align to the strategic plan of R & D for research center. The Fig. 2 shows and example of lessons learned registered in social network twitter.

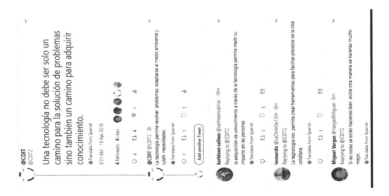

Fig. 2. Example of lessons learned registered in social network twitter.

To carry out the information extraction process, an application has been implemented for these three social networks; the application based on Python-social-auth technology allows the development in an agile way and provides the connection to numerous social networks with little configuration of parameters. The framework is integrated with certain profiles, this application allows access to tweets, retweets and mentions that refer to textual structures of topics related to R & D lessons, the text structures are identified with a # hashtag that will be defined by the research group or groups of researchers associated with the R + D centers.

The mathematical model applied to obtain the associated trends (A, P, D) is showed in (1). The model analyze each lesson learned as an entity named defined "category" taken in ontology R&D [20]. An example of this category can be resources, dates, places or processes.

$$A_x = \sum_{n=1}^{\infty} (A, P, D) \quad \forall_n > 0 \tag{1}$$

Where:

$P \rightarrow$ *Weight (I like it, comments)*: evaluate the number of Likes or retweets mad linked to each lesson registered.

$D \rightarrow$ *Registration time* = Determine the line time from lesson registered to first response; e.g. hours, days, minutes.

$n \rightarrow$ Number of arcs = Represent the thread or sequence for each lesson learnt.

$Ac \rightarrow$ Relevant publications = Similarity R&D terms for P, e.g. Synonyms, folksonomies, Hashtags.

$A\chi \rightarrow$ Identify the content relevance for extracting. If the relation is equal to zero, then the lesson learnt is not candidate for acquisition.

A scenario of analysis is give in the Table 1. In this case, the lesson "*#CDDI Una tecnología no debe ser solo un camino para la solución de problemas sino también un camino para adquirir conocimiento.*" is retrieved from twitter social network, see Fig. 2.

The relevance result is (Table 2):

Table 2. Analysis of relevance for lessons learnt acquisition process.

Lesson	Social net	P	D	Ac	n	Aχ
1	Twitter	1	1 h	3	4	3
Thread 1.1	Twitter	1	3 min	2	1	2
Thread 1.2	Twitter	0	11 min	1	0	0
Thread 1.3	Twitter/Facebook	0	0	1	0	0

The results can then be used to calculate aggregations, identify trends and produce reports, dashboards and performance measures.

Retrieval and Integrating

This component of the computational architecture makes it possible to determine the set of categories, groups, and trends related to the current status of knowledge acquisition and management on R&D-related issues from lessons learned that have been structured through web service extraction. This process requires the application of linguistic techniques, using natural language processing [1].

However, the source data for this process is nominal data and unstructured text containing information on the concepts, profiles, categories, description, codes, events, and control, along with the terminology of the set of lessons learned in knowledge management for R&D.

The information integration process involves a level of processing in which the application of ontology is crucial, given that the ontology enables the integration of specialized vocabulary into the knowledge domain. The tasks of indexing terms and linguistic concepts involved in ontologies make it possible to classify the topics, categories, entities (persons), and attributes of the entities mentioned in the lessons learned that are extracted.

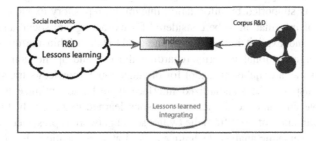

Fig. 3. R&D organizational learning process.

Figure 3 shows how the vocabulary "corpus" of data ontology allows the semantic indexing of scenarios such as: HR training, prototypes, patents, scientific articles, software registers. After the retrieval process all lessons learned are integrated and stored in a NoSQL structure.

For example, the word "management" can be changed in the word "administration"; To solve this lexical problem, this research adapts two approaches to the method of lexical variation ontological "lexical variation ontology". First, the method is applied in the English language corpus; in this case the variation must be made to a new corpus adaptable to the Spanish language since the language in which the lessons learned are recorded is Spanish. The main objective is to present a lexical ontology acquisition method that allows the variation of the noun and the verb through the generation of the corpus and the integration with the ontology of R + D data.

The other hand, the grammatical decomposition aims to understand the semantic behavior of each word as an entity contained in the R & D data ontology; Terms such as articles, connectors, links are discarded in the analysis process since they are not part of the set of terms included in the Ontology.

The model requires machine learning techniques for social analysis is a mechanism that is thought-out to implementation in the second stage of this project, this is a We Development an experimental non-probabilistic prediction prototype focused unstructured information lexical analysis; lessons recorded in social networks for corporative environments, which can be used and extended to other types of organizational R&D structures, either government or private.

The application of Natural language processing like method of information extracting enable the latent semantic indexing; and the ontology help to semantic enrichment for each of the lessons learnt analyzed. This process are the next step and future work for this research.

Information Management (I. M)

This component involves the storage subsystem that offers the opportunity to integrate the necessary repositories and supports about the structural conformation of the lesson learned into the computational architecture. The information initially captured on corporative social networks allows real time collection of lessons learned and documents from each social network [2]. In the architecture, the I.M proposes the collection of information packages from Research gate, blogs, LinkedIn, and digital repositories; this workflow is supported by information integrating repository explained in Fig. 3.

The type of information to be considered for extracting and social analysis stems from the tacit and explicit knowledge of the R&D staff. Within the organization, is relevant the organizational maturity regarding the use and application of corporate social networks as a collaborative tool for organizational knowledge transfer.

Figure 4 displays the standardized interface in order to optimize the ability to search, retrieve and analyze the texts of lessons learned extracted. In this case, the capture and extraction of texts from the twitter social network is presented. Through the use of text and semantic analysis techniques, like Latent Semantic Indexing, LSI, [22], it is possible to learn about the trends and reality of the knowledge that is being generated by the work teams, using the dissemination of lessons learned from each member of these teams. The result involves entities and concepts that are analyzed lexically and syntactically. Meanwhile, the semantic (structural) analysis given to each

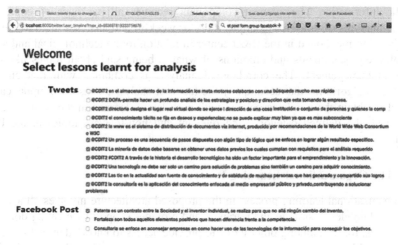

Fig. 4. Standardized interface of lessons learnt extracted using crawling

learned lesson make it possible to identify entities (see Sect. 4.2) that are or are not contained within the R + D vocabulary.

After extracting and filtering the lessons learned from unstructured sources, such as blogs, tweets, and organizational forums, the next stage is to create an information management component for constructing and organizing the organizational memory (OM). This is a continuous process and is at the core of the proposed platform. The lessons learnt filtering is supported by use of semantic indexing, in our approach the tool applied was ontology R&D [1].

The tasks of filtering and integrating information or lessons learned are based on the R&D ontology. The task of populating the organizational memory will be based on topics related to innovation and technological development for an R&D center. The purpose of designing the OM is to structure informal, case-based information. The OM also facilitates the automatic capture, retrieval, transfer, and reuse of knowledge. In information management, OM is defined as a flexible structure that enables the consolidation [23], in one sole repository, of all lessons learned on issues relevant to the R&D knowledge domain. Therefore, the design of the OM begins with the individual memory of each member of the R&D center and concludes with the creation of the collective memory.

In view of the above, organizational learning allows us to understand the impact of the opinions and perceptions of the human resources of the R&D center in relation to certain knowledge or experiences, for example, technological management. The R&D center can carry out periodic, offline analyses, through reports prepared on the basis of an analysis of the data from the OM obtained and formalized in real time. The framework allows for the incorporation into this analysis of an immense amount of spontaneous and real time information from social networks, forums, and blogs, to assess their impact on the thematic trends and behaviors and, thus, rapidly reveal both critical events and competitive advantages.

The Information Management component receives all packages of content in specific intervals of time (for example, daily or weekly) and analyses them to identify what is being mentioned in the R&D center in relation to the technological and social variables, e.g. sentiments and emotions of what is being said about topics like technological management. The correlational analysis is combined with mathematical models and algorithms that accompany the factorial analysis. These two inputs can be applied to obtain the trends associated with each lesson learned in terms of the entity mentioned, the defined category, and relevant and non-relevant topics at the R&D center.

4.2 The Organizational Learning Process

The organizational learning process in the proposed architecture involves all activities related to knowledge storage and retrieval, and provides support by creating document repositories, forums, among other tools, to provide access to knowledge that serves for decision-making purposes at any given moment; thus, running the organizational memory like a cycle of Knowledge Management processes. The way the organizational memory is structured can establish six (6) categories of organizational memory of Sect. 3.

From the perspective of business modelling language, ontologies provide a precise description of the concepts of the R&D domain and the relationships between these concepts. Therefore, in organizational learning processes, ontology offers a basic vocabulary that is useful for strategic knowledge management and establishes two levels of abstraction: for knowledge management and for the representation of knowledge.

The most important function of an ontology is the need to reach a consensus on the knowledge of the domain within an organization, so that the knowledge represented is not the subjective perspective of an individual but, rather, is shared and accepted by a community committed to the principle of organizational culture, facilitating communication and interoperability amongst the members of the R&D Centre.

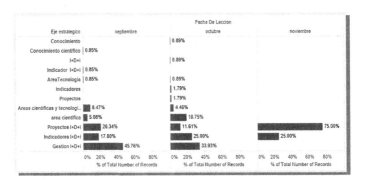

Fig. 5. Querying of the trends of lessons learned.

Finally, Fig. 5 shows an of example dashboard obtained of the information that we have obtained from the previous processes and that feed the "tableau tool" for the comparison of the trends of lessons learned regarding the strategic axes of the R + D centres in period time one month. The analysis shows that in September 2017 there was a greater opinion tendency on R & D Management (45.76%) as in the month of October 2017 (33.93%) and the trend of publications with respect to R + D projects is greater with 75.00%.

5   Conclusions and Future Research

In this paper is proposed the design of general architecture of a computational model driven to extraction, integrating and analysis not structured information obtained from scientific and academic social networks. The aim in this research is development an organizational learning system that apply new computational algorithms like natural language processing that allow organizational learning to be more effective and specific in R&D centres.

Organizational learning is considered a strategic objective for the long-term success of an organization. Earlier organizational learning models responded to more general needs; for example, were applied algorithms for information extracting from Facebook and twitter, also we used document management or information systems to support global management decision-making in research groups.

Organizational learning requires the development of new techniques to make knowledge management more effective. The incorporation and application of semantics to organizational knowledge acquired through ontologies (metadata) provides a solution for more effective organizational knowledge transfer and consultation, as organizational learning has a positive effect on performance within the organization. Ontology makes it possible to group together terms and concepts in a single management structure. Therefore, this tool facilitates the analysis of data and information obtained in social networks, by providing inputs for strategic planning and decision-making on issues related to Innovation and Technological Development in the above-mentioned centers.

References

1. Pico, B., Suárez, M.: Organizational memory construction supported in semantically tagged. Int. J. Appl. Eng. Res. 41744–41748 (2015)
2. Kirwan, C.: Making Sense of Organizational Learning: Putting Theory into Practice. Gower Publishing Limited, Farnham (2013)
3. Chiha, R., Ben Ayed, M.: Towards an approach based on ontology for semantic-temporal modeling of social network data. In: Madureira, A.M., Abraham, A., Gamboa, D., Novais, P. (eds.) ISDA 2016. AISC, vol. 557, pp. 708–717. Springer, Cham (2017). https://doi.org/10.1007/978-3-319-53480-0_70
4. Fam, D.: Facilitating communities of practice as social learning systems: a case study of trialling sustainable sanitation at the University of Technology Sydney (UTS). Knowl. Manag. Res. Pract. 15, 391–399 (2017)

5. Haas, M.R., Hansen, M.T.: Different knowledge, different benefits: toward a productivity perspective on knowledge sharing in organizations. Strateg. Manag. J. **28**, 1133–1153 (2010)

6. Razmerita, L., Kirchner, K., Sudzina, F.: Personal knowledge management: the role of Web 2.0 tools for managing knowledge at individual and organisational levels. Online Inf. Rev. **33**(6) 1021–1039 (2009). https://doi.org/10.1108/14684520911010981

7. Tan, W., Blake, M.B., Saleh, I., Dustdar, S.: Social-network-sourced big data analytics. IEEE Internet Comput. **17**(5), 62–69 (2013)

8. Sinclaire, J.K., Vogus, C.E.: Adoption of social networking sites: an exploratory adaptive structuration perspective for global organizations. Inf. Technol. Manag. **12**(4), 293–314 (2011)

9. Chow, W.S., Chan, L.S.: Social network, social trust and shared goals in organizational knowledge sharing. Inf. Manag. **45**(7), 458–465 (2008)

10. Takeuchi, R.: A critical review of expatriate adjustment research through a multiple stakeholder view: progress, emerging trends, and prospects. J. Manag. **36**(4), 1040–1064. First Published January 26 (2010). https://doi.org/10.1177/0149206309349308

11. Pirró, G., Mastroianni, C., Talia, D.: A framework for distributed knowledge management: design and implementation. Futur. Gener. Comput. Syst. **26**, 38–49 (2010). https://doi.org/10.1016/j.future.2009.06.004

12. Myong-Hun, C., Harrington, J.: Individual learning and social learning: endogenous division of cognitive labor in a population of co-evolving problem-solvers. Adm. Sci. **3**, 53–75 (2013)

13. Breslin, J., Decker, S.: The future of social networks on the internet: the need for semantics. IEEE Internet Comput. **11**(6), 86–90 (2007). https://doi.org/10.1109/MIC.2007.138

14. Fernández-Mesa, A., Ferreras-Méndez, J., Alegre, J., Chiva, R.: Shedding new lights on organisational learning, knowledge and capabilities. Cambridge Scholars Publishing, Newcastle (2014)

15. López-Quintero, J., Cueva Lovelle, J., González Crespo, R., García-Díaz, V.: A personal knowledge management metamodel based on semantic analysis and social information. Soft Comput. 1–10 (2016)

16. Kamasat, R., Yozgat, U., Yavuz, M.: Knowledge process capabilities and innovation: testing the moderating effects of environmental dynamism and strategic flexibility. Knowl. Manag. Res. Pract. **15**, 356–368 (2017)

17. Espinoza Mejía, M., Saquicela, V., Palacio Baus, K., Albán, H.: Extracción de preferencias televisivas desde los perfiles de redes sociales. Politécnico **34**(2), 1–9 (2014)

18. Peis, E., Herrera Viedma, E., Montero, Y.H., Herrera Torres, J.C.: Análisis de la web semántica: estado actual y requisitos futuros. El Prof. Inf. **12**(5), 368–376 (2003)

19. Abecker, A., Bernardi, A., Hinkelmann, K., Kuhn, O.: Toward a technology for organizational memories. IEEE Intell. **13**(3), 40–48 (1998). https://doi.org/10.1109/5254.683209

20. Barón, M.J.S.: Applying social analysis for construction of organizational memory of R&D centers from lessons learned. In: Proceedings of the 9th International Conference on Information Management and Engineering (ICIME 2017), pp. 217–220. ACM, New York. https://doi.org/10.1145/3149572.3149604

21. Barão, A., de Vasconcelos, J., Rocha, Á., Pereira, R.: Research note: a knowledge management approach to capture organizational learning networks. Int. J. Inf. Manag. (2017). https://doi.org/10.1016/j.ijinfomgt.2017.07.013

22. Różewski, P., Jankowski, J., Bródka, P., Michalski, R.: Knowledge workers' collaborative learning behavior modeling in an organizational social network. Comput. Hum. Behav. **51**, 1248–1260 (2015)

23. Van Grinsven, M., Visser, M.: Empowerment, knowledge conversion and dimensions of organizational learning. Learn. organ. **18**(5), 378–391 (2011)

Storm Runoff Prediction Using Rainfall Radar Map Supported by Global Optimization Methodology

Yoshitomo Yonese[1]([⊠]), Akira Kawamura[2], and Hideo Amaguchi[2]

[1] CTI Engineering Co., Ltd., Tokyo, Japan
yonese@ctie.co.jp
[2] Faculty of Urban Environmental Sciences, Tokyo Metropolitan University,
Tokyo, Japan

Abstract. In Tokyo metropolitan area, flood risk is increasing due to social and environmental conditions including concentration of population and industry etc. Small urban watersheds are at a high risk of inundation by river flooding and/or inner water induced by heavy rainfall in a short time. To estimate river water level accurately in urban small rivers, it is critically important to conduct precise runoff analysis by using spatiotemporally distributed rainfall data. In this study, a runoff analysis was conducted with spatiotemporally densely distributed X-band MP Radar (X-band multi-parameter radar) data as input for storm events occurred in upper Kanda River, a typical urban small river in Tokyo. Then, SCE-UA method, one of global optimization methodologies, was applied to identify the parameters of the storm runoff model. The results revealed that urban storm runoff was predicted accurately using X-band MP radar map supported by optimized runoff model.

Keywords: Urban runoff · X-band MP radar · Small urban watershed
SCE-UA method

1 Introduction

In recent years, locally concentrated heavy rainfall, known as guerrilla-type rainstorms, has frequently brought about flood damages in Japan. Especially, Tokyo Metropolis is at an increasing risk of flooding due to its social and environmental conditions such as population and industry concentration, and urbanization or climate change which increase storm runoff. Small urban watersheds are prone to be caused inundation by river flooding or inner water because heavy rainfall even for a short while can bring about a sudden increase in storm runoff volume. Based on these backgrounds, it is expected to conduct precise runoff analysis by using detailed spatiotemporally distributed rainfall data.

X-band MP radar network (XRAIN), deployed by the Ministry of Land, Infrastructure, Transportation, and Tourism of Japan (MLIT), was started its full operation in March 2014 after the trial operation since 2010. The system provides detailed spatiotemporally distributed rainfall data. Earlier studies on the X-band MP radar data

© Springer Nature Switzerland AG 2018
G. R. Simari et al. (Eds.): IBERAMIA 2018, LNAI 11238, pp. 507–517, 2018.
https://doi.org/10.1007/978-3-030-03928-8_41

include; characteristics of the data and precise estimation methods of radar rainfall [1], and the precision evaluation of X-band MP radar rainfall [2].

However, storm runoff prediction using X-band MP radar data has not been carried out for small urban watershed. In addition, there is no method for calibrating urban runoff models. X-band MP Radar data, having sixteen times higher resolution and five times higher frequency compared to conventional radar data, are a large set of rainfall data, so-called big data. To make the best use of these detailed data, it is expected that runoff analysis models convert rainfall into precise storm runoff.

Thus, in this study, the authors built a storm runoff model using X-band MP radar data, and applied a global optimization method, the Shuffled Complex Evolution University of Arizona, SCE-UA, [3] for optimization of the runoff model. With the model, the authors evaluated the hydrograph reproducibility. Storm events in upper Kanda River, one of representing urban small rivers in Tokyo, were selected as the target.

2   Target Watershed and Storm Events

2.1   Target Watershed

The Kanda River, an urban watershed in western Tokyo, Japan, was selected as the target watershed. It originates in Inokashira Pond in Mitaka City and flows into Nakano Ward, then, into Shinjuku Ward after merging with the Zenpukuji River. With the basin area of 105.0 km^2 and the length of 25.48 km, it is one of typical small rivers in Tokyo and is designated as one of Japanese first-class rivers. In this study, Koyo Bridge, shown in Fig. 1, was selected as the site to determine the reproducibility of the model, and upper Kanda River basin, having a catchment area of 7.7 km^2 at Koyo Bridge, was selected as the target basin.

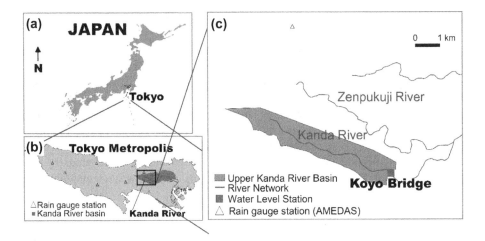

Fig. 1. Index map of (a) Japan, (b) Kanda river basin in Tokyo and (c) target area upper Kanda basin at Koyo Bridge.

2.2   Target Storm Events

Five target events were selected from the ones occurred in 2013. Since heavy rainfalls during a short period are capable of rising water level in small rivers, rainfall over 25 mm in 30 min were selected as the target events [4].

Storm events were defined as sequential rainfalls with no longer than 1 h intervals. Table 1 shows the five target events. In the table, 30 min maximum rainfall, the period of rainfall data used in runoff analysis, and rainfall causes are also listed.

Table 1. Target rainfall events

Rainfall event	Rainfall (mm/30 min)	Period of rainfall data used for runoff analysis	Cause of rainfall
Ev.1	36	9/15 03:20–9/15 17:20 (841 min.)	Typhoon No.18
Ev.2	35	8/12 17:14–8/12 23:39 (386 min.)	Atmospheric instability
Ev.3	31	6/25 11:38–6/25 18:10 (393 min.)	Atmospheric instability
Ev.4	26	9/04 22:51–9/05 14:27 (937 min.)	Low pressure
Ev.5	25	4/06 14:48–4/07 04:53 (846 min.)	Low pressure

2.3   Overview of the Rainfall Data

X-band MP Radar provides detailed rainfall data in every 250 m × 250 m mesh in every 1 min. The target area is only 7.7 km^2 and consisted of as much as 138 mesh data (see Fig. 2). The basin average rainfall applied to the runoff analysis was created from X-band MP Radar data.

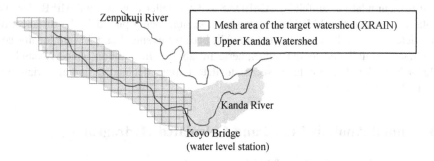

Fig. 2. Mesh area of the target watershed

Figure 3 shows hyetographs and cumulative rainfall by X-band MP Radar. For comparison, ground rainfall observation data, called AMEDAS data, is also shown in Fig. 3. AMEDAS observation stations are deployed by the Japan Meteorological Agency (JMA), and the nearest station from the target basin is located 5 km distant from the target watershed (see Fig. 1). Figure 3 shows the time series of rainfall for events from 1 to 3 out of the five target events.

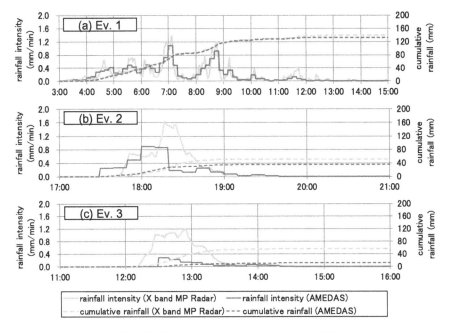

Fig. 3. Hyetographs and cumulative rainfall

In Fig. 3(a), X-band MP Radar and AMEDAS show nearly the same hyetograph and cumulative rainfall. In contrast, these hyetographs seem differences in Fig. 3(b) and (c): cumulative rainfall by AMEDAS is far smaller than X-band MP Radar. The data implies that the AMEDAS observation station, being placed in the distance, did not detect the locally concentrated rainfall, because events 2 and 3 were locally concentrated rainfall due to the atmospheric instability. In addition, since X-band MP Radar provides 1-min data, it seems to detect more detailed temporal variation of rainfall than AMEDAS data.

3   Runoff Analysis Model and Calculated Hydrograph

3.1   Overview of the Runoff Model

The runoff model used in this study is called Urban Storage Function (USF) model (see Fig. 4) with governing Eqs. (1)–(4) [5]. It is a lumped runoff analysis model in which urban runoff mechanism is incorporated. In USF model, users do not have to separate effective rainfall and runoff components, because runoff components are conceptually expressed to incorporate urban-specific runoff mechanism such as outflow to other basins through combined sewer system or leakage from water distribution pipes.

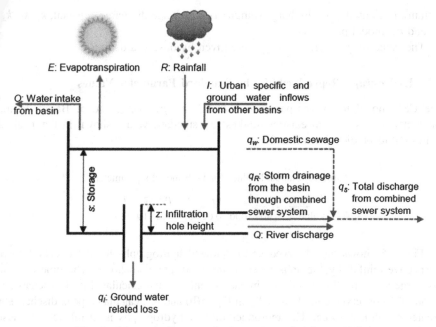

Fig. 4. Schematic diagram of urban storage function model

The Eq. (1) is the relation between runoff from the basin and the total storage within the basin, whose continuous equation leads to the Eq. (2). The Eq. (3) is groundwater-related loss. The Eq. (4) expresses the relation between river discharge and storm drainage to other basins through the combined sewer system.

$$s = k_1(Q + q_R)^{p_1} + k_2 \frac{d}{dt}\{(Q + q_R)^{p_2}\} \tag{1}$$

$$\frac{ds}{dt} = R + I - E - O - Q - q_R - q_l \tag{2}$$

$$q_l = \begin{cases} k_3(s - z) & (s \geq z) \\ 0 & (s < z) \end{cases} \tag{3}$$

$$q_R = \begin{cases} \alpha(Q + q_R - Q_o) & (\alpha(Q + q_R - Q_o) < q_{Rmax}) \\ q_{Rmax} & (\alpha(Q + q_R - Q_o) \geq q_{Rmax}) \end{cases} \tag{4}$$

Where s: total stored height (mm), t: time (min), Q: river discharge (mm/min), q_R: storm drainage to other basins through the combined sewer system, q_{Rmax}: maximum storm drainage, q_l: groundwater-related loss (mm/min), R: rainfall intensity (mm/min), I: urban-specific and ground water inflows from other basins (mm/min), E: evapotranspiration (mm/min), O: water intake (mm/min), z: infiltration hole height for

q_l (mm), Q_o: initial river discharge (mm/min), α: sewage discharge constant, k_1, k_2, k_3 p_1, and p_2: model parameters.

The value of q_{Rmax}, I, E, O, Q_0 were given by observed data.

3.2 Hydrograph Reproducibility by Standard Parameter Values

The USF model has seven-parameters: k_1, k_2, k_3, p_1, p_2, z, and α. Based on the parameter values used in existing studies [5], standard values shown in the Table 2 were used to predict storm runoff.

Table 2. Standard values for USF model's parameters

Parameter	k_1	k_2	k_3	p_1	p_2	z	a
Value	40	1000	0.02	0.4	0.2	10	0.5

Figure 5 shows the observed and calculated hydrographs for the events 1 to 3. Respective rainfall hyetographs given as the input are also shown. The time of peak discharge were mostly reproduced in each event, but the calculated peak discharge is greater than observed data. Especially in Fig. 5(b) and (c), calculated peak discharge is greater by almost twice. The reproducibility of hydrographs is insufficient because rainfall or runoff characteristics, which are different in each event, were not expressed appropriately.

4 Optimization of the Storm Runoff Model by Global Optimization Methodology

4.1 Procedure to Setting Parameters of Storm Runoff Analysis Model by SCE-UA Method

In this section, SCE-UA method was applied to optimize USF model's seven parameters.

SCE-UA method is a global search method with an algorithm based on the synthesis of four concepts: competitive evolution, controlled random search, simplex method, and complex shuffling. It is an effective and efficient automated optimization method for calibrating model parameters [3, 6–8].

According to Kanazuka's study [9], in which he compared the effectiveness of parameter identification between USE-UA method, Particle Swarm Optimization (PSO), and Cuckoo search, it was found that SCE-UA method was the most effective in applying to USF models.

So, the authors applied SCE-UA method for parameter estimation of the USF models for the five selected storm events in the target watershed. Root mean square error (RMSE) was used as the objective function in evaluating the reproducibility of the model. The model parameters are identified by calibration using the average watershed rainfall compiled from X-band MP Radar and the observed river discharge. SCE-UA method requires a number of runs and generations for optimizing parameters to be converged.

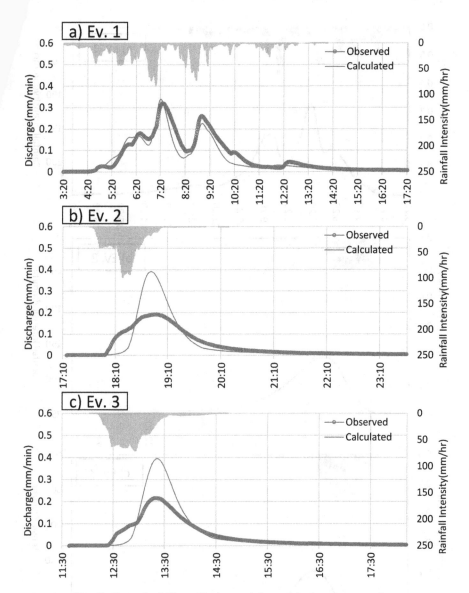

Fig. 5. Reproducibility of hydrograph by standard parameter values

4.2 Reproducibility of Runoff Hydrographs by Optimal Parameters

Figure 6 shows runoff analysis results of events 1–3 from 1st generation to 40th generation by SCE-UA method. RMSE values for each generation and event are shown in Table 3.

Calculated runoff hydrographs shown in Fig. 6 indicates that, for each event, the calculated hydrographs reproduces the shape of the observed hydrograph more precisely as generation numbers increase. Also, as shown in Table 3, the RMSE values

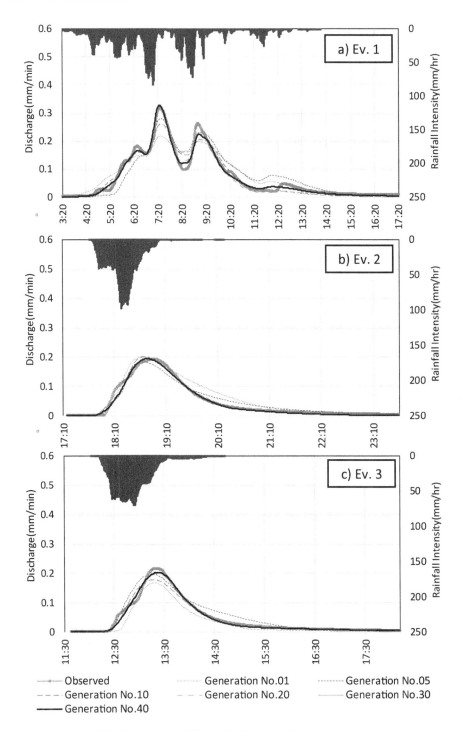

Fig. 6. Reproducibility of hydrograph of each generation

Table 3. RMSE for each generation

	Generation No.01	Generation No.05	Generation No.10	Generation No.20	Generation No.30	Generation No.40
Ev.1	0.029	0.028	0.019	0.012	0.011	0.011
Ev.2	0.013	0.010	0.006	0.005	0.004	0.004
Ev.3	0.013	0.012	0.008	0.005	0.004	0.004
Ev.4	0.020	0.018	0.013	0.010	0.008	0.008
Ev.5	0.033	0.032	0.026	0.024	0.024	0.024

decrease with the increase of generation numbers. They converge mostly to the minimum value when the calibration was proceeding between 30th to 40th generations.

Percentage errors in peak discharge, PEP, are shown in Table 4. The data depicts a similar trend as RMSE; PEP values become lower, closer to zero, as generation numbers increases, and become the closest to zero at 40th generation.

Table 4. PEP for each generation

	Generation No.01	Generation No.05	Generation No.10	Generation No.20	Generation No.30	Generation No.40
Ev.1	−32%	−13%	−18%	−3%	2%	2%
Ev.2	4%	−3%	6%	0%	1%	1%
Ev.3	−22%	−9%	−17%	−8%	−6%	−5%
Ev.4	−46%	−20%	−20%	−5%	−6%	−4%
Ev.5	−48%	−57%	−34%	−37%	−37%	−37%

In this section, USF model's seven parameters were optimized by SCE-UA method with X-band MP Radar data and observed river discharge. The result revealed that the calculated discharge nearly reproduces the observed hydrograph, which implies that the hydrograph reproducibility of USF model with optimal parameters is sufficiently high.

4.3   Comparing Best Parameters Between Events

In the last section, the optimal parameters of USF model were identified for each storm event. As shown in Fig. 7, the parameter values in 40th generation fluctuates substantially among different events, for k_1 ranges from 40 to 190, k_2 from 300 to 2800, k_3 from 0.007 to 0.022, p_1 from 0.1 to 1.4, p_2 from 0.2 to 1.5, z from 3 to 105, and α from 0.2 to 0.9. It implies that, by giving different parameter values to different events, the model incorporates the event-based characteristics of observed X-band MP Radar and river discharge. Thus, RMSE is minimized, and the reproducibility of USF model's runoff analysis is highly accurate.

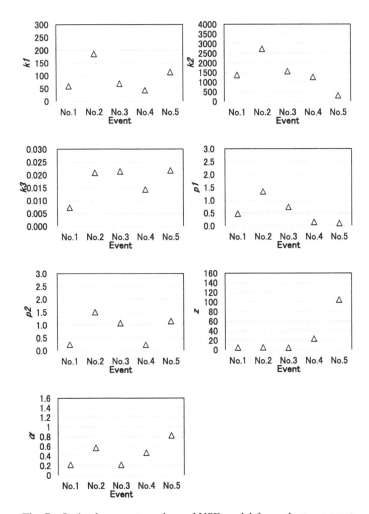

Fig. 7. Optimal parameter values of USF model for each storm event

5   Conclusion

X-band MP radar data, which has high spatiotemporal resolution, was used to predict storm runoff in urban watershed in upper Kanda river basin, western Tokyo, Japan. SCE-UA Global Optimization method was applied to optimize USF model parameters for urban storm events. The results revealed that, although the hydrograph reproducibility was not sufficient with standard parameter values, urban storm runoff was predicted accurately with parameters optimized by SCE-UA method.

It implies that the SCE-UA method successfully identified the optimal values for USF model's seven parameters. In addition, it is concluded that, at least, 30 generations of SCE-UA method were enough to identify parameters of required preciseness.

In runoff prediction in urban small watersheds, practical use of X-band MP Radar data and USF model is one of a future challenge. It is important to improve reproducibility of runoff analysis models by optimizing multiple parameters by global optimization method such as SCE-UA with detailed rainfall information provided by X-band MP Radar.

References

1. Tsuchiya, S., Kawasaki, M., Godo, H.: Improvement of the radar rainfall accuracy of XRAIN by modifying of rainfall attenuation correction and compositing radar rainfall. J. Jpn. Soc. Civ. Eng. Ser. B1 (Hydraul. Eng.) **71**(4), I_457–I_462 (2015)
2. Yonese, Y., Kawamura, A., Amaguchi, H., Tonotsuka, A.: Precision evaluation of X-band MP radar rainfall in a small urban watershed by comparison to 1-minute ground observation rainfall data. J. Jpn. Soc. Civ. Eng. Ser. B1 (Hydraul. Eng.) **72**(4), I_217–I_222 (2016)
3. Duan, Q.Y., Gupta, V.K., Sorooshian, S.: Shuffled complex evolution approach for effective and efficient global minimization. J. Optim. Theory Appl. **76**, 501–521 (1993). https://doi.org/10.1007/BF00939380
4. Yonese, Y., Kawamura, A., Amaguchi, H., Tonotsuka, A.: Spatiotemporal charactaristic analysis of X-band MP radar rainfall in a small urban watershed focused on the movement of rainfall area. J. Jpn. Soc. Civ. Eng. Ser. B1 (Hydraul. Eng.) **73**(4), I_217–I_222 (2017)
5. Takasaki, T., Kawamura, A., Amaguchi, H., Araki, K.: New storage function model considering urban runoff process. J. Jpn. Soc. Civ. Eng. Ser. B **65**(3), 217–230 (2009)
6. Kawamura, A., Morinaga, Y., Jinno, K., Dandy, G.C.: The comparison of runoff prediction accuracy among the various storage function models with loss mechanisms. In: Proceedings of the 2nd Asia Pacific Association of Hydrology and Water Resources Conference, vol. II, pp. 43–50 (2004)
7. Tanakamaru, H., Burges, S.J.: Application of global optimization to parameter estimation of the tank model. In: Proceedings of the International Conference on Water Resources and Environment Research, vol. II, pp. 39–46 (1996)
8. Saritha, P.G., Akira, K., Tadakatsu, T., Hideo, A., Gubash, A.: An effective storage function model for an urban watershed in terms of hydrograph reproducibility and Akaike information criterion. J. Hydrol. **563**, 657–668 (2018)
9. Kanazuka, T.: Parameter identification of urban Storage function model by evolutionary computing methods. Master's Thesis, Tokyo Metropolitan University, Graduate School of Urban Environmental Sciences (2017)

Retraction Note to: Encouraging the Recycling Process of Urban Waste by Means of Game Theory Techniques Using a Multi-agent Architecture

Alfonso González-Briones⊙, Pablo Chamoso⊙, Sara Rodríguez⊙,
Angélica González-Arrieta⊙, and Juan M. Corchado⊙

Retraction Note to:
Chapter 10 in: G. R. Simari et al. (Eds.): *Advances in Artificial Intelligence – IBERAMIA 2018*, LNAI 11238,
https://doi.org/10.1007/978-3-030-03928-8_10

The Series Editor and the publisher have retracted this chapter. An investigation by the publisher found that a number of chapters, including this one, from multiple conference proceedings raise various concerns, including but not limited to inappropriate or unusual citation behavior and undisclosed competing interests. Based on the findings of the investigation, the Series Editor and the publisher no longer have confidence in the results and conclusions of this chapter.

The authors disagree with this retraction.

The retracted version of this chapter can be found at
https://doi.org/10.1007/978-3-030-03928-8_10

Author Index

Printed in the United States
by Baker & Taylor Publisher Services